Modern Exterior Ballistics

Carl B. Freidhoff

Modern Exterior Ballistics

The Launch and Flight Dynamics of Symmetric Projectiles

Robert L. McCoy

Schiffer Military History
Atglen, PA

Dedication and Acknowledgments

This book is dedicated to my many friends and colleagues in exterior ballistics, who have encouraged me over the years to undertake such an effort. The book is also dedicated to my wife, Carolyn, and my daughters Amy and Kelly, who gave up large amounts of time with their husband and father, so the work could be completed. Finally, this book is dedicated to my mentors, C. H. Murphy, L. C. MacAllister, and A. S. Platou of the U.S. Army Ballistic Research Laboratory (BRL) at Aberdeen Proving Ground, Maryland, from whom I learned much about exterior ballistics.

Additional thanks are due my technical reviewers, P. Plostins of the Propulsion & Flight Division of the Army Research Laboratory (formerly the BRL), and J. W. Bradley, who retired from the BRL several years ago. I also wish to thank D. G. Miller of Livermore, California, and W. J. Chase of the Firing Tables Branch at Aberdeen Proving Ground, for many helpful comments and suggestions.

All photographs are courtesy of the U.S. Army Research Laboratory, at Aberdeen Proving Ground, Maryland.

Robert L. McCoy
March 1998

Book Design by Ian C. Robertson.

Library of Congress Catalog Number: 98-87583.

Printed in China.
ISBN: 0-7643-0720-7

We are interested in hearing from authors with book ideas on related topics.

Published by Schiffer Publishing Ltd.
4880 Lower Valley Road
Atglen, PA 19310
Phone: (610) 593-1777
FAX: (610) 593-2002
E-mail: schifferbk@aol.com.
Please write for a free catalog.
This book may be purchased from the publisher.
Please include $3.95 postage.
Try your bookstore first.

Contents

A Dedication to Robert L. McCoy

This book on exterior ballistics represents the life work and passion of Bob McCoy. It was his wish ~~toeave~~ to leave a historical perspective as well as an accurate technical treatise for both the engineering community and the sporting arms industry. Bob was in fact an aerospace engineer, but he always referred to himself as a "ballistician." He was very proud to have worked for and served the American people for 30 years at the U.S. Army Ballistic Research Laboratory while truly enjoying his passion. Bob was one of the most respected members of the staff of the U.S. Army Ballistic Research Laboratory and had an international reputation in aeroballistics. We will always remember his professionalism, his enthusiasm, his boisterous laugh, his passion for ballistics, and most of all, his friendship. We his students, his coworkers, his peers, and his friends dedicate this book to the memory of the last true ballistician of the 20th century.

Vural Oskay
Bob Whyte
Keith Soencksen
Fred J Brandon
André J. Sowa
Joyce V. Smith
James E. Danberg
Kevin S. Fansler
John H. Whiteside
Robert T. [illegible] Jr.
Mary K. McDonald
John Kineke
[illegible]
Fran Mirabelle

Cynthia A. Miller
Edward M. Hauck
Margaret M. Sullivan
James A. Matts
Barbara A. Tilghman
Elizabeth A. Laurie
Betty Jo Icker
James W. Bradley
Lyle D. Kayser
[illegible]
Joe Kochenderfer
William J. Chase
Andrew Mark
[illegible] Patton
[illegible]

Peter Plostins
Donald G. Miller
[illegible]
Wayne Hathaway
Ed Schmidt
Mark L. Bundy
Carrie L. Sharpless
Jubaraj Sahu
Raymond Von Wahlde
Paul Weinacht
Ameer G. Mikhail
Gene R. Cooper
Charles J. Nietubicz
Jo A. Panamarou
James M Garner
[illegible]
Joseph M. Wall
Charlie Murphy
Jonathan A Bornstein
Bradford S. Davis
Nathan Gerber
William P. D'Amico, Jr.
Robert F. Lieske
Charles H. Lebegern, Jr.
Walt Sturek

Preface

This book is primarily designed to be a self-teaching aid to the entry-level professional exterior ballistician, who has searched in vain for courses in exterior ballistics among the formal university science and engineering curricula. It is intentionally written in an informal style, to gain and hold the reader's interest and attention. The book is specifically aimed at those with an undergraduate background in mathematics, physics, or the mechanical and aerospace engineering sciences, all of which are suitable fields of study for a career in exterior ballistics.

The layman who is a shooter, hunter, or amateur ballistician will also find this book interesting and useful. The historical perspective on exterior ballistics fills an existing need, since the more recent developments that have occurred since the Second World War are not well documented in any generally available publication. The layman who lacks the prerequisite background in mathematics, physics, or engineering science will have difficulty in following some of the highly mathematical derivations in this book; however, many of the final results are simple enough to be used by anyone who is equipped with a modern scientific hand-held calculator. The amateur ballistician with a home computer can take better advantage of the growing commercial market in exterior ballistic software, some of which cannot be used intelligently without a general understanding of the basic principles of exterior ballistics.

This is a book about *modern* exterior ballistics. The fundamentals of the classical science are presented, but special emphasis is placed on the new technologies that emerged during and after the Second World War, and their contributions to the modern science. In the mid-twentieth century, the simultaneous advent of continuous-flow supersonic wind tunnels, operational spark photography ranges, and modern high-speed digital computers revolutionized the science of exterior ballistics. A major purpose of this book is to illustrate how the modern measurements augment the classical results; another is to update the information available in older published textbooks.

Robert L. McCoy
March 1998

1

A Brief History of Exterior Ballistics

1.1 INTRODUCTION

Ballistics is the science that deals with the motion of projectiles. The word ballistics was derived from the Latin "ballista," which was an ancient machine designed to hurl a javelin. Modern writers divide the subject into interior, exterior, and terminal ballistics, which describe, respectively, the propulsion, atmospheric flight, and target impact action of projectiles. The modern science of exterior ballistics has evolved as a specialized branch of the dynamics of rigid bodies, moving under the influence of gravitational and aerodynamic forces. A comprehensive history of exterior ballistics would fill several volumes, and only a few highlights can be included in this chapter. Some of the terms and concepts mentioned in this history may be unfamiliar to the reader. The essential ones are reintroduced and defined in succeeding chapters.

1.2 EARLY BEGINNINGS

Exterior ballistics existed for centuries as an art before its first beginnings as a science. Although a number of sixteenth and seventeenth century European investigators contributed to the growing body of renaissance knowledge, Isaac Newton of England (1642-1727) was probably the greatest of the modern founders of exterior ballistics. Newton's laws of motion established the framework of modern classical mechanics, without which ballistics could not have advanced from an art to a science.

Newton was interested in the motion of a projectile in a resisting medium, and advanced the theory that fluid resistance is proportional to the fluid density, to the projectile cross-sectional area, and to the square of the velocity. He timed the fall of spheres in St. Paul's Cathedral, and confirmed his resistance law for low velocities.

Newton conceived an aerodynamic drag that was particulate in nature. He envisioned particles of air colliding with the projectile, and giving up the normal (perpendicular to the surface) component of their momentum; after impact the particles would continue moving parallel to the projectile surface. Newton could not have anticipated the shock waves that accompany transonic and supersonic flows, thus his particle theory of drag is, in general, an oversimplification. However, at very high (hypersonic) velocities, where the bow shock lies close to the projectile surface, the behavior of air becomes similar to the picture conceived by Newton, and Newtonian impact theory actually predicts some aspects of hypersonic flows rather well.

Benjamin Robins of England (1707-1751) developed the first successful ballistic pendulum in 1740, based on an idea proposed by the younger Cassini in 1707. Between 1740 and 1742, Robins measured the drag of 12-gauge lead musket balls (approximately 3/4 inch diameter) at velocities in the neighborhood of 1600 feet per second, and observed retardations over one hundred times the acceleration of gravity. Although most ballisticians of that day did not believe his data, modern sphere drag measurements show that Robins' ballistic pendulum gave essentially correct results. Charles Hutton (1737-1823), who succeeded Robins at Woolwich, obtained drag results for spheres between 1787 and 1791 that showed close agreement with Robins' measurements.

Rifled gun barrels first appeared in significant numbers around the middle of the seventeenth century, but the development of elongated bullets did not occur until about 1825. In 1851, Captain Minié of France invented the "Minié Ball," an ogival-cylindrical bullet with a conical base cavity to provide obturation in a rifled barrel. Cast iron artillery shell of elongated form, with pre-engraved rotating bands to provide both spin and obturation, began to appear at about the same time. The elongated bullets and shell gave significant increases in range, compared with the spherical shot previously used.

1.3 EXTERIOR BALLISTICS IN THE NINETEENTH CENTURY

After about 1850, ballisticians of many countries began experiments to improve the accuracy of drag measurements. Francis Bashforth of England invented the Bashforth electro-mechanical chronograph, based on circuitry developed by Charles Wheatstone, inventor of the Wheatstone bridge. From 1865 to 1880, Bashforth measured the retardations of English artillery shell in use at that time. A typical English projectile used in Bashforth's very extensive experiments was a short ogival-cylindrical design with about a 1.5 caliber radius head. The test velocities ranged from 430 to 2780 feet per second, and were obtained using the same multiple-station concept used in modern spark ranges.

General Mayevski of Russia conducted resistance firings at St. Petersburg in 1868 and 1869. His projectiles had essentially the

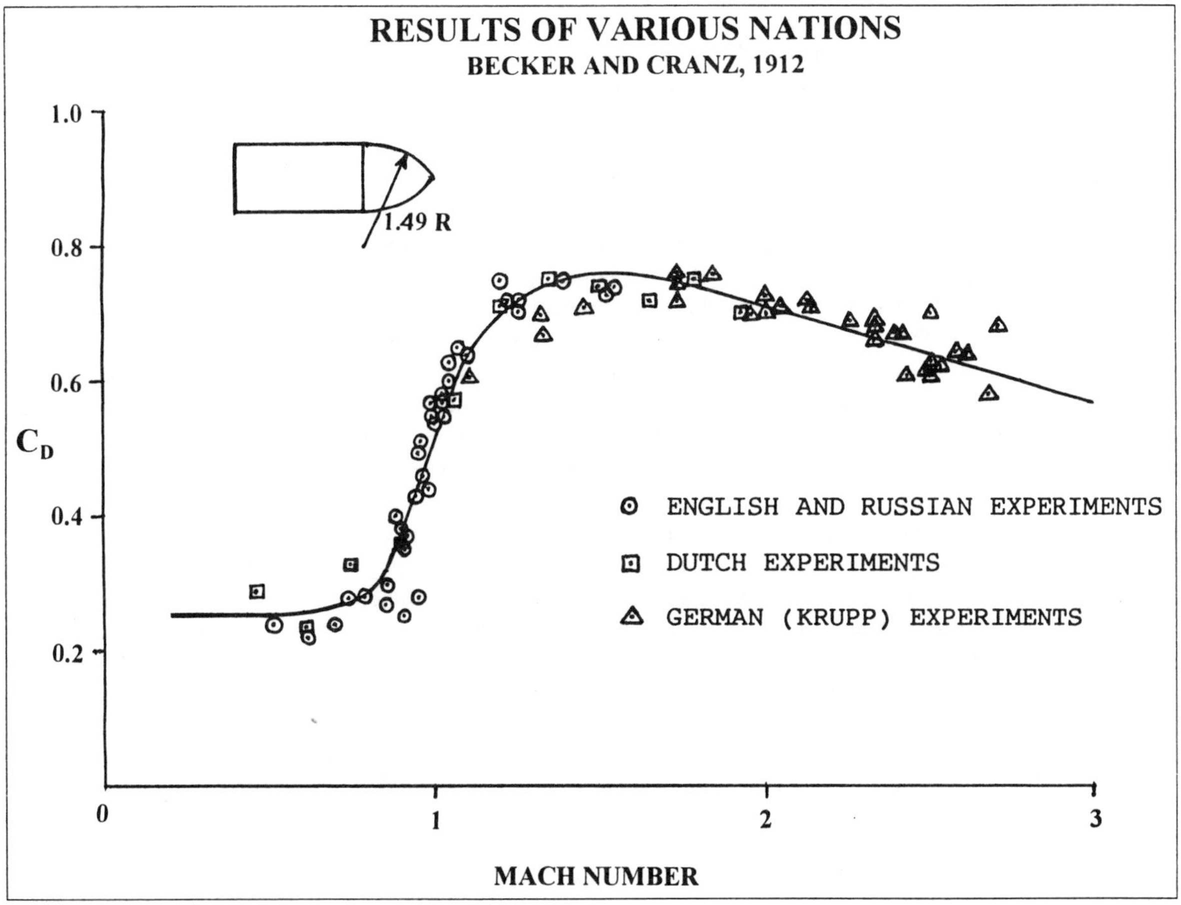

Figure 1.1 Nineteenth Century Drag Coefficients

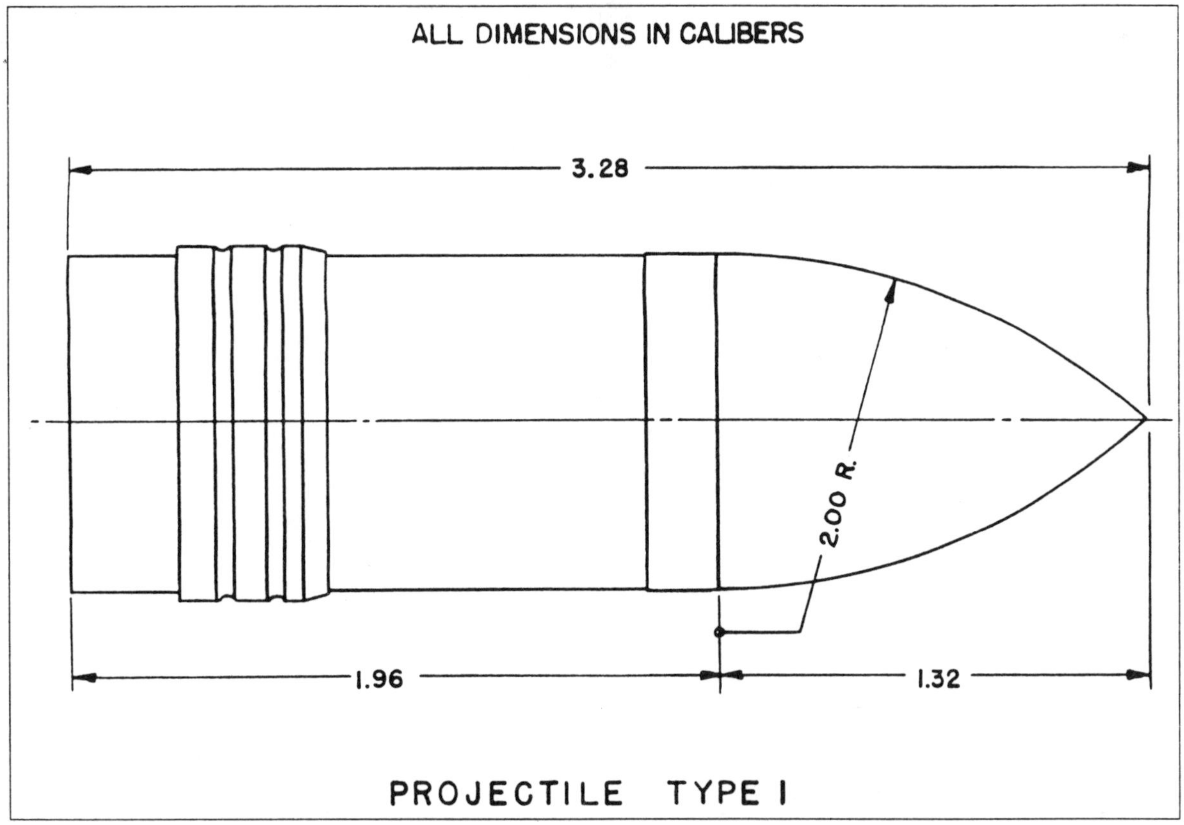

Figure 1.2 Sketch of Profile Type 1.

same form as Bashforth's. Mayevski's firings covered the velocity range from 560 to 1340 feet per second. Colonel Hojel of Holland also did some resistance firings in 1883 and 1884, using shell of nearly the same form as the English and Russian designs, over a velocity range of 490 to 2130 feet per second.

From 1875 to 1881, the Krupp factory at Meppen Proving Ground, Germany, conducted a large number of air resistance firings, using three different projectile shapes. One shape was similar to that used in the Russian and English experiments, with a 1.49 caliber radius head; the other shell types had longer ogives. The velocities of the Krupp firings varied from 1200 to 3000 feet per second. In a report published in 1912, Becker and Cranz (Ref. 1) summarized the results obtained by various nations for the 1.49 caliber radius head artillery shell; their graph, converted to modern aeroballistic nomenclature and plotted against Mach number, is illustrated here as Figure 1.1.

In 1883, General Mayevski analyzed the Krupp firing data and formulated his "zone" laws of air resistance for a projectile about 3 calibers long, having a flat base and an ogival head with a 2 caliber radius. Mayevski's projectile shape is essentially identical to that of Projectile Type 1, shown in Figure 1.2. Colonel James M. Ingalls of the U. S. Artillery converted Mayevski's results into English units, and based his tables (Ref. 2) on them. *Ingalls' Tables* were first published as *Artillery Circular M*, in 1900. An abbreviated version of *Ingalls' Tables* was published by General Julian S. Hatcher (Ref. 3), in *Hatcher's Notebook*, which is well known to American riflemen. Colonel F. Siacci of Italy, who around 1880 proposed the "Siacci Method" for flat-fire trajectory calculations, also published the results of the Krupp firings in the *Rivista di artiglieria e genio* for March, 1896.

From 1873 to 1898, the Gâvre Commission of the French Naval Artillery conducted numerous air resistance firings at the Gâvre Proving Ground, utilizing the Boulengé chronograph which had been developed in Belgium around 1864. Most of the French test projectiles were ogival-cylindrical shapes, with ogival caliber radii of 1.64, 1.98, or 3.34 calibers. Test velocities ranged from 390 to 3800 feet per second. In 1893, the Gâvre Commission traced curves for the resistance functions corresponding to the test projectile shapes. In 1917, Chief Engineer M. Garnier of the Gâvre Commission published a table of the resistance function for Projectile Type 1. The Ordnance Department of the U. S. Army prepared a table of the logarithm of the Gâvre resistance function in 1918 (Ref. 4), and a slight modification of this function, with extension to higher velocities by E. E. Herrmann (Ref. 5) of the U. S. Naval Academy, is referred to today as the G_1 Drag Function. Note that the Ingalls Drag Function and the G_1 Drag Function reflect two different sets of test data and analysis for essentially identical projectile shapes. Figure 1.3 illustrates the difference between the Ingalls and the G_1 drag curves.

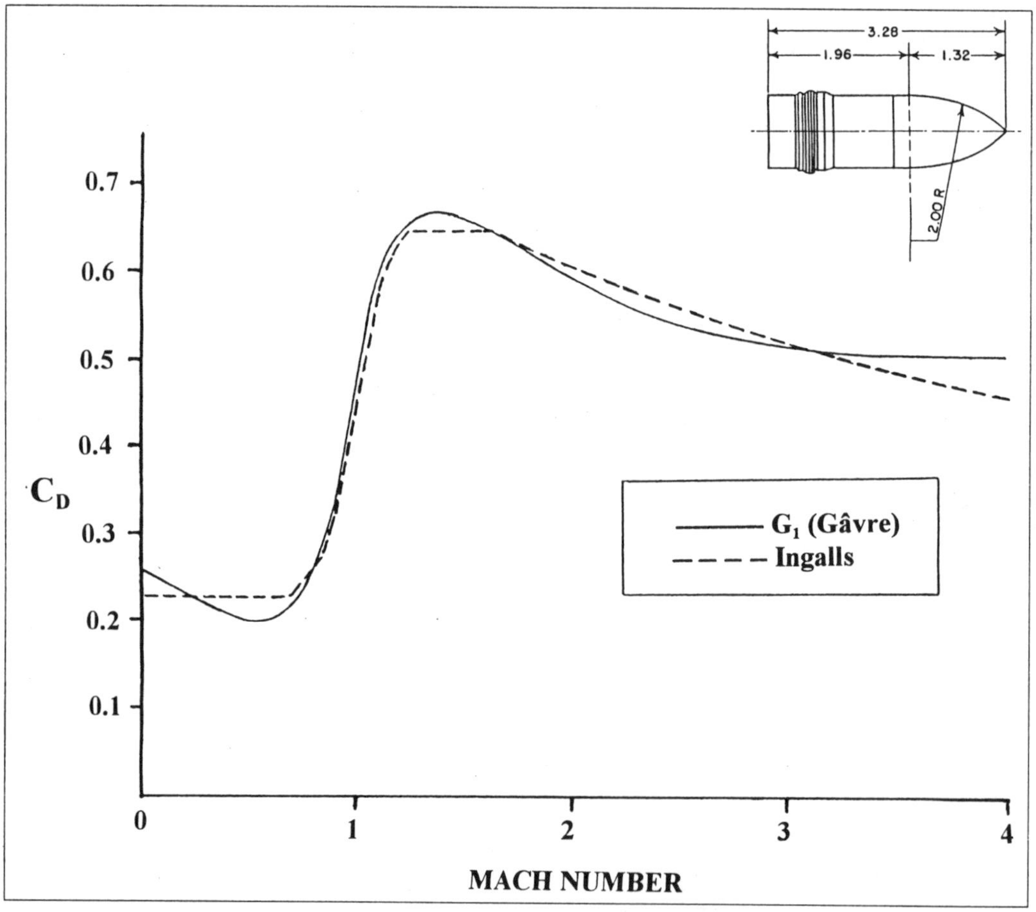

Figure 1.3 Comparison of the Ingalls and Gâvre Drag Coefficients.

1.4 EARLY TWENTIETH CENTURY DEVELOPMENTS

During the first decade of the twentieth century, the German firm of Krupp investigated the effect of long slender ogives on the drag of small caliber projectiles. The tangent ogives of most nineteenth century projectile designs were generated using radii of 1.5 to 3 calibers; Krupp tested long tangent ogive noses with generating radii up to 10 calibers. The long, slender ogives were found to reduce drag by nearly 50 percent at supersonic speeds. The German army adopted a lighter weight bullet with the new low drag "spitzer" shape for their 8mm service rifle cartridge, and the U. S. Army subsequently adopted the 150 grain M1906 spitzer bullet for the M1903 Springfield rifle. During the First World War, the Krupp firm used the 10 caliber radius ogive design for the 210mm Paris Gun (Wilhelmgeschütze) projectile, which was used to bombard Paris from 120 kilometers (75 miles) range.

Two additional series of resistance firings were conducted by the British, early in the twentieth century. The British *Ballistic Tables of 1909* (Ref. 6) were based on extensive firings carried out from 1904 to 1906. The British 1909 tables are essentially identical to those of Ingalls. In 1921, F. W. Jones conducted resistance firings at Hodsock, England, for a .303 caliber flat-based spitzer bullet, using a ballistic pendulum designed by Colonel H. Mellish and Lord Cottesloe. The results of Jones' tests were published as the *Hodsock Tables* (Ref. 7), which are reprinted in the last chapter of Major Gerald Burrard's *Notes on Sporting Rifles* (Ref. 8). Neither the British Tables of 1909 nor the *Hodsock Tables* have been used extensively in the United States. The later British *Textbook of Small Arms, 1929* (Ref. 9), contains exterior ballistic tables similar to those of Hodsock.

All the European ballisticians of the late nineteenth century made a fundamental error in their analysis of drag test data; experimental retardation coefficients should have been combined at equal Mach numbers instead of at equal velocities. The distinction is not of great importance except at transonic speeds. However, the transonic slopes of both the Ingalls and G_1 drag curves are now known to be too low; the error results from statistical dispersion introduced by neglect of the influence of the speed of sound.

By the end of the First World War, ballisticians of many countries had recognized the fact that the longer ogives and boattails of projectiles then in current use were not accurately represented by the Ingalls or G_1 drag functions. In 1922 and 1923, the Gâvre Commission, under the direction of Chairman J. Dupuis, conducted resistance firings of five projectile shapes, using 138mm shell fired at speeds from 900 to 2900 feet per second. The Type I projectile was slightly longer than G_1, but nearly identical in shape. Type I-BT was similar to Type I, except for a boattailed base, with 5 degree boattail angle, and a boattail length of 0.67 caliber. The Type II and Type III shell had longer ogives; Type II had a head length of 2.32 calibers, and was tested in both flat base and boattailed versions. The Type III shell had a 2.78 caliber head, and only a boattailed design was tested. The 1922-1923 Gâvre Commission firing results were published in 1928 and 1929 in the *Mémorial de l'Artillerie Française*, and were extensively used in France until about 1950, but were not generally available in the United States.

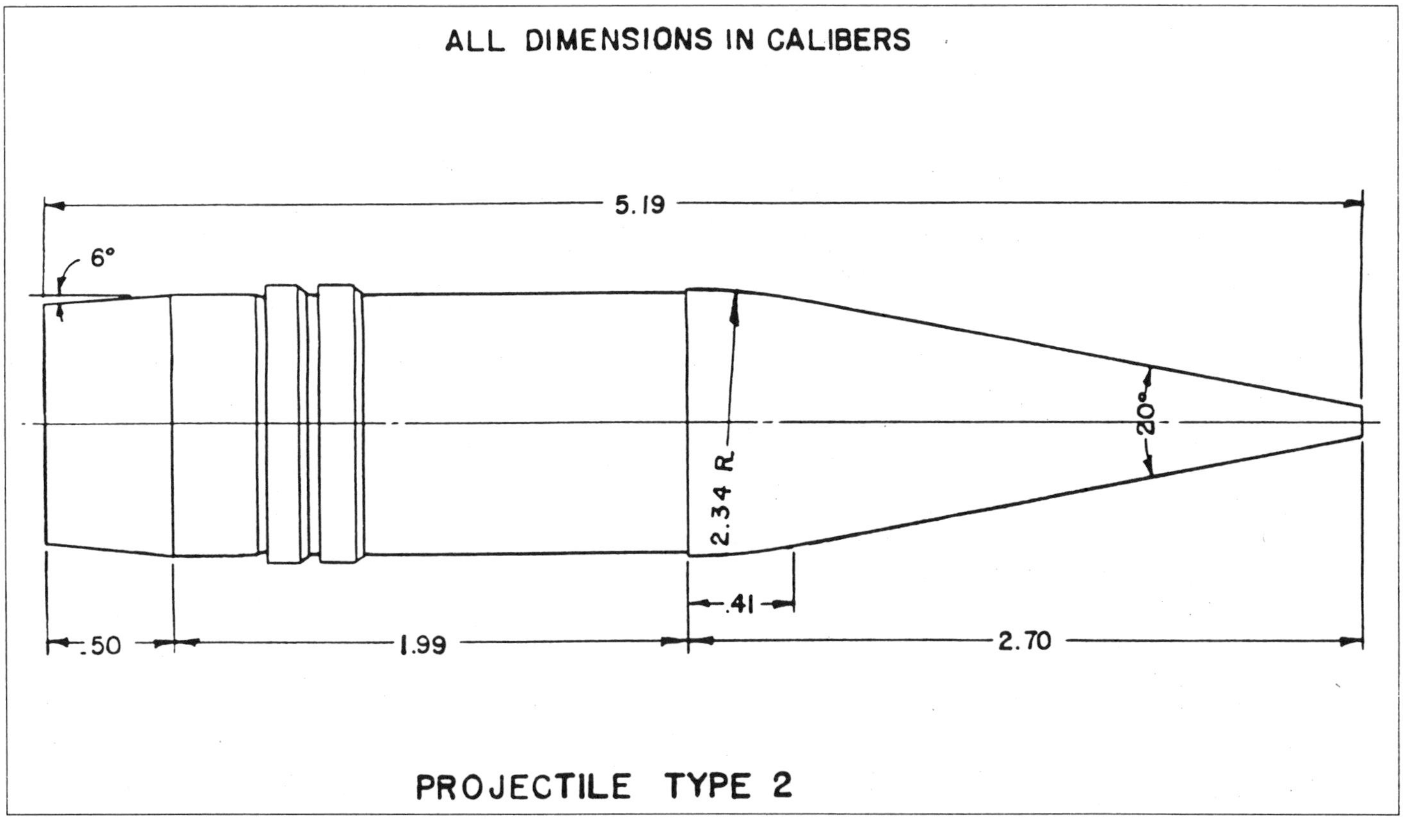

Figure 1.4 Sketch of Projectile Type 2.

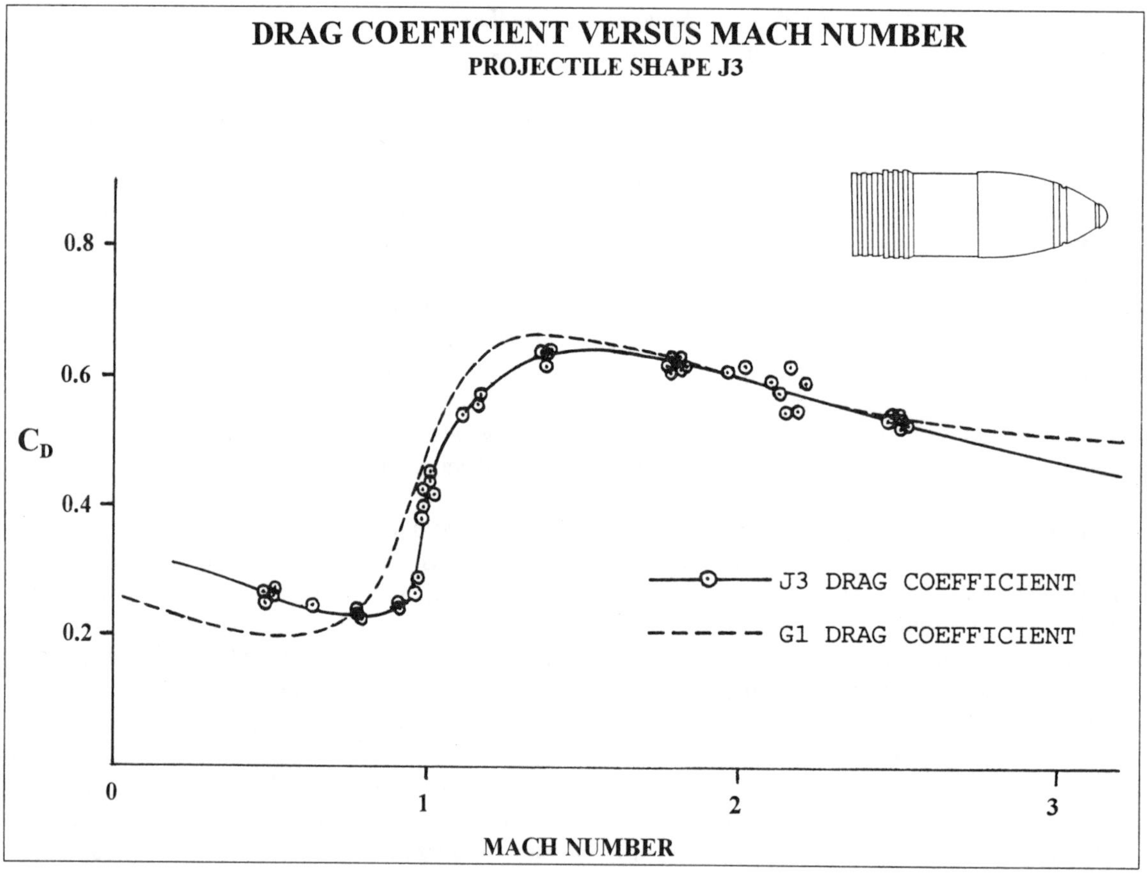

Figure 1.5 Comparison of J3 and G1 Drag Coefficients.

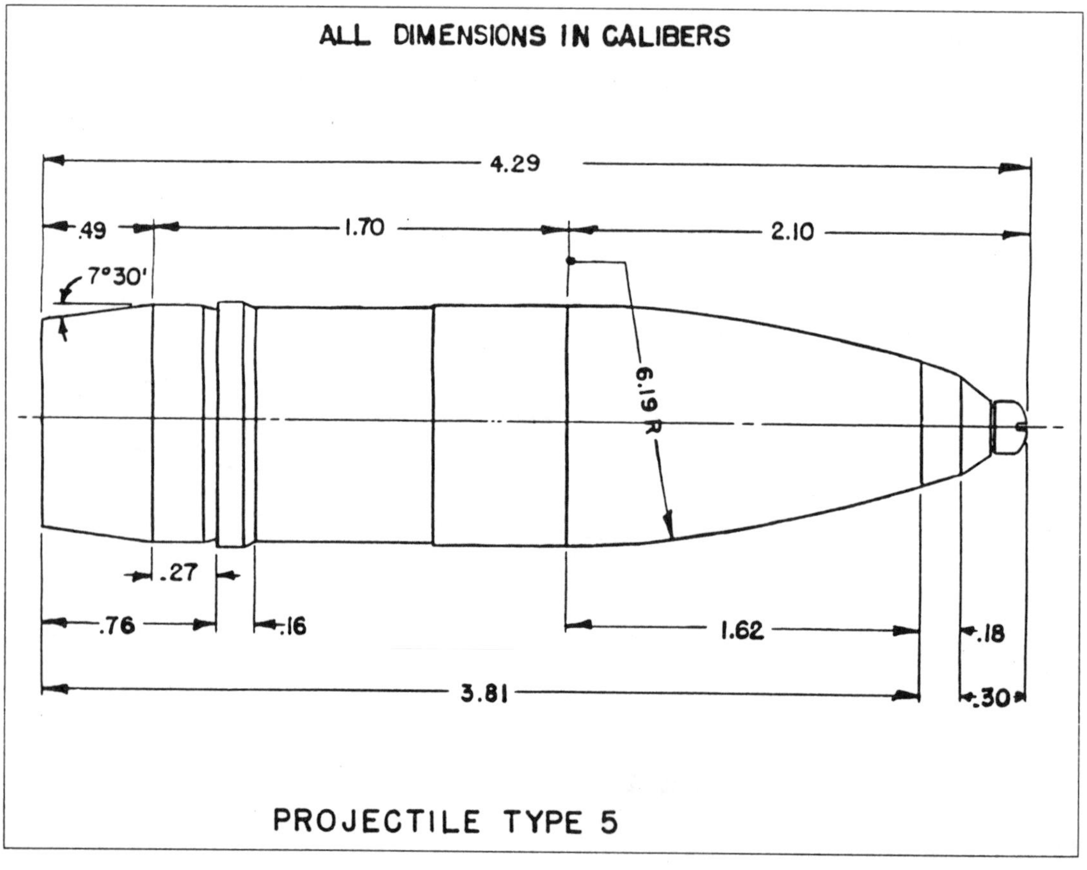

Figure 1.6 Sketch of Projectile Type 5.

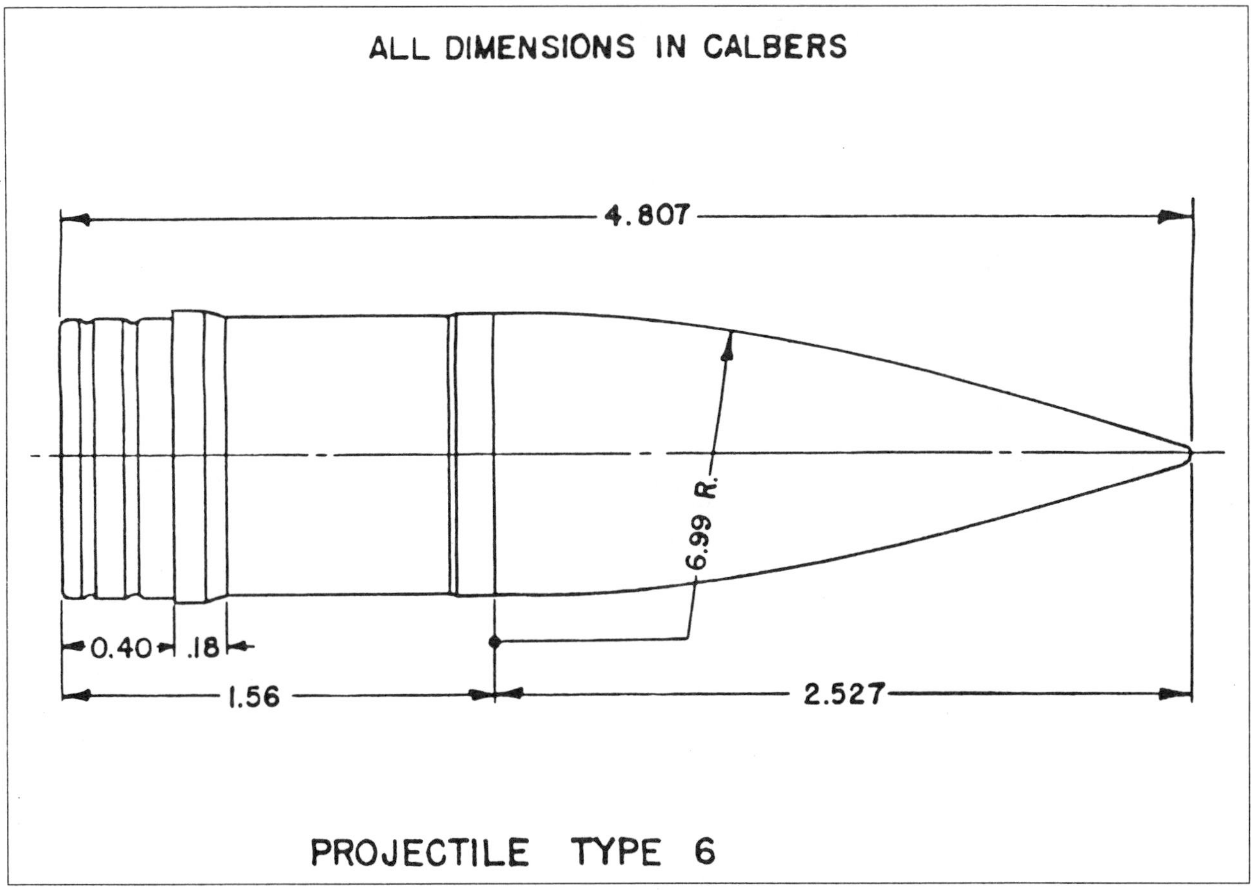

Figure 1.7 Sketch of Projectile Type 6.

From 1922 to 1925, R. H. Kent and H. P. Hitchcock (Ref.10) of the Ballistics Section, Aberdeen Proving Ground, Maryland, conducted resistance firings of a 3.3 inch shell called "Type J," which we now refer to as G_2, or Projectile Type 2. The G_2 projectile had a long, conical head shape, and a 6 degree boattail; Figure 1.4 shows the G_2 projectile shape. The Aberdeen Rotating Drum chronograph was used, with inductance coils for the start-stop signals. Velocities tested varied from 650 to 3190 feet per second. The drag data for these tests and thereafter at Aberdeen Proving Ground, were properly plotted against Mach number.

In 1926, Kent and Hitchcock conducted resistance firings of the 3 inch shell, Mark IX, with the Mark III time fuze. This projectile was known as J_3, and was almost identical in form to Projectile Type 1. Firings of the J_3 shape were performed as a check on the accuracy of the G_1 drag function. The general form of the J_3 drag coefficient was similar to that of G_1, as shown in Figure 1.5. Thus the J_3 drag function was not used after 1927.

Kent and Hitchcock conducted resistance firings of the 75mm high explosive shell, Mark IV with the Mark III PD (point-detonating) fuze, between 1927 and 1933. The Mark III PD fuze was a long spike-nosed fuze extending about 1.5 calibers ahead of the ogive. Ballistic tables were prepared for this shell, which was referred to as J_4, but the unusual J_4 projectile shape is of little interest today.

Resistance firings of the 75mm Mark IV shell with the Mark V fuze were conducted at the same time as those above, and this projectile was referred to as J_5; the later designation is G_5, or Projectile Type 5, which is shown in Figure 1.6. Velocities tested ranged from 600 to 2230 feet per second. The G_5 projectile shape was frequently used in U. S. Ordnance as a reference standard drag shape as late as 1960.

The J_6 (G_6), or Projectile Type 6 was tested from 1929 to 1931 at Aberdeen Proving Ground. The resistance firings were conducted using the 3 inch M1915 shell, at velocities from 600 to 3000 feet per second. Projectile Type 6 (G_6) is shown in Figure 1.7. The G_6 shape was also used as a reference standard drag shape until about 1960.

Two later designs included as reference shapes were G_7 and G_8, obtained from the External Ballistics Department, Ordnance Board of the War Office, England (Ref. 11) in 1940. Projectile Type 7 (G_7) was referred to as the British Standard Streamline Projectile, and Projectile Type 8 (G_8) was called the British Streamline Projectile with Cylindrical Base. U. S. versions of G_7 and G_8 Ballistic Tables were compiled by Kent and Hitchcock in 1943, and were extensively used for firing table calculations during the Second World War. The Type 7 and Type 8 projectiles are illustrated in Figures 1.8 and 1.9, respectively.

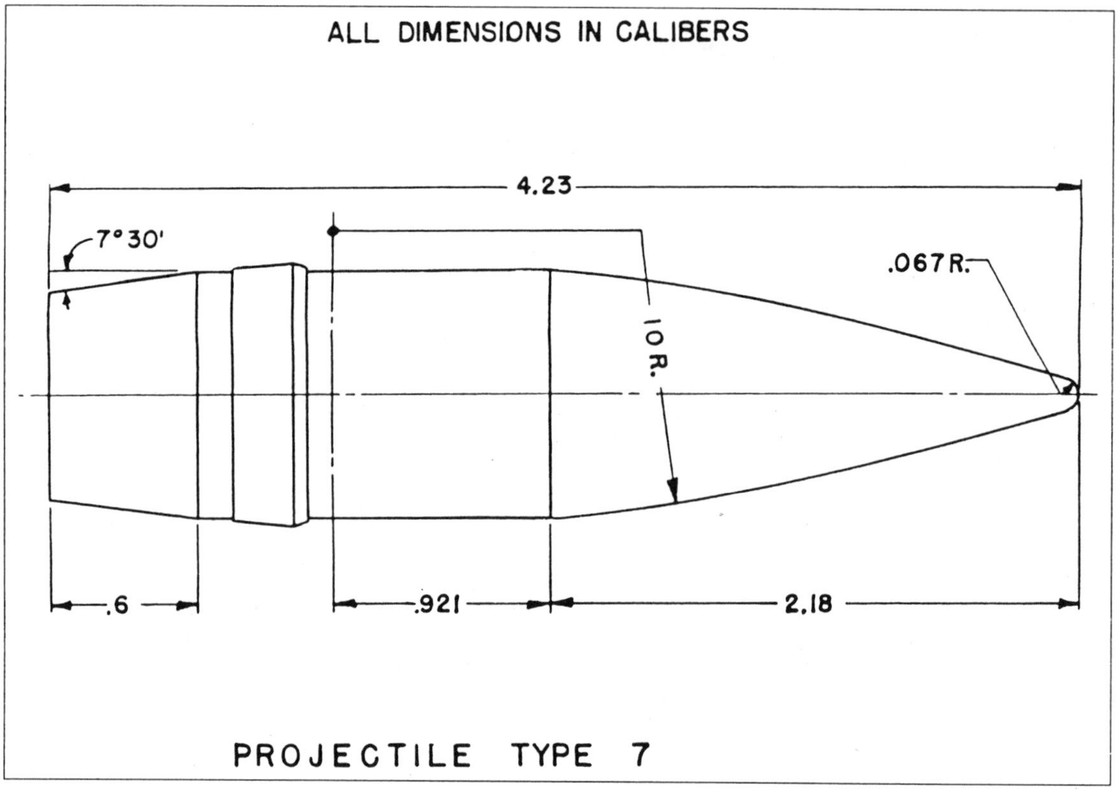

Figure 1.8 Sketch of Projectile Type 7.

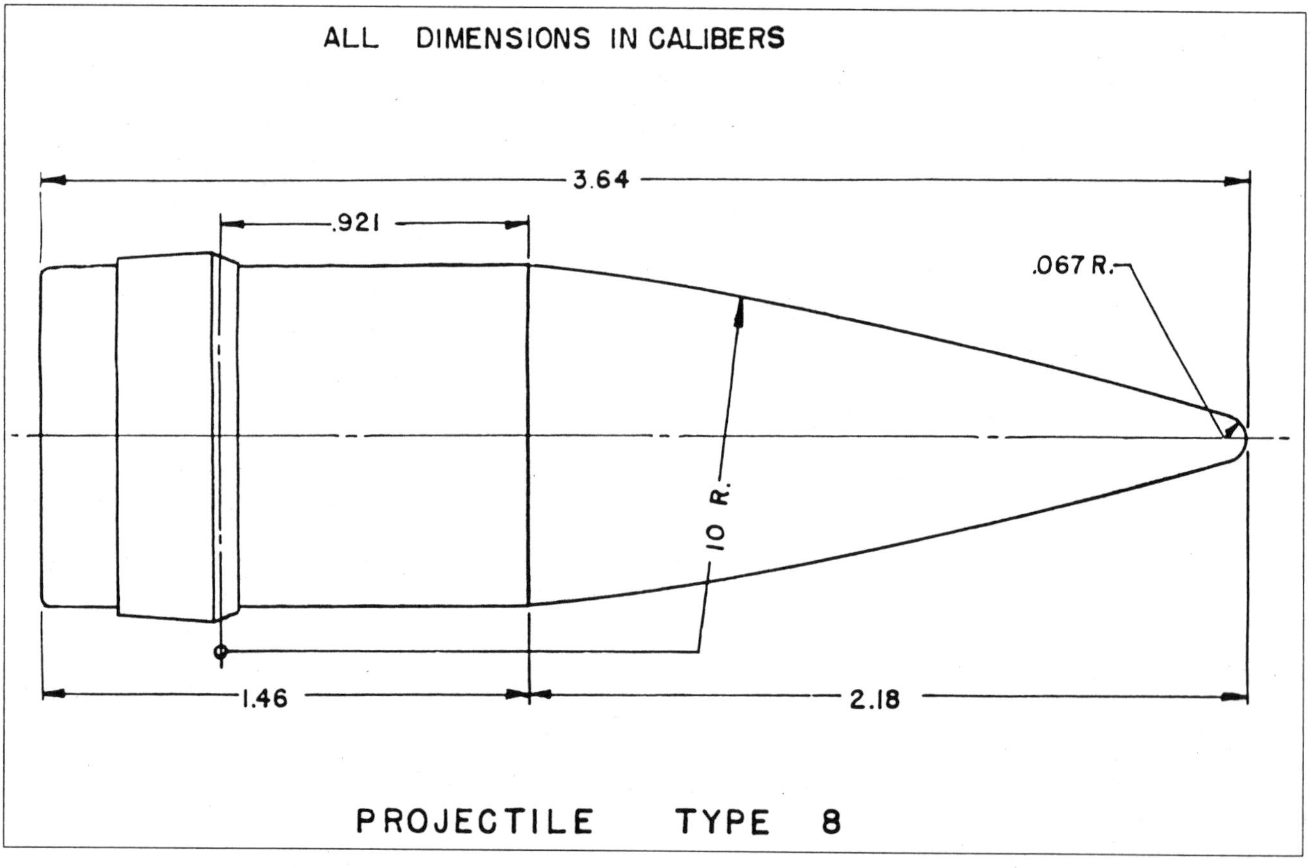

Figure 1.9 Sketch of Projectile Type 8.

The modern exterior ballistician might well ask why reference standard drag shapes were required prior to and during the Second World War. The answer is that they were a matter of practical necessity. The labor involved in manual computation of a single long range trajectory was so enormous that only a few such trajectories could be done. However, if complete ballistic tables were available for several reference standard projectiles, trajectories for a new design could be obtained by means of a "form factor" relating the new shell to one of the reference standards, and the method of differential corrections. A task requiring several weeks of manual computation was thereby reduced to a few days. Modern ballisticians with ready access to high speed digital computers can hardly appreciate the drudgery involved in the manual computation of trajectories.

Thus far, our historical development has considered only the problem of the aerodynamic drag (resistance) acting on projectiles. Nineteenth century investigators concentrated their efforts on the drag, and generally made the assumption that an elongated projectile, if given sufficient spin from a rifled barrel, would always fly with small yaw. Since the projectile shapes in common use at that time were short and relatively blunt, the assumption of stable flight was usually justified. The selection of a proper twist of rifling for a given projectile was more of an art than a science in the nineteenth century; rules of thumb such as Greenhill's Rule (Ref. 9), derived in 1879, were commonly used. It is probable that both George Greenhill in England and Carl Cranz in Germany understood the concept we now refer to as gyroscopic stability. However, the nineteenth century ballisticians had no means for measurement of the aerodynamic overturning moment acting on the projectile, which is a necessary input to the gyroscopic stability equation.

1.5 THE FIRST MODERN AERODYNAMIC FORCE-MOMENT SYSTEM FOR PROJECTILES

A number of early European investigators had experimented with firing projectiles through several yaw cards as a check on the gyroscopic stability. In the first decade of the twentieth century, a remarkable independent effort was made by F. W. Mann of Massachusetts (Ref. 12), who conducted extensive yaw card tests of various turn-of-the-century military and sporting rifle bullets. Mann was a painstaking and careful experimenter, and he made the first reasonably accurate measurements of the epicyclic yaw and swerve of spin-stabilized projectiles. He investigated the effects of static and dynamic unbalance on the flight of rifle bullets, and correctly identified the quantities we refer to today as lateral throwoff and aerodynamic jump. Although Mann lacked the aeronautical background necessary to properly interpret some of his findings, he did pioneer the experimental yaw-card technique that was successfully used for the next forty years.

The nature of the total aerodynamic force and moment system which acts on a projectile in flight was first recognized with the advent of aircraft. Low speed wind tunnel measurements of the drag, lift, and overturning moment acting on airplanes were first made in the early years of the twentieth century. Two pioneering English aerodynamicists, F. W. Lanchester and G. H. Bryan, studied the forces and moments acting on aircraft, and included a pitch damping moment, which acted to reduce the pitching angular velocity. In 1919, R. H. Fowler, E. G. Gallop, C. N. H. Lock and H. W. Richmond conducted an extensive series of yaw-card firings at Portsmouth, England, using 3 inch English naval guns and projectiles. Fowler formulated the first reasonably complete aerodynamic force-moment system for spinning projectiles, extending the work of Lanchester and Bryan to include Magnus forces and moments, and a spin damping moment. An approximate analytical solution of the resulting differential equations showed that the yawing motion of a spinning shell is epicyclic, with two characteristic frequencies. The aerodynamic forces and moments acting on the 3 inch naval shell were inferred by graphically fitting the epicyclic solution to the yaw-card measurements, and Fowler's work is thus considered to be the first modern free-flight ballistic range experiment. The four English investigators published their work as a paper of the Royal Society of London (Ref. 13) in 1920; the title of the paper was *The Aerodynamics of a Spinning Shell*, and it is now considered a classic.

From about 1925 until the end of the Second World War, Kent and Hitchcock conducted numerous yaw card firings at Aberdeen Proving Ground, Maryland. The projectiles tested included everything from small arms bullets to large caliber artillery shell. Kent and Hitchcock used Fowler's graphical data reduction methods. Many good results were obtained from these yaw-card firings, in spite of the crude measurements and the limitations of graphical data reduction.

J. L. Synge of Canada recognized in 1942 that Fowler's aerodynamic force-moment system for spinning projectiles was logically incomplete, and in 1943 Nielsen and Synge (Ref. 14) introduced the complete aerodynamic system in use today. Kent studied the gyroscopic and dynamic stability criteria (Ref. 15) implied in Fowler's work. J. L. Kelley and E. J. McShane, who worked at the U.S. Army Ballistic Research Laboratory (BRL) during the Second World War, revised and updated the work of Fowler and Synge in a BRL report (Ref. 16) titled *On the Motion of a Projectile with Small or Slowly Changing Yaw*. Kelley and McShane derived the complete dynamic stability criteria used today, and established the fact that gyroscopic stability is a necessary but not a sufficient condition for dynamic stability. In layman's language, this means that the yaw can, in certain cases, increase along the trajectory, even though the projectile is everywhere gyroscopically stable! The work of Kelley and McShane was later incorporated in their classical textbook, *Exterior Ballistics* (Ref. 17), published in 1953.

1.6 THE BEGINNINGS OF COMPUTATIONAL AERODYNAMICS

The modern science of computational aerodynamics traces its origins to the eighteenth century with the work of Johann and Daniel Bernoulli and Leonhard Euler. Daniel Bernoulli first derived the equation we now refer to as "Bernoulli's equation" in 1738. Euler is recognized as the founder of hydromechanics; he was the first to advance the modern concept of fluid pressure, and later formulated what we refer to today as the "Euler equations" that describe the flow of an inviscid (frictionless) fluid.

The nineteenth century produced many technical achievements in applied fluid mechanics which left scientific knowledge far behind. In an incompressible, frictionless fluid, there can be no drag, or resistance to motion; thus theoretical hydrodynamics appeared useless to nineteenth century engineers and ballisticians. The effects of viscosity on fluid flow were studied by several nineteenth century investigators, including Poiseuille, Stokes, and Osborne Reynolds, with whom the Reynolds Number is now identified. By the middle of the nineteenth century, Navier and Stokes had independently derived the Navier-Stokes equations, which describe the flow of viscous fluids. A few special analytical solutions of the Navier-Stokes equations have been found for very simple cases, but general solutions of these non-linear partial differential equations are possible only by numerical methods, coupled with modern large scale supercomputers.

The foundations of thermodynamics were also laid in the nineteenth century, with the work of Rumford, Joule, Lord Kelvin, Clausius, Rankine and others. The theory of shock waves was developed at about the same time. Ernst Mach of Germany (for whom the Mach Number was later named) made the first spark shadowgraphs of a bullet in supersonic flight in 1885. Mach's shadowgraphs provided visual illustrations of shock waves on projectiles flying at supersonic speeds. Rankine of Scotland and Hugoniot of France had independently derived the equations governing changes in flow properties across shock waves in the late nineteenth century, and in 1910, Lord Rayleigh and G. I. Taylor of England independently used the second law of thermodynamics to prove that only compression shocks are physically possible.

In 1904, L. Prandtl (Ref. 18) advanced his boundary layer theory. Prandtl's concept envisioned a thin layer of fluid near the surface, in which all the effects of viscosity are concentrated; outside the boundary layer, the fluid behaves essentially as if it were frictionless. Although Prandtl's boundary layer theory is only an approximation, its general validity and usefulness in applied aerodynamics is well established today.

Max Munk introduced his "airship theory" (Ref. 19) in 1924. Munk's apparent mass method for estimating the aerodynamic characteristics of airship hulls has gradually grown into the modern generalized slender body theory of Ward (Ref. 20), Bryson (Ref. 21), Sacks (Ref. 22) and others. J. N. Nielsen, in his book *Missile Aerodynamics* (Ref. 23), states his belief that modern slender body theory, which includes both finned missiles and rotationally symmetric projectiles, is the backbone of missile aerodynamics. The same statement could well be made for the general class of modern projectiles commonly encountered in exterior ballistics.

The development of high-energy smokeless propellants in the early years of the twentieth century pushed the velocities of projectiles up to high supersonic speeds. Again, scientific knowledge lagged far behind the progress being made along experimental lines. Modern development of axisymmetric supersonic flow theory did not begin until about 1930, with the work of von Kármán and Moore (Ref. 24), and Taylor and Maccoll (Ref. 25). By 1937, Courant and Hilbert (Ref. 26) had outlined a method for solving the differential equations for the supersonic flow of air past planar and axisymmetric bodies, but the extreme tediousness of the numerical calculations discouraged all attempts at solutions, except for elementary shapes. The German school of Prandtl, Busemann, Sauer, Tollmien, Guderley and others had developed approximate graphical methods of solution in the decade immediately before the Second World War. The U. S. and British efforts were primarily directed toward linearization of the hydrodynamical equations. Linearization permits closed-form analytical solutions of the approximate equations, and are usually restricted to small disturbances and limited Mach number regions. However, the analytical solutions provide insight into the physical nature of the flow, and are therefore useful, even though some accuracy has been sacrificed.

The advent of high speed electronic digital computers after the Second World War shifted the emphasis to numerical solutions of the exact hydrodynamical equations. In 1950, Clippinger and Gerber (Ref. 27) programmed the ENIAC computer at BRL to solve supersonic flowfields past projectiles by the method of characteristics, and computational aerodynamics at last began to catch up with experimental results.

1.7 EXTERIOR BALLISTICS RESEARCH DURING THE SECOND WORLD WAR

The beginning of the Second World War spawned an unprecedented growth in science and technology. The science of exterior ballistics experienced rapid progress as a direct result of three particular wartime developments: (1) fully operational supersonic wind tunnels, (2) free-flight spark photography ranges, and (3) high speed electronic computers. Supersonic wind tunnels permitted direct measurements of the static aerodynamic forces and moments acting on high speed projectiles; the effects of parametric variations in projectile shape were readily investigated with the new wind tunnel facilities. Spark photography ranges permitted the precise, interference-free measurement of the drag, spin, yaw and swerve of a projectile in flight; with the help of the complete ballistic theory simultaneously advanced by Kelley and McShane, all significant aerodynamic forces and moments acting on the projectile could be determined from a set of firings through the spark photography range. The high-speed electronic computer was an enormous help in the reduction and analysis of both wind tunnel and spark photography range data; in addition, the electronic computer rapidly solved both the ordinary differential equations of the projectile's trajectory, and the partial differential equations of the flowfield around the projectile.

German and U. S. research in exterior ballistics during the Second World War were essentially parallel efforts, with the German development leading the U. S. initially; the U. S. effort caught up, and surpassed the German technology by the end of the war. Germany had several operational supersonic blowdown wind tunnels, and a number of good subsonic tunnels early in the war; the U. S. effort was directed toward closed-return, continuous-flow supersonic wind tunnels, which are much more expensive to build, but allow more efficient operation. The Weapons Institute of the Hermann Göring Luftwaffe Research Establishment constructed a spark photography range at Braunschweig, Germany, which was larger in size but less precise in instrumentation than the Aerodynamics Range at BRL. The German spark range facility used break-wire technology for initiating the spark light sources, and the outdated Boulengé chronograph was used for velocity measurement. The director of the range facility, Karl Schussler, described the range operation and instrumentation (Ref. 28) in a 1942 technical report. Although a number of spark stations were planned, only eight had been completed and installed by the end of the war, and the German spark photography range was never fully utilized for its intended purpose as an aerodynamics research facility.

The first spark shadowgraph of a projectile in flight was taken by E. Mach of Germany in 1885. In 1893, the British physicist V. Boys improved on Mach's technique, by means of a pure shadow process without lenses or mirrors. The late nineteenth century investigators used either the muzzle blast or the recoil of the gun to trigger the electric spark discharge, and they could obtain only one shadowgraph, near the muzzle, for each shot fired. The British built a small research spark photography range in 1924, at their National Physical Laboratory. This range was 150 feet long, used break-wire triggering, and eventually had nineteen spark photography stations. Around 1938, Kent attempted to construct a spark photography range at Aberdeen Proving Ground, in which a succession of downrange shadowgraphs could be obtained for each shot fired. Kent used the recoil of the gun to initiate a succession of electronic trigger pulses, which would discharge the sequence of sparks at the proper times. The method did not work, but an important result was obtained from this experiment; the projectile itself would have to electronically trigger the spark discharge at each station, before a reliable spark photography range could be built.

The six fundamental requirements for a modern ballistic spark photography range were apparent by 1940: (1) a light source one-millionth of a second in duration and of sufficient intensity to expose a photographic plate, (2) syncronization of the triggering of the light source with the passage of the projectile to be photographed, (3) no interference with the free flight of the projectile, (4) an array of photographic stations arranged along the trajectory in sufficient density to provide useful data, (5) a survey technique to locate the position of each station along the trajectory to an accuracy of 0.01 inch (note that the distance survey for very large ranges does not have to be quite this accurate), and (6) a chronograph system to record the times of the spark discharges to an accuracy of one-millionth of a second.

Colonel H. H. Zornig and Kent assigned the task of the design and construction of such a range to A. C. Charters, on his arrival at the BRL. Charters' efforts were successful, and the BRL Aerodynamics Range was first put into operation in 1943. A number of ballistic spark photography ranges are in current use today, in the U. S., Canada, and Europe; all of these trace their ancestry to A. C. Charters' pioneering efforts during the Second World War.

Figure 1.10 is a photograph of the original BRL Aerodynamics Range (circa 1943), looking uprange toward the gun firing position, and it shows the first six operational spark photography stations. By 1958, the range looked as shown in Figure 1.11 (looking downrange), with much improved instrumentation, and many more spark stations added. The row of cylindrical cans to the left of the stations are the spark light sources, and the square frames in front of the stations support coils of fine electrical wire, used for electrostatic triggering. Today, infra-red light screens have replaced the electrostatic inductance coils, and even more stations have been added.

Figure 1.12 illustrates the local and master coordinate systems used in the BRL Aerodynamics Range. The mirror at each station enables both horizontal and vertical shadowgraphs to be obtained from a single spark light source.

Several spark shadowgraphs from the BRL Aerodynamics Range, showing the flowfields around typical research projectile shapes, are illustrated in Figures 1.13 through 1.22. Figure 1.13 is

Figure 1.10 Photograph of original BRL Aerodynamics Range, 1944.

Figure 1.11 Photograph of BRL Aerodynamics Range, 1958.

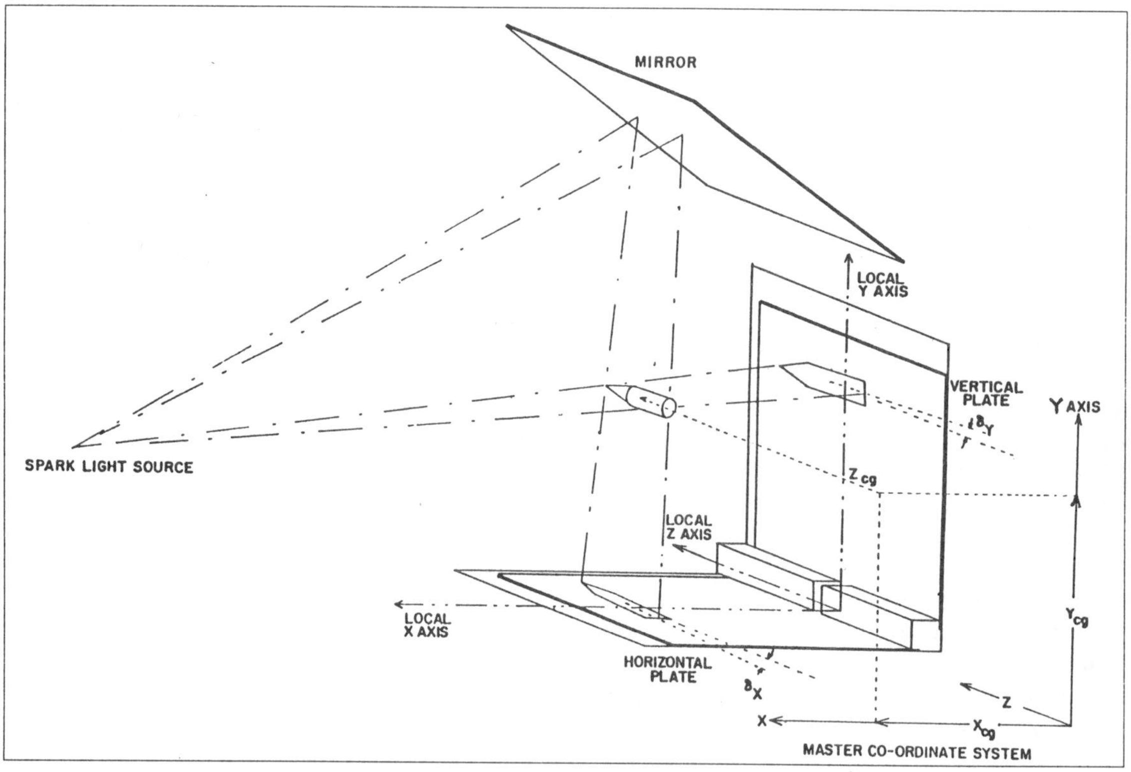

Figure 1.12 Coordinate System for the BRL Aerodynamics Range.

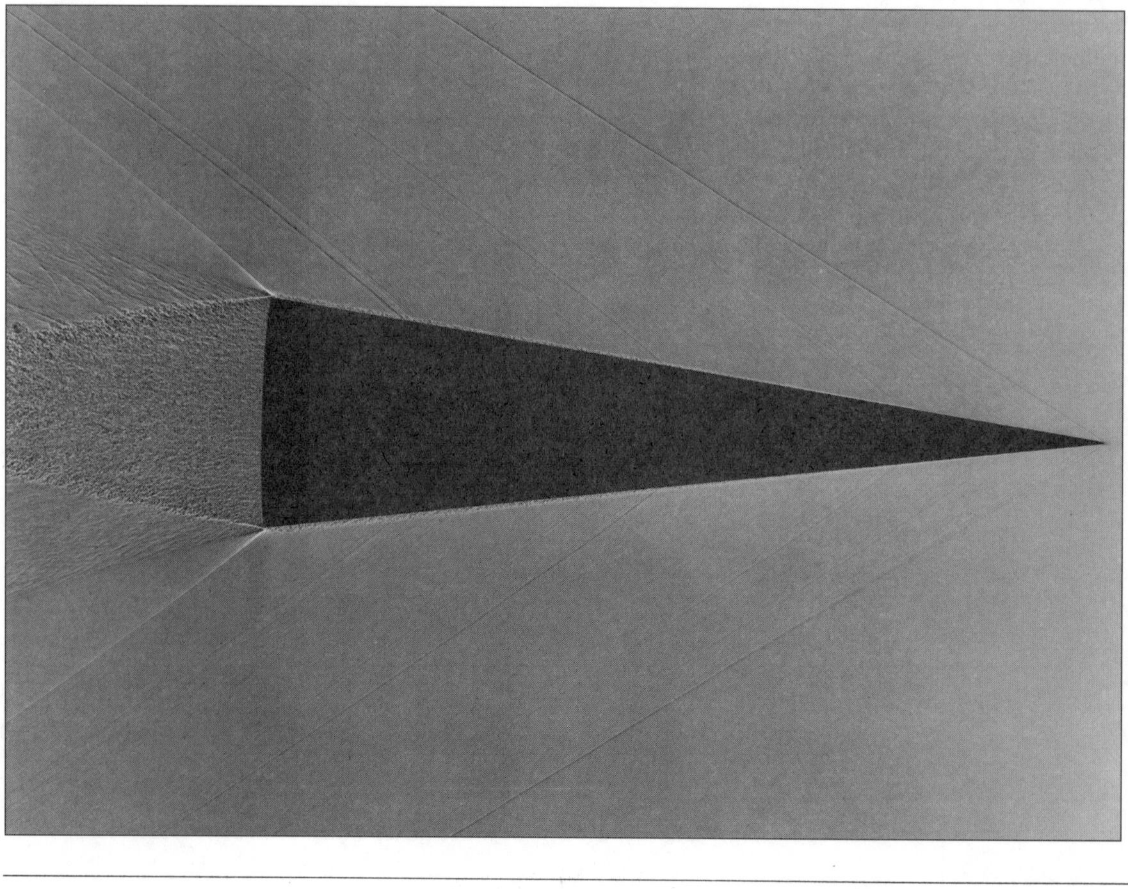

Figure 1.13 Shadowgraph of 3.8 Caliber Long Cone at Mach 1.98.

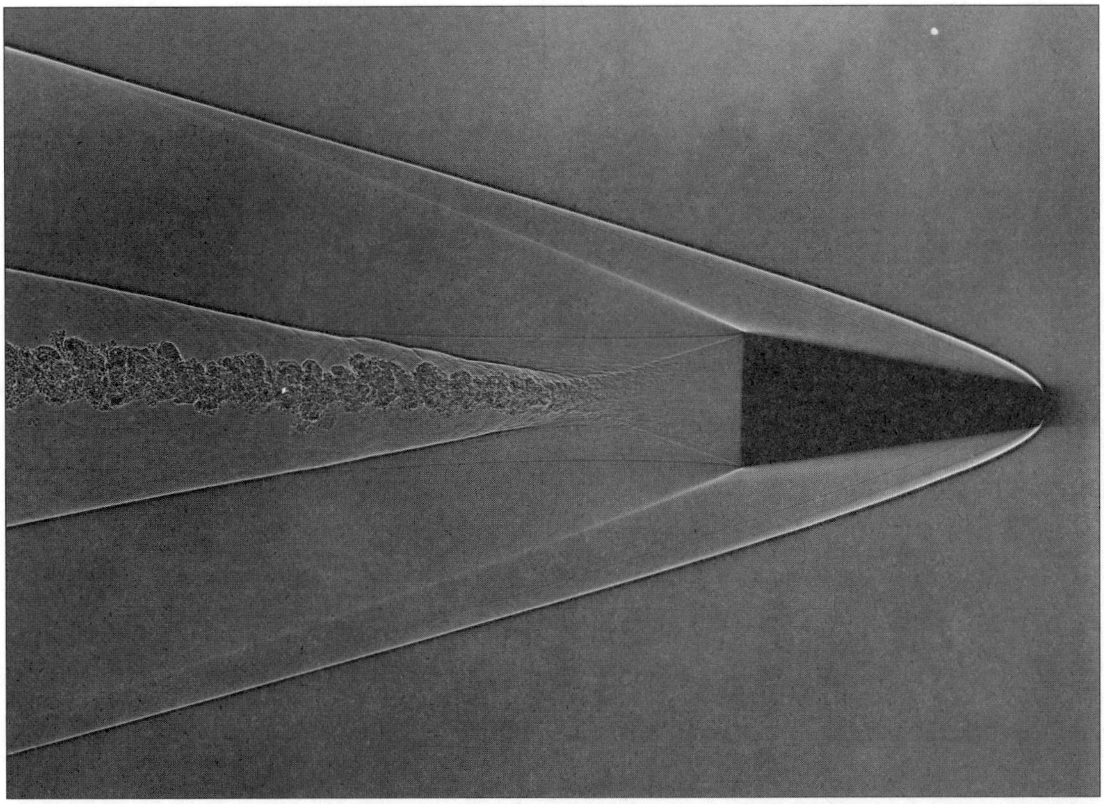

Figure 1.14 Shadowgraph of Spherically Blunted Cone at Mach 4.2.

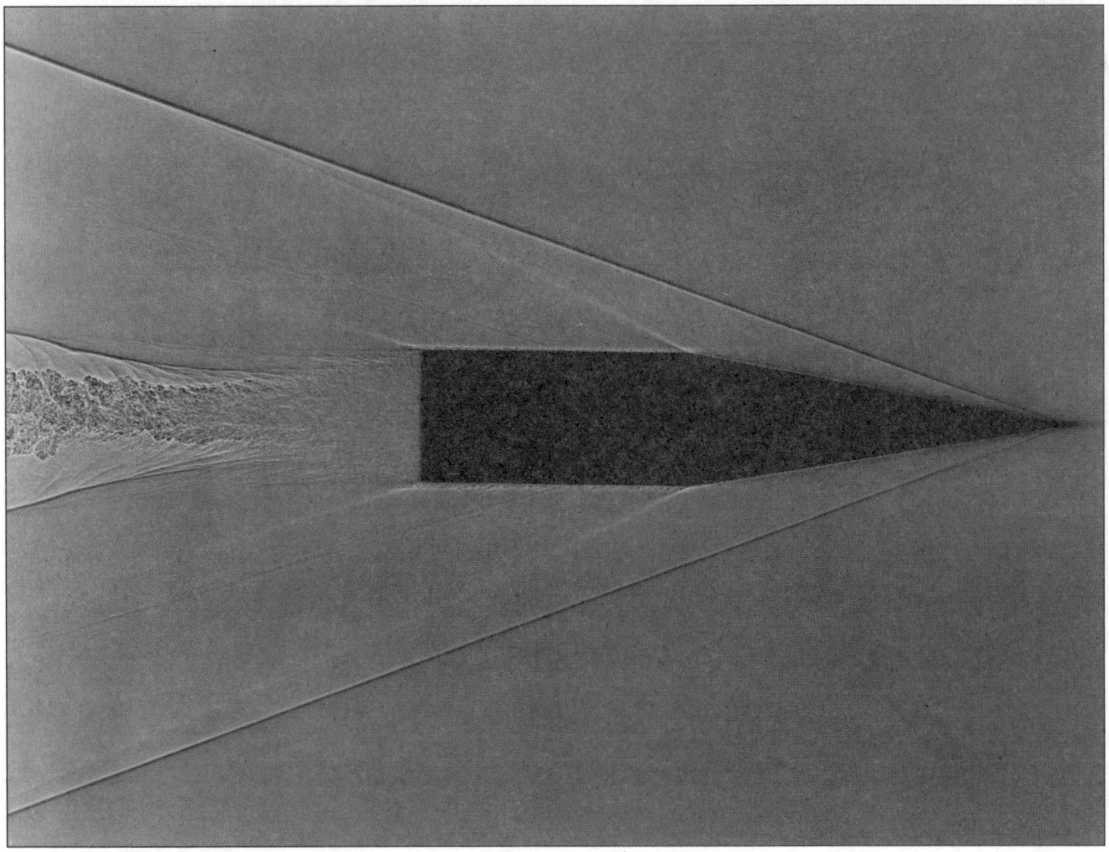

Figure 1.15 Shadowgraph of 5.12 Caliber Long Cone-Cylinder at Mach 3.43.

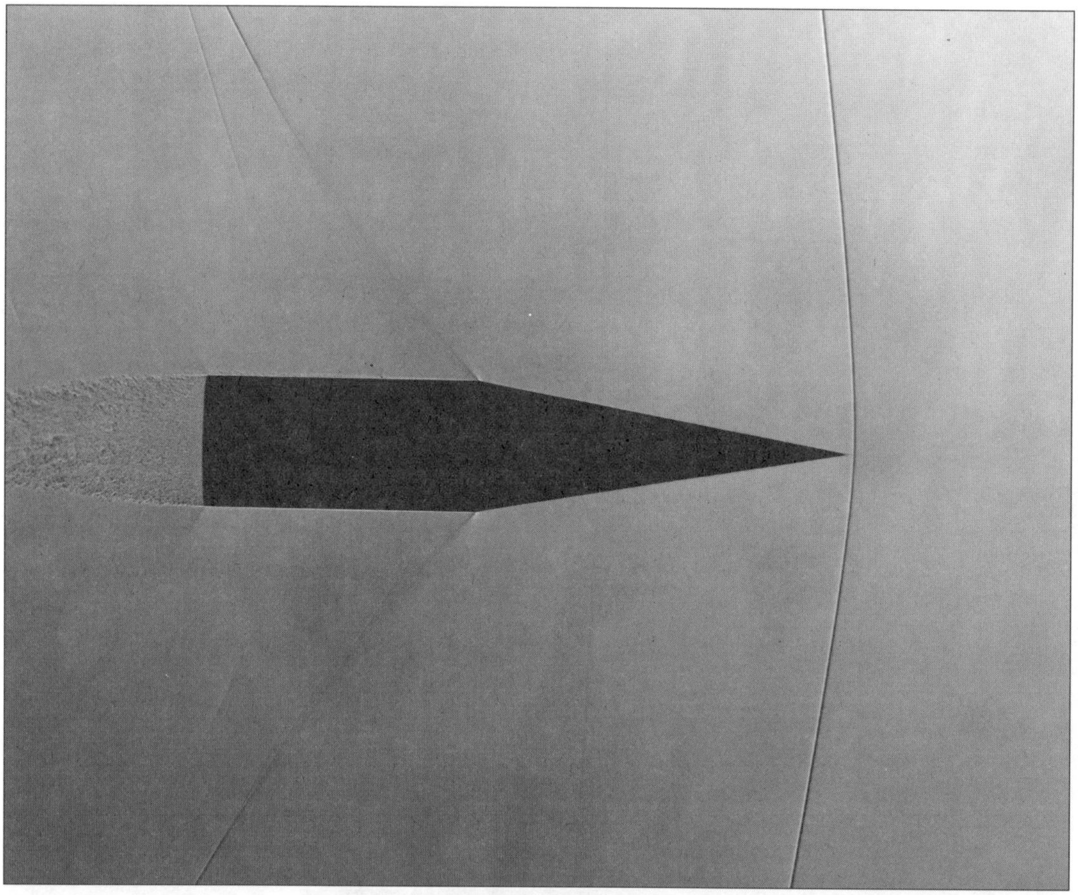

Figure 1.16 Shadowgraph of 5.12 Caliber Long Cone-Cylinder at Mach 1.02.

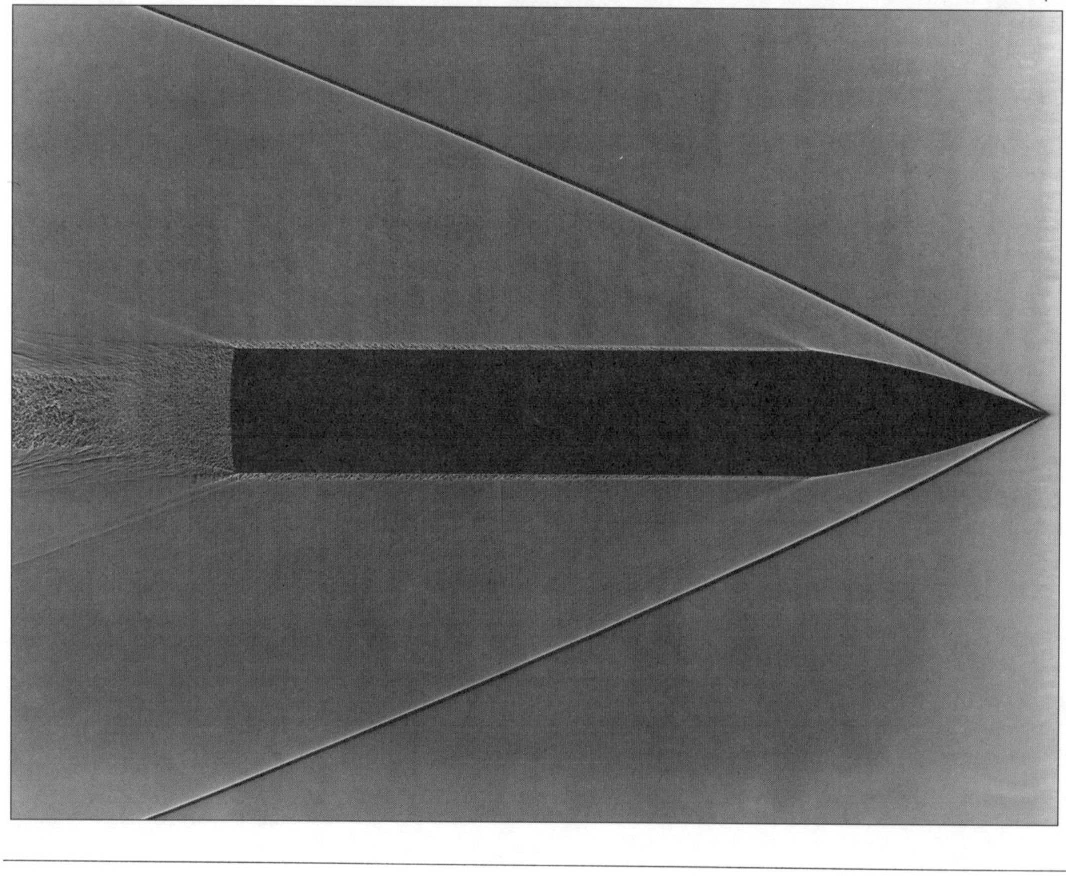

Figure 1.17 Shadowgraph of 7 Caliber ANSR with 2 Caliber Nose at Mach 3.18.

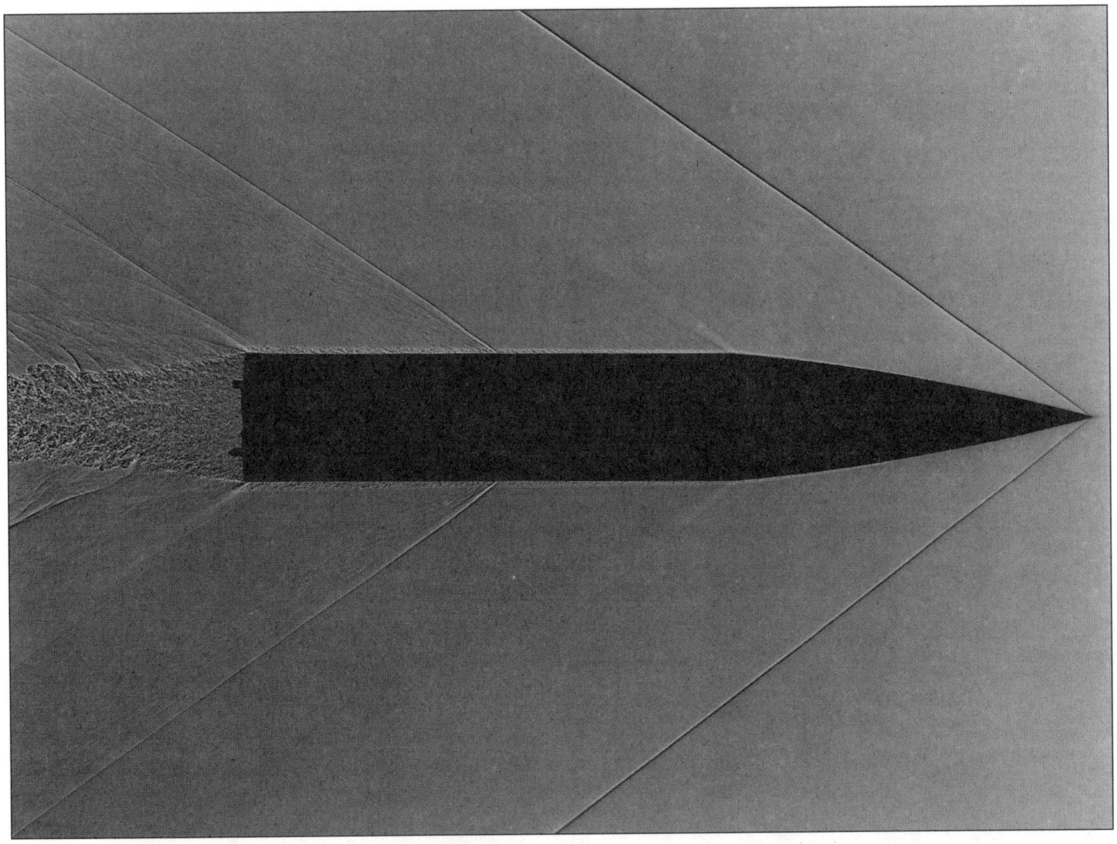

Figure 1.18 Shadowgraph of 7 Caliber ANSR with 3 Caliber Nose at Mach 1.83.

a shadowgraph of a pointed right-circular cone, whose base diameter is 37mm and whose length is 3.8 calibers, at Mach 1.98. Note the conical bow shock attached to the pointed tip of the cone. The boundary layer is laminar along the cone surface for about one caliber, then transition to a turbulent boundary layer occurs (looks like tiny bubbles). The thickness of the boundary layer grows with increasing distance along the projectile. The wake behind the cone is a region of turbulent free shear flow, and the pressure in the wake is below free stream static pressure, which gives rise to base drag.

Figure 1.14 shows the flowfield around a spherically blunted cone at Mach 4.2. Note the high curvature of the strong bow shock wave near the rounded tip of the cone, and the diminishing shock curvature far downstream of the tip. A second strong shock wave occurs at the neck of the wake, a little over one caliber downstream of the base; the wake shock returns the supersonic flow outside the wake back to the streamwise direction.

Figures 1.15 and 1.16 illustrate the flowfields around a 5.12 caliber long, sharp pointed cone-cylinder projectile at Mach 3.43 and 1.02, respectively. Note the pronounced differences in shock wave patterns as the flow changes from high to very low supersonic speed.

Figure 1.17 is a shadowgraph of the 7 caliber long Army-Navy Spinner Rocket (ANSR) model, at Mach 3.18. This projectile has a 2 caliber long pointed secant ogive nose, and a 5 caliber long cylindrical afterbody. Note the thick turbulent boundary layer near the base of this 20mm diameter model. Figure 1.18, taken at Mach 1.83, shows the flowfield around a modified 7 caliber ANSR model, with a 3 caliber long pointed secant ogive nose, and a 4 caliber long afterbody. Note the weak shock about halfway back along the cylindrical afterbody; this shock is caused by a bi-metallic joint in the model. Also note the two small pins protruding from the base of this model; these roll pins are used to measure the spin of the projectile as it travels downrange.

Figure 1.19 shows the flowfield around a 7/8 inch diameter smooth steel sphere, at Mach 1.24. Note the very strong, detached, curved bow shock wave in front of the sphere. The boundary layer separates just aft of the equatorial plane (the plane perpendicular to the flight path, containing the maximum diameter of the sphere), and a weak oblique shock wave forms at the boundary layer separation point. Almost the entire rear hemisphere lies in the turbulent wake. Note the wake recompression shock about one and one half calibers downstream of the sphere trailing edge.

The flow around a 3 caliber long cylinder (wadcutter) at Mach 1.04 is shown in Figure 1.20. The bow shock wave stands approximately two and one half calibers upstream of the blunt leading edge of the projectile, and there is very little shock curvature. As the flight velocity decreases toward Mach 1.00, the shock will become a true normal shock wave with no curvature, and will move far out in front of the bullet. Note that the sharp leading edge causes the boundary layer to separate immediately behind the upstream face of the blunt wadcutter projectile.

Figure 1.21 is a shadowgraph of the 10 caliber long Basic Finner model, at Mach 1.62. This projectile consists of a 10 caliber long cone-cylinder projectile with four single-wedge, square planform

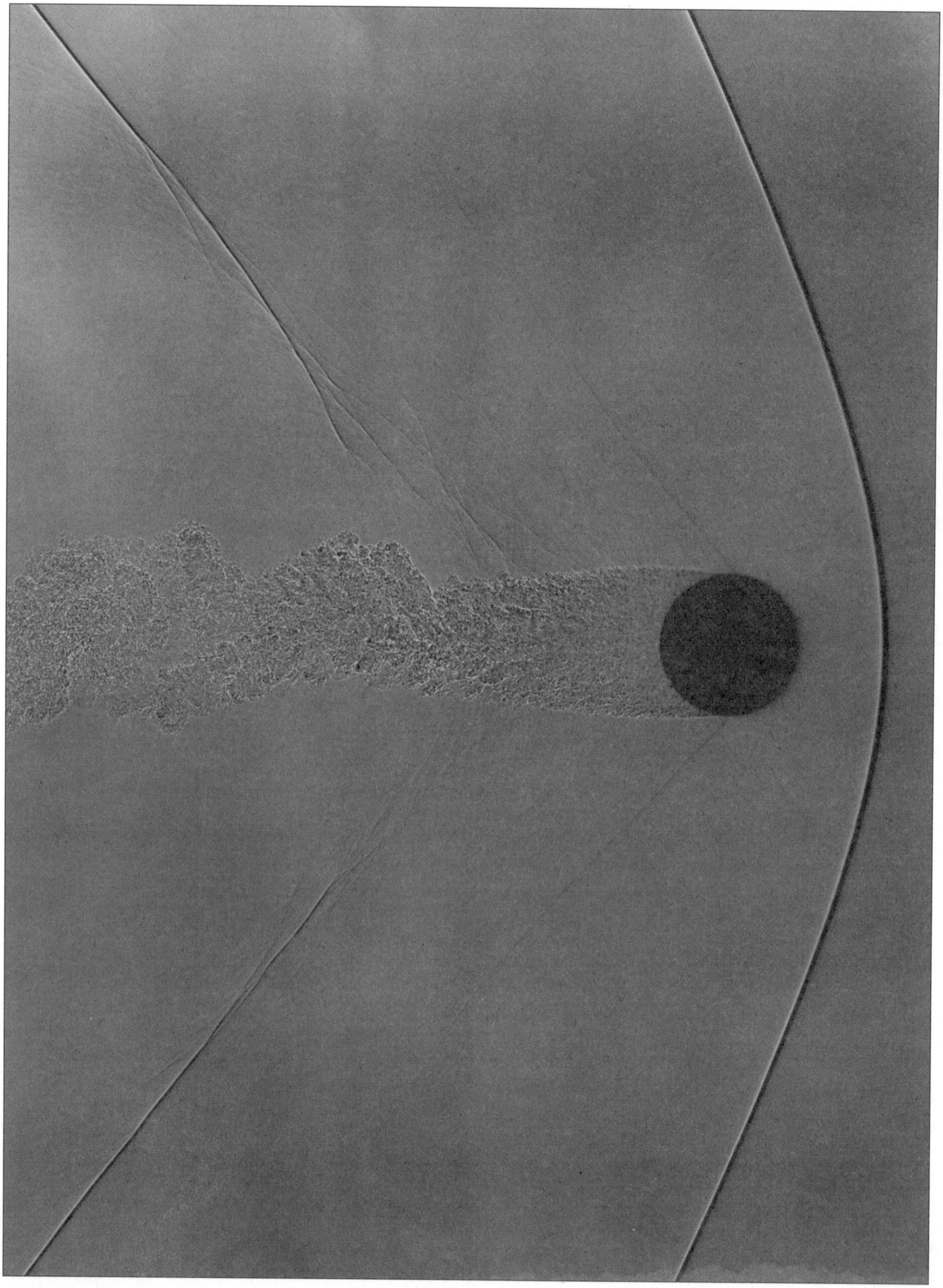

Figure 1.19 Shadowgraph of 7/8 Inch Smooth Sphere at Mach 1.24.

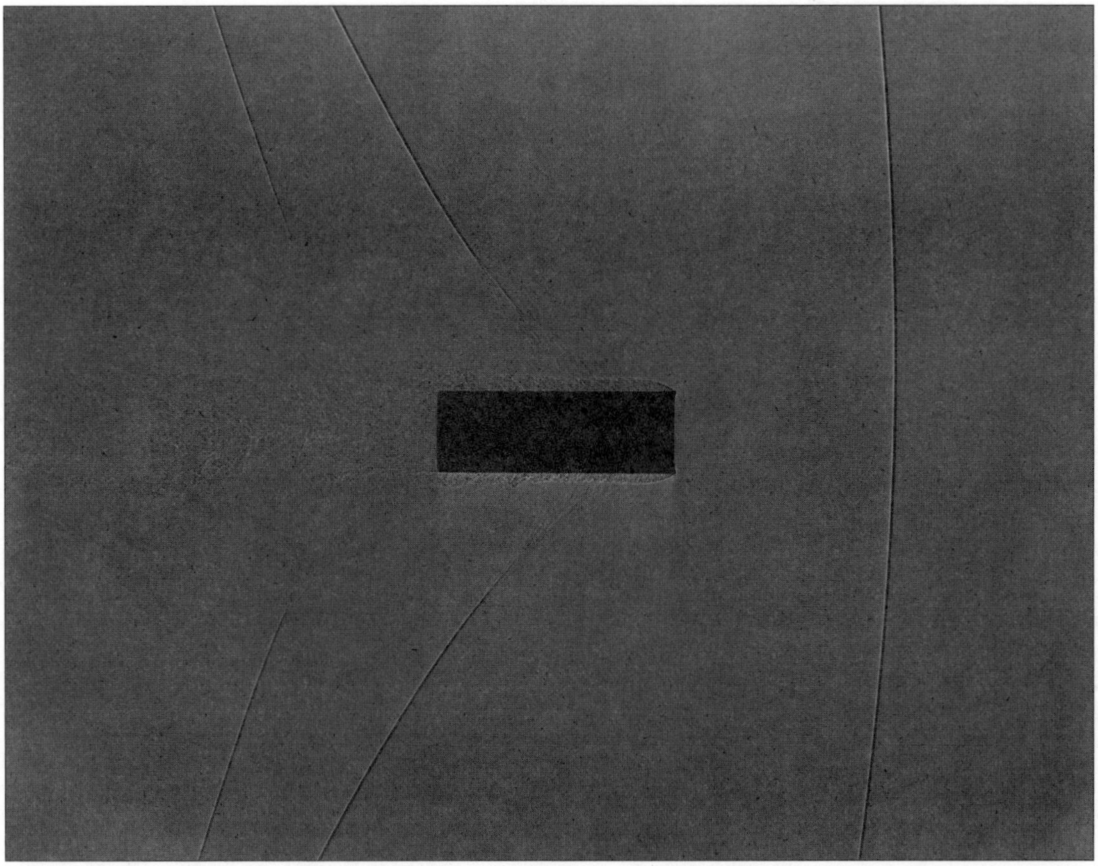

Figure 1.20 Shadowgraph of 3 Caliber Long Cylinder (Wadcutter) at Mach 1.04.

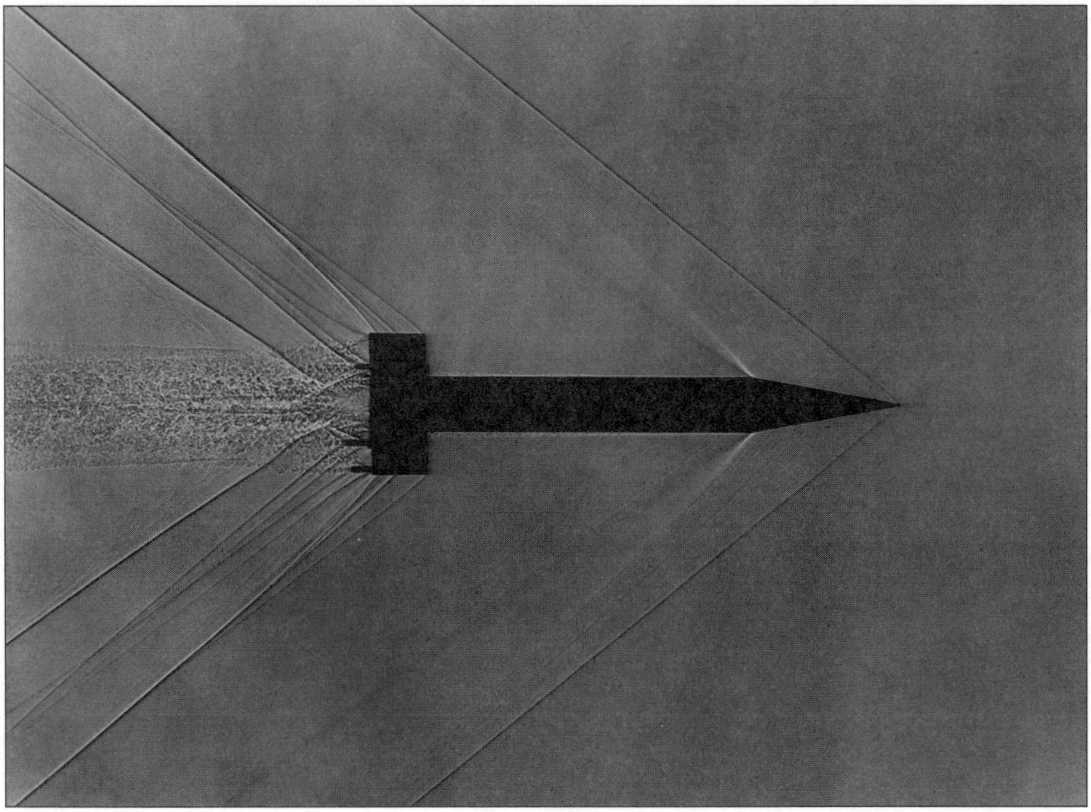

Figure 1.21 Shadowgraph of 10 Caliber Long Basic Finner at Mach 1.62.

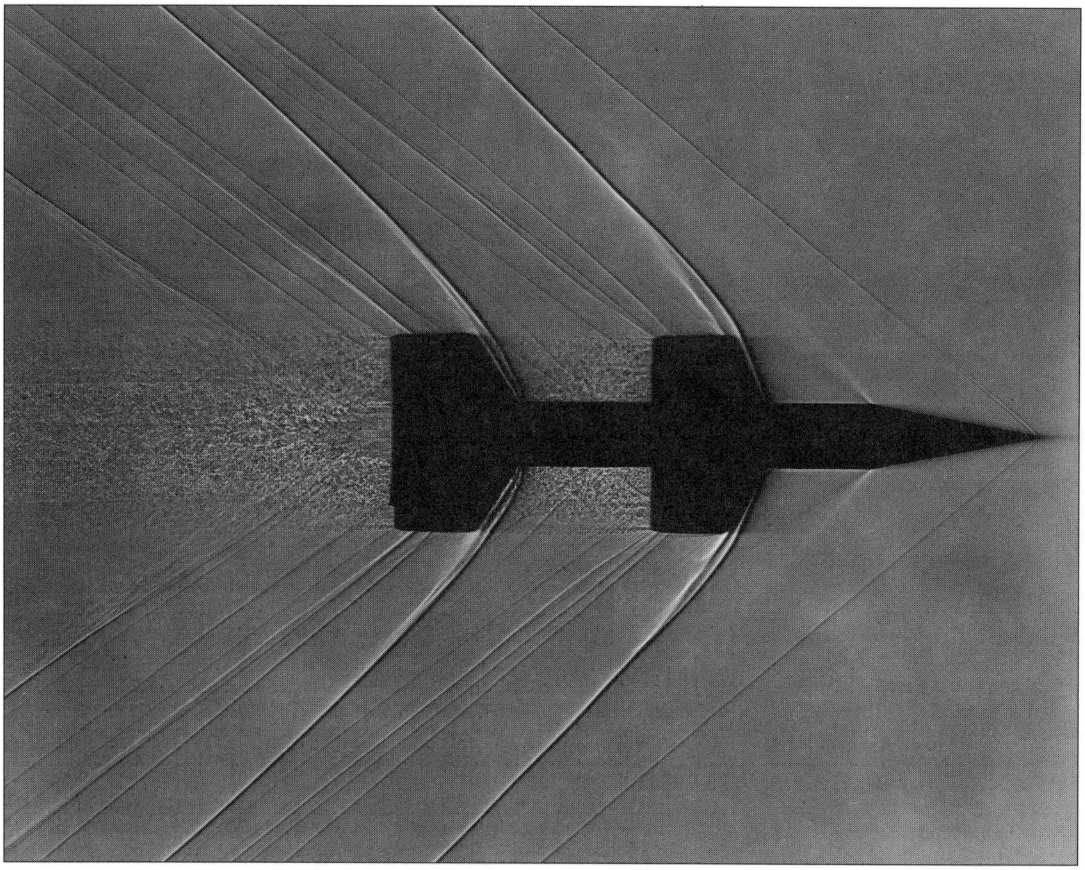

Figure 1.22 Shadowgraph of 20 mm Missile Model with Wings and Fins at Mach 1.6.

fins spaced symmetrically around the aft end of the body, to provide static stability. Note the roll pins protruding from the fin trailing edges (for spin measurement), and the two-dimensional vortex sheets shed into the wake, from the trailing edges of the four fins.

Figure 1.22 is the last shadowgraph in our series; it shows the flowfield at Mach 1.60 around a cone-cylinder guided missile model, with four wings mounted symmetrically around the mid-body, and four tail fins symmetrically spaced around the back end of the cylindrical afterbody. Both wings and fins are often used on guided missiles, to provide movable control surfaces for guidance, as well as the large aerodynamic lift required to execute high speed maneuvers in flight.

The BRL Aerodynamics Range (Ref. 29) is still in continuous operation, and the instrumentation has been progressively improved over the years. The technical characteristics and measurement capability of the range will be discussed in a later chapter. For historical purposes, it is sufficient to state that modern free-flight spark photography ranges routinely achieve an order of magnitude (ten times) higher precision in drag and stability measurements than were possible with solenoid chronographs and yaw-card ranges. The spark photography range has thus evolved into one of the most powerful tools available to the modern exterior ballistician.

The BRL Transonic Range was designed in 1944, and primary construction was finished in 1947. The instrumention was completed, and full scale operation began in the summer of 1950. Photographs of the exterior and interior views of the Transonic Range are shown as Figures 1.23 and 1.24, respectively. The design and operation of the range is described in BRL Report No. 1044, titled *The Transonic Free Flight Range*, published in 1958. This large (22 ft. by 22 ft.) free-flight spark photography range was designed to satisfy von Kármán's ratio for 3-inch diameter projectiles. (Theodore von Kármán had derived the theoretical result, that for no choking at transonic speeds, the ratio of test sectional area to projectile cross-sectional area should be 10,000 to one). Although the range building is 1000 feet long, only 680 feet are fully instrumented. The same basic data reduction methods are used for both of the BRL free-flight spark photography ranges.

In 1940, Professor Theodore von Kármán of the California Institute of Technology, who was a scientific advisor to the BRL during the war, recommended the construction of a wind tunnel at Aberdeen Proving Ground, Maryland, for Ordnance Department ballistic research. Professor von Kármán's proposal was approved, and construction of the new wind tunnel was completed in November 1944. Fitted with both subsonic and supersonic nozzles, the latter capable of test section velocities up to Mach 1.7, the first BRL wind tunnel was promptly put to work in the acquisition of basic aerodynamic design information for bombs, rockets, and other fin-stabilized projectiles.

In 1946, the need for changing test section velocity easily and rapidly from one supersonic level to another had become apparent, and the BRL began construction of a flexible nozzle tunnel. The new wind tunnel was completed late in 1947, and it was the first

Figure 1.23 Photograph of BRL Transonic Range exterior view.

Figure 1.24 Photograph of BRL Transonic Range, interior view.

flexible nozzle, continuous flow tunnel in the world to achieve airspeeds exceeding Mach 4. A schematic of this wind tunnel is shown in Figure 1.25. In 1954, another flexible nozzle wind tunnel was constructed, with a speed range from Mach 1.25 to Mach 5. Figure 1.26 shows the nozzle section of this tunnel with the sidewall removed, to show the throat plates set for Mach 5, and a model of a cone-flare stabilized re-entry vehicle mounted in the test section. In 1961, a hypersonic research tunnel was completed at the BRL. This tunnel used three interchangable fixed nozzles, and operated at speeds of Mach 6.0, Mach 7.5, and Mach 9.2.

The first modern high speed electronic computer, ENIAC (Electronic Numerical Integrator and Computer), was built at the BRL during the Second World War by the Moore School of Electrical Engineering of the University of Pennsylvania, under contract to the U. S. Army Chief of Ordnance. The ENIAC (Ref. 30) was the outgrowth of the pre-war research of a number of mathematicians

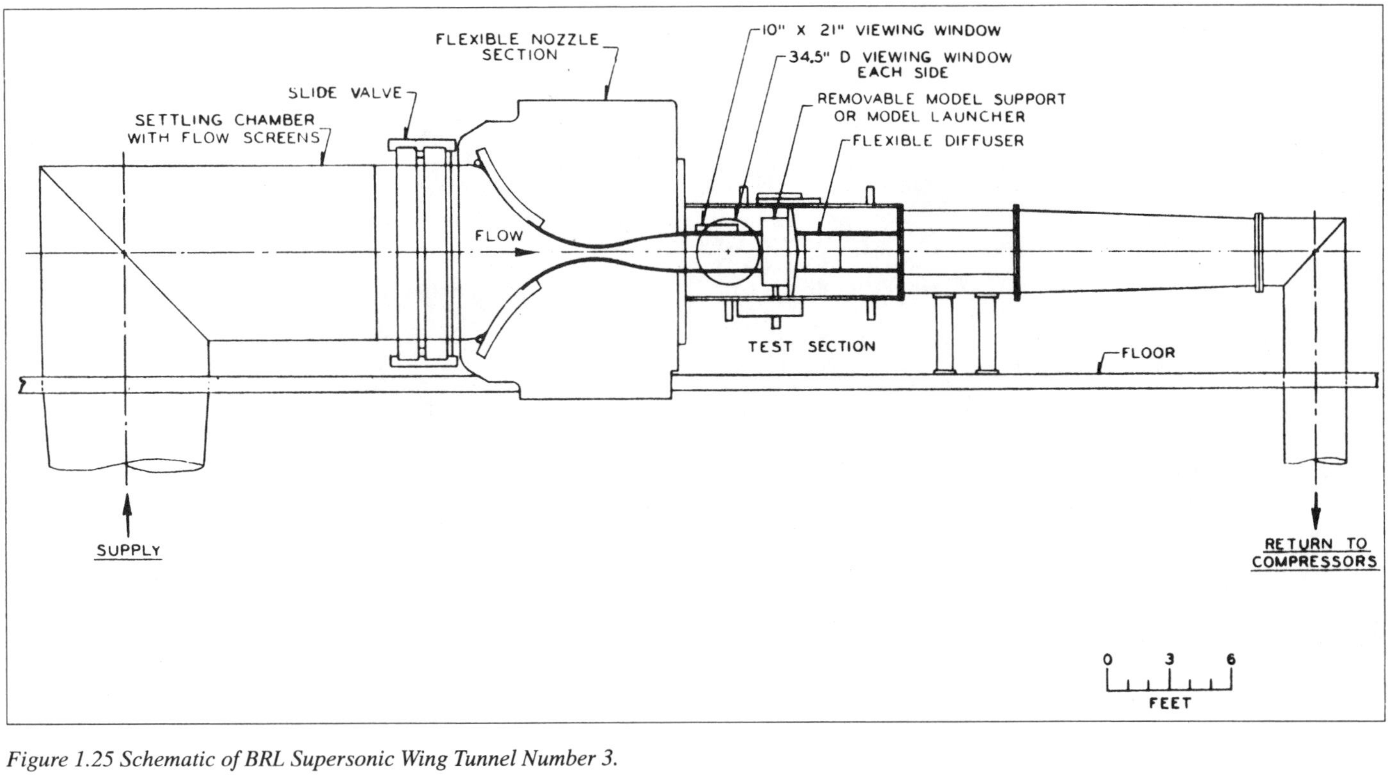

Figure 1.25 Schematic of BRL Supersonic Wing Tunnel Number 3.

and scientists both at the BRL and at several universities. ENIAC was completed in 1945, and was a decimal machine utilizing 19,000 vacuum tubes, 1500 relays, and hundreds of thousands of resistors, capacitors and inductors. It weighed over 30 tons, and consumed nearly 200 kilowatts of electrical power. Although the ENIAC had much less computing power than most modern microcomputers, it was an enormous technical achievement in 1945, and it enabled ballisticians to solve problems that were previously considered impossible.

Larger and faster electronic computers such as EDVAC, ORDVAC and UNIVAC followed the ENIAC, and further expanded the horizons of exterior ballisticians. The first reasonably complete solutions for the supersonic airflow around a projectile were done on the ENIAC, and successive generations of high speed computers permitted solutions of increasingly more difficult problems. Today, supercomputer technology is attacking the most difficult problem in computational aerodynamics: the three-dimensional, time-dependent, compressible Navier-Stokes equations.

1.8 POST-WAR PROGRESS IN EXTERIOR BALLISTICS

The rapid progress in exterior ballistics brought about by the Second World War has continued, and even accelerated during the past fifty years, as a result of the cold war threat. Hypersonic, supersonic, and transonic wind tunnels proliferated throughout the United States Army, Navy, Air Force, the National Aeronautics and Space Administration (NASA), and a number of aircraft companies and universities. Several European countries developed advanced modern wind tunnel facilities. A number of additional spark photography ranges were built, and several nations now have operational spark ranges. High speed digital computer technology has achieved performance beyond the fondest hope of the scientists who developed the ENIAC, and computational aerodynamics has finally caught up with modern experimental capability. Exterior ballistics has become a mature engineering science; it is often referred to today as "aeroballistics."

The Second World War had made the lack of a systematic aerodynamic database painfully obvious to both projectile and missile designers, and the new experimental facilities were quickly employed in a number of basic research programs designed to investigate the effects of configuration changes on the aerodynamic forces and moments in various speed regions. References 31 through 40 are examples of the experimental investigations conducted in free-flight spark photography ranges and supersonic wind tunnels during the two decades after the Second World War. Many additional test programs have been conducted over the years, and a rather substantial aerodynamic database exists today, although some of it is not easy to find unless one knows where to look.

In 1953-54, C. H. Murphy revised and improved both the Kelley-McShane dynamic stability criteria (Ref. 41), and the data reduction techniques for free-flight spark photography ranges (Ref. 42). J. D. Nicolaides introduced the tricyclic theory (Ref.43) in 1953, which accounted for the effect of small configurational or

Figure 1.26 Photograph of BRL Supersonic Wing Tunnel Number 1, with sidewall removed and throat plates set for Mach 5.

mass asymmetries on the epicyclic yawing motion of projectiles. In 1956, Murphy advanced his quasi-linear theory (Ref. 44) which permitted the determination of nonlinear aerodynamic forces and moments from free-flight spark photography range tests. Comparison of the nonlinear spark range measurements with those obtained from large angle of attack testing in wind tunnels showed excellent agreement. The quasi-linear technique was augmented in 1970 by the work of Chapman and Kirk (Ref. 45), who advanced a method of nonlinear spark range data reduction based on numerical integration of the six-degrees-of-freedom differential equations of motion. Good agreement between the two methods has been observed on a number of experimental programs. Modern exterior ballisticians now recognize the fact that the aerodynamic force-moment systems acting on all projectiles are to some extent nonlinear, and current test methodology usually requires the determination of both linear and nonlinear aerodynamic coefficients.

The practical calculation of supersonic flowfields past projectiles was extended by the work of M. D. Van Dyke (Ref. 46) in 1951, and that of Syvertson and Dennis (Ref. 47) in 1955. Van Dyke's second-order supersonic flow theory and Syvertson and Dennis' second-order shock expansion theory are still used today in fast design codes for engineering parametric design studies. Van Driest's theory of turbulent boundary layers in high speed compressible flow (Ref. 48), and Chapman's investigation of base pressure effects (Ref. 49) provided additional tools for the engineer working in computational aerodynamics.

By 1980, the size and speed of digital computers had advanced to the stage at which an attack on the Navier-Stokes equations could be attempted. References 50 through 52 are modern examples of computational aerodynamics using supercomputer technology. Even with the largest and fastest computers available today, many hours of computer time are required to solve a single flowfield past a given configuration.

Since the beginning of exterior ballistics as a science, ballisticians have searched for methods to quickly and accurately estimate the drag and stability of projectiles in flight. Many modern ballisticians do not have access to wind tunnels, spark photography ranges, or large-scale supercomputer facilities, and must therefore rely on estimation methods for projectile design studies. Prior to about 1970 estimation methods in aeroballistics were, for the most part, based on handbook techniques. In 1969, R. H. Whyte of the General Electric Company developed a computer program called "SPINNER," which used empirical correlation of a large data base from twenty-five years of spark photography range firings to provide fast and reasonably accurate estimates of the aerodynamic characteristics of ordnance projectiles. Whyte's computer code was revised and updated in 1973 (Ref. 53), and again in 1979. The SPINNER program is currently incorporated into Whyte's "Projectile Design and Analysis System" (PRODAS) code, which contains several interior and exterior ballistic computer programs.

F. G. Moore, of the Naval Surface Weapons Laboratory at Dahlgren, Virginia, advanced a different method (Ref. 54) in 1972; Moore's approach used an approximate solution of the flowfield past the projectile, with semi-empirical corrections for the second-order effects neglected in the simplified flowfield solution. In 1974, the author developed a computer program called "MCDRAG" (Ref. 55), which was based on the use of aerodynamic similarity laws to correlate a large volume of high-quality drag coefficient data, accumulated over thirty years of firings in the BRL spark photography ranges.

Moore's computer code (AP95) has now evolved into a general predictive method (Ref. 56-58) for either fin or spin stabilized projectiles. References 59 and 60 are additional examples of modern data-based aeroprediction codes. All of the above computer programs are referred to today as "fast design codes," because they run quickly even on very small computers, and provide reasonably accurate estimates that are useful in projectile design studies.

The calculation of a projectile's trajectory was the classical exterior ballistics problem, and the entire modern science of exterior ballistics has evolved because of a continuous need to improve the accuracy of trajectory calculations. The vacuum trajectory, which assumed gravity was the only significant force acting on the projectile, was superseded by the Siacci method which, although restricted to flat fire, did account for the effect of aerodynamic drag. The Siacci method was, in turn, replaced by numerical integration of the point-mass differential equations, after the Second World War.

By 1960, the size and speed of digital computers had advanced to a level that permitted the first practical modern six-degrees-of-freedom (6-DOF) trajectory calculations. The 6-DOF trajectory calculation numerically solves six simultaneous second-order differential equations, to yield a complete description of the position, velocity, time, and angular (pitching, yawing and spinning) motion of the projectile, from the muzzle of the gun to the target. 6-DOF trajectory programs have proliferated throughout the exterior ballistics community today, and are routinely used in ordnance engineering.

Modern 6-DOF trajectory calculations, based on measured physical properties, complete aerodynamic forces and moments, and all required initial conditions, have demonstrated excellent agreement with the results of numerous instrumented field firings. There are, of course, many situations in which the older methods are entirely sufficient for all practical purposes. One broad class for which this is generally true are the small-yaw, flat-fire trajectories typical of ground-launched small arms. However, if the rifle or machine gun is to be fired sideways from a high-speed aircraft, the consequent large-yaw flight cannot be correctly calculated by any method less sophisticated than a complete 6-DOF trajectory program. Artillery and mortar fire at very high gun elevation angles also require 6-DOF calculations, although simpler methods are sufficiently accurate for artillery shell fired at lower angles of departure.

1.9 FUTURE DEVELOPMENTS

Exterior ballistics has made great progress over the three centuries of its scientific existence. More progress has been achieved in the last fifty years than occurred in all previous centuries, as is true of most modern engineering sciences. It is interesting to speculate about the future of exterior ballistics. New technologies such as laser holography and the electronic shadowgraph hold the promise of automated data collection and reduction for free-flight ballistic ranges. Computational aerodynamics is waiting for the next generation of supercomputers to permit complete flowfield solutions in minutes instead of the many hours now required. The current trend in gun-launched munitions is toward ever-increasing muzzle velocities, and exterior ballisticians of the future will have to devise new experimental facilities to test hypervelocity projectiles.

Exterior ballisticians have traditionally focused their efforts on unguided, rigid, rotationally symmetric, single-body projectiles. Future work in this field will expand into such areas as (a) maneuvering (also called "smart") projectiles, with in-flight course corrections, (b) high angle of attack flight, (c) sub-munition dispensing and dispersal, and (d) the aeroballistics of complex multi-body systems. Whatever the future may bring, it is hoped that exterior ballisticians of the twenty-first century will find the career field as exciting and challenging as have those of us fortunate enough to have worked in exterior ballistics in the last half of the twentieth century.

REFERENCES

1. Becker, K., and C. Cranz, "Messungen Uber den Luftwiderstand für Grosse Geschwindigkeiten," Artilleristische Monatshefte, 1912, II.

2. Ingalls, J. M., *Ingalls' Ballistic Tables, Artillery Circular M*, U.S. Army Ordnance Board, ~~1893~~ 1900 (Revised 1917).

3. Hatcher, J. S., *Hatcher's Notebook*, Second Edition, The Stackpole Company, 1957.

4. *Exterior Ballistic Tables Based on Numerical Integration*, Ordnance Department, U. S. Army, 1924.

5. Herrmann, E. E., *Range and Ballistic Tables*, U. S. Naval Ordnance, 1926 (Revised 1930, 1935).

6. *Ballistic Tables, 1909*, War Office, England, 1909.

7. Jones, F. W., *The Hodsock Ballistic Tables for Rifles*, Edward Arnold & Company, London, 1925.

8. Burrard, G., *Notes on Sporting Rifles*, Edward Arnold & Company, London, 4th Edition, 1953.

9. *Textbook of Small Arms*, War Office, England, 1929.

10. Hitchcock, H. P., "Resistance Functions of Various Types of Projectiles," Ballistic Research Laboratories Report No. 27, 1935.

11. *Ballistic Tables, 1940*, External Ballistics Department, Ordnance Board, War Office, England, 1940.

12. Mann, F. W., *The Bullet's Flight from Powder to Target*, Munn & Company, New York, New York, 1909. (Reprinted 1942, 1952).

13. Fowler, R. H., E. G. Gallop, C. N. H. Lock and H. W. Richmond, "The Aerodynamics of a Spinning Shell," *Philosophical Transactions of the Royal Society of London*, Series A, Volume 221, 1920; Part II, ibid., Series A, Volume 222, 1922.

14. Nielsen, K. L., and J. L. Synge, "On the Motion of a Spinning Shell," Ballistic Research Laboratories Report No. X-116, 1943.

15. Kent, R. H., "An Elementary Treatment of the Motion of a Spinning Projectile About its Center of Gravity," Ballistic Research Laboratories Report No. 85, 1937.

16. Kelley, J. L., and E. J. McShane, "On the Motion of a Projectile With Small or Slowly Changing Yaw," Ballistic Research Laboratories Report No. 446, 1944.

17. McShane, E. J., J. L. Kelley, and F. V. Reno, *Exterior Ballistics*, University of Denver Press, 1953.

18. Prandtl, L., "Ueber Fluesigkeitsbewegung bei sehr kliener Reibung," *Proceedings of the Third International Mathematics Congress*, Heidelberg, Germany, 1904.

19. Munk, M. M., "The Aerodynamic Forces on Airship Hulls," National Advisory Committee for Aeronautics Technical Report No. 184, 1924.

20. Ward, G. N., "Supersonic Flow Past Slender Pointed Bodies," *Quarterly Journal of Mechanics and Applied Mathematics*, Vol. 2, Part 1, 1949.

21. Bryson, A. E., Jr., "Evaluation of the Inertia Coefficients of the Cross-Section of a Slender Body," *Journal of the Aeronautical Sciences*, Vol. 21, No. 6, 1954.

22. Sacks, A. H., "Aerodynamic Forces, Moments, and Stability Derivatives for Slender Bodies of General Cross Section," National Advisory Committee for Aeronautics Technical Note No. 3283, 1954.

23. Nielsen, J. N., *Missile Aerodynamics*, McGraw-Hill Book Company, Inc., 1960.

24. von Kármán, T., and N. B. Moore, "Resistance of Slender Bodies Moving with Supersonic Velocities, with Special Reference to Projectiles," *Transactions of the American Society of Mechanical Engineers (Applied Mechanics)*, 54, 1932.

25. Taylor, G. I., and J. W. Maccoll, "The Air Pressure on a Cone Moving at High Speeds," *Proceedings of the Royal Society of London*, Series A, Volume 139, 1933.

26. Courant, R., and D. Hilbert, *Methoden der Mathematischen Physik, II*, Julius Springer, Berlin, 1937.

27. Clippinger, R. F., and N. Gerber, "Supersonic Flow Over Bodies of Revolution (With Special Reference to High Speed Computing)," Ballistic Research Laboratories Report No. 719, 1950.

28. Schussler, K., "Die Ballistischen Versuchs-und Messenlagen der Luftfahrtforschungsanstalt Hermann Göring," *Deutsche Akademie der Luftfahrtforschung*, Berlin, 1942.

29. Braun, W. F., "The Free Flight Aerodynamics Range," Ballistic Research Laboratories Report No. 1048, 1958.

30. "The ENIAC Story," *Ordnance*, January-February, 1961.

31. Murphy, C. H., and L. E. Schmidt, "The Effect of Length on the Aerodynamic Characteristics of Bodies of Revolution in Supersonic Flight," Ballistic Research Laboratories Report No. 876, 1953.

32. Dickinson, E. R., "Some Aerodynamic Effects of Headshape Variation at Mach Number 2.44," Ballistic Research Laboratories Memorandum Report No. 838, 1954.

33. Dickinson, E. R., "The Effect of Boattailing on the Drag Coefficient of Cone-Cylinder Projectiles at Supersonic Velocities," Ballistic Research Laboratories Memorandum Report No. 842, 1954.

34. Buford, W. E., "The Effects of Afterbody Length and Mach Number on the Normal Force and Center of Pressure of Conical and Ogival Nose Bodies," *Journal of the Aeronautical Sciences*, Vol. 25, No. 2, 1958.

35. Schmidt, L. E., "The Dynamic Properties of Pure Cones and Cone Cylinders," Ballistic Research Laboratories Memorandum Report No. 759, 1954.

36. MacAllister, L. C., "The Aerodynamic Properties of a Simple Non-Rolling Finned Cone-Cylinder Configuration Between Mach Numbers 1.0 and 2.5," Ballistic Research Laboratories Report No. 934, 1955.

37. Perkins, E. W., L. H. Jorgensen and S. C. Sommer, "Investigation of the Drag of Various Axially Symmetric Nose Shapes of Fineness Ratio 3 for Mach Numbers from 1.24 to 7.4," National Advisory Committee for Aeronautics Report No. 1386, 1958.

38. Dickinson, E. R., "Some Aerodynamic Effects of Blunting a Projectile Nose," Ballistic Research Laboratories Memorandum Report No. 1596, 1964.

39. Dickinson, E. R., "Some Aerodynamic Effects of Varying the Body Length and Head Length of a Spinning Projectile," Ballistic Research Laboratories Memorandum Report No. 1664, 1965.

40. Karpov, B. G., "The Effect of Various Boattail Shapes on Base Pressure and Other Aerodynamic Characteristics of a 7-Caliber Long Body of Revolution at M=1.70," Ballistic Research Laboratories Report No. 1295, 1965.

41. Murphy, C. H., "On Stability Criteria of the Kelley-McShane Linearized Theory of Yawing Motion," Ballistic Research Laboratories Report No. 853, 1953.

42. Murphy, C. H., "Data Reduction for the Free Flight Spark Ranges," Ballistic Research Laboratories Report No. 900, 1954.

43. Nicolaides, J. D., "On the Free Flight Motion of Missiles Having Slight Configurational Asymmetries," Ballistic Research Laboratories Report No. 858, 1953.

44. Murphy, C. H., "The Measurement of Non-Linear Forces and Moments by Means of Free Flight Tests," Ballistic Research Laboratories Report No. 974, 1956.

45. Chapman, G. T., and D. B. Kirk, "A Method of Extracting Aerodynamic Coefficients from Free-Flight Data," AIAA Journal, 8, No. 4, 1970.

46. Van Dyke, M. D., "First and Second Order Theory of Supersonic Flow Past Bodies of Revolution," *Journal of the Aeronautical Sciences*, Vol. 18, No. 3, 1951.

47. Syvertson, C. A., and D. H. Dennis, "A Second-Order Shock Expansion Method Applicable to Bodies of Revolution Near Zero Lift," National Advisory Committee for Aeronautics Technical Report No. 1328, 1955.

48. Van Driest, E. R., "Turbulent Boundary Layers in Compressible Fluids," *Journal of the Aeronautical Sciences*, Vol. 18, No. 3, 1951.

49. Chapman, D. R., "An Analysis of Base Pressure at Supersonic Velocities and Comparison With Experiment," National Advisory Committee for Aeronautics Report No. 1051, 1951.

50. Sturek, W. B., "Application of CFD to the Aerodynamics of Spinning Shell," AIAA Paper 84.0323, 1984.

51. Nietubicz, C. J., and W. B. Sturek, "Navier-Stokes Code Verification for Projectile Configurations at Supersonic and Transonic Velocities," AIAA Paper No. 88-1995, AIAA 15th Aerodynamic Testing Conference, 1988.

52. Patel, N. R., W. B. Sturek and G. A. Smith, "Parallel Computation of Supersonic Flows Using a Three-Dimensional, Zonal, Navier-Stokes Code," Ballistic Research Laboratory Technical Report No. BRL-TR-3049, 1989.

53. Whyte, R. H., "SPIN-73, An Updated Version of the SPINNER Computer Program," Picatinny Arsenal Contractor Report TR-4588, 1973.

54. Moore, F. G., "Body Alone Aerodynamics of Guided and Unguided Projectiles at Subsonic, Transonic and Supersonic Mach Numbers," Naval Weapons Laboratory Technical Report TR-2796, 1972.

55. McCoy, R. L., "MCDRAG - A Computer Program for Estimating the Drag Coefficients of Projectiles," Ballistic Research Laboratories Technical Report ARBRL-TR-02293, 1981.

56. Moore, F. G., R. M. McInville, and T. Hymer, "The 1995 Version of the NSWC Aeroprediction Code: Part I - Summary of New Theoretical Methodology," Naval Surface Weapons Center, NSWCD/TR-94/379, 1995.

57. Moore, F. G., T. C. Hymer, and R. M. McInville, "The 1995 Version of the NSWC Aeroprediction Code: Part II - Computer Program User's Guide and Listing," Naval Surface Weapons Center, NSWCD/TR-95/5, 1995.

58. Hymer, T. C. and F. G. Moore, "Users Guide for an Interactive Personal Computer Interface for the Aeroprediction Code," Naval Surface Weapons Center, NSWCD/TR-94/107, 1994.

59. Morris, M. A., "A Computer Program to Predict the Major Aerodynamic Coefficients of Conventional Shell and Bullet Body Shapes," RARDE Branch Memorandum 9/81, England, 1981.

60. Burns, K. A., K. J. Deters, S. L. Story, S. R. Vukelich, and W. B. Blake, "MISSILE DATCOM Users Manual - Revision 6/93," McDonnell Douglas Aerospace, St. Louis, MO, Wright Laboratory Report WL-TR-93-3043, 1993.

2

Aerodynamic Forces and Moments Acting on Projectiles

2.1 INTRODUCTION

The modern aerodynamic force-moment system acting on symmetric projectiles traces its origin to the formulation by Fowler, Gallop, Lock and Richmond (Ref. 1) in 1920. Nielsen and Synge (Ref. 2) added the forces and moments required to bring Fowler's system into logical consistency. Kent (Ref. 3) and Kelley and McShane (Ref. 4) refined the ballistic force-moment system and studied the two stability criteria predicted by the complete ballistic theory. Maple and Synge (Ref. 5) explored the consequences of rotational symmetry on the aerodynamic forces and moments acting on spinning projectiles.

By the end of the Second World War, the ballistic system for spinning shell and the aerodynamic system used in aircraft dynamics had developed along very different lines. Aerodynamicists involved with ballistics found the classical ballistic system and nomenclature confusing, and ballisticians found aircraft aerodynamics unfamiliar and incomplete. McShane, Kelley and Reno (Ref. 6), in their 1953 textbook *Exterior Ballistics*, summarized the highest development of the classical ballistic system. An excellent description of the aircraft aerodynamic system was given by Perkins and Hage (Ref. 7) in 1949.

Bolz (Ref. 8), Nicolaides (Ref. 9) and Charters (Ref. 10) attempted to reconcile and unify the ballistic and aerodynamic force-moment systems into a single, generalized aeroballistic system. The American Society of Mechanical Engineers published a proposed standard aeroballistic system (Ref. 11) for the aeronautical sciences in 1954. In 1963, Murphy advanced his aeroballistic force-moment system (Ref. 12), which differs from that of Reference 11 by a factor of two for the aeroballistic coefficients which involve angular velocities. Reference 11 is referred to today as the NACA (National Advisory Committee for Aeronautics) Aeroballistic System, and Reference 12 defines the BRL (Ballistic Research Laboratory) Aeroballistic System. Both systems are currently in common use in the aeroballistics community.

A rational argument can be made for one aeroballistic system over the other, in certain specific instances. However, there is no significant difference in practice, because the conversion of results between the two systems is straightforward. The author is predisposed toward the BRL system through long association with C. H. Murphy, and the BRL Aeroballistic System is therefore adopted throughout this book.

Before we can specify an aeroballistic force-moment system that takes full advantage of the Maple-Synge consequences of symmetry, some restrictions must be placed on the projectile geometric and inertial properties. The projectile is assumed to be either a body of revolution whose spin axis coincides with a principal axis of inertia, or a finned missile with three or more identical fins spaced symmetrically around the circumference of a body of revolution; exterior ballisticians refer to such a missile as possesing "at least trigonal symmetry." In addition to the requirements of configurational and mass symmetry, the projectile is also restricted to small yaw flight along its trajectory. In later chapters, both the symmetry and the small yaw restrictions will be somewhat relaxed.

Classical exterior ballistics uses the terms "yaw" or "yawing motion" to describe any angular motion of the projectile axis of rotational symmetry relative to the trajectory. In conventional aircraft aerodynamics, the terms "pitch" or "angle of attack" refer to the aircraft's nose pointing above or below its flight path; the terms "yaw" or "angle of sideslip" refer to the nose pointing to the left or right of the flight path. Most modern aeroballisticians often use the classical expression "yawing motion" to describe any combined pitching and yawing motion, and this book follows the modern practice, wherever no ambiguity is present. Occasionally a distinction in terminology will be drawn, to clarify a situation in which possible confusion could arise.

The next nine sections of this chapter illustrate all the significant aerodynamic forces and moments acting on symmetric projectiles. The directions illustrated in the Figures are those considered positive under the sign convention of the BRL Aeroballistic System. Some forces and moments usually act in a direction opposite to the illustration; the spin damping moment is one example. Thus the spin damping moment coefficient is *always* negative. Other coefficients may be positive or negative, such as the Magnus moment coefficient. By referring to the illustrations in the next nine sections, with proper regard to the signs of coefficients, the reader will always be able to ascertain the correct directions of the aerodynamic forces and moments. All equations that define the aerodynamic forces and moments are stated in two forms: (a) the *vector* formulation, and (b) the *scalar magnitude* of each force or moment.

2.2 DRAG FORCE

The aerodynamic drag force opposes the forward velocity of the projectile, as illustrated in Figure 2.1. Drag is the classical aerodynamic force of exterior ballistics; early investigators referred to it as the "air resistance." A modern vector statement of the drag force is given as equation (2.1-a), and the scalar magnitude of the force is stated as equation (2.1-b):

Vector Drag Force = $$-\frac{1}{2}\rho S C_D \vec{V} V = -\frac{1}{2}\rho V^2 S C_D \vec{i} \qquad \textbf{(2.1-a)}$$

Drag Force = $$-\frac{1}{2}\rho V^2 S C_D \qquad \textbf{(2.1-b)}$$

where ρ = air density

$\vec{V}$ = the vector velocity

V = the scalar magnitude of the vector velocity

$\vec{i} = \frac{\vec{V}}{V}$, which is a unit vector in the direction of the vector velocity

S = projectile reference area

C_D = drag coefficient

We note that in fluid dynamics, the quantity $1/2\rho V^2$ that appears in equations (2.1-a) and (2.1-b) is called the *dynamic pressure*. In practice, the reference area, S, is defined as:

$$S = \frac{\pi d^2}{4} \qquad \textbf{(2.2)}$$

where d = the projectile reference diameter

The reference diameter of a projectile is *usually taken* as the diameter of the cylindrical section immediately following the end of the ogive. It is permissible, however, to use any convenient value as the reference diameter, as long as the selected dimension is clearly stated and illustrated.

Note that the drag force is directed opposite to the velocity, regardless of the direction in which the projectile is pointing. The effect of yawing motion on drag is accounted for by allowing the drag coefficient to vary with yaw. If the total yaw angle is α_t, as illustrated in Figure 2.1 (*top right*), the drag coefficient is usually well approximated by:

$$C_D = C_{D_0} + C_{D_{\delta^2}}\delta^2 \qquad \textbf{(2.3)}$$

where C_{D_0} = zero-yaw drag coefficient (which usually varies with Mach number)

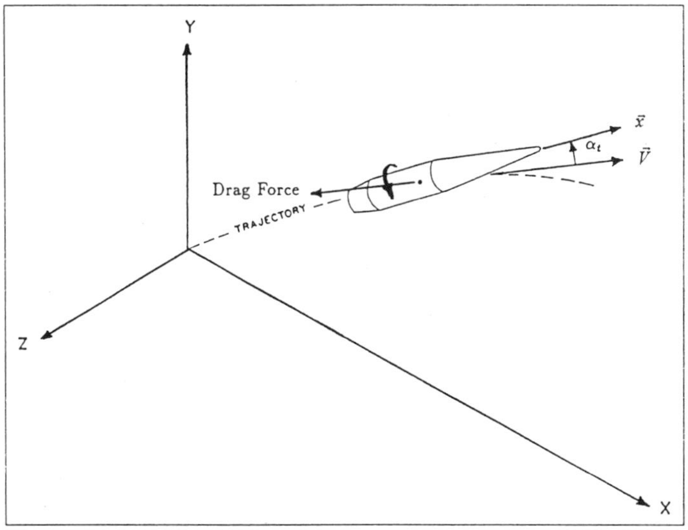

Figure 2.1 Drag Force

$C_{D_{\delta^2}}$ = yaw drag coefficient (which also varies with Mach number)

$\delta = \sin\alpha_t$

$\alpha_t \approx \sqrt{\alpha^2 + \beta^2}$, a good approximation to the total yaw angle (see note below)

α = angle of attack (pitch)

β = angle of sideslip (yaw)

Note that a strictly correct definition of the total angle of attack is given by the equation:

$$\sin\alpha_t = \sqrt{\left(\frac{\sin\alpha}{\cos\beta}\right)^2 + \sin^2\beta}$$

However, for small total angles of attack (α_t < 15 degrees), the difference between the exact and the approximate definitions is insignificant.

The drag coefficient varies quadratically with total yaw angle, thus drag increases rapidly with large yawing motion. Since low drag is generally desirable, the yaw drag effect requires that the yawing motion be as small as possible. As will be seen later, α_t varies along the trajectory, due to the epicyclic ("rosette") motion of the projectile's axis about the flight path. Consequently the drag coefficient changes during the flight, with both velocity and yaw level.

2.3 SPIN DAMPING MOMENT

The spin damping moment opposes the spin of the projectile; it always reduces the axial spin. Figure 2.2 shows a positive spin damping moment, which would cause the magnitude of spin to increase.

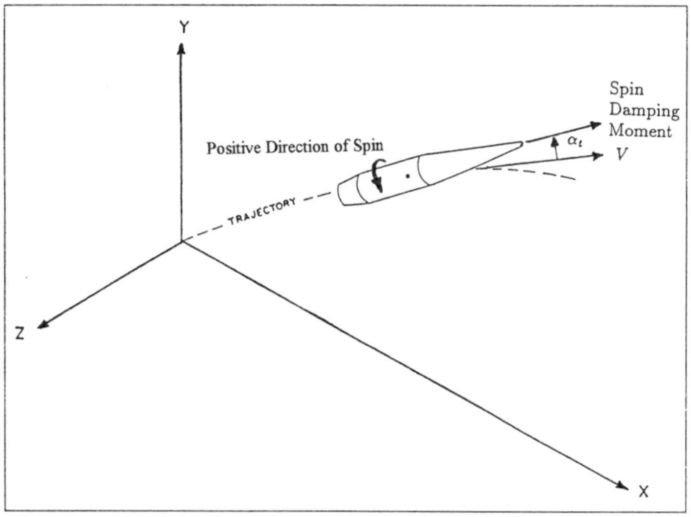

Figure 2.2 Spin Damping Moment

Thus the spin damping moment coefficient must always be negative. The vector spin damping moment is defined as equation (2.4-a), and the scalar magnitude is given by equation (2.4-b):

$$\textit{Vector Spin Damping Moment} = \frac{1}{2}\rho V^2 Sd\left(\frac{pd}{V}\right)C_{l_p}\vec{x} \quad \textbf{(2.4-a)}$$

$$\textit{Spin Damping Moment} = \frac{1}{2}\rho V^2 Sd\left(\frac{pd}{V}\right)C_{l_p} \quad \textbf{(2.4-b)}$$

where ρ = air density

V = projectile velocity

S = projectile reference area

d = projectile reference diameter

p = axial spin (usually measured in radians per second, positive for right-hand spin)

C_{l_p} = spin damping moment coefficient

$\vec{x}$ = a unit vector along the projectile's axis of symmetry (see Figure 2.1)

The quantity *(pd/V)* has a special significance in exterior ballistics; it is the spin per caliber of travel, or in non-dimensional units, the ratio of axial spin to forward velocity. The spin damping moment coefficient is always negative, and both the axial spin and the forward velocity decrease along the trajectory, for typical spin stabilized projectiles. However, the spin damping is much smaller than the effect of drag on velocity, and the ratio *(pd/V)* usually increases along a flat-fire trajectory for a spin stabilized projectile. Note that the NACA aeroballistic system uses *(pd/2V)* instead of *(pd/V)*, which accounts for the factor of two difference in coefficients that depend on angular velocity.

2.4 ROLLING MOMENT FOR CANTED FIN PROJECTILES

If a finned missile has differentially canted fins, a rolling moment tending to increase axial spin is present. The positive direction of the rolling moment due to canted fins is the same as that shown in Figure 2.2 (*left*), and the rolling moment is given by our usual vector and scalar equations:

$$\textit{Vector Rolling Moment} = \frac{1}{2}\rho V^2 Sd\delta_F C_{l_\delta}\vec{x} \quad \textbf{(2.5-a)}$$

$$\textit{Rolling Moment} = \frac{1}{2}\rho V^2 Sd\delta_F C_{l_\delta} \quad \textbf{(2.5-b)}$$

where δ_F = fin cant angle

C_{l_δ} = rolling moment coefficient

The remaining symbols were previously defined.

For positive, or right-hand fin cant (looking downrange from the gun), the rolling moment coefficient is positive (clockwise); a left hand fin cant produces a negative rolling moment, which leads to a counterclockwise rolling motion. If the fins are uncanted (parallel to the axis of symmetry), the fin cant angle is zero and there is no rolling moment.

For a finned missile with canted fins, the rolling moment causes increasing spin at the same time the spin damping moment tends to decrease the spin. The two moments therefore oppose each other, and the usual result is that the spin approaches a steady-state value, after which it neither increases nor decreases. A slow steady-state spin is often advantageous for a finned missile, since the slow spin averages the effect of small configurational or mass asymmetries over long trajectories.

2.5 LIFT AND NORMAL FORCES

Aerodynamic lift is the force perpendicular to the trajectory, tending to pull the projectile in the direction its nose is pointed. If the nose of the projectile is above its trajectory, as illustrated in Figure 2.3 (*top p. 35*), the lift force causes the projectile to climb. The lift force is stated in vector and scalar forms:

Vector
Vecto Lift Force =

$$\frac{1}{2}\rho SC_{L_\alpha}\left[\vec{V}\times\left(\vec{x}\times\vec{V}\right)\right] = \frac{1}{2}\rho SC_{L_\alpha}V^2\left[\vec{i}\times\left(\vec{x}\times\vec{i}\right)\right] \quad \textbf{(2.6-a)}$$

Lift Force =

$$\frac{1}{2}\rho V^2 SC_{L_\alpha}\sin\alpha_t \quad \textbf{(2.6-b)}$$

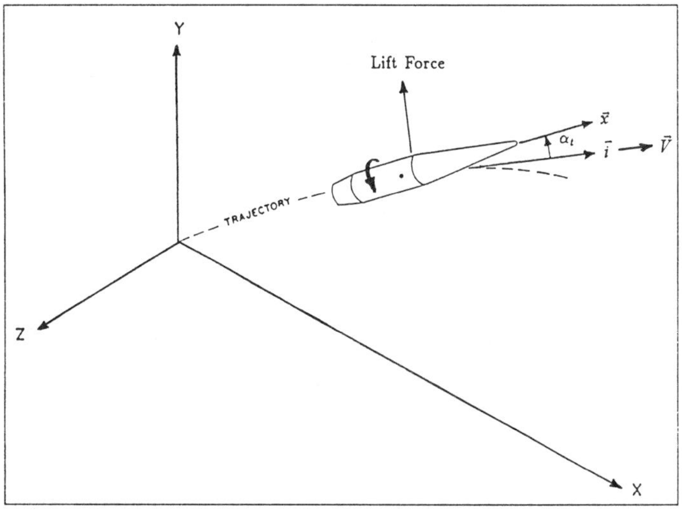

Figure 2.3 Lift Force

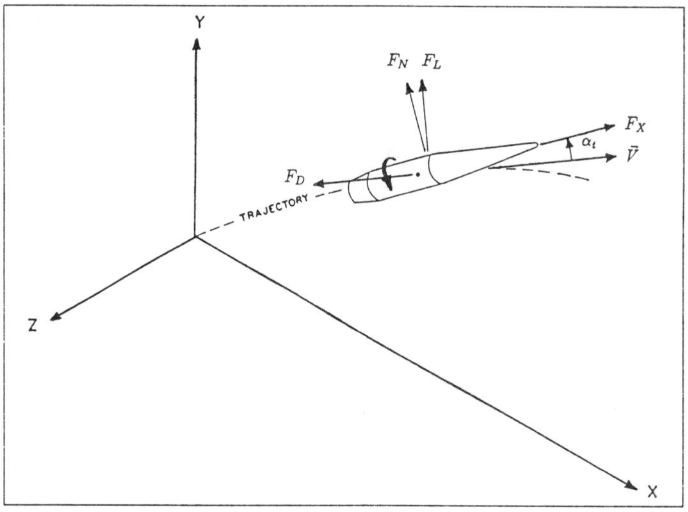

Figure 2.4 Drag, Lift, Axial and Normal Forces

where C_{L_α} = lift force coefficient

The lift force is proportional to the sine of the total yaw angle, and always acts *perpendicular to the trajectory*, in the plane containing both the trajectory and the projectile axis of rotational symmetry. The lift force vanishes only if the total yaw angle is zero.

Aerodynamic lift is the force that produces the drift of spin stabilized projectiles at long ranges. Lift also causes such effects as aerodynamic jump and epicyclic swerve, which will be addressed in later chapters.

The lift force coefficient often exhibits nonlinear behavior, e.g., the coefficient varies with yaw level. The nonlinear lift coefficient is usually well described by:

$$C_{L_\alpha} = C_{L_{\alpha_0}} + C_{L_{\alpha_2}} \delta^2 \qquad \textbf{(2.7)}$$

where $C_{L_{\alpha_0}}$ = linear lift force coefficient

$C_{L_{\alpha_2}}$ = cubic lift force coefficient

The coefficients $C_{L_{\alpha_0}}$ and $C_{L_{\alpha_2}}$ in Equation (2.7) are referred to as linear and cubic coefficients because in the lift force definition (2.6-a) and (2.6-b), the variation of lift force with total yaw angle includes a term proportional to ($\sin\alpha_t$), and a second term proportional to ($\sin^3 \alpha_t$).

Some authors prefer to work in body axes (parallel and perpendicular to the *projectile axis of symmetry*) rather than wind axes (parallel and perpendicular to the *trajectory*). In a body axis system, the drag and lift forces are replaced by the axial force and the normal force. Figure 2.4 illustrates the four forces involved.

Axial
Avial Force =

$$\frac{1}{2}\rho V^2 S C_x \qquad \textbf{(2.8)}$$

Normal Force =

$$\frac{1}{2}\rho V^2 S C_{N_\alpha} \sin\alpha_t \qquad \textbf{(2.9)}$$

where C_X = axial force coefficient

C_{N_α} = normal force coefficient

The total aerodynamic force acting on the projectile is independent of our decision to resolve the component forces in body axes or in wind axes. If F_D is the drag force, F_L is the lift force, F_X is the axial force and F_N is the normal force, the four forces shown in Figure 2.4 are interrelated by the pair of equations:

$$F_D = F_N \sin\alpha_t - F_X \cos\alpha_t \qquad \textbf{(2.10)}$$

$$F_L = F_N \cos\alpha_t + F_X \sin\alpha_t \qquad \textbf{(2.11)}$$

If equations (2.1), (2.6), (2.8) and (2.9) are substituted in (2.10) and (2.11), and common factors are cancelled, the following pair of equations results:

$$C_D = C_{N_\alpha} \sin^2\alpha_t - C_X \cos\alpha_t \qquad \textbf{(2.12)}$$

$$C_{L_\alpha} = C_{N_\alpha} \cos\alpha_t + C_X \qquad \textbf{(2.13)}$$

For small yaw, $\cos\alpha_t \approx 1$ and $\sin^2\alpha_t \langle\langle 1$. Substituting the small yaw approximations into (2.12) and (2.13) provides the useful results:

$$C_X \approx -C_D \qquad \textbf{(2.14)}$$

$$C_{N_\alpha} \approx C_{L_\alpha} + C_D \qquad \textbf{(2.15)}$$

Equations (2.14) and (2.15) provide a simple means of conversion between body axes and wind axes force components. Equation (2.15) is particularly useful, since it allows direct comparison of wind tunnel results, which measure the normal force, with spark photography range results, which infer the lift force from the measured center-of-mass swerving motion.

The normal force coefficient also exhibits nonlinear behavior, similar to that observed in the lift force coefficient. A good approximation to the nonlinear normal force coefficient is:

$$C_{N_\alpha} = C_{N_{\alpha_0}} + C_{N_{\alpha 2}} \delta^2 \quad \textbf{(2.16)}$$

where $C_{N_{\alpha_0}}$ = linear normal force coefficient

$C_{N_{\alpha 2}}$ = cubic normal force coefficient

The axial force coefficient also varies with yaw level, in a similar manner to the drag coefficient, but will not be discussed, since the axial force is not used in the remainder of this book.

2.6 OVERTURNING MOMENT

The overturning moment is the aerodynamic moment associated with the lift or normal force. If the projectile's nose lies above its trajectory, as illustrated in Figure 2.5, a positive overturning moment acts to increase the yaw angle. The overturning moment is given by the vector and scalar equations:

Vector Overturning Moment = $\frac{1}{2}\rho S d C_{M_\alpha} V^2 (\vec{i} \times \vec{x})$ **(2.19-a)**

Overturning Moment = $\frac{1}{2}\rho V^2 S d C_{M_\alpha} \sin\alpha_t$ **(2.19-b)**

where C_{M_α} = overturning moment coefficient

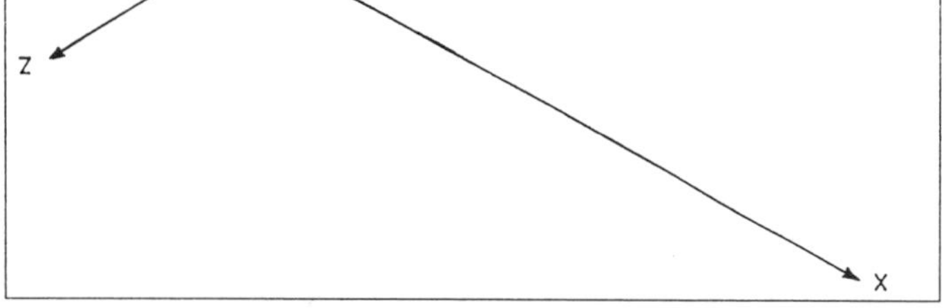

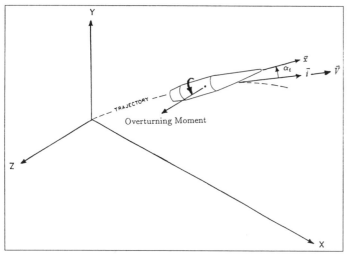

Figure 2.5 Overturning (Pitching) Moment

Some authors refer to the overturning moment as the "pitching moment" or "static moment," and the terms are often used interchangeably in the literature. The overturning moment varies with the sine of the total yaw angle, and for a positive coefficient, always acts to increase the yaw. Thus a non-spinning projectile with positive C_{M_α} is usually unstable.

If sufficiently large fins are added to the tail of a projectile, the large tail lift due to the fins overpowers the smaller lift due to the nose, and the result is a negative C_{M_α}, which acts to decrease the yaw. It is intuitively obvious that such a projectile should be stable without spin, and this result will be demonstrated in a later chapter.

For a projectile with positive C_{M_α}, axial spin is imparted to counteract the destabilizing effect of the overturning moment. In a later chapter, the question of how much spin is required will lead to the concept of gyroscopic stability.

The overturning moment coefficient usually exhibits nonlinear behavior, and the coefficient variation with yaw level is generally well described by:

$$C_{M_\alpha} = C_{M_{\alpha_0}} + C_{M_{\alpha 2}} \delta^2 \quad \textbf{(2.20)}$$

where $C_{M_{\alpha_0}}$ = linear overturning moment coefficient

$C_{M_{\alpha_2}}$ = cubic overturning moment coefficient

2.7 MAGNUS FORCE

The Magnus force was first identified by Benjamin Robins in 1742, but was named for the German scientist who re-discovered it in 1852. It is produced by unequal pressures on opposite sides of a spinning body. The unequal pressures are the result of viscous interaction between the fluid and the spinning surface. Anyone who has observed the curved flight of a spinning golf ball, tennis ball or baseball has seen a demonstration of the Magnus force. We will merely note here that Magnus forces acting on spinning projectiles are *much smaller* than those observed for low-velocity spinning spheres.

Figure 2.6 (*top p. 37*) shows the Magnus force acting in the direction considered positive under the sign convention of the BRL Aeroballistic System. In practice, the Magnus force nearly always acts in the opposite direction to that illustrated in Figure 2.6, thus the Magnus force coefficient, $C_{N_{p\alpha}}$, is usually a small negative quantity. Note that the Magnus force always acts in a direction perpendicular to the plane of yaw; aeroballisticians often refer to it as a "side force." The vector and scalar equations defining the Magnus force are:

Vector Magnus Force = $\frac{1}{2}\rho V^2 S \left(\frac{pd}{V}\right) C_{N_{p\alpha}} (\vec{i} \times \vec{x})$ **(2.21-a)**

Magnus Force = $\frac{1}{2}\rho V^2 S \left(\frac{pd}{V}\right) C_{N_{p\alpha}} \sin\alpha_t$ **(2.21-b)**

where $C_{N_{p\alpha}}$ = Magnus force coefficient

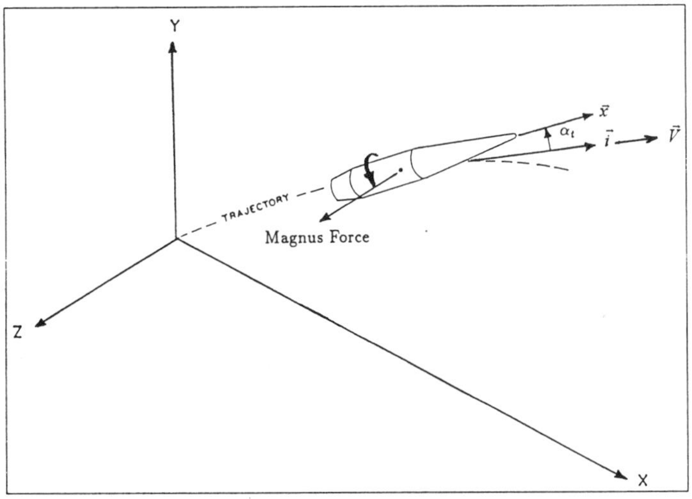

Figure 2.6 Magnus Force

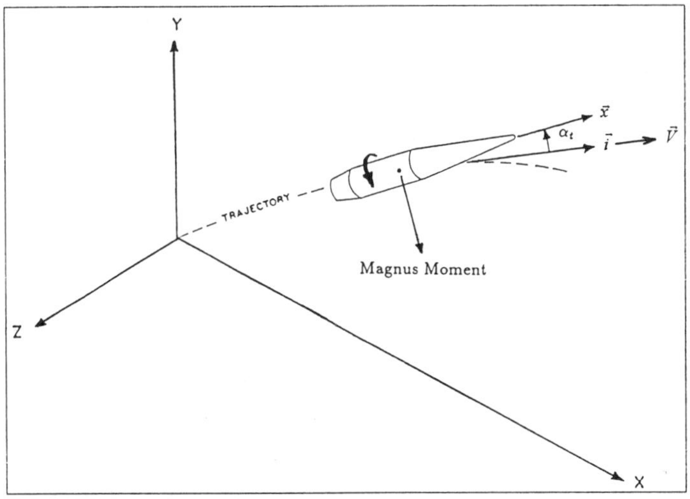

Figure 2.7 Magnus Moment

The Magnus force is proportional to the product of the spin and the sine of the yaw angle, thus the force vanishes for either zero spin or zero yaw. The Magnus force is often nonlinear with yaw level, and the variation is described by:

$$C_{N_{p\alpha}} = C_{N_{p\alpha_o}} + C_{N_{p\alpha_2}} \delta^2 \qquad \textbf{(2.22)}$$

where $C_{N_{p\alpha_o}}$ = linear Magnus force coefficient

$C_{N_{p\alpha_2}}$ = cubic Magnus force coefficient

At very low velocities, the Magnus force also displays nonlinear variation with spin, but such velocities are below the region of interest for most practical exterior ballistics problems.

2.8 MAGNUS MOMENT

The Magnus moment is illustrated in Figure 2.7 (*top right*), which shows the positive direction in the BRL Aeroballistic System. The Magnus moment coefficient can be either positive or negative, depending on the projectile shape, the center of gravity location, the amplitude of yawing motion and the flight Mach number. The Magnus moment is defined by the vector and scalar equations:

Vector Magnus Moment =

$$\frac{1}{2}\rho S d V^2 S\left(\frac{pd}{V}\right) C_{M_{p\alpha}} \left[\vec{x} \times \left(\vec{i} \times \vec{x}\right)\right] \qquad \textbf{(2.23-a)}$$

Magnus Moment =

$$\frac{1}{2}\rho V^2 S d\left(\frac{pd}{V}\right) C_{M_{p\alpha}} \sin\alpha_t \qquad \textbf{(2.23-b)}$$

where $C_{M_{p\alpha}}$ = Magnus moment coefficient

Although the Magnus *force* acting on a spinning projectile is usually small enough to be neglected, the Magnus ***moment*** must always be considered, because a large value of $C_{M_{p\alpha}}$ can have a disasterous effect on the dynamic stability. In a later chapter, the relationship between the Magnus moment coefficient and the dynamic stability will be addressed.

The Magnus moment is often strongly nonlinear with yaw level, and the nonlinear behavior is well represented by:

$$C_{M_{p\alpha}} = C_{M_{p\alpha_o}} + C_{M_{p\alpha_2}} \delta^2 \qquad \textbf{(2.24)}$$

where $C_{M_{p\alpha_o}}$ = linear Magnus moment coefficient

$C_{M_{p\alpha_2}}$ = cubic Magnus moment coefficient

In many cases, particularly at transonic and subsonic speeds, a simple cubic dependence of the Magnus moment on is insufficient to describe the strongly nonlinear behavior observed. Higher order terms, such as a quintic in angle of attack are sometimes required, or a bi-cubic representation may be used, in which two different simple cubic approximations are applied over the small yaw and the larger yaw regions. The nonlinear Magnus moment is the *primary cause* of limit-cycle yaw behavior, which will also be discussed in a later chapter.

2.9 CENTERS OF PRESSURE OF THE NORMAL FORCE AND THE MAGNUS FORCE

The overturning moment may be defined as the product of the normal force and a "moment arm," which is the distance between the projectile's center of gravity and its *normal force center of pressure*. The center of pressure is actually a fictitious quantity, which is defined as the point at which the observed normal force would have to act, in order to produce the observed overturning moment. The mathematical relationship between the overturning moment coefficient, the normal force coefficient, the center of gravity, and the *normal force center of pressure* is:

$$C_{M_\alpha} = C_{N_\alpha}\left(CG - CP_N\right) \qquad \textbf{(2.25)}$$

where CG = distance from projectile nose to center of gravity

CP_N = distance from projectile nose to the normal force center of pressure

In a similar manner, the relationship between the Magnus moment coefficient, the Magnus force coefficient, the center of gravity, and the *Magnus force center of pressure* is:

$$C_{M_{p\alpha}} = C_{N_{p\alpha}}\left(CG - CP_F\right) \qquad \textbf{(2.26)}$$

where CP_F = distance from projectile nose to the Magnus force center of pressure

It is important to note that the *normal force center of pressure* and the *Magnus force center of pressure* are *not the same*. For spin-stabilized projectiles, the normal force CP_N is usually located ahead (toward the nose) of the center of gravity, whereas the Magnus force CP_F generally lies aft of the CG. A few examples of the normal and Magnus force centers of pressure will be illustrated in later chapters of this book.

Most modern aeroballisticians do not use the center of pressure concept very much today. However, it is still useful as an illustrative tool, to assist in understanding the effect of center of gravity changes on the aerodynamic moment coefficients. In addition, several modern fast-design aeroprediction computer codes still print out estimated force coefficients and centers of pressure, at various Mach numbers and yaw levels, and equations (2.25) and (2.26) are still useful in obtaining estimates of the associated moment coefficients.

2.10 PITCH DAMPING FORCE

Figure 2.8 (*top right*)shows the positive direction of the pitch damping force for a positive pitching angular velocity, q. The pitch damping force acts in the plane of transverse angular velocity, which is not necessarily the same as the yaw plane. The pitch damping force contains two parts; one part proportional to transverse angular velocity (pitching velocity), and a second part proportional to the rate of change of total angle of attack. The vector and scalar expressions for the pitch damping force are:

Vector Pitch Damping Force =

$$\frac{1}{2}\rho S d C_{M_q} V\left(\frac{d\vec{x}}{dt}\right) + \frac{1}{2}\rho S d C_{M\dot{\alpha}} V\left[\left(\frac{d\vec{x}}{dt}\right) - \left(\frac{d\vec{i}}{dt}\right)\right] \qquad \textbf{(2.27-a)}$$

Pitch Damping Force =

$$\frac{1}{2}\rho V^2 S\left[\left(\frac{q_t d}{V}\right)C_{N_q} + \left(\frac{\dot{\alpha}_t d}{V}\right)C_{N\dot{\alpha}}\right] \qquad \textbf{(2.27-b)}$$

where $q_t = \sqrt{q^2 + r^2}$, total transverse angular velocity

q = pitching angular velocity

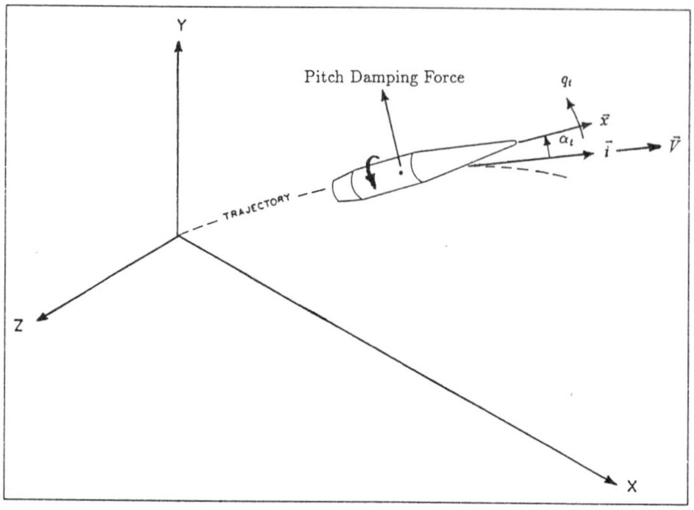

Figure 2.8 Pitch Damping Force

r = yawing (sideslip) angular velocity

$\dot{\alpha}_t = \dfrac{d\alpha_t}{dt}$ = rate of change of total yaw angle

C_{N_q} = pitch damping force coefficient due to q_t

$C_{N_{\dot{\alpha}}}$ = pitch damping force coefficient due to $\dot{\alpha}_t$

$\dfrac{d\vec{x}}{dt}$ = rate of change of the unit vector . (Note that the transverse angular velocities q and r are contained in the vector $\dfrac{d\vec{x}}{dt}$).

For flat-fire trajectories, q_t and $\dot{\alpha}_t$ are virtually identical, and the pitch damping force is well approximated by the simpler expressions:

Vector Pitch Damping Force ≅

$$\frac{1}{2}\rho S d\left(C_{N_q} + C_{N_{\dot{\alpha}}}\right)V\left(\frac{d\vec{x}}{dt}\right) \qquad \textbf{(2.28-a)}$$

Pitch Damping Force ≅

$$\frac{1}{2}\rho V^2 S d\left(\frac{q_t d}{V}\right)\left(C_{N_q} + C_{N_{\dot{\alpha}}}\right) \qquad \textbf{(2.28-b)}$$

The pitch damping force acting on spin-stabilized projectiles is generally *much smaller* than the normal force, and few direct measurements of it have ever been made in spark photography ranges. The pitch damping force, like the Magnus force, must be retained for logical completeness, but it is usually neglected in practice.

2.11 PITCH DAMPING MOMENT

The pitch damping moment is illustrated in Figure 2.9 for a positive pitching angular velocity. The pitch damping moment also contains two parts, one proportional to q_t and one proportional to α_t. The total pitch damping moment is given by the vector and scalar equations:

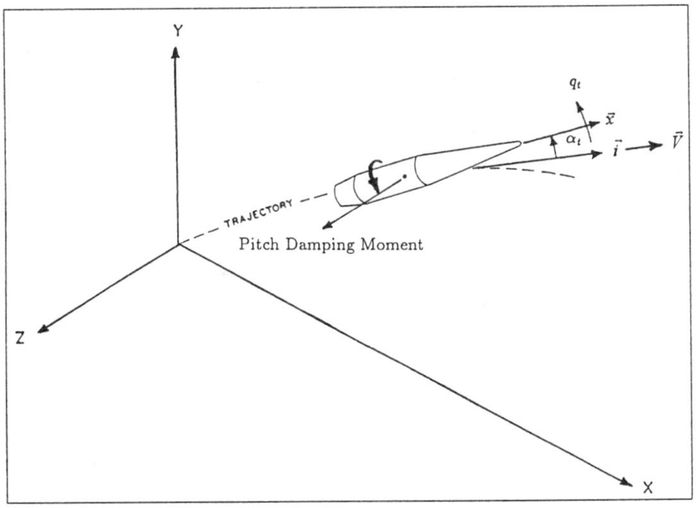

Figure 2.9 Pitch Damping Moment

Vector Pitch Damping Moment =

$$\frac{1}{2}\rho Sd^2 C_{M_q} V\left(\vec{x}\times\frac{d\vec{x}}{dt}\right)+\frac{1}{2}\rho Sd^2 C_{M_{\dot{\alpha}}} V\left[\left(\vec{x}\times\frac{d\vec{x}}{dt}\right)-\left(\vec{x}\times\frac{d\vec{i}}{dt}\right)\right] \quad \textbf{(2.29-a)}$$

Pitch Damping Moment =

$$\frac{1}{2}\rho V^2 Sd\left[\left(\frac{q_t d}{V}\right)C_{M_q}+\left(\frac{\dot{\alpha}_t d}{V}\right)C_{M\dot{\alpha}}\right] \quad \textbf{(2.29-b)}$$

As we noted in the previous section on the pitch damping force, q_t and $\dot{\alpha}_t$ are virtually identical in practice, and the simpler vector and scalar approximations are generally used:

Vector Pitch Damping Moment =

$$\frac{1}{2}\rho Sd^2\left(C_{M_q}+C_{M_{\dot{\alpha}}}\right)V\left(\vec{x}\times\frac{d\vec{x}}{dt}\right) \quad \textbf{(2.30-a)}$$

Pitch Damping Moment =

$$\frac{1}{2}\rho V^2 Sd\left(\frac{q_t d}{V}\right)\left(C_{M_q}+C_{M_{\dot{\alpha}}}\right) \quad \textbf{(2.30-b)}$$

where C_{M_q} = pitch damping moment coefficient due to q_t

$C_{M_{\dot{\alpha}}}$ = pitch damping moment coefficient due to $\dot{\alpha}_t$

Although the pitch damping ***force*** is generally negligible, the pitch damping ***moment*** must always be retained because of its influence on the dynamic stability. In general, a positive pitch damping moment acts to increase total transverse angular velocity, and is therefore destabilizing. For dynamic stability, the pitch damping moment coefficient sum, $\left(C_{M_q}+C_{M_{\dot{\alpha}}}\right)$, should be negative; fortunately for ballisticians and projectile designers, it usually is. Positive pitch damping moment coefficient sums have been observed for a number of projectile shapes at transonic and subsonic speeds, and are usually troublesome. (Slender-body theory tells us that C_{M_q} cannot ever be positive; on the other hand, the same theory shows that $C_{M_{\dot{\alpha}}}$ *may be positive* for some center of gravity locations. More research is needed to explore the physical cause of observed positive pitch damping moment coefficient sums at transonic and subsonic speeds.) The combined effects of Magnus and pitch damping moments on the dynamic stability will be closely examined in Chapter 10 of this book.

There is some evidence that the pitch damping moment can vary with yaw level at transonic and subsonic speeds; such behavior has not been observed at supersonic speeds. In most cases where nonlinear pitch damping has been measured, its influence on the yawing motion is much smaller than that of the nonlinear Magnus moment.

2.12 NEGLECTED FORCES AND MOMENTS

Nielsen and Synge (Ref. 2) first showed that the Magnus cross force and cross moment must be retained in order to preserve logical consistency in our aerodynamic force-moment system for spinning symmetric projectiles. However, free-flight spark range tests have never been able to measure this force or moment; they produce such insignificant effects on the trajectory that even a high precision spark range facility cannot detect them. The Magnus cross force and cross moment will be defined but not illustrated, since they are included only to preserve logical consistency.

Magnus Cross Force =

$$\frac{1}{2}\rho V^2 S\left(\frac{pd}{V}\right)\left(\frac{q_t d}{V}\right)C_{N_{pq}} \quad \textbf{(2.31)}$$

Magnus Cross Moment =

$$\frac{1}{2}\rho V^2 Sd\left(\frac{pd}{V}\right)\left(\frac{q_t d}{V}\right)C_{M_{pq}} \quad \textbf{(2.32)}$$

where $C_{N_{pq}}$ = Magnus cross force coefficient

$C_{M_{pq}}$ = Magnus cross moment coefficient

Other neglected aerodynamic forces and moments include terms proportional to linear and angular accelerations, which are negligible except at extremely low velocities. Forces and moments due to buoyancy are important for dirigibles and torpedos, but are insignificant for conventional projectiles, and are therefore neglected.

2.13 THE EFFECT OF CENTER OF GRAVITY LOCATION ON THE AERODYNAMIC FORCES AND MOMENTS

The effect of a shift in the projectile center of gravity location on the aerodynamic force-moment system is determined by application of the laws of mechanics to the total force and moment. If two projectiles are identical in size and shape, but the center of gravity of the second projectile lies farther aft (toward the tail) than does the center of gravity of the first projectile, the laws of mechanics state that the total aerodynamic force acting on the two projectiles is identical, but the total aerodynamic moment for the second projectile must equal the moment for the first projectile plus the product of the total force and the shift in center of gravity.

Table 2.1
The Effect of a Center of Gravity Shift on the Aerodynamic Coefficients

$$\hat{C}_D = C_D$$
$$\hat{C}_X = C_X$$
$$\hat{C}_{l_p} = C_{l_p}$$
$$\hat{C}_{l_\alpha} = C_{l_\alpha}$$
$$\hat{C}_{L_\alpha} = C_{L_\alpha}$$
$$\hat{C}_{N_\alpha} = C_{N_\alpha}$$
$$\hat{C}_{M_\alpha} = C_{M_\alpha} + \Delta_{CG} C_{N_\alpha}$$
$$\hat{C}_{N_{p\alpha}} = C_{N_{p\alpha}}$$
$$\hat{C}_{M_{p\alpha}} = C_{M_{p\alpha}} + \Delta_{CG} C_{N_{p\alpha}}$$
$$\hat{C}_{N_q} = C_{N_q} - \Delta_{CG} C_{N_\alpha}$$
$$\hat{C}_{N_{\dot\alpha}} = C_{N_{\dot\alpha}}$$
$$\hat{C}_{M_q} = C_{M_q} + \Delta_{CG}\left(C_{N_q} - C_{M_\alpha}\right) - \Delta^2{}_{CG} C_{N_\alpha}$$
$$\hat{C}_{M_{\dot\alpha}} = C_{M_{\dot\alpha}} + \Delta_{CG} C_{N_{\dot\alpha}}$$
$$\hat{C}_{N_{pq}} = C_{N_{pq}} + \Delta_{CG} C_{N_{p\alpha}}$$
$$\hat{C}_{M_{pq}} = C_{M_{pq}} + \Delta_{CG}\left(C_{N_{pq}} + C_{M_{p\alpha}}\right) + \Delta^2{}_{CG} C_{N_{p\alpha}}$$

Table 2.2
Conversion from Ballistic to BRL Aeroballistic Nomenclature

Coefficient	Conversion Equation
Drag Coefficient	$C_D = \frac{8}{\pi} K_D$
Spin Damping Moment Coefficient	$C_{l_p} = \frac{-8}{\pi} K_A$
Lift Force Coefficient	$C_{L_\alpha} = \frac{8}{\pi} K_L$
Normal Force Coefficient	$C_{N_\alpha} = \frac{8}{\pi} K_N$
Overturning Moment Coefficient	$C_{M_\alpha} = \frac{8}{\pi} K_M$
Magnus Force Coefficient	$C_{N_{p\alpha}} = \frac{-8}{\pi} K_F$
Magnus Moment Coefficient	$C_{M_{p\alpha}} = \frac{-8}{\pi} K_T$
Pitch Damping Force Coefficient	$\left(C_{N_q} + C_{N_{\dot\alpha}}\right) = -\frac{8}{\pi} K_S$
Pitch Damping Moment Coefficient	$\left(C_{M_q} + C_{M_{\dot\alpha}}\right) = -\frac{8}{\pi} K_H$
Magnus Cross Force Coefficient	$C_{N_{pq}} = -\frac{8}{\pi} K_{XF}$
Magnus Cross Moment Coefficient	$C_{M_{pq}} = -\frac{8}{\pi} K_{XT}$

The algebraic operations involved in deriving the center of gravity transformation equations are both lengthy and tedious, and will not be presented here. McShane, Kelley and Reno (Ref. 6) and Murphy (Ref. 13) give complete derivations of the transformation equations, and the interested reader is referred to these sources.

Table 2.1 lists the center of gravity transformation equations for all significant aerodynamic forces and moments acting on symmetric spinning and finned projectiles. The coefficients with a circumflex (^) overscript are the values after a center of gravity shift of Δ_{CG} (measured in calibers); Δ_{CG} is considered positive if the shift is *toward the tail* of the projectile.

2.14 MODERN AEROBALLISTIC AND OLDER BALLISTIC NOMENCLATURES

McShane, Kelley and Reno (Ref.6) used the older ballistic nomenclature (etc.) in their textbook "Exterior Ballistics." This text has been used for forty years as a standard, and a considerable amount (K_D, K_L, K_M, etc.) of aerodynamic data has been published in the older nomenclature. Table 2.2 lists the conversion equations between the older ballistic and the modern BRL Aeroballistic nomenclatures.

The other commonly used aeroballistic system is the NACA (National Advisory Committee for Aeronautics) aeroballistic system (Ref. 11), which was standardized in 1954 by the American Society of Mechanical Engineers. Table 2.3 lists the conversion equations relating the BRL and the NACA aeroballistic coefficients.

2.15 SUMMARY

In this chapter, all the significant aerodynamic forces and moments which act on spinning and non-spinning rotationally symmetric projectiles have been defined and illustrated. A brief description of the physical nature and the important variables associated with each force and moment are presented. Some aerodynamic forces and moments are much smaller than others, and our discussion identifies the particular forces and moments which are usually small enough to be neglected.

Table 2.3
Conversion from NACA to BRL Aeroballistic Nomenclature

Coefficient	BRL NACA
Normal Force Coefficient	$C_{N_\alpha} = -C_{Z_\alpha}$
Pitching Moment Coefficient	$C_{M_\alpha} = C_{m_\alpha}$
Spin Damping Moment Coefficient	$C_{l_p} = \frac{1}{2}C_{l_p}$
Magnus Force Coefficient	$C_{N_{p\alpha}} = \frac{1}{2}C_{Y_{p\alpha}}$
Magnus Moment Coefficient	$C_{M_{p\alpha}} = \frac{1}{2}C_{n_{p\alpha}}$
Pitch Damping Force Coefficient	$\left(C_{N_q} + C_{N_{\dot{\alpha}}}\right) = -\frac{1}{2}\left(C_{Z_q} + C_{Z_{\dot{\alpha}}}\right)$
Pitch Damping Moment Coefficient	$\left(C_{M_q} + C_{M_{\dot{\alpha}}}\right) = \frac{1}{2}\left(C_{m_q} + C_{m_{\dot{\alpha}}}\right)$
Magnus Cross Force Coefficient	$C_{N_{pq}} = -\frac{1}{4}C_{Y_{pq}}$
Magnus Cross Moment Coefficient	$C_{M_{pq}} = -\frac{1}{4}C_{n_{pq}}$

The fact that most aerodynamic forces and moments are nonlinear has been emphasized in this chapter. The older classical textbooks on exterior ballistics did not address nonlinear forces and moments; full realization of the dependence of aerodynamic forces and moments on yaw level did not occur until the decade after the Second World War, and the widespread modern use of wind tunnels and spark photography ranges. In later chapters, we will investigate some of the interesting projectile flight dynamic characteristics which result from nonlinear aerodynamic force-moment systems.

REFERENCES

1. Fowler, R. H., E. G. Gallop, C. N. H. Lock and H. W. Richmond, "The Aerodynamics of a Spinning Shell," *Philosophical Transactions of the Royal Society of London*, Series A, Volume 221, 1920.

2. Nielsen, K. L., and J. L. Synge, "On the Motion of a Spinning Shell," Ballistic Research Laboratories Report No. X-116, 1943. [Also published in the *Quarterly of Applied Mathematics*, Vol. 4, No. 3, 1946].

3. Kent, R. H., "An Elementary Treatment of the Motion of a Spinning Projectile About its Center of Gravity," Ballistic Research Laboratories Report No. 85, 1937.

4. Kelley, J. L., and E. J. McShane, "On the Motion of a Projectile With Small or Slowly Changing Yaw," Ballistic Research Laboratories Report No. 446, 1944.

5. Maple, C. G., and J. L. Synge, "Aerodynamic Symmetry of Projectiles," *Quarterly of Applied Mathematics*, Volume 4, 1949.

6. McShane, E. J., J. L. Kelley and F. V. Reno, *Exterior Ballistics*, University of Denver Press, 1953.

7. Perkins, C. D., and R. E. Hage, *Airplane Performance Stability and Control*, John Wiley & Sons, Inc., 1949.

8. Bolz, R., "Dynamic Stability of a Missile in Rolling Flight," *Journal of the Aeronautical Sciences*, Vol. 19, No. 6, 1952.

9. Nicolaides, J. D., "On the Free Flight Motion of Missiles Having Slight Configurational Asymmetries," Ballistic Research Laboratories Report No. 858, 1953.

10. Charters, A. C., "The Linearized Equations of Motion Underlying the Dynamic Stability of Aircraft, Spinning Projectiles, and Symmetrical Missiles," National Advisory Committee for Aeronautics Technical Note 3350, 1955.

11. "Americal Standard Letter Symbols for Aeronautical Sciences," ASA X10.7-1954, *American Society of Mechanical Engineers*, New York, 1954.

12. Murphy, C. H., "Free Flight Motion of Symmetric Missiles," Ballistic Research Laboratories Report No. 1216, 1963.

13. Murphy, C. H., "On the Stability Criteria of the Kelley-McShane Linearized Theory of Yawing Motion," Ballistic Research Laboratories Report No. 853, 1953.

3

The Vacuum Trajectory

3.1 INTRODUCTION

The vacuum trajectory (the case where all the aerodynamic forces and moments are zero), was first stated in correct mathematical form by Galileo Galilei of Italy (1564-1642). Galileo had studied uniform horizontal motion and gravity-accelerated vertical motion, and he showed that a combination of these two motions is an accurate description of the trajectory, for a low velocity projectile. Galileo was the first to demonstrate that the vacuum trajectory is a parabola, and he could have correctly computed vacuum trajectories if accurate methods of measuring the muzzle velocity and the gravitational acceleration had been available. He understood that air resistance was important at higher speeds, and stated that the vacuum trajectory provided useful results for heavy projectiles shot from bows or arbalistas, but not for the higher velocities attained by firearms.

Although the vacuum trajectory is seldom used in modern exterior ballistics, it still provides a useful introduction to the subject, because it highlights many of the important physical aspects of the trajectory problem, yet reduces to simple mathematical solutions. In addition to its simplicity, the vacuum trajectory exhibits many of the properties of atmospheric trajectories, and thus provides background for the higher order approximations which will be presented in later chapters.

3.2 EQUATIONS OF MOTION

We will adopt a rectangular coordinate system with the origin located at the gun muzzle. The X-axis is chosen tangent to the earth's surface at the launch point, and is directed along the line of fire. The Y-axis is directed vertically upward, through the launch point.

Newton's second law of motion for the projectile states that the rate of change of momentum must equal the sum of all the externally applied forces. Figure 3.1 illustrates the coordinate system, a typical vacuum trajectory, and the pertinent variables.

For constant projectile mass, Newton's second law gives the general vector differential equation of motion as:

$$m\frac{d\vec{V}}{dt} = \sum \vec{F} + m\vec{g} + m\vec{\Lambda} \tag{3.1}$$

where m = projectile mass

$\vec{V}$ = vector velocity

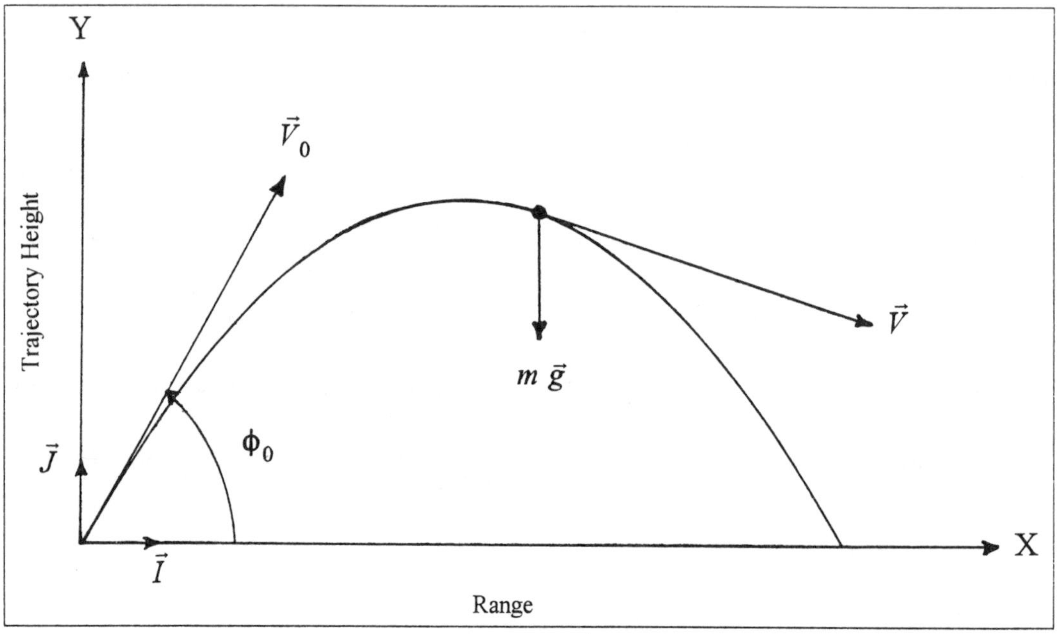

Figure 3.1 Coordinate system for the Vacuum Trajectory.

t = time

$\frac{d\vec{V}}{dt}$ = vector acceleration

$\sum \vec{F}$ = vector sum of all the aerodynamic forces

$\vec{g}$ = vector acceleration due to gravity

$\vec{\Lambda}$ = vector Coriolis acceleration due to the earth's rotation

The small Coriolis acceleration term appearing in equation (3.1) is the price we pay for adopting a convenient earth-fixed coordinate system, instead of more cumbersome inertial (star-fixed) coordinates. Coriolis acceleration has a significant effect on long range artillery fire, and will be discussed in a later chapter. For the modest velocities and ranges considered in this chapter, Coriolis effects are negligible in comparison with the acceleration due to gravity.

No aerodynamic forces can exist in a vacuum, and setting $\sum \vec{F} = 0$ in equation (3.1) leads to the classical form of the vacuum trajectory differential equation:

$$\frac{d\vec{V}}{dt} = \vec{g} \tag{3.2}$$

Before we can solve equation (3.2), the vector quantities must be resolved into components along the X and Y axes. The vector velocity and acceleration are given by:

$$\vec{V} = V_x\vec{I} + V_y\vec{J} \tag{3.3}$$

$$\frac{d\vec{V}}{dt} = \dot{V}_x\vec{I} + \dot{V}_y\vec{J} \tag{3.4}$$

where $\vec{I}$ is a unit vector along the X-axis

$\vec{J}$ is a unit vector along the Y-axis

V_x = X-component of velocity

V_y = Y-component of velocity

$\dot{V}_x = \frac{dV_x}{dt}$ = X-component of acceleration

$\dot{V}_y = \frac{dV_y}{dt}$ = Y-component of acceleration

The superscript dot $(\dot{\ })$ is a convenient mathematical notation for the derivative of a quantity with respect to time.

We assume that the gravitational acceleration vector, $\vec{g}$, is a constant, with scalar magnitude g = 32.174 feet per second squared (the world-wide sea level average), and is directed vertically downward, in the $-\vec{J}$ direction.

$$\vec{g} = -g\vec{J} \tag{3.5}$$

We now substitute equations (3.4) and (3.5) into equation (3.2):

$$\dot{V}_x\vec{I} + \dot{V}_y\vec{J} = -g\vec{J} \tag{3.6}$$

Now, if two vectors are equal, their respective components must also be equal. Collecting coefficients of the two unit vectors in equation (3.6) yields the pair of scalar differential equations:

$$\dot{V}_x = 0 \tag{3.7}$$

$$\dot{V}_y = -g \tag{3.8}$$

These simple linear differential equations may be directly integrated. The first integration gives:

$$V_x = V_{x_o} = V_o \cos\phi_o \tag{3.9}$$

$$V_y = V_{y_o} - gt = V_o \sin\phi_o - gt \tag{3.10}$$

where $V_{x_o} = V_o \cos\phi_o$ = X-component of velocity at launch

$V_{y_o} = V_o \sin\phi_o$ = Y-component of velocity at launch

$V_o = \sqrt{V_{x_o}^{\ 2} + V_{y_o}^{\ 2}}$ = scalar magnitude of muzzle velocity

ϕ_o = gun elevation angle above horizontal

t = time

A second integration gives:

$$X = \int V_x dt = V_o t \cos\phi_o \tag{3.11}$$

$$Y = \int V_y dt = V_o t \sin\phi_o - \frac{1}{2}gt^2 \tag{3.12}$$

where X = range at time t

Y = trajectory height at time t

Equations (3.11) and (3.12) are the parametric equations of the vacuum trajectory, with time as the parameter. The standard form is obtained by eliminating time between the two equations. If we solve equation (3.11) for time and substitute into equation (3.12):

$$t = \frac{X}{V_o \cos\phi_o} \tag{3.13}$$

$$Y = X\tan\phi_o - \frac{gX^2}{2V^2_o\cos^2\phi_o} \qquad \textbf{(3.14)}$$

Equation (3.14) is the mathematical equation of a parabola. A graph of trajectory height versus range for any non-trivial vacuum trajectory will therefore show the characteristic parabolic shape.

3.3 DISCUSSION OF THE VACUUM TRAJECTORY

Vacuum trajectories have many interesting properties, and we will illustrate several of them in this section. Other properties will be mentioned, but the details will be left as exercises for the interested reader.

Range and Elevation on Level Ground

The range of a projectile fired to level ground impact in a vacuum is obtained by setting Y = 0 in equation (3.14) and solving for X:

$$X\left(\tan\phi_o - \frac{gX}{2V_o^2\cos^2\phi_o}\right) = 0 \qquad \textbf{(3.15)}$$

The trivial solution, X = 0, verifies that the trajectory passes through the launch point. The non-trivial solution is:

$$X = R = \frac{V_o^2}{g}\sin 2\phi_o \qquad \textbf{(3.16)}$$

where R = range to impact on level ground

The elevation angle required to hit a target at range R is found by solving equation (3.16) for ϕ_o :

$$\phi_o = \frac{1}{2}\sin^{-1}\left(\frac{gR}{V_o^2}\right) \qquad \textbf{(3.17)}$$

where a capital letter on the inverse trigonometric function denotes the principal value.

Example 3.1

An arrow shot from a modern compound bow was chronographed at 200 feet per second muzzle velocity. Assuming the vacuum trajectory to be a good approximation, what elevation angles are required to hit level ground targets at ranges of 50 and 100 yards?

For the 50 yards (150 feet) range, equation (3.17) gives:

$$\phi_o = \frac{1}{2}\sin^{-1}\left(\frac{(32.174)(150)}{(200)^2}\right) = 3.46°$$

and for the 100 yards (300 feet) range:

$$\phi_o = \frac{1}{2}\sin^{-1}\left(\frac{(32.174)(300)}{(200)^2}\right) = 6.98°$$

We observe that for short range trajectories (more precisely, for $gR/V_o^2 << 1$), doubling the gun elevation angle approximately doubles the range.

Gun Elevation for Maximum Range

The gun elevation angle giving maximum range is found by differentiating equation (3.16) with respect to ϕ_o , setting the derivative equal to zero, and solving for ϕ_o :

$$\frac{dR}{d\phi_o} = \frac{2V_o^2}{g}\cos 2\phi_o = 0 \qquad \textbf{(3.18)}$$

The solution of equation (3.18) gives $\cos 2\phi_o = 0$, so that:

$$2\phi_o = 90 \text{ degrees, or } \boxed{\phi_o = 45°} \qquad (3.19)$$

Equation (3.19) shows that a gun elevation angle of 45 degrees always gives maximum range on level ground for any vacuum trajectory. As an historical note, this result had been verified experimentally even before Galileo's time.

Example 3.2

What would be the maximum expected range on level ground, for the arrow of example 3.1 ?

At $\phi_o = 45°$, equation (3.16) gives:

$$R = \frac{(200)^2}{32.174}(1) = 1243 \text{ feet, or } 414 \text{ yards}$$

Since the vacuum trajectory is always an upper bound for the actual atmospheric trajectory, we might reasonably expect that the actual maximum range of the arrow at the given velocity is somewhat less than 400 yards.

High-Angle Fire

In section 3.3 we derived the gun elevation angle required to achieve a given range on level ground. There are actually two elevation angles which satisfy equation (3.16); only the low angle solution is given by equation (3.17). The high-angle solution (denoted by $\hat{\phi}_o$) is:

$$\hat{\phi}_o = 90° - \phi_o = 90° - \frac{1}{2}\sin^{-1}\left(\frac{gR}{V_o^2}\right) \qquad \textbf{(3.20)}$$

The derivation of this result is left to the interested reader. [Hint: Use the trigonometric identity, $\sin\alpha = \sin(180° - \alpha)$].

High-angle, or indirect fire, is commonly encountered in the use of mortars. Mortars are often used to attack targets inaccessible to direct fire weapons, such as a target on the opposite side of a hill. In addition, mortars are low pressure, low velocity weapons, and the vacuum trajectory is often a good approximation to the actual flight of a heavy, low velocity mortar projectile.

Example 3.3

An infantry officer in charge of a mortar platoon has been ordered to attack an enemy bunker on the other side of a low ridge. A topographic map shows the bunker to be at the same altitude as the mortar platoon. The level ground range to the target is 600 meters; the top of the ridge is 300 meters from the gun site, and the ridge crest is 150 meters above the gun-target altitude. A propellant charge is selected that gives a muzzle velocity of 80 meters/second. Can the gunner hit his target?

This problem is more difficult than those in the two preceding examples. Not only must the gunner solve the range-elevation problem, but the trajectory must clear the ridge line, and then descend on the target.

The first step in the solution is to find the two gun elevation angles that give a level ground range of 600 meters. The value of g in the metric system is 9.807 meters per second squared, and the two elevation angles are found from equations (3.17) and (3.20):

$$\phi = \frac{1}{2} Sin^{-1}\left[\frac{(9.807)(600)}{(80)^2}\right] = 33.42°$$

$$\hat{\phi}_o = 90° - 33.42° = 56.58°$$

The gunner must now determine if either of these elevations will permit the trajectory to clear the ridge line. To answer this question, we must go back to equations (3.10) and (3.12). The summit of the vacuum trajectory occurs where the vertical component of velocity, V_{yo}, is zero. If equation (3.10) is set equal to zero, solved for t, and the result substituted into equation (3.12):

$$Y_S = \frac{V_o^2 \sin^2 \phi_o}{2g} \qquad \textbf{(3.21)}$$

where Y_S is the summital height, or maximum ordinate of the trajectory.

Substituting the low-angle solution into equation (3.21):

$$Y_S = \frac{[80\sin(33.42°)]^2}{2(9.807)} = 99 \text{ meters}$$

The low-angle solution will not clear the 150 meter crest of the ridge. Substituting the high-angle solution into equation (3.21):

$$Y_S = \frac{[80\sin(56.58°)]^2}{2(9.807)} = 227 \text{ meters}$$

Thus the gunner can hit the bunker by setting the mortar elevation angle at 56.58 degrees.

Maximum Ordinate of the Trajectory

A useful alternative form of equation (3.21) is easily obtained in terms of the time of flight to impact on level ground. If equation (3.12) is set equal to zero and solved for the time of flight to impact, t_I :

$$t_I = \frac{2V_o \sin\phi_o}{g} \qquad \textbf{(3.22)}$$

From equation (3.22) we find:

$$V_o^2 \sin^2 \phi_o = \frac{1}{4} g^2 t_I^2 \qquad \textbf{(3.23)}$$

Substituting equation (3.23) into equation (3.21):

$$\boxed{Y_S = \frac{g}{8} t_I^2} \qquad \textbf{(3.24)}$$

Equation (3.24) is frequently used as an upper-bound estimate for metrological data collection in artillery firing. For the flat-fire trajectories typical of ground launched small arms, equation (3.24) usually predicts the maximum ordinate to within one percent error.

An exercise for the interested reader is to show that the trajectory summit occurs at $X_s = R/2$.

Angle of Fall

The angle between the horizontal and the descending branch of the vacuum trajectory, at impact on level ground, is found from the slope of the trajectory at impact. Differentiating equation (3.14) with respect to X:

$$\frac{dY}{dX} = \tan\phi_o - \frac{gX}{V_o^2 \cos^2 \phi_o} \qquad \textbf{(3.25)}$$

At impact, $X = \frac{V_o^2}{g} \sin 2\phi_o$, from equation (3.16). Substituting this result in equation (3.25), we have:

$$\left(\frac{dY}{dX}\right)_I = \tan\phi_I = \tan\phi_o - \frac{\sin 2\phi_o}{\cos^2 \phi_o} \qquad \textbf{(3.26)}$$

With the help of the trigonometric identity*, equation (3.26) reduces to: *$\sin 2\phi_o = 2\sin\phi_o \cos\phi_o$

$$\boxed{\tan\phi_I = -\tan\phi_o} \qquad \textbf{(3.27)}$$

Thus the angle of fall on level ground is always the negative of the angle of departure, for any vacuum trajectory. This result can be generalized to show that the ascending and descending branches of any vacuum trajectory are symmetric about a vertical line passing through the summit. This exercise is left to the interested reader.

The Envelope of Vacuum Trajectories

For a fixed muzzle velocity, every vacuum trajectory will, at some point, be tangent to a curve that we define as the envelope of trajectories. The equation of the envelope is:

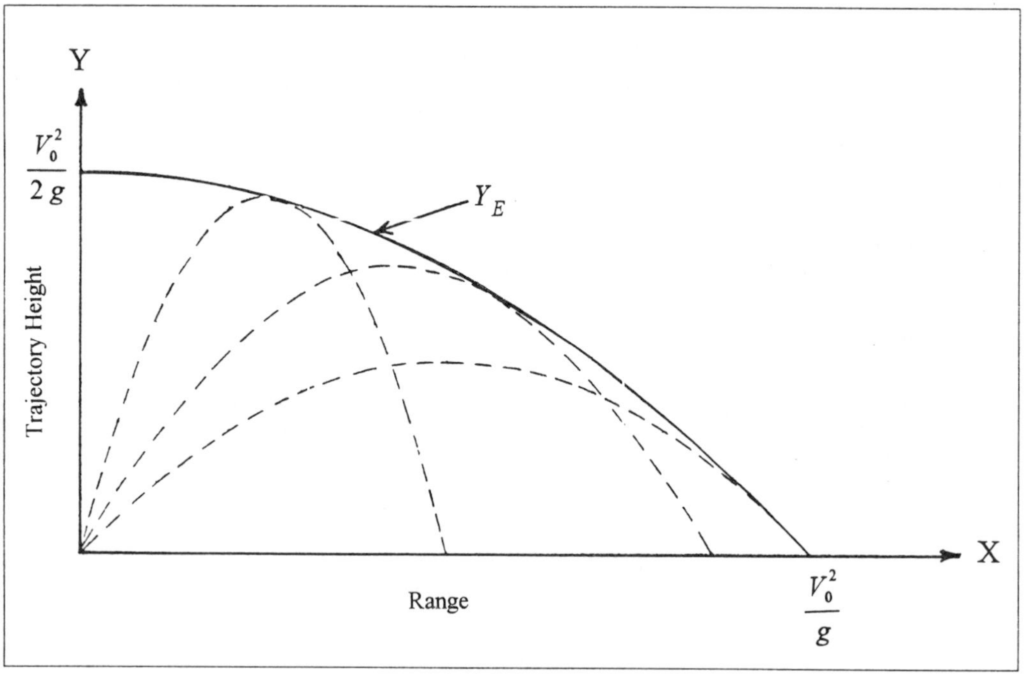

Figure 3.2 Envelope of Vacuum Trajectories.

$$Y_E = \frac{V_o^2}{2g} - \frac{gX^2}{2V_o^2} \qquad (3.28)$$

The derivation of equation (3.28) is rather long and tedious, and is therefore omitted. Figure 3.2 illustrates the envelope of vacuum trajectories for a fixed muzzle velocity.

The envelope of trajectories is a useful curve, because it defines the danger space associated with a firing range. Although actual projectiles will travel neither as far nor as high as the vacuum envelope, the curve of an actual envelope is strikingly similar in appearance to that of Figure 3.2. The envelope of trajectories is usually required for the design of gunnery training ranges, because accidental firing at any elevation angle could occur, and the danger to low flying aircraft must be considered, as well as the danger to personnel on the ground.

The Flat-Fire Approximation to the Vacuum Trajectory

Equation (3.14) may be written in the equivalent form:

$$Y = X\tan\phi_o - \frac{gX^2}{2V_o^2}\sec^2\phi_o \qquad (3.29)$$

The derivative of the trajectory height with respect to elevation angle, at a fixed range, is:

$$\frac{dY}{d\phi_o} = X\left(1 - \frac{gX}{V_o^2}\tan\phi_o\right)\sec^2\phi_o \qquad (3.30)$$

If $\tan^2\phi_o << 1$, then $\sec^2\phi_o$ may be replaced by unity with no more than one percent error. The restriction, $\tan^2\phi_o << 1$, will therefore be taken as the flat-fire approximation to the vacuum trajectory. Vacuum trajectories for which $\phi_o < 5$ degrees, i.e., for which $\tan\phi_o < 0.1$, may be treated as flat-fire trajectories.

If we introduce the flat-fire approximation into equations (3.29) and (3.30):

$$Y \approxeq X\tan\phi_o - \frac{gX^2}{2V_o^2} \qquad (3.31)$$

$$\frac{dY}{d\phi_o} \approxeq X\left(1 - \frac{gX}{V_o^2}\tan\phi_o\right) \qquad (3.32)$$

For short ranges, where $\frac{gX}{V_o^2}\tan\phi_o << 1$, equation (3.32) may be further approximated as:

$$\frac{dY}{d\phi_o} \approxeq X \qquad (3.33)$$

Equation (3.33) is usually referred to as the "rigid trajectory" approximation, because a change in elevation angle produces a change in trajectory height that increases in direct proportion to increasing range, and the trajectory appears to rotate "rigidly" about the origin. The restriction under which the rigid trajectory approximation is formally valid for a vacuum trajectory is:

$$\frac{gX}{V_o^2}\tan\phi_o << 1 \qquad (3.34)$$

The error in trajectory height due to the flat-fire approximation is the difference between equations (3.31) and (3.29). That is, the approximation (3.31) is too high by the amount:

$$\varepsilon_Y = \frac{gX^2}{2V_o^2}\tan^2\phi_o \tag{3.35}$$

The vertical error in the flat-fire approximation to the vacuum trajectory increases rapidly with increasing range and elevation angle.

Example 3.4

What errors would result from using the flat-fire approximation in the arrow problem of example 3.1? Use equation (3.35) to evaluate the errors.

For the 50 yards range:

$$\varepsilon_Y = \frac{(32.174)(150)^2}{2(200)^2}\tan^2(3.46°) = 0.03 \text{ foot} = 0.4 \text{ inch}$$

The error at 50 yards range is negligible.

For the 100 yards range:

$$\varepsilon_Y = \frac{(32.174)(300)^2}{2(200)^2}\tan^2(6.98°) = 0.54 \text{ foot} = 6.5 \text{ inches}$$

The much larger error in the flat-fire approximation at 100 yards range is not surprising, since the elevation angle required to hit the 100 yard target violates the vacuum trajectory flat-fire restriction. One purpose of this example is to illustrate what happens when the flat-fire approximation is pushed beyond the limit of its validity.

The observant reader might correctly point out that there is no need for the flat-fire approximation to the vacuum trajectory, since the exact solution is simple and straightforward. In later chapters, the flat-fire approximation will be used in cases where no exact analytical solution is possible, and the flat-fire vacuum trajectory is introduced here to provide a background for future development.

3.4 FIRING UPHILL AND DOWNHILL

For uphill or downhill firing, the gun-target line is not horizontal. Figure 3.3 illustrates the problem of firing at a target whose altitude is higher than that of the gun. The gun-target line is inclined at an angle A, relative to the horizontal; in military terminology, A is the "angle of site." The gun elevation angle above the line of site is ϕ_o, and the angle ϕ_o is usually referred to as "superelevation." The angle of site is considered positive for uphill firing, and negative for a downhill slope.

A new coordinate system is introduced, with both the $\tilde{X}$ and $\tilde{Y}$ axes rotated through the angle A, so that the $\tilde{X}$-axis now lies along the gun-target line, and the $\tilde{Y}$-axis remains perpendicular to the $\tilde{X}$-axis. Relative to the $\tilde{X}$, $\tilde{Y}$ coordinates, the gravitational acceleration vector has components (-g sin A, -g cos A). The new differential equations of motion are:

$$\frac{d\tilde{V}_x}{dt} = -g\sin A \tag{3.36}$$

$$\frac{d\tilde{V}_y}{dt} = -g\cos A \tag{3.37}$$

Note that for A = 0, equations (3.36) and (3.37) reduce to equations (3.7) and (3.8). Integrating equations (3.36) and (3.37) yields:

$$\tilde{V}_x = V_o\cos\phi_o - gt\sin A \tag{3.38}$$

$$\tilde{V}_y = V_o\sin\phi_o - gt\cos A \tag{3.39}$$

$$\tilde{X} = V_o t\cos\phi_o - \frac{1}{2}gt^2\sin A \tag{3.40}$$

$$\tilde{Y} = V_o t\sin\phi_o - \frac{1}{2}gt^2\cos A \tag{3.41}$$

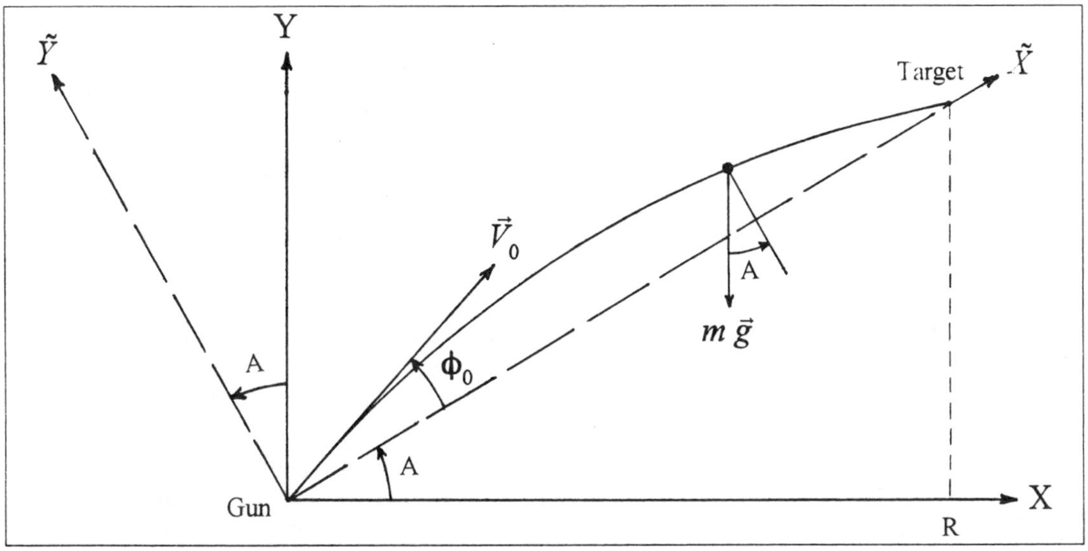

Figure 3.3 Uphill Coordinate System for the Vacuum Trajectory

Equations (3.40) and (3.41) are the parametric equations of the vacuum trajectory for uphill and downhill firing. Note that for A = 0 these equations reduce to equations (3.11) and (3.12).

The elimination of time between the parametric equations (3.40) and (3.41) is not as simple as it was for the level ground trajectory, because both $\tilde{X}$ and $\tilde{Y}$ vary quadratically with time. The equation stating the explicit dependence of $\tilde{X}$ on $\tilde{Y}$ is too cumbersome to be of any practical value, and the parametric form is ordinarily used instead. However, there are two special cases of the uphill-downhill vacuum trajectory problem that reduce to relatively simple analytical forms, and these special cases readily illustrate the interesting nature of the problem.

The first special case involves an expression for the dependence of slant range to impact, R_S, on the two angles, A and ϕ_o. At the impact point, $\tilde{Y} = 0$, and equation (3.41) gives:

$$t\left(V_o \sin\phi_o - \frac{1}{2} g t \cos A\right) = 0 \tag{3.42}$$

The non-trivial solution is:

$$t = \frac{2V_o \sin\phi_o}{g\cos A} \tag{3.43}$$

Substituting equation (3.43) into equation (3.40) and simplifying:

$$\tilde{X} = R_S = \frac{V_o^2}{g}\left[\sin 2\phi_o - 2\sin^2\phi_o \tan A\right]\sec A \tag{3.44}$$

With the help of the trigonometric identities:

$$2\sin^2\phi_o = 1 - \cos 2\phi_o = \sin 2\phi_o \tan\phi_o \tag{3.45}$$

Equation (3.44) can be written as:

$$R_S = \frac{V_o^2}{g}\sin 2\phi_o\left[1 - \tan\phi_o \tan A\right]\sec A \tag{3.46}$$

But $\frac{V_o^2}{g}\sin 2\phi_o = R$, the level ground range to impact, from equation (3.16). Substituting equation (3.16) into equation (3.46):

$$\boxed{R_S/R = \left[1 - \tan\phi_o \tan A\right]\sec A} \tag{3.47}$$

For a fixed superelevation angle, equation (3.47) states the relationship between the angle of site, A, and the ratio of slant range to level ground range. If $R_S/R > 1$, the slant range to impact along the incline exceeds the level ground range, and $R_S/R < 1$ means the slant range will be less than the level ground range. Equation (3.47) illustrates some very interesting properties of vacuum trajectories for uphill and downhill firing.

We first observe that since tan (-A) = -tan A, and sec (-A) = sec A, $R_S/R > 1$ for -90° < A < 0. Thus the slant range always exceeds the level ground range for downhill firing. For uphill firing where 90°> A > 0, with very small ϕ_o, $R_S/R > 1$. However, for larger superelevation angles, can be less than one, and the slant range will then be less than the level ground range. There is one (and only one) particular value of ϕ_o for which $R_S/R = 1$ at any given positive angle of site, and this critical value is obtained by setting $R_S/R = 1$ in equation (3.47) and solving for $\phi_{o_{cr}}$:

$$\boxed{\phi_{o_{cr}} = \tan^{-1}\left[(1 - \cos A)\cot A\right]} \tag{3.48}$$

where $\phi_{o_{cr}}$ = critical superelevation angle for $R_S/R = 1$

Some values of the critical superelevation angle at various angles of site, calculated by means of equation (3.48), are listed in Table 3.1. [Note that equation (3.48) is indeterminate at A = 0, and L' Hospital's rule must be used to find $\phi_{o_{cr}}$ at A = 0].

Table 3.1

A (Degrees)	$\phi_{o_{cr}}$ (Degrees)
0	0
15	7.25
30	13.06
45	16.33
60	16.10
75	11.23
90	0

For uphill vacuum trajectories, note that if $\phi_o < \phi_{o_{cr}}$, then $R_S/R > 1$; if $\phi_o = \phi_{o_{cr}}$, then $R_S/R = 1$; and if $\phi_o > \phi_{o_{cr}}$, then $R_S/R < 1$. Figures 3.4 and 3.5 are plots of equation (3.47) for uphill and downhill firing, respectively, and illustrate the interesting effect of various angles of site on the vacuum trajectory.

The flat-fire approximation to equation (3.47) provides another interesting and useful result. For $|\tan\phi_o \tan A|$ << 1, equation (3.47) reduces to the simple form:

$$\boxed{R_S/R \approx \sec A, or \quad (R_S \cos A)/R \approx 1} \tag{3.49}$$

The second form of equation (3.49) is referred to as the rifleman's rule for uphill and downhill firing; if the slant range to the target is R_S, the rifle sights should be set for the equivalent horizontal range $R_S \cos A$, in order to hit the target. However, the flat-fire approximation for uphill and downhill firing is more restrictive than for the level ground case. For moderate angles of site, tan A is of order unity, which requires that $\tan\phi_o$ << 1. Thus the flat-fire approximation to the vacuum trajectory, for uphill and downhill firing, is more restrictive than the corresponding condition, $\tan^2\phi_o$ << 1, for flat-fire across level ground.

The second special case of the uphill-downhill problem is an expression for the height of impact, $\tilde{Y}_I$, of the vacuum trajectory, at a slant range equal to the corresponding level ground impact range.

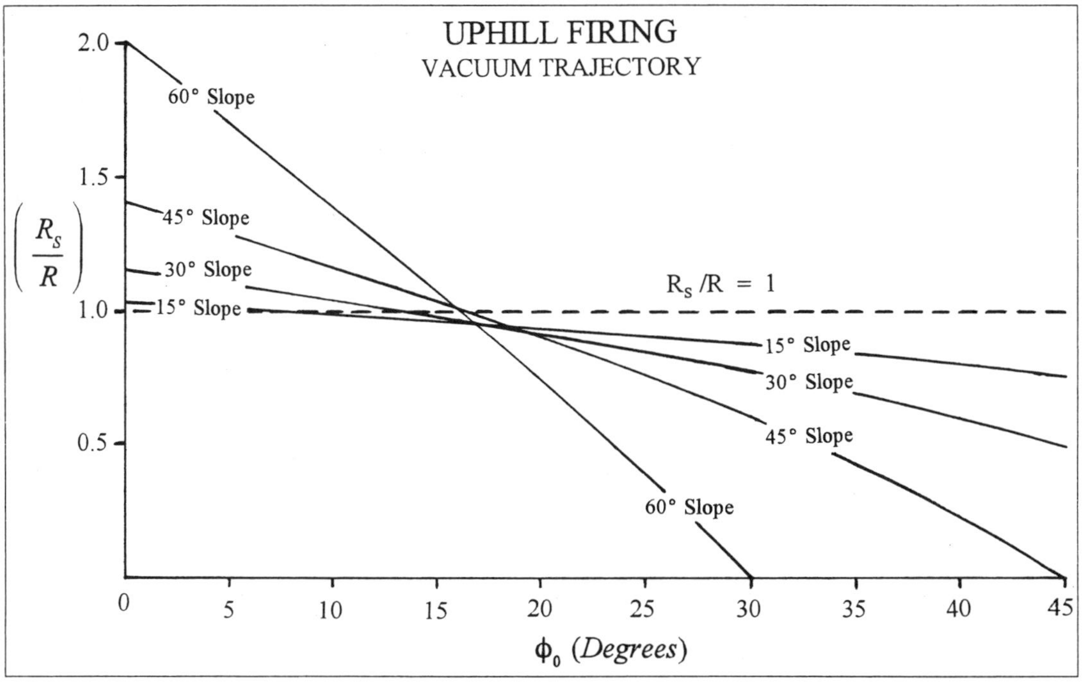

Figure 3.4 Ratio of Slant Range to Ground Range versus Superelevation.

We will solve equation (3.40) for time, substitute the solution into equation (3.41), and evaluate $\tilde{Y}_I$ for $\tilde{X}$ equal to the level ground range.

Equation (3.40) is solved for time by means of the quadratic formula:

$$t = \frac{V_o \cos\phi_o}{g\sin A}\left(1 \pm \sqrt{1 - \frac{2g\tilde{X}\sin A}{V_o^2 \cos^2\phi_o}}\right) \qquad \textbf{(3.50)}$$

The root corresponding to the negative sign before the radical in equation (3.50) is the correct solution. After some algebraic manipulation, equation (3.50) may be written in the alternative form:

$$t = \frac{2\tilde{X}}{V_o \cos\phi_o\left(1 + \sqrt{1 - \frac{2g\tilde{X}\sin A}{V_o^2 \cos^2\phi_o}}\right)} \qquad \textbf{(3.51)}$$

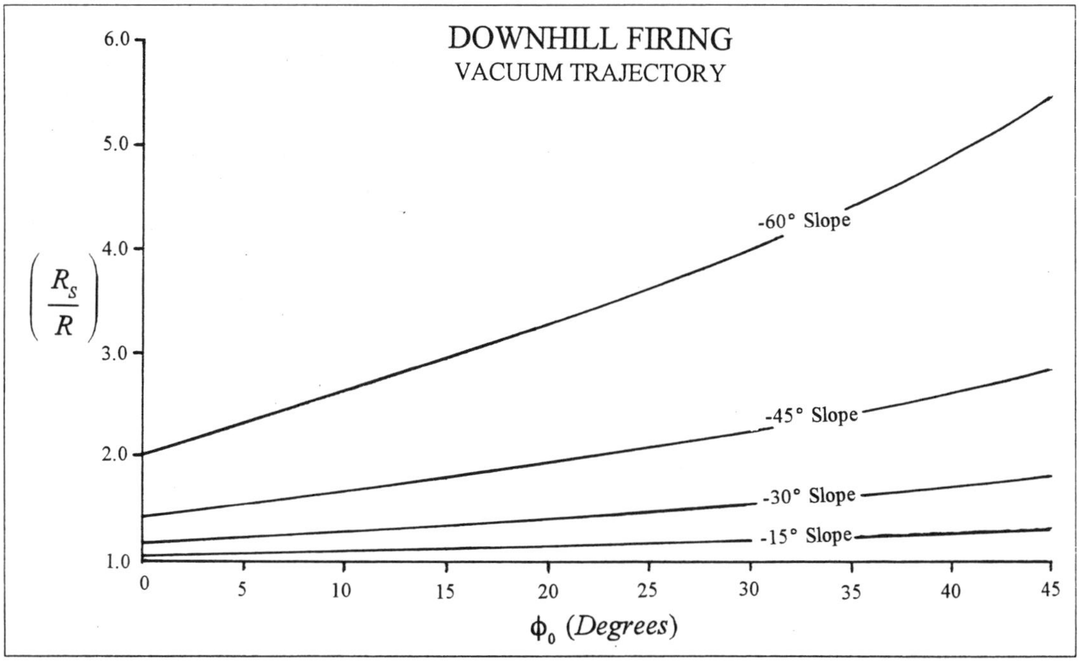

Figure 3.5 Ratio of Slant Range to Ground Range versus Superelevation.

Now, for $\tilde{X} = R = \frac{V_o^2}{g}\sin 2\phi_o$:

$$t = \frac{4V_o \sin\phi_o}{g(1+\nu)} \qquad \textbf{(3.52)}$$

where

$$\nu = \sqrt{1 - 4\tan\phi_o \sin A} \qquad \textbf{(3.53)}$$

Substituting equation (3.52) into equation (3.41):

$$\tilde{Y}_I = \frac{4V_o^2 \sin^2\phi_o}{g(1+\nu)}\left[1 - \frac{2\cos A}{1+\nu}\right] \qquad \textbf{(3.54)}$$

A number of intermediate algebraic steps have been omitted in the above derivation; these are left as an exercise for the interested reader.

Before we explore the properties of equations (3.53) and (3.54), we must first address the restriction implied in the ν equation. The parameter ν can be real only if the quantity $4\tan\phi_o \sin A < 1$. For downhill firing, sin (-A) = -sin A, thus ν is always real for any A < 0. However, for firing uphill, the parameter ν can be real only if $\tan\phi_o < \frac{1}{4}\csc A$. This inequality defines another restriction on ϕ_o; the projectile cannot reach an uphill target if the superelevation angle exceeds a maximum value, given by:

$$\phi_{o_{MAX}} = \tan^{-1}\left[\frac{1}{4}\csc A\right] \qquad \textbf{(3.55)}$$

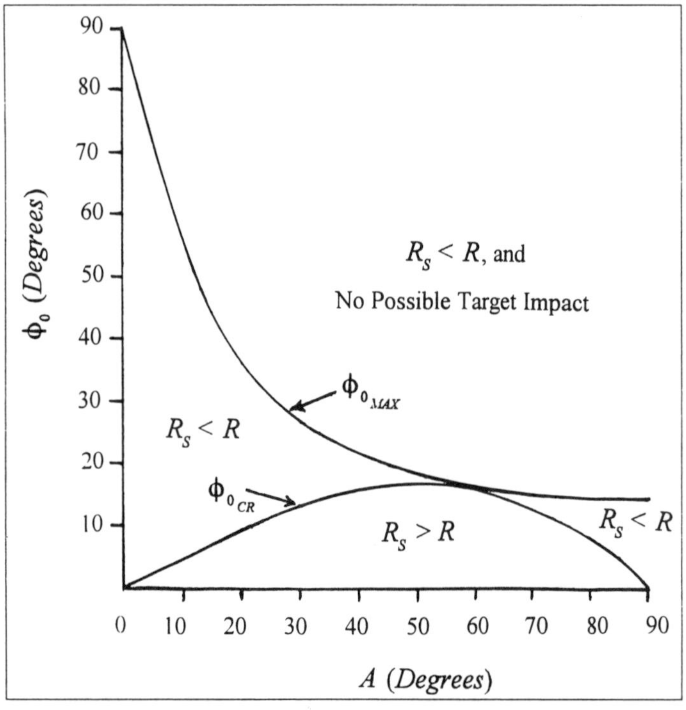

Figure 3.6 Critical Superelevation Angles versus Angle of Site

The angle $\phi_{o_{MAX}}$ is the superelevation angle above which the uphill vacuum trajectory can never reach the target. Figure 3.6 illustrates the variation of the two critical superelevation angles, $\phi_{o_{cr}}$ and $\phi_{o_{MAX}}$, with uphill angle of site, A, and shows how the two curves bound the various solution regions for vacuum trajectories.

Several interesting properties of equations (3.53) and (3.54) are listed below:

(a) If A = 0, then $\nu = 1$, and $\tilde{Y}_I = 0$. The impact height vanishes, as it should, for level ground firing.

(b) If $\phi_o = \phi_{o_{cr}} = \tan^{-1}\left[(1-\cos A)\cot A\right]$, $\nu = 2\cos A - 1$, and $\tilde{Y}_I = 0$. The impact height correctly vanishes for the critical superelevation angle, where $R_S/R = 1$.

(c) For flat-fire ($\tan\phi_o << 1$), $\nu \approx 1$, and the approximate impact height is given by:

$$\tilde{Y}_I = \frac{2V_o^2 \sin^2\phi_o}{g}\left[1 - \cos A\right] \qquad \textbf{(3.56)}$$

Now, cos (-A) = cos A, and we observe that for flat-fire, the trajectory will always intersect the target above center, and the projectile will strike equally high for either uphill or downhill firing.

Example 3.5

An air gun fires a heavy projectile at a muzzle velocity of 250 feet per second. Sight settings have been obtained for ranges between 50 yards and 400 yards, on level ground. Determine the impact locations on targets placed at the same ranges, but along a 30 degree uphill incline.

The first step in the solution is to find the gun elevation angles required to hit the level ground targets, using equation (3.17). For A = 30 degrees, equation (3.47) is then used to find the ratio of slant range to level ground range. Table 3.2 illustrates the calculations.

The projectile will hit high on the 50, 100 and 200 yard uphill targets, and low on the 300 and 400 yard targets. To find how high or low the impacts will be, we will use the exact parametric equations (3.53) and (3.54). The flat-fire approximation to the impact height, from equation (3.56), is also included for comparison.

At 50 yards range, flat-fire is a valid assumption for the low velocity air gun, and the error in equation (3.56) is less than one inch in impact height. For the longer ranges, all of which violate the flat-fire restriction, the accuracy of equation (3.56) degrades rapidly, and at the two longest ranges, it predicts a high impact on the target, when in fact, the impact will be low.

Table 3.2

R (Yards)	ϕ_o (Degrees)	R_S/R	R_S (Yards)
50	2.21	1.129	56
100	4.44	1.103	110
200	9.00	1.049	210
300	13.80	0.991	297
400	19.08	0.924	370

Example 3.6

Repeat the calculations of example 3.5 for firing downhill along a minus 30 degree incline. This exercise is left to the interested reader.

Enough detail has been included in this section to demonstrate that firing uphill and downhill is not a trivial problem, even with the simplifying assumption of a vacuum trajectory. The fact that actual atmospheric trajectories behave in a remarkably similar fashion is sufficient reason to understand the behavior of uphill and downhill vacuum trajectories.

3.5 SUMMARY

A number of interesting properties of vacuum trajectories have been presented in this chapter. Actual atmospheric trajectories display many of these same properties, but lack the convenience of a simple analytical solution. Although there are very few practical applications of the vacuum trajectory in modern exterior ballistics, the mathematical methods introduced in this chapter form the framework on which the higher approximations of later chapters are based.

Table 3.3

R_S (Yards)	[Equation (3.53)] ν	[Equation (3.54)] $\tilde{Y}_I$ (Inches)	[Equation (3.56)] $\tilde{Y}_I$(Inches)
50	0.961	8.5	9.3
100	0.919	28.4	37.5
200	0.827	64.6	153
300	0.713	-33.8	355
400	0.555	-727	667

4

Notes on Aerodynamic Drag

4.1 INTRODUCTION

The importance of aerodynamic drag to exterior ballistics was first realized in the eighteenth century, when Benjamin Robins of England invented the ballistic pendulum, and used his invention to make the first reasonably accurate velocity measurements. Robins chronographed the velocity of twelve-gauge (3/4 inch) lead spheres at various ranges, and showed that the aerodynamic drag force acting on a high velocity spherical projectile was many times larger than the force of gravity.

The modern concept of aerodynamic drag has gradually evolved over the past 250 years, and some of the milestones in that evolution were noted in Chapter 1. The experimental high water mark occurred about fifty years ago, with the advent of modern high speed wind tunnels and spark photography ranges. The precise measurements made possible by modern facilities have significantly advanced the current state of knowledge of the aerodynamic forces and moments that act on projectiles. This chapter presents some of the aerodynamic drag results obtained in modern wind tunnels and spark photography ranges, and updates the information published in the older classical textbooks on exterior ballistics.

4.2 CLASSICAL DRAG MEASUREMENTS

A brief history of the aerodynamic drag measurements made during the last third of the nineteenth century was given in section 1.3 of Chapter 1. Figure 1.1 illustrates some of the earliest results obtained by various nations for the drag coefficient of a flat-based artillery shell with a short tangent ogive nose. Figures 1.2 and 1.3 show the slightly improved Projectile Type 1 design, and the drag results obtained for this shape by General Mayevski from firings done at the Krupp factory in Germany (on which Ingalls' Tables were based), and by the French Naval Artillery from firings done at the Gâvre Proving Ground (on which the later G_1 Tables were based). Both the Ingalls (Ref.1) and the Gâvre (Ref. 2) drag functions, and

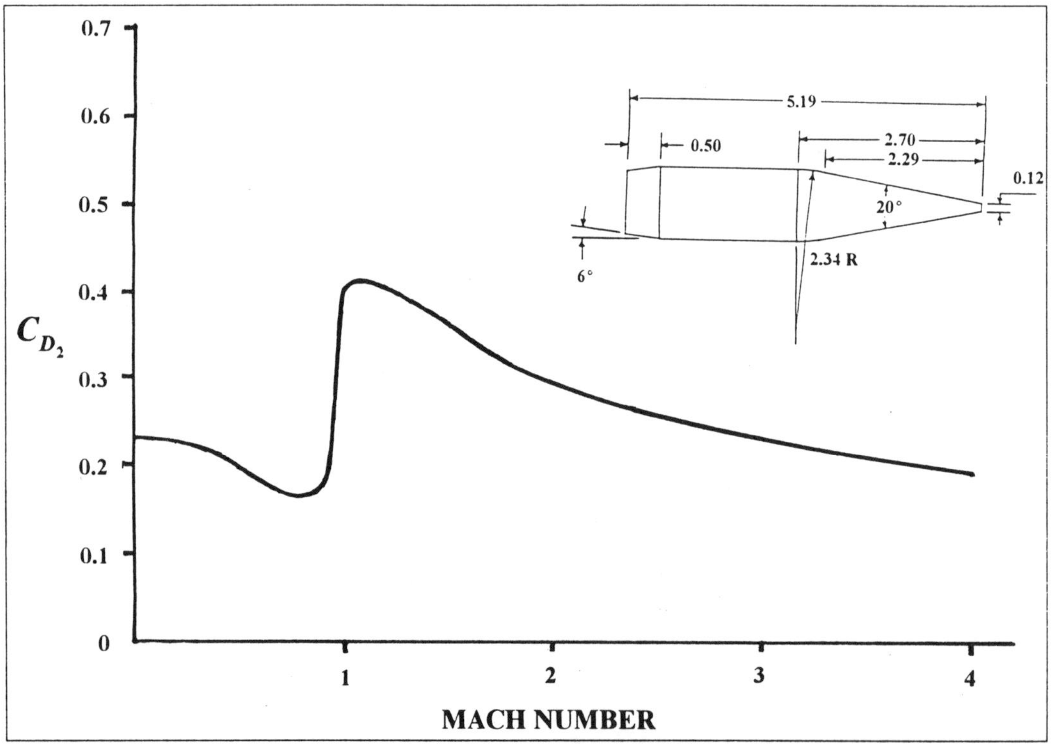

Figure 4.1 Drag Coefficient versus Mach Number for Projectile Type 2.

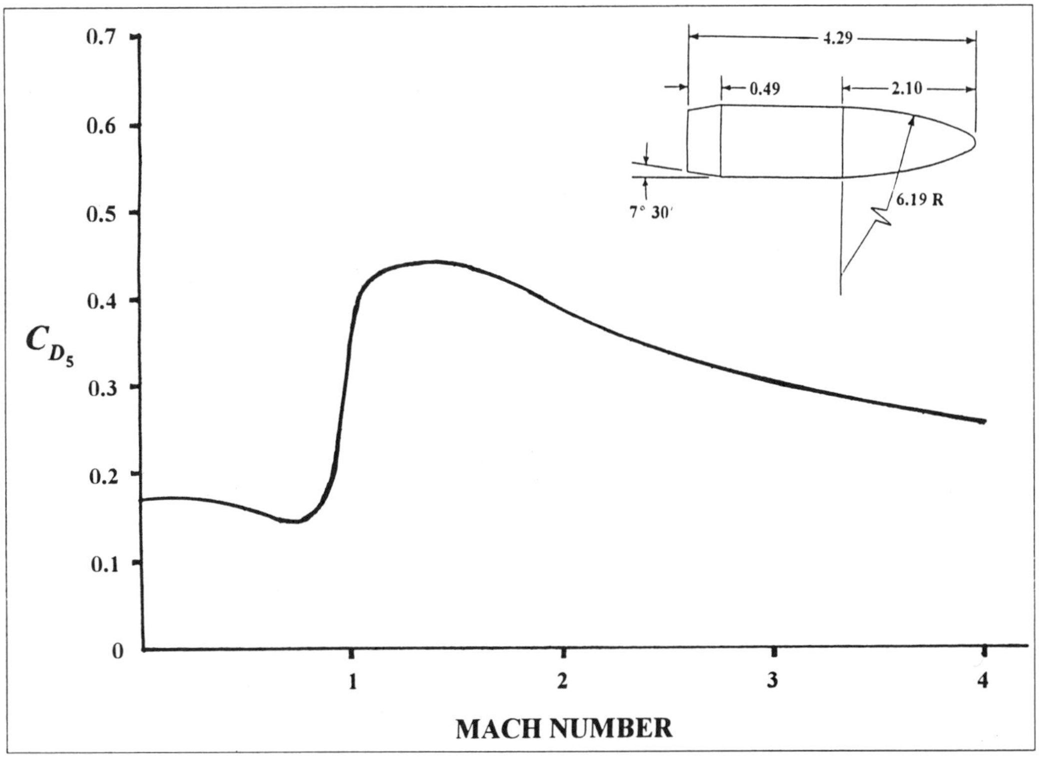

Figure 4.2 Drag Coefficient versus Mach Number for Projectile Type 5.

the related exterior ballistic tables based on them, were first published between 1895 and 1900, and have been widely distributed and used ever since. Until the end of the First World War, virtually all nations used either the Ingalls or the G_1 tables for most exterior ballistic calculations.

The Ingalls and G_1 drag functions, and their associated exterior ballistic tables, were often used to calculate trajectories for projectiles that were quite different in shape from Projectile Type 1. The effect of a different projectile shape on the drag was accounted for by means of a form factor "i," that adjusted the Ingalls or G_1

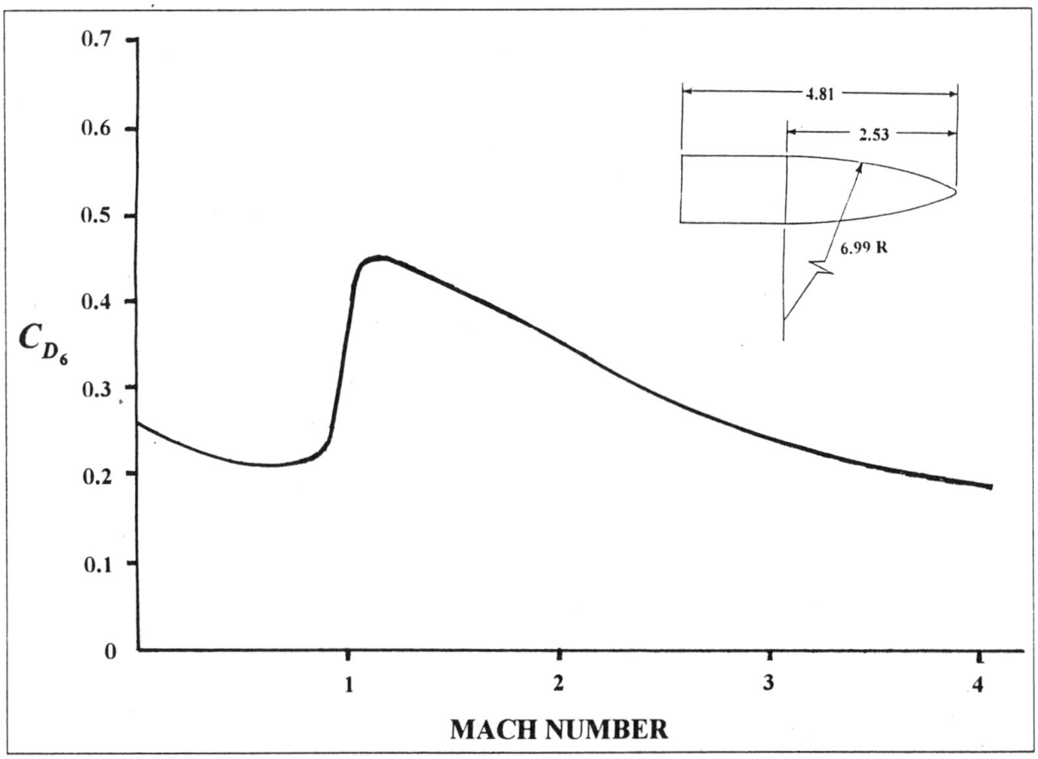

Figure 4.3 Drag Coefficient versus Mach Number for Projectile Type 6.

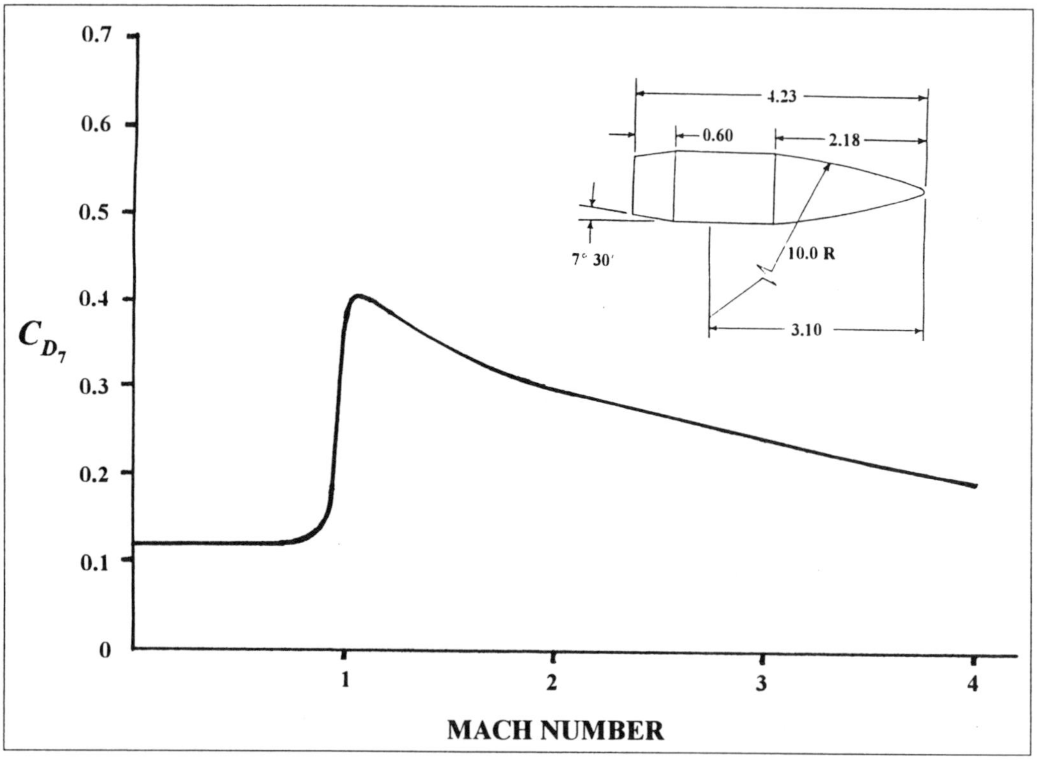

Figure 4.4 Drag Coefficient versus Mach Number for Projectile Type 7.

drag curve so it more or less agreed with the actual projectile drag. We will illustrate the technique in Chapter 6 of this book. As a slightly humorous note, H. P. Hitchcock (Ref. 3) observed, not entirely in jest, that the form factor was denoted by "i" because it was sometimes called the coefficient of ignorance!

During the period between the First and the Second World Wars, a number of advances were made in the science of aerodynamic drag determination. Ballistic instrumentation was significantly improved, projectile design was evolving toward longer, lower drag configurations and the emerging new science of modern supersonic

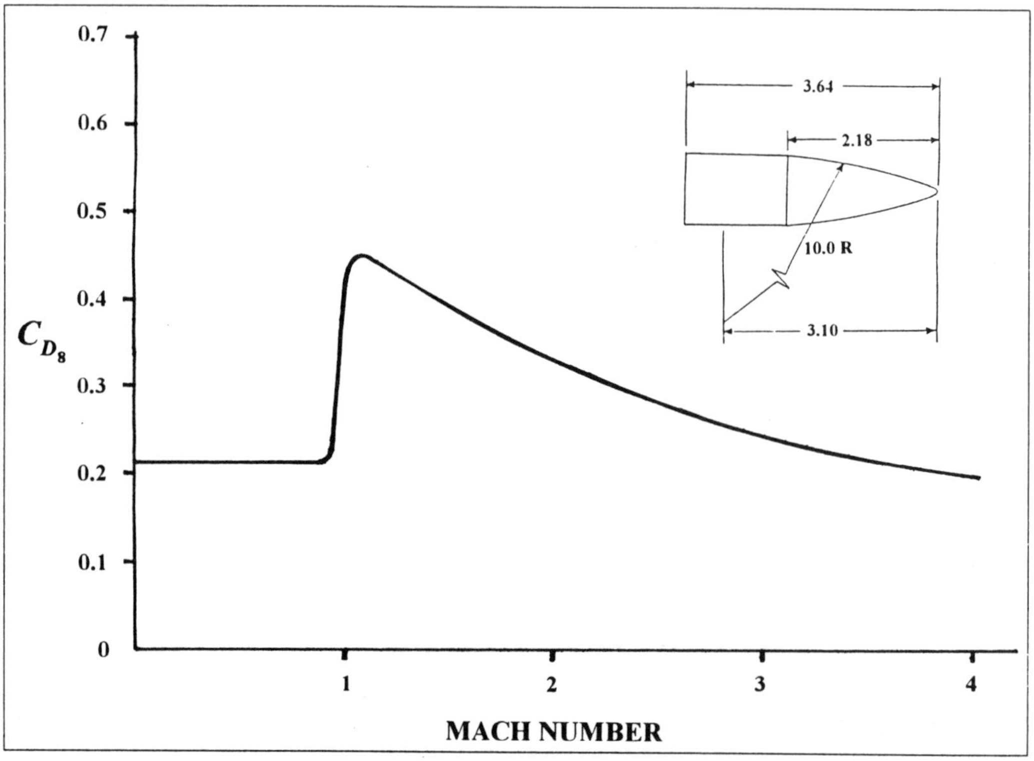

Figure 4.5 Drag Coefficient versus Mach Number for Projectile Type 8.

aerodynamics was beginning to provide a better theoretical understanding of the nature of drag. Various nations began experimental programs to accurately measure the drag of the new improved projectile designs (see section 1.4 of Chapter 1). In this section, we will highlight the results of investigations conducted by R. H. Kent and H. P. Hitchcock at Aberdeen Proving Ground, Maryland.

Figures 4.1 through 4.5 illustrate the drag results obtained by Kent and Hitchcock for the projectile shapes we now refer to as Projectile Type 2 (G_2), Projectile Type 5 (G_5), Projectile Type 6 (G_6), Projectile Type 7 (G_7) and Projectile Type 8 (G_8). The dimensions of these projectiles were given in Figures 1.4 through 1.8 of Chapter 1. Projectile Type 2 was referred to as "Type J" in References 3, 4 and 5.

Various revisions of the drag coefficients and related ballistic tables exist for the G_2 through G_8 projectile shapes. Generally, the last revisions, which were done during or shortly after the Second World War, are the curves presented in this chapter. (One exception is the G_2 drag curve; the second revision, G_2 Rev 2, is less accurate than the first, and therefore G_2 Rev 1 is used). The following table lists the projectile types, the drag function and revision used, the BRL File number in which the drag table is found, and the year of adoption:

Table 4.1

Projectile Type	Drag Function	BRL File Number	Year
1	G_1	N-I-50	1942
2	G_2 Rev 1	N-I-86	1945
5	G_5 Rev 1	N-I-79	1945
6	G_6 Rev 1	N-I-87	1945
7	G_7 Rev 2	N-I-119	1952
8	G_8 Rev 1	N-I-89	1945

After about 1950, the use of reference standard projectile drag shapes began to disappear in U. S. Army Ordnance, due to the simultaneous advent of modern supersonic wind tunnels, spark photography ranges and high-speed digital computers. The classical G_2 through G_8 projectile shapes, drag coefficients, and ballistic tables now take their place beside the Ingalls and G_1 functions which served exterior ballisticians very well in an even earlier time.

4.3 THE PHYSICAL NATURE OF DRAG

A modern definition of the aerodynamic drag force was stated in equations (2.1-a) and (2.1-b) of Chapter 2. Note that the quantity $\frac{1}{2}\rho V^2 S$ has the dimensions of a force, and the drag coefficient, , is therefore dimensionless, i.e., independent of the system of units chosen.

The dimensionless drag coefficient, in turn, depends on a number of other dimensionless variables. For the general class of projectiles typically used in exterior ballistics, these include the Mach number, the Reynolds number, the yaw level, and various non-dimensional shape parameters, which collectively specify the projectile shape. The Mach number, V/a, where *a* is the speed of sound, is the ratio of projectile speed to the speed of sound in air, and is therefore a nondimensional speed. The Reynolds number, $\rho Vl/\mu$, where μ is the viscosity of air and *l* is the projectile length, is the ratio of inertia forces to viscous forces. [Note: the reference diameter, *d*, is sometimes used instead of the length, *l*, in defining the Reynolds number]. The effect of projectile size on the drag coefficient is related to the Reynolds number. In general, the dependence of the drag on Reynolds number is slight, and both the zero-yaw drag coefficient C_{D_0}, and the yaw-drag coefficient $C_{D_{\delta^2}}$, are usually regarded as depending only on Mach number. There are exceptions to this general rule, as we will note later in this chapter.

The fluid mechanism that transmits the drag force to the projectile consists of two parts; surface pressure and surface shear stress. The pressure drag acting on the projectile forebody is often called "wave drag," and the pressure drag acting on the projectile base is simply called "base drag". The viscous contribution to drag arises from the surface shear stress, and is usually called "skin friction drag". For all practical purposes, the wave drag depends only on the Mach number. The base drag depends primarily on Mach number, but the Reynolds number effect on base drag is not entirely negligible. The skin friction drag shows a significant dependence on both Mach number and Reynolds number. The various components of the aerodynamic drag force behave in significantly different ways in different speed regions, which gives rise to some of the interesting drag coefficient plots we will discuss later in this chapter.

4.4 AIRFLOW REGIMES

Some effects of projectile shape on the drag coefficient at various Mach numbers are illustrated in Figure 4.6 (*top p. 56*). The lowest curve is a plot of the drag coefficient versus Mach number for the very low drag 5.56mm BRL-1 projectile (Ref. 6), which has a three-caliber long secant ogive nose, and a one-caliber long conical boattail. The middle curve shows the drag coefficient of a short, flat-based bullet with an ogive length of 1.3 calibers, and a méplat

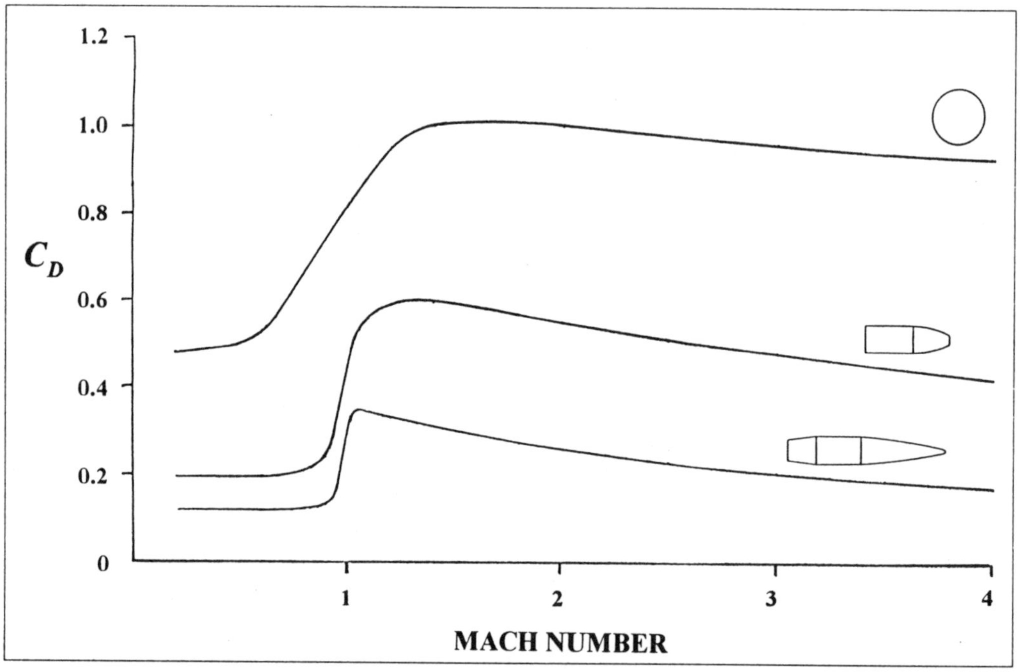

Figure 4.6 Drag Coefficients for Three Projectile Shapes.

(nose-tip flat) diameter of 0.35 caliber. This projectile has approximately twice the drag coefficient of the BRL-1 shape, at all speeds. The upper curve in Figure 4.6 is a plot of the drag coefficient versus Mach number for a 9/16 inch diameter smooth steel sphere. The sphere drag coefficient is nearly four times that of the very low drag BRL-1 shape!

The three drag coefficient plots shown in Figure 4.6 have some common characteristics. At subsonic flight speeds (Mach numbers well below 1.0), the drag coefficients are essentially constant. The drag coefficient rises sharply near Mach 1.0, then slowly decreases at higher supersonic speeds. The sudden rise in C_D that occurs at flight speeds just below the speed of sound is caused by the formation of shock waves in the flowfield around the projectile.

The nature of subsonic, transonic and supersonic flow is clearly illustrated by a series of twelve spark shadowgraphs recently taken in the BRL Aerodynamics Range (Ref. 7) for the caliber .50 Ball M33 bullet (Ref. 8). The M33 is a typical boattailed small arms projectile, whose dimensions are shown in Figure 4.7; the measured zero-yaw drag coefficient variation with Mach number is plotted in Figure 4.8.

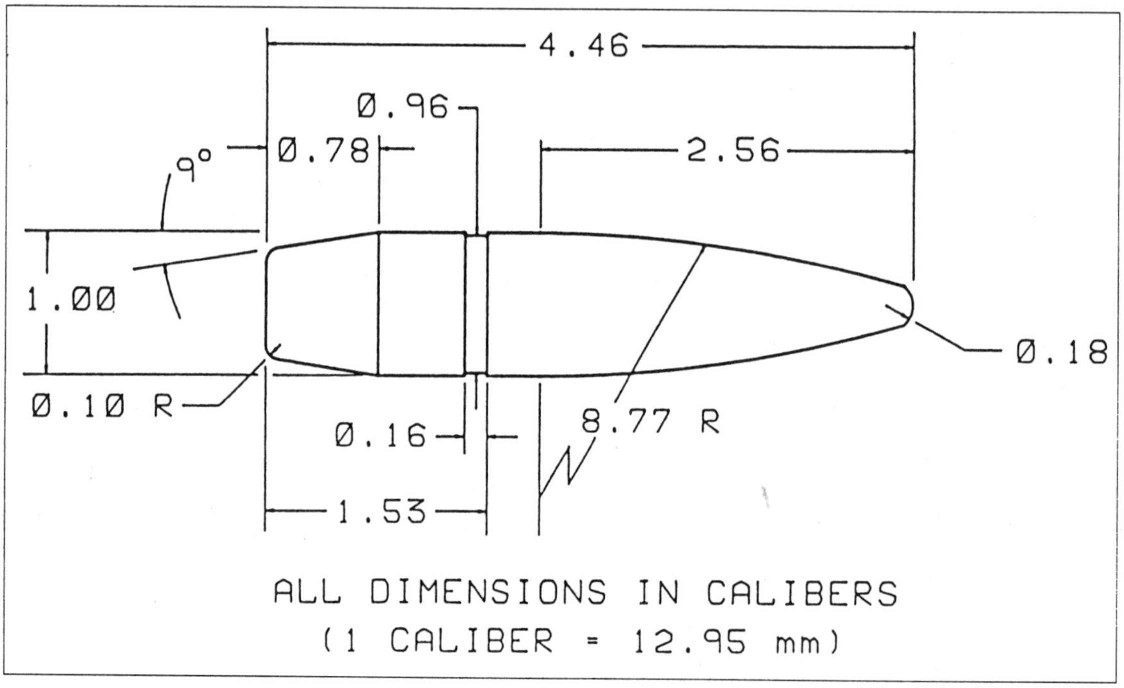

Figure 4.7 Sketch of the Caliber .50 Ball M33 Projectile.

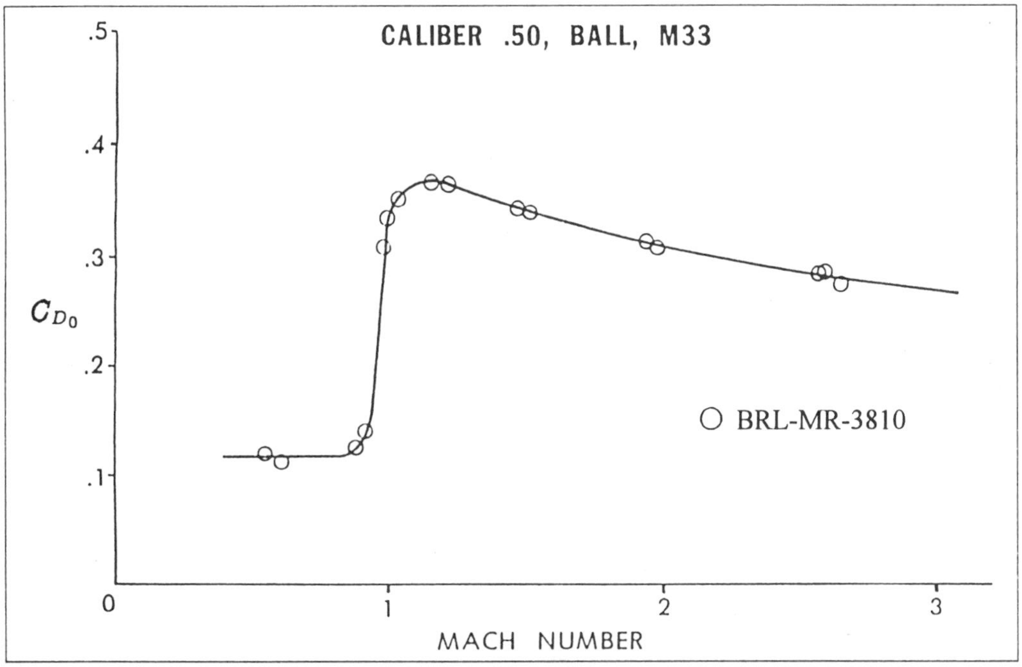

Figure 4.8 Zero-Yaw Drag Coefficient versus Mach Number for the Caliber .50 Ball M33 Projectile.

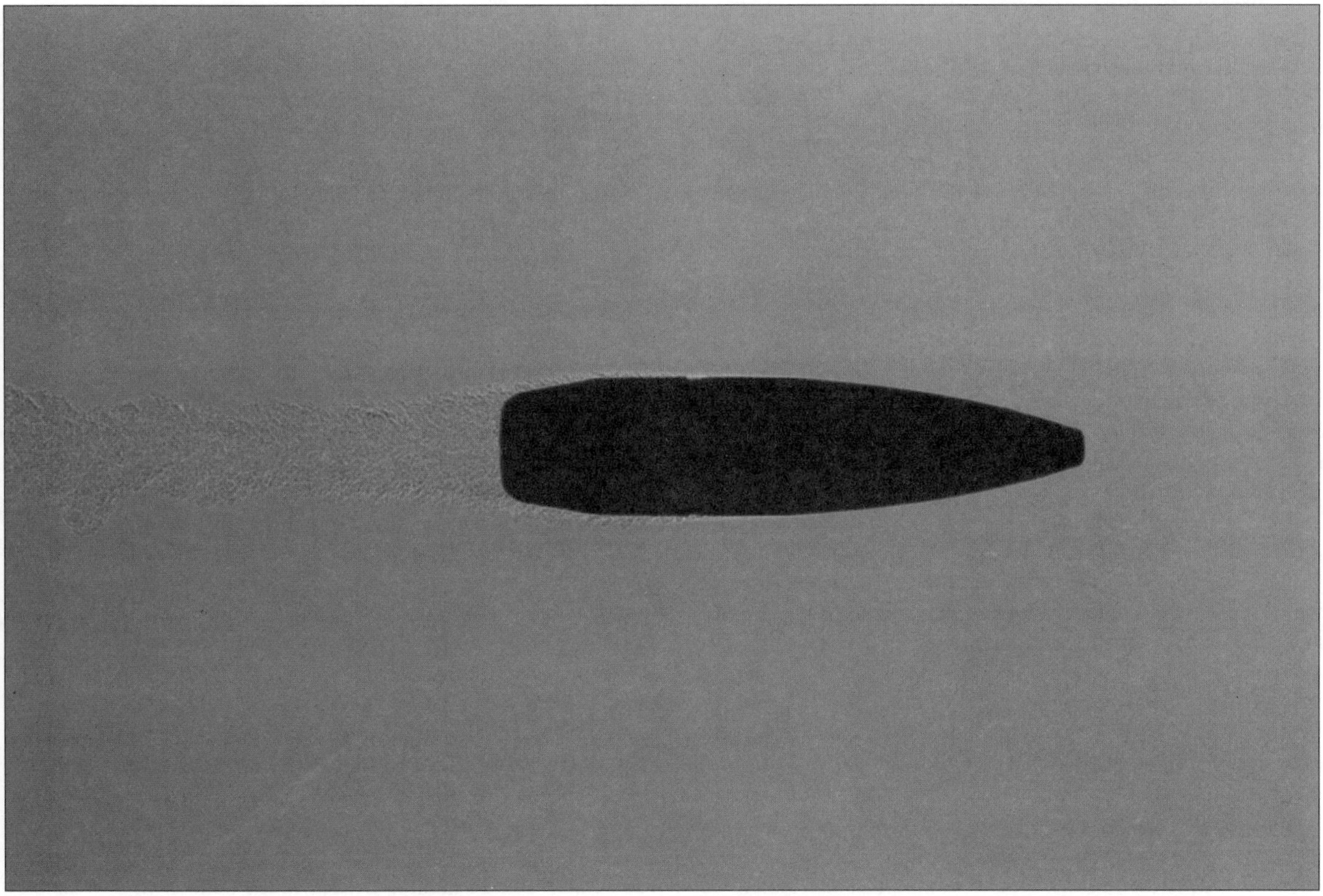

Figure 4.9 Shadowgraph of Flowfield at Mach 0.75.

Figure 4.9 is a spark shadowgraph of the Ball M33 projectile taken at Mach 0.75; the flowfield at this speed is everywhere subsonic, as is confirmed by the absence of shock waves. The boundary layer over the ogive is laminar, with transition to turbulence (looks like bubbles) just aft of the ogive-cylinder junction. Note the increase in turbulent boundary layer thickness caused by the boattail. The general character of the boundary layer and the turbulent wake, which is a region of low pressure behind the projectile base, are common to all the shadowgraphs in this series. The measured drag coefficient is 0.118, for Mach numbers below 0.80.

In Figure 4.10, taken at Mach 0.89, the projectile is at the low end of the transonic flow region. The flow over most of the surface is subsonic; the expansion caused by the boattail is just sufficient to generate a tiny region of locally supersonic flow, which shocks down to subsonic speed approximately one-third of the way down the boattail. The drag coefficient at Mach 0.89 is 0.126, which is only slightly above the subsonic value.

At Mach 0.92, illustrated in Figure 4.11, the flow over most of the ogive is subsonic. Expansion around the ogive onto the cylindrical center section generates a very small region of locally supersonic flow, which shocks down to subsonic speed almost immediately. The flow between the ogive-cylinder shock and the start of the boattail is subsonic. The expansion around the boattail corner causes locally supersonic flow, which shocks down to subsonic speed roughly half way down the boattail. The shock waves at Mach 0.92 are visibly stronger than the very weak boattail shock observed in Figure 4.10. The measured drag coefficient at Mach 0.92 has increased to 0.139.

Figure 4.12 shows the flowfield at Mach 0.96. The flow over the front half of the ogive is subsonic, after which expansion causes locally supersonic flow back onto the cylinder. The flow shocks down to subsonic speed just ahead of the cannelure (crimping groove). A region of locally subsonic flow exists from the cannelure to the start of the boattail. Expansion caused by the boattail corner produces locally supersonic flow, which shocks down to subsonic speed about two-thirds of the way down the boattail. The shock waves are becoming stronger as the flight Mach number is increased. Note the increase in the turbulent boundary layer thickness caused by the strong boattail shock. The drag coefficient at Mach 0.96 has increased to 0.202.

In Figure 4.13, at Mach 0.98, the presence of Mach waves indicates that the flow is locally supersonic over much of the bullet surface. The flow over the front half of the ogive is subsonic, after which it accelerates to form a small supersonic zone, then immediately shocks back down to subsonic speed. Local expansion at the ogive-cylinder junction again accelerates the flow to supersonic speed, and it remains supersonic over the rest of the projectile. Note the optical refraction (vertical white lines) behind the projectile, caused by the light passing edgewise through the strong three-dimensional, saucer-shaped trailing shock wave. The drag coefficient is rising rapidly, and has increased to 0.263 at Mach 0.98. The rapid increase in drag coefficient at high transonic speed is the phenomenon often described in the popular literature as the "sound barrier."

Figure 4.14, taken at Mach 1.00, shows a rather similar flowfield to that observed at Mach 0.98. Theoretically, a true normal shock now stands infinitely far ahead of the nose; in reality the shock is a finite distance ahead, but far out of the field of view of the shadowgraph. The drag coefficient is still rising very sharply, and has increased to 0.323 at Mach 1.00.

Figure 4.15, taken at Mach 1.02, shows a strong, slightly curved bow shock standing about 1.5 calibers ahead of the nose tip. The front one-half of the ogive shows locally subsonic flow, with no indication of Mach waves; the flow over the aft part of the projectile is supersonic. Note the oblique shock at the forward-facing step of the cannelure, the trailing shock near the end of the boattail, and the downstream wake recompression shock that forms at the neck of the wake, where the supersonic flow returns to the streamwise direction. The trailing shock and the wake recompression shock eventually coalesce, as Figure 4.15 shows. The drag coefficient at Mach 1.02 has increased to 0.344.

Figure 4.16, taken at Mach 1.06, illustrates the rapidly decreasing bow shock standoff, and the increasing shock curvature near the nose tip, as the Mach number increases at low supersonic speed. The flow over the front one-third of the ogive is locally subsonic, as indicated by the absence of Mach waves, and the shock wave patterns are very similar to those observed at Mach 1.02. The measured drag coefficient at Mach 1.06 is 0.357.

In Figure 4.17, at Mach 1.24, the bow shock has moved closer to the nose tip, the shock curvature near the tip is greater, and except for a very small region around the blunt nose tip, the flowfield around the projectile is everywhere supersonic. The drag coefficient at Mach 1.24 is 0.365, which is nearly its maximum value.

At Mach 1.53, illustrated in Figure 4.18, the bow shock standoff at the nose tip has virtually disappeared. The initially high curvature of the shock near the blunt projectile nose tip is quickly attenuated, and the bow shock becomes essentially an oblique shock wave at large distances from the projectile. The flowfield at this speed and all higher speeds is everywhere supersonic. The drag coefficient at Mach 1.53 is 0.342.

Figures 4.19 and 4.20, taken at Mach 1.99 and Mach 2.66, respectively, illustrate the flowfield around the caliber .50 Ball M33 projectile at high supersonic speeds. The shock waves are swept farther back with increasing flight Mach number, in accordance with supersonic oblique shock wave theory. The measured drag coefficient at Mach 1.99 has decreased to 0.311; at Mach 2.66 the drag coefficient has dropped to 0.282.

The hypersonic flow regime is not illustrated in our shadowgraph series. At hypersonic speeds, the shock waves are similar in appearance to those of Figure 4.20, but are swept even farther back. One characteristic of hypersonic flow is that the bow shock wave lies essentially adjacent to the projectile surface. The thin region between the shock and the surface is referred to as the "shock layer," and the very high temperature, pressure and density of air in the shock layer is another characteristic of hypersonic flow. There is no exact dividing point between supersonic and hypersonic speed. As a rough rule of thumb, a flight Mach number of 5 is usually taken as the beginning of the hypersonic flow regime.

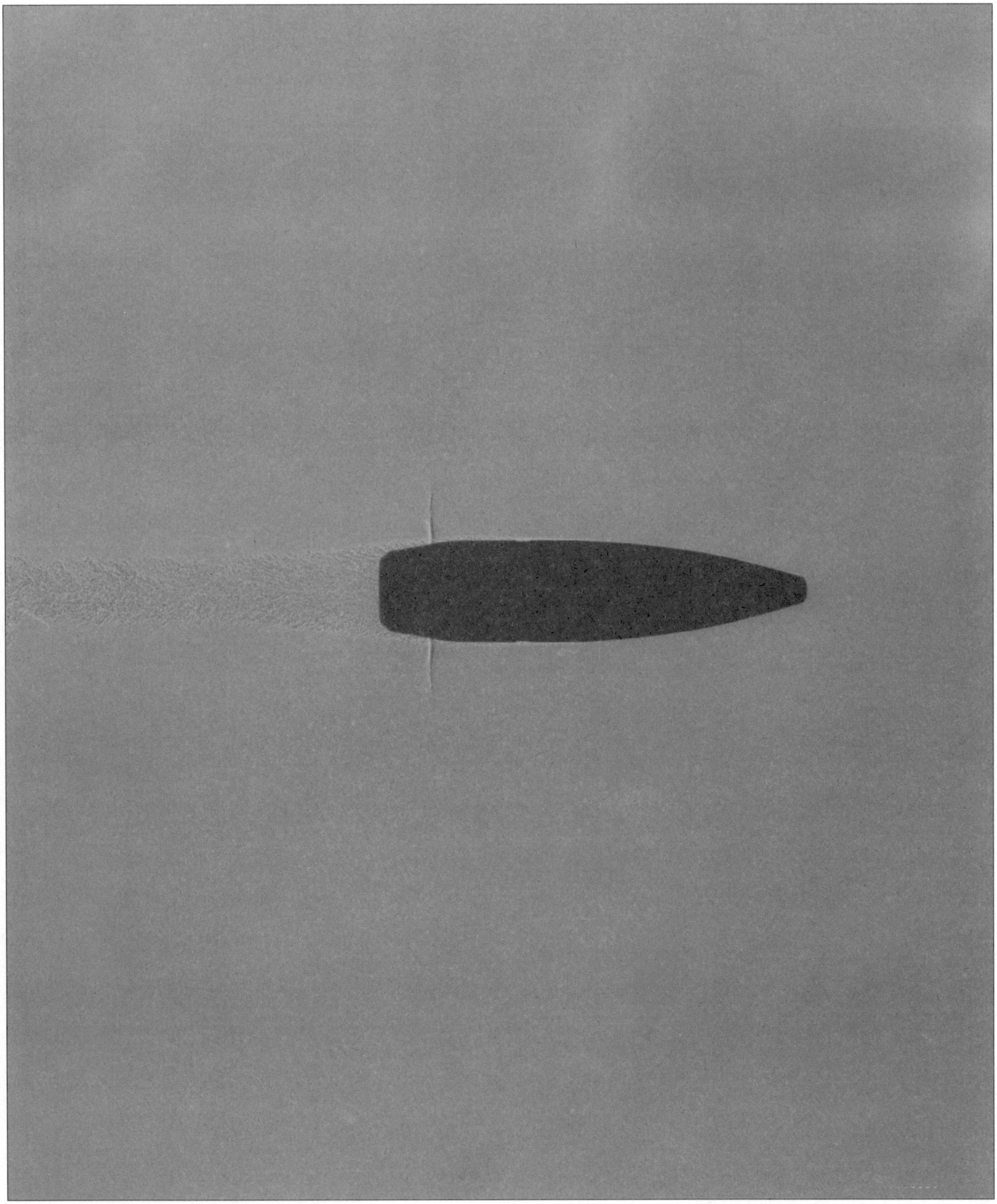

Figure 4.10 Shadowgraph of Flowfield at Mach 0.89.

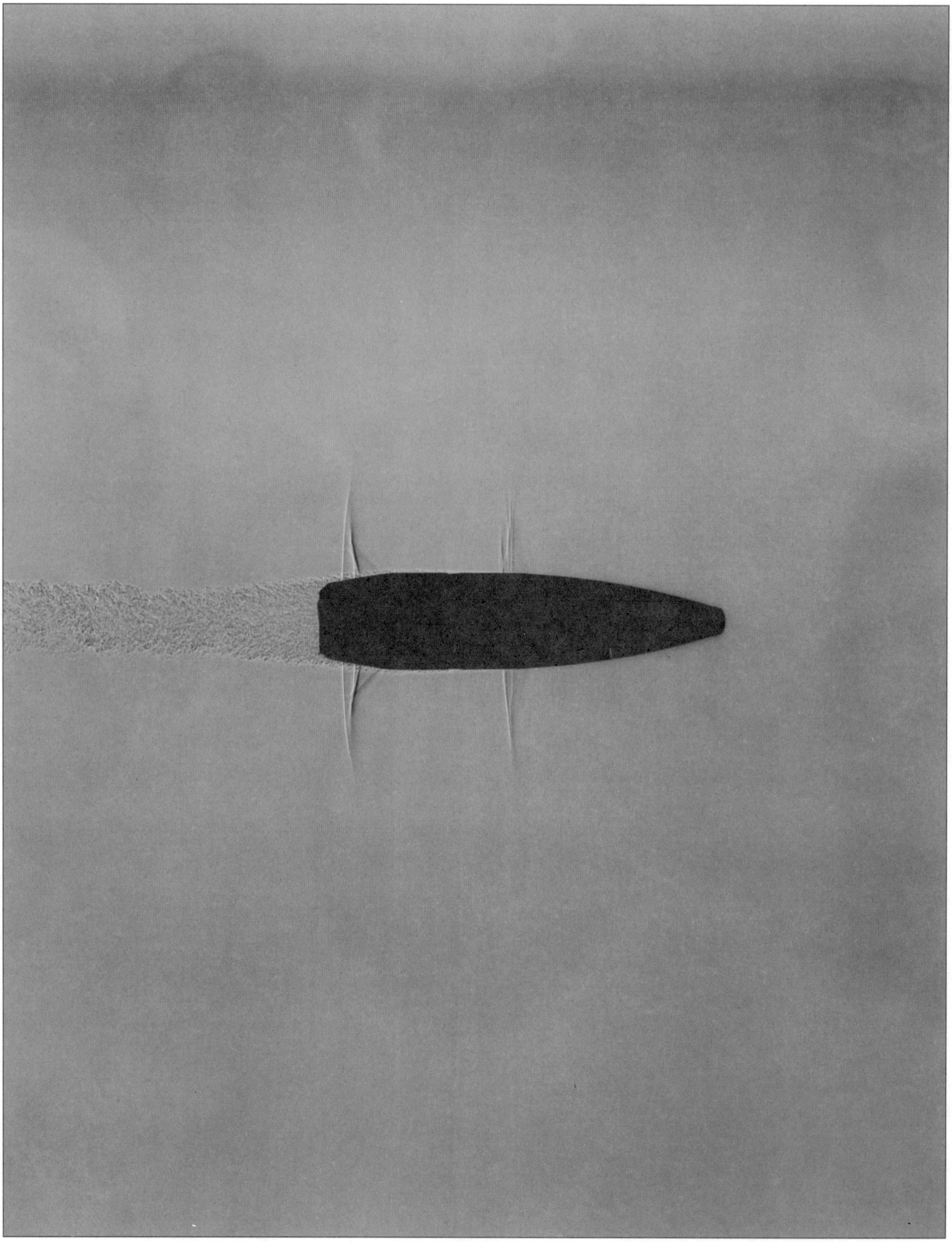

Figure 4.11 Shadowgraph of Flowfield at Mach 0.92.

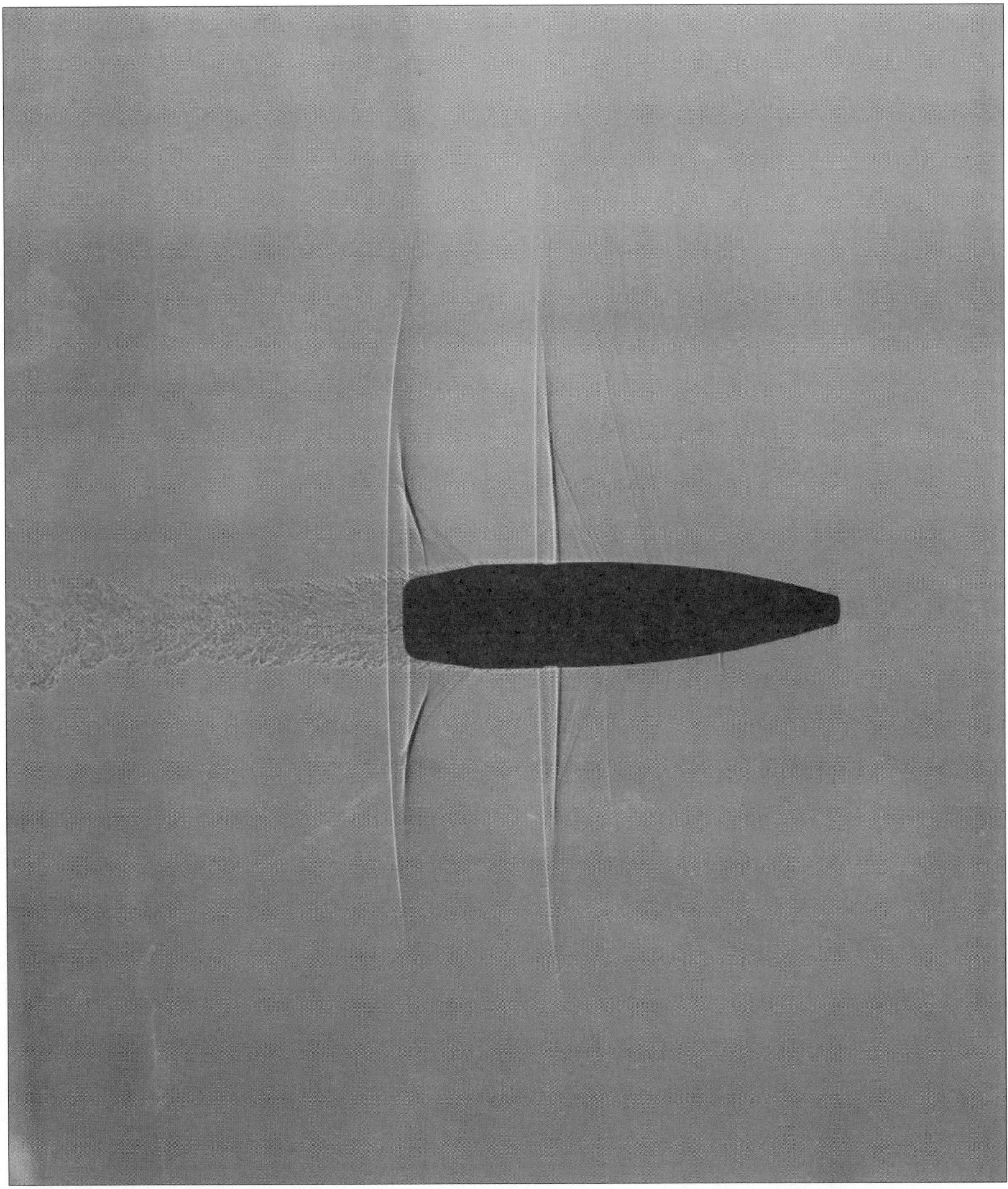

Figure 4.12 Shadowgraph of Flowfield at Mach 0.96.

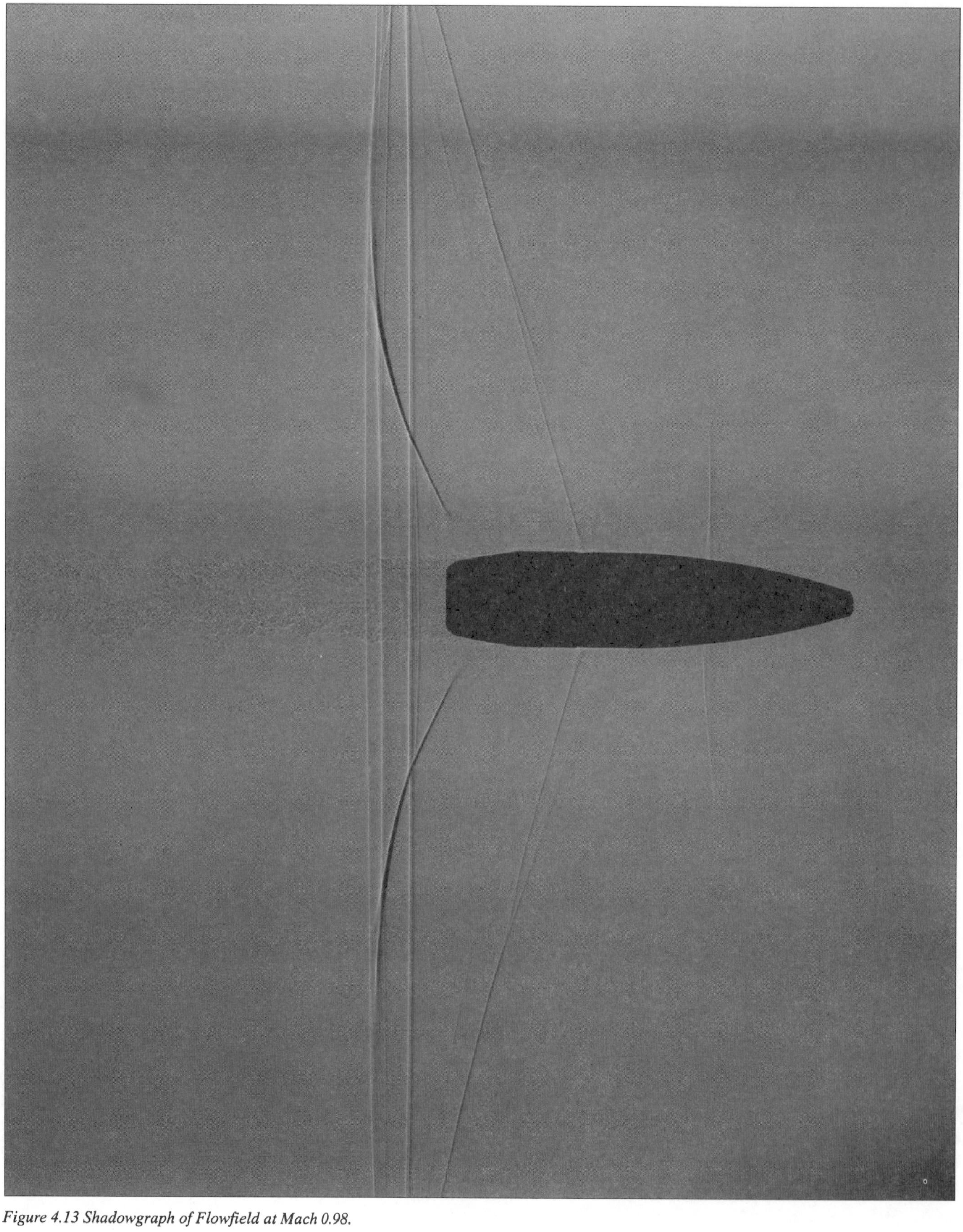

Figure 4.13 Shadowgraph of Flowfield at Mach 0.98.

Figure 4.14 Shadowgraph of Flowfield at Mach 1.00.

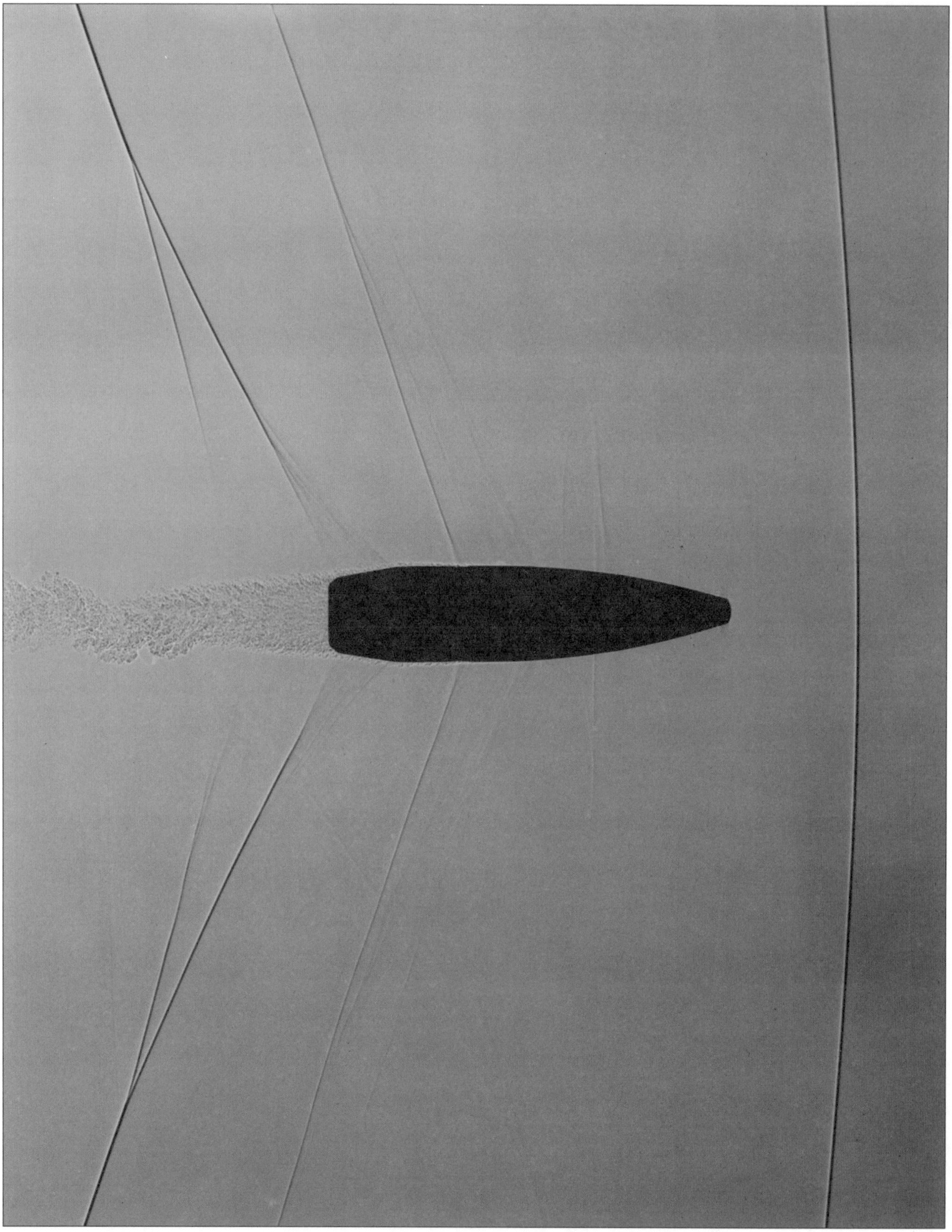

Figure 4.15 Shadowgraph of Flowfield at Mach 1.02.

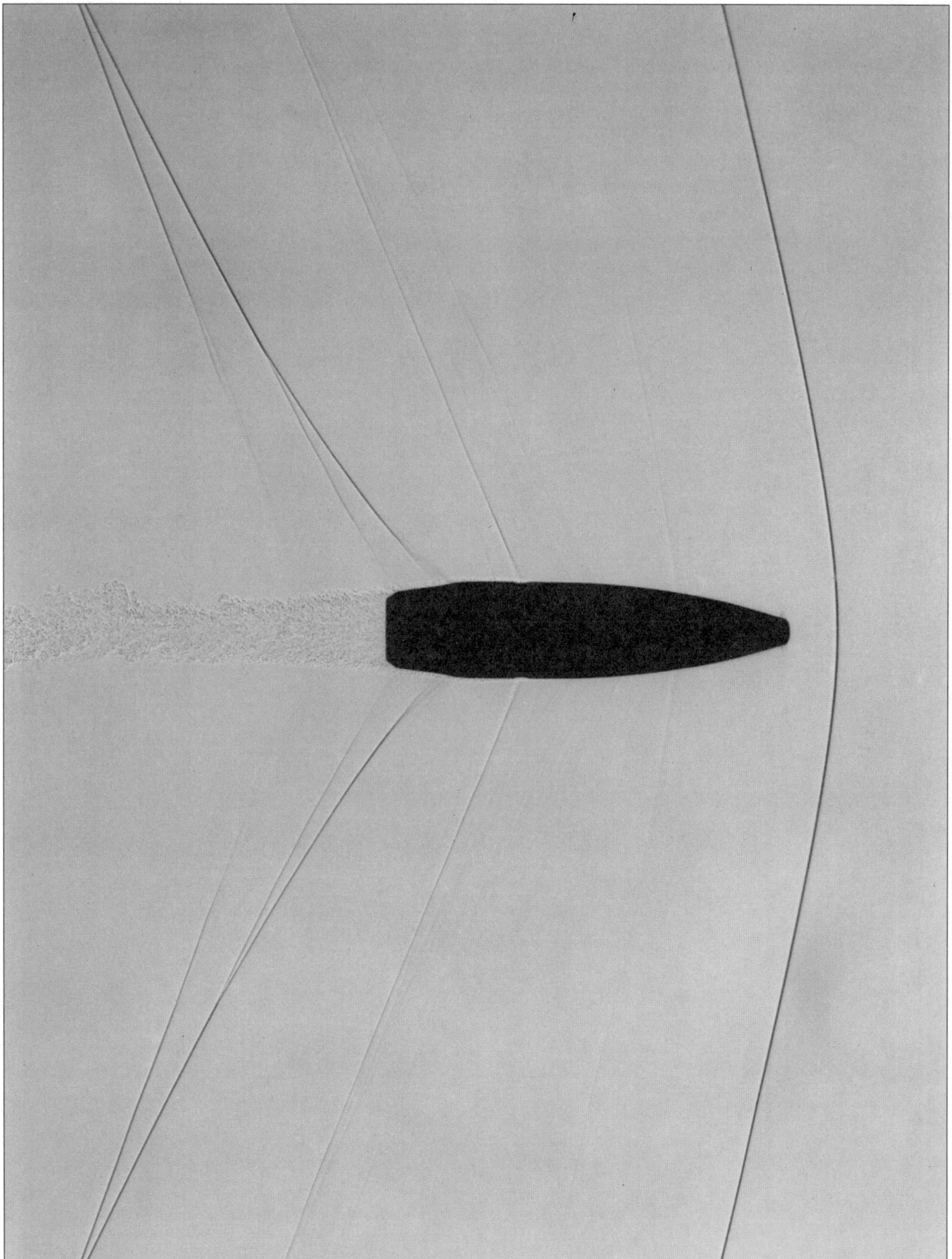

Figure 4.16 Shadowgraph of Flowfield at Mach 1.06.

Figure 4.17 Shadowgraph of Flowfield at Mach 1.24.

Figure 4.18 Shadowgraph of Flowfield at Mach 1.53.

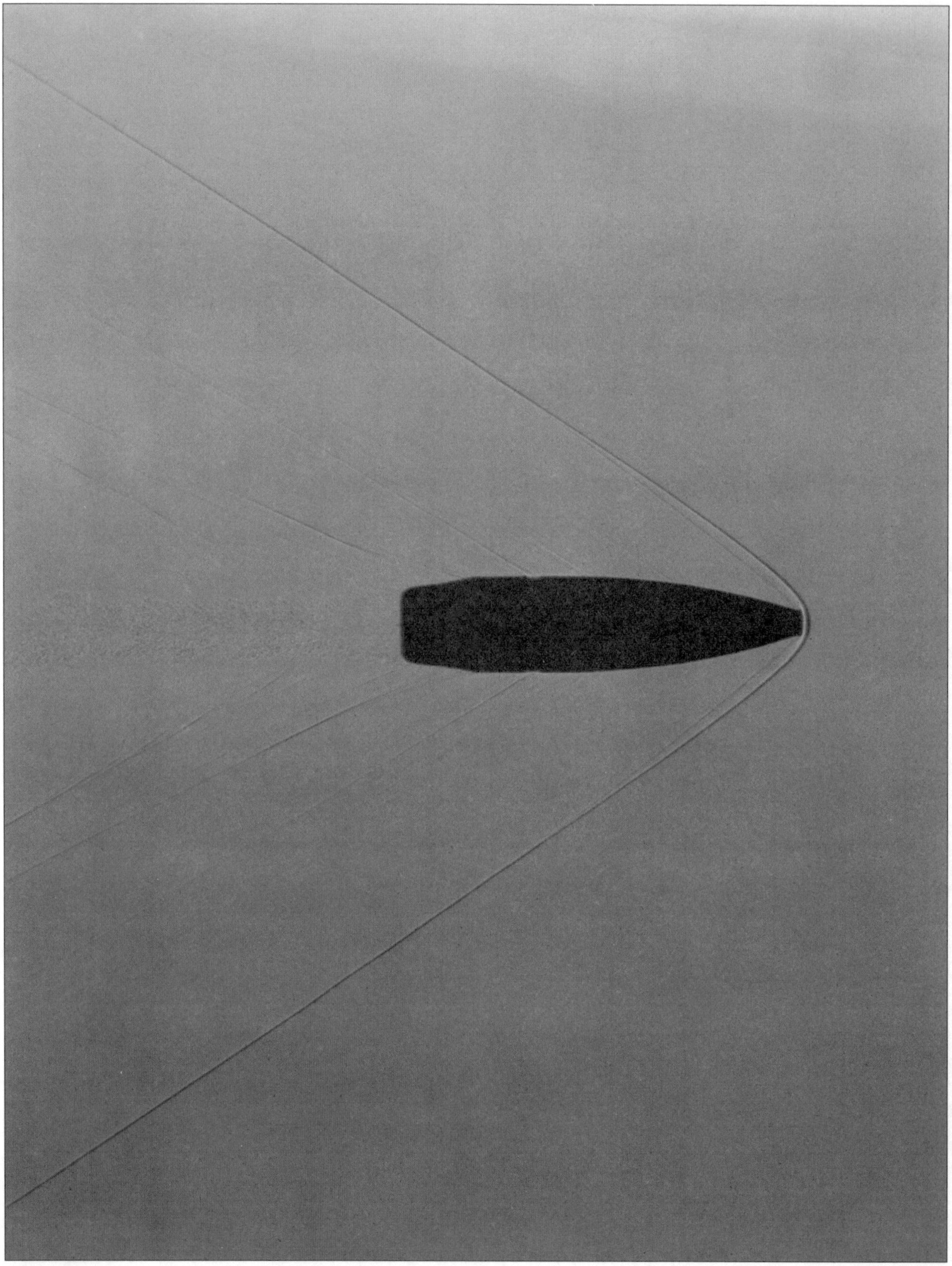

Figure 4.19 Shadowgraph of Flowfield at Mach 1.99.

Figure 4.20 Shadowgraph of Flowfield at Mach 2.66.

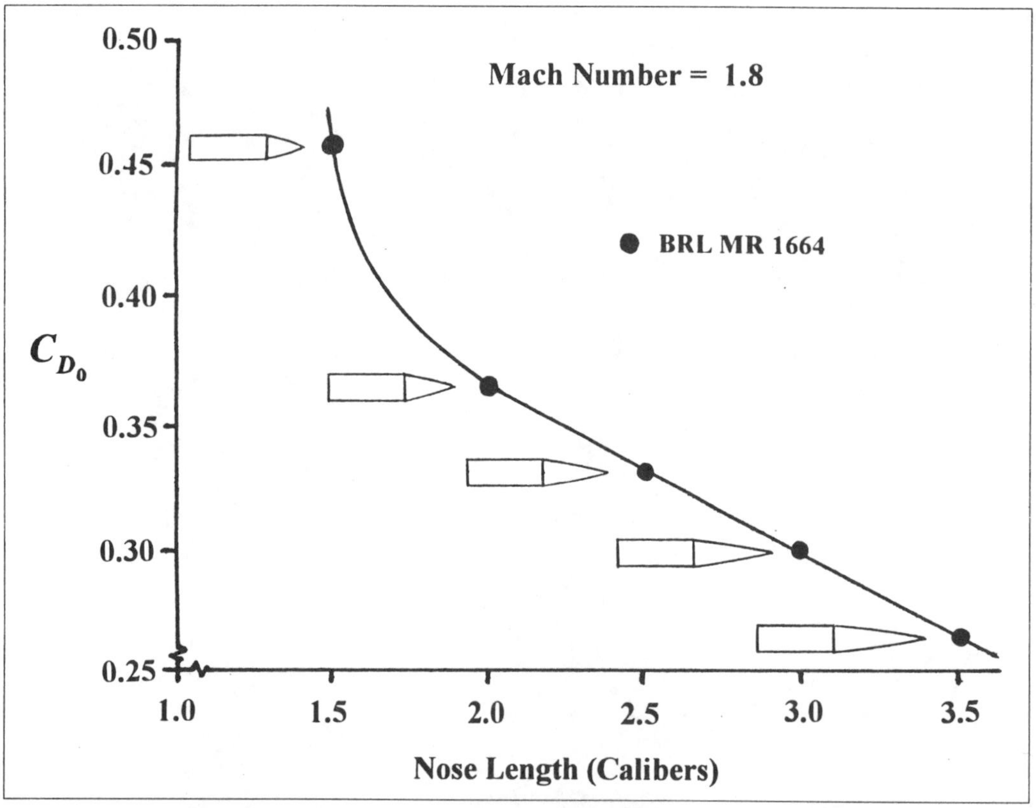

Figure 4.21 Zero-Yaw Drag Coefficient versus Nose Length.

No attempt is made in this chapter to discuss the basic fluid dynamic and thermodynamic processes involved in the formation of boundary layers and shock waves. This book is about exterior ballistics, and space does not permit even a cursory review of the modern science of aerodynamics. References 9 through 12 are recommended to the reader who is interested in a more complete understanding of compressible flow, shock waves, and boundary layer theory.

4.5 THE EFFECT OF PROJECTILE SHAPE ON DRAG

Figure 4.6 illustrated the fact that short, blunt projectiles are higher drag shapes than are longer, more streamlined configurations. In this section, we will take a closer look at several of the more important projectile shape parameters, and their effect on the drag coefficient in various speed regions.

The first shape parameter effect we will investigate is the effect of projectile nose length on the drag. Figure 4.21 illustrates the effect of varying the nose length of a secant-ogive projectile (Ref. 13) at Mach 1.8, and shows that short nose lengths dramatically increase the drag at this speed. Theoretical and experimental results confirm that the shape of the curve in Figure 4.21 is also typical for other projectile nose shapes, at both lower and higher supersonic speeds.

All ogival nose shapes are generated by circular arcs, and the radius of the arc, denoted by R, has a distinct effect on the drag. [Note that the symbol R was used to denote the range in Chapter 3. There should be no confusion, however, because the symbol R in this chapter always means the radius of an ogive]. The nose shape (headshape) parameter used to quantify the drag effect is R_T/R, where R_T is the radius of a tangent ogive nose whose length is the same as the actual nose. For any tangent ogive nose, $R = R_T$, thus the headshape parameter $R_T/R = 1$ for all tangent ogive noses. A conical nose may be considered as an ogive with an infinite generating radius, thus $R_T/R = 0$ for any conical (spire-pointed) nose shape. Every secant ogive is generated by an arc whose radius lies somewhere between these two extremes; therefore $0 < R_T/R < 1$ for any secant ogive nose.

Figure 4.22 shows the effect on the drag coefficient of varying the nose shape (Ref. 14) at Mach 2.44, and illustrates the fact that a secant ogive design has less drag at high supersonic speed than either the conical or tangent ogive shapes. The lowest drag circular arc ogive at supersonic speed (i.e. $R_T/R = 0.5$), is a secant ogive design whose generating radius is twice that of the corresponding tangent ogive radius for the same nose length. The upper curve of Figure 4.23 shows a similar result at low supersonic speed. However, the lower curve of Figure 4.23 shows that the tangent ogive, which gives the highest drag at supersonic speeds, is lower in drag than either the conical or the secant ogive shapes at Mach 0.80. (The reader is cautioned not to draw the erroneous conclusion that the low-drag nose shapes indicated in Figures 4.22 and 4.23 are absolute least-drag shapes; they are merely the lowest drag members of the family of circular-arc ogival noses).

A projectile nose may be blunted in two distinct ways: (1) by truncating a sharp pointed nose, or (2) by opening up the nose contour, while holding the nose length constant. The first approach (truncation) always increases the drag, although the effect of small

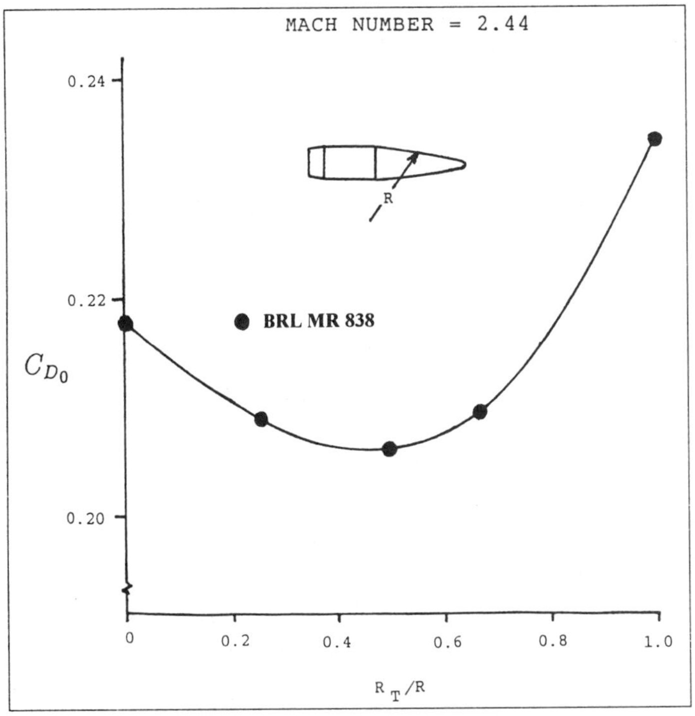

Figure 4.22 Zero-Yaw Drag Coefficient versus Headshape Parameter

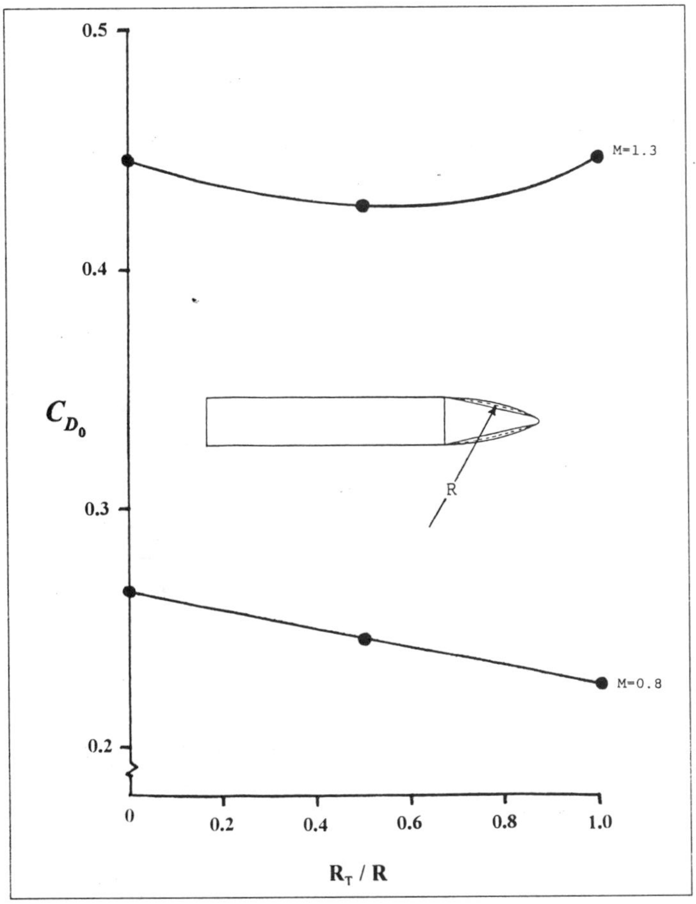

Figure 4.23 Zero-Yaw Drag Coefficient versus Headshape Parameter.

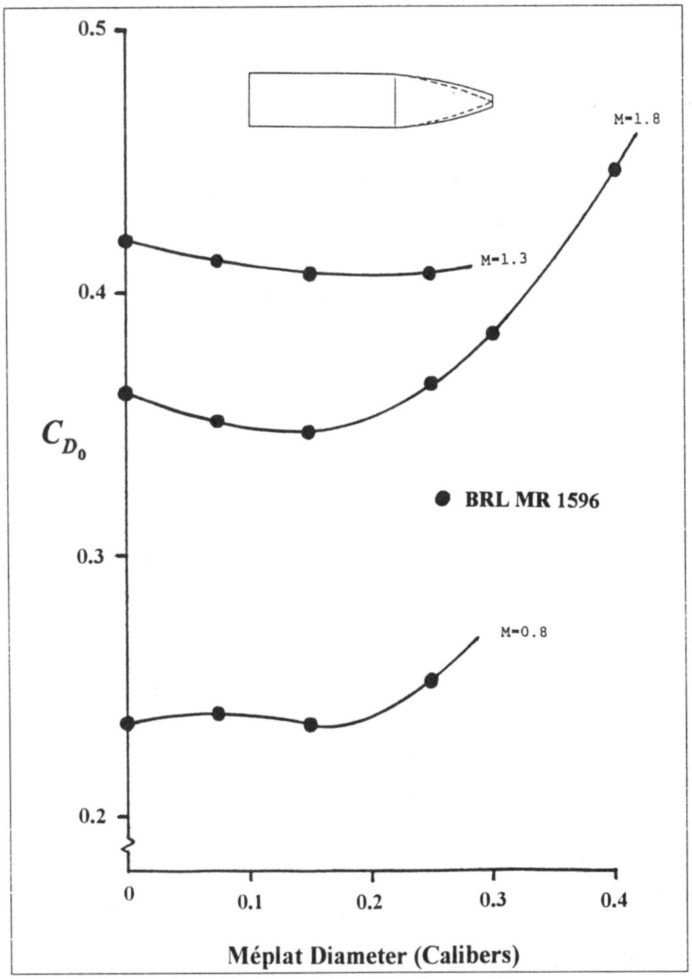

Figure 4.24 The effect of Nose Bluntness on the Drag Coefficient.

bluntness [méplat (nose-tip flat) diameter less than 0.1 caliber] is insignificant.

Figure 4.24 illustrates the effect on drag of blunting the projectile nose (Ref. 15) by opening up the nose contour. For a fixed nose length at supersonic speeds, opening up the nose contour to a small méplat gives lower drag than the sharp pointed nose! This fact is indeed fortunate for the projectile designer who strives for low drag designs, since sharp pointed ogives are utterly impractical for either ordnance or sporting use.

The méplat diameter that gives lowest drag varies with the flight Mach number, the nose length, and the nose shape. In general, a méplat diameter of 0.10 to 0.15 caliber is a good design choice over a wide range of flight speeds. For a fixed nose length at supersonic speeds, an inscribed hemispherical tip, instead of a méplat, gives a slight further reduction in drag.

Figure 4.25 shows the effect of boattailing on the drag coefficient at high supersonic speeds (Ref. 16). For a seven-degree boattail angle, lengthening the boattail systematically reduces the drag at supersonic speeds. Unfortunately, very long boattails usually cause flight dynamic instability, which will be discussed in a later chap-

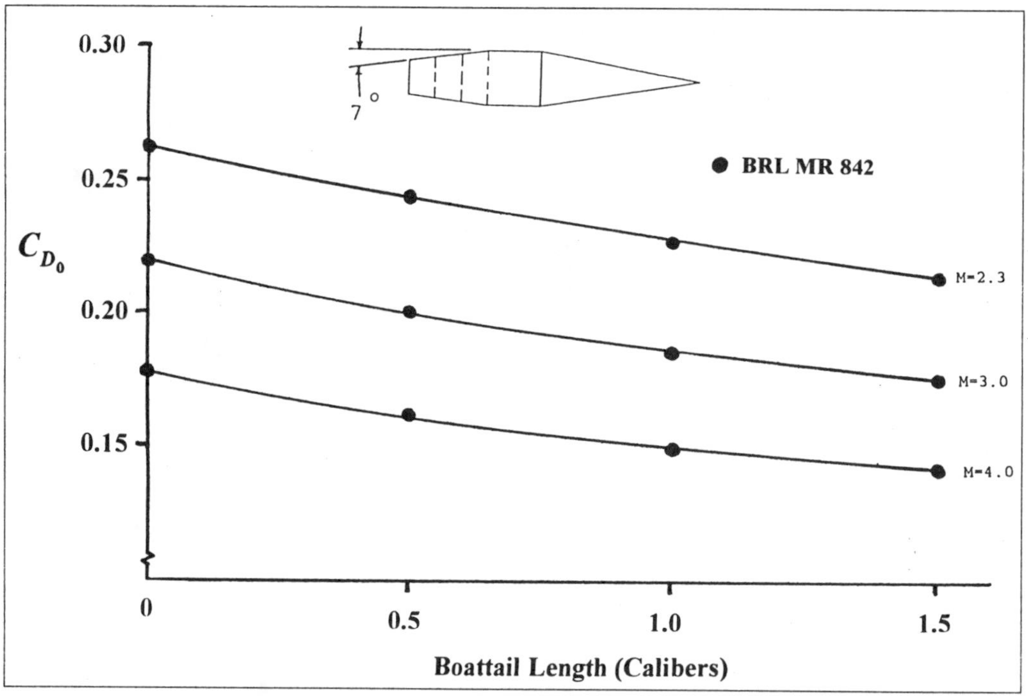

Figure 4.25 The effect of Boattail Length on the Drag Coefficient at Supersonic Speeds.

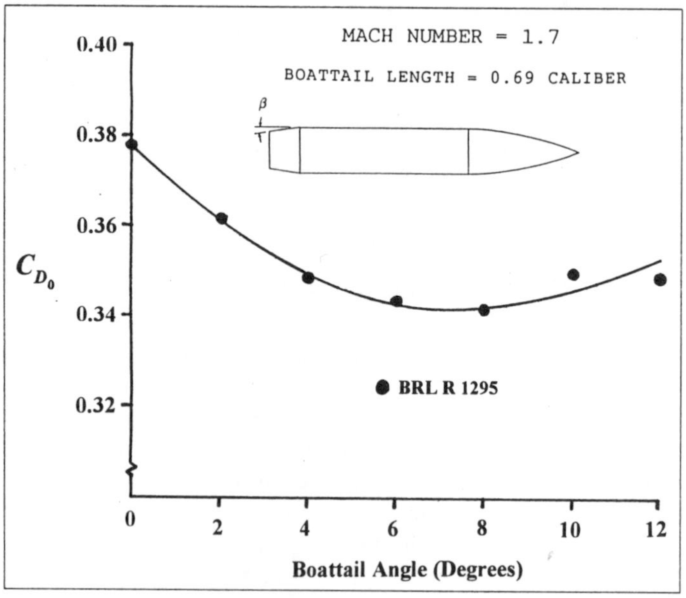

Figure 4.26 The effect of Boattail Angle on the Drag Coefficient.

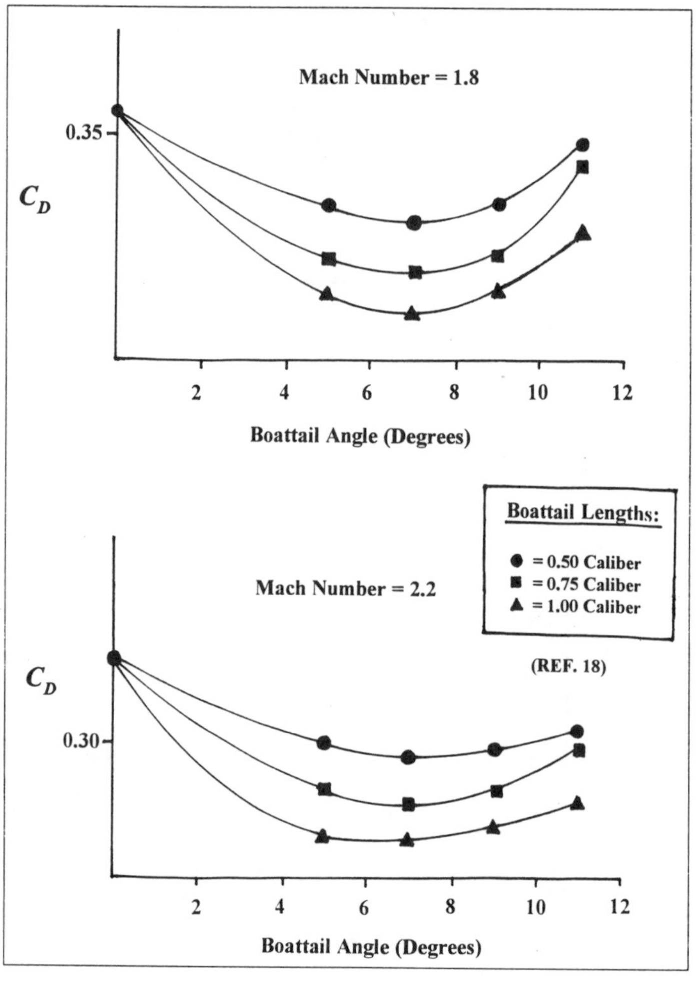

Figure 4.27 The effect of Boattail Angle on the Drag Coefficient.

ter. Practical boattails generally lie between one-half and one caliber in length at supersonic speeds.

The effect on drag of varying the boattail angle, with the boattail length held constant, is shown in the next two figures. Figure 4.26, at Mach 1.7, shows that a boattail angle of approximately seven degrees gives the lowest drag at moderate supersonic speeds (Ref. 17). Figure 4.27, from a 1983 paper presented by B. Kneubühl of Switzerland (Ref. 18), shows a very similar result for some experimental .25 caliber small arms bullets at two supersonic Mach numbers.

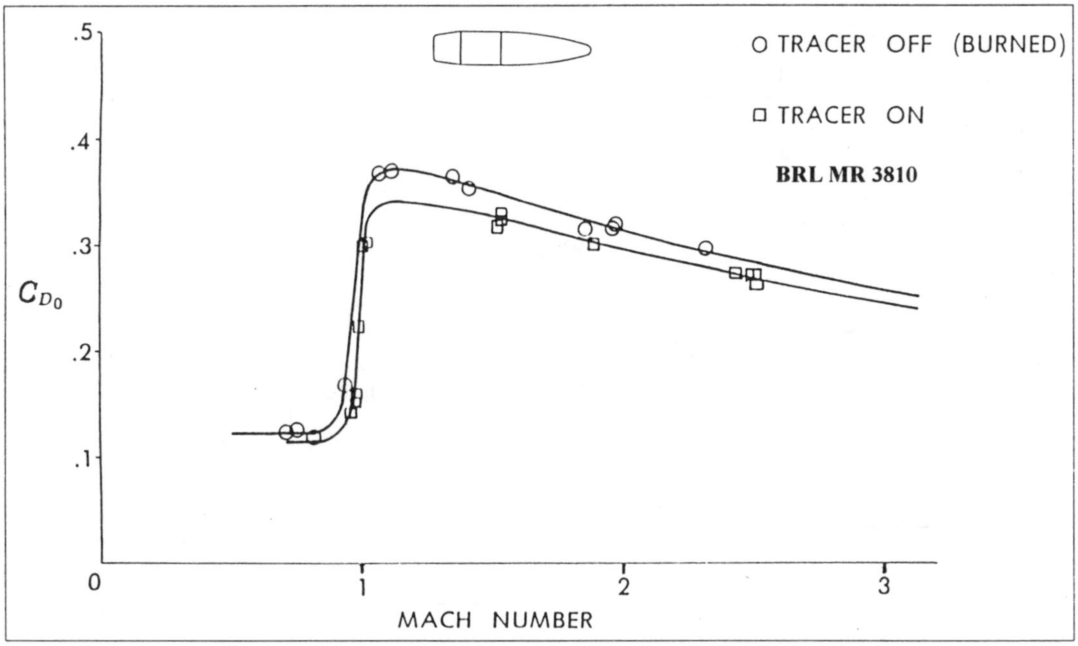

Figure 4.28 The effect of a Burning Tracer on the Drag Coefficient.

The curves of Figures 4.26 and 4.27 are relatively flat for boattail angles between five and nine degrees. The popular nine-degree boattail, which has been used for many good projectile designs, gives about two percent higher total drag than does an optimum seven-degree boattail angle. However, boattail angles steeper than ten degrees usually cause boundary layer separation, which destroys the boattail effectiveness as a drag-reducing device.

4.6 THE EFFECT OF A BURNING TRACER ON DRAG

Tracers are often used with ordnance projectiles to provide a visual trajectory indicator to the gunner. The pyrotechnic tracer mixture, which is pressed into a cavity in the projectile base, is ignited in the barrel of the gun by the burning propellant, and the in-flight burning time of the tracer is controlled by the amount and the burning rate of the pyrotechnic mixture.

In flight, the burning tracer injects hot gas into the turbulent wake behind the projectile, which raises the base pressure and thereby lowers the drag. Since the trajectory of the tracer round is usually required to ballistically match the flight of a companion high explosive or armor piercing projectile, the exterior ballistician must know, at least approximately, how much the burning tracer reduces the drag.

Some typical effects of burning tracers on the drag of small caliber projectiles are illustrated in Figures 4.28 and 4.29. The tracer-

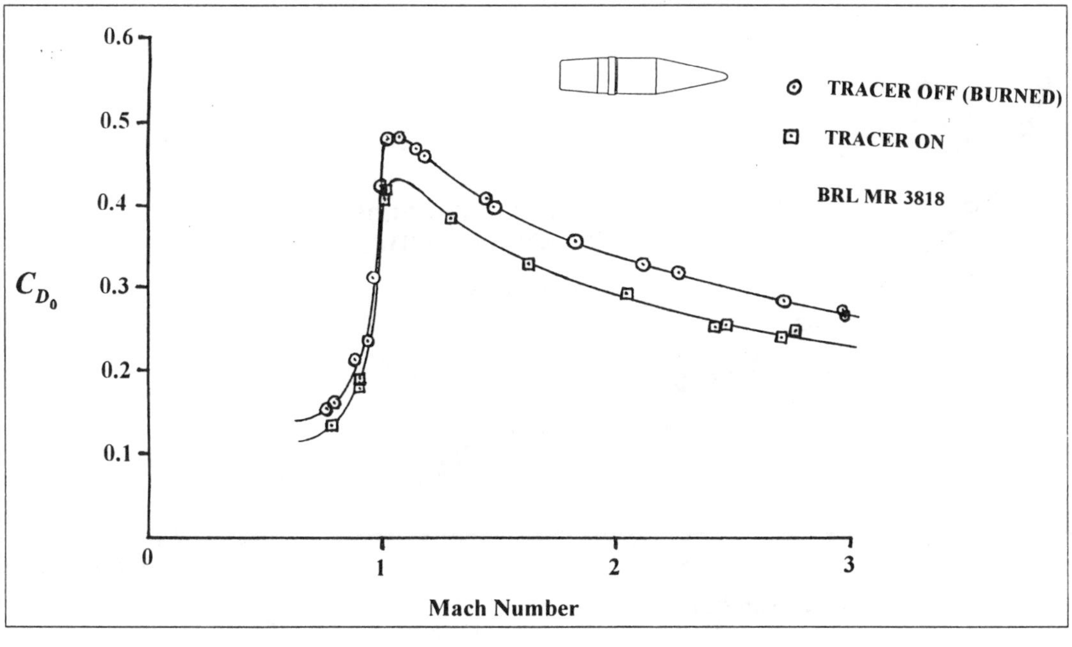

Figure 4.29 The effect of a Burning Tracer on the Drag Coefficient.

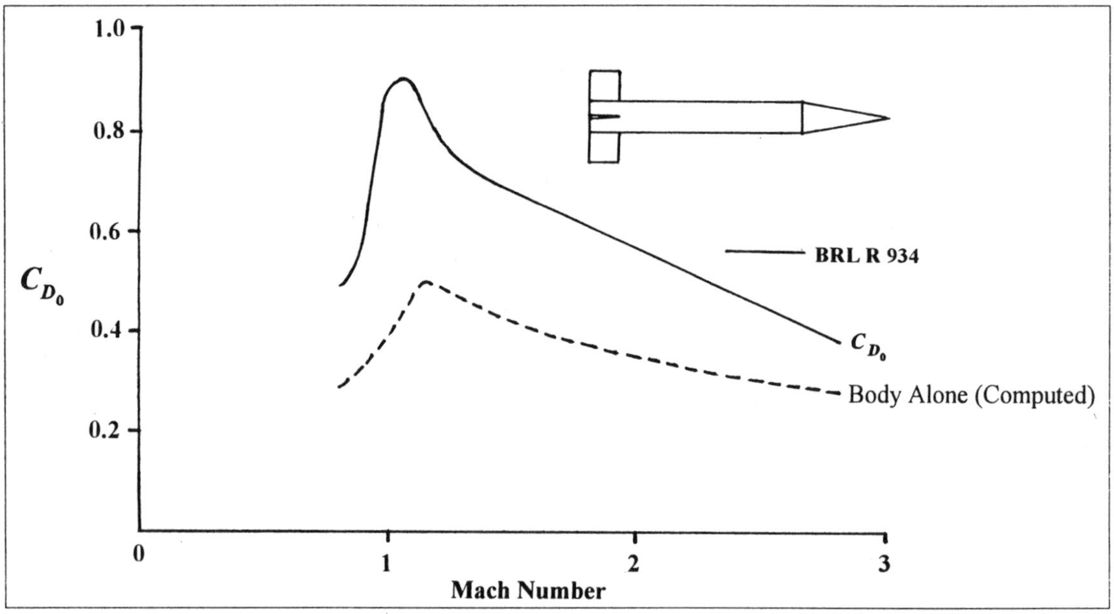

Figure 4.30 The effect of Rectangular, Single-Wedge Fins on the Drag Coefficient.

drag effect is determined by firing one group of test rounds with burned-out or inert tracers, and another group of rounds with burning tracers, in a modern facility such as the BRL Aerodynamics Range. Figure 4.28 shows that the burning tracer reduces the drag of the caliber .50 APIT M20 projectile (Ref. 8) by approximately seven percent at supersonic speeds. The tracer effect on the drag coefficient of an anti-aircraft 20mm projectile is shown in Figure 4.29; this higher burning rate tracer reduces the drag by about twelve percent at supersonic speeds.

The concept of a very high burning rate tracer has evolved into the modern base-burn projectile design, in which a high energy fuel is used instead of a pyrotechnic mixture. Drag reductions approaching thirty percent have recently been achieved with optimized base-burn configurations. It is probable that long-range artillery will be the primary future application of base-burn technology.

4.7 THE EFFECT OF FINS ON THE DRAG

Fin-stabilized projectiles are frequently employed in modern ordnance design. Mortars, flechettes, long-rod kinetic energy penetrators and rocket-powered missiles are typical examples of projectiles that are not suitable for spin stabilization. This section illustrates the experimental drag coefficients obtained for several typical finned ordnance designs.

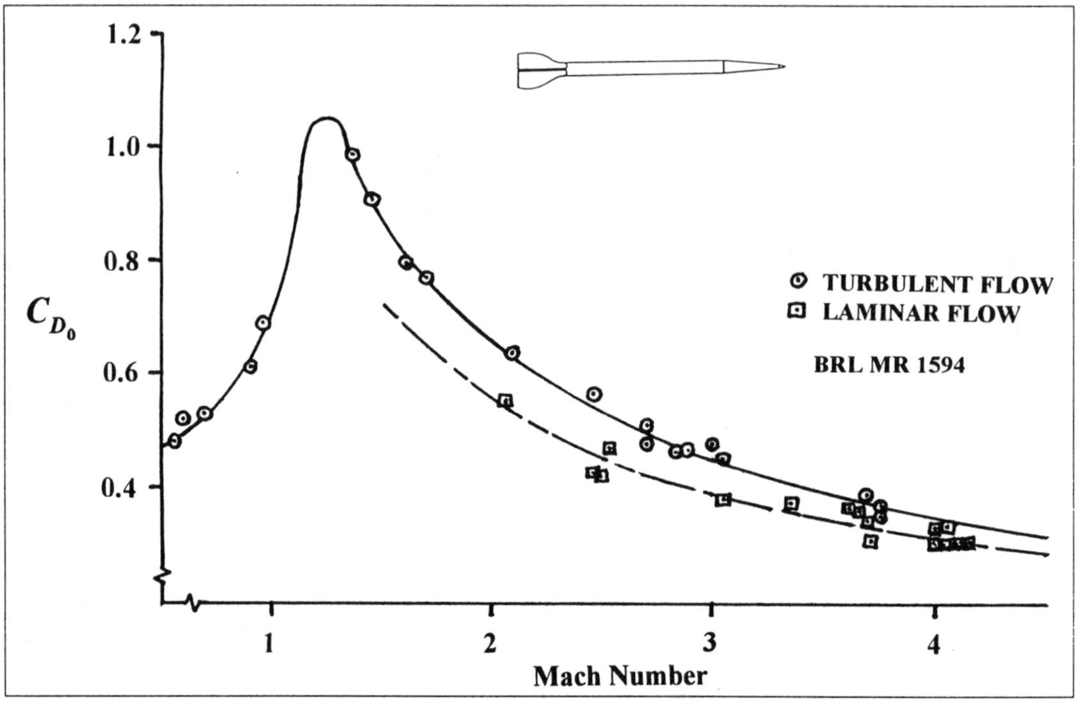

Figure 4.31 The Drag Coefficient of a Flechette with Laminar and Turbulent Boundary Layer.

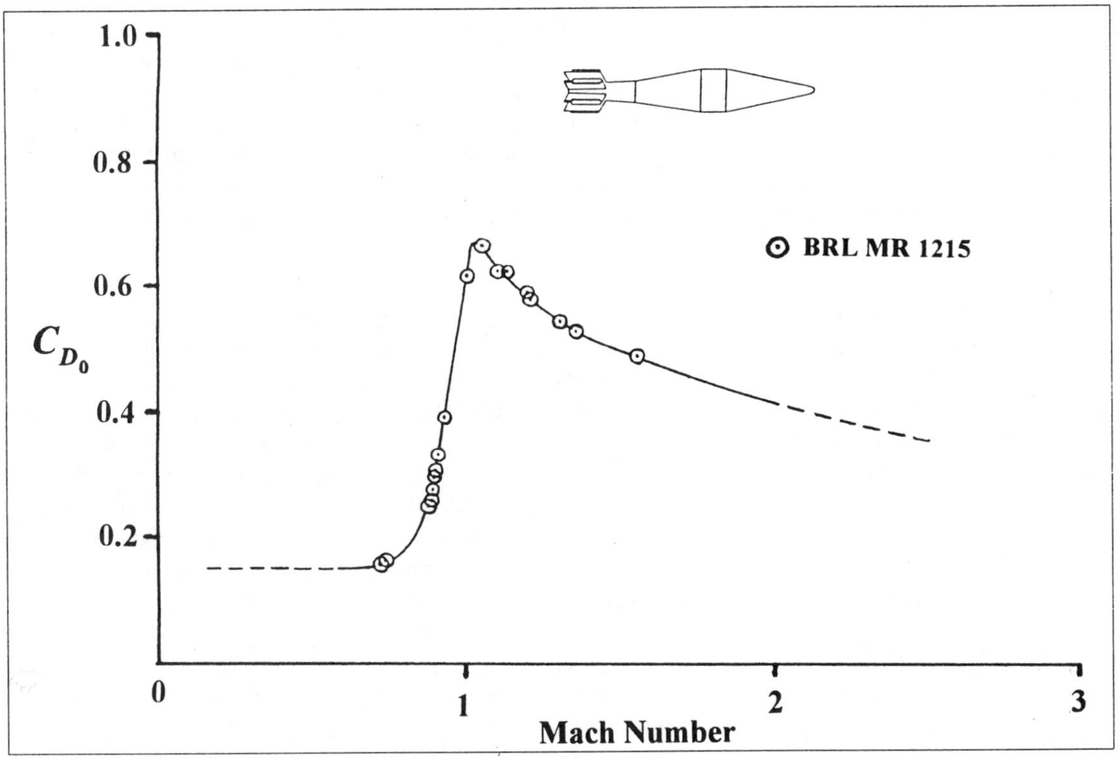

Figure 4.32 The Drag Coefficient of a Typical Fin-Stabilized Ordnance Projectile.

Figure 4.30 shows the total drag coefficient and the body-alone contribution for the 20mm Basic Finner model (Ref. 19). The Basic Finner is a ten-caliber long cone-cylinder projectile, with four square planform, single-wedge, 0.08 caliber thickness fins. Approximately forty percent of the total Basic Finner drag is due to the fins.

The drag coefficient of a ten-grain steel flechette (Ref. 6) is illustrated in Figure 4.31. The flechette has a cone-cylinder body whose diameter is 1.79mm (0.0705 inch); the total length is 23.5 calibers. Four flat-plate fins with an average fin thickness of 0.10 caliber, and a three-caliber total span, are used to stabilize the flechette.

In section 4.3 we noted that the Reynolds number effect on drag is usually small enough to be neglected; however, the flechette of Figure 4.31 is an exception to that general rule. At flight speeds

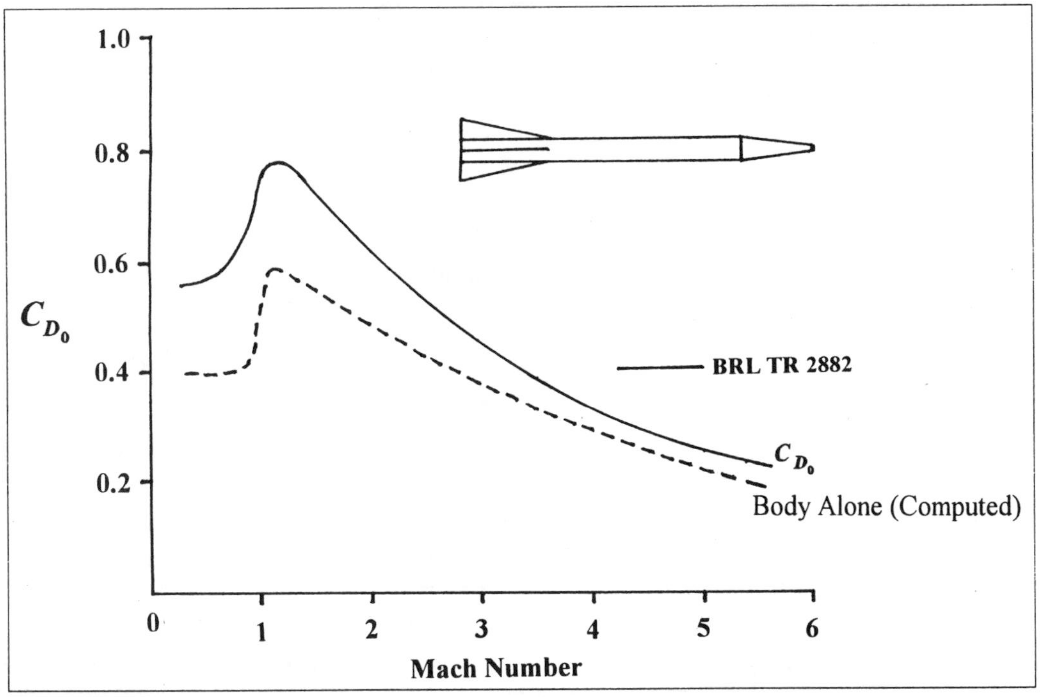

Figure 4.33 The effect of Swept Triangular, Flat-Plate Fins on the Drag Coefficient.

between subsonic and high supersonic, the flechette Reynolds numbers, based on projectile length, range from one million at low speed to about four million at high speed. Boundary layer theory (Ref. 12) tells us that for such transition Reynolds numbers, the flow may be either laminar or turbulent.

Figure 4.31 indicates that slightly over half of the flechette rounds fired at supersonic speeds exhibit laminar boundary layers; the remainder show turbulent boundary layer flow. The type of flow present on any given flechette depends on small round-to-round differences in surface roughness, and on the average yaw level of the flight, with increasing yaw and roughness leading to a higher probability of turbulence. At supersonic speeds, the flechettes with turbulent boundary layers show about fifteen percent higher drag than those with laminar boundary layer flow, which is in generally good agreement with the predictions (Ref. 12) of boundary layer theory.

The drag coefficient of a typical fin-stabilized ordnance projectile (Ref. 20) is illustrated in Figure 4.32. The reference diameter is 105mm (4.134 inches), and six shrouded fins, each of which are 0.04 caliber thick, are symmetrically spaced about the afterbody. This projectile shape is characteristic of fin-stabilized mortars, rifle grenades, and shaped-charge munitions for anti-tank use. The tapered afterbody and the thin, one-caliber span tail fins help reduce the drag below that of the other finned projectile shapes illustrated in this chapter.

Figure 4.33 shows the drag coefficient and the body-alone curve, for a typical finned, long-rod kinetic energy penetrator. The penetrator has a cone-cylinder body, whose diameter is 8.3mm; the total body length is slightly over sixteen calibers. Four triangular planform, flat-plate fins are symmetrically spaced around the projectile afterbody. The fin chord is 4.3 calibers, the total span is 2.5 calibers, and each fin is 0.11 caliber thick. The fins account for about twenty percent of the total drag at supersonic speeds, and about thirty percent at transonic and subsonic speeds. Note the highly swept fin leading edges. The effect of leading edge sweepback in reducing the supersonic drag of wings and fins was first recognized by the German scientist Adolph Busemann in 1935, and practically all modern supersonic finned projectiles use highly swept fins, such as those shown in Figure 4.33.

4.8 THE DRAG OF SMOOTH SPHERES

In section (4.3) we noted that the effect of Reynolds number on aerodynamic drag is usually insignificant in comparison with the Mach number effect. The drag of smooth spheres is another notable exception to this general rule, and some of the interesting drag properties of spherical projectiles are illustrated in this section.

The drag of smooth spheres has been measured in several modern facilities, and some of the results are shown in Figure 4.34. The solid curve is based on firings of 9/16" diameter steel spheres (Ref. 21). The drag of a 0.10" diameter sphere is everywhere lower than that of a 9/16" sphere. However, the drag of the 1.50" diameter sphere does not follow any expected trend. The large sphere shows the highest drag at transonic and low supersonic speeds, but its subsonic drag behavior appears to be anomalous. These anomalous subsonic effects are even more dramatic for 2-inch and 4-inch diameter spheres at atmospheric pressure (Ref. 21a). The explanation of the apparent anomaly lies in the effect of Reynolds number on the drag of spheres.

Figure 4.35 is a plot of the drag coefficient for a smooth sphere against the common logarithm of the Reynolds number, at three flight Mach numbers. At typical projectile flight speeds, Reynolds numbers of order 10^5 to 10^6 are observed, and the logarithm is generally used to avoid working with such very large numbers.

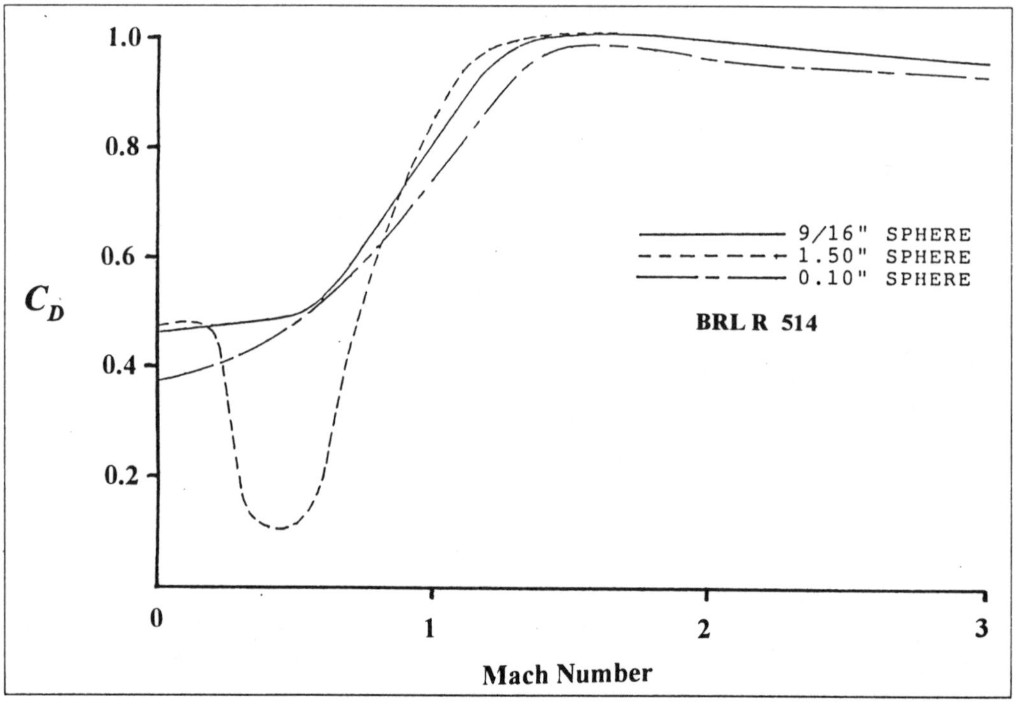

Figure 4.34 Drag Coefficient versus Mach Number for Smooth Spheres.

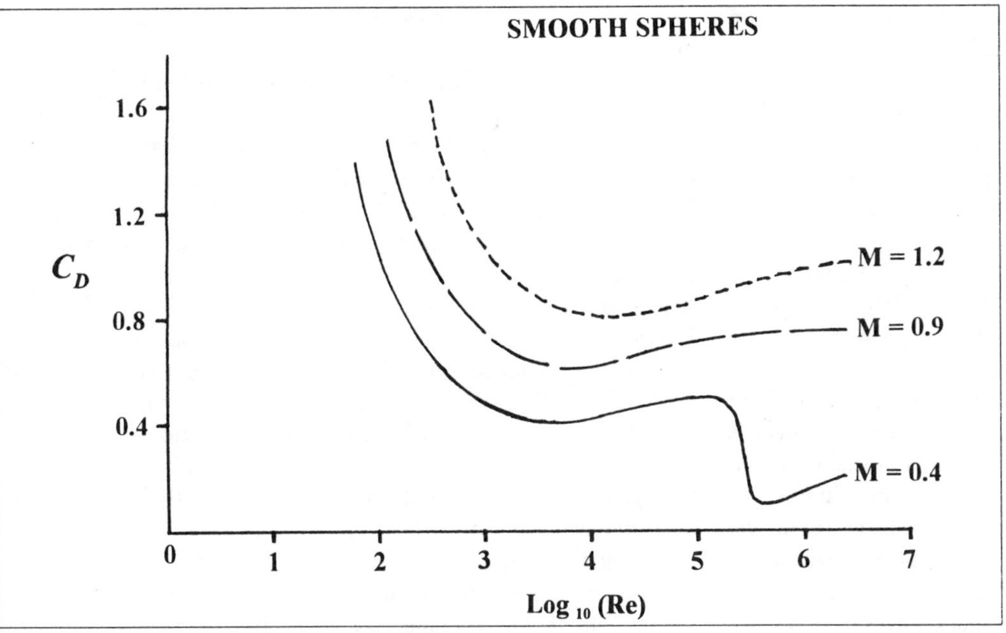

Figure 4.35 Sphere Drag Coefficient versus Reynolds Number.

The bottom curve in Figure 4.35, at Mach 0.4, shows a sudden drop in drag at a Reynolds number of about 250,000 ($\log_{10} Re$ 5.4), which is the critical Reynolds number for smooth spheres. The sudden decrease in drag at the critical Reynolds number is due to boundary layer transition; the boundary layer changes from laminar to turbulent flow as the speed increases through the critical Reynolds number. Note that there is no evidence of a critical Reynolds number at either Mach 0.9 or Mach 1.2; we will return to this fact presently.

Figure 4.36 illustrates the subsonic effect of a laminar versus a turbulent boundary layer on the separation point for a smooth sphere. The laminar boundary layer separates just ahead of the point at which the maximum diameter of the sphere occurs. A turbulent boundary layer has much higher kinetic energy than does a laminar boundary layer, and the turbulent boundary layer is thus better able to withstand the large adverse pressure gradient along the rearward surface of the sphere. The result, as shown in Figure 4.36, is that a turbulent boundary layer remains attached to the sphere surface well aft of the point of maximum diameter, and thereby significantly reduces the base drag. The drag coefficient at Mach 0.4 drops from approximately 0.5 to 0.1, with transition from a laminar to a turbulent boundary layer.

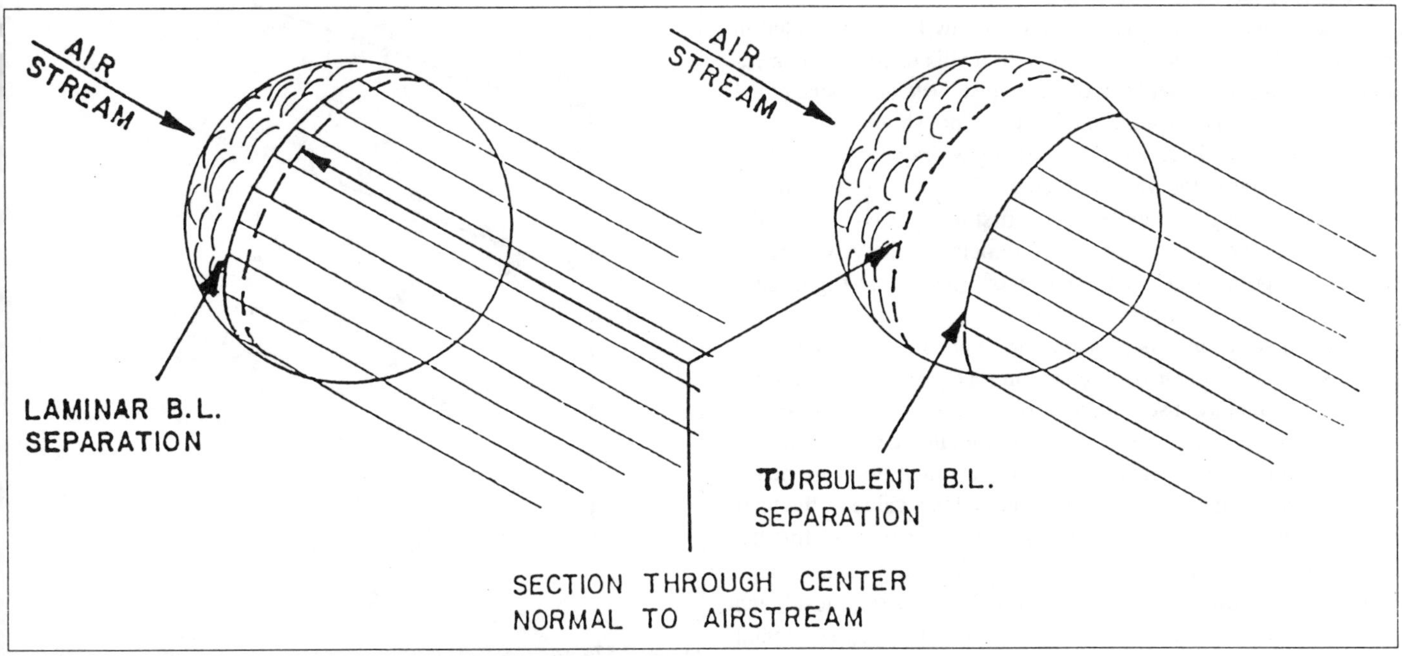

Figure 4.36 Illustration of Laminar and Turbulent Flow Around Spheres.

We will now re-examine the subsonic drag characteristics of the three sphere sizes shown in Figure 4.34. For the 0.10" diameter sphere, the Reynolds number at Mach 0.4 is approximately 25,000 at sea-level standard atmospheric conditions, thus $\log_{10} Re$=5.6 for the 1.50" diameter sphere at Mach 0.4, which is above the critical value, and the boundary layer on the large sphere is therefore turbulent. In fact, the boundary layer on the 1.50" diameter sphere is turbulent for all flight speeds above Mach 0.2, which explains the subsonic drag behavior observed in Figure 4.34. At all flight Mach numbers between Mach 0.2 and Mach 0.8, the drag of the 1.50" diameter sphere is well below that of the 9/16" sphere.

Figure 4.35 explains why the smaller spheres show no evidence of a critical Reynolds number. The 9/16" sphere does not reach the critical Reynolds number until its flight speed approaches Mach 0.9, and the 0.10" diameter sphere is at high supersonic speed before its Reynolds number reaches the critical value. Figure 4.35 shows no critical Reynolds number behavior at Mach 0.9 and above. At transonic and supersonic speeds, boundary layer separation is dominated by the shock wave system rather than by Reynolds number. At flight speeds above Mach 0.8, the shock waves force boundary layer separation to occur at or before the point of maximum sphere diameter, regardless of whether the boundary layer is laminar or turbulent.

The addition of surface roughness to a smooth sphere causes subsonic boundary layer transition to occur at lower Reynolds numbers; very rough spheres show critical Reynolds numbers around 100,000 ($\log_{10} Re$=5.0). However, surface roughness causes slight drag increases at all speeds. At subsonic speeds, large surface roughness increases the drag approximately ten percent above the value for a smooth sphere. At supersonic speeds, very rough spheres show approximately five percent more drag than do smooth spheres.

4.9 THE EFFECT OF YAW ON DRAG

The dependence of aerodynamic drag on yaw level was stated in equation (2.3) of Chapter 2. This equation tells us that if the measured total drag coefficient is plotted against the squared sine of the total yaw angle, the experimental data points should lie along a straight line whose intercept is the zero-yaw drag coefficient, C_{D_o}, and whose slope is the yaw-drag coefficient, $C_{D_{\delta^2}}$. The quadratic dependence of drag on yaw level was first recognized early in the twentieth century, but accurate measurements of the yaw-drag effect were not possible before the advent of modern free-flight spark photography ranges and wind tunnels.

Modern wind tunnels measure the drag force at various discrete yaw angles, and the data reduction for C_{D_o} and $C_{D_{\delta^2}}$ is straightforward. The method used in spark photography ranges is somewhat more complicated. For each round fired in the range, both the total drag and the epicyclic pitching and yawing motion are determined. Thus the firing of a single round yields a value of the total drag coefficient, and a corresponding average yaw level for that flight. The determination of both C_{D_o} and $C_{D_{\delta^2}}$ from spark range testing involves firing several rounds (Ref. 22) at the same test Mach number, but at different average yaw levels. Several experimental techniques used to induce various yaw levels will be discussed in a later chapter.

The relative simplicity of the wind tunnel method for determination of C_{D_o} and $C_{D_{\delta^2}}$ is offset by the need for a model support system in the wind tunnel test section, and the fact that the presence of the support system affects the flowfield and therefore the drag. Free-flight ranges are thus preferred over wind tunnels for precise drag measurements, despite the more complicated experimental procedures required. (The superiority of free-flight ranges over wind tunnels is not universal; the determination of the lift force and pitching moment in wind tunnels is usually very good, because the flowfield interference caused by the model support system has an insignificant effect on the static transverse forces and moments).

The next nine figures in this chapter illustrate the yaw-drag results obtained for three different test projectiles from spark photography range firings, and show how the free-flight total drag measurements are used to separate the drag into its zero-yaw and yaw-drag components.

Figure 4.37 is a plot of the total drag coefficient against the squared sine of the average yaw angle, for the 7-Caliber Army-

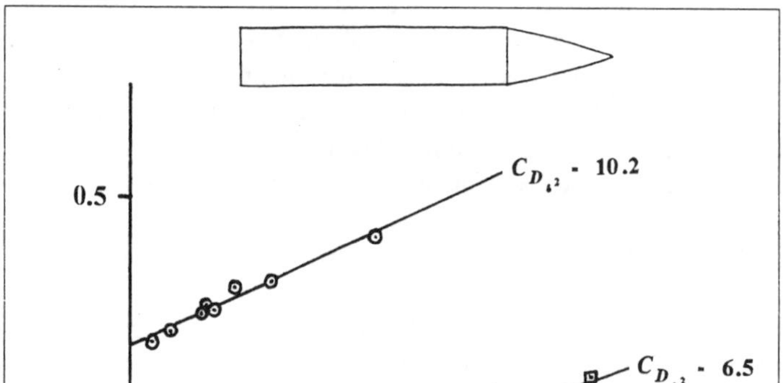

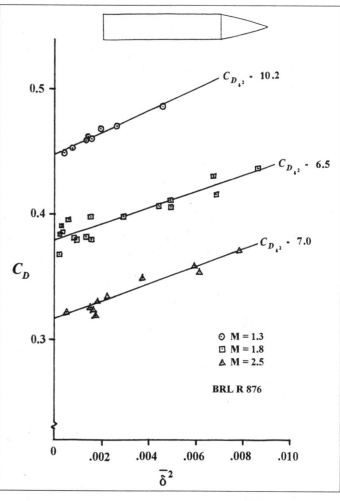

Figure 4.37 Drag Coefficient versus Average Squared Yaw for the Army-Navy Spinner Rocket Shape.

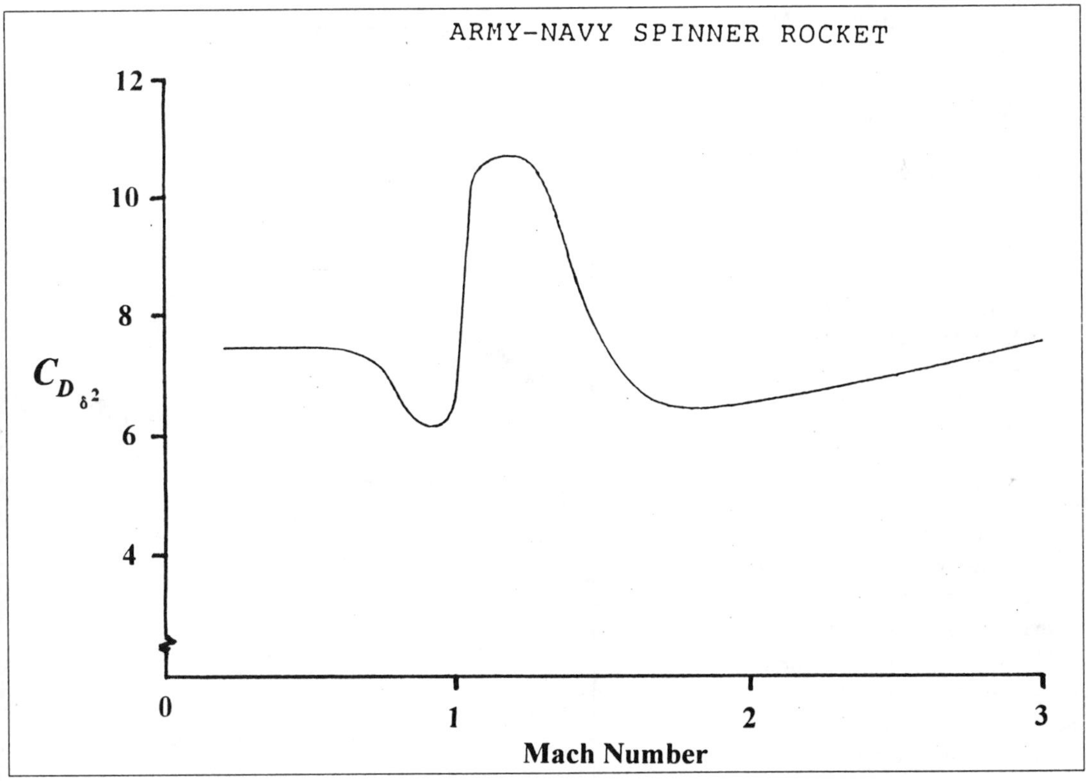

Figure 4.38 Yaw-Drag Coefficient versus Mach Number.

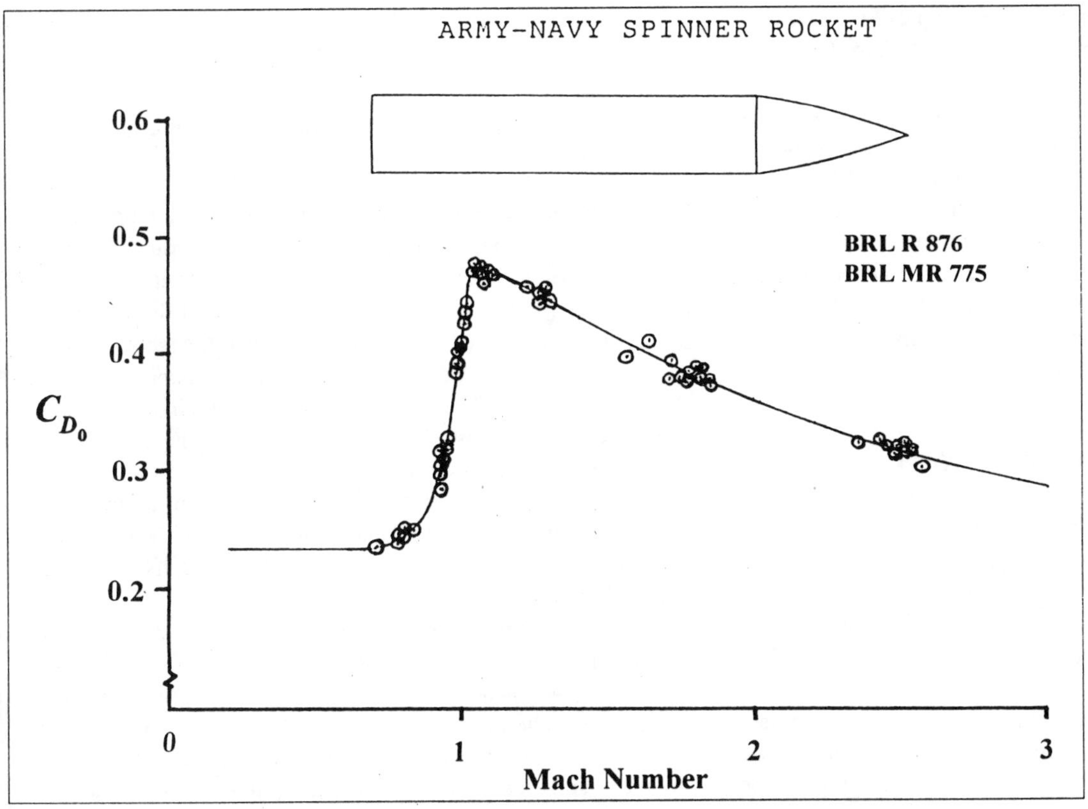

Figure ~~4.38~~ 4.39 Zero-Yaw Drag Coefficient versus Mach Number.

Navy Spinner Rocket shape (Ref. 23) at three supersonic Mach numbers. The model is seven calibers long, and it has a two-caliber long, pointed, secant ogive nose. The straight lines shown in Figure 4.37 are linear regression lines determined from least-squares fitting of the observed data points, and the values of $C_{D_{\delta^2}}$ obtained as the slopes of the lines are indicated. Although there is some scatter of the data points about the regression line, a straight line obviously fits the data very well, and confirms the quadratic dependence of drag on yaw level.

Figure 4.37 presents only a representative sample of the data available for the 7-Caliber Army-Navy Spinner Rocket shape. Similar correlations were done for other test Mach numbers (Ref. 24), and Figure 4.38 shows a smooth curve connecting all the values of $C_{D_{\delta^2}}$ obtained. The curve of Figure 4.38 is then used to correct the range values of total drag coefficient to C_{D_0} values, for each round fired in the test program. The result is shown in Figure 4.39, which is a plot of C_{D_0} against Mach number for the Army-Navy Spinner Rocket. Note that the variation of $C_{D_{\delta^2}}$ with Mach number is significantly different from the Mach number dependence observed for C_{D_0}. Other than the fact that both curves show rapid change in the vicinity of Mach 1.0, there is little similarity between the behavior of the zero-yaw drag and the yaw-drag coefficients.

Figures 4.40 through 4.42 illustrate the results of a similar analysis for a cone-cylinder projectile (Ref. 25), whose nose length is approximately three calibers, and whose overall length is slightly over five calibers. The behavior of the yaw-drag coefficient for the cone-cylinder projectile is rather different from that observed for the Army-Navy Spinner Rocket, although the two curves are obviously of the same order of magnitude.

Figure 4.43 illustrates a representative sample of the yaw-drag analysis for the caliber .50 Armor Piercing Incendiary (API) M8 projectile (Ref. 8). The API M8 is essentially identical in exterior contour to the Ball M33 projectile, whose dimensions were shown in Figure 4.7. The API M8 bullet was fired at various yaw levels, but the Ball M33 was tested only at small yaw. Since the two configurations are virtually identical, the yaw-drag coefficient shown in Figure 4.44 was used to correct the data for both round types to zero-yaw values. Figures 4.45 and 4.8 (see section 4.4) show the variation of C_{D_0} with Mach number for the API M8 and Ball M33, respectively. The two bullets are intended to be ballistically matched, and comparison of these two figures shows that a ballistic match has indeed been achieved.

4.10 MINIMUM DRAG PROJECTILE SHAPES

The effect of projectile shape on the drag coefficient at various speeds was discussed at length in section 4.5 of this chapter. Particular values of certain projectile shape parameters were noted that give low aerodynamic drag in various flight speed regions. It is intuitively obvious that a proper combination of optimum values of all the significant shape parameters might lead to a minimum drag projectile shape.

A number of theoretical studies have considered the problem of ogive shapes for minimum supersonic wave drag. One of the earliest attempts to find a theoretical minimum drag nose shape

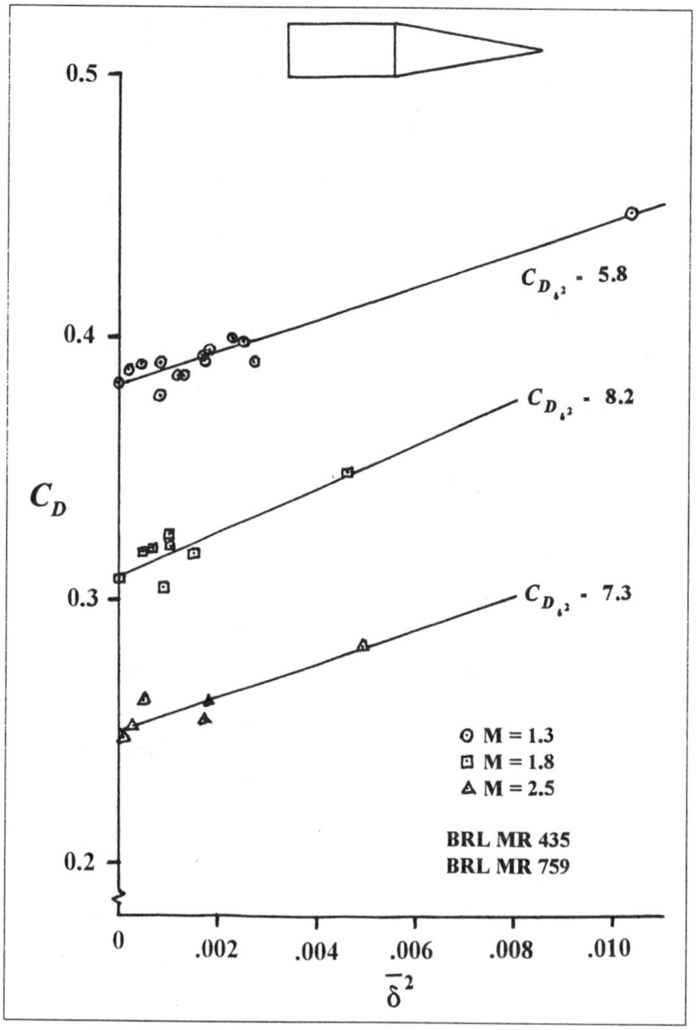

Figure 4.40 Drag Coefficient versus Average Squared Yaw for a 20 mm Cone-Cylinder Projectile.

was made by von Kármán (Ref. 26), who derived an integral equation for the wave drag of slender bodies of revolution at moderate supersonic speeds. The work of von Kármán was later extended by Sears (Ref. 27), Haack (Ref. 28) and others, and the theoretical optimum nose shape for slender ogives at moderate supersonic Mach numbers is referred to today as the Sears-Haack shape.

Eggers, Resnikoff and Dennis (Ref. 29) obtained theoretical hypersonic optimum nose shapes from Newtonian theory. The theoretical least-drag hypersonic nose shape is described by a very complicated equation, which differs only slightly from a simple 3/4 power-law shape. The Sears-Haack and the 3/4 power-law nose shapes are illustrated in Figure 4.46, for nose lengths of two and three calibers.

In 1958, Perkins, Jorgensen and Sommer (Ref. 30) measured the forebody drag (wave drag plus viscous skin friction) of various three-caliber long nose shapes in the Ames Laboratory supersonic wind tunnels. The nose shapes tested included the Sears-Haack contour, a family of power-law noses, and cones with various amounts of spherical tip bluntness. Figures 4.47 and 4.48 illustrate

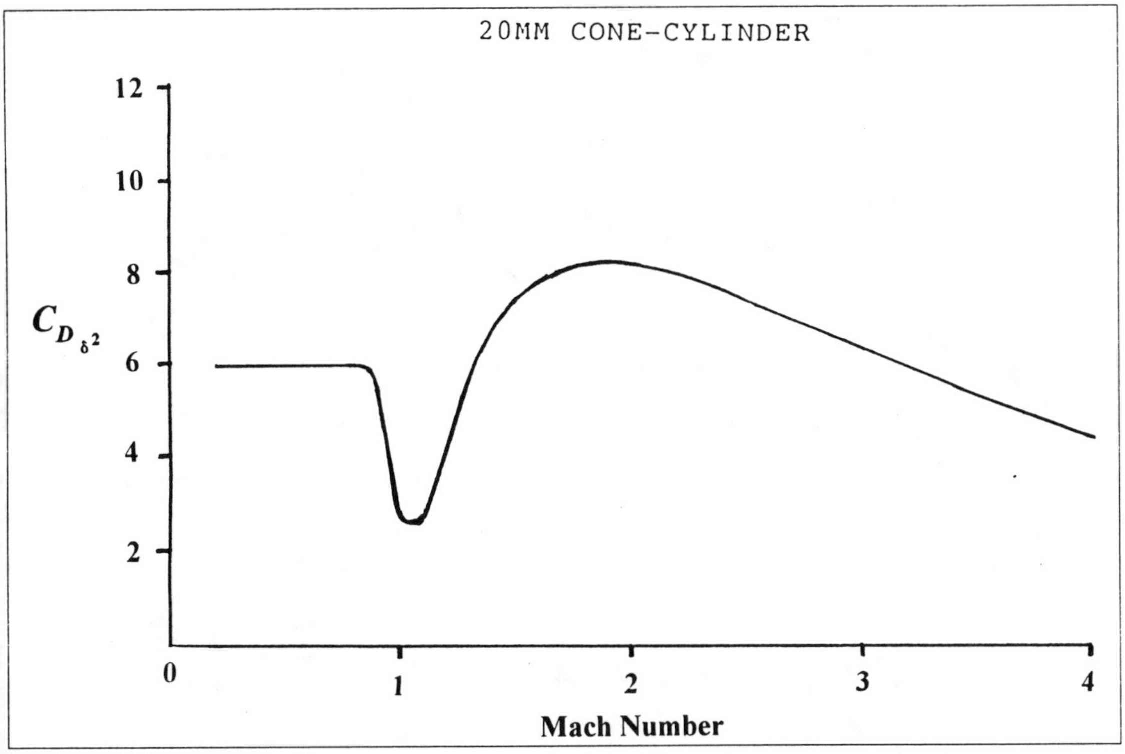

Figure 4.41 Yaw-Drag Coefficient versus Mach Number.

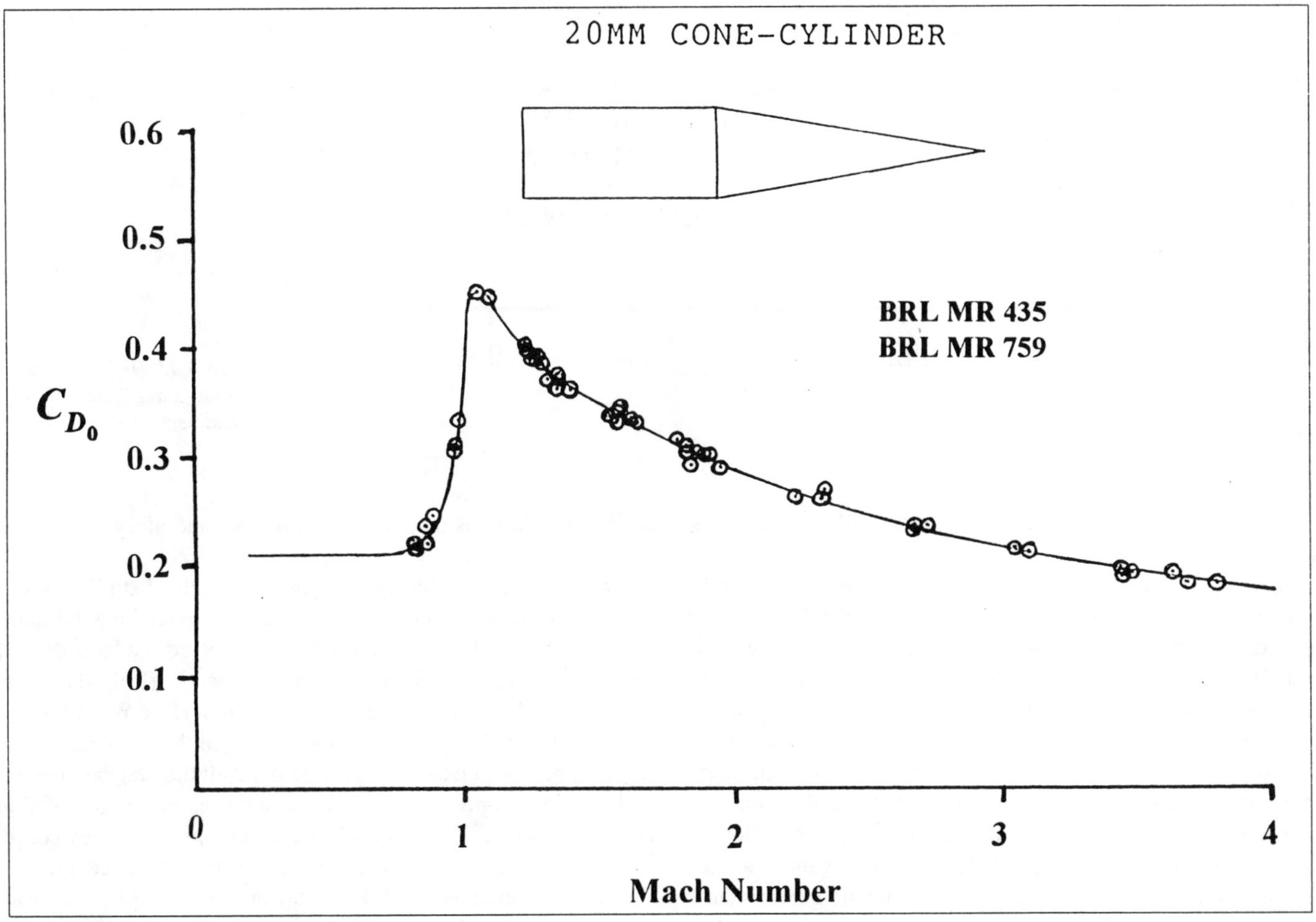

Figure 4.42 Zero Yaw Drag Coefficient versus Mach Number.

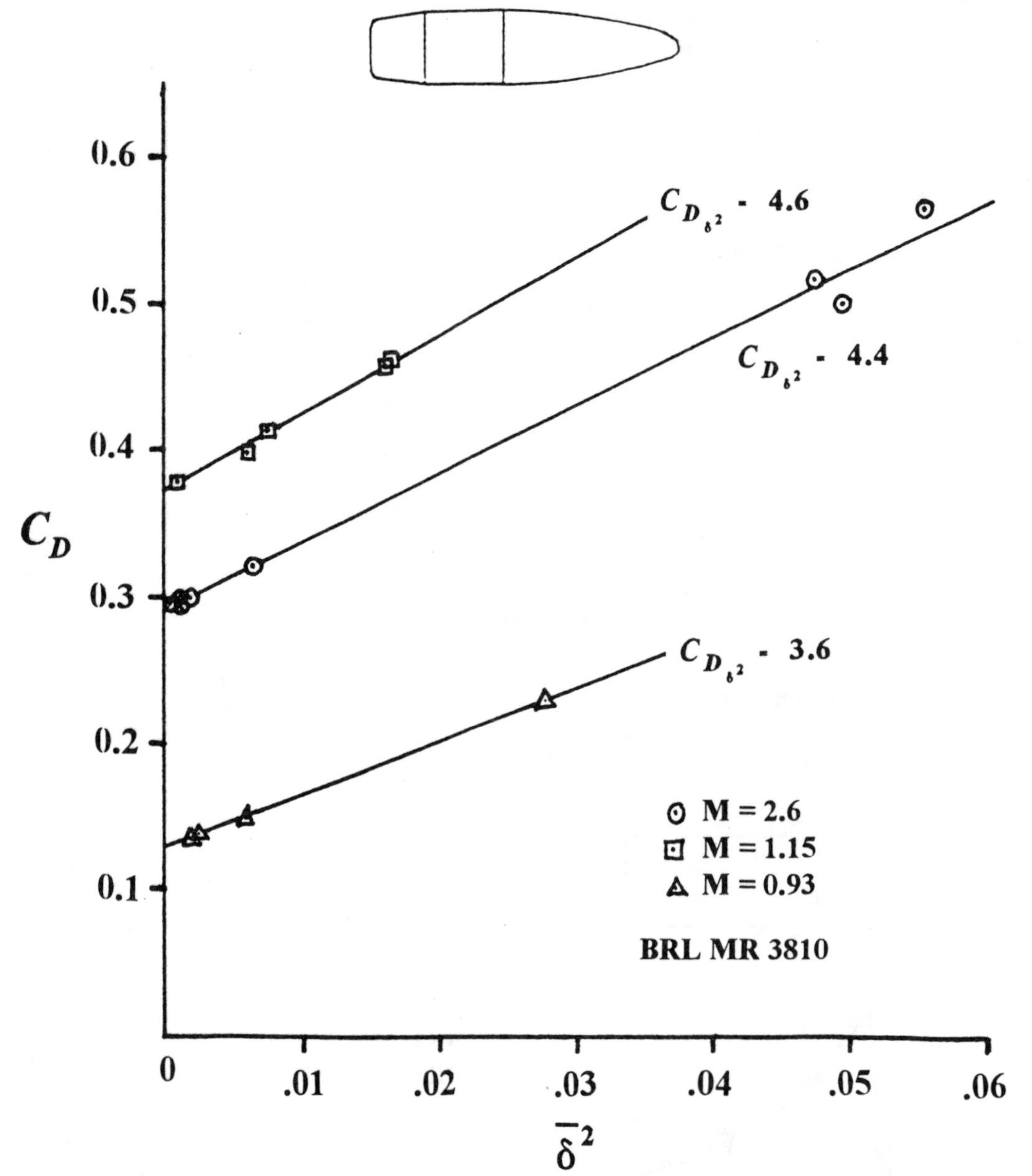

Figure 4.43 Drag Coefficient versus Average Squared Yaw for the Caliber .50 API M8 Projectile.

some of the wind tunnel results for the four lowest drag nose shapes tested.

Figure 4.48 shows the measured foredrag coefficients (total drag coefficient minus the base drag coefficient) for the four nose shapes of Figure 4.47. The lowest drag nose at high supersonic speeds is the 3/4 power-law shape, which is often referred to as the "hypersonic optimum" shape. The lowest drag nose at low supersonic speeds is the more blunt paraboloid (1/2 power-law shape), which gives the highest drag of the four designs at Mach numbers greater than 2.4. Contrary to theoretical predictions, the wind tunnel test results indicate that the Sears-Haack nose is not the lowest drag shape at any supersonic speed! The reader is again cautioned not to draw the incorrect conclusion that the low drag nose shapes of Figure 4.48 are absolute least-drag shapes; they are merely the lowest drag designs included in the Ames Laboratory wind tunnel tests.

None of the previously mentioned theoretical studies considered either the skin friction or the base drag; even the wind tunnel test results presented in Reference 30 neglected the base drag effect. More recently Hager, De Jarnette and Moore (Ref. 31), Mason (Ref. 32), and Moga (Ref. 33), of the Naval Surface Weapons Center (NSWC) at Dahlgren, Virginia, addressed the problem of finding minimum supersonic drag shapes with all the drag components included in the optimization. The method used in Reference 33 included a numerical iteration scheme to determine the body coordinates that minimize total drag, based on modified second-order shock-expansion theory (Ref. 34) for the ogive and boattail wave drag, the Van Driest theory (Ref. 35) for turbulent skin friction drag,

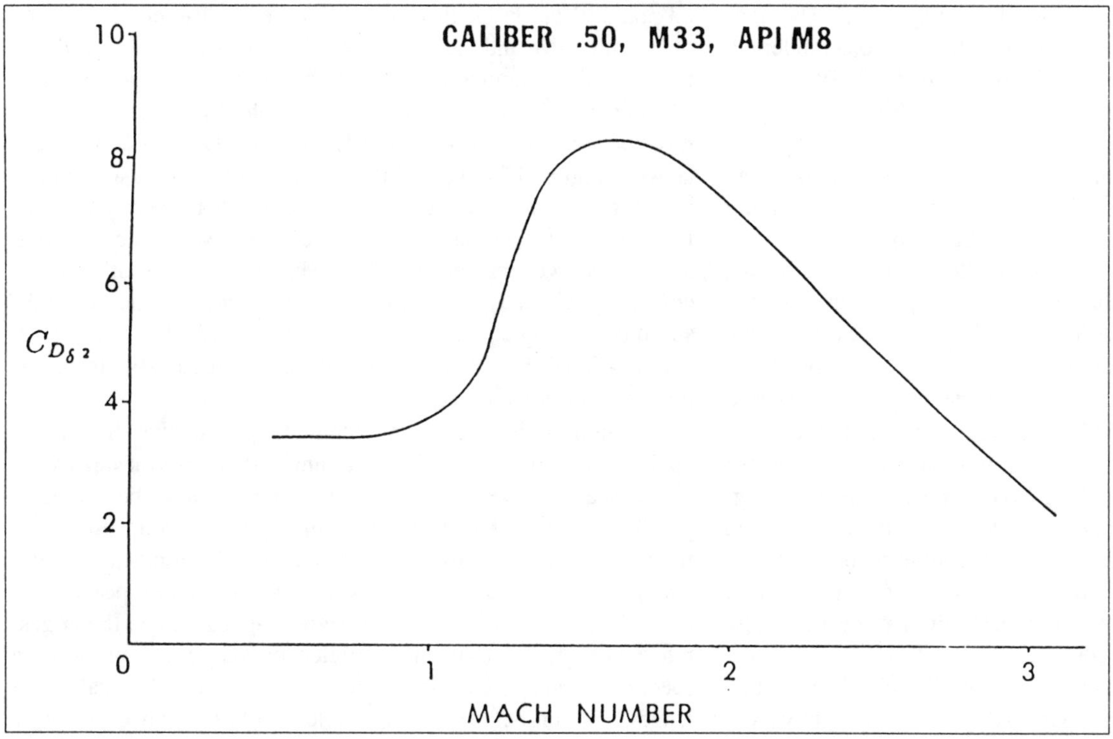

Figure 4.44 Yaw-Drag Coefficient versus Mach Number.

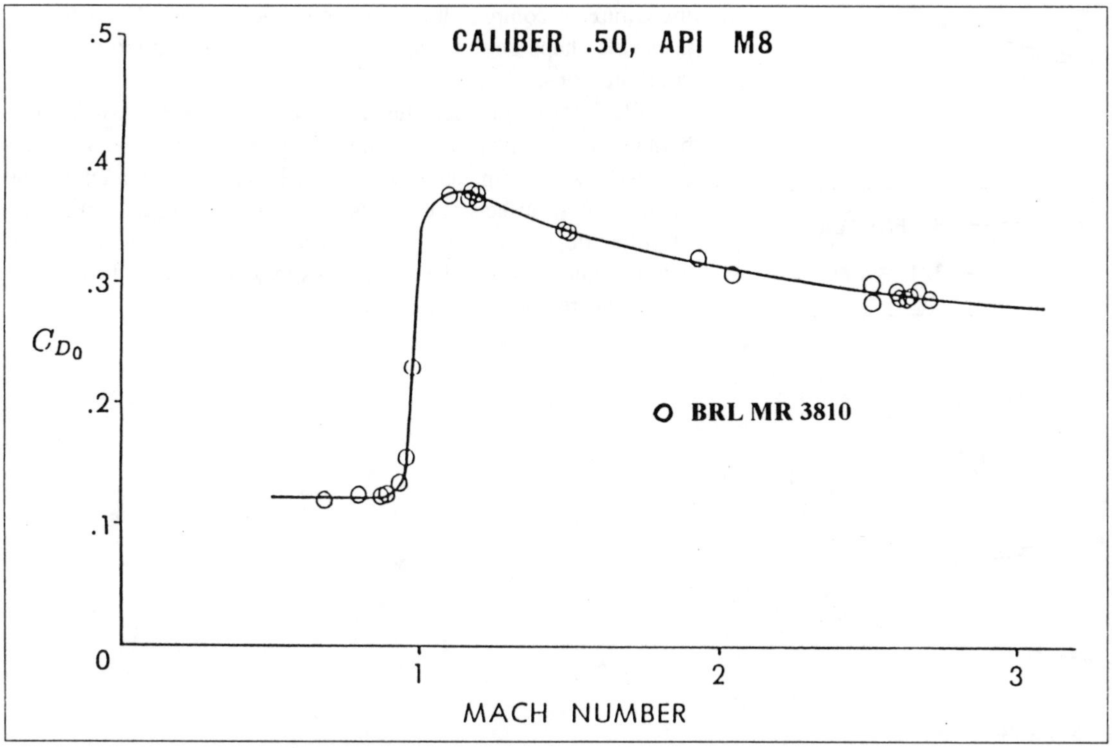

4.45

Figure 4.44 Zero Yaw Drag Coefficient versus Mach Number for the Caliber .50 API M8 Projectile.

and Moore's (Ref. 36) semi-empirical base drag model. The optimum shape was observed to vary with both total projectile length and the flight Mach number. An illustration of the NSWC least-drag shapes for 4, 5 and 6-caliber long projectiles at high supersonic speeds is shown in Figure 4.49.

All the NSWC minimum-drag designs consist of a low drag nose shape that differs only slightly from the hypersonic optimum (3/4 power-law) profile, followed immediately by a boattail that terminates in a base diameter of approximately 0.70 caliber. Such a projectile design, with no cylindrical centerbody section, has been successfully launched from a rifled gun barrel by means of front bore-riding nubs, located well forward on the ogive section. Modern sabot technology, in which the sub-caliber projectile is encased in a discarding sabot and fired from a larger caliber gun, is another alternative. An estimate of the zero-yaw drag coefficient versus Mach number for the 5-caliber long NSWC model is shown in Figure 4.50. If such a design could be made to fly with small yaw, it would indeed be an extremely low drag configuration. Unfortunately, the long boattails selected by the NSWC drag optimization process usually cause severe dynamic instability, particularly at low supersonic and transonic speeds.

The optimum secant ogive nose shape $R_T/R = 0.5$, with a small méplat or inscribed hemispherical nose tip, gives slightly more drag than the optimum nose shapes illustrated in Figure 4.49. For all practical purposes, there is no significant difference, and both the secant ogive and the 3/4 power-law shapes may be considered to be practical minimum drag nose shapes at supersonic speeds.

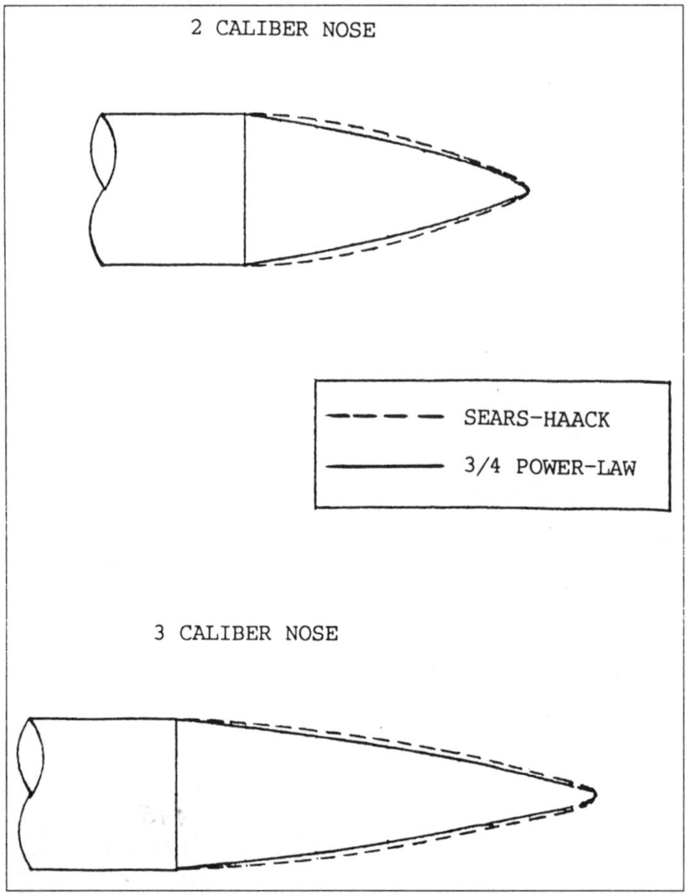

Figure 4.46 Theoretical Nose Shapes for Minimum Wave Drag.

Figure 4.48 suggests that the paraboloid is a very low drag nose shape at low supersonic speeds, and possibly at transonic speeds as well. Figure 4.23 showed that the tangent ogive is a low drag nose shape at subsonic speeds. It is not possible to specify an absolute least-drag nose shape at the lower speeds, without conducting a low-speed version of the NSWC study; to the author's knowledge, no such study has been done. The next generation of high-speed computing equipment may have the capability to solve such computational fluid dynamics problems in a reasonable length of time at an affordable cost.

Boattailing is an efficient technique for reducing drag, especially at subsonic speeds. The optimum boattail angle at supersonic speeds is about seven degrees, and the boattail should be as long as possible, consistent with the requirement for dynamically stable flight. Dynamic stability considerations usually limit the boattail length to about a one-caliber maximum at supersonic speeds.

A boattail angle around ten degrees appears to be the largest practical angle for an attached turbulent boundary layer at subsonic speeds, provided the boattail is not much over one-half caliber in length. The ten-degree boattail angle should be reduced for very small caliber bullets, whose boundary layers are predominantly laminar. The effect of boattailing on the dynamic stability at transonic and subsonic speeds is generally negative, and long or steep boattails are usually very difficult to stabilize at these lower speeds.

4.11 SUMMARY

The physical nature and the behavior of the aerodynamic drag force are highlighted in this chapter. Some emphasis has been placed on the nature of compressible flow and shock waves. The effect of projectile shape on the drag is illustrated for a number of typical configurations.

The information presented in this chapter will prove helpful to both the reader who is interested in the general nature and behavior of aerodynamic drag, and to the professional ballistician who must understand the effects of configuration design changes on the drag of projectiles. In addition, a basic understanding of the nature of aerodynamic drag provides a good background for the study of point-mass trajectories in the next four chapters.

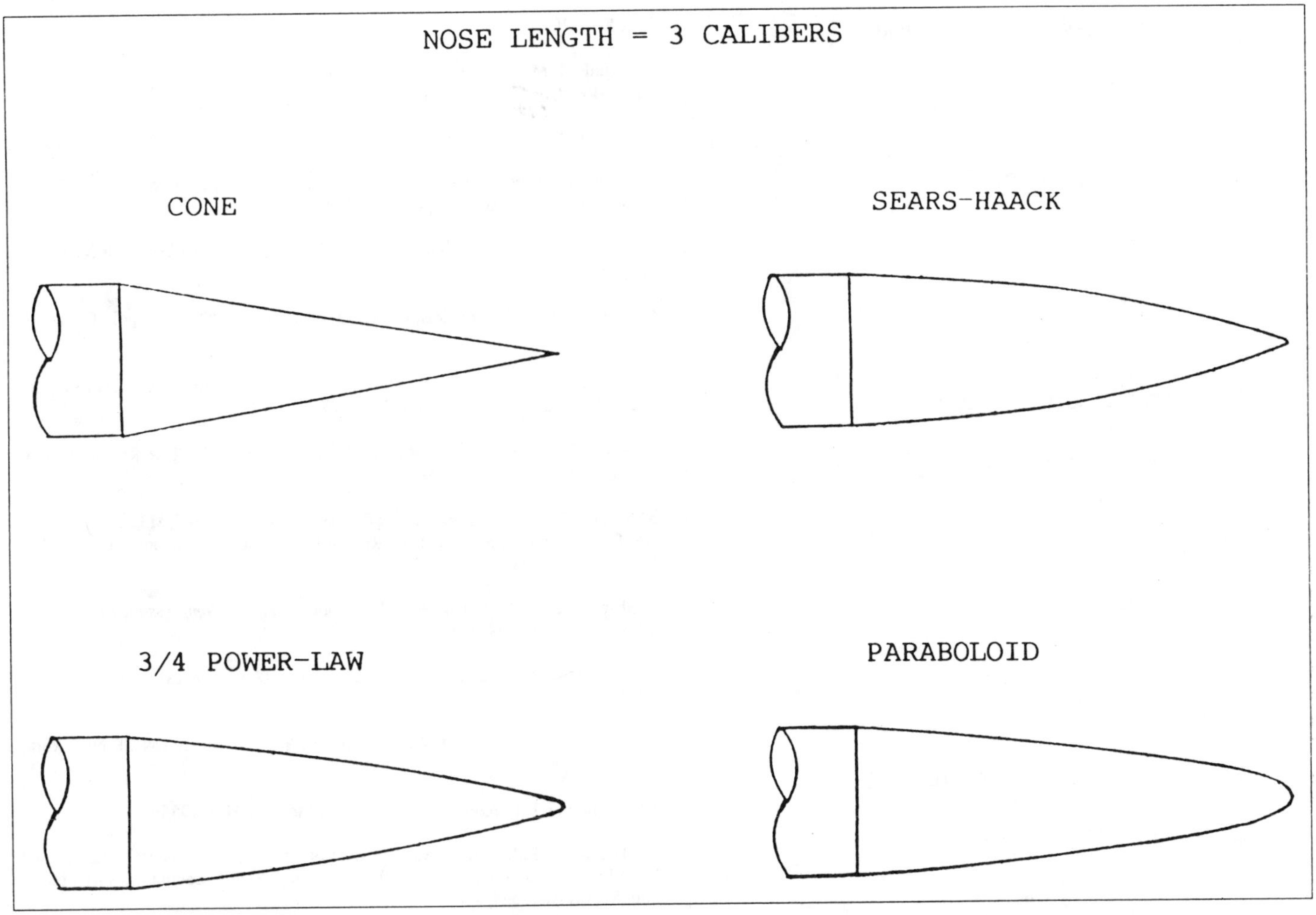

Figure 4.47 Theoretical Nose Shapes for Minimum Wave Drag.

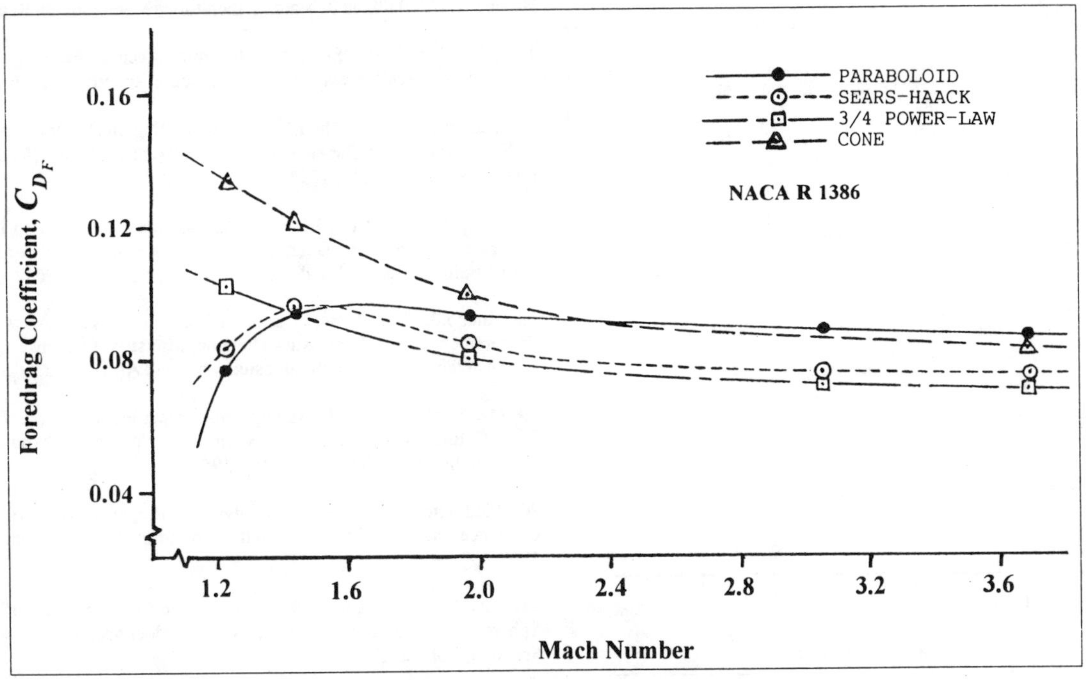

Figure 4.48 Wind Tunnel Foredrag Coefficient versus Mach Number.

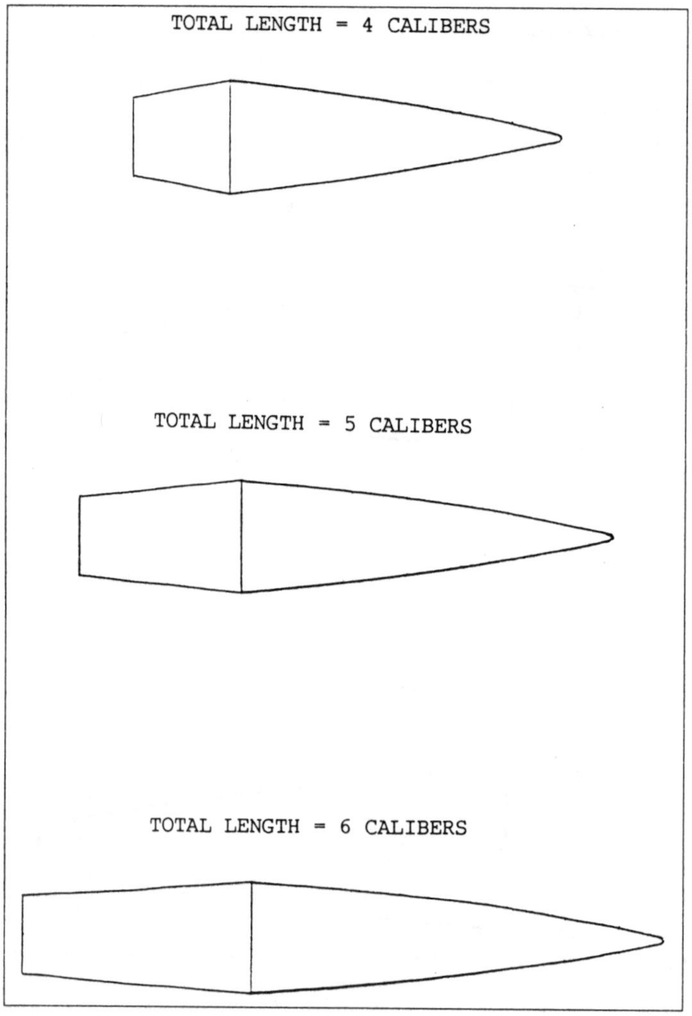

Figure 4.49 NSWC Minimum Drag Projectile Shapes.

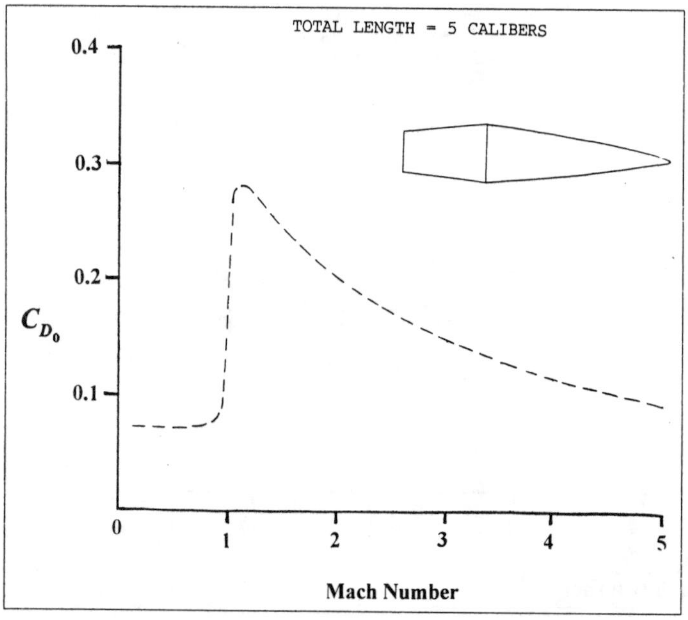

Figure 4.50 Estimated Zero-Yaw Drag Coefficient versus Mach Number.

REFERENCES

1. Ingalls, J. M., *Ingalls' Ballistic Tables*, Artillery Circular M, U. S. Army Ordnance Board, ~~1893~~ 1900 (Revised 1917).

2. Capt. Lalune, Gâvre Commission Report Numbers 1414 and 1429, 1897-1898.

3. Hitchcock, H. P., "Resistance Functions of Various Types of Projectiles," Ballistic Research Laboratories Report No. 27, 1935.

4. McShane, E. J., J. L. Kelley, and F. V. Reno, *Exterior Ballistics*, University of Denver Press, 1953.

5. Hatcher, J. S., *Hatcher's Notebook*, Second Edition, The Stackpole Company, 1957.

6. Braun, W. F., "Aerodynamic Data for Small Arms Projectiles," Ballistic Research Laboratories Report No. 1630, 1973.

7. Braun, W. F., "The Free Flight Aerodynamics Range," Ballistic Research Laboratories Report No. 1048, 1958.

8. McCoy, R. L., "The Aerodynamic Characteristics of .50 Ball, M33, API, M8, and APIT, M20 Ammunition," Ballistic Research Laboratory Memorandum Report No. BRL-MR-3810, 1990.

9. Shapiro, A. H., *The Dynamics and Thermodynamics of Compressible Fluid Flows*, 2 Volumes, Roland, New York, 1953.

10. Liepmann, H. W., and A. Roshko, *Elements of Gasdynamics*, Wiley, New York, 1957.

11. Anderson, J. D., Jr., *Modern Compressible Flow*, McGraw-Hill, New York, 1982.

12. Schlicting, H., *Boundary Layer Theory*, McGraw-Hill, 1955.

13. Dickinson, E. R., "Some Aerodynamic Effects of Varying the Body Length and Head Length of a Spinning Projectile," Ballistic Research Laboratories Memorandum Report No. 1664, 1965.

14. Dickinson, E. R., "Some Aerodynamic Effects of Headshape Variation at Mach Number 2.44," Ballistic Research Laboratories Memorandum Report No. 838, 1954.

15. Dickinson, E. R., "Some Aerodynamic Effects of Blunting a Projectile Nose," Ballistic Research Laboratories Memorandum Report No. 1596, 1964.

16. Dickinson, E. R., "The Effect of Boattailing on the Drag Coefficient of Cone-Cylinder Projectiles at Supersonic Velocities," Ballistic Research Laboratories Memorandum Report No. 842, 1954.

17. Karpov, B. G., "The Effect of Various Boattail Shapes on Base Pressure and Other Aerodynamic Characteristics of a 7-Caliber Long Body of Revolution at M = 1.70," Ballistic Research Laboratories Report No. 1295, 1965.

18. Kneubühl, B. P., "Optimization of Boattails for Small Arms Bullets," Defense Procurement Group 2, Ballistics Division, Ministry of Defense, Switzerland. (Presented at the International Symposium on Small Arms at Quantico, Virginia, 1983).

19. MacAllister, L. C., "The Aerodynamic Properties of a Simple Non-Rolling Finned Cone-Cylinder Configuration Between Mach Numbers 1.0 and 2.5," Ballistic Research Laboratories Report No. 934, 1955.

20. Piddington, M. J., "Some Aerodynamic Properties of a Typical Fin Stabilized Ordnance Shell," Ballistic Research Laboratories Memorandum Report No. 1215, 1959.

21. Charters, A. C., and R. N. Thomas, "The Aerodynamic Performance of Small Spheres from Subsonic to High Supersonic Velocities," *Journal of the Aeronautical Sciences*, Vol. 12, 1945.

21a. Miller, D. G., and A. B. Bailey, "Sphere Drag at Mach Numbers from 0.3 to 2.0 at Reynolds Numbers Approaching 10^7," *Journal of Fluid Mechanics*, Vol. 93 (Part 3), 1979.

22. Murphy, C. H., "The Measurement of Non-Linear Forces and Moments by Means of Free Flight Tests," Ballistic Research Laboratories Report No. 974, 1956.

23. Murphy, C. H., and L. E. Schmidt, "The Effect of Length on the Aerodynamic Characteristics of Bodies of Revolution in Supersonic Flight," Ballistic Research Laboratories Report No. 876, 1953.

24. Schmidt, L. E., and C. H. Murphy, "The Aerodynamic Properties of the 7-Caliber Army-Navy Spinner Rocket in Transonic Flight," Ballistic Research Laboratories Memorandum Report No. 775, 1954.

25. Schmidt, L. E., "The Dynamic Properties of Pure Cones and Cone Cylinders," Ballistic Research Laboratories Memorandum Report No 759, 1954.

26. von Kármán, T., "The Problem of Resistance in Compressible Fluids," Fifth Volta Congress, held in Rome, Italy, 1935.

27. Sears, W. R., "On Projectiles of Minimum Wave Drag," *Quarterly of Applied Mathematics*, Vol. 4, No. 4, 1947.

28. Haack, W., "Projectile Forms of Minimum Wave Resistance," (Translation) Douglas Aircraft Company Report No. 288, 1946.

29. Eggers, A. J., Jr., M. M. Resnikoff and D. H. Dennis, "Bodies of Revolution for Minimum Drag at High Supersonic Airspeeds," NACA Report No. 1306, 1957.

30. Perkins, E. W., L. H. Jorgensen and S. C. Sommer, "Investigation of the Drag of Various Axially Symmetric Nose Shapes of Fineness Ratio 3 for Mach Numbers from 1.24 to 7.4," NACA Report No. 1386, 1958.

31. Hager, W. W., F. R. De Jarnette and F. G. Moore, "Optimal Projectile Shapes for Minimum Total Drag," NSWC/DL TR-3597, Dahlgren, Virginia, 1977.

32. Mason, L. A., "Theoretical and Experimental Results for 25mm and 30mm Optimum and Low-Drag Projectile Shapes," NSWC TR-79-18, Dalhgren, Virginia, 1979.

33. Moga, N. J., "Optimal Bodies for Minimum Total Drag at Supersonic Speeds," NSWC TR-80-208, Dahlgren, Virginia, 1980.

34. Jackson, C. M., Jr., W. C. Sawyer and R. S. Smith, "A Method for Determining Surface Pressure on Blunt Bodies of Revolution at Small Angles of Attack in Supersonic Flow," NASA TN D-4865, 1968.

35. Van Driest, E. R., "Turbulent Boundary Layer in Compressible Fluids," *Journal of the Aeronautical Sciences,* Vol. 18, No. 3, 1951.

36. Moore, F. G., "Body Alone Aerodynamics of Guided and Unguided Projectiles at Subsonic, Transonic, and Supersonic Mach Numbers," NWL TR-2796, Dahlgren, Virginia, 1972.

5

The Flat-Fire Point Mass Trajectory

5.1 INTRODUCTION

The first known analytical solution of the differential equations describing a point-mass trajectory was obtained in 1711, by Johann Bernoulli (1667-1748) of Switzerland. Bernoulli's solution assumed constant air density and constant drag coefficient, thus it was valid only for low velocity, flat-fire trajectories. About forty years later another Swiss mathematician, Leonhard Euler (1707-1783), developed the mean-value, short-arc method for solving systems of ordinary differential equations, and used his method to solve elementary point-mass trajectories. Euler's method is applicable to trajectories with variable drag coefficients and variable air densities and temperatures and thus represents, in principle, the first general solution of the point-mass trajectory problem.

Both the Bernoulli and the Euler methods required the use of quadratures (the approximation of definite integrals by the sum of small squares); such methods would be described today as "labor-intensive." Although Euler's method was successfully used from about 1750 until the latter part of the nineteenth century, the extreme tediousness of the manual arithmetic computations eventually forced exterior ballisticians to develop simpler approximate methods for practical trajectory calculation.

One of the most useful approximate methods was devised around 1880 by F. Siacci of Italy. Siacci's method (Ref. 1), which is described in the next chapter, reduces any flat-fire trajectory to easily tabulated quadratures, given in terms of the "pseudo-velocity," which is the product of the horizontal component of velocity and the secant of the angle of departure. Although the Siacci method was abandoned as impractical for artillery fire by the end of the First World War, its use in direct-fire weapons such as small arms and tank gunnery persisted in U. S. Army Ordnance until the middle of the twentieth century. The Siacci method is still in almost universal use throughout the U. S. sporting arms and ammunition industry, and for the short-range, flat-fire trajectories of typical sporting projectiles, its accuracy is sufficient for most practical purposes.

In this chapter, the differential equations of the point-mass trajectory are derived, then simplified using the flat-fire approximation. Several special analytical solutions of flat-fire trajectories are obtained, for cases of practical interest.

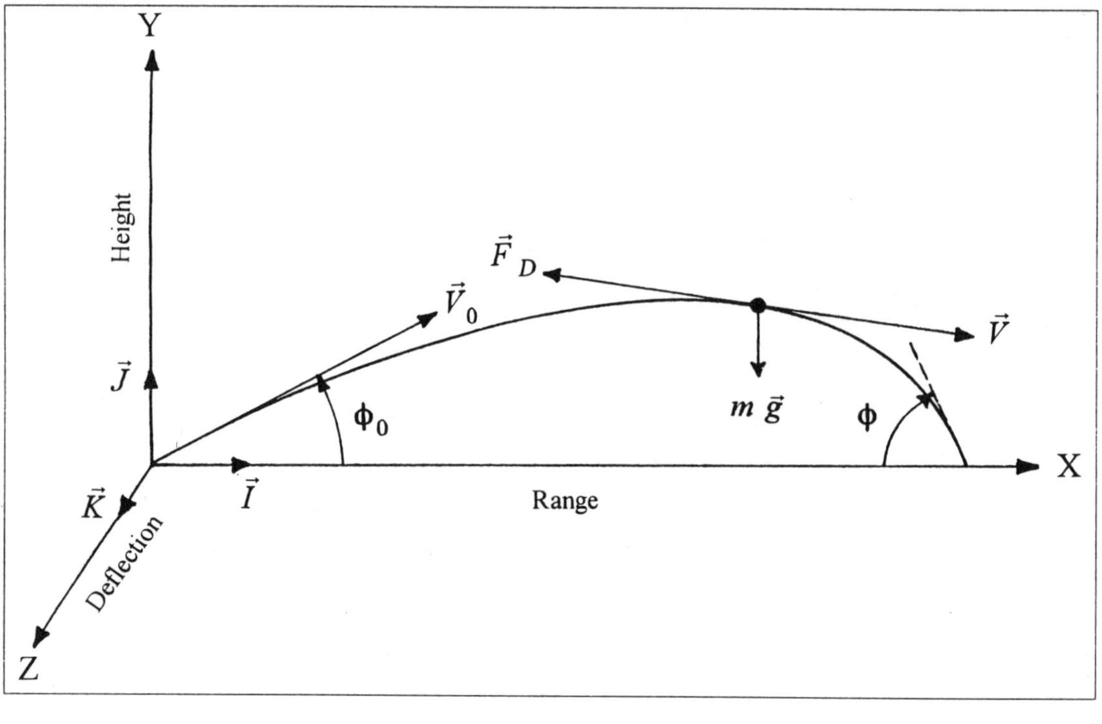

Figure 5.1 Coordinate System for the Point-Mass Trajectory.

5.2 EQUATIONS OF MOTION

We will adopt a right-handed rectangular coordinate system, similar to the coordinates chosen for the vacuum trajectory in Chapter 3. The X-axis is tangent to the earth's surface at the launch point, and is directed from the gun toward the target. The Y-axis is directed vertically upward, through the launch point. The Z-axis lies in the plane tangent to the earth's surface at the launch point, and is directed to the right when looking downrange. Figure 5.1 illustrates the coordinate system, a typical point-mass trajectory, and the pertinent variables.

Newton's second law of motion for a projectile with constant mass was stated as equation (3.1) of Chapter 3. If the very small Coriolis acceleration due to the earth's rotation is neglected, equation (3.1) reduces to:

$$m\frac{d\vec{V}}{dt} = \sum\vec{F} + m\vec{g} \qquad (5.1)$$

where
- m = projectile mass
- $\vec{V}$ = vector velocity
- t = time
- $\dfrac{d\vec{V}}{dt}$ = vector acceleration
- $\sum\vec{F}$ = vector sum of all the aerodynamic forces
- $\vec{g}$ = vector acceleration due to gravity

The reader will recall from Chapter 2 that the only significant aerodynamic forces acting on symmetric projectiles are the drag force, the lift force, and the Magnus force. If the total yaw angle is everywhere small along the trajectory, equations (2.6) and (2.21) tell us that the lift and Magnus forces are also very small, and may therefore be neglected in comparison with the drag force stated in equation (2.1). The fundamental assumption of the point-mass trajectory approximation (i.e., aerodynamic drag and gravity are the only significant forces acting on the projectile), is thus equivalent to the assumption that the total yaw is everywhere small along the trajectory.

The term "particle trajectory" is often found in classical exterior ballistic literature; its meaning is synonymous with our term "point-mass trajectory." Either term implies a non-spinning, nonlifting projectile, whose mass is concentrated at a mathematical point in space. Such a projectile could experience no aerodynamic force other than drag. Exterior ballisticians of the nineteenth and early twentieth centuries therefore referred to any trajectory produced solely by the forces of aerodynamic drag and gravity as a "point-mass" or "particle" trajectory.

The magnitude of the aerodynamic drag force is $\left(\frac{1}{2}\right)\rho V^2 S C_D$, and the direction of the force is $-\vec{V}$, so the drag opposes the vector velocity. The vector form of the drag force is therefore given by:

$$\vec{F}_D = -\frac{1}{2}\rho S C_D V\vec{V} \qquad (5.2)$$

where
- $\vec{F}_D$ = vector aerodynamic drag force
- ρ = air density
- S = projectile reference area
- C_D = dimensionless drag coefficient
- $\vec{V}$ = vector velocity
- V = scalar magnitude of velocity (speed)

Substituting the vector drag force for in equation (5.1), and dividing both sides by the projectile mass, yields the vector differential equation of motion of the point-mass trajectory:

$$\frac{d\vec{V}}{dt} = -\frac{\rho S C_D}{2m} V\vec{V} + \vec{g} \qquad (5.3)$$

The vector quantities are now resolved into components along the coordinate axes. The vector velocity and acceleration are given by:

$$\vec{V} = V_x\vec{I} + V_y\vec{J} + V_z\vec{K} \qquad (5.4)$$

$$\frac{d\vec{V}}{dt} = \dot{V}_x\vec{I} + \dot{V}_y\vec{J} + \dot{V}_z\vec{K} \qquad (5.5)$$

where
- $\vec{I}$ is a unit vector along the X-axis
- $\vec{J}$ is a unit vector along the Y-axis
- $\vec{K}$ is a unit vector along the Z-axis
- V_x = X-component of velocity
- V_y = Y-component of velocity
- V_z = Z-component of velocity
- $\dot{V}_x$ = X-component of acceleration
- $\dot{V}_y$ = Y-component of acceleration
- $\dot{V}_z$ = Z-component of acceleration

The gravitational acceleration vector, $\vec{g}$, has standard scalar magnitude 32.174 feet per second squared (9.807 meters per second squared) at sea level, and is directed vertically downward, in the $-\vec{J}$ direction.

$$\vec{g} = -g\vec{J} \qquad (5.6)$$

The quantity $\dfrac{\rho S C_D}{2m}$ appears so often in this chapter, it is convenient to define a special symbol:

$$\boxed{\hat{C}_D^* = \frac{\rho S C_D}{2m} = \frac{\rho\pi}{8}\frac{C_D}{C}} \qquad (5.7)$$

where $C = m/d^2$, the ballistic coefficient of the projectile.

[Note that the quantity $\hat{C}_D^*$ is not dimensionless; it has the units of (1/length). In later chapters we will introduce another dimensionless quantity C_D^*, defined as $C_D^* = \hat{C}_D^* d$, for use with distance measured in nondimensional units (calibers)].

Substitution of equations (5.4) through (5.7) into equation (5.3), and collection of coefficients of the three unit vectors yields the three scalar differential equations:

$$\boxed{\dot{V}_x = -\hat{C}_D^* V V_x} \qquad (5.8)$$

$$\boxed{\dot{V}_y = -\hat{C}_D^* V V_y - g} \qquad (5.9)$$

$$\boxed{\dot{V}_z = -\hat{C}_D^* V V_z} \qquad (5.10)$$

The scalar magnitude of velocity, or speed, is found from the vector dot product of with itself:

$$V^2 = \vec{V} \bullet \vec{V} = V_x^2 + V_y^2 + V_z^2 \qquad (5.11)$$

Taking the square root of both sides of equation (5.11):

$$\boxed{V = \sqrt{V_x^2 + V_y^2 + V_z^2}} \qquad (5.12)$$

Equations (5.8), (5.9) and (5.10), together with equation (5.12), are an exact statement of Newton's second law of motion for a projectile acted on only by the forces of aerodynamic drag and gravity.

Note that equations (5.8) through (5.10) all contain the scalar magnitude of velocity, V, and the three differential equations are therefore non-linearly coupled to each other through equation (5.12). This nonlinear coupling is the cause of the analytical intractability of the point-mass differential equations. In Chapter 3, we observed that a simple, analytical solution for the vacuum trajectory was easily obtained; however, no such analytical solution exists for the point-mass trajectory. Thus two options are available for point-mass trajectories: (1) the equations can be linearized (approximated) in such a manner as to permit an analytical solution, or (2) the full nonlinear equations can be solved numerically. Classical exterior ballistics of the nineteenth and early twentieth centuries was dominated by the first option, due to the labor-intensive nature of manually-computed numerical solutions. In modern practice, whenever maximum accuracy is desired, the full nonlinear point-mass differential equations are readily solved numerically on a high-speed digital computer, and now even with "personal computers."

One of the most useful linearized forms of the point-mass trajectory equations is the flat-fire approximation, which we will consider in the remaining sections of this chapter. Modern methods using numerical integration are described in Chapter 8.

5.3 THE FLAT-FIRE APPROXIMATION

A flat-fire trajectory is defined as a trajectory that is restricted to lie everywhere close to the X-axis. It is intuitively obvious that the velocity components and are much smaller than the component for any flat-fire trajectory. If there is no crosswind, may be dropped with no loss in generality, and equation (5.12) reduces to:

$$V = \sqrt{V_x^2 + V_y^2} = V_x\sqrt{1 + \left(V_y/V_x\right)^2} \qquad (5.13)$$

The right-hand side of equation (5.13) is now expanded in a binomial series:

$$V = V_x\left[1 + \frac{1}{2}\left(V_y/V_x\right)^2 - \frac{1}{8}\left(V_y/V_x\right)^4 + \cdots\right] \qquad (5.14)$$

Equation (5.14) shows that V and V_x differ by less than 1/2 of one percent if the following inequality is satisfied:

$$\left|V_y/V_x\right| < 10^{-1} \qquad (5.15)$$

Inequality (5.15) tells us that since $V_y/V_x = \tan\phi$, a strict mathematical definition of flat-fire requires both the angle of departure and the angle of fall of the trajectory to be less than 5.7 degrees above the horizontal. (In practice, angles as large as fifteen degrees can be tolerated without incurring serious trajectory errors).

Substituting the flat-fire approximation $V \approx V_x$ into equations (5.8) and (5.9) yields the differential equations of motion for a flat-fire trajectory:

$$\boxed{\dot{V}_x = -\hat{C}_D^* V_x^2} \qquad (5.16)$$

$$\boxed{\dot{V}_y = -\hat{C}_D^* V_x V_y - g} \qquad (5.17)$$

The independent variable in equations (5.16) and (5.17) is time. However, downrange distance, X, is frequently a more convenient independent variable than is the time. Equations (5.16) and (5.17) are readily transformed into new equations with distance X as the independent variable:

$$X = \int_0^t V_x ds_1 \text{, by definition.} \qquad (5.18)$$

$$\dot{V}_x = \frac{dV_x}{dt} = \frac{dV_x}{dX} \bullet \frac{dX}{dt} = V_x\frac{dV_x}{dX} = V_x V_x' \qquad (5.19)$$

$$\dot{V}_y = \frac{dV_y}{dt} = \frac{dV_y}{dX} \bullet \frac{dX}{dt} = V_x\frac{dV_y}{dX} = V_x V_y' \qquad (5.20)$$

where
$$V_x' = \frac{dV_x}{dX}$$
$$V_y' = \frac{dV_y}{dX}$$

Substituting equations (5.19) and (5.20) into equations (5.16) and (5.17):

$$\boxed{V_x' = -\hat{C}_D^* V_x} \qquad (5.21)$$

$$\boxed{V_y' = -\hat{C}_D^* V_y - \frac{g}{V_x}} \qquad (5.22)$$

Equations (5.21) and (5.22) are the flat-fire differential equations of motion, with downrange distance as the independent variable. An exact analytical solution of equations (5.21) and (5.22) exists, and it is given by:

$$V_x = V_{x_o} e^{-\int_0^X \hat{C}_D^* ds_1} \qquad (5.23)$$

$$V_y = e^{-\int_0^X \hat{C}_D^* ds_1} \left[V_{y_o} - \int_0^X \left(\frac{g}{V_x} \right) e^{\int_0^{s_2} \hat{C}_D^* ds_1} ds_2 \right] \qquad (5.24)$$

$$\frac{V_y}{V_x} = \tan\phi = \tan\phi_o - \frac{1}{V_{x_o}} \int_0^X \left(\frac{g}{V_x} \right) e^{\int_0^{s_2} \hat{C}_D^* ds_1} ds_2 \qquad (5.25)$$

$$Y = Y_o + X\tan\phi_o - \frac{gX^2}{2V_{x_o}^2} \left[\frac{2}{X^2} \int_0^X \int_0^{s_3} e^{2\int_0^{s_2} \hat{C}_D^* ds_1} ds_2 ds_3 \right] \qquad (5.26)$$

$$t = \frac{1}{V_{x_o}} \int_0^X e^{\int_0^{s_2} \hat{C}_D^* ds_1} ds_2 \qquad (5.27)$$

where ϕ = angle of fall (inclination) of the trajectory

ϕ_o = gun elevation angle above horizontal

Y = trajectory height at range X

Y_o = initial trajectory height

t = time of flight to range X

s_1 s_2 s_3 (lower case)

S_1, S_2, and S_3 are dummy variables of integration

Equations (5.23) through (5.27) are called "quadrature solutions." If the variation of aerodynamic drag is known at all points along the trajectory, the definite integrals, or quadratures can be evaluated. However, the disadvantage of quadrature solutions is obvious; unless the variation in $\hat{C}_D^*$ is restricted to elementary functions, the evaluation of the definite integrals does not result in a closed form analytical solution, and thus requires numerical integration methods. The exact quadrature solution of the flat-fire equations is therefore of little practical value in exterior ballistics. In the next sections of this chapter, we will look at some special analytical forms of drag coefficient variation with Mach number that have been found to be useful in the calculation of flat-fire trajectories, precisely because they give closed form, analytical solutions.

5.4 SPECIAL ANALYTICAL SOLUTIONS OF THE FLAT-FIRE EQUATIONS

In this section we will consider three special forms of drag coefficient variation with Mach number that have proved to be both simple and useful in flat-fire trajectory analysis. The three special forms are: (1) constant drag coefficient, (2) drag coefficient inversely proportional to Mach number, and (3) drag coefficient inversely proportional to the square root of Mach number. All of these are useful, but in different flight speed regions, as we shall see presently.

The difference in height between the lowest and highest points of a flat-fire trajectory is so small that both air density and air temperature may be assumed to be constant everywhere along the flight path. The speed of sound in air is also constant, since it depends only on the temperature.

The differential equations for which we will need solutions are equations (5.16), (5.17) and (5.21) of the previous section. The solution of (5.21) was given as equation (5.23), and the required solutions of equations (5.16) and (5.17) are:

$$V_x = \frac{V_{x_o}}{1 + V_{x_o} \int_0^t \hat{C}_D^* ds_1} \qquad (5.28)$$

$$V_y = \left(\frac{V_{y_o}}{V_{x_o}} \right) V_x - gV_x \int_0^t \frac{ds_1}{V_x} \qquad (5.29)$$

Inverting equation (5.23) gives:

$$\frac{dt}{dX} = \frac{1}{V_{x_o}} e^{\int_0^X \hat{C}_D^* ds_1} \qquad (5.30)$$

Integrating equation (5.30) yields:

$$t = \frac{1}{V_{x_o}} \int_0^X e^{\int_0^{s_2} \hat{C}_D^* ds_1} ds_2 \qquad (5.31)$$

The inclination along the trajectory is given by the ratio of V_y to V_x, from equations (5.28) and (5.29):

$$\tan\phi = \frac{V_y}{V_x} = \tan\phi_o - g\int_0^t \frac{ds_1}{V_x} \qquad (5.32)$$

Finally, the height at any point along the trajectory is found from the integral of equation (5.29):

$$Y = Y_o + X\tan\phi_o - g\int_0^t\left(V_x\int_0^t \frac{ds_1}{V_x}\right)ds_2 \tag{5.33}$$

The quadrature solutions given by equations (5.28) through (5.33) are now evaluated for the three special forms of drag coefficient variation with Mach number. These equations retain both X and t as independent variables, because it will simplify the notation later in this chapter.

5.5 CONSTANT DRAG COEFFICIENT (SQUARE LAW OF AIR RESISTANCE)

Let $C_D = K_1$, a constant value **(5.34)**

$$\text{Then}\quad \hat{C}_D^* = \frac{\rho S}{2m}C_D = \frac{\rho S}{2m}K_1 = k_1 \tag{5.35}$$

Substituting these definitions into equations (5.23), (5.27), (5.29), (5.32) and (5.33) gives:

$$V_x = V_{x_o}e^{-k_1 X} = \frac{V_{x_o}}{1 + V_{x_o}k_1 t} \tag{5.36}$$

$$V_y = V_x\left[\tan\phi_o - \frac{gt}{V_{x_o}}\left(1 + \frac{1}{2}V_{x_o}k_1 t\right)\right] \tag{5.37}$$

$$\tan\phi = \frac{V_y}{V_x} = \tan\phi_o - \frac{gt}{V_{x_o}}\left(1 + \frac{1}{2}V_{x_o}k_1 t\right) \tag{5.38}$$

$$Y = Y_o + X\tan\phi_o - \frac{1}{2}gt^2\left[\frac{1}{2} + \frac{1}{V_{x_o}k_1 t} - \frac{\ln(1+V_{x_o}k_1 t)}{(V_{x_o}k_1 t)^2}\right] \tag{5.39}$$

The time of flight is obtained from equation (5.31):

$$t = \frac{1}{V_{x_o}k_1}\left[e^{k_1 X} - 1\right] \tag{5.40}$$

Equation (5.36) is now used to eliminate k_1 from equations (5.37) through (5.40). The final results are summarized below for any flat-fire trajectory with constant drag coefficient:

$$V_x = V_{x_o}e^{-k_1 X} \tag{5.41}$$

$$k_1 = \frac{\rho S}{2m}C_D \quad \text{, where } C_D \text{ is constant} \tag{5.42}$$

$$t = \frac{X}{V_{x_o}}\left(\frac{V_{x_o}}{V_x} - 1\right)\Big/\ln\left(\frac{V_{x_o}}{V_x}\right) \tag{5.43}$$

$$\tan\phi = \tan\phi_o - \frac{gt}{V_{x_o}}\left[\frac{1}{2}\left(1 + \frac{V_{x_o}}{V_x}\right)\right] \tag{5.44}$$

$$Y = Y_o + X\tan\phi_o - \frac{1}{2}gt^2\left[\frac{1}{2} + \left(\frac{V_{x_o}}{V_x} - 1\right)^{-1} - \left(\frac{V_{x_o}}{V_x} - 1\right)^{-2}\ln\left(\frac{V_{x_o}}{V_x}\right)\right] \tag{5.45}$$

The flat-fire trajectory with constant drag coefficient is often a useful approximation in modern exterior ballistics. Most subsonic projectiles have nearly constant drag coefficients, as we observed in Chapter 4. Constant drag coefficients are also characteristic of projectiles flying at hypersonic speeds. Over a short distance, the variation in drag coefficient is usually small for any projectile at any flight speed, and a constant drag coefficient is often an adequate approximation in free-flight ballistic range work.

Example 5.1

The standard military load for the Caliber .45 M1911A1 pistol is the Ball M1911 round, which contains a 230 grain round nose full metal jacketed bullet loaded to a muzzle velocity of approximately 860 feet per second. The projectile reference diameter is 0.452", the ICAO sea-level standard air density is approximately 0.0765 pounds per cubic foot, and the average measured value (Ref. 2) of the M1911 drag coefficient at subsonic speeds is 0.205. Use equations (5.41) through (5.43) to construct a ballistic table of striking velocity and time of flight out to 200 yards range, in 25 yard intervals.

The reference area, S, and the projectile mass, m, are:

$$S = \frac{\pi}{4}d^2 = \frac{\pi}{4}\left(\frac{.452}{12}\right)^2 = 0.001114\,ft^2$$

$$m = \frac{230}{7000} = 0.03286 \text{ pound}$$

$$\text{Then}\quad k_1 = \frac{(.0765)(.001114)}{2(.03286)}(.205) = 0.0002658\,ft^{-1}$$

The downrange striking velocity and time of flight are:

$$V_x = 860e^{-.0002658X} \tag{5.46}$$

$$t = \frac{X}{860}\left(\frac{860}{V_x} - 1\right)\Big/\ln\left(\frac{860}{V_x}\right) \tag{5.47}$$

Substituting the appropriate values of X in equation (5.46), and both X and V_x in equation (5.47) yields the values listed in Table 5.1:

Table 5.1

Range (Yards)	X (Feet)	V_x (ft./sec.)	t (sec.)
0	0	860	0
25	75	843	0.088
50	150	826	0.178
75	225	810	0.270
100	300	794	0.363
125	375	779	0.459
150	450	763	0.556
175	525	748	0.655
200	600	733	0.756

Example 5.2

The top of the front sight blade on the M1911A1 pistol is 0.56" above the bore centerline. We will take g = 32.174 feet per second squared, and Y_o = -0.56" = -0.0467 foot, relative to line-of-sight coordinates. Use equation (5.45) and the results of Table 5.1 to find the gun elevation angle required to zero the pistol at 50 yards range. Given a 50 yard zero, where will the bullet strike at the other ranges?

Since the pistol is to be zeroed at 50 yards, Y = 0 when X = 150 feet. The time of flight to 50 yards is 0.178 second, and V_x = 826 feet per second. We substitute the appropriate values in equation (5.45) and solve for ϕ_o :

$$0 = -.0467 + 150\tan\phi_o - \frac{1}{2}(32.174)(.178)^2\left[\frac{1}{2} + 24.294 - 23.807\right]$$

$$150\tan\phi_o = 0.5496,\ or\ \tan\phi_o = 0.003664$$

The required elevation angle for a 50 yard zero is:

$$\phi_o = \tan^{-1}(0.003664) = 12.6 \quad \text{minutes}$$

The trajectory height at the other ranges is now obtained from equation (5.45), and the results are listed in Table 5.2:

Table 5.2

Range (Yards)	X (Feet)	Y (Feet)	Y (Inches)
0	0	-0.05	-0.6
25	75	0.10	1.2
50	150	0	0
75	225	-0.37	-4.4
100	300	-1.02	-12.2
125	375	-1.95	-23.4
150	450	-3.18	-38.1
175	525	-4.72	-56.6
200	600	-6.58	-79.0

Table 5.2 shows that if the caliber .45 pistol is zeroed at 50 yards range with military ball ammunition, the bullet will strike about 1.2 inches above point of aim at 25 yards, and about one foot low at 100 yards. The gravity drop of the low velocity projectile increases rapidly for ranges beyond 100 yards.

5.6 DRAG COEFFICIENT INVERSELY PROPORTIONAL TO MACH NUMBER (LINEAR LAW OF AIR RESISTANCE)

Let $C_D = K_2/M$, where M is Mach number, and K_2 is a constant. **(5.48)**

$$\text{Then } \hat{C}_D^* = \frac{\rho S}{2m}C_D = \frac{\rho S}{2m}\frac{K_2}{M} \quad \textbf{(5.49)}$$

For flat-fire, $M = V_x/a$, where a = speed of sound **(5.50)**

$$\text{We define } k_2 = \frac{\rho S}{2m}K_2 a \quad \textbf{(5.51)}$$

$$\text{Then} \quad \hat{C}_D^* = \frac{\rho S}{2m}\frac{K_2 a}{V_x} = \frac{k_2}{V_x} \quad \textbf{(5.52)}$$

Substituting these definitions into equations (5.16), (5.17) and (5.21):

$$\dot{V}_x = -k_2 V_x \quad \textbf{(5.53)}$$

$$\dot{V}_y = -k_2 V_y - g \quad \textbf{(5.54)}$$

$$V_x' = \frac{dV_x}{dX} = -k_2 \quad \textbf{(5.55)}$$

Integrating equations (5.53) through (5.55), and eliminating k_2 between the solution equations yields the results summarized below. The details are left as an exercise for the interested reader.

$$V_x = V_{x_o} - k_2 X, \quad \textbf{(5.56)}$$

where the definition of k_2 is given by equation (5.51).

$$t = \frac{X}{V_{x_o}}\ln\left(\frac{V_{x_o}}{V_x}\right)\bigg/\left(1 - \frac{V_x}{V_{x_o}}\right) \quad \textbf{(5.57)}$$

$$\tan\phi = \tan\phi_o - \frac{gt}{V_{x_o}}\left[\left(\frac{V_{x_o}}{V_x} - 1\right)\bigg/\ln\left(1 - \frac{V_{x_o}}{V_x}\right)\right] \quad \textbf{(5.58)}$$

$$Y = Y_o + X\tan\phi_o - \frac{1}{2}gt^2\left[2\bigg/\ln\left(\frac{V_{x_o}}{V_x}\right)\right]\left[1 - \left(1 - \frac{V_x}{V_{x_o}}\right)\bigg/\ln\left(\frac{V_{x_o}}{V_x}\right)\right] \quad \textbf{(5.59)}$$

The flat-fire trajectory with drag coefficient inversely proportional to Mach number is often useful at very high supersonic speeds. Celmins (Ref. 3) has recently noted the utility of this approximation in the reduction of free-flight range data for modern high velocity kinetic energy penetrator projectiles. Celmins observed that if the entire useful flight of the projectile lies above Mach 2.5, equation (5.48) is an accurate description of the variation of the drag coefficient with Mach number. Thus equations (5.56) through (5.59), with the definitions of equations (5.48) and (5.51), give a good approximation to the flat-fire trajectories of many projectiles that fly at high supersonic speeds.

5.7 DRAG COEFFICIENT INVERSELY PROPORTIONAL TO THE SQUARE ROOT OF MACH NUMBER (3/2 POWER LAW OF AIR RESISTANCE)

Let $C_D = K_3/\sqrt{M}$, where M = Mach number, and K_3 is a constant. **(5.60)**

Then $$\hat{C}_D^* = \frac{\rho S}{2m} C_D = \frac{\rho S}{2m} \frac{K_3}{\sqrt{M}} \qquad \textbf{(5.61)}$$

We define $$k_3 = \frac{\rho S}{2m} K_3 \sqrt{a} \qquad \textbf{(5.62)}$$

$$\hat{C}_D^* = \frac{\rho S}{2m} K_3 \sqrt{\frac{a}{V_x}} = \frac{k_3}{\sqrt{M}} \qquad (5.63)$$

If these definitions are substituted into equations (5.16), (5.17) and (5.21):

$$\dot{V}_x = -k_3 V_x^{3/2} \qquad \textbf{(5.64)}$$

$$\dot{V}_y = -k_3 \sqrt{V_x} V_y - g \qquad \textbf{(5.65)}$$

$$V_x' = \frac{dV_x}{dX} = -k_3 \sqrt{V_x} \qquad \textbf{(5.66)}$$

Integrating equations (5.64) through (5.66), and eliminating k_3 among the solution equations, gives the results summarized below:

$$V_x = \left[\sqrt{V_{x_o}} - \frac{1}{2} k_3 X\right]^2, \qquad \textbf{(5.67)}$$

where equation (5.62) is the definition of k_3.

$$t = \frac{X}{V_{x_o}} \sqrt{\frac{V_{x_o}}{V_x}} \qquad \textbf{(5.68)}$$

$$\tan\phi = \tan\phi_o - \frac{gt}{V_{x_o}} \left[\frac{1}{3}\left(1 + \sqrt{\frac{V_{x_o}}{V_x}} + \frac{V_{x_o}}{V_x}\right)\right] \qquad \textbf{(5.69)}$$

$$Y = Y_o + X \tan\phi_o - \frac{1}{2} g t^2 \left[\frac{1}{3}\left(1 + 2\sqrt{\frac{V_x}{V_{x_o}}}\right)\right] \qquad \textbf{(5.70)}$$

Equation (5.70) was derived by McShane, Kelley and Reno (Ref. 4) in their classical textbook "Exterior Ballistics." The authors noted the usefulness of this approximation in computing the gravity drop of flat-fire trajectories. A. J. Pejsa's recent book "Mod-

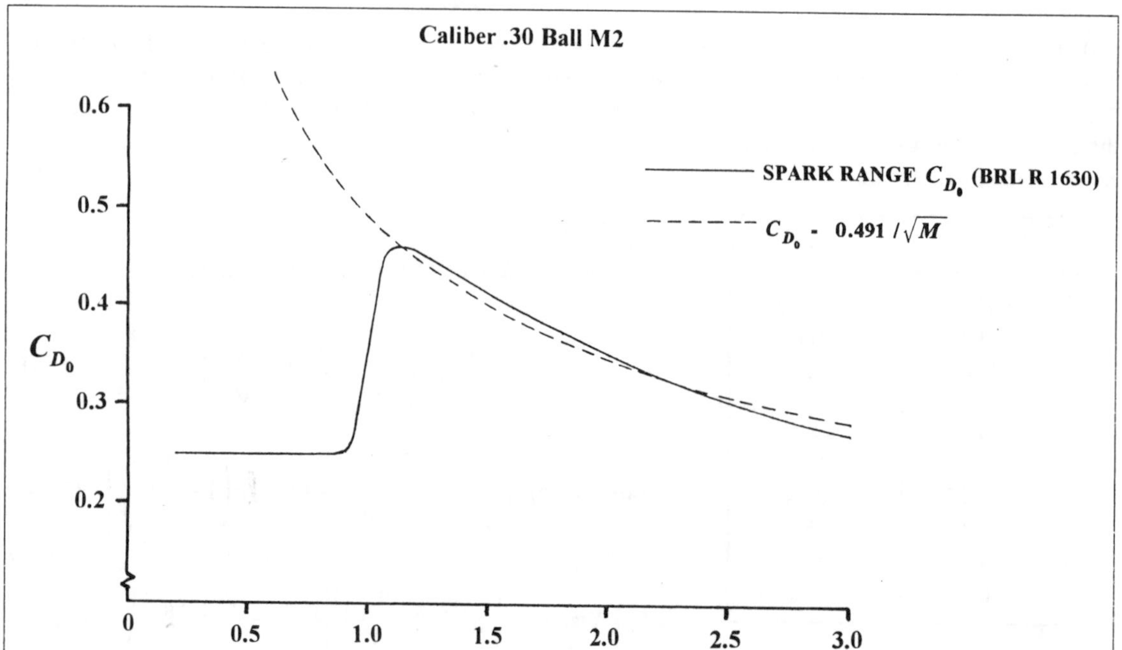

Figure 5.2 Zero-Yaw Drag Coefficient versus Mach Number.

ern Practical Ballistics" (Ref. 5) also takes advantage of the fact that the drag coefficients of many modern small arms projectiles are accurately described by equation (5.60) over most of the supersonic flight regime.

Example 5.3

The service rifle cartridge used by U. S. infantry forces in the Second World War was the caliber .30 Ball M2, which fired a 150 grain flat-based spitzer bullet at a muzzle velocity of approximately 2800 feet per second. Over the Mach number range 1.2 to 3, Figure 5.2 shows that for K_3= 0.491, equation (5.60) agrees closely with the spark range measured drag coefficient curve for the .30 Ball M2 bullet. Using Army Standard Metro values of 0.0751 pounds per cubic foot for air density and 1120 feet per second for the speed of sound in air, calculate a table of striking velocity, time of flight, gun elevation angle, and terminal angle of fall out to 600 yards range, in 100 yard intervals.

The reference area, S, and the projectile mass, m, are:

$$S = \frac{\pi}{4}d^2 = \frac{\pi}{4}\left(\frac{.308}{12}\right)^2 = 0.0005174\, ft^2$$

$$m = \frac{150}{7000} = 0.02143 \text{ pound}$$

Then $k_3 = \dfrac{(.0751)(.0005174)}{2(.02143)}(.491)\sqrt{1120} = 0.0149(ft-\sec)^{-1/2}$

The downrange striking velocity and time of flight are found from equations (5.67) and (5.68). Equation (5.70) with Y_o = 0 is then solved for $\tan\phi_o$ when Y= 0, and finally, equation (5.69) is used to determine the angles of fall at the various ranges. The results are summarized in Table 5.3:

Table 5.3

Range (Yards)	V (fps)	t (sec.)	ϕ_o (Minutes)	ϕ (Minutes)
0	2800	0	0	0
100	2568	0.112	2.2	-2.4
200	2347	0.234	4.8	-5.3
300	2135	0.368	7.6	-9.1
400	1934	0.516	10.9	-13.9
500	1742	0.679	14.6	-20.0
600	1561	0.861	18.9	-28.0

The approximate values given in Table 5.3 for the caliber .30 Ball M2 projectile agree very closely with those obtained by modern numerical integration methods, at ranges out to 600 yards. At longer ranges, where the velocity drops to transonic and subsonic speeds, the agreement is less satisfactory, as would be expected from Figure 5.2. However, Examples 5.1 through 5.3 demonstrate the practical utility of the various approximations in the calculation of flat-fire trajectories over moderate ranges.

5.8 COMPARISON OF FLAT-FIRE TRAJECTORY APPROXIMATIONS

The time of flight, angle of fall, and trajectory height equations of the previous three sections may be written in the general form:

$$t = \frac{X}{V_{x_o}}T \tag{5.71}$$

$$\tan\phi = \tan\phi_o - \frac{gt}{V_{x_o}}P \tag{5.72}$$

$$Y = Y_o + X\tan\phi_o - \frac{1}{2}gt^2Q \tag{5.73}$$

The function T in equation (5.71) is the ratio of actual time of flight to the time of flight in a vacuum. Likewise, the function P in equation (5.72) is the ratio of the actual angle of inclination to the vacuum angle of inclination. The function Q in equation (5.73) is the ratio of of the actual trajectory drop to the drop that would be observed for a flat-fire vacuum trajectory. The functions T, P, and Q are obtained by inspection of equations (5.43) through (5.45), (5.57) through (5.59), and (5.68) through (5.70), for the three special analytical forms of drag coefficient variation with Mach number. The results are summarized in Tables 5.4 through 5.6:

Table 5.4

Drag Coefficient Variation	T
Constant C_D	$\left[\left(V_{x_o}/V_x\right)-1\right]/\ln\left(V_{x_o}/V_x\right)$
$C_D = K_2/M$	$\ln\left(V_{x_o}/V_x\right)/\left[1-\left(V_x/V_{x_o}\right)\right]$
$C_D = K_3/\sqrt{M}$	$\sqrt{V_{x_o}/V_x}$

Table 5.5	
Drag Coefficient Variation	P
Constant C_D	$\left[1+\left(V_{x_o}/V_x\right)\right]/2$
$C_D = K_2/M$	$\left[\left(V_{x_o}/V_x\right)-1\right]/\ln\left(V_{x_o}/V_x\right)$
$C_D = K_3/\sqrt{M}$	$\left[1+\sqrt{V_{x_o}/V_x}+\left(V_{x_o}/V_x\right)\right]/3$

The functions T, P, and Q for the three different drag coefficient variations appear to be totally unrelated to each other. However, if we evaluate the functions for various values of V_x/V_{x_o}, a somewhat surprising (and useful) result is obtained; for all values of $V_x/V_{x_o} > 0.5$, the functions T, P, and Q are practically independent of the particular form we choose for the drag coefficient variation with Mach number. Tables 5.7 through 5.9 illustrate the results:

Table 5.6	
Drag Coefficient Variation	Q
Constant C_D	$\frac{1}{2}+\left(\frac{V_{x_o}}{V_x}-1\right)^{-1}-\left(\frac{V_{x_o}}{V_x}-1\right)^{-2}\ln\left(\frac{V_{x_o}}{V_x}\right)$
$C_D = K_2/M$	$\left[2/\ln\left(\frac{V_{x_o}}{V_x}\right)\right]\left[1-\left(1-\frac{V_x}{V_{x_o}}\right)/\ln\left(\frac{V_{x_o}}{V_x}\right)\right]$
$C_D = K_3/\sqrt{M}$	$\frac{1}{3}\left(1+2\sqrt{\frac{V_x}{V_{x_o}}}\right)$

Tables 5.7 and 5.8 show that the differences between the highest and lowest values of the time of flight and angle of fall functions are less than 4 percent, for all $V_x/V_{x_o} > 0.5$. The trajectory height (or gravity drop) function shows even less difference between the highest and lowest values; for $V_x/V_{x_o} > 0.5$, the largest difference in Q is less than 0.5 percent. The time of flight, angle of fall, and gravity drop for flat-fire trajectories are thus observed to be relatively insensitive to the variation of drag coefficient with Mach number, out to the range at which the velocity has decayed to one-half the muzzle velocity. Furthermore, the last column in Tables 5.7 through 5.9 is nearly the average of the second and third, and we see that a drag coefficient which varies inversely as the square root of the Mach number is an excellent choice for all-around use in flat-fire trajectory approximations.

5.9 SUMMARY

The exact differential equations of motion for a point-mass trajectory are derived in this chapter. The exact equations are then linearized by means of the flat-fire assumption, and several of the classical flat-fire approximations are derived. A particularly useful result is obtained for the special case in which the drag coefficient varies inversely as the square root of the Mach number.

A useful rule of thumb for practical application of the flat-fire equations is suggested by Tables 5.7 through 5.9. For ranges beyond the point at which the striking velocity has decayed to one-half the muzzle velocity, the flat-fire results become increasingly more sensitive to the variation of the drag coefficient with Mach number. Thus the flat-fire equations should only be used out to the range at which the remaining velocity is at least one-half the muzzle velocity $V_x \geq V_{x_o}/2$.

Table 5.7

V_x/V_{x_o}	T [C_D= *constant*]	T $[C_D = K_2/M]$	T $[C_D = K_3/\sqrt{M}]$
1.0	1.000	1.000	1.000
0.9	1.055	1.054	1.054
0.8	1.120	1.116	1.118
0.7	1.202	1.189	1.195
0.6	1.305	1.277	1.291
0.5	1.443	1.386	1.414
0.4	1.637	1.527	1.581
0.3	1.938	1.720	1.826
0.2	2.485	2.012	2.236

Table 5.8

V_x/V_{x_o}	P [C_D= *constant*]	P $[C_D = K_2/M]$	P $[C_D = K_3/\sqrt{M}]$
1.0	1.000	1.000	1.000
0.9	1.056	1.055	1.055
0.8	1.125	1.120	1.123
0.7	1.214	1.202	1.208
0.6	1.333	1.305	1.319
0.5	1.500	1.443	1.471
0.4	1.750	1.637	1.694
0.3	2.167	1.938	2.053
0.2	3.000	2.485	2.745

Table 5.9

V_x/V_{x_o}	Q [C_D= *constant*]	Q $[C_D = K_2/M]$	Q $[C_D = K_3/\sqrt{M}]$
1.0	1.0000	1.0000	1.0000
0.9	0.9658	0.9658	0.9658
0.8	0.9297	0.9296	0.9296
0.7	0.8914	0.8910	0.8911
0.6	0.8506	0.8494	0.8497
0.5	0.8069	0.8040	0.8047
0.4	0.7594	0.7534	0.7550
0.3	0.7074	0.6954	0.6985
0.2	0.6494	0.6250	0.6315

REFERENCES

1a. Siacci, F., "Balistica e pratica," *Giornale di artiglieria e genio*, parte 2° (non ufficiale), 1° volume, 1880.

1b. Siacci, F., "Perfezionamenti Vari al Nuovo Metodo di Resolvere i Problemi del Tiro," *Rivista di artiglieria e genio*, Volume III, parte 1°, 1886.

2. Braun, W. F., "Aerodynamic Data for Small Arms Projectiles," Ballistic Research Laboratory Report No. 1630, 1973.

3. Celmins, I., "Projectile Supersonic Drag Characteristics," Ballistic Research Laboratory Memorandum Report No. BRL-MR-3843, 1990.

4. McShane, E. J., J. L. Kelley and F. V. Reno, *Exterior Ballistics*, University of Denver Press, 1953.

5. Pejsa, A. J., *Modern Practical Ballistics*, Kenwood Publishing, Minneapolis, Minnesota, Second Edition, 1991.

6

The Siacci Method for Flat-Fire Trajectories

6.1 INTRODUCTION

In section 5.1 of the previous chapter, we observed that one of the most useful approximate methods for flat-fire trajectory calculation was introduced in 1880 (and in improved form in 1886) by Col. Francesco Siacci of Italy (Ref. 1a, Ref. 1b). The Siacci method is designed for trajectories with angles of departure less than fifteen degrees, and it reduces any flat-fire trajectory to easily tabulated quadratures giving distance, time, inclination (flight path angle) and altitude (height) in terms of a "pseudo-velocity," which will be defined in the next section.

In America, the most widely known set of ballistic tables based on Siacci's method are the Ingalls' Tables (Ref. 2b), first published in 1900 as "Artillery Circular M," by Col. James M. Ingalls of the U. S. Artillery. Ingalls' Tables used the Mayevski-Zaboudski drag function (Ref. 2c), which was based on firings done by the German firm of Krupp at Meppen Proving Ground, Germany, from about 1875 to 1881.

The Siacci method is no longer used in U. S. Army Ordnance, as modern numerical integration has now replaced all the classical approximate methods. However, Siacci's method is still in widespread use throughout the U. S. sporting arms and ammunition industry, and for the short ranges common to sporting projectile trajectories, its accuracy is sufficient for nearly all practical purposes.

6.2 SIACCI ASSUMPTIONS AND APPROXIMATIONS

The three fundamental assumptions made in the Siacci method are: (1) the difference in height of the lowest and highest points of the trajectory is small enough that the air density may be assumed to be constant along the trajectory, (2) the air temperature along the trajectory is also constant, and differs insignificantly from the standard air temperature, and (3) the value of the velocity, V, is very well approximated by $V_x \sec\phi_o$ along the entire trajectory, where V_x is the horizontal component of velocity and ϕ_o is the angle of departure in the vertical plane.

The first of the above assumptions is straightforward; the second is a little more subtle. The drag coefficient depends on Mach number, not on velocity. However, if the air temperature remains everywhere close to the standard value, the drag dependence on Mach number may be replaced with a dependence on velocity, without incurring significant error.

The author's friend and colleague, W. C. Davis, Jr., of the Tioga Engineering Company, has recently pointed out that modern Siacci calculations make a temperature (speed of sound) correction to the velocities before entering the tables. Thus the independent variable used is actually equivalent to the Mach number, and the second assumption made above is no longer required.

Siacci's quantity $V_x \sec\phi_o$ is called the "pseudo-velocity," and is defined as the product of the horizontal component of velocity and the secant of the angle of departure.

$$V \approx V_x \sec\phi_o, \text{ or } V_x \approx V\cos\phi_o \qquad (6.1)$$

The expression $V_x = V\cos\phi$ is exact everywhere along the trajectory, and we observe that the third Siacci assumption is equivalent to the flat-fire condition, i.e., the change in $\cos\phi$ along the flight path is everywhere very small.

6.3 DERIVATION OF THE SIACCI FUNCTIONS

Equations (5.8) and (5.9) from the previous chapter are an exact statement of Newton's second law of motion for a planar trajectory acted on by the forces of aerodynamic drag and gravity:

$$\dot{V}_x = \frac{dV_x}{dt} = -\hat{C}_D^* V V_x \qquad (5.8)$$

$$\dot{V}_y = \frac{dV_y}{dt} = -\hat{C}_D^* V V_y - g \qquad (5.9)$$

Substituting the second equation of (6.1) into equation (5.8):

$$\dot{V}\cos\phi_o = -\hat{C}_D^* V^2 \cos\phi_o, \qquad (6.2)$$

$$\text{or,} \quad \frac{dV}{dt} = -\hat{C}_D^* V^2 \qquad (6.3)$$

The reference area, S, is defined in the usual way:

$$S = \frac{\pi}{4} d^2 \qquad (6.4)$$

$$\text{Then,} \quad \hat{C}_D^* = \frac{\rho\pi d^2 C_D}{8m} = \frac{\rho\pi C_D}{8C}, \qquad (6.5)$$

where $C = \dfrac{m}{d^2}$ (in American practice, C has the units lb./in.2) **(6.6)**

Let $G(V) = \dfrac{\rho \pi C_D V}{8}$ **(6.7)**

Then, $\hat{C}_D^* = \dfrac{G(V)}{CV}$ **(6.8)**

Substituting equation (6.8) into equation (6.3) and inverting:

$$\boxed{\frac{dt}{dV} = \frac{-C}{VG(V)}} \quad \textbf{(6.9)}$$

Equation (6.9) is the differential equation of the Siacci time of flight function. The space, or distance equation is now readily obtained:

$$\frac{dX}{dV} = \frac{dX}{dt} \bullet \frac{dt}{dV} = V_x \frac{dt}{dV} = V\cos\phi_o\left(\frac{-C}{VG(V)}\right) \quad \textbf{(6.10)}$$

$$\boxed{\frac{dX}{dV} = \frac{-C\cos\phi_o}{G(V)}} \quad \textbf{(6.11)}$$

Equation (6.11) is the differential equation of the Siacci space function. The inclination equation is now derived:

$$\tan\phi = \frac{dY}{dX} = \frac{V_y}{V_x} = \frac{V_y}{V}\sec\phi_o \quad \textbf{(6.12)}$$

$$V' = \frac{dV}{dX} = \frac{\dot{V}}{V}\sec\phi_o = -\hat{C}_D^* V \sec\phi_o \quad \textbf{(6.13)}$$

$$V_y' = \frac{dV_y}{dX} = \frac{\dot{V}_y}{V}\sec\phi_o = -(\hat{C}_D^* V_y + g/V)\sec\phi_o \quad \textbf{(6.14)}$$

$$\frac{d(\tan\phi)}{dX} = \left[\frac{VV_y' - V_yV'}{V^2}\right]\sec\phi_o \quad \textbf{(6.15)}$$

Substituting equations (6.13) and (6.14) into equation (6.15) and simplifying:

$$\frac{d(\tan\phi)}{dX} = -\frac{g}{V^2}\sec^2\phi_o \quad \textbf{(6.16)}$$

$$\frac{d(\tan\phi)}{dV} = \frac{d(\tan\phi)}{dX} \bullet \frac{dX}{dV} \quad \textbf{(6.17)}$$

We now substitute equations (6.11) and (6.16) into (6.17), and the differential equation of the Siacci inclination function is:

$$\boxed{\frac{d(\tan\phi)}{dV} = \frac{gC\sec\phi_o}{V^2G(V)}} \quad \textbf{(6.18)}$$

The differential equation for the Siacci altitude function is now readily obtained, with the help of equations (6.11) and (6.12):

$$\boxed{\frac{dY}{dV} = \frac{dY}{dX} \bullet \frac{dX}{dV} = \frac{-C\cos\phi_o\tan\phi}{G(V)}} \quad \textbf{(6.19)}$$

The utility of the Siacci method is based on the use of numerical quadrature to tabulate four primary functions, which are the solutions of equations (6.9), (6.11), (6.18), and (6.19). A value V_{max}, greater than the largest expected value of muzzle velocity, is selected. The definitions of the four tabulated Siacci functions are:

$$T(V) = \int_V^{V_{max}} \frac{dV}{VG(V)}$$ [the units of *T(V)* are sec.-in.²/lb.] **(6.20)**

$$S(V) = \int_V^{V_{max}} \frac{dV}{G(V)}$$ [the units of S(V) are ft.-in.²/lb.] **(6.21)**

$$I(V) = \int_V^{V_{max}} \frac{2gdV}{V^2G(V)}$$ [the units of I(V) are in.²/lb.] **(6.22)**

$$A(V) = \int_V^{V_{max}} \frac{I(V)dV}{G(V)}$$ [the units of A(V) are ft.-in.⁴/lb.²] **(6.23)**

The above integrals are the four primary Siacci functions, for the drag function G(V).

The function S(V) is the downrange distance travelled, or space function, T(V) is the time of flight function, I(V) is the trajectory inclination function, and A(V) is the altitude, or trajectory height function. The solutions of equations (6.9), (6.11), (6.18) and (6.19) are now obtained, and the results are expressed in terms of the four tabulated primary Siacci functions.

Integrating equation (6.9) and substituting equation (6.20) yields:

$$t = -C\int_{V_o}^{V} \frac{dV}{VG(V)} = C\left[T(V) - T(V_o)\right] \quad \textbf{(6.24)}$$

A similar integration of equation (6.11), with the definition of equation (6.21) gives:

$$X = -C\cos\phi_o\int_{V_o}^{V} \frac{dV}{G(V)} = C\cos\phi_o\left[S(V) - S(V_o)\right] \quad \textbf{(6.25)}$$

Integrating (6.18) and substituting equation (6.22):

$$\tan\phi = \tan\phi_o + C\sec\phi_o\int_{V_o}^{V} \frac{gdV}{V^2G(V)} \quad \textbf{(6.26)}$$

$$\tan\phi = \tan\phi_o - \frac{1}{2}C\sec\phi_o\left[I(V) - I(V_o)\right] \quad \textbf{(6.27)}$$

Finally, we integrate equation (6.19) with the help of equation (6.25), and substitute equations (6.22) and (6.23):

$$Y = X\left[\tan\phi_o + \frac{1}{2}CI(V_o)\sec\phi_o\right] - \frac{1}{2}C^2\left[A(V) - A(V_o)\right] \quad \textbf{(6.28)}$$

Dividing both sides of equation (6.28) by equation (6.25) and rearranging terms:

$$Y/X = \tan\phi_o - \frac{1}{2} C \sec\phi_o \left[\frac{A(V) - A(V_o)}{S(V) - S(V_o)} - I(V_o) \right] \quad \textbf{(6.29)}$$

The four equations (6.24), (6.25), (6.27) and (6.29) may now be used with a set of tables for the primary Siacci functions, to calculate flat-fire trajectories for any projectile whose aerodynamic drag is well approximated by the drag function G(V).

These equations (in a rearranged order) are collected below for easy reference:

$$X = C\cos\phi_o\left[S(V) - S(V_o)\right] \quad \textbf{(6.30)}$$

$$t = C\left[T(V) - T(V_o)\right] \quad \textbf{(6.31)}$$

$$Y = Y_o + X\tan\phi_o - \frac{1}{2} CX \sec\phi_o \left[\frac{A(V) - A(V_o)}{S(V) - S(V_o)} - I(V_o) \right] \quad \textbf{(6.32)}$$

$$\tan\phi = \tan\phi_o - \frac{1}{2} C \sec\phi_o \left[I(V) - I(V_o)\right] \quad \textbf{(6.33)}$$

Note the alternative form of equation (6.29), in which both sides are multiplied by the range, X. The initial height, Y_o, has been added to generalize the trajectory altitude function, and the result is equation (6.32).

The derivation given above for the primary Siacci functions follows that of McShane, Kelley, and Reno (Ref. 3); it also gives essentially the same results as the Kent-Hitchcock method (Ref. 4). A more general derivation, provided by D. G. Miller, of Livermore, California in a private communication to the author, gives the results expressed below as equations (6.34)-(6.37): (also see Ref. 5a,b,c)

$$X = \frac{C}{\beta}\left[S(V) - S(V_o)\right] \quad \textbf{(6.34)}$$

$$t = \frac{C}{\beta\cos\phi_o}\left[T(V) - T(V_o)\right] \quad \textbf{(6.35)}$$

$$Y = Y_o + X\tan\phi_o - \frac{CX}{2\beta\cos^2\phi_o} \left[\frac{A(V) - A(V_o)}{S(V) - S(V_o)} - I(V_o) \right] \quad \textbf{(6.36)}$$

$$\tan\phi = \tan\phi_o - \frac{CX}{2\beta\cos^2\phi_o}\left[I(V) - I(V_o)\right] \quad \textbf{(6.37)}$$

Col. Ingalls described the factor β as an "integrating factor" that was intended to compensate for the errors introduced by several approximations made in Siacci's method. Various choices may be made for the factor, β. If we choose $\beta = \sec\phi_o$, we get the same results as given in equations (6.30-6.33). Col. Ingalls chose to use $\beta = \sqrt{\sec\phi_o}$, which turns out to be an excellent all-around value, as we will demonstrate in a later chapter. For short ranges and very flat-fire trajectories, where ϕ_o < 5 degrees, $\cos\phi_o \approx 1$, $\sec\phi_o \approx 1$, and $\beta \approx 1$. The following approximations with β = 1 are therefore generally used in calculating short range trajectories for sporting use:

$$X = C\left[S(V) - S(V_o)\right] \quad \textbf{(6.38)}$$

$$t = C\left[T(V) - T(V_o)\right] \quad \textbf{(6.39)}$$

$$Y = Y_o + X\tan\phi_o - \frac{1}{2} CX \left[\frac{A(V) - A(V_o)}{S(V) - S(V_o)} - I(V_o) \right] \quad \textbf{(6.40)}$$

$$\tan\phi = \tan\phi_o - \frac{1}{2} C\left[I(V) - I(V_o)\right] \quad \textbf{(6.41)}$$

The definitions of symbols in the above equations are collected below for the reader's convenience:

X = downrange distance, or range (feet)

t = time of flight (seconds)

Y = trajectory height, or altitude (feet)

Y_o = initial trajectory height (feet)

ϕ = trajectory inclination angle

ϕ_o = angle of departure (gun elevation angle)

V = velocity at range X (feet per second)

V_o = muzzle velocity (feet per second)

C = ballistic coefficient (pounds per square inch)

S(V) = Siacci space function (ft.-in.²/lb.)

T(V) = Siacci time of flight function (sec.-in.²/lb.)

I(V) = Siacci inclination function (in.²/lb.)

A(V) = Siacci altitude (height) function (ft.-in.⁴/lb.²)

β = dimensionless Siacci correction factor (generally, a function of $\cos\phi_o$)

6.4 THE COMPUTATION OF SIACCI BALLISTIC TABLES

The four primary Siacci functions, as defined by the integrals of equations (6.20) through (6.23), are tabulated at the end of this chapter, for the Ingalls and G_1 drag functions illustrated in Chapter 1, and the G_2, G_5, G_6, G_7 and G_8 drag functions shown in Chapter 4. Siacci tables are also included for "G_{SP}" (G-SPhere), which is the drag function shown in Chapter 4 for a 9/16-inch diameter smooth steel sphere.

All the above ballistic tables were computed using a standard numerical integration method (Simpson's Rule) on a modern micro-computer, and are tabulated for velocities from 4500 feet per second (fps) down to 100 fps, in 10 fps intervals. In order to maintain consistency with classical published tables, the Army Standard Metro sea-level atmospheric and gravity values were used:

ρ_o = 0.075126 pound per cubic foot

a_0 = 1120.27 feet per second (speed of sound in air at 59_F)

g = 32.16 feet per second per second

The present ballistic tables agree to within the numerical round-off error with Ingalls' Tables (Ref. 2), (Ref. 6), and with those on file for G2 through G8 (Ref. 7), (Ref. 8), at the Ballistic Research Laboratory. Most of the tables included in this chapter have not previously been published in any forum available to the general public. The reader who is interested in Siacci methods is encouraged to take advantage of the flexibility offered by available ballistic tables for a variety of aerodynamic drag functions.

6.5 THE PRACTICAL USE OF THE BALLISTIC TABLES

The generalized ballistic coefficient for use with the tables of this chapter is given by:

$$C_j = \left(\frac{m}{i_j d^2}\right)\left(\frac{\rho_o}{\rho}\right) \qquad \textbf{(6.42)}$$

where C_j = ballistic coefficient, relative to drag function “j”

i_j = form factor, relative to drag function “j”

j = ING, 1, 2, 5, 6, 7, 8 or SP for the present tables

m = projectile mass (pounds)

d = projectile reference diameter (inches)

ρ = local air density (pounds per cubic foot)

ρ_o = standard sea-level air density (0.075126 lb/ft^3)

The air density correction is useful for calculating trajectories at various altitudes above sea level, and will be described later. If $\rho = \rho_o$, the ballistic coefficient for sea-level standard air density reduces to the classical form:

$$C_j = \frac{m}{i_j d^2} \qquad \textbf{(6.43)}$$

The form factor of any given projectile relative to one of the standard shapes is simply the average ratio of the actual projectile drag coefficient to that of the standard shape, over a suitable Mach number range:

$$i_j = \left[\frac{C_D}{C_{D_j}}\right]_{AVE} \qquad \textbf{(6.44)}$$

The practical application of equation (6.44) requires a table of the drag coefficients versus Mach number for all eight of the reference standard drag functions used in this chapter. Table 6.1 at the end of this chapter lists the required values.

Example 6.1

The variation of the zero-yaw drag coefficient with Mach number for the caliber .30 Ball M2 bullet (Ref. 9) is illustrated in Figure 6.1. Selected values from the Ball M2 drag curve are listed in Table 6.2:

Table 6.2
Drag Coefficient Table for the Caliber .30 Ball M2 Projectile

Mach No.	C_D	Mach No.	C_D	Mach No.	C_D
0	.250	1.05	.443	1.8	.373
0.8	.250	1.1	.464	2.0	.351
0.9	.252	1.2	.456	2.2	.331
0.95	.288	1.4	.427	2.5	.305
1.0	.362	1.6	.399	3.0	.271

The reference diameter of the caliber .30 Ball M2 bullet is 0.308" and its nominal weight is 150 grains. Use the results of Tables 6.1 and 6.2 to determine the best drag function and sea-level ballistic coefficient, from Mach 3.0 down to Mach 1.4. Try the Ingalls, G_1, G_6 and G_8 drag curves, which are for flat-based projectile shapes.

The form factors of the caliber .30 Ball M2 bullet, relative to the four drag functions, are computed by means of equation (6.44), and are listed in Table 6.3 for selected supersonic Mach numbers:

Table 6.3
Form Factors for the Caliber .30 Ball M2 Projectile

Mach Number	i_{ING}	i_1	i_6	i_8
1.4	.665	.644	.998	1.052
1.6	.621	.617	.988	1.056
1.8	.601	.601	.984	1.060
2.0	.583	.592	.997	1.067
2.2	.566	.582	1.018	1.075
2.5	.547	.565	1.059	1.089
3.0	.527	.528	1.124	1.115
AVERAGE	.587	.590	1.024	1.073
Std. Dev.	.047	.037	.051	.022

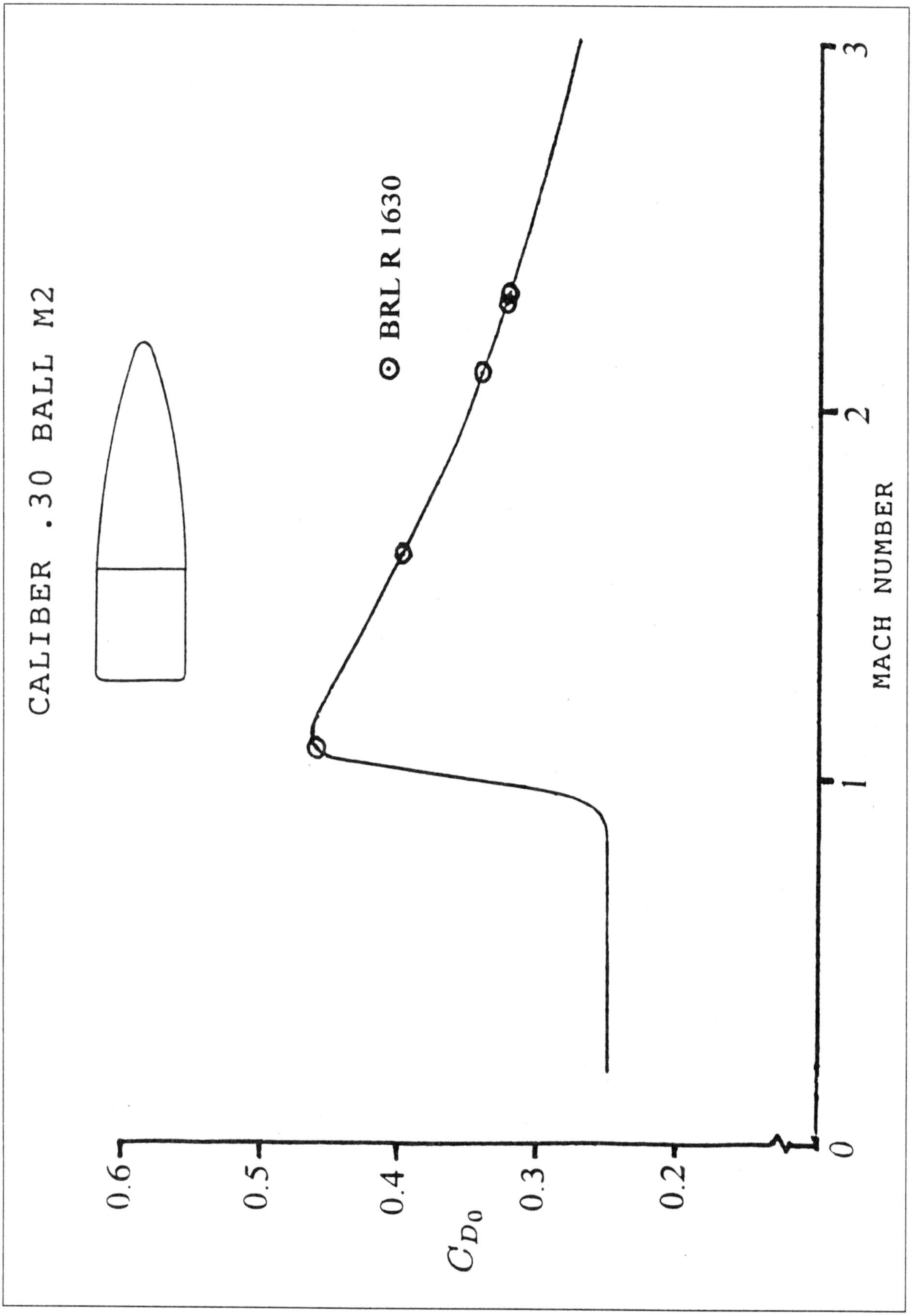

Figure 6.1 Zero-Yaw Drag Coefficient versus Mach Number.

The average form factors and the standard deviations are obtained with the help of a modern scientific hand-held calculator. It is evident that the G_8 drag function is the best of the four considered for the caliber .30 Ball M2 projectile at supersonic speeds; the standard deviation in i_8 is the smallest of the four form factors.

The fact that the G8 drag function gives the best approximation for the caliber .30 Ball M2 bullet is somewhat surprising, because the Ball M2 shape is very close to that of Projectile Type 6. The G_8 drag function is often superior to G_6 for flat-based tangent ogive rifle bullets, as we will note in a later section of this chapter.

The ballistic coefficient to be used with the G_8 ballistic tables is found from equation (6.43) and the average value of i_8 from Table 6.3:

$$C_8 = \frac{150}{(1.073)(7000)(.308)^2} = 0.210\, lb./in.^2$$

Example 6.2

Use the results of Example 6.1 and the G_8 ballistic tables at the end of this chapter to calculate the trajectory of the caliber .30 Ball M2 bullet out to 600 yards range, if the muzzle velocity is 2800 feet per second and the angle of departure is 19 minutes. Tabulate the results in 100 yard intervals.

From the G_8 tables we find:

$S(V_0) = 10006.1$ ft.-in.^{2}/lb.

$T(V_0) = 2.804$ sec.-in.^{2}/lb.

$I(V_0) = 0.05149$ in.^{2}/lb.

$A(V_0) = 217.19$ ft.-in.^{4}/lb.^{2}

$\tan\phi_o = \tan$ (19 minutes) = 0.005527

Equation (6.38) is first solved for S(V):

$$S(V) = S(V_0) + X/C = 10006.1 + X/(0.210) \qquad \textbf{(6.45)}$$

$$t = 0.210\,[T(V) - 2.804] \qquad \textbf{(6.46)}$$

$$Y = X\left(0.005227 - 0.105\left[\frac{A(V) - 217.9}{S(V) - 10006.1} - 0.05149\right]\right) \qquad \textbf{(6.47)}$$

The trajectory computation proceeds as follows:

Values of *S(V)* are computed from equation (6.45), and recorded in the third column of Table 6.4. Since our Siacci values are tabulated every ten feet per second, the corresponding values of velocity, V, must be obtained from the G_8 table by linear interpolation. The interpolation process is illustrated below, for the 100 yard values of *V*, *T(V)* and *A(V)*. The usual units of *S(V)*, *T(V)*, *I(V)* and *A(V)* apply, and for the sake of brevity, will not be carried along throughout the calculations.

S(V) = 11434.7 lies between 11388.0 (V = 2580 fps), and 11451.5 (V = 2570 fps). The method of linear interpolation gives:

V = 2580 + [(2570-2580)/(11451.5 - 11388.0)] (11434.7-11388.0)

V = 2572.6 fps

The values of *T(V)* and *A(V)* for V = 2572.6 fps are now found by two additional linear interpolations.

V = 2572.6 fps lies between V = 2580 fps and V = 2570 fps.

T(V) = 3.318 + [(3.343 - 3.318)/(2570 - 2580)] (2572.6 - 2580)

T(V) = 3.337, for V = 2572.6 fps

A(V) = 296.61 + [(300.68 - 296.61)/(2570 - 2580)] (2572.6 - 2580)

A(V) = 299.62, for V = 2572.6 fps

Similar linear interpolations are used to compute the remaining values of V, *T(V)* and *A(V)*, for ranges from 200 to 600 yards. The complete results are shown in Table 6.4, below:

Table 6.4
Caliber .30 Ball M2 - G8 Ballistic Tables

Range (Yds.)	X(Feet)	S(V)	V(fps)	T(V)	A(V)
0	0	10006.1	2800	2.804	217.19
100	300	11434.7	2573	3.337	299.62
200	600	12863.2	2351	3.916	401.90
300	900	14291.8	2135	4.555	528.12
400	1200	15720.4	1927	5.259	683.18
500	1500	17149.0	1727	6.042	873.77
600	1800	18577.5	1537	6.919	1108.73

The values of T(V) and A(V) from Table 6.4 are now substituted into equations (6.46) and (6.47) to give the results shown in Table 6.5:

Table 6.5
Caliber .30 Ball M2 - G8 Ballistic Tables

Range (Yards)	X (Feet)	t (seconds)	Y (Feet)	Y (Inches)
0	0	0	0	0
100	300	.112	1.46	17.6
200	600	.234	2.49	29.8
300	900	.368	2.98	35.8
400	1200	.516	2.85	34.1
500	1500	.680	1.92	23.1
600	1800	.864	0.02	0.3

The results of modern numerical integration for the same case are shown in Table 6.6:

Table 6.6
Caliber .30 Ball M2 - Numerical Integration

Range (Yards)	V (fps)	t (seconds)	Y (Inches)
0	2800	0	0
100	2571	.112	17.6
200	2349	.234	29.8
300	2135	.368	35.8
400	1930	.516	34.1
500	1733	.680	23.0
600	1547	.863	0.3

The largest difference in velocity is 10 feet per second; the times of flight agree to within 0.001 second, and the largest difference in trajectory height is 0.1 inch. In general, the Siacci method agrees very well with the results of modern numerical methods.

The next example illustrates the determination of the ballistic coefficient and the form factor from a known velocity-distance table.

Example 6.3

A table of striking velocity versus range for the 7.62mm Ball M80 bullet, fired at a muzzle velocity of 2810 feet per second, is given in Table 6.7. The reference diameter is 0.308" and the nominal bullet weight is 147 grains. A plot of the Ball M80 zero-yaw drag coefficient versus Mach number, from spark photography range firings (Ref. 9), is illustrated in Figure 6.2. Army Standard Metro, and the drag coefficient shown in Figure 6.2, were used to calculate Table 6.7. The 7.62mm Ball M80 bullet is very similar in shape to Projectile Type 7. Use the G_7 ballistic tables to determine the ballistic coefficient, C_7, and the form factor, i_7, for the Ball M80 bullet.

Table 6.7
7.62mm Ball M80 - Numerical Integration

Range (Yards)	Striking Velocity (fps)
0	2810
100	2590
200	2370
300	2160
400	1960
500	1765
600	1580

The velocities in Table 6.7 are recorded to the nearest five feet per second. The values of S(V) in the G_7 ballistic table are easily obtained for five feet per second intervals, by averaging the tabulated values. For example, S(V) at V = 1765 fps is the average of the tabulated S(V) values at V = 1760 fps and V = 1770 fps.

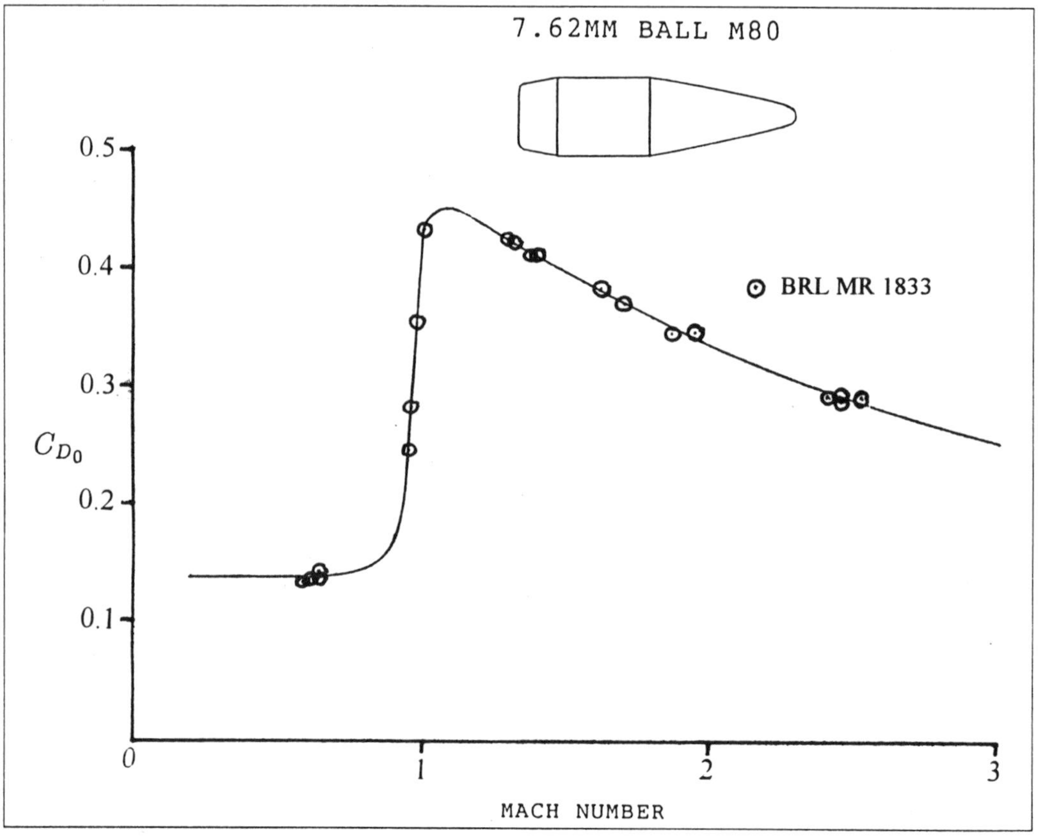

Figure 6.2 Zero-Yaw Drag Coefficient versus Mach Number.

The ballistic coefficient is obtained by solving equation (6.38) for C:

$$C = X/[S(V) - S(V_0)] \quad \textbf{(6.44)}$$

The work is shown in Table 6.8:

Table 6.8
7.62mm Ball M80 - G7 Ballistic Tables

Range (Yards)	X (Feet)	V (fps)	S(V)	C_7
0	0	2810	10002.2	---
100	300	2590	11450.9	.207
200	600	2370	12967.9	.202
300	900	2160	14493.6	.200
400	1200	1960	16029.1	.199
500	1500	1765	17603.3	.197
600	1800	1580	19169.0	.196

The average value of C_7 for the Ball M80 bullet from the muzzle to 600 yards range is 0.200 pounds per square inch, with a standard deviation of 0.004. The sectional density is:

$m/d^2 = 147/[(7000)(.308)^2] = 0.221$ pounds per square inch

Solving equation (6.43) for the form factor:

$$i_j = \left(\frac{m}{d^2}\right) \Big/ C_j \quad \textbf{(6.49)}$$

For the 7.62mm Ball M80 bullet:

$i_7 = 0.221/0.200 = 1.105$

Example 6.4

A .270 Winchester rifle is used for hunting in the mountains, at high altitudes above sea level. The ammunition used contains a flat-based 130 grain spitzer bullet, which chronographs at 3040 feet per second muzzle velocity, and the form factor of the bullet relative to Projectile Type 8 is known to be 1.25. The line of sight through the scope is 1.8" above the bore centerline, and the rifle-ammunition combination is sighted to strike 3 inches above the point of aim at 100 yards. Use the G_8 ballistic tables to determine the sea-level trajectory in 100 yard increments out to 500 yards range. How much would the trajectory differ at 9000 feet altitude above sea level? (The air density at 9000 feet altitude is 75% of the value at sea level).

At sea level, the ballistic coefficient is:

$C_8 = 130/[(1.25)(7000)(.277)2\,] = 0.194$ lb./in^2

Initial values of $S(V_0)$, $I(V_0)$, and $A(V_0)$ are found from the G_8 ballistic tables for $V_0 = 3040$ fps:

$S(V_0) = 8528.0$

$I(V_0) = 0.04032$

$A(V_0) = 149.57$

Equation (6.34) is now solved for S(V):

$$S(V) = S(V_0) + X/C = 8528.0 + X/(0.194) \quad \textbf{(6.50)}$$

The first five columns of Table 6.9 are now constructed. First, values of S(V) are determined from equation (6.50), and entered in the third column of the table. Corresponding values of downrange velocity, V, and A(V) are then obtained by the same linear interpolation methods illustrated for the construction of Table 6.4. The first five columns of data in Table 6.9 are now complete; we will return and fill in the values of Y presently.

The next task is to find the required angle of departure such that the bullet strikes 3" above the point of aim at 100 yards range. The values of Y_0 and Y at 100 yards are:

$Y_0 = -1.8" = -0.15$ foot

$Y = 3.0" = 0.25$ foot, at $X = 300$ feet

Table 6.9
.270 Winchester - 130 Grain Bullet - Sea Level - G8 Ballistic Tables

R (Yards)	X (Feet)	S(V)	V (fps)	A(V)	Y (Feet)	Y(Inches)
0	0	8528.0	3040	149.57	-.15	-1.8
100	300	10074.4	2789	220.74	.25	3.0
200	600	11620.8	2543	311.73	.28	3.3
300	900	13167.2	2304	426.63	-.15	-1.8
400	1200	14713.6	2073	570.59	-1.12	-13.4
500	1500	16260.0	1850	750.60	-2.76	-33.2

Note that the value of Y_0 is negative, because the X-axis is taken as the line of sight, and the trajectory starts below the line of sight.

Equation (6.40) is now solved for tan :

$$\tan\phi_o = (Y - Y_o)/X + \frac{1}{2}C\left[\frac{A(V) - A(V_o)}{S(V) - S(V_o)} - I(V_o)\right] \quad \textbf{(6.51)}$$

Substituting the appropriate values into equation (6.51):

$$\tan\phi_o = \frac{0.40}{300} + 0.097\left[\frac{220.74 - 149.57}{10074.4 - 8528.0} - 0.04032\right]$$

$$\tan\phi_o = 0.001333 + 0.000553 = 0.001886$$

Thus, $\phi_o = \tan^{-1}(0.001886) = 6.5$ minutes

Equation (6.40) is now used to finish the computation of Table 6.9:

$$Y = -0.15 + 0.001886X - 0.097X\left[\frac{A(V) - 149.57}{S(V) - 8528.0} - 0.04032\right] \quad \textbf{(6.52)}$$

The value of Y in equation (6.52) is in feet. Substituting the appropriate values into equation (6.52), and converting the results into inches gives the last two columns of Table 6.9.

For the second part of example 6.4, the above computations are repeated for an air density corresponding to 9000 feet altitude above sea level. We will assume the hunter re-sights his rifle at the high altitude, so the shot group again prints 3 inches high at 100 yards range. The assumption is also made that the air temperature and the muzzle velocity are unchanged by the increase in altitude (this is probably not true, in general).

At 9000 feet altitude above sea level, the ratio of standard to local air density, (ρ_o/ρ), is $\frac{1}{0.75} = 1.333$. From equation (6.42) we find:

C_8 = (.194) (1.333) = 0.259 lb./in^2, at 9000 feet altitude

The trajectory calculations for the high altitude case are done in the same manner as those for sea level, and the results are listed in Table 6.10. The details are left to the reader, who is encouraged to work through this problem and verify the results.

A comparison of the results listed in Tables 6.9 and 6.10 shows that 9000 feet altitude affects the vertical strike of the bullet by 5.7 inches at 500 yards range; at 400 yards the difference in trajectory height is only 2.5 inches. Such small trajectory differences are insignificant, for any practical purpose.

An even more simple flat-fire trajectory approximation consists of the Siacci method for calculation of the velocity and time of flight values, followed by the application of equations (5.69) and (5.70) from the previous chapter to determine the inclination and altitude values along the flight path. Such hybrid trajectory computation methods were very popular in U.S. Army Ordnance until the middle of the twentieth century, and are often used today by the U.S. sporting arms and ammunition industry.

6.6 FORM FACTORS OF TYPICAL SMALL ARMS PROJECTILES

The previous section covered the practical use of Siacci ballistic tables for the calculation of flat-fire small arms trajectories over moderate ranges. Examples of the determination of form factors and ballistic coefficients from known drag coefficients and velocity-distance tables were presented, as illustrations of the general method.

Table 6.11 at the end of this chapter (page 113) lists the form factors and ballistic coefficients of a number of past and present military small arms bullets, and a few sporting and match bullets. The results given in Table 6.11 are all based on modern spark photography range firing data. The G_1 and Ingalls drag functions give the best results for blunt projectiles with short nose lengths. For modern rifle bullets with longer ogives, the G_7 and G_8 drag functions give the best overall approximations for boattailed and flat-based bullets, respectively.

6.7 THE EFFECT OF PROJECTILE SHAPE ON THE FORM FACTOR

In 1939, H. P. Hitchcock wrote a BRL Report (Ref. 10) entitled "A Study of Form Factors of Spinning Projectiles," in which the effects of variations in projectile nose length and boattail dimensions on the form factors of projectiles were analyzed. Hitchcock's data included form factors for projectiles ranging in size from caliber .30 small arms bullets up to the enormous 16-inch gun projectiles.

Reference 10 was revised in 1942, and again in 1951 and 1952, in three additional reports (Ref. 11), (Ref. 12), and (Ref. 13), by the

Table 6.10
.270 Winchester - 130 Grain Bullet - 9000 Feet Altitude - G8 Ballistic Tables

R(Yards)	X (Feet)	S(V)	V (fps)	A(V)	Y (Feet)	Y (Inches)
0	0	8528.0	3040	149.57	-.15	-1.8
100	300	9686.3	2852	201.15	.25	3.0
200	600	10844.6	2666	263.34	.29	3.5
300	900	12002.9	2484	337.73	-.08	-0.9
400	1200	13161.2	2305	426.14	-.91	-10.9
500	1500	14319.5	2131	530.82	-2.29	-27.5

same author. A set of empirical rules were obtained for estimating form factors of projectiles relative to the G_1, G_2, G_5 and G_6 projectile shapes. Hitchcock found that the caliber of the projectile appeared to have no appreciable effect on the form factor (i.e., Reynolds number effects were negligible), and that any observed differences in the form factors for large and small calibers were due more to minor shape variations than to size.

Form factors are very useful in small arms ballistics. It is not cost-effective to conduct spark range or wind tunnel tests on all of the many hundreds (perhaps thousands!) of small arms bullet designs in existence. Furthermore, many of these designs are generically similar to each other, and the use of reference standard drag shapes with an appropriate set of form factors, is a sufficiently good drag approximation for most practical purposes.

For this chapter, a modern study of the form factors of small arms bullets at supersonic speeds was done. The method used for the study was a blending of high quality experimental drag data from spark photography range firings (Ref. 9), and modern theoretical techniques (Ref. 14), (Ref. 15), for estimating the drag of projectiles. The theoretical methods were first run for many of the projectile shapes in Reference 9, and small correction factors were obtained, to bring the theoretical results into very close agreement with the experimental data. The corrected theoretical techniques were then used to generate a series of six form factor curves for modern rifle bullets.

Four baseline projectile shapes were selected for the study: (1) four-caliber long flat-based designs, with tangent ogive noses, (2) the same as (1), but with secant ogive noses, (3) 4.5-caliber long boattailed designs, with a 9-degree, 0.5 caliber long boattail, and tangent ogive noses, and (4) the same as (3), but with secant ogive noses. Nose lengths for all models were varied between 1.0 and 3.0 calibers, and méplat diameters were varied between zero (sharp-pointed) and 0.4 calibers. The very blunt méplats ($d_M > 0.25$ caliber) show non-systematic drag behavior, and are not accurately represented by a form factor approach. Very blunt noses (such as most pistol bullets) are thus excluded from the present study. The form factors for all méplats up to 0.25 caliber diameter differed by only a few percent, and average values of the form factors for all the smaller méplat diameters are therefore adopted.

The form factors from the present study are plotted against the projectile nose length, in calibers, in Figures 6.3 through 6.8. Figure 6.3 illustrates the variation of the form factor relative to G_1 (or Ingalls) with projectile nose length, for flat-based projectiles with tangent ogive and secant ogive nose shapes. The effect of nose length on form factor is much more significant than the effect of nose shape. Figure 6.4 shows the form factor relative to G_6 versus nose length, for flat-based bullets with tangent ogive noses. Figure 6.5 gives the form factor variation relative to the G_8 projectile shape, for flat-based designs with both tangent ogive and secant ogive noses.

Figures 6.6 through 6.8 are similar plots for boattailed small arms bullets. Figure 6.6 shows the variation of the form factor relative to G_1 (or Ingalls) with projectile nose length, for boattailed configurations whose nose shapes are tangent ogives or secant ogives. Projectile Type 1 is a flat-based design, and the Ingalls or G_1 ballistic tables are often not the best choice for boattailed bul-

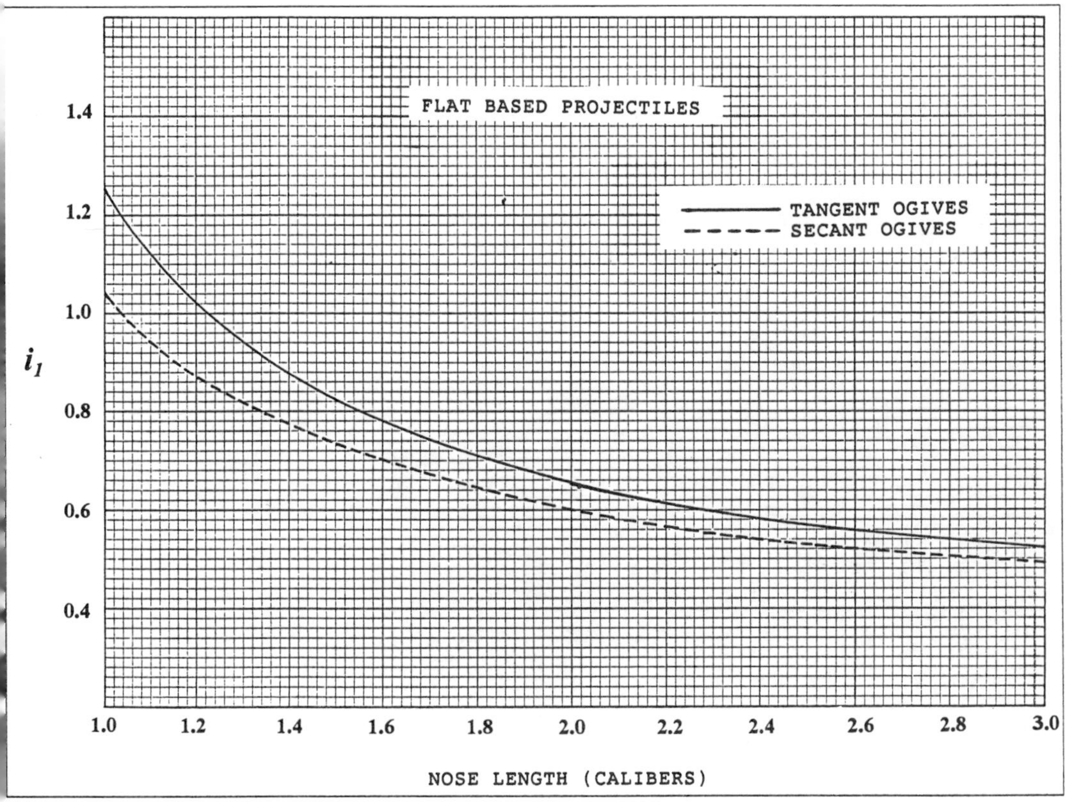

Figure 6.3 Form Factor versus Nose Length for Ingalls and G_1 Drag Functions.

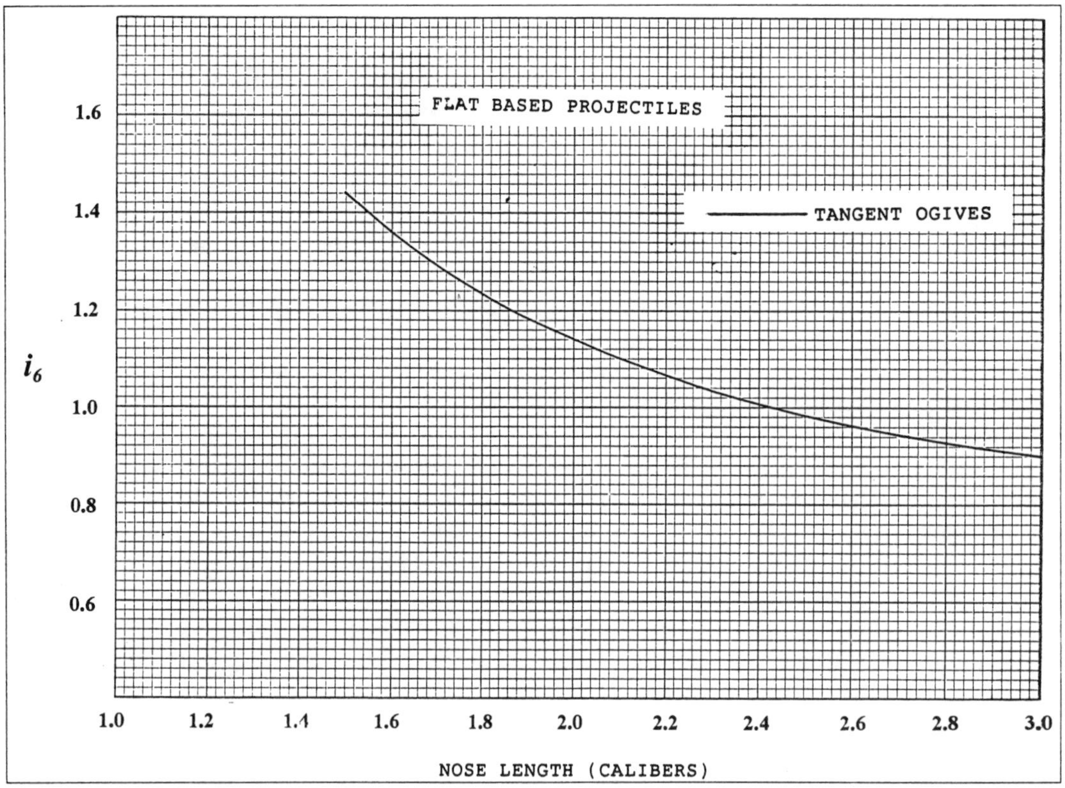

Figure 6.4 Form Factor versus Nose Length for G_6 Drag Functions.

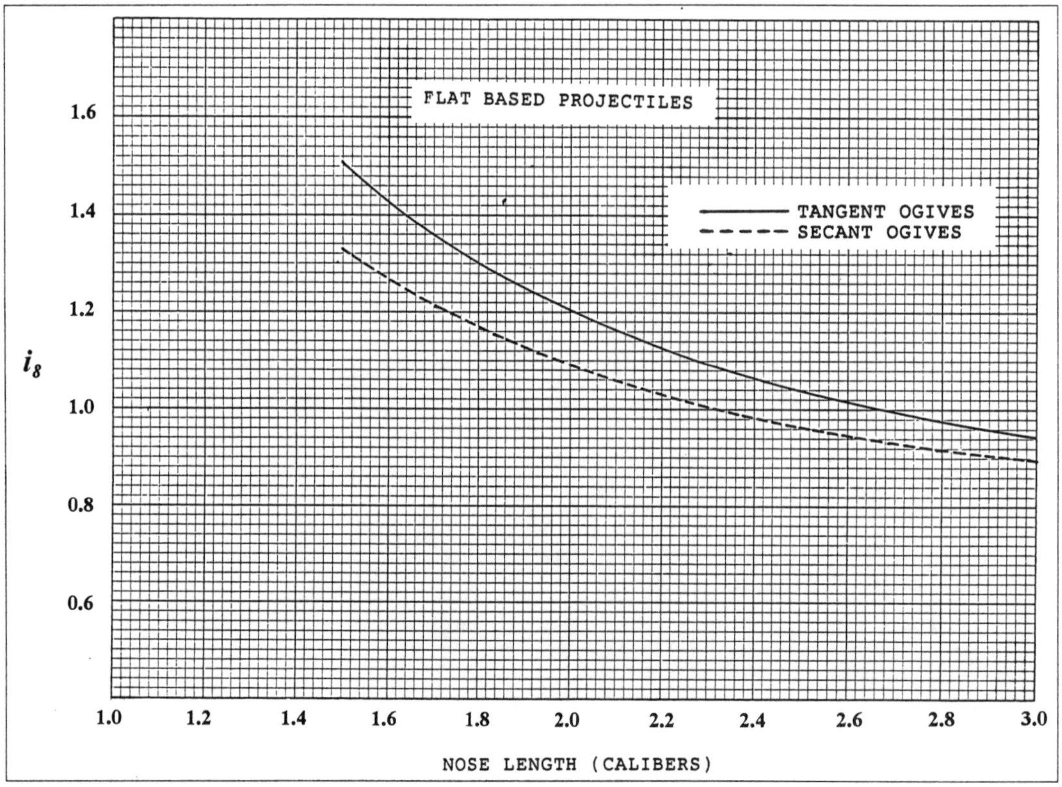

Figure 6.5 Form Factor versus Nose Length for G_8 Drag Functions.

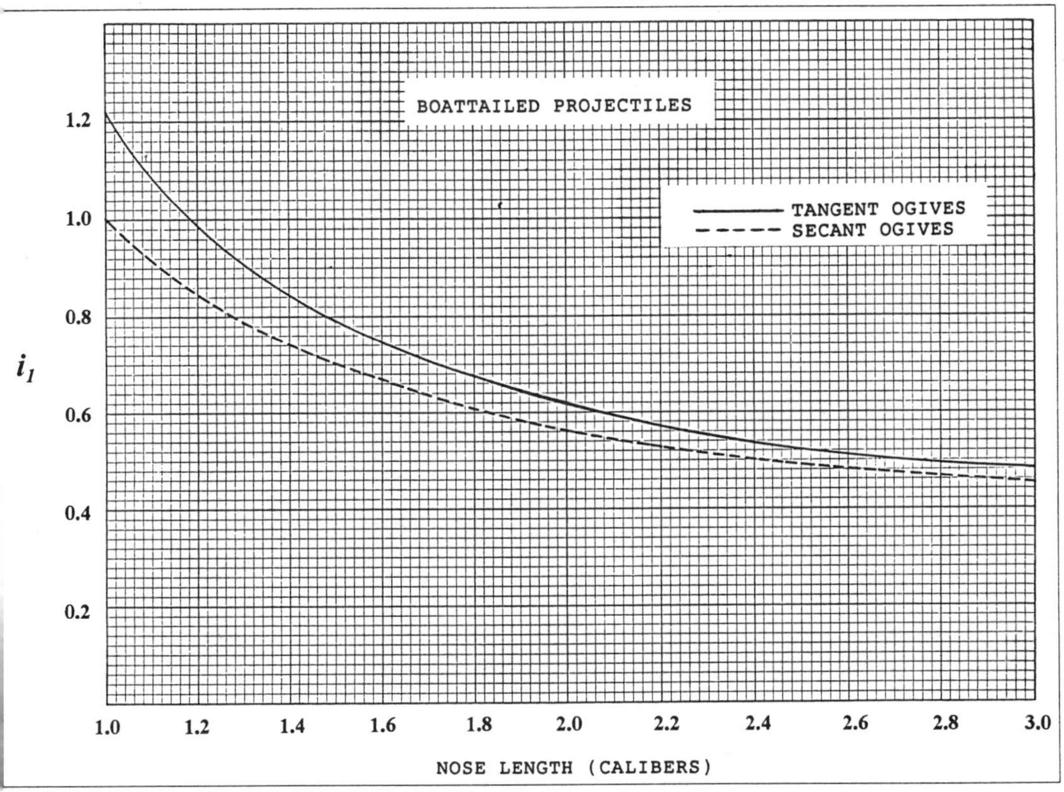

Figure 6.6 Form Factor versus Nose Length for Ingalls and G_1 Drag Functions.

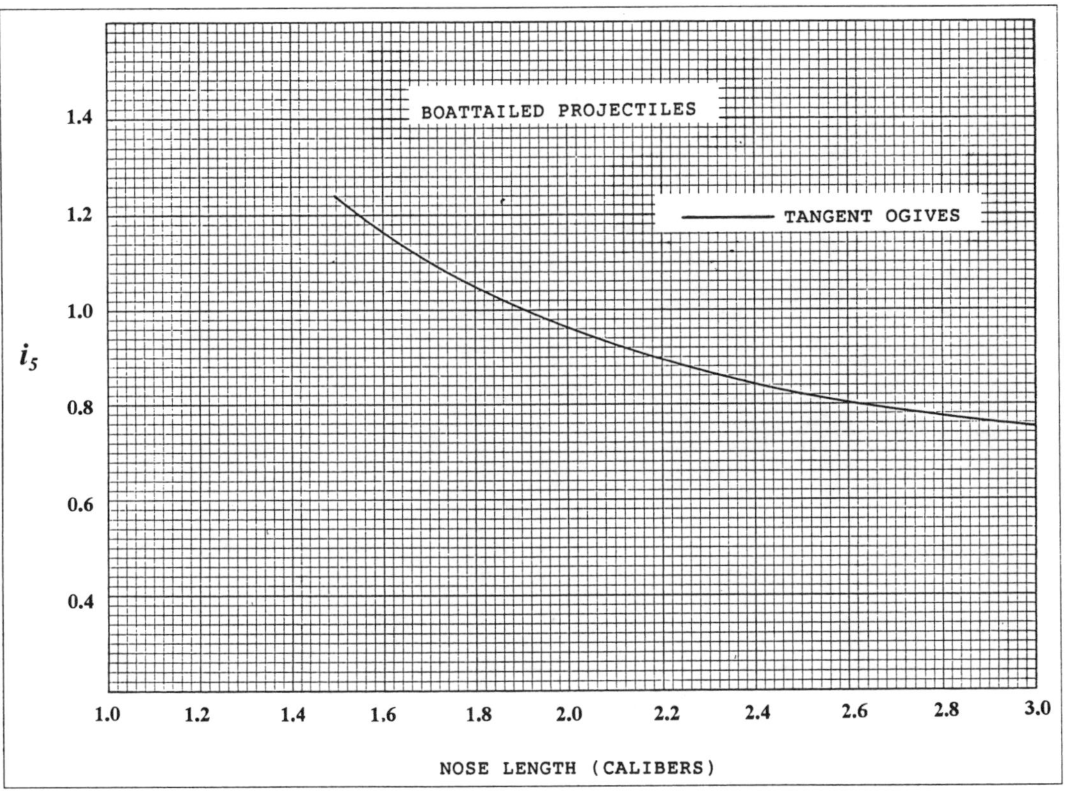

Figure 6.7 Form Factor versus Nose Length for G_5 Drag Functions.

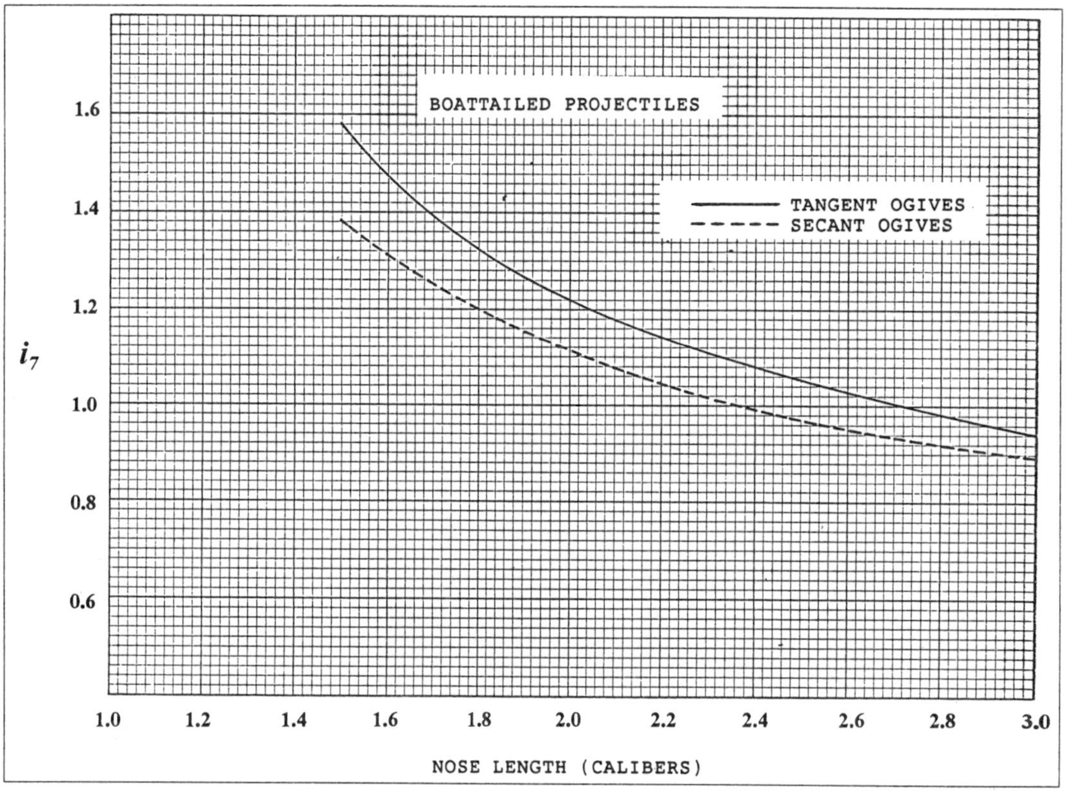

Figure 6.8 Form Factor versus Nose Length for G_7 Drag Functions.

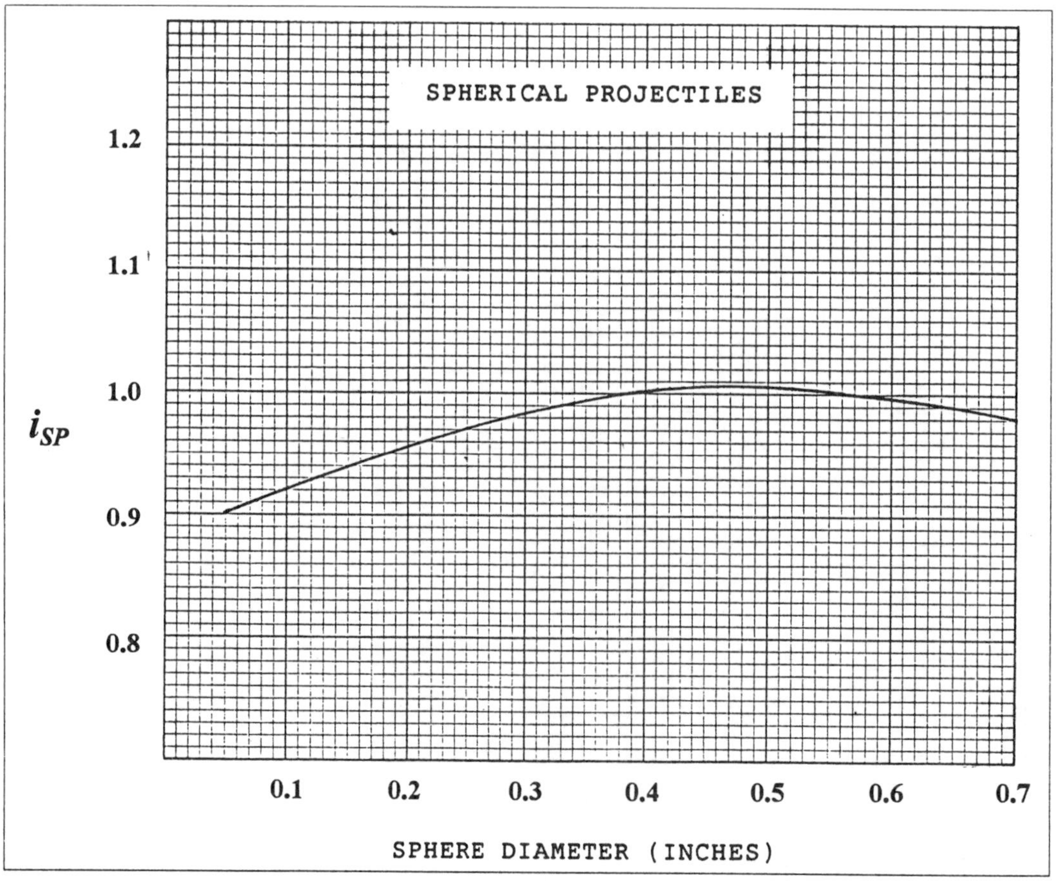

Figure 6.9 Form Factor versus Sphere Diameter for GSP Drag Function.

lets. However, these tables have been in service for nearly a century, and their use for small arms projectiles in general is traditional among many riflemen. The use of a form factor from Figure 6.6 will provide a reasonably good ballistic coefficient for use with Ingalls or G_1 tables and boattailed small arms bullets.

Figure 6.7 shows the form factor relative to G_5 versus nose length, for boattailed bullets with tangent ogive noses. Figure 6.8 illustrates the variation of the form factor relative to G_7 with nose length, for boattailed bullets with tangent ogive and secant ogive nose shapes. Since most boattailed projectiles have nose lengths greater than 1.5 calibers, the use of G_5 or G_7 ballistic tables, with form factors from Figures 6.7 or 6.8, are generally preferred over Figure 6.6 and the older Ingalls or G_1 tables.

An additional form factor curve, plotted as Figure 6.9, is used with the G_{SP} ballistic tables for spherical, or round ball trajectories. Figure 6.9 shows the variation of the form factor with the diameter of the spherical projectile, for diameters between 0.05 inch and 0.70 inch. The behavior of aerodynamic drag for larger spheres is non-systematic (see Chapter 4), and cannot be accurately represented by a simple form factor approach. The curve of Figure 6.9 is valid for all velocities under 2000 feet per second, and is thus useful for the calculation of flat-fire trajectories, for both fine shot and black powder muzzle loading rifles firing round ball projectiles.

6.8 RULES FOR THE USE OF THE FORM FACTOR CHARTS

Some general rules are recommended for the use of Figures 6.3 through 6.8 in estimating the form factors of modern rifle bullets at supersonic velocities. These rules are approximate, and are intended to be used only as guidelines.

For flat-based bullets, with nose lengths between 1.0 and 1.7 calibers, use Figure 6.3 to estimate a form factor for the G_1 or Ingalls ballistic tables. The top (solid) curve is for tangent ogives, and the lower (dashed) curve is for secant ogive nose shapes. (If a conical, or spire-point nose shape is encountered, always select the tangent ogive curve).

For flat-based bullets with either tangent or secant ogive nose shapes, and nose lengths greater than 1.7 calibers, use Figure 6.5 to estimate a form factor for the G_8 ballistic tables. The top (solid) curve is for tangent ogives, and the bottom (dashed) curve is for secant ogive noses. An alternate choice for tangent ogives is to use Figure 6.4 and the G_6 ballistic tables; practical experience with modern rifle bullets indicates that G_8 is usually a better choice for both tangent and secant ogive nose shapes.

For the infrequent case of a boattailed bullet with nose length less than 1.7 calibers, use Figure 6.6 to estimate a form factor for the G_1 or Ingalls ballistic tables. The top (solid) curve is for tangent ogives, and the bottom (dashed) curve is for secant ogive shapes.

For boattailed bullets with either tangent or secant ogive nose shapes, and nose lengths greater than 1.7 calibers, use Figure 6.8 to estimate a form factor for the G_7 ballistic tables. The top (solid) curve is for tangent ogives, and the bottom (dashed) curve is for secant ogive shapes. Figure 6.7 and the G_5 ballistic tables may be used for boattailed bullets with tangent ogive noses, but G_7 is usually a better choice for both tangent and secant ogive nose shapes.

Example 6.5

The caliber .30 Ball M2 projectile is a flat-based tangent ogive design, with a nominal nose length of 2.37 calibers. Use the upper curve of Figure 6.5 to estimate a form factor relative to G_8.

From Figure 6.5, $i_8 = 1.07$, for $L_N = 2.37$ calibers. Table 6.11 lists $i_8 = 1.076$ for the same bullet, based on modern spark photography range drag measurements (Ref. 9). The two results are virtually identical for the caliber .30 Ball M2 bullet.

Example 6.6

The caliber .50 Ball M33 bullet is a boattailed tangent ogive design, with a nominal nose length (see Figure 4.7 of Chapter 4) of 2.56 calibers. Use the top (solid) curve of Figure 6.8 to estimate a form factor relative to G_7.

From Figure 6.8, $i_7 = 1.04$, for $L_N = 2.56$ calibers. Table 6.11 lists $i_7 = 1.050$ for the caliber .50 Ball M33 projectile (Ref. 16). The two results disagree by one percent, which is an insignificant difference.

6.9 ADDITIONAL NOTES ON FORM FACTORS

The U.S. Standard Atmosphere of 1962 (Ref. 17), which is based on the International Civil Aviation Organization (ICAO) atmosphere of 1954 (Ref. 18), has become the world-wide standard atmosphere, for both aviation and ballistics use. Prior to about 1960, practically all U.S. ballistic calculations and firing tables were based on the older Army Standard Metro atmosphere. For the flat-fire trajectories considered in this chapter, the only significant difference between the two atmospheres is a 1.8 percent difference in sea-level standard air density. The ICAO value is 0.076474 pounds per cubic foot, and the Army Standard Metro value, as stated in section 6.4, is 0.075126 pounds per cubic foot.

The ballistic tables of this chapter may be used to compute flat-fire trajectories for the ICAO atmosphere. If the form factor based on Army Standard Metro is known, multiply the form factor by 1.018, and use the corrected value to calculate a ballistic coefficient for the ICAO atmosphere.

No definite rules appear possible for estimating form factors at transonic or subsonic speeds. A suitable estimate can often be made by comparison of the projectile shape with that of a similarly shaped design, whose form factor is known.

Table 6.1

Reference Standard Drag Coefficients versus Mach Number								
Mach Number	$C_{D_{ING}}$	C_{D_1}	C_{D_2}	C_{D_5}	C_{D_6}	C_{D_7}	C_{D_8}	$C_{D_{SP}}$
0	.228	.263	.230	.171	.262	.120	.211	.466
0.5	.228	.203	.198	.160	.216	.119	.210	.497
0.6	.228	.203	.183	.153	.213	.119	.210	.526
0.7	.228	.217	.170	.147	.212	.120	.210	.592
0.8	.260	.255	.167	.149	.215	.124	.210	.661
0.9	.317	.342	.183	.182	.230	.146	.211	.737
0.95	.373	.408	.259	.241	.273	.205	.257	.776
1.0	.435	.481	.398	.338	.360	.380	.407	.814
1.05	.503	.543	.410	.403	.426	.404	.448	.851
1.1	.576	.588	.411	.420	.447	.401	.448	.887
1.2	.628	.639	.402	.434	.448	.388	.435	.951
1.3	.642	.659	.390	.439	.439	.373	.421	.991
1.4	.642	.663	.376	.441	.428	.358	.406	1.003
1.5	.642	.657	.359	.439	.416	.344	.392	1.008
1.6	.642	.647	.343	.433	.404	.332	.378	1.009
1.8	.621	.621	.315	.412	.379	.312	.352	1.007
2.0	.602	.593	.293	.386	.352	.298	.329	1.001
2.2	.585	.569	.277	.363	.325	.286	.308	.994
2.5	.558	.540	.257	.335	.288	.270	.280	.981
3.0	.514	.513	.231	.300	.241	.242	.243	.961
3.5	.479	.504	.209	.275	.209	.215	.215	.943
4.0	.451	.501	.191	.255	.187	.194	.195	.928

Table 6.11

Form Factors and Ballistic Coefficients of Small Arms Projectiles

Reference Diameter (Inches)	Projectile	Nominal Weight (Grains)	Velocity ~~Weight~~ Interval ~~Interval~~ ~~(Grains)~~ (fps)	Form Factor ~~(fps)~~ i	Ballistic Coefficient C (lb/in^2) ~~C (lb./in.^{2})~~	Drag Function
.224	.22 Long Rifle Match	40	1090-1000	.765	.149	G1
.224	.22 Long Rifle Match	40	1090-940	.776	.147	G1
.224	5.56mm M193	55	3270-1280	1.308	.120	G7
.224	5.56mm M855	62	3110-1470	1.172	.151	G7
.221	5.45 X 39mm Soviet	53.5	2950-1520	.929	.168	G7
.224	5.56mm BRL-1	66	3200-1340	.858	.219	G7
.264	6.5mm Norma BT Match	139	3070-2200	.922	.309	G7
.277	Sierra 90 Gr. HP	90	3360-1400	.812	.207	G1
.277	Sierra 110 Gr. SP	110	3200-1600	1.242	.165	G8
.277	Sierra 130 Gr. SP	130	3050-1700	1.192	.203	G8
.277	Barnes 180 Gr. RN	180	2550-1350	1.124	.298	G1
.308	.30 Ball M2	150	2800-1550	1.076	.210	G8
.308	7.62mm M80	147	2810-1580	1.105	.200	G7
.308	7.62mm M118 Match	174	2600-1620	1.096	.239	G7
.308	7.62mm M852 HPBT	168	2650-1560	1.177	.215	G7
.308	7.62mm M852 HPBT	168	2600-1600	.595	.425	G1
.308	Sierra 190 Gr. HPBT	190	2490-1570	1.135	.252	G7
.355	9mm Ball 124 Gr. RN	124	1360-1060	1.044	.135	G1
.355	9mm Ball 124 Gr. FN	124	1360-1050	1.102	.128	G1
.452	.45 Ball M1911	230	860-800	.866	.186	G1
.510	.50 Ball M33	650	2950-1540	1.050	.340	G7

Notes: HP = Hollow Point
SP = Spitzer Soft Point
RN = Round Nose
FN = Flat Nose
HPBT = Hollow Point Boattail

pp. 114-156

V: velocity
S(V): space function
A(V): altitude function
I(V): trajectory inclination function
T(V): time of flight function

Tables of the Primary Siacci Functions

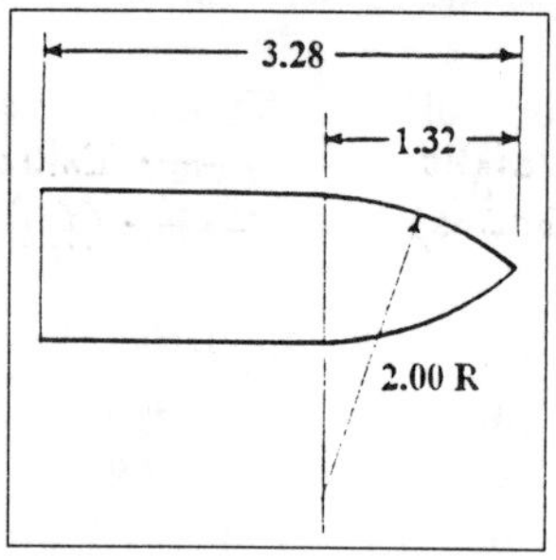

Ingalls Drag Function

Quantity	Units
V	ft./sec.
S(V)	ft.-in.^{2}/lb.
A(V)	ft.-in.^{4}/lb.^{2}
I(V)	in.^{2}/lb.
T(V)	sec.-in.^{2}/lb.

V	S(V)	A(V)	I(V)	T(V)
4500	0.0	0.00	0.00000	0.000
4490	24.1	0.00	0.00008	0.005
4480	48.2	0.00	0.00015	0.011
4470	72.4	0.01	0.00023	0.016
4460	96.6	0.01	0.00031	0.022
4450	120.8	0.02	0.00039	0.027
4440	145.0	0.03	0.00047	0.032
4430	169.3	0.05	0.00055	0.038
4420	193.6	0.06	0.00063	0.043
4410	217.9	0.08	0.00071	0.049
4400	242.3	0.09	0.00079	0.054
4390	266.7	0.11	0.00087	0.060
4380	291.1	0.14	0.00095	0.066
4370	315.6	0.16	0.00103	0.071
4360	340.1	0.19	0.00111	0.077
4350	364.6	0.22	0.00120	0.082
4340	389.1	0.25	0.00128	0.088
4330	413.7	0.28	0.00137	0.094
4320	438.3	0.31	0.00145	0.099
4310	463.0	0.35	0.00154	0.105
4300	487.7	0.39	0.00162	0.111
4290	512.4	0.43	0.00171	0.117
4280	537.1	0.47	0.00179	0.122
4270	561.9	0.52	0.00188	0.128
4260	586.7	0.57	0.00197	0.134
4250	611.5	0.62	0.00206	0.140
4240	636.4	0.67	0.00215	0.146
4230	661.3	0.72	0.00224	0.152
4220	686.2	0.78	0.00233	0.157
4210	711.2	0.84	0.00242	0.163
4200	736.2	0.90	0.00251	0.169
4190	761.2	0.97	0.00260	0.175
4180	786.3	1.03	0.00269	0.181
4170	811.4	1.10	0.00278	0.187
4160	836.5	1.17	0.00288	0.193
4150	861.6	1.24	0.00297	0.199
4140	886.8	1.32	0.00306	0.205
4130	912.1	1.40	0.00316	0.212
4120	937.3	1.48	0.00325	0.218
4110	962.6	1.56	0.00335	0.224
4100	988.0	1.65	0.00345	0.230
4090	1013.3	1.74	0.00354	0.236
4080	1038.7	1.83	0.00364	0.242
4070	1064.2	1.92	0.00374	0.249
4060	1089.6	2.02	0.00384	0.255
4050	1115.1	2.12	0.00394	0.261
4040	1140.7	2.22	0.00404	0.268
4030	1166.2	2.33	0.00414	0.274
4020	1191.8	2.43	0.00424	0.280
4010	1217.5	2.54	0.00434	0.287
4000	1243.1	2.66	0.00445	0.293
3990	1268.9	2.77	0.00455	0.299
3980	1294.6	2.89	0.00466	0.306
3970	1320.4	3.01	0.00476	0.312
3960	1346.2	3.14	0.00487	0.319
3950	1372.1	3.26	0.00497	0.325

V	S(V)	A(V)	I(V)	T(V)
3940	1397.9	3.39	0.00508	0.332
3930	1423.9	3.53	0.00519	0.339
3920	1449.8	3.66	0.00530	0.345
3910	1475.8	3.80	0.00540	0.352
3900	1501.9	3.94	0.00551	0.359
3890	1527.9	4.09	0.00563	0.365
3880	1554.0	4.24	0.00574	0.372
3870	1580.2	4.39	0.00585	0.379
3860	1606.4	4.54	0.00596	0.385
3850	1632.6	4.70	0.00607	0.392
3840	1658.9	4.86	0.00619	0.399
3830	1685.2	5.03	0.00630	0.406
3820	1711.5	5.19	0.00642	0.413
3810	1737.9	5.36	0.00654	0.420
3800	1764.3	5.54	0.00665	0.427
3790	1790.7	5.72	0.00677	0.434
3780	1817.2	5.90	0.00689	0.441
3770	1843.7	6.08	0.00701	0.448
3760	1870.3	6.27	0.00713	0.455
3750	1896.9	6.46	0.00725	0.462
3740	1923.5	6.66	0.00737	0.469
3730	1950.2	6.85	0.00750	0.476
3720	1976.9	7.06	0.00762	0.483
3710	2003.7	7.26	0.00775	0.490
3700	2030.5	7.47	0.00787	0.498
3690	2057.3	7.68	0.00800	0.505
3680	2084.2	7.90	0.00813	0.512
3670	2111.1	8.12	0.00825	0.520
3660	2138.1	8.35	0.00838	0.527
3650	2165.1	8.57	0.00851	0.534
3640	2192.1	8.81	0.00864	0.542
3630	2219.2	9.04	0.00878	0.549
3620	2246.3	9.28	0.00891	0.557
3610	2273.5	9.52	0.00904	0.564
3600	2300.7	9.77	0.00918	0.572
3590	2327.9	10.02	0.00931	0.579
3580	2355.2	10.28	0.00945	0.587
3570	2382.6	10.54	0.00959	0.595
3560	2409.9	10.80	0.00972	0.602
3550	2437.4	11.07	0.00986	0.610
3540	2464.8	11.35	0.01000	0.618
3530	2492.3	11.62	0.01015	0.625
3520	2519.9	11.90	0.01029	0.633
3510	2547.4	12.19	0.01043	0.641
3500	2575.1	12.48	0.01058	0.649
3490	2602.7	12.78	0.01072	0.657

V	S(V)	A(V)	I(V)	T(V)
3480	2630.5	13.07	0.01087	0.665
3470	2658.2	13.38	0.01102	0.673
3460	2686.0	13.69	0.01117	0.681
3450	2713.9	14.00	0.01132	0.689
3440	2741.8	14.32	0.01147	0.697
3430	2769.7	14.64	0.01162	0.705
3420	2797.7	14.97	0.01177	0.713
3410	2825.7	15.30	0.01193	0.722
3400	2853.8	15.64	0.01208	0.730
3390	2881.9	15.98	0.01224	0.738
3380	2910.1	16.33	0.01240	0.746
3370	2938.3	16.68	0.01256	0.755
3360	2966.5	17.03	0.01272	0.763
3350	2994.8	17.40	0.01288	0.772
3340	3023.2	17.76	0.01304	0.780
3330	3051.6	18.14	0.01321	0.789
3320	3080.0	18.52	0.01337	0.797
3310	3108.5	18.90	0.01354	0.806
3300	3137.1	19.29	0.01371	0.814
3290	3165.6	19.68	0.01388	0.823
3280	3194.3	20.08	0.01405	0.832
3270	3222.9	20.49	0.01422	0.841
3260	3251.7	20.90	0.01439	0.849
3250	3280.5	21.31	0.01457	0.858
3240	3309.3	21.74	0.01474	0.867
3230	3338.2	22.16	0.01492	0.876
3220	3367.1	22.60	0.01510	0.885
3210	3396.1	23.04	0.01528	0.894
3200	3425.1	23.49	0.01546	0.903
3190	3454.1	23.94	0.01565	0.912
3180	3483.3	24.40	0.01583	0.921
3170	3512.4	24.86	0.01602	0.930
3160	3541.7	25.33	0.01620	0.940
3150	3570.9	25.81	0.01639	0.949
3140	3600.3	26.29	0.01658	0.958
3130	3629.7	26.78	0.01678	0.968
3120	3659.1	27.28	0.01697	0.977
3110	3688.6	27.78	0.01717	0.987
3100	3718.1	28.29	0.01736	0.996
3090	3747.7	28.81	0.01756	1.006
3080	3777.3	29.33	0.01776	1.015
3070	3807.0	29.86	0.01796	1.025
3060	3836.8	30.40	0.01817	1.035
3050	3866.6	30.94	0.01837	1.044
3040	3896.4	31.50	0.01858	1.054
3030	3926.3	32.05	0.01879	1.064
3020	3956.3	32.62	0.01900	1.074

V	S(V)	A(V)	I(V)	T(V)
3010	3986.3	33.19	0.01921	1.084
3000	4016.4	33.77	0.01943	1.094
2990	4046.5	34.36	0.01964	1.104
2980	4076.7	34.96	0.01986	1.114
2970	4106.9	35.56	0.02008	1.124
2960	4137.2	36.17	0.02030	1.134
2950	4167.5	36.79	0.02052	1.145
2940	4198.0	37.42	0.02075	1.155
2930	4228.4	38.06	0.02098	1.165
2920	4258.9	38.70	0.02121	1.176
2910	4289.5	39.35	0.02144	1.186
2900	4320.1	40.01	0.02167	1.197
2890	4350.8	40.68	0.02191	1.207
2880	4381.6	41.36	0.02214	1.218
2870	4412.4	42.04	0.02238	1.229
2860	4443.3	42.74	0.02263	1.240
2850	4474.2	43.44	0.02287	1.250
2840	4505.2	44.16	0.02312	1.261
2830	4536.2	44.88	0.02337	1.272
2820	4567.4	45.61	0.02362	1.283
2810	4598.5	46.35	0.02387	1.294
2800	4629.8	47.10	0.02412	1.306
2790	4661.0	47.86	0.02438	1.317
2780	4692.4	48.63	0.02464	1.328
2770	4723.8	49.40	0.02490	1.339
2760	4755.3	50.19	0.02517	1.351
2750	4786.8	50.99	0.02544	1.362
2740	4818.4	51.80	0.02571	1.374
2730	4850.1	52.62	0.02598	1.385
2720	4881.8	53.44	0.02625	1.397
2710	4913.6	54.28	0.02653	1.409
2700	4945.5	55.13	0.02681	1.420
2690	4977.4	55.99	0.02709	1.432
2680	5009.4	56.87	0.02738	1.444
2670	5041.5	57.75	0.02767	1.456
2660	5073.6	58.64	0.02796	1.468
2650	5105.8	59.55	0.02825	1.480
2640	5138.0	60.46	0.02855	1.492
2630	5170.4	61.39	0.02885	1.505
2620	5202.8	62.33	0.02915	1.517
2610	5235.2	63.28	0.02946	1.529
2600	5267.8	64.24	0.02976	1.542
2590	5300.4	65.22	0.03008	1.555
2580	5333.2	66.21	0.03039	1.567
2570	5366.0	67.21	0.03071	1.580
2560	5398.9	68.23	0.03103	1.593

V	S(V)	A(V)	I(V)	T(V)
2550	5431.9	69.26	0.03136	1.606
2540	5465.0	70.30	0.03169	1.619
2530	5498.2	71.36	0.03202	1.632
2520	5531.5	72.43	0.03235	1.645
2510	5564.9	73.52	0.03269	1.658
2500	5598.3	74.62	0.03304	1.672
2490	5631.9	75.73	0.03338	1.685
2480	5665.6	76.86	0.03373	1.699
2470	5699.3	78.01	0.03409	1.712
2460	5733.2	79.17	0.03445	1.726
2450	5767.1	80.34	0.03481	1.740
2440	5801.1	81.53	0.03517	1.754
2430	5835.3	82.74	0.03554	1.768
2420	5869.5	83.96	0.03592	1.782
2410	5903.9	85.20	0.03630	1.796
2400	5938.3	86.46	0.03668	1.810
2390	5972.8	87.73	0.03707	1.825
2380	6007.5	89.02	0.03746	1.839
2370	6042.2	90.33	0.03786	1.854
2360	6077.1	91.66	0.03826	1.869
2350	6112.0	93.00	0.03866	1.884
2340	6147.1	94.36	0.03907	1.899
2330	6182.2	95.74	0.03949	1.914
2320	6217.5	97.14	0.03991	1.929
2310	6252.8	98.56	0.04033	1.944
2300	6288.3	100.00	0.04076	1.959
2290	6323.9	101.46	0.04119	1.975
2280	6359.6	102.94	0.04163	1.991
2270	6395.4	104.44	0.04208	2.006
2260	6431.3	105.96	0.04253	2.022
2250	6467.3	107.50	0.04299	2.038
2240	6503.5	109.06	0.04345	2.054
2230	6539.7	110.64	0.04391	2.070
2220	6576.1	112.25	0.04439	2.087
2210	6612.6	113.87	0.04486	2.103
2200	6649.2	115.52	0.04535	2.120
2190	6685.9	117.20	0.04584	2.137
2180	6722.7	118.90	0.04633	2.153
2170	6759.6	120.62	0.04684	2.170
2160	6796.7	122.36	0.04735	2.188
2150	6833.9	124.13	0.04786	2.205
2140	6871.2	125.93	0.04838	2.222
2130	6908.6	127.75	0.04891	2.240
2120	6946.2	129.60	0.04944	2.257
2110	6983.9	131.47	0.04999	2.275
2100	7021.7	133.37	0.05054	2.293

V	S(V)	A(V)	I(V)	T(V)
2090	7059.6	135.30	0.05109	2.311
2080	7097.7	137.25	0.05165	2.330
2070	7135.8	139.23	0.05222	2.348
2060	7174.2	141.25	0.05280	2.366
2050	7212.6	143.29	0.05339	2.385
2040	7251.2	145.36	0.05398	2.404
2030	7289.9	147.46	0.05458	2.423
2020	7328.7	149.59	0.05519	2.442
2010	7367.7	151.76	0.05581	2.462
2000	7406.8	153.95	0.05644	2.481
1990	7446.1	156.18	0.05707	2.501
1980	7485.5	158.44	0.05771	2.521
1970	7525.0	160.73	0.05836	2.541
1960	7564.7	163.06	0.05903	2.561
1950	7604.5	165.42	0.05970	2.581
1940	7644.4	167.82	0.06037	2.602
1930	7684.5	170.26	0.06106	2.622
1920	7724.8	172.73	0.06176	2.643
1910	7765.2	175.24	0.06247	2.664
1900	7805.7	177.78	0.06319	2.686
1890	7846.4	180.37	0.06392	2.707
1880	7887.2	183.00	0.06466	2.729
1870	7928.2	185.66	0.06541	2.751
1860	7969.4	188.37	0.06617	2.773
1850	8010.7	191.12	0.06694	2.795
1840	8052.1	193.91	0.06772	2.818
1830	8093.7	196.74	0.06852	2.840
1820	8135.5	199.62	0.06932	2.863
1810	8177.4	202.55	0.07014	2.886
1800	8219.6	205.52	0.07097	2.910
1790	8261.9	208.54	0.07182	2.933
1780	8304.5	211.62	0.07268	2.957
1770	8347.3	214.75	0.07355	2.981
1760	8390.3	217.93	0.07444	3.005
1750	8433.6	221.17	0.07535	3.030
1740	8477.2	224.48	0.07627	3.055
1730	8521.0	227.84	0.07720	3.080
1720	8565.0	231.26	0.07815	3.106
1710	8609.3	234.74	0.07912	3.132
1700	8653.9	238.29	0.08011	3.158
1690	8698.7	241.90	0.08111	3.184
1680	8743.8	245.59	0.08213	3.211
1670	8789.2	249.33	0.08317	3.238
1660	8834.8	253.15	0.08423	3.266
1650	8880.7	257.05	0.08531	3.293
1640	8926.9	261.01	0.08641	3.321

V	S(V)	A(V)	I(V)	T(V)
1630	8973.4	265.05	0.08753	3.350
1620	9020.2	269.17	0.08867	3.379
1610	9067.2	273.37	0.08983	3.408
1600	9114.6	277.65	0.09101	3.437
1590	9162.2	282.02	0.09221	3.467
1580	9210.1	286.47	0.09344	3.497
1570	9258.4	291.01	0.09469	3.528
1560	9306.9	295.64	0.09597	3.559
1550	9355.8	300.36	0.09727	3.590
1540	9405.0	305.17	0.09859	3.622
1530	9454.5	310.09	0.09994	3.654
1520	9504.3	315.10	0.10132	3.687
1510	9554.5	320.22	0.10273	3.720
1500	9605.0	325.44	0.10416	3.754
1490	9655.8	330.77	0.10562	3.788
1480	9707.0	336.22	0.10712	3.822
1470	9758.5	341.77	0.10864	3.857
1460	9810.3	347.45	0.11019	3.893
1450	9862.6	353.25	0.11178	3.929
1440	9915.2	359.17	0.11340	3.965
1430	9968.1	365.21	0.11506	4.002
1420	10021.4	371.39	0.11674	4.039
1410	10075.1	377.71	0.11847	4.077
1400	10129.2	384.17	0.12023	4.116
1390	10183.7	390.76	0.12203	4.155
1380	10238.6	397.51	0.12387	4.194
1370	10293.8	404.41	0.12575	4.235
1360	10349.9	411.51	0.12769	4.276
1350	10406.8	418.84	0.12968	4.318
1340	10464.6	426.39	0.13174	4.361
1330	10523.2	434.17	0.13385	4.404
1320	10582.7	442.21	0.13603	4.449
1310	10643.2	450.49	0.13828	4.495
1300	10704.5	459.05	0.14060	4.542
1290	10766.8	467.88	0.14299	4.590
1280	10830.1	477.01	0.14545	4.640
1270	10894.4	486.44	0.14800	4.690
1260	10959.7	496.19	0.15062	4.742
1250	11026.1	506.27	0.15333	4.795
1240	11093.5	516.71	0.15613	4.849
1230	11162.0	527.50	0.15902	4.904
1220	11232.1	538.75	0.16202	4.961
1210	11304.5	550.60	0.16518	5.021
1200	11379.3	563.09	0.16849	5.083
1190	11456.7	576.26	0.17198	5.148
1180	11536.8	590.17	0.17565	5.216

V	S(V)	A(V)	I(V)	T(V)
1170	11619.6	604.87	0.17950	5.286
1160	11705.2	620.43	0.18356	5.360
1150	11793.9	636.89	0.18784	5.436
1140	11885.7	654.35	0.19234	5.517
1130	11980.8	672.86	0.19709	5.600
1120	12079.4	692.53	0.20210	5.688
1110	12181.5	713.43	0.20738	5.779
1100	12287.3	735.68	0.21296	5.875
1090	12397.1	759.38	0.21885	5.976
1080	12511.0	784.66	0.22507	6.080
1070	12629.2	811.64	0.23165	6.190
1060	12751.8	840.48	0.23861	6.306
1050	12879.2	871.35	0.24597	6.426
1040	13011.6	904.42	0.25377	6.553
1030	13149.1	939.88	0.26202	6.686
1020	13292.1	977.97	0.27078	6.825
1010	13440.8	1018.92	0.28006	6.972
1000	13595.5	1063.01	0.28992	7.126
990	13756.5	1110.53	0.30038	7.288
980	13924.1	1161.82	0.31149	7.458
970	14098.8	1217.25	0.32331	7.637
960	14279.7	1276.85	0.33580	7.824
950	14464.4	1340.09	0.34883	8.018
940	14653.1	1407.18	0.36242	8.218
930	14845.8	1478.39	0.37660	8.424
920	15042.7	1554.01	0.39141	8.637
910	15244.0	1634.33	0.40687	8.857
900	15449.7	1719.68	0.42303	9.084
890	15660.0	1810.43	0.43992	9.319
880	15875.2	1906.96	0.45759	9.562
870	16095.2	2009.69	0.47608	9.813
860	16320.4	2119.06	0.49543	10.074
850	16550.9	2235.58	0.51572	10.343
840	16786.9	2359.77	0.53697	10.623
830	17028.5	2492.22	0.55927	10.912
820	17276.1	2633.55	0.58266	11.212
810	17529.7	2784.46	0.60723	11.523
800	17789.7	2945.68	0.63304	11.846
790	18056.3	3118.06	0.66017	12.182
780	18328.6	3301.67	0.68860	12.529
770	18604.6	3495.74	0.71815	12.885
760	18884.1	3700.77	0.74888	13.250
750	19167.4	3917.40	0.78084	13.625
740	19454.4	4146.29	0.81411	14.011
730	19745.4	4388.18	0.84875	14.407
720	20040.4	4643.83	0.88485	14.813

V	S(V)	A(V)	I(V)	T(V)
710	20339.4	4914.09	0.92248	15.232
700	20642.8	5199.84	0.96174	15.662
690	20950.5	5502.04	1.00272	16.105
680	21262.7	5821.73	1.04552	16.561
670	21579.5	6160.03	1.09025	17.030
660	21901.1	6518.12	1.13702	17.514
650	22227.6	6897.30	1.18598	18.012
640	22559.1	7298.97	1.23724	18.526
630	22895.9	7724.65	1.29097	19.056
620	23238.1	8175.96	1.34732	19.604
610	23585.8	8654.69	1.40646	20.169
600	23939.3	9162.77	1.46858	20.754
590	24298.7	9702.27	1.53389	21.358
580	24664.3	10275.50	1.60260	21.983
570	25036.2	10884.92	1.67497	22.630
560	25414.7	11533.25	1.75124	23.299
550	25800.0	12223.46	1.83171	23.994
540	26192.4	12958.79	1.91670	24.714
530	26592.2	13742.79	2.00654	25.461
520	26999.5	14579.39	2.10161	26.237
510	27414.8	15472.87	2.20233	27.043
500	27838.2	16427.98	2.30915	27.882
490	28270.3	17449.95	2.42258	28.755
480	28711.2	18544.57	2.54317	29.664
470	29161.4	19718.27	2.67155	30.612
460	29621.3	20978.18	2.80838	31.601
450	30091.4	22332.25	2.95444	32.634
440	30571.9	23789.33	3.11057	33.714
430	31063.6	25359.35	3.27772	34.845
420	31566.8	27053.44	3.45695	36.029
410	32082.1	28884.09	3.64945	37.271
400	32610.2	30865.42	3.85657	38.574
390	33151.6	33013.38	4.07982	39.945
380	33707.1	35346.05	4.32094	41.388
370	34277.4	37884.02	4.58186	42.909
360	34863.3	40650.79	4.86483	44.515
350	35465.7	43673.30	5.17240	46.212
340	36085.6	46982.52	5.50750	48.009
330	36724.0	50614.22	5.87353	49.915
320	37382.1	54609.85	6.27441	51.940
310	38061.0	59017.71	6.71470	54.096
300	38762.2	63894.33	7.19975	56.395
290	39487.2	69306.16	7.73584	58.853
280	40237.6	75331.82	8.33039	61.487
270	41015.4	82064.79	8.99222	64.316
260	41822.4	89616.91	9.73187	67.362

V	S(V)	A(V)	I(V)	T(V)
250	42661.2	98122.96	10.56204	70.652
240	43534.1	107746.42	11.49813	74.216
230	44444.3	118687.19	12.55896	78.090
220	45394.9	131191.74	13.76771	82.316
210	46389.7	145566.75	15.15322	86.945
200	47433.1	162197.62	16.75171	92.037
190	48530.0	181573.99	18.60918	97.665
180	49686.2	204325.48	20.78476	103.917

V	S(V)	A(V)	I(V)	T(V)
170	50908.6	231272.53	23.35545	110.906
160	52205.0	263500.18	26.42307	118.768
150	53585.2	302467.41	30.12445	127.679
140	55060.6	350172.97	34.64701	137.862
130	56645.4	409413.87	40.25291	149.612
120	58357.1	484200.65	47.31797	163.320
110	60217.8	580448.23	56.39627	179.521
100	62256.0	707173.24	68.33227	198.962

Tables of the Primary Siacci Functions

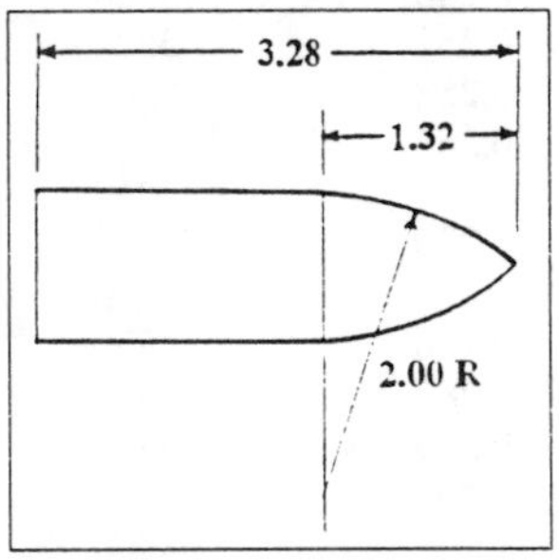

G_1 Drag Function

Quantity	Units
V	ft./sec.
S(V)	ft.-in.^{2}/lb.
A(V)	ft.-in.^{4}/lb.^{2}
I(V)	in.^{2}/lb.
T(V)	sec.-in.^{2}/lb.

V	S(V)	A(V)	~~T(V)~~ I(v)	T(V)
4500	0.0	0.00	0.00000	0.000
4490	21.7	0.00	0.00007	0.005
4480	43.4	0.00	0.00014	0.010
4470	65.2	0.01	0.00021	0.015
4460	87.1	0.01	0.00028	0.019
4450	108.9	0.02	0.00035	0.024
4440	130.9	0.03	0.00042	0.029
4430	152.8	0.04	0.00049	0.034
4420	174.9	0.05	0.00057	0.039
4410	196.9	0.06	0.00064	0.044
4400	219.1	0.08	0.00071	0.049
4390	241.2	0.09	0.00079	0.054
4380	263.4	0.11	0.00086	0.059
4370	285.7	0.13	0. 00093	0.064
4360	308.0	0.15	0.00101	0.070
4350	330.4	0.18	0.00109	0.075
4340	352.8	0.20	0.00116	0.080
4330	375.3	0.23	0.00124	0.085

V	S(V)	A(V)	~~T(V)~~ I(v)	T(V)
4320	397.8	0.26	0.00132	0.090
4310	420.4	0.29	0.00139	0.095
4300	443.0	0.32	0.00147	0.101
4290	465.6	0.36	0.00155	0.106
4280	488.3	0.39	0.00163	0.111
4270	511.1	0.43	0.00171	0.117
4260	533.9	0.47	0.00179	0.122
4250	556.8	0.51	0.00187	0.127
4240	579.7	0.56	0.00196	0.133
4230	602.7	0.60	0.00204	0.138
4220	625.7	0.65	0.00212	0.144
4210	648.8	0.70	0.00220	0.149
4200	671.9	0.75	0.00229	0.155
4190	695.1	0.81	0.00237	0.160
4180	718.3	0.86	0.00246	0.166
4170	741.6	0.92	0.00254	0.171
4160	765.0	0.98	0.00263	0.177
4150	788.4	1.04	0.00272	0.182

V	S(V)	A(V)	~~T(V)~~ I(v)	T(V)
4140	811.8	1.11	0.00281	0.188
4130	835.3	1.17	0.00289	0.194
4120	858.9	1.24	0.00298	0.200
4110	882.5	1.31	0.00307	0.205
4100	906.1	1.39	0.00316	0.211
4090	929.8	1.46	0.00325	0.217
4080	953.6	1.54	0.00335	0.223
4070	977.5	1.62	0.00344	0.228
4060	1001.3	1.71	0.00353	0.234
4050	1025.3	1.79	0.00362	0.240
4040	1049.3	1.88	0.00372	0.246
4030	1073.3	1.97	0.00381	0.252
4020	1097.4	2.06	0.00391	0.258
4010	1121.6	2.16	0.00401	0.264
4000	1145.8	2.26	0.00410	0.270
3990	1170.1	2.36	0.00420	0.276
3980	1194.4	2.46	0.00430	0.282
3970	1218.8	2.57	0.00440	0.289
3960	1243.3	2.68	0.00450	0.295
3950	1267.8	2.79	0.00460	0.301
3940	1292.3	2.90	0.00470	0.307
3930	1316.9	3.02	0.00480	0.313
3920	1341.6	3.14	0.00491	0.320
3910	1366.4	3.26	0.00501	0.326
3900	1391.1	3.39	0.00512	0.332
3890	1416.0	3.52	0.00522	0.339
3880	1440.9	3.65	0.00533	0.345
3870	1465.8	3.78	0.00543	0.352
3860	1490.9	3.92	0.00554	0.358
3850	1515.9	4.06	0.00565	0.365
3840	1541.1	4.20	0.00576	0.371
3830	1566.3	4.35	0.00587	0.378
3820	1591.5	4.50	0.00598	0.384
3810	1616.9	4.65	0.00609	0.391
3800	1642.2	4.81	0.00620	0.398
3790	1667.7	4.97	0.00632	0.404
3780	1693.2	5.13	0.00643	0.411
3770	1718.7	5.30	0.00655	0.418
3760	1744.4	5.47	0.00666	0.425
3750	1770.0	5.64	0.00678	0.431
3740	1795.8	5.81	0.00690	0.438
3730	1821.6	5.99	0.00702	0.445
3720	1847.5	6.18	0.00714	0.452
3710	1873.4	6.36	0.00726	0.459
3700	1899.4	6.55	0.00738	0.466
3690	1925.5	6.75	0.00750	0.473

V	S(V)	A(V)	~~T(V)~~ I(v)	T(V)
3680	1951.6	6.95	0.00763	0.480
3670	1977.8	7.15	0.00775	0.487
3660	2004.1	7.35	0.00788	0.495
3650	2030.4	7.56	0.00801	0.502
3640	2056.8	7.77	0.00813	0.509
3630	2083.3	7.99	0.00826	0.516
3620	2109.8	8.21	0.00839	0.524
3610	2136.4	8.44	0.00852	0.531
3600	2163.0	8.67	0.00865	0.538
3590	2189.7	8.90	0.00879	0.546
3580	2216.5	9.14	0.00892	0.553
3570	2243.4	9.38	0.00906	0.561
3560	2270.3	9.62	0.00919	0.568
3550	2297.2	9.87	0.00933	0.576
3540	2324.3	10.13	0.00947	0.584
3530	2351.4	10.39	0.00961	0.591
3520	2378.6	10.65	0.00975	0.599
3510	2405.8	10.92	0.00989	0.607
3500	2433.1	11.19	0.01003	0.614
3490	2460.5	11.47	0.01018	0.622
3480	2488.0	11.75	0.01032	0.630
3470	2515.5	12.03	0.01047	0.638
3460	2543.1	12.32	0.01062	0.646
3450	2570.7	12.62	0.01077	0.654
3440	2598.4	12.92	0.01092	0.662
3430	2626.2	13.22	0.01107	0.670
3420	2654.1	13.54	0.01122	0.678
3410	2682.0	13.85	0.01137	0.687
3400	2710.0	14.17	0.01153	0.695
3390	2738.0	14.50	0.01169	0.703
3380	2766.2	14.83	0.01184	0.711
3370	2794.4	15.16	0.01200	0.720
3360	2822.6	15.51	0.01216	0.728
3350	2851.0	15.85	0.01233	0.737
3340	2879.4	16.21	0.01249	0.745
3330	2907.8	16.56	0.01265	0.754
3320	2936.4	16.93	0.01282	0.762
3310	2965.0	17.30	0.01299	0.771
3300	2993.7	17.67	0.01316	0.779
3290	3022.4	18.05	0.01333	0.788
3280	3051.2	18.44	0.01350	0.797
3270	3080.1	18.83	0.01367	0.806
3260	3109.1	19.23	0.01385	0.815
3250	3138.1	19.63	0.01402	0.824
3240	3167.2	20.04	0.01420	0.832
3230	3196.4	20.46	0.01438	0.842

V	S(V)	A(V)	~~T(V)~~ I(V)	T(V)
3220	3225.6	20.88	0.01456	0.851
3210	3254.9	21.31	0.01474	0.860
3200	3284.3	21.75	0.01493	0.869
3190	3313.8	22.19	0.01511	0.878
3180	3343.3	22.64	0.01530	0.887
3170	3372.9	23.10	0.01549	0.897
3160	3402.5	23.56	0.01568	0.906
3150	3432.3	24.03	0.01587	0.915
3140	3462.1	24.50	0.01607	0.925
3130	3492.0	24.99	0.01626	0.934
3120	3521.9	25.48	0.01646	0.944
3110	3551.9	25.97	0.01666	0.954
3100	3582.0	26.48	0.01686	0.963
3090	3612.2	26.99	0.01706	0.973
3080	3642.4	27.51	0.01726	0.983
3070	3672.7	28.03	0.01747	0.993
3060	3703.1	28.57	0.01768	1.003
3050	3733.5	29.11	0.01789	1.013
3040	3764.0	29.66	0.01810	1.023
3030	3794.6	30.21	0.01831	1.033
3020	3825.2	30.78	0.01853	1.043
3010	3856.0	31.35	0.01875	1.053
3000	3886.8	31.93	0.01897	1.063
2990	3917.6	32.52	0.01919	1.074
2980	3948.6	33.12	0.01941	1.084
2970	3979.6	33.72	0.01964	1.094
2960	4010.7	34.34	0.01986	1.105
2950	4041.9	34.96	0.02009	1.115
2940	4073.1	35.59	0.02032	1.126
2930	4104.4	36.23	0.02056	1.137
2920	4135.8	36.88	0.02079	1.147
2910	4167.2	37.54	0.02103	1.158
2900	4198.8	38.21	0.02127	1.169
2890	4230.4	38.88	0.02151	1.180
2880	4262.0	39.57	0.02176	1.191
2870	4293.8	40.26	0.02201	1.202
2860	4325.6	40.97	0.02226	1.213
2850	4357.5	41.68	0.02251	1.224
2840	4389.4	42.40	0.02276	1.236
2830	4421.5	43.14	0.02302	1.247
2820	4453.6	43.88	0.02328	1.258
2810	4485.8	44.63	0.02354	1.270
2800	4518.0	45.40	0.02380	1.281
2790	4550.3	46.17	0.02407	1.293
2780	4582.8	46.95	0.02434	1.304
2770	4615.2	47.75	0.02461	1.316
2760	4647.8	48.55	0.02488	1.328
2750	4680.4	49.37	0.02516	1.340
2740	4713.1	50.20	0.02544	1.352
2730	4745.9	51.04	0.02572	1.364
2720	4778.7	51.89	0.02600	1.376
2710	4811.7	52.75	0.02629	1.388
2700	4844.7	53.62	0.02658	1.400
2690	4877.7	54.50	0.02687	1.412
2680	4910.9	55.40	0.02717	1.425
2670	4944.1	56.31	0.02747	1.437
2660	4977.4	57.23	0.02777	1.449
2650	5010.8	58.16	0.02807	1.462
2640	5044.2	59.10	0.02838	1.475
2630	5077.8	60.06	0.02869	1.487
2620	5111.4	61.03	0.02901	1.500
2610	5145.0	62.01	0.02932	1.513
2600	5178.8	63.01	0.02964	1.526
2590	5212.6	64.01	0.02997	1.539
2580	5246.5	65.04	0.03029	1.552
2570	5280.5	66.07	0.03062	1.565
2560	5314.6	67.12	0.03096	1.579
2550	5348.7	68.18	0.03129	1.592
2540	5382.9	69.26	0.03163	1.605
2530	5417.2	70.35	0.03197	1.619
2520	5451.6	71.45	0.03232	1.633
2510	5486.0	72.57	0.03267	1.646
2500	5520.5	73.71	0.03303	1.660
2490	5555.1	74.85	0.03338	1.674
2480	5589.8	76.02	0.03374	1.688
2470	5624.5	77.20	0.03411	1.702
2460	5659.4	78.39	0.03448	1.716
2450	5694.3	79.60	0.03485	1.730
2440	5729.3	80.83	0.03523	1.745
2430	5764.4	82.07	0.03561	1.759
2420	5799.5	83.33	0.03599	1.774
2410	5834.7	84.60	0.03638	1.788
2400	5870.1	85.90	0.03677	1.803
2390	5905.4	87.20	0.03717	1.818
2380	5940.9	88.53	0.03757	1.832
2370	5976.5	89.87	0.03798	1.847
2360	6012.1	91.23	0.03839	1.862
2350	6047.9	92.61	0.03880	1.878
2340	6083.7	94.01	0.03922	1.893
2330	6119.6	95.42	0.03964	1.908
2320	6155.5	96.86	0.04007	1.924
2310	6191.6	98.31	0.04050	1.939

V	S(V)	A(V)	~~T(V)~~ I(V)	T(V)
2300	6227.8	99.78	0.04094	1.955
2290	6264.0	101.28	0.04138	1.971
2280	6300.3	102.79	0.04183	1.987
2270	6336.7	104.32	0.04228	2.003
2260	6373.2	105.87	0.04274	2.019
2250	6409.8	107.44	0.04320	2.035
2240	6446.5	109.04	0.04367	2.051
2230	6483.3	110.65	0.04415	2.068
2220	6520.1	112.29	0.04462	2.084
2210	6557.1	113.94	0.04511	2.101
2200	6594.1	115.62	0.04560	2.118
2190	6631.2	117.32	0.04609	2.135
2180	6668.4	119.05	0.04660	2.152
2170	6705.7	120.80	0.04710	2.169
2160	6743.2	122.57	0.04762	2.186
2150	6780.7	124.37	0.04814	2.204
2140	6818.3	126.18	0.04866	2.221
2130	6856.0	128.03	0.04919	2.239
2120	6893.8	129.90	0.04973	2.257
2110	6931.7	131.79	0.05028	2.275
2100	6969.7	133.72	0.05083	2.293
2090	7007.8	135.66	0.05139	2.311
2080	7046.0	137.64	0.05195	2.329
2070	7084.3	139.64	0.05253	2.348
2060	7122.8	141.67	0.05311	2.366
2050	7161.3	143.73	0.05369	2.385
2040	7200.0	145.82	0.05429	2.404
2030	7238.7	147.93	0.05489	2.423
2020	7277.6	150.08	0.05550	2.442
2010	7316.6	152.25	0.05612	2.461
2000	7355.7	154.46	0.05674	2.481
1990	7394.9	156.70	0.05738	2.501
1980	7434.3	158.97	0.05802	2.520
1970	7473.8	161.27	0.05867	2.540
1960	7513.3	163.61	0.05933	2.561
1950	7553.1	165.98	0.06000	2.581
1940	7592.9	168.38	0.06067	2.601
1930	7632.9	170.82	0.06136	2.622
1920	7673.0	173.29	0.06206	2.643
1910	7713.2	175.81	0.06276	2.664
1900	7753.6	178.35	0.06348	2.685
1890	7794.1	180.94	0.06420	2.706
1880	7834.7	183.56	0.06494	2.728
1870	7875.5	186.23	0.06569	2.750
1860	7916.5	188.93	0.06644	2.772
1850	7957.5	191.68	0.06721	2.794

V	S(V)	A(V)	~~T(V)~~ I(V)	T(V)
1840	7998.8	194.47	0.06799	2.816
1830	8040.2	197.29	0.06878	2.839
1820	8081.7	200.17	0.06958	2.862
1810	8123.4	203.09	0.07040	2.885
1800	8165.2	206.05	0.07122	2.908
1790	8207.3	209.06	0.07206	2.931
1780	8249.4	212.12	0.07291	2.955
1770	8291.8	215.22	0.07378	2.979
1760	8334.3	218.38	0.07466	3.003
1750	8377.0	221.59	0.07555	3.027
1740	8419.9	224.85	0.07645	3.052
1730	8463.0	228.16	0.07738	3.076
1720	8506.3	231.53	0.07831	3.102
1710	8549.8	234.96	0.07926	3.127
1700	8593.4	238.44	0.08023	3.153
1690	8637.3	241.98	0.08121	3.178
1680	8681.4	245.58	0.08221	3.205
1670	8725.7	249.25	0.08322	3.231
1660	8770.3	252.98	0.08426	3.258
1650	8815.0	256.77	0.08531	3.285
1640	8860.0	260.63	0.08638	3.312
1630	8905.2	264.56	0.08747	3.340
1620	8950.7	268.57	0.08857	3.368
1610	8996.4	272.64	0.08970	3.396
1600	9042.3	276.79	0.09085	3.425
1590	9088.6	281.02	0.09202	3.454
1580	9135.1	285.32	0.09321	3.483
1570	9181.9	289.71	0.09442	3.513
1560	9228.9	294.19	0.09566	3.543
1550	9276.3	298.75	0.09692	3.573
1540	9324.0	303.40	0.09820	3.604
1530	9372.0	308.14	0.09951	3.635
1520	9420.3	312.99	0.10085	3.667
1510	9469.0	317.92	0.10221	3.699
1500	9518.0	322.97	0.10360	3.732
1490	9567.3	328.12	0.10502	3.765
1480	9617.1	333.38	0.10647	3.798
1470	9667.2	338.75	0.10796	3.832
1460	9717.7	344.24	0.10947	3.867
1450	9768.6	349.85	0.11102	3.902
1440	9820.0	355.59	0.11260	3.937
1430	9871.8	361.47	0.11422	3.973
1420	9924.0	367.48	0.11587	4.010
1410	9976.7	373.63	0.11757	4.047
1400	10030.0	379.94	0.11930	4.085
1390	10083.7	386.40	0.12108	4.124

V	S(V)	A(V)	~~T(V)~~ I(V)	T(V)
1380	10138.1	393.03	0.12290	4.163
1370	10192.9	399.82	0.12477	4.203
1360	10248.4	406.79	0.12668	4.244
1350	10304.5	413.96	0.12865	4.285
1340	10361.2	421.31	0.13066	4.327
1330	10418.7	428.88	0.13274	4.370
1320	10476.8	436.66	0.13487	4.414
1310	10535.8	444.67	0.13706	4.459
1300	10595.5	452.93	0.13932	4.505
1290	10656.1	461.44	0.14164	4.551
1280	10717.6	470.22	0.14404	4.599
1270	10780.1	479.30	0.14651	4.648
1260	10843.6	488.68	0.14906	4.698
1250	10908.1	498.39	0.15170	4.750
1240	10973.9	508.45	0.15442	4.803
1230	11040.8	518.89	0.15725	4.857
1220	11109.2	529.73	0.16018	4.913
1210	11178.9	541.01	0.16322	4.970
1200	11250.2	552.76	0.16637	5.029
1190	11323.2	565.02	0.16966	5.090
1180	11397.9	577.83	0.17309	5.153
1170	11474.7	591.25	0.17666	5.219
1160	11553.5	605.32	0.18040	5.286
1150	11634.6	620.12	0.18431	5.357
1140	11718.3	635.70	0.18841	5.430
1130	11804.6	652.15	0.19272	5.506
1120	11893.8	669.54	0.19726	5.585
1110	11986.2	687.99	0.20204	5.668
1100	12081.9	707.58	0.20708	5.755
1090	12181.4	728.43	0.21242	5.845
1080	12284.7	750.67	0.21806	5.941
1070	12392.2	774.44	0.22405	6.041
1060	12504.2	799.88	0.23040	6.146
1050	12620.9	827.16	0.23714	6.256
1040	12742.5	856.44	0.24431	6.373
1030	12869.3	887.90	0.25192	6.495
1020	13001.6	921.76	0.26002	6.624
1010	13139.5	958.20	0.26863	6.760
1000	13283.2	997.45	0.27778	6.903
990	13432.9	1039.75	0.28750	7.054
980	13588.7	1085.35	0.29784	7.212
970	13750.7	1134.51	0.30880	7.378
960	13919.2	1187.50	0.32044	7.553
950	14094.1	1244.62	0.33277	7.736
940	14275.5	1306.18	0.34584	7.928
930	14463.6	1372.51	0.35968	8.129

V	S(V)	A(V)	~~T(V)~~ I(V)	T(V)
920	14658.2	1443.94	0.37431	8.339
910	14859.5	1520.86	0.38978	8.559
900	15067.6	1603.63	0.40612	8.789
890	15282.3	1692.66	0.42336	9.029
880	15503.6	1788.38	0.44154	9.279
870	15731.7	1891.26	0.46070	9.540
860	15966.4	2001.77	0.48088	9.811
850	16207.8	2120.38	0.50212	10.094
840	16455.7	2247.64	0.52446	10.387
830	16710.3	2384.11	0.54794	10.692
820	16971.4	2530.39	0.57262	11.008
810	17239.0	2687.08	0.59853	11.337
800	17513.1	2854.86	0.62574	11.677
790	17793.7	3034.46	0.65431	12.030
780	18080.7	3226.53	0.68427	12.396
770	18374.1	3431.85	0.71568	12.774
760	18673.7	3651.20	0.74862	13.166
750	18979.6	3885.44	0.78313	13.571
740	19291.9	4135.61	0.81933	13.991
730	19610.3	4402.52	0.85724	14.424
720	19934.8	4687.16	0.89696	14.871
710	20265.8	4990.83	0.93860	15.334
700	20602.8	5314.48	0.98222	15.812
690	20945.9	5659.28	1.02791	16.306
68Q	21295.1	6026.52	1.07578	16.816
670	21650.4	6417.65	1.12594	17.342
660	22011.9	6834.19	1.17854	17.886
650	22379.7	7277.66	1.23367	18.447
640	22753.6	7749.77	1.29150	19.027
630	23133.9	8252.30	1.35215	19.626
620	23520.4	8787.21	1.41581	20.245
610	23913.2	9356.37	1.48261	20.883
600	24312.2	9961.86	1.55274	21.543
590	24717.8	10606.42	1.62643	22.224
580	25129.8	11292.50	1.70388	22.929
570	25548.5	12022.83	1.78534	23.657
560	25974.0	12800.60	1.87108	24.410
550	26406.4	13629.01	1.96138	25.189
540	26845.7	14511.39	2.05652	25.995
530	27292.1	15451.88	2.15687	26.830
520	27746.0	16454.57	2.26279	27.694
510	28207.2	17523.87	2.37466	28.590
500	28676.2	18665.25	2.49297	29.519
490	29153.3	19884.20	2.61822	30.483
480	29638.5	21186.60	2.75092	31.483
470	30132.1	22579.06	2.89167	32.522

V	S(V)	A(V)	~~T(V)~~ I(V)	T(V)
460	30634.5	24068.83	3.04112	33.603
450	31145.8	25664.10	3.20000	34.727
440	31666.6	27374.42	3.36920	35.897
430	32197.3	29209.99	3.54963	37.117
420	32738.1	31181.36	3.74225	38.390
410	33289.4	33300.78	3.94819	39.718
400	33851.7	35582.49	4.16876	41.107
390	34425.8	38042.90	4.40546	42.560
380	35012.0	40699.44	4.65991	44.083
370	35610.9	43571.71	4.93393	45.681
360	36223.5	46684.05	5.22977	47.359
350	36850.6	50062.99	5.54992	49.126
340	37492.7	53737.04	5.89703	50.987
330	38150.5	57738.65	6.27414	52.951
320	38825.0	62107.80	6.68503	55.027
310	39517.4	66890.15	7.13402	57.225
300	40228.6	72137.30	7.62601	59.557
290	40960.3	77912.52	8.16701	62.038

V	S(V)	A(V)	~~T(V)~~ I(V)	T(V)
280	41713.9	84289.54	8.76406	64.683
270	42490.9	91353.04	9.42526	67.509
260	43292.9	99203.33	10.16025	70.536
250	44122.2	107965.08	10.98106	73.789
240	44980.6	117780.64	11.90145	77.293
230	45870.9	128832.00	12.93914	81.083
220	46796.8	141349.35	14.11645	85.199
210	47759.7	155577.02	15.45735	89.679
200	48764.2	171864.78	16.99629	94.581
190	49816.1	190664.44	18.77751	99.978
180	50919.0	212498.28	20.85269	105.942
170	52079.3	238080.69	23.29266	112.576
160	53303.4	268331.66	26.18905	119.999
150	54598.7	304455.56	29.66263	128.362
140	55976.6	348169.75	33.88602	137.872
130	57449.5	401823.63	39.09586	148.792
120	59033.8	468802.18	45.63452	161.479
110	60745.6	553860.03	53.98517	176.382
100	62608.0	664239.15	64.89125	194.146

Tables of the Primary Siacci Functions

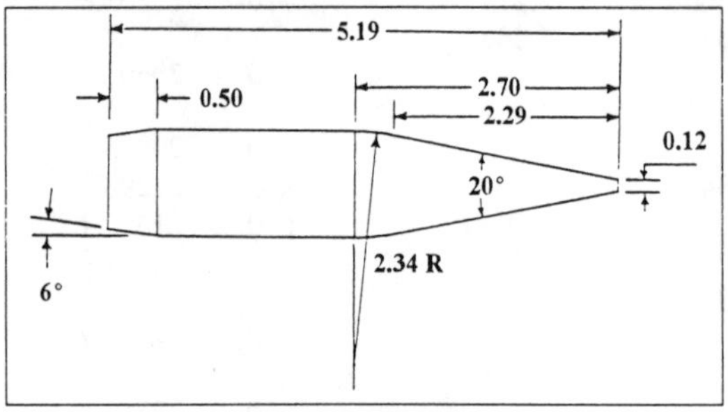

G_2 Drag Function

Quantity	Units
V	ft./sec.
S(V)	ft.-in.²/lb.
A(V)	ft.-in.⁴/lb.²
I(V)	in.²/lb.
T(V)	sec.-in.²/lb.

V	S(V)	A(V)	I(V)	T(V)
4500	0.0	0.00	0.00000	0.000
4490	56.9	0.01	0.00018	0.013
4480	113.9	0.02	0.00036	0.025
4470	170.9	0.05	0.00055	0.038
4460	227.9	0.08	0.00073	0.051
4450	285.0	0.13	0.00092	0.064
4440	342.1	0.19	0.00110	0.077
4430	399.3	0.26	0.00129	0.089

V	S(V)	A(V)	I(V)	T(V)
4420	456.5	0.33	0.00148	0.102
4410	513.8	0.42	0.00167	0.115
4400	571.1	0.53	0.00186	0.128
4390	628.5	0.64	0.00205	0.141
4380	685.9	0.76	0.00224	0.154
4370	743.3	0.89	0.00243	0.168
4360	800.8	1.04	0.00263	0.181
4350	858.3	1.20	0.00282	0.194

V	S(V)	A(V)	I(V)	T(V)
4340	915.9	1.36	0.00302	0.207
4330	973.5	1.54	0.00321	0.221
4320	1031.2	1.74	0.00341	0.234
4310	1088.9	1.94	0.00361	0.247
4300	1146.7	2.15	0.00381	0.261
4290	1204.5	2.38	0.00401	0.274
4280	1262.4	2.62	0.00422	0.288
4270	1320.3	2.87	0.00442	0.301
4260	1378.2	3.13	0.00463	0.315
4250	1436.2	3.40	0.00483	0.328
4240	1494.2	3.69	0.00504	0.342
4230	1552.3	3.99	0.00525	0.356
4220	1610.4	4.30	0.00546	0.370
4210	1668.6	4.62	0.00567	0.383
4200	1726.8	4.96	0.00588	0.397
4190	1785.0	5.31	0.00609	0.411
4180	1843.3	5.67	0.00631	0.425
4170	1901.7	6.04	0.00652	0.439
4160	1960.1	6.43	0.00674	0.453
4150	2018.5	6.83	0.00695	0.467
4140	2077.0	7.24	0.00717	0.481
4130	2135.5	7.67	0.00739	0.495
4120	2194.0	8.11	0.00761	0.509
4110	2252.7	8.56	0.00784	0.524
4100	2311.3	9.03	0.00806	0.538
4090	2370.0	9.51	0.00829	0.552
4080	2428.8	10.00	0.00851	0.567
4070	2487.5	10.51	0.00874	0.581
4060	2546.4	11.03	0.00897	0.596
4050	2605.3	11.56	0.00920	0.610
4040	2664.2	12.11	0.00943	0.625
4030	2723.2	12.68	0.00966	0.639
4020	2782.2	13.25	0.00990	0.654
4010	2841.3	13.84	0.01013	0.669
4000	2900.4	14.45	0.01037	0.683
3990	2959.6	15.07	0.01061	0.698
3980	3018.8	15.71	0.01085	0.713
3970	3078.0	16.36	0.01109	0.728
3960	3137.4	17.02	0.01133	0.743
3950	3196.7	17.70	0.01158	0.758
3940	3256.1	18.40	0.01182	0.773
3930	3315.6	19.11	0.01207	0.788
3920	3375.1	19.83	0.01232	0.803
3910	3434.7	20.58	0.01257	0.819
3900	3494.3	21.33	0.01282	0.834
3890	3553.9	22.10	0.01307	0.849

V	S(V)	A(V)	I(V)	T(V)
3880	3613.6	22.89	0.01333	0.865
3870	3673.4	23.70	0.01358	0.880
3860	3733.2	24.52	0.01384	0.895
3850	3793.1	25.35	0.01410	0.911
3840	3853.0	26.21	0.01436	0.927
3830	3913.0	27.08	0.01462	0.942
3820	3973.0	27.96	0.01489	0.958
3810	4033.1	28.86	0.01515	0.974
3800	4093.2	29.78	0.01542	0.989
3790	4153.4	30.72	0.01569	1.005
3780	4213.7	31.67	0.01596	1.021
3770	4274.0	32.64	0.01623	1.037
3760	4334.3	33.63	0.01651	1.053
3750	4394.8	34.64	0.01678	1.069
3740	4455.2	35.66	0.01706	1.085
3730	4515.7	36.70	0.01734	1.102
3720	4576.3	37.76	0.01762	1.118
3710	4637.0	38.84	0.01790	1.134
3700	4697.7	39.93	0.01819	1.151
3690	4758.4	41.05	0.01847	1.167
3680	4819.2	42.18	0.01876	1.184
3670	4880.1	43.33	0.01905	1.200
3660	4941.1	44.50	0.01934	1.217
3650	5002.1	45.69	0.01964	1.233
3640	5063.1	46.89	0.01993	1.250
3630	5124.2	48.12	0.02023	1.267
3620	5185.4	49.37	0.02053	1.284
3610	5246.6	50.63	0.02083	1.301
3600	5307.9	51.92	0.02113	1.318
3590	5369.3	53.23	0.02144	1.335
3580	5430.7	54.55	0.02175	1.352
3570	5492.2	55.90	0.02205	1.369
3560	5553.7	57.27	0.02237	1.387
3550	5615.4	58.65	0.02268	1.404
3540	5677.0	60.06	0.02300	1.421
3530	5738.8	61.49	0.02331	1.439
3520	5800.6	62.94	0.02363	1.456
3510	5862.4	64.41	0.02396	1.474
3500	5924.4	65.91	0.02428	1.492
3490	5986.4	67.42	0.02461	1.509
3480	6048.4	68.96	0.02493	1.527
3470	6110.6	70.52	0.02527	1.545
3460	6172.7	72.10	0.02560	1.563
3450	6235.0	73.71	0.02593	1.581
3440	6297.3	75.33	0.02627	1.599
3430	6359.7	76.98	0.02661	1.617

V	S(V)	A(V)	I(V)	T(V)
3420	6422.2	78.66	0.02695	1.635
3410	6484.7	80.35	0.02730	1.654
3400	6547.3	82.07	0.02765	1.672
3390	6610.0	83.82	0.02800	1.691
3380	6672.7	85.58	0.02835	1.709
3370	6735.5	87.37	0.02870	1.728
3360	6798.4	89.19	0.02906	1.746
3350	6861.4	91.03	0.02942	1.765
3340	6924.4	92.90	0.02978	1.784
3330	6987.5	94.79	0.03015	1.803
3320	7050.7	96.70	0.03051	1.822
3310	7113.9	98.64	0.03088	1.841
3300	7177.2	100.61	0.03126	1.860
3290	7240.6	102.61	0.03163	1.879
3280	7304.1	104.62	0.03201	1.899
3270	7367.6	106.67	0.03239	1.918
3260	7431.2	108.74	0.03278	1.938
3250	7494.9	110.84	0.03316	1.957
3240	7558.6	112.97	0.03355	1.977
3230	7622.5	115.12	0.03394	1.997
3220	7686.4	117.31	0.03434	2.016
3210	7750.4	119.52	0.03474	2.036
3200	7814.5	121.76	0.03514	2.056
3190	7878.6	124.02	0.03554	2.076
3180	7942.9	126.32	0.03595	2.096
3170	8007.2	128.65	0.03636	2.117
3160	8071.6	131.00	0.03678	2.137
3150	8136.1	133.38	0.03719	2.158
3140	8200.6	135.80	0.03761	2.178
3130	8265.3	138.25	0.03803	2.199
3120	8330.0	140.72	0.03846	2.219
3110	8394.8	143.23	0.03889	2.240
3100	8459.7	145.77	0.03932	2.261
3090	8524.7	148.34	0.03976	2.282
3080	8589.8	150.94	0.04020	2.303
3070	8655.0	153.57	0.04064	2.324
3060	8720.2	156.24	0.04109	2.346
3050	8785.5	158.94	0.04154	2.367
3040	8851.0	161.67	0.04199	2.389
3030	8916.5	164.43	0.04245	2.410
3020	8982.1	167.23	0.04291	2.432
3010	9047.8	170.07	0.04338	2.454
3000	9113.5	172.94	0.04385	2.475
2990	9179.4	175.84	0.04432	2.497
2980	9245.4	178.78	0.04479	2.520

V	S(V)	A(V)	I(V)	T(V)
2970	9311.4	181.75	0.04527	2.542
2960	9377.6	184.77	0.04576	2.564
2950	9443.8	187.81	0.04625	2.587
2940	9510.1	190.90	0.04674	2.609
2930	9576.6	194.02	0.04723	2.632
2920	9643.1	197.18	0.04773	2.654
2910	9709.7	200.37	0.04824	2.677
2900	9776.4	203.61	0.04875	2.700
2890	9843.2	206.88	0.04926	2.723
2880	9910.1	210.20	0.04978	2.746
2870	9977.1	213.55	0.05030	2.770
2860	10044.3	216.94	0.05082	2.793
2850	10111.5	220.37	0.05135	2.817
2840	10178.8	223.85	0.05189	2.840
2830	10246.2	227.36	0.05243	2.864
2820	10313.7	230.92	0.05297	2.888
2810	10381.3	234.52	0.05352	2.912
2800	10449.0	238.17	0.05408	2.936
2790	10516.8	241.85	0.05463	2.961
2780	10584.8	245.58	0.05520	2.985
2770	10652.8	249.36	0.05576	3.009
2760	10720.9	253.18	0.05634	3.034
2750	10789.2	257.04	0.05692	3.059
2740	10857.5	260.95	0.05750	3.084
2730	10926.0	264.91	0.05809	3.109
2720	10994.6	268.91	0.05868	3.134
2710	11063.3	272.96	0.05928	3.159
2700	11132.1	277.06	0.05989	3.185
2690	11201.0	281.21	0.06050	3.210
2680	11270.0	285.41	0.06111	3.236
2670	11339.1	289.65	0.06173	3.262
2660	11408.4	293.95	0.06236	3.288
2650	11477.7	298.30	0.06299	3.314
2640	11547.2	302.70	0.06363	3.340
2630	11616.8	307.15	0.06428	3.367
2620	11686.5	311.65	0.06493	3.393
2610	11756.4	316.21	0.06559	3.420
2600	11826.3	320.82	0.06625	3.447
2590	11896.3	325.48	0.06692	3.474
2580	11966.5	330.20	0.06759	3.503
2570	12036.8	334.98	0.06827	3.528
2560	12107.2	339.81	0.06896	3.556
2550	12177.7	344.69	0.06966	3.583
2540	12248.3	349.64	0.07036	3.611
2530	12319.1	354.64	0.07107	3.635
2520	12389.9	359.70	0.07178	3.667

V	S(V)	A(V)	I(V)	T(V)
2510	12460.9	364.82	0.07250	3.695
2500	12532.0	370.00	0.07323	3.723
2490	12603.2	375.24	0.07397	3.752
2480	12674.5	380.54	0.07471	3.781
2470	12745.9	385.91	0.07546	3.810
2460	12817.5	391.33	0.07622	3.839
2450	12889.2	396.82	0.07698	3.868
2440	12961.0	402.38	0.07776	3.897
2430	13032.9	408.00	0.07854	3.927
2420	13104.9	413.68	0.07932	3.956
2410	13177.0	419.43	0.08012	3.986
2400	13249.3	425.25	0.08092	4.016
2390	13321.7	431.14	0.08173	4.047
2380	13394.2	437.09	0.08255	4.077
2370	13466.8	443.12	0.08338	4.108
2360	13539.5	449.22	0.08422	4.138
2350	13612.4	455.38	0.08506	4.169
2340	13685.4	461.62	0.08592	4.200
2330	13758.5	467.93	0.08678	4.232
2320	13831.7	474.32	0.08765	4.263
2310	13905.1	480.78	0.08853	4.295
2300	13978.5	487.32	0.08942	4.327
2290	14052.1	493.93	0.09032	4.359
2280	14125.9	500.63	0.09123	4.391
2270	14199.7	507.40	0.09215	4.424
2260	14273.7	514.25	0.09307	4.456
2250	14347.8	521.18	0.09401	4.489
2240	14422.0	528.19	0.09496	4.522
2230	14496.3	535.28	0.09591	4.555
2220	14570.8	542.46	0.09688	4.589
2210	14645.3	549.72	0.09786	4.622
2200	14720.0	557.07	0.09885	4.656
2190	14794.8	564.50	0.09985	4.690
2180	14869.8	572.02	0.10086	4.725
2170	14944.8	579.63	0.10188	4.759
2160	15020.0	587.32	0.10291	4.794
2150	15095.3	595.11	0.10395	4.829
2140	15170.7	602.99	0.10500	4.864
2130	15246.2	610.96	0.10607	4.899
2120	15321.9	619.03	0.10715	4.935
2110	15397.6	627.19	0.10824	4.971
2100	15473.5	635.44	0.10934	5.007
2090	15549.5	643.79	0.11045	5.043
2080	15625.6	652.24	0.11158	5.080
2070	15701.9	660.79	0.11272	5.116
2060	15778.2	669.44	0.11387	5.153

V	S(V)	A(V)	I(V)	T(V)
2050	15854.7	678.19	0.11503	5.191
2040	15931.2	687.04	0.11621	5.228
2030	16007.9	696.00	0.11740	5.266
2020	16084.7	705.06	0.11861	5.304
2010	16161.6	714.22	0.11982	5.342
2000	16238.6	723.50	0.12106	5.380
1990	16315.7	732.88	0.12230	5.419
1980	16392.9	742.37	0.12356	5.458
1970	16470.2	751.97	0.12484	5.497
1960	16547.6	761.69	0.12613	5.536
1950	16625.2	771.52	0.12743	5.576
1940	16702.8	781.47	0.12875	5.616
1930	16780.6	791.53	0.13009	5.656
1920	16858.4	801.71	0.13144	5.696
1910	16936.4	812.01	0.13281	5.737
1900	17014.5	822.44	0.13419	5.778
1890	17092.7	832.98	0.13559	5.819
1880	17171.0	843.65	0.13701	5.861
1870	17249.4	854.45	0.13844	5.903
1860	17327.9	865.38	0.13990	5.945
1850	17406.5	876.43	0.14136	5.987
1840	17485.2	887.62	0.14285	6.030
1830	17564.1	898.94	0.14436	6.073
1820	17643.0	910.40	0.14588	6.116
1810	17722.1	922.00	0. i4743	6.160
1800	17801.3	933.73	0.14899	6.204
1790	17880.6	945.61	0.15057	6.248
1780	17960.0	957.63	0.15218	6.292
1770	18039.5	969.80	0.15380	6.337
1760	18119.2	982.12	0.15545	6.382
1750	18199.0	994.59	0.15711	6.428
1740	18278.9	1007.22	0.15880	6.474
1730	18359.0	1020.00	0.16051	6.520
1720	18439.2	1032.94	0.16224	6.566
1710	18519.5	1046.04	0.16400	6.613
1700	18600.0	1059.31	0.16578	6.660
1690	18680.6	1072.74	0.16759	6.708
1680	18761.3	1086.35	0.16941	6.756
1670	18842.2	1100.13	0.17127	6.804
1660	18923.2	1114.08	0.17315	6.853
1650	19004.4	1128.22	0.17506	6.902
1640	19085.8	1142.54	0.17699	6.951
1630	19167.3	1157.05	0.17895	7.001
1620	19249.0	1171.75	0.18094	7.051
1610	19330.9	1186.64	0.18296	7.102
1600	19412.9	1201.74	0.18501	7.153

V	S(V)	A(V)	I(V)	T(V)
1590	19495.1	1217.04	0.18709	7.205
1580	19577.6	1232.55	0.18920	7.257
1570	19660.2	1248.27	0.19134	7.309
1560	19743.1	1264.22	0.19352	7.362
1550	19826.2	1280.39	0.19573	7.415
1540	19909.5	1296.79	0.19797	7.469
1530	19993.1	1313.43	0.20025	7.524
1520	20076.9	1330.31	0.20257	7.579
1510	20161.0	1347.44	0.20493	7.634
1500	20245.3	1364.83	0.20733	7.690
1490	20330.0	1382.49	0.20976	7.747
1480	20414.9	1400.41	0.21224	7.804
1470	20500.2	1418.61	0.21476	7.862
1460	20585.8	1437.10	0.21732	7.920
1450	20671.7	1455.88	0.21993	7.979
1440	20757.9	1474.95	0.22259	8.039
1430	20844.5	1494.34	0.22529	8.099
1420	20931.4	1514.05	0.22805	8.160
1410	21018.7	1534.08	0.23085	8.222
1400	21106.4	1554.45	0.23371	8.285
1390	21194.5	1575.17	0.23662	8.348
1380	21283.0	1596.24	0.23959	8.412
1370	21371.9	1617.68	0.24261	8.476
1360	21461.3	1639.50	0.24570	8.542
1350	21551.1	1661.70	0.24885	8.608
1340	21641.4	1684.31	0.25205	8.675
1330	21732.1	1707.33	0.25533	8.743
1320	21823.3	1730.77	0.25867	8.812
1310	21915.0	1754.65	0.26208	8.882
1300	22007.3	1778.98	0.26557	8.952
1290	22100.0	1803.78	0.26912	9.024
1280	22193.3	1829.06	0.27276	9.097
1270	22287.2	1854.84	0.27647	9.170
1260	22381.6	1881.13	0.28027	9.245
1250	22476.7	1907.95	0.28415	9.321
1240	22572.3	1935.32	0.28812	9.397
1230	22668.6	1963.26	0.29218	9.475
1220	22765.6	1991.80	0.29634	9.555
1210	22863.3	2020.95	0.30059	9.635
1200	22961.8	2050.76	0.30496	9.717
1190	23061.1	2081.27	0.30943	9.800
1180	23161.3	2112.52	0.31402	9.884
1170	23262.6	2144.56	0.31874	9.971
1160	23364.9	2177.43	0.32359	10.058
1150	23468.4	2211.18	0.32858	10.148
1140	23573.2	2245.87	0.33372	10.240

V	S(V)	A(V)	I(V)	T(V)
1130	23679.4	2281.59	0.33902	10.333
1120	23787.6	2318.56	0.34452	10.429
1110	23898.9	2357.23	0.35028	10.529
1100	24015.5	2398.44	0.35642	10.635
1090	24140.7	2443.46	0.36314	10.749
1080	24278.4	2494.01	0.37067	10.876
1070	24433.2	2552.06	0.37929	11.020
1060	24608.8	2619.52	0.38924	11.185
1050	24806.9	2697.75	0.40069	11.373
1040	25026.2	2787.05	0.41361	11.583
1030	25262.9	2886.64	0.42783	11.811
1020	25512.6	2995.34	0.44311	12.055
1010	25771.6	3112.23	0.45929	12.310
1000	26038.2	3236.93	0.47627	12.575
990	26311.6	3369.53	0.49403	12.850
980	26591.4	3510.33	0.51258	13.134
970	26877.4	3659.73	0.53193	13.428
960	27169.6	3818.07	0.55211	13.730
950	27467.5	3985.69	0.57313	14.042
940	27770.9	4162.89	0.59498	14.363
930	28079.6	4350.01	0.61769	14.693
920	28393.1	4547.37	0.64126	15.032
910	28711.4	4755.35	0.66572	15.380
900	29034.2	4974.32	0.69107	15.737
890	29361.3	5204.67	0.71734	16.103
880	29692.6	5446.82	0.74455	16.477
870	30028.0	5701.18	0.77272	16.860
860	30367.1	5968.17	0.80187	17.252
850	30709.9	6248.23	0.83204	17.653
840	31056.3	6541.82	0.86324	18.063
830	31406.1	6849.40	0.89551	18.482
820	31759.2	7171.47	0.92888	18.910
810	32115.5	7508.56	0.96339	19.347
800	32474.9	7861.21	0.99907	19.794
790	32837.4	8230.00	1.03596	20.250
780	33202.9	8615.53	1.07410	20.715
770	33571.2	9018.42	1.11355	21.191
760	33942.4	9439.32	1.15435	21.676
750	34316.4	9878.91	1.19656	22.171
740	34693.2	10337.90	1.24022	22.677
730	35072.7	10817.07	1.28540	23.193
720	35454.9	11317.25	1.33218	23.720
710	35839.8	11839.34	1.38061	24.259
700	36227.5	12384.30	1.43079	24.809
690	36618.1	12953.18	1.48280	25.371
680	37011.5	13547.11	1.53673	25.945

V	S(V)	A(V)	I(V)	T(V)
670	37407.9	14167.27	1.59269	26.532
660	37807.3	14814.96	1.65079	27.133
650	38209.8	15491.56	1.71114	27.748
640	38615.6	16198.56	1.77388	28.377
630	39024.7	16937.59	1.83915	29.021
620	39437.4	17710.42	1.90710	29.681
610	39853.7	18519.01	1.97790	30.358
600	40273.8	19365.47	2.05174	31.053
590	40698.0	20252.12	2.12882	31.766
580	41126.5	21181.47	2.20936	32.498
570	41559.5	22156.26	2.29361	33.251
560	41997.3	23179.47	2.38182	34.026
550	42440.0	24254.34	2.47428	34.824
540	42888.0	25384.42	2.57131	35.646
530	43341.6	26573.61	2.67324	36.494
520	43801.0	27826.16	2.78046	37.369
510	44266.5	29146.81	2.89338	38.273
500	44738.7	30540.74	3.01247	39.208
490	45217.7	32013.69	3.13824	40.176
480	45704.0	33571.99	3.27124	41.178
470	46198.0	35222.65	3.41210	42.218
460	46700.2	36973.42	3.56151	43.299
450	47211.0	38832.88	3.72024	44.421
440	47730.9	40810.58	3.88913	45.590
430	48260.4	42917.12	4.06915	46.807
420	48800.0	45164.39	4.26135	48.077
410	49350.4	47565.72	4.46693	49.403
400	49912.1	50136.14	4.68725	50.790

V	S(V)	A(V)	I(V)	T(V)
390	50485.8	52892.60	4.92382	52.243
380	51072.3	55854.29	5.17837	53.766
370	51672.3	59043.00	5.45289	55.366
360	52286.7	62483.55	5.74960	57.050
350	52916.4	66204.31	6.07109	58.824
340	53562.4	70237.83	6.42029	60.696
330	54225.7	74621.57	6.80061	62.677
320	54907.6	79398.86	7.21599	64.775
310	55609.2	84620.01	7.67101	67.003
300	56332.1	90343.75	8.17102	69.374
290	57077.6	96638.98	8.72233	71.901
280	57847.6	103586.94	9.33235	74.603
270	58643.8	111284.01	10.00990	77.499
260	59468.4	119845.21	10.76555	80.612
250	60323.5	129408.74	11.61198	83.966
240	61211.9	140141.87	12.56457	87.593
230	62136.4	152248.60	13.64210	91.528
220	63100.3	165979.83	14.86772	95.813
210	64107.3	181646.96	16.27017	100.499
200	65161.7	199640.30	17.88555	105.644
190	66268.4	220454.54	19.75967	111.323
180	67433.3	244724.28	21.95137	117.622
170	68662.8	273274.63	24.53726	124.652
160	69965.1	307194.52	27.61859	132.549
150	71349.5	347945.28	31.33138	141.487
140	72827,6	397525.08	35.86189	151.688
130	74413.2	458725.09	41.47061	163.444
120	76123.7	535540.53	48.53081	177.143
110	77981.1	633854.08	57.59275	193.315
100	80013.6	762619.22	69.49482	212.701

Tables of the Primary Siacci Functions

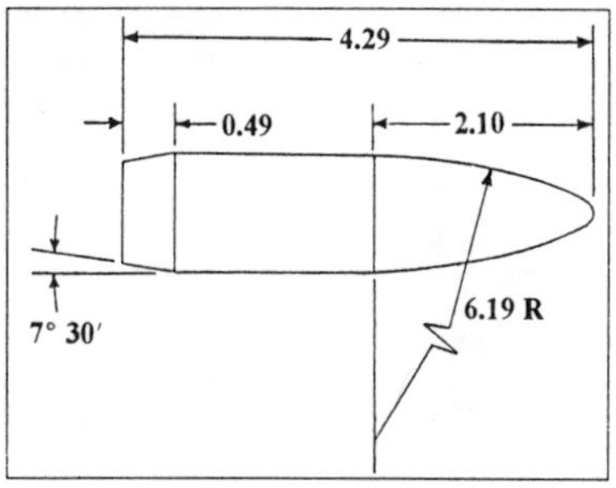

G_5 Drag Function

Quantity	Units
V	ft./sec.
S(V)	ft.-in.^{2}/lb.
A(V)	ft.-in.^{4}/lb.^{2}
I(V)	in.^{2}/lb.
T(V)	sec.-in.^{2}/lb.

V	S(V)	A(V)	I(V)	T(V)
4500	0.0	0.00	0.00000	0.000
4490	42.6	0.00	0.00014	0.009
4480	85.3	0.01	0.00027	0.019
4470	127.9	0.03	0.00041	0.029
4460	170.7	0.05	0.00055	0.038
4450	213.5	0.07	0.00069	0.048
4440	256.3	0.11	0.00083	0.057
4430	299.2	0.14	0.00097	0.067
4420	342.1	0.19	0.00111	0.077
4410	385.1	0.24	0.00125	0.086
4400	428.1	0.30	0.00139	0.096
4390	471.1	0.36	0.00153	0.106
4380	514.2	0.43	0.00168	0.116
4370	557.4	0.50	0.00182	0.126
4360	600.6	0.59	0.00197	0.136
4350	643.8	0.67	0.00212	0.146
4340	687.1	0.77	0.00226	0.155
4330	730.4	0.87	0.00241	0.165
4320	773.8	0.98	0.00256	0.175
4310	817.2	1.09	0.00271	0.186
4300	860.7	1.21	0.00286	0.196
4290	904.2	1.34	0.00301	0.206
4280	947.8	1.48	0.00317	0.216
4270	991.4	1.62	0.00332	0.226
4260	1035.0	1.76	0.00347	0.236
4250	1078.7	1.92	0.00363	0.247
4240	1122.5	2.08	0.00379	0.257
4230	1166.3	2.25	0.00394	0.267

V	S(V)	A(V)	I(V)	T(V)
4220	1210.1	2.43	0.00410	0.278
4210	1254.0	2.61	0.00426	0.288
4200	1298.0	2.80	0.00442	0.299
4190	1342.0	3.00	0.00458	0.309
4180	1386.0	3.20	0.00474	0.320
4170	1430.1	3.42	0.00490	0.330
4160	1474.2	3.64	0.00507	0.341
4150	1518.4	3.87	0.00523	0.351
4140	1562.6	4.10	0.00540	0.362
4130	1606.9	4.34	0.00556	0.373
4120	1651.2	4.59	0.00573	0.383
4110	1695.6	4.85	0.00590	0.394
4100	1740.0	5.12	0.00607	0.405
4090	1784.5	5.39	0.00624	0.416
4080	1829.0	5.67	0.00641	0.427
4070	1873.6	5.96	0.00658	0.438
4060	1918.2	6.26	0.00676	0.449
4050	1962.9	6.57	0.00693	0.460
4040	2007.6	6.88	0.00711	0.471
4030	2052.4	7.20	0.00729	0.482
4020	2097.2	7.53	0.00746	0.493
4010	2142.1	7.87	0.00764	0.504
4000	2187.0	8.22	0.00782	0.515
3990	2231.9	8.57	0.00800	0.527
3980	2277.0	8.94	0.00819	0.538
3970	2322.0	9.31	0.00837	0.549
3960	2367.1	9.69	0.00855	0.561
3950	2412.3	10.08	0.00874	0.572

V	S(V)	A(V)	I(V)	T(V)
3940	2457.5	10.48	0.00893	0.584
3930	2502.8	10.89	0.00912	0.595
3920	2548.1	11.31	0.00930	0.607
3910	2593.5	11.74	0.00949	0.618
3900	2638.9	12.17	0.00969	0.630
3890	2684.4	12.62	0.00988	0.642
3880	2729.9	13.07	0.01007	0.653
3870	2775.5	13.53	0.01027	0.665
3860	2821.1	14.01	0.01047	0.677
3850	2866.8	14.49	0.01066	0.689
3840	2912.6	14.98	0.01086	0.701
3830	2958.3	15.48	0.01106	0.713
3820	3004.2	16.00	0.01126	0.725
3810	3050.1	16.52	0.01147	0.737
3800	3096.0	17.05	0.01167	0.749
3790	3142.0	17.59	0.01188	0.761
3780	3188.1	18.14	0.01208	0.773
3770	3234.2	18.70	0.01229	0.785
3760	3280.3	19.28	0.01250	0.797
3750	3326.5	19.86	0.01271	0.810
3740	3372.8	20.45	0.01292	0.822
3730	3419.1	21.06	0.01314	0.834
3720	3465.5	21.67	0.01335	0.847
3710	3511.9	22.29	0.01357	0.859
3700	3558.4	22.93	0.01379	0.872
3690	3604.9	23.58	0.01400	0.885
3680	3651.5	24.23	0.01423	0.897
3670	3698.1	24.90	0.01445	0.910
3660	3744.8	25.58	0.01467	0.923
3650	3791.6	26.27	0.01490	0.935
3640	3838.4	26.98	0.01512	0.948
3630	3885.2	27.69	0.01535	0.961
3620	3932.1	28.42	0.01558	0.974
3610	3979.1	29.15	0.01581	0.987
3600	4026.1	29.90	0.01604	1.000
3590	4073.2	30.66	0.01628	1.013
3580	4120.4	31.44	0.01651	1.026
3570	4167.5	32.22	0.01675	1.040
3560	4214.8	33.02	0.01699	1.053
3550	4262.1	33.83	0.01723	1.066
3540	4309.5	34.65	0.01747	1.079
3530	4356.9	35.48	0.01772	1.093
3520	4404.3	36.33	0.01796	1.106
3510	4451.9	37.19	0.01821	1.120
3500	4499.5	38.06	0.01846	1.133
3490	4547.1	38.95	0.01871	1.147

V	S(V)	A(V)	I(V)	T(V)
3480	4594.8	39.85	0.01896	1.161
3470	4642.6	40.76	0.01922	1.174
3460	4690.4	41.68	0.01947	1.188
3450	4738.2	42.62	0.01973	1.202
3440	4786.2	43.57	0.01999	1.216
3430	4834.2	44.54	0.02025	1.230
3420	4882.2	45.52	0.02052	1.244
3410	4930.3	46.51	0.02078	1.258
3400	4978.5	47.52	0.02105	1.272
3390	5026.7	48.54	0.02132	1.286
3380	5075.0	49.58	0.02159	1.301
3370	5123.3	50.63	0.02186	1.315
3360	5171.7	51.69	0.02214	1.329
3350	5220.2	52.77	0.02242	1.344
3340	5268.7	53.87	0.02269	1.358
3330	5317.3	54.98	0.02297	1.373
3320	5365.9	56.10	0.02326	1.388
3310	5414.6	57.24	0.02354	1.402
3300	5463.4	58.39	0.02383	1.417
3290	5512.2	59.56	0.02412	1.432
3280	5561.1	60.75	0.02441	1.447
3270	5610.0	61.95	0.02470	1.462
3260	5659.0	63.17	0.02500	1.477
3250	5708.1	64.40	0.02530	1.492
3240	5757.2	65.65	0.02560	1.507
3230	5806.4	66.92	0.02590	1.522
3220	5855.6	68.20	0.02620	1.537
3210	5904.9	69.50	0.02651	1.553
3200	5954.3	70.82	0.02682	1.568
3190	6003.7	72.15	0.02713	1.584
3180	6053.2	73.50	0.02745	1.599
3170	6102.8	74.87	0.02776	1.615
3160	6152.4	76.26	0.02808	1.630
3150	6202.1	77.66	0.02840	1.646
3140	6251.8	79.08	0.02873	1.662
3130	6301.6	80.52	0.02905	1.678
3120	6351.5	81.98	0.02938	1.694
3110	6401.4	83.45	0.02971	1.710
3100	6451.4	84.95	0.03004	1.726
3090	6501.5	86.46	0.03038	1.742
3080	6551.6	87.99	0.03072	1.758
3070	6601.8	89.54	0.03106	1.775
3060	6652.1	91.11	0.03140	1.791
3050	6702.4	92.70	0.03175	1.808
3040	6752.8	94.31	0.03210	1.824
3030	6803.3	95.94	0.03245	1.841

V	S(V)	A(V)	I(V)	T(V)
3020	6853.8	97.58	0.03281	1.857
3010	6904.4	99.25	0.03317	1.874
3000	6955.0	100.94	0.03353	1.891
2990	7005.7	102.65	0.03389	1.908
2980	7056.5	104.38	0.03426	1.925
2970	7107.3	106.13	0.03463	1.942
2960	7158.3	107.91	0.03500	1.959
2950	7209.2	109.70	0.03537	1.977
2940	7260.3	111.51	0.03575	1.994
2930	7311.4	113.35	0.03614	2.011
2920	7362.6	115.21	0.03652	2.029
2910	7413.8	117.09	0.03691	2.046
2900	7465.1	119.00	0.03730	2.064
2890	7516.5	120.92	0.03769	2.082
2880	7568.0	122.87	0.03809	2.100
2870	7619.5	124.85	0.03849	2.118
2860	7671.1	126.84	0.03890	2.136
2850	7722.8	128.86	0.03930	2.154
2840	7774.5	130.91	0.03971	2.172
2830	7826.3	132.97	0.04013	2.190
2820	7878.2	135.07	0.04055	2.208
2810	7930.1	137.18	0.04097	2.227
2800	7982.1	139.33	0.04139	2.245
2790	8034.2	141.49	0.04182	2.264
2780	8086.3	143.69	0.04226	2.283
2770	8138.6	145.90	0.04269	2.302
2760	8190.9	148.15	0.04313	2.321
2750	8243.2	150.42	0.04358	2.340
2740	8295.7	152.71	0.04402	2.359
2730	8348.2	155.04	0.04447	2.378
2720	8400.8	157.39	0.04493	2.397
2710	8453.4	159.77	0.04539	2.417
2700	8506.2	162.17	0.04585	2.436
2690	8559.0	164.61	0.04632	2.456
2680	8611.8	167.07	0.04679	2.475
2670	8664.8	169.56	0.04727	2.495
2660	8717.8	172.08	0.04775	2.515
2650	8770.9	174.62	0.04823	2.535
2640	8824. 1	177.20	0.04872	2.555
2630	8877.3	179.81	0.04922	2.575
2620	8930.6	182.45	0.04971	2.596
2610	8984.0	185.11	0.05022	2.616
2600	9037.5	187.81	0.05072	2.637
2590	9091.0	190.54	0.05123	2.657
2580	9144.7	193.30	0.05175	2.678
2570	9198.4	196.10	0.05227	2.699

V	S(V)	A(V)	I(V)	T(V)
2560	9252.1	198.92	0.05280	2.720
2550	9306.0	201.78	0.05333	2.741
2540	9359.9	204.67	0.05386	2.762
2530	9413.9	207.59	0.05440	2.783
2520	9468.0	210.55	0.05495	2.805
2510	9522.1	213.54	0.05550	2.826
2500	9576.4	216.56	0.05605	2.848
2490	9630.7	219.62	0.05662	2.870
2480	9685.1	222.72	0.05718	2.892
2470	9739.6	225.85	0.05775	2.914
2460	9794.1	229.01	0.05833	2.936
2450	9848.7	232.22	0.05891	2.958
2440	9903.4	235.46	0.05950	2.980
2430	9958.2	238.73	0.06010	3.003
2420	10013.1	242.05	0.06070	3.025
2410	10068.1	245.40	0.06130	3.048
2400	10123.1	248.79	0.06192	3.071
2390	10178.2	252.22	0.06253	3.094
2380	10233.4	255.69	0.06316	3.117
2370	10288.7	259.20	0.06379	3.141
2360	10344.0	262.75	0.06443	3.164
2350	10399.5	266.34	0.06507	3.188
2340	10455.0	269.97	0.06572	3.211
2330	10510.6	273.64	0.06637	3.235
2320	10566.3	277.36	0.06704	3.259
2310	10622.1	281.11	0.06771	3.283
2300	10678.0	284.91	0.06838	3.307
2290	10733.9	288.76	0.06907	3.332
2280	10789.9	292.65	0.06976	3.356
2270	10846.1	296.58	0.07045	3.381
2260	10902.3	300.56	0.07116	3.406
2250	10958.6	304.59	0.07187	3.431
2240	11014.9	308.66	0.07259	3.456
2230	11071.4	312.78	0.07332	3.481
2220	11128.0	316.95	0.07405	3.506
2210	11184.6	321.16	0.07479	3.532
2200	11241.3	325.43	0.07554	3.558
2190	11298.1	329.74	0.07630	3.584
2180	11355.1	334.10	0.07707	3.610
2170	11412.1	338.52	0.07784	3.636
2160	11469.1	342.99	0.07863	3.662
2150	11526.3	347.51	0.07942	3.689
2140	11583.6	352.08	0.08022	3.715
2130	11641.0	356.70	0.08103	3.742
2120	11698.5	361.39	0.08185	3.769
2110	11756.1	366.12	0.08268	3.797

V	S(V)	A(V)	I(V)	T(V)
2100	11813.8	370.92	0.08352	3.824
2090	11871.6	375.77	0.08436	3.852
2080	11929.5	380.68	0.08522	3.879
2070	11987.5	385.65	0.08609	3.907
2060	12045.7	390.68	0.08696	3.936
2050	12103.9	395.77	0.08785	3.964
2040	12162.3	400.93	0.08875	3.992
2030	12220.8	406.14	0.08966	4.021
2020	12279.4	411.43	0.09058	4.050
2010	12338.2	416.78	0.09151	4.079
2000	12397.1	422.19	0.09245	4.109
1990	12456.1	427.68	0.09340	4.138
1980	12515.3	433.23	0.09437	4.168
1970	12574.6	438.86	0.09535	4.198
1960	12634.0	444.56	0.09634	4.228
1950	12693.7	450.33	0.09734	4.259
1940	12753.5	456.18	0.09836	4.290
1930	12813.4	462.11	0.09939	4.321
1920	12873.5	468.12	0.10043	4.352
1910	12933.8	474.21	0.10149	4.383
1900	12994.3	480.38	0.10256	4.415
1890	13055.0	486.63	0.10365	4.447
1880	13115.8	492.97	0.10475	4.479
1870	13176.9	499.40	0.10587	4.512
1860	13238.1	505.92	0.10700	4.545
1850	13299.6	512.53	0.10815	4.578
1840	13361.3	519.24	0.10931	4.611
1830	13423.2	526.04	0.11050	4.645
1820	13485.3	532.94	0.11170	4.679
1810	13547.7	539.95	0.11291	4.713
1800	13610.3	547.05	0.11415	4.748
1790	13673.1	554.27	0.11540	4.783
1780	13736.2	561.59	0.11668	4.819
1770	13799.6	569.03	0.11797	4.854
1760	13863.2	576.58	0.11929	4.890
1750	13927.2	584.24	0.12062	4.927
1740	13991.4	592.03	0.12198	4.963
1730	14055.8	599.94	0.12335	5.001
1720	14120.6	607.98	0.12475	5.038
1710	14185.7	616.14	0.12618	5.076
1700	14251.1	624.44	0.12762	5.115
1690	14316.9	632.88	0.12910	5.153
1680	14382.9	641.46	0.13059	5.193
1670	14449.3	650.18	0.13212	5.232
1660	14516.1	659.05	0.13366	5.272
1650	14583.2	668.08	0.13524	5.313

V	S(V)	A(V)	I(V)	T(V)
1640	14650.7	677.26	0.13684	5.354
1630	14718.5	686.60	0.13848	5.395
1620	14786.8	696.10	0.14014	5.437
1610	14855.4	705.78	0.14183	5.480
1600	14924.5	715.64	0.14356	5.523
1590	14993.9	725.67	0.14531	5.566
1580	15063.8	735.89	0.14710	5.611
1570	15134.2	746.30	0.14893	5.655
1560	15205.0	756.90	0.15078	5.700
1550	15276.2	767.71	0.15268	5.746
1540	15347.9	778.73	0.15461	5.793
1530	15420.1	789.96	0.15658	5.840
1520	15492.7	801.41	0.15859	5.887
1510	15565.9	813.09	0.16064	5.936
1500	15639.6	825.00	0.16273	5.985
1490	15713.8	837.16	0.16487	6.034
1480	15788.5	849.56	0.16705	6.084
1470	15863.8	862.21	0.16927	6.135
1460	15939.6	875.13	0.17155	6.187
1450	16016.0	888.32	0.17387	6.240
1440	16092.9	901.80	0.17624	6.293
1430	16170.5	915.56	0.17866	6.347
1420	16248.6	929.62	0.18114	6.402
1410	16327.4	943.99	0.18367	6.458
1400	16406.8	958.67	0.18625	6.514
1390	16486.9	973.69	0.18890	6.571
1380	16567.6	989.05	0.19161	6.630
1370	16649.1	1004.77	0.19438	6.689
1360	16731.2	1020.85	0.19721	6.749
1350	16814.1	1037.32	0.20012	6.810
1340	16897.7	1054.18	0.20309	6.873
1330	16982.2	1071.46	0.20614	6.936
1320	17067.4	1089.17	0.20926	7.000
1310	17153.5	1107.33	0.21247	7.066
1300	17240.6	1125.95	0.21575	7.132
1290	17328.5	1145.07	0.21913	7.200
1280	17417.4	1164.71	0.22259	7.269
1270	17507.2	1184.87	0.22614	7.340
1260	17598.1	1205.58	0.22980	7.412
1250	17690.0	1226.87	0.23355	7.485
1240	17782.9	1248.75	0.23740	7.560
1230	17876.9	1271.25	0.24137	7.636
1220	17972.0	1294.39	0.24544	7.713
1210	18068.3	1318.23	0.24964	7.793
1200	18165.9	1342.81	0.25397	7.874
1190	18265.1	1368.22	0.25843	7.957

V	S(V)	A(V)	I(V)	T(V)
1180	18366.1	1394.55	0.26306	8.042
1170	18469.3	1421.96	0.26787	8.130
1160	18575.4	1450.63	0.27289	8.221
1150	18684.9	1480.81	0.27818	8.316
1140	18798.8	1512.80	0.28376	8.415
1130	18917.9	1546.97	0.28971	8.520
1120	19043.5	1583.74	0.29609	8.632
1110	19176.6	1623.62	0.30298	8.751
1100	19318.5	1667.15	0.31046	8.879
1090	19470.6	1714.97	0.31862	9.018
1080	19633.9	1767.74	0.32754	9.169
1070	19809.7	1826.16	0.33733	9.332
1060	19998.8	1890.96	0.34805	9.510
1050	20201.8	1962.82	0.35979	9.702
1040	20419.1	2042.38	0.37259	9.910
1030	20650.5	2130.22	0.38648	10.134
1020	20895.7	2226.81	0.40150	10.373
1010	21154.0	2332.58	0.41762	10.628
1000	21424.6	2447.90	0.43485	10.897
990	21706.7	2573.15	0.45318	11.180
980	21999.5	2708.70	0.47260	11.478
970	22302.5	2854.96	0.49310	11.788
960	22614.9	3012.37	0.51468	12.112
950	22936.2	3181.40	0.53734	12.449
940	23266.1	3362.58	0.56111	12.798
930	23604.2	3556.43	0.58598	13.159
920	23949.9	3763.51	0.61197	13.533
910	24303.0	3984.36	0.63910	13.919
900	24663.1	4219.55	0.66738	14.317
890	25029.7	4469.61	0.69682	14.727
880	25402.6	4735.11	0.72744	15.148
870	25781.3	5016.62	0.75926	15.581
860	26165.6	5314.72	0.79230	16.025
850	26555.1	5630.02	0.82657	16.481
840	26949.8	5963.19	0.86212	16.948
830	27349.3	6314.94	0.89898	17.426
820	27753.5	6686.01	0.93718	17.916
810	28162.3	7077.23	0.97677	18.418
800	28575.7	7489.45	1.01781	18.931
790	28993.6	7923.61	1.06034	19.457
780	29415.9	8380.68	1.10442	19.995
770	29842.6	8861.72	1.15012	20.546
760	30273.9	9367.85	1.19752	21.109
750	30709.6	9900.27	1.24669	21.686
740	31149.8	10460.24	1.29770	22.277
730	31594.5	11049.12	1.35066	22.882

V	S(V)	A(V)	I(V)	T(V)
720	32043.9	11668.35	1.40565	23.502
710	32497.9	12319.47	1.46278	24.137
700	32956.7	13004.12	1.52215	24.788
690	33420.3	13724.03	1.58389	25.455
680	33888.8	14481.10	1.64812	26.139
670	34362.4	15277.31	1.71498	26.841
660	34841.0	16114.81	1.78460	27.561
650	35325.0	16995.92	1.85716	28.299
640	35814.3	17923.13	1.93283	29.058
630	36309.2	18899.13	2.01178	29.837
620	36809.9	19926.84	2.09422	30.639
610	37316.4	21009.44	2.18038	31.462
600	37829.2	22150.37	2.27049	32.310
590	38348.3	23353.40	2.36481	33.182
580	38874.1	24622.62	2.46365	34.081
570	39406.8	25962.52	2.56729	35.008
560	39946.8	27377.98	2.67610	35.963
550	40494.3	28874.35	2.79045	36.950
540	41049.8	30457.45	2.91074	37.969
530	41613.4	32133.68	3.03743	39.023
520	42185.8	33910.02	3.17100	40.113
510	42767.1	35794.13	3.31200	41.242
500	43357.8	37794.39	3.46102	42.412
490	43958.4	39920.02	3.61870	43.625
480	44569.3	42181.19	3.78576	44.885
470	45190.9	44589.11	3.96299	46.193
460	45823.7	47156.18	4.15127	47.554
450	46468.3	49896.19	4.35158	48.971
440	47125.2	52824.52	4.56500	50.448
430	47795.1	55958.33	4.79276	51.988
420	48478.7	59316.90	5.03622	53.596
410	49176.6	62921.91	5.29692	55.278
400	49889.6	66797.82	5.57660	57.039
390	50618.7	70972.34	5.87724	58.885
380	51364.8	75476.91	6.20107	60.823
370	52128.9	80347.29	6.55064	62.861
360	52912.0	85624.34	6.92887	65.007
350	53715.5	91354.89	7.33908	67.270
340	54540.6	97592.77	7.78512	69.662
330	55388.8	104400.19	8.27142	72.194
320	56261.7	111849.33	8.80313	74.881
310	57160.8	120024.30	9.38624	77.736
300	58088.3	129023.66	10.02778	80.777
290	59046.0	138963.39	10.73600	84.024
280	60036.5	149980.78	11.52070	87.500
270	61062.1	162239.17	12.39351	91.231

V	S(V)	A(V)	I(V)	T(V)
260	62125.8	175934.14	13.36835	95.245
250	63230.8	191301.34	14.46198	99.580
240	64380.4	208626.75	15.69476	104.273
230	65578.8	228260.04	17.09155	109.374
220	66830.4	250632.41	18.68300	114.939
210	68140.2	276280.38	20.50723	121.033
200	69514.1	305878.26	22.61213	127.738
190	70958.8	340282.87	25.05855	135.150

V	S(V)	A(V)	I(V)	T(V)
180	72482.0	380596.13	27.92468	143.388
170	74092.9	428254.33	31.31242	152.597
160	75802.0	485157.66	35.35651	162.962
150	77622.2	553862.18	40.23816	174.714
140	79569.0	637871.42	46.20558	188.150
130	81661.2	742091.01	53.60620	203.662
120	83922.1	873559.38	62.93824	221.769
110	86381.3	1042664.68	74.93663	243.181
100	89076.8	1265254.84	90.72194	268.891

Tables of the Primary Siacci Functions

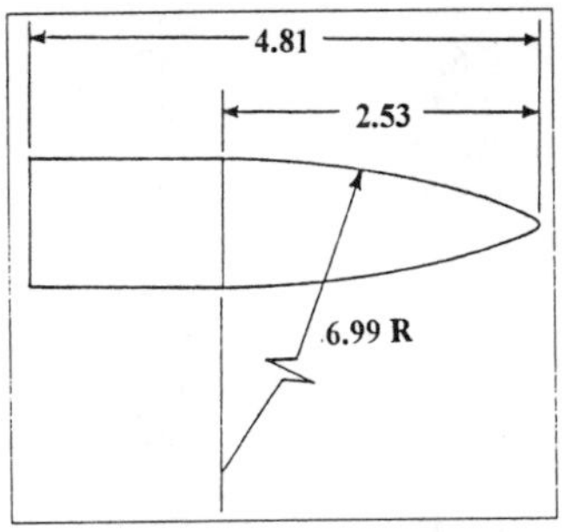

G_6 Drag Function

Quantity	Units
V	ft./sec.
S(V)	ft.-in.^{2}/lb.
A(V)	ft.-in.^{4}/lb.^{2}
I(V)	in.^{2}/lb.
T(V)	sec.-in.^{2}/lb.

V	S(V)	A(V)	~~T(V)~~ I(V)	T(V)
4500	0.0	0.00	0.00000	0.000
4490	58.3	0.01	0.00019	0.013
4480	116.7	0.02	0.00037	0.026
4470	175.1	0.05	0.00056	0.039
4460	233.5	0.09	0.00075	0.052
4450	292.0	0.14	0.00094	0.065
4440	350.4	0.20	0.00113	0.078
4430	408.9	0.27	0.00132	0.092
4420	467.4	0.35	0.00151	0.105
4410	525.9	0.45	0.00170	0.118
4400	584.5	0.55	0.00190	0.131
4390	643.1	0.67	0.00209	0.145
4380	701.7	0.80	0.00229	0.158
4370	760.3	0.94	0.00249	0.171
4360	819.0	1.09	0.00268	0.185
4350	877.6	1.25	0.00288	0.198
4340	936.3	1.43	0.00308	0.212

V	S(V)	A(V)	~~T(V)~~ I(V)	T(V)
4330	995.1	1.61	0.00328	0.225
4320	1053.8	1.81	0.00349	0.239
4310	1112.6	2.02	0.00369	0.253
4300	1171.4	2.25	0.00389	0.266
4290	1230.2	2.48	0.00410	0.280
4280	1289.0	2.73	0.00431	0.294
4270	1347.9	2.99	0.00451	0.307
4260	1406.7	3.26	0.00472	0.321
4250	1465.6	3.54	0.00493	0.335
4240	1524.6	3.84	0.00514	0.349
4230	1583.5	4.15	0.00535	0.363
4220	1642.5	4.47	0.00556	0.377
4210	1701.5	4.81	0.00578	0.391
4200	1760.5	5.15	0.00599	0.405
4190	1819.5	5.51	0.00621	0.419
4180	1878.6	5.89	0.00642	0.433
4170	1937.6	6.27	0.00664	0.447
4160	1996.7	6.67	0.00686	0.461

V	S(V)	A(V)	I(V) ~~T(V)~~	T(V)
4150	2055.9	7.08	0.00708	0.476
4140	2115.0	7.51	0.00730	0.490
4130	2174.2	7.95	0.00753	0.504
4120	2233.3	8.40	0.00775	0.519
4110	2292.5	8.86	0.00797	0.533
4100	2351.8	9.34	0.00820	0.547
4090	2411.0	9.84	0.00843	0.562
4080	2470.2	10.34	0.00866	0.576
4070	2529.5	10.86	0.00889	0.591
4060	2588.8	11.40	0.00912	0.605
4050	2648.1	11.94	0.00935	0.620
4040	2707.5	12.51	0.00958	0.635
4030	2766.8	13.08	0.00982	0.649
4020	2826.2	13.67	0.01005	0.664
4010	2885.6	14.27	0.01029	0.679
4000	2945.0	14.89	0.01053	0.694
3990	3004.4	15.53	0.01077	0.709
3980	3063.9	16.17	0.01101	0.724
3970	3123.4	16.84	0.01125	0.739
3960	3182.9	17.51	0.01149	0.754
3950	3242.4	18.20	0.01174	0.769
3940	3301.9	18.91	0.01198	0.784
3930	3361.5	19.63	0.01223	0.799
3920	3421.0	20.37	0.01248	0.814
3910	3480.6	21.12	0.01273	0.829
3900	3540.2	21.88	0.01298	0.845
3890	3599.9	22.67	0.01323	0.860
3880	3659.5	23.46	0.01349	0.875
3870	3719.2	24.27	0.01374	0.891
3860	3778.8	25.10	0.01400	0.906
3850	3838.5	25.95	0.01426	0.922
3840	3898.3	26.81	0.01452	0.937
3830	3958.0	27.68	0.01478	0.953
3820	4017.7	28.57	0.01504	0.968
3810	4077.5	29.48	0.01531	0.984
3800	4137.3	30.40	0.01557	1.000
3790	4197.1	31.34	0.01584	1.015
3780	4256.9	32.30	0.01611	1.031
3770	4316.8	33.27	0.01638	1.047
3760	4376.6	34.26	0.01665	1.063
3750	4436.5	35.26	0.01692	1.079
3740	4496.4	36.28	0.01720	1.095
3730	4556.3	37.32	0.01747	1.111
3720	4616.2	38.38	0.01775	1.127
3710	4676.1	39.45	0.01803	1.143
3700	4736.1	40.54	0.01831	1.159

V	S(V)	A(V)	I(V) ~~T(V)~~	T(V)
3690	4796.0	41.65	0.01859	1.176
3680	4856.0	42.77	0.01888	1.192
3670	4916.0	43.91	0.01916	1.208
3660	4976.0	45.07	0.01945	1.225
3650	5036.0	46.24	0.01974	1.241
3640	5096.0	47.44	0.02003	1.257
3630	5156.1	48.65	0.02032	1.274
3620	5216.1	49.88	0.02062	1.291
3610	5276.2	51.13	0.02091	1.307
3600	5336.3	52.39	0.02121	1.324
3590	5396.3	53.67	0.02151	1.341
3580	5456.5	54.98	0.02181	1.357
3570	5516.6	56.30	0.02211	1.374
3560	5576.7	57.64	0.02242	1.391
3550	5636.8	58.99	0.02272	1.408
3540	5697.0	60.37	0.02303	1.425
3530	5757.2	61.76	0.02334	1.442
3520	5817.4	63.18	0.02365	1.459
3510	5877.5	64.61	0.02397	1.476
3500	5937.8	66.06	0.02428	1.493
3490	5998.0	67.54	0.02460	1.510
3480	6058.2	69.03	0.02492	1.528
3470	6118.4	70.54	0.02524	1.545
3460	6178.7	72.07	0.02556	1.562
3450	6238.9	73.62	0.02589	1.580
3440	6299.2	75.19	0.02621	1.597
3430	6359.5	76.78	0.02654	1.615
3420	6419.8	78.39	0.02687	1.633
3410	6480.0	80.02	0.02720	1.650
3400	6540.4	81.67	0.02754	1.668
3390	6600.7	83.34	0.02787	1.686
3380	6661.0	85.03	0.02821	1.704
3370	6721.3	86.74	0.02855	1.721
3360	6781.6	88.48	0.02890	1.739
3350	6842.0	90.23	0.02924	1.757
3340	6902.3	92.00	0.02959	1.775
3330	6962.7	93.80	0.02994	1.793
3320	7023.1	95.62	0.03029	1.812
3310	7083.5	97.46	0.03064	1.830
3300	7143.8	99.32	0.03100	1.848
3290	7204.2	101.20	0.03136	1.866
3280	7264.6	103.11	0.03172	1.885
3270	7325.0	105.03	0.03208	1.903
3260	7385.4	106.98	0.03244	1.922
3250	7445.8	108.95	0.03281	1.940
3240	7506.3	110.95	0.03318	1.959

V	S(V)	A(V)	I(V) ~~T(V)~~	T(V)
3230	7566.7	112.96	0.03355	1.978
3220	7627.1	115.00	0.03392	1.996
3210	7687.5	117.06	0.03430	2.015
3200	7748.0	119.15	0.03468	2.034
3190	7808.4	121.25	0.03506	2.053
3180	7868.8	123.38	0.03544	2.072
3170	7929.3	125.54	0.03583	2.091
3160	7989.7	127.71	0.03621	2.110
3150	8050.2	129.92	0.03661	2.129
3140	8110.6	132.14	0.03700	2.148
3130	8171.1	134.39	0.03739	2.168
3120	8231.6	136.66	0.03779	2.187
3110	8292.0	138.96	0.03819	2.206
3100	8352.5	141.28	0.03860	2.226
3090	8413.0	143.63	0.03900	2.245
3080	8473.5	146.00	0.03941	2.265
3070	8533.9	148.40	0.03982	2.285
3060	8594.4	150.82	0.04024	2.304
3050	8654.9	153.26	0.04065	2.324
3040	8715.4	155.73	0.04107	2.344
3030	8775.8	158.23	0.04150	2.364
3020	8836.3	160.75	0.04192	2.384
3010	8896.8	163.30	0.04235	2.404
3000	8957.3	165.88	0.04278	2.424
2990	9017.7	168.48	0.04321	2.444
2980	9078.2	171.10	0.04365	2.465
2970	9138.7	173.75	0.04409	2.485
2960	9199.1	176.43	0.04453	2.505
2950	9259.6	179.14	0.04498	2.526
2940	9320.1	181.87	0.04543	2.546
2930	9380.5	184.63	0.04588	2.567
2920	9441.0	187.42	0.04633	2.588
2910	9501.5	190.24	0.04679	2.608
2900	9561.9	193.08	0.04725	2.629
2890	9622.4	195.95	0.04771	2.650
2880	9682.8	198.85	0.04818	2.671
2870	9743.3	201.78	0.04865	2.692
2860	9803.8	204.73	0.04913	2.713
2850	9864.2	207.72	0.04960	2.734
2840	9924.7	210.73	0.05008	2.756
2830	9985.1	213.77	0.05057	2.777
2820	10045.6	216.84	0.05105	2.798
2810	10106.0	219.94	0.05154	2.820
2800	10166.5	223.08	0.05204	2.841
2790	10227.0	226.24	0.05254	2.863
2780	10287.4	229.43	0.05304	2.885

V	S(V)	A(V)	I(V) ~~T(V)~~	T(V)
2770	10347.9	232.65	0.05354	2.906
2760	10408.3	235.90	0.05405	2.928
2750	10468.8	239.19	0.05456	2.950
2740	10529.3	242.50	0.05508	2.972
2730	10589.8	245.85	0.05560	2.994
2720	10650.3	249.23	0.05612	3.017
2710	10710.8	252.64	0.05665	3.039
2700	10771.3	256.08	0.05718	3.061
2690	10831.8	259.56	0.05772	3.084
2680	10892.3	263.07	0.05826	3.106
2670	10952.8	266.61	0.05880	3.129
2660	11013.4	270.19	0.05935	3.152
2650	11073.9	273.80	0.05990	3.174
2640	11134.5	277.45	0.06046	3.197
2630	11195.1	281.12	0.06102	3.220
2620	11255.7	284.84	0.06159	3.243
2610	11316.3	288.59	0.06216	3.267
2600	11376.9	292.38	0.06273	3.290
2590	11437.5	296.20	0.06331	3.313
2580	11498,2	300.06	0.06390	3.337
2570	11558.9	303.95	0.06449	3.360
2560	11619.6	307.88	0.06508	3.384
2550	11680.3	311.85	0.06568	3.408
2540	11741.1	315.86	0.06628	3.432
2530	11801.8	319.91	0.06689	3.456
2520	11862.6	323.99	0.06750	3.480
2510	11923.4	328.12	0.06812	3.504
2500	11984.3	332.28	0.06874	3.528
2490	12045.1	336.48	0.06937	3.552
2480	12106.0	340.73	0.07001	3.577
2470	12167.0	345.01	0.07065	3.602
2460	12227.9	349.34	0.07129	3.626
2450	12288.9	353.70	0.07194	3.651
2440	12349.9	358.11	0.07260	3.676
2430	12411.0	362.57	0.07326	3.701
2420	12472.0	367.06	0.07393	3.726
2410	12533.2	371.60	0.07460	3.752
2400	12594.3	376.18	0.07528	3.777
2390	12655.5	380.81	0.07597	3.803
2380	12716.8	385.49	0.07666	3.828
2370	12778.0	390.20	0.07736	3.854
2360	12839.3	394.97	0.07807	3.880
2350	12900.7	399.78	0.07878	3.906
2340	12962.1	404.64	0.07950	3.932
2330	13023.6	409.55	0.08022	3.959
2320	13085.1	414.51	0.08095	3.985

V	S(V)	A(V)	I(V) ~~T(V)~~	T(V)
2310	13146.6	419.51	0.08169	4.012
2300	13208.2	424.57	0.08244	4.038
2290	13269.9	429.67	0.08319	4.065
2280	13331.6	434.83	0.08395	4.092
2270	13393.4	440.04	0.08472	4.119
2260	13455.2	445.30	0.08549	4.147
2250	13517.1	450.62	0.08628	4.174
2240	13579.1	455.99	0.08707	4.202
2230	13641.1	461.41	0.08787	4.230
2220	13703.2	466.90	0.08867	4.257
2210	13765.4	472.43	0.08949	4.286
2200	13827.6	478.03	0.09031	4.314
2190	13889.9	483.68	0.09114	4.3,42
2180	13952.2	489.39	0.09198	4.371
2170	14014.7	495.16	0.09283	4.399
2160	14077.2	500.99	0.09369	4.428
2150	14139.8	506.88	0.09456	4.457
2140	14202.4	512.83	0.09543	4.486
2130	14265.2	518.84	0.09632	4.516
2120	14328.0	524.92	0.09721	4.545
2110	14390.9	531.07	0.09812	4.575
2100	14453.9	537.28	0.09903	4.605
2090	14517.0	543.55	0.09996	4.635
2080	14580.2	549.90	0.10089	4.666
2070	14643.4	556.31	0.10184	4.696
2060	14706.8	562.80	0.10279	4.727
2050	14770.3	569.35	0.10376	4.758
2040	14833.9	575.98	0.10474	4.789
2030	14897.5	582.68	0.10573	4.820
2020	14961.3	589.46	0.10673	4.851
2010	15025.2	596.31	0.10774	4.883
2000	15089.3	603.24	0.10876	4.915
1990	15153.4	610.25	0.10980	4.947
1980	15217.7	617.34	0.11085	4.980
1970	15282.1	624.52	0.11191	5.012
1960	15346.6	631.77	0.11299	5.045
1950	15411.3	639.11	0.11407	5.078
1940	15476.1	646.54	0.11518	5.112
1930	15541.0	654.06	0.11629	5.145
1920	15606.1	661.66	0.11742	5.179
1910	15671.4	669.36	0.11857	5.213
1900	15736.8	677.15	0.11972	5.247
1890	15802.3	685.04	0.12090	5.282
1880	15868.0	693.02	0.12209	5.317
1870	15933.9	701.11	0.12329	5.352
1860	16000.0	709.29	0.12451	5.387

V	S(V)	A(V)	I(V) ~~T(V)~~	T(V)
1850	16066.2	717.57	0.12575	5.423
1840	16132.6	725.96	0.12701	5.459
1830	16199.1	734.46	0.12828	5.495
1820	16265.9	743.07	0.12957	5.532
1810	16332.8	751.78	0.13087	5.569
1800	16399.9	760.61	0.13220	5.606
1790	16467.2	769.56	0.13354	5.643
1780	16534.8	778.62	0.13491	5.681
1770	16602.5	787.80	0.13629	5.719
1760	16670.4	797.10	0.13769	5.758
1750	16738.5	806.53	0.13911	5.797
1740	16806.9	816.09	0.14056	5.836
1730	16875.4	825.77	0.14202	5.875
1720	16944.2	835.59	0.14351	5.915
1710	17013.2	845.54	0.14502	5.955
1700	17082.4	855.63	0.14655	5.996
1690	17151.8	865.87	0.14810	6.037
1680	17221.5	876.24	0.14968	6.078
1670	17291.5	886.76	0.15129	6.120
1660	17361.6	897.44	0.15291	6.162
1650	17432.0	908.26	0.15457	6.205
1640	17502.7	919.24	0.15625	6.248
1630	17573.6	930.39	0.15795	6.291
1620	17644.8	941.69	0.15969	6.335
1610	17716.2	953.16	0.16145	6.379
1600	17787.9	964.80	0.16324	6.424
1590	17859.9	976.62	0.16506	6.469
1580	17932.2	988.61	0.16691	6.515
1570	18004.7	1000.79	0.16879	6.561
1560	18077.6	1013.15	0.17070	6.607
1550	18150.7	1025.71	0.17265	6.654
1540	18224.1	1038.46	0.17463	6.702
1530	18297.8	1051.40	0.17664	6.750
1520	18371.9	1064.56	0.17869	6.798
1510	18446.2	1077.92	0.18077	6.847
1500	18520.9	1091.50	0.18289	6.897
1490	18595.9	1105.30	0.18505	6.947
1480	18671.3	1119.32	0.18725	6.998
1470	18747.0	1133.58	0.18949	7.049
1460	18823.0	1148.08	0.19176	7.101
1450	18899.4	1162.82	0.19409	7.154
1440	18976.2	1177.80	0.19645	7.207
1430	19053.3	1193.05	0.19886	7.260
1420	19130.8	1208.56	0.20131	7.315
1410	19208.7	1224.34	0.20382	7.370
1400	19287.0	1240.40	0.20637	7.426

V	S(V)	A(V)	~~T(V)~~ I(v)	T(V)
1390	19365.7	1256.74	0.20897	7.482
1380	19444.9	1273.38	0.21162	7.539
1370	19524.4	1290.33	0.21433	7.597
1360	19604.4	1307.59	0.21709	7.656
1350	19684.9	1325.17	0.21991	7.715
1340	19765.9	1343.10	0.22279	7.775
1330	19847.4	1361.37	0.22573	7.836
1320	19929.4	1380.01	0.22874	7.898
1310	20012.0	1399.02	0.23181	7.961
1300	20095.1	1418.43	0.23495	8.025
1290	20179.0	1438.26	0.23816	8.090
1280	20263.4	1458.51	0.24145	8.155
1270	20348.6	1479.22	0.24482	8.222
1260	20434.5	1500.40	0.24828	8.290
1250	20521.2	1522.08	0.25182	8.359
1240	20608.7	1544.28	0.25545	8.429
1230	20697.2	1567.04	0.25918	8.501
1220	20786.6	1590.40	0.26302	8.574
1210	20877.3	1614.41	0.26696	8.649
1200	20969.2	1639.15	0.27104	8.725
1190	21062.8	1664.71	0.27525	8.803
1180	21158.2	1691.18	0.27962	8.884
1170	21255.9	1718.73	0.28418	8.967
1160	21356.4	1747.52	0.28894	9.053
1150	21460.2	1777.78	0.29395	9.143
1140	21568.1	1809.77	0.29924	9.237
1130	216BO.7	1843.78	0.30486	9.336
1120	21798.9	1880.17	0.31087	9.442
1110	21923.6	1919.32	0.31732	9.553
1100	22055.5	1961.64	0.32427	9.673
1090	22195.5	2007.56	0.33178	9.801
1080	22344.2	2057.49	0.33990	9.938
1070	22502.0	2111.83	0.34869	10.084
1060	22669.2	2170.91	0.35817	10.241
1050	22845.6	2234.99	0.36836	10.409
1040	23030.8	2304.21	0.37927	10.586
1030	23224.1	2378.64	0.39088	10.773
1020	23424.6	2458.25	0.40316	10.968
1010	23631.5	2542.98	0.41607	11.172
1000	23843.8	2632.79	0.42960	11.383
990	24061.1	2727.63	0.44371	11.602
980	24282.6	2827.53	0.45840	11.827
970	24508.0	2932.58	0.47365	12.058
960	24737.1	3042.90	0.48948	12.295
950	24969.7	3158.68	0.50588	12.539
940	25205.8	3280.11	0.52289	12.789

V	S(V)	A(V)	~~T(V)~~ I(v)	T(V)
930	25445.3	3407.45	0.54051	13.045
920	25688.3	3540.97	0.55877	13.308
910	25934.6	3680.94	0.57770	13.577
900	26184.4	3827.67	0.59732	13.853
890	26437.6	3981.49	0.61765	14.136
880	26694.2	4142.71	0.63873	14.426
870	26954.4	4311.71	0.66059	14.723
860	27218.0	4488.84	0.68325	15.028
850	27485.2	4674.51	0.70676	15.340
840	27755.9	4869.13	0.73115	15.661
830	28030.2	5073.14	0.75645	15.989
820	28308.2	5287.03	0.78272	16.326
810	28589.8	5511.29	0.80999	16.672
800	28875.1	5746.44	0.83832	17.026
790	29164.3	5993.07	0.86775	17.390
780	29457.3	6251.77	0.89833	17.763
770	29754.2	6523.18	0.93013	18.146
760	30055.0	6807.98	0.96320	18.539
750	30359.9	7106.89	0.99760	18.943
740	30669.0	7420.68	1.03342	19.358
730	30982.2	7750.17	1.07071	19.784
720	31299.6	8096.23	1.10956	20.222
710	31621.5	8459.80	1.15006	20.672
700	31947.7	8841.88	1.19228	21.135
690	32278.5	9243.53	1.23633	21.611
680	32613.9	9665.90	1.28232	22.101
670	32954.1	10110.22	1.33034	22.605
660	33299.1	10577.81	1.38053	23.124
650	33649.1	11070.10	1.43300	23.658
640	34004.2	11588.60	1.48790	24.208
630	34364.4	12134.97	1.54538	24.776
620	34730.1	12710.98	1.60559	25.361
610	35101.2	13318.56	1.66871	25.964
600	35478.1	13959.77	1.73494	26.587
590	35860.7	14636.87	1.80447	27.230
580	36249.4	15352.28	1.87752	27.895
570	36644.2	16108.65	1.95434	28.581
560	37045.4	16908.84	2.03518	29.292
550	37453.1	17755.97	2.12034	30.026
540	37867.7	18653.43	2.21012	30.787
530	38289.2	19604.94	2.30486	31.575
520	38718.0	20614.53	2.40494	32.392
510	39154.3	21686.65	2.51075	33.239
500	39598.3	22826.16	2.62276	34.118
490	40050.3	24038.39	2.74144	35.031
480	40510.7	25329.24	2.86734	35.981

V	S(V)	A(V)	I(V) ~~T(V)~~	T(V)
470	40979.7	26705.20	3.00107	36.968
460	41457.7	28173.44	3.14328	37.996
450	41945.0	29741.92	3.29472	39.067
440	42442.1	31419.45	3.45621	40.184
430	42949.3	33215.87	3.62865	41.351
420	43467.1	35142.13	3.81307	42.569
410	43995.9	37210.49	4.01063	43.843
400	44536.4	39434.70	4.22259	45.178
390	45088.9	41830.21	4.45043	46.577
380	45654.1	44414.46	4.69577	48.045
370	46232.7	47207.19	4.96047	49.588
360	46825.3	50230.80	5.24666	51.212
350	47432.7	53510.80	5.55675	52.923
340	48055.6	57076.39	5.89351	54.729
330	48695.1	60961.07	6.26013	56.638
320	49352.0	65203.46	6.66030	58.660
310	50027.4	69848.27	7.09830	60.804
300	50722.5	74947.53	7.57911	63.084

V	S(V)	A(V)	I(V) ~~T(V)~~	T(V)
290	51438.6	80562.06	8.10859	65.511
280	52177.0	86763.37	8.69364	68.103
270	52939.5	93636.02	9.34244	70.876
260	53727.6	101280.63	10.06476	73.851
250	54543.6	109817.72	10.87232	77.051
240	55389.4	119392.69	11.77932	80.505
230	56267.8	130182.33	12.80308	84.244
220	57181.5	142403.36	13.96487	88.306
210	58133.8	156323.90	15.29111	92.737
200	59128.4	172278.95	16.81492	97.590
190	60169.8	190691.67	18.57826	102.933
180	61262.9	212103.01	20.63494	108.844
170	62413.6	237213.70	23.05491	115.423
160	63628.9	266944.97	25.93044	122.793
150	64917.2	302528.09	29.38526	131.110
140	66288.5	345639.77	33.58848	140.575
130	67755.1	398612.08	38.77614	151.448
120	69332.4	464768.47	45.28582	164.079
110	71039.5	548980.36	53.61421	178.942
100	72901.3	658627.61	64.51656	196.700

Tables of the Primary Siacci Functions

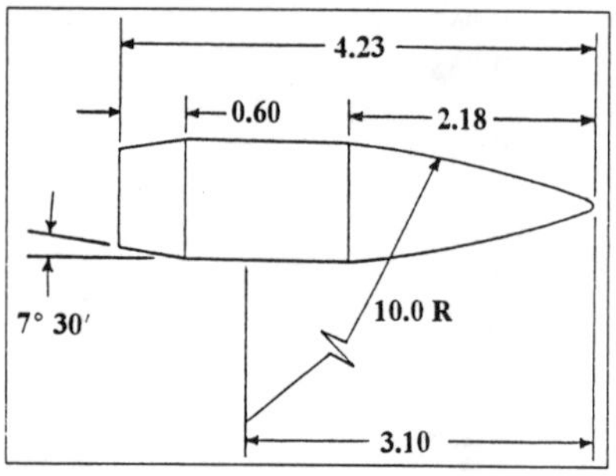

G_7 Drag Function

Quantity	Units
V	ft./sec.
S(V)	ft.-in.^{2}/lb.
A(V)	ft.-in.^{4}/lb.^{2}
I(V)	in.^{2}/lb.
T(V)	sec.-in.^{2}/lb.

V	S(V)	A(V)	I(V) ~~T(V)~~	T(V)
4500	0.0	0.00	0.00000	0.000
4490	56.3	0.01	0.00018	0.013
4480	112.5	0.02	0.00036	0.025
4470	168.8	0.05	0.00054	0.038
4460	225.2	0.08	0.00072	0.050
4450	281.5	0.13	0.00090	0.063
4440	337.9	0.18	0.00109	0.076

V	S(V)	A(V)	I(V) ~~T(V)~~	T(V)
4430	394.3	0.25	0.00127	0.088
4420	450.7	0.33	0.00146	0.101
4410	507.2	0.41	0.00164	0.114
4400	563.7	0.51	0.00183	0.127
4390	620.2	0.62	0.00202	0.140
4380	676.7	0.74	0.00221	0.152
4370	733.2	0.87	0.00240	0.165
4360	789.8	1.01	0.00259	0.178

V	S(V)	A(V)	I(V) ~~T(V)~~	T(V)
4350	846.4	1.16	0.00278	0.191
4340	903.1	1.33	0.00297	0.204
4330	959.7	1.50	0.00317	0.217
4320	1016.4	1.69	0.00336	0.231
4310	1073.1	1.88	0.00356	0.244
4300	1129.9	2.09	0.00376	0.257
4290	1186.6	2.31	0.00395	0.270
4280	1243.4	2.54	0.00415	0.283
4270	1300.2	2.78	0.00435	0.297
4260	1357.1	3.03	0.00455	0.310
4250	1413.9	3.30	0.00476	0.323
4240	1470.8	3.57	0.00496	0.337
4230	1527.7	3.86	0.00516	0.350
4220	1584.7	4.16	0.00537	0.364
4210	1641.6	4.47	0.00557	0.377
4200	1698.6	4.80	0.00578	0.391
4190	1755.7	5.13	0.00599	0.404
4180	1812.7	5.48	0.00620	0.418
4170	1869.8	5.84	0.00641	0.432
4160	1926.9	6.21	0.00662	0.445
4150	1984.0	6.60	0.00683	0.459
4140	2041.2	6.99	0.00705	0.473
4130	2098.4	7.40	0.00726	0.487
4120	2155.6	7.83	0.00748	0.501
4110	2212.8	8.26	0.00770	0.514
4100	2270.1	8.71	0.00792	0.528
4090	2327.4	9.17	0.00814	0.542
4080	2384.7	9.64	0.00836	0.556
4070	2442.1	10.12	0.00858	0.570
4060	2499.5	10.62	0.00880	0.585
4050	2556.9	11.14	0.00903	0.599
4040	2614.3	11.66	0.00925	0.613
4030	2671.8	12.20	0.00948	0.627
4020	2729.3	12.75	0.00971	0.641
4010	2786.8	13.32	0.00994	0.656
4000	2844.3	13.89	0.01017	0.670
3990	2901.9	14.49	0.01040	0.685
3980	2959.5	15.09	0.01063	0.699
3970	3017.1	15.71	0.01087	0.714
3960	3074.8	16.34	0.01110	0.728
3950	3132.5	16.99	0.01134	0.743
3940	3190.2	17.65	0.01158	0.757
3930	3248.0	18.33	0.01182	0.772
3920	3305.7	19.02	0.01206	0.787
3910	3363.5	19.72	0.01230	0.801
3900	3421.4	20.44	0.01255	0.816

V	S(V)	A(V)	I(V) ~~T(V)~~	T(V)
3890	3479.2	21.18	0.01279	0.831
3880	3537.1	21.92	0.01304	0.846
3870	3595.1	22.69	0.01329	0.861
3860	3653.0	23.46	0.01354	0.876
3850	3711.0	24.25	0.01379	0.891
3840	3769.0	25.06	0.01404	0.906
3830	3827.1	25.88	0.01429	0.921
3820	3885.1	26.72	0.01455	0.936
3810	3943.2	27.57	0.01481	0.952
3800	4001.4	28.44	0.01506	0.967
3790	4059.5	29.33	0.01532	0.982
3780	4117.7	30.23	0.01559	0.998
3770	4175.9	31.14	0.01585	1.013
3760	4234.2	32.07	0.01611	1.029
3750	4292.5	33.02	0.01638	1.044
3740	4350.8	33.98	0.01665	1.060
3730	4409.2	34.96	0.01692	1.075
3720	4467.5	35.96	0.01719	1.091
3710	4525.9	36.97	0.01746	1.107
3700	4584.4	38.00	0.01773	1.122
3690	4642.8	39.04	0.01801	1.138
3680	4701.3	40.10	0.01828	1.154
3670	4759.9	41.18	0.01856	1.170
3660	4818.4	42.28	0.01884	1.186
3650	4877.0	43.39	0.01913	1.202
3640	4935.7	44.52	0.01941	1.218
3630	4994.3	45.67	0.01970	1.234
3620	5053.0	46.83	0.01998	1.250
3610	5111.8	48.01	0.02027	1.267
3600	5170.6	49.21	0.02056	1.283
3590	5229.4	50.43	0.02086	1.299
3580	5288.3	51.67	0.02115	1.316
3570	5347.2	52.92	0.02145	1.332
3560	5406.1	54.19	0.02174	1.349
3550	5465.1	55.49	0.02204	1.365
3540	5524.1	56.80	0.02235	1.382
3530	5583.2	58.13	0.02265	1.399
3520	5642.3	59.47	0.02296	1.416
3510	5701.4	60.84	0.02327	1.432
3500	5760.6	62.23	0.02357	1.449
3490	5819.9	63.63	0.02389	1.466
3480	5879.1	65.06	0.02420	1.483
3470	5938.5	66.50	0.02452	1.500
3460	5997.9	67.97	0.02483	1.517
3450	6057.3	69.45	0.02516	1.535
3440	6116.7	70.96	0.02548	1.552

V	S(V)	A(V)	I(V) ~~T(V)~~	T(V)
3430	6176.3	72.49	0.02580	1.569
3420	6235.8	74.03	0.02613	1.587
3410	6295.5	75.60	0.02646	1.604
3400	6355.1	77.19	0.02679	1.622
3390	6414.9	78.80	0.02712	1.639
3380	6474.6	80.43	0.02746	1.657
3370	6534.5	82.08	0.02780	1.675
3360	6594.4	83.76	0.02814	1.692
3350	6654.3	85.45	0.02848	1.710
3340	6714.3	87.17	0.02882	1.728
3330	6774.4	88.91	0.02917	1.746
3320	6834.5	90.68	0.02952	1.764
3310	6894.7	92.47	0.02987	1.782
3300	6954.9	94.28	0.03023	1.801
3290	7015.3	96.11	0.03058	1.819
3280	7075.6	97.97	0.03094	1.837
3270	7136.1	99.85	0.03131	1.856
3260	7196.6	101.75	0.03167	1.874
3250	7257.1	103.68	0.03204	1.893
3240	7317.8	105.64	0.03241	1.912
3230	7378.5	107.62	0.03278	1.930
3220	7439.3	109.62	0.03316	1.949
3210	7500.1	111.65	0.03354	1.968
3200	7561.0	113.70	0.03392	1.987
3190	7622.0	115.78	0.03430	2.006
3180	7683.1	117.89	0.03469	2.025
3170	7744.2	120.02	0.03508	2.045
3160	7805.4	122.18	0.03547	2.064
3150	7866.7	124.37	0.03587	2.083
3140	7928.1	126.58	0.03627	2.103
3130	7989.5	128.82	0.03667	2.123
3120	8051.0	131.09	0.03708	2.142
3110	8112.6	133.39	0.03748	2.162
3100	8174.3	135.71	0.03790	2.182
3090	8236.0	138.06	0.03831	2.202
3080	8297.9	140.45	0.03873	2.222
3070	8359.8	142.86	0.03915	2.242
3060	8421.8	145.30	0.03957	2.262
3050	8483.9	147.77	0.04000	2.283
3040	8546.1	150.27	0.04043	2.303
3030	8608.3	152.80	0.04087	2.323
3020	8670.7	155.36	0.04131	2.344
3010	8733.1	157.95	0.04175	2.365
3000	8795.6	160.58	0.04219	2.386
2990	8858.3	163.24	0.04264	2.407
2980	8921.0	165.92	0.04309	2.428
2970	8983.8	168.64	0.04355	2.449
2960	9046.7	171.40	0.04401	2.470
2950	9109.7	174.19	0.04448	2.491
2940	9172.8	177.01	0.04494	2.513
2930	9236.0	179.86	0.04542	2.534
2920	9299.2	182.75	0.04589	2.556
2910	9362.6	185.67	0.04637	2.578
2900	9426.1	188.63	0.04685	2.599
2890	9489.7	191.63	0.04734	2.621
2880	9553.4	194.66	0.04783	2.643
2870	9617.2	197.73	0.04833	2.666
2860	9681.1	200.83	0.04883	2.688
2850	9745.1	203.97	0.04934	2.710
2840	9809.2	207.15	0.04985	2.733
2830	9873.5	210.37	0.05036	2.756
2820	9937.8	213.63	0.05088	2.778
2810	10002.2	216.92	0.05140	2.801
2800	10066.8	220.26	0.05193	2.824
2790	10131.5	223.64	0.05246	2.847
2780	10196.3	227.05	0.05300	2.871
2770	10261.2	230.51	0.05354	2.894
2760	10326.2	234.01	0.05409	2.918
2750	10391.3	237.55	0.05464	2.941
2740	10456.6	241.13	0.05520	2.965
2730	10522.0	244.76	0.05576	2.989
2720	10587.5	248.43	0.05633	3.013
2710	10653.1	252.15	0.05690	3.037
2700	10718.9	255.91	0.05748	3.061
2690	10784.8	259.72	0.05806	3.086
2680	10850.8	263.57	0.05865	3.110
2670	10916.9	267.47	0.05925	3.135
2660	10983.2	271.41	0.05985	3.160
2650	11049.6	275.41	0.06045	3.185
2640	11116.1	279.45	0.06106	3.210
2630	11182.8	283.54	0.06168	3.235
2620	11249.7	287.69	0.06231	3.261
2610	11316.6	291.88	0.06293	3.287
2600	11383.7	296.12	0.06357	3.312
2590	11450.9	300.42	0.06421	3.338
2580	11518.3	304.77	0.06486	3.364
2570	11585.8	309.17	0.06552	3.390
2560	11653.5	313.62	0.06618	3.417
2550	11721.3	318.13	0.06685	3.443
2540	11789.2	322.70	0.06752	3.470
2530	11857.3	327.32	0.06820	3.497
2520	11925.6	332.00	0.06889	3.524

V	S(V)	A(V)	I(V)	T(V)
2510	11994.0	336.73	0.06959	3.551
2500	12062.5	341.53	0.07029	3.579
2490	12131.2	346.38	0.07100	3.606
2480	12200.1	351.29	0.07172	3.634
2470	12269.1	356.26	0.07244	3.662
2460	12338.2	361.30	0.07317	3.690
2450	12407.5	366.40	0.07391	3.718
2440	12477.0	371.56	0.07466	3.746
2430	12546.6	376.78	0.07541	3.775
2420	12616.4	382.07	0.07618	3.804
2410	12686.4	387.43	0.07695	3.833
2400	12756.5	392.85	0.07773	3.862
2390	12826.8	398.34	0.07852	3.891
2380	12897.3	403.90	0.07931	3.921
2370	12967.9	409.53	0.08012	3.950
2360	13038.7	415.23	0.08093	3.980
2350	13109.6	421.01	0.08176	4.011
2340	13180.8	426.85	0.08259	4.041
2330	13252.1	432.77	0.08343	4.071
2320	13323.6	438.77	0.08428	4.102
2310	13395.3	444.84	0.08514	4.133
2300	13467.1	450.99	0.08601	4.164
2290	13539.2	457.22	0.08689	4.196
2280	13611.4	463.53	0.08778	4.227
2270	13683.9	469.92	0.08868	4.259
2260	13756.5	476.39	0.08959	4.291
2250	13829.3	482.95	0.09051	4.324
2240	13902.3	489.59	0.09144	4.356
2230	13975.5	496.32	0.09239	4.389
2220	14048.9	503.13	0.09334	4.422
2210	14122.5	510.04	0.09431	4.455
2200	14196.3	517.04	0.09528	4.488
2190	14270.3	524.12	0.09627	4.522
2180	14344.5	531.31	0.09727	4.556
2170	14419.0	538.58	0.09828	4.590
2160	14493.6	545.96	0.09931	4.625
2150	14568.4	553.43	0.10034	4.660
2140	14643.5	561.00	0.10139	4.695
2130	14718.8	568.67	0.10245	4.730
2120	14794.2	576.44	0.10353	q .765
2110	14869.9	584.32	0.10462	4.801
2100	14945.8	592,30	0.10572	4.837
2090	15021.8	600.38	0.10683	4.873
2080	15098.1	608.57	0.10796	4.910
2070	15174.6	616.87	0.10910	4.947
2060	15251.2	625.28	0.11026	4.984

V	S(V)	A(V)	I(V)	T(V)
2050	15328.1	633.80	0.11143	5.021
2040	15405.2	642.44	0.11262	5.059
2030	15482.5	651.18	0.11382	5.097
2020	15559.9	660.05	0.11503	5.135
2010	15637.6	669.03	0.11626	5.174
2000	15715.5	678.14	0.11751	5.213
1990	15793.6	687.36	0.11877	5.252
1980	15871.9	696.71	0.12005	5.291
1970	15950.4	706.19	0.12134	5.331
1960	16029.1	715.79	0.12265	5.371
1950	16108.0	725.52	0.12398	5.412
1940	16187.1	735.38	0.12533	5.452
1930	16266.4	745.37	0.12669	5.493
1920	16345.9	755.49	0.12807	5.534
1910	16425.5	765.75	0.12947	5.576
1900	16505.4	776.15	0.13088	5.618
1890	16585.5	786.68	0.13232	5.660
1880	16665.7	797.36	0.13377	5.703
1870	16746.2	808.18	0.13524	5.746
1860	16826.9	819.15	0.13673	5.789
1850	16907.7	830.27	0.13824	5.833
1840	16988.8	841.54	0.13978	5.877
1830	17070.1	852.97	0.14133	5.921
1820	17151.6	864.54	0.14290	5.965
1810	17233.2	876.28	0.14450	6.010
1800	17315.1	888.18	0.14611	6.056
1790	17397.2	900.24	0.14775	6.102
1780	17479.5	912.47	0.14941	6.148
1770	17562.0	924.86	0.15110	6.194
1760	17644.6	937.42	0.15280	6.241
1750	17727.5	950.16	0.15453	6.288
1740	17810.6	963.07	0.15629	6.336
1730	17893.9	976.16	0.15807	6.384
1720	17977.4	989.44	0.15987	6.432
1710	18061.1	1002.90	0.16171	6.481
1700	18145.0	1016.55	0.16356	6.530
1690	18229.2	1030.39	0.16545	6.580
1680	18313.5	1044.42	0.16736	6.630
1670	18398.1	1058.65	0.16930	6.680
1660	18482.9	1073.09	0.17126	6.731
1650	18567.9	1087.73	0.17326	6.783
1640	18653.1	1102.58	0.17528	6.834
1630	18738.5	1117.64	0.17734	6.887
1620	18824.1	1132.92	0.17943	6.939
1610	18910.0	1148.42	0.18154	6.993
1600	18996.1	1164.14	0.18369	7.046

V	S(V)	A(V)	I(V)	T(V)
1590	19082.4	1180.09	0.18588	7.100
1580	19169.0	1196.27	0.18809	7.155
1570	19255.7	1212.69	0.19034	7.210
1560	19342.7	1229.35	0.19263	7.266
1550	19430.0	1246.26	0.19495	7.322
1540	19517.4	1263.41	0.19730	7.378
1530	19605.1	1280.82	0.19970	7.436
1520	19693.1	1298.49	0.20213	7.493
1510	19781.3	1316.42	0.20460	7.551
1500	19869.7	1334.63	0.20711	7.610
1490	19958.5	1353.12	0.20967	7.670
1480	20047.5	1371.90	0.21226	7.729
1470	20136.8	1390.98	0.21490	7.790
1460	20226.4	1410.34	0.21759	7.851
1450	20316.2	1430.01	0.22032	7.913
1440	20406.3	1449.99	0.22309	7.975
1430	20496.7	1470.29	0.22592	8.038
1420	20587.5	1490.92	0.22879	8.102
1410	20678.5	1511.88	0.23172	8.166
1400	20769.8	1533.18	0.23469	8.231
1390	20861.5	1554.83	0.23772	8.297
1380	20953.5	1576.85	0.24081	8.363
1370	21045.9	1599.24	0.24395	8.431
1360	21138.6	1622.00	0.24715	8.499
1350	21231.7	1645.16	0.25041	8.567
1340	21325.1	1668.71	0.25373	8.637
1330	21419.0	1692.68	0.25712	8.707
1320	21513.2	1717.07	0.26057	8.778
1310	21607.8	1741.90	0.26409	8.850
1300	21702.9	1767.17	0.26768	8.923
1290	21798.4	1792.91	0.27135	8.997
1280	21894.4	1819.13	0.27508	9.071
1270	21990.8	1845.84	0.27890	9.147
1260	22087.7	1873.06	0.28279	9.224
1250	22185.1	1900.80	0.28677	9.301
1240	22283.1	1929.09	0.29084	9.380
1230	22381.6	1957.94	0.29499	9.460
1220	22480.7	1987.38	0.29924	9.541
1210	22580.4	2017.44	0.30359	9.623
1200	22680.8	2048.15	0.30803	9.706
1190	22782.0	2079.54	0.31259	9.791
1180	22883.9	2111.63	0.31726	9.877
1170	22986.6	2144.47	0.32204	9.964
1160	23090.3	2178.11	0.32696	10.053
1150	23195.2	2212.68	0.33202	10.144
1140	23301.7	2248.31	0.33724	10.237
1130	23410.4	2285.28	0.34267	10.333
1120	23522.7	2324.08	0.34838	10.433
1110	23640.8	2365.57	0.35449	10.538
1100	23768.5	2411.28	0.36122	10.654
1090	23912.4	2463.81	0.36894	10.785
1080	24079.8	2526.32	0.37808	10.940
1070	24275.0	2601.17	0.38895	11.121
1060	24496.3	2688.64	0.40150	11.329
1050	24740.9	2788.58	0.41564	11.561
1040	25007.0	2901.27	0.43132	11.816
1030	25293.2	3027.13	0.44850	12.092
1020	25597.6	3166.49	0.46714	12.389
1010	25918.5	3319.60	0.48718	12.705
1000	26253.4	3486.34	0.50851	13.039
990	26601.0	3666.99	0.53109	13.388
980	26959.9	3861.84	0.55488	13.752
970	27329.5	4071.53	0.57989	14.131
960	27709.4	4296.83	0.60614	14.525
950	28099.4	4538.54	0.63364	14.934
940	28498.6	4797.24	0.66240	15.356
930	28906.5	5073.55	0.69241	15.792
920	29323.0	5368.38	0.72372	16.243
910	29747.4	5682.43	0.75633	16.706
900	30179.3	6016.42	0.79025	17.184
890	30618.6	6371.29	0.82553	17.675
880	31065.1	6748.01	0.86219	18.179
870	31518.6	7147.68	0.90030	18.697
860	31979.4	7571.57	0.93991	19.230
850	32447.0	8020.71	0.98106	19.777
840	32921.9	8496.65	1.02383	20.339
830	33403.6	9000.54	1.06828	20.916
820	33892.4	9533.92	1.11447	21.508
810	34388.3	10098.47	1.16250	22.117
800	34891.3	10695.69	1.21242	22.742
790	35401.4	11327.38	1.26434	23.383
780	35918.5	11995.09	1.31832	24.042
770	36443.1	12701.27	1.37450	24.719
760	36975.1	13447.98	1.43297	25.414
750	37514.4	14237.22	1.49384	26.129
740	38061.4	15071.50	1.55722	26.863
730	38616.1	15953.55	1.62327	27.618
720	39178.7	16886.17	1.69213	28.394
710	39749.5	17872.36	1.76395	29.192
700	40328.6	18915.43	1.83889	30.014
690	40916.2	20018.91	1.91715	30.859
680	41512.6	21186.57	1.99891	31.730

V	S(V)	A(V)	~~T(V)~~ I(v)	T(V)
670	42118.0	22422.51	2.08438	32.627
660	42732.7	23731.17	2.17380	33.551
650	43357.0	25117.32	2.26740	34.504
640	43991.2	26586.09	2.36546	35.488
630	44635.3	28142.65	2.46821	36.502
620	45289.8	29793.17	2.57599	37.549
610	45954.9	31543.98	2.68912	38.631
600	46631.0	33401.95	2.80793	39.748
590	47318.4	35374.84	2.93284	40.904
580	48017.5	37470.95	3.06425	42.099
570	48728.8	39699.35	3.20264	43.336
560	49452.6	42070.07	3.34851	44.617
550	50189.5	44593.88	3.50240	45.945
540	50939.9	47282.48	3.66491	47.322
530	51704.3	50149.33	3.83671	48.751
520	52483.4	53208.99	4.01856	50.235
510	53277.7	56476.82	4.21121	51.777
500	54087.8	59970.65	4.41556	53.381
490	54914.4	63709.65	4.63259	55.051
480	55758.0	67714.42	4.86330	56.791
470	56619.4	72008.61	5.10891	58.605
460	57499.3	76618.34	5.37070	60.497
450	58398.5	81572.36	5.65013	62.473
440	59317.8	86902.62	5.94878	64.539
430	60258.2	92646.31	6.26852	66.701
420	61220.8	98843.66	6.61135	68.966
410	62206.4	105540.17	6.97955	71.342
400	63216.5	112788.57	7.37574	73.836
390	64252.0	120645.11	7.80272	76.458
380	65314.2	129175.88	8.26377	79.217
370	66404.9	138458.72	8.76278	82.126
360	67525.3	148576.88	9.30387	85.196
350	68677.2	159629.57	9.89197	88.441
340	69862.4	171729.57	10.53266	91.877
330	71082.7	185005.89	11.23235	95.520
320	72340.8	199613.58	11.99872	99.392
310	73638.7	215727.27	12.84041	103.513
300	74979.0	233552.77	13.76760	107.908
290	76364.5	253329.07	14.79208	112.606
280	77798.9	275352.24	15.92853	117.640
270	79286.0	299968.85	17.19401	123.048
260	80829.4	327583.99	18.60848	128.874
250	82434.2	358705.78	20.19695	135.169
240	84104.5	393915.47	21.98797	141.988
230	85845.1	433928.26	24.01675	149.397
220	87663.6	479673.31	26.32906	157.482
210	89566.7	532263.11	28.97952	166.337
200	91562.5	593102.11	32.03717	176.077
190	93660.4	663977.09	35.58976	186.840
180	95871.3	747176.92	39.74976	198.796
170	98208.3	845706.55	44.66474	212.158
160	100687.3	963554.45	50.53047	227.192
150	103325.5	1105995.39	57.60565	244.224
140	106144.1	1280262.24	66.24562	263.678
130	109172.3	1496682.11	76.95717	286.130
120	112442.5	1769829.85	90.45480	312.319
110	115995.3	2121094.56	107.78827	343.252
100	119886.9	2583497.40	130.57802	380.371

Tables of the Primary Siacci Functions

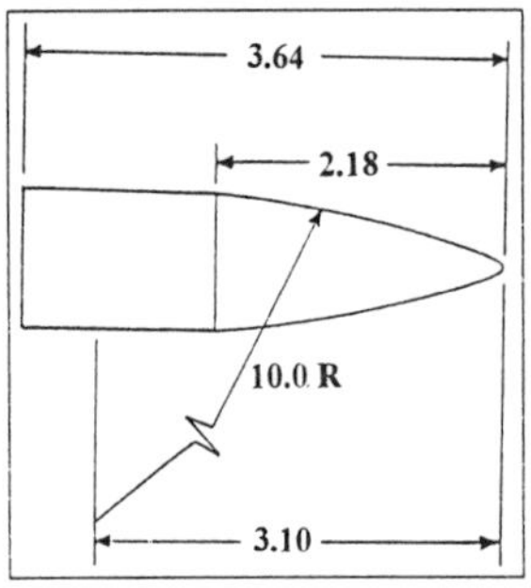

G_8 Drag Function

Quantity	Units
V	ft./sec.
S(V)	ft.-in.^{2}/lb.
A(V)	ft.-in.^{4}/lb.^{2}
I(V)	in.^{2}/lb.
T(V)	sec.-in.^{2}/lb.

V	S(V)	A(V)	I(V)	T(V)
4500	0.0	0.00	0.00000	0.000
4490	55.8	0.00	0.00018	0.012
4480	111.6	0.02	0.00036	0.025
4470	167.5	0.04	0.00054	0.037
4460	223.5	0.08	0.00072	0.050
4450	279.4	0.12	0.00090	0.062
4440	335.4	0.18	0.00108	0.075
4430	391.5	0.25	0.00126	0.088
4420	447.6	0.32	0.00145	0.100
4410	503.7	0.41	0.00163	0.113
4400	559.9	0.51	0.00182	0.126
4390	616.1	0.61	0.00201	0.139
4380	672.4	0.73	0.00219	0.151
4370	728.7	0.86	0.00238	0.164
4360	785.0	1.00	0.00257	0.177
4350	841.4	1.15	0.00276	0.190
4340	897.8	1.31	0.00296	0.203
4330	954.3	1.48	0.00315	0.216
4320	1010.8	1.67	0.00334	0.229
4310	1067.4	1.86	0.00354	0.242
4300	1124.0	2.07	0.00374	0.256
4290	1180.6	2.29	0.00393	0.269
4280	1237.3	2.51	0.00413	0.282
4270	1294.0	2.75	0.00433	0.295
4260	1350.7	3.01	0.00453	0.308
4250	1407.5	3.27	0.00473	0.322
4240	1464.4	3.54	0.00494	0.335
4230	1521.2	3.83	0.00514	0.349

V	S(V)	A(V)	I(V)	T(V)
4220	1578.1	4.13	0.00535	0.362
4210	1635.1	4.44	0.00555	0.376
4200	1692.1	4.76	0.00576	0.389
4190	1749.1	5.10	0.00597	0.403
4180	1806.2	5.44	0.00618	0.416
4170	1863.3	5.80	0.00639	0.430
4160	1920.4	6.17	0.00660	0.444
4150	1977.6	6.56	0.00681	0.458
4140	2034.8	6.95	0.00703	0.471
4130	2092.1	7.36	0.00724	0.485
4120	2149.4	7.78	0.00746	0.499
4110	2206.7	8.21	0.00768	0.513
4100	2264.0	8.66	0.00790	0.527
4090	2321.4	9.12	0.00812	0.541
4080	2378.9	9.59	0.00834	0.555
4070	2436.3	10.08	0.00856	0.569
4060	2493.8	10.58	0.00878	0.583
4050	2551.4	11.09	0.00901	0.598
4040	2608.9	11.61	0.00924	0.612
4030	2666.5	12.15	0.00946	0.626
4020	2724.2	12.71	0.00969	0.640
4010	2781.9	13.27	0.00992	0.655
4000	2839.6	13.85	0.01015	0.669
3990	2897.3	14.44	0.01039	0.684
3980	2955.1	15.05	0.01062	0.698
3970	3012.9	15.67	0.01086	0.713
3960	3070.7	16.31	0.01109	0.727
3950	3128.6	16.95	0.01133	0.742

V	S(V)	A(V)	I(V)	T(V)
3940	3186.5	17.62	0.01157	0.757
3930	3244.4	18.29	0.01181	0.771
3920	3302.4	18.99	0.01205	0.786
3910	3360.3	19.69	0.01230	0.801
3900	3418.4	20.41	0.01254	0.816
3890	3476.4	21.15	0.01279	0.831
3880	3534.5	21.90	0.01303	0.846
3870	3592.6	22.66	0.01328	0.861
3860	3650.8	23.44	0.01353	0.876
3850	3709.0	24.24	0.01378	0.891
3840	3767.2	25.05	0.01404	0.906
3830	3825.4	25.87	0.01429	0.921
3820	3883.7	26.71	0.01455	0.936
3810	3942.0	27.57	0.01481	0.952
3800	4000.3	28.44	0.01507	0.967
3790	4058.7	29.33	0.01533	0.982
3780	4117.1	30.23	0.01559	0.998
3770	4175.5	31.15	0.01585	1.013
3760	4234.0	32.08	0.01612	1.029
3750	4292.5	33.03	0.01638	1.044
3740	4351.0	34.00	0.01665	1.060
3730	4409.5	34.98	0.01692	1.076
3720	4468 1	35.98	0.01719	1.091
3710	4526 7	37.00	0.01747	1.107
3700	4585.4	38.03	0.01774	1.123
3690	4644.0	39.08	0.01802	1.139
3680	4702.7	40.14	0.01830	1.155
3670	4761.5	41.23	0.01858	1.171
3660	4820.2	42.33	0.01886	1.187
3650	4879.0	43.44	0.01914	1.203
3640	4937.8	44.58	0.01943	1.219
3630	4996.7	45.73	0.01971	1.235
3620	5055.5	46.90	0.02000	1.251
3610	5114.5	48.08	0.02029	1.268
3600	5173.4	49.29	0.02058	1.284
3590	5232.4	50.51	0.02088	1.300
3580	5291.4	51.75	0.02117	1.317
3570	5350.4	53.01	0.02147	1.333
3560	5409.4	54.29	0.02177	1.350
3550	5468.5	55.58	0.02207	1.367
3540	5527.6	56.89	0.02237	1.383
3530	5586.8	58.23	0.02267	1.400
3520	5646.0	59.58	0.02298	1.417
3510	5705.2	60.95	0.02329	1.434
3500	5764.4	62.34	0.02360	1.450
3490	5823.7	63.75	0.02391	1.467
3480	5883.0	65.17	0.02423	1.484

V	S(V)	A(V)	I(V)	T(V)
3470	5942.4	66.62	0.02454	1.502
3460	6001.8	68.09	0.02486	1.519
3450	6061.2	69.57	0.02518	1.536
3440	6120.6	71.08	0.02550	1.553
3430	6180.1	72.60	0.02583	1.570
3420	6239.6	74.15	0.02615	1.588
3410	6299.1	75.72	0.02648	1.605
3400	6358.7	77.31	0.02681	1.623
3390	6418.3	78.91	0.02714	1.640
3380	6477.9	80.54	0.02748	1.658
3370	6537.6	82.19	0.02782	1.676
3360	6597.3	83.86	0.02815	1.693
3350	6657.0	85.55	0.02850	1.711
3340	6716.8	87.27	0.02884	1.729
3330	6776.6	89.00	0.02919	1.747
3320	6836.5	90.76	0.02953	1.765
3310	6896.4	92.54	0.02988	1.783
3300	6956.3	94.34	0.03024	1.801
3290	7016.2	96.16	0.03059	1.819
3280	7076.2	98.01	0.03095	1.838
3270	7136.2	99.88	0.03131	1.856
3260	7196.3	101.77	0.03167	1.874
3250	7256.4	103.68	0.03204	1.893
3240	7316.5	105.62	0.03240	1.911
3230	7376.7	107.58	0.03277	1.930
3220	7436.9	109.57	0.03315	1.949
3210	7497.2	111.58	0.03352	1.967
3200	7557.5	113.61	0.03390	1.986
3190	7617.8	115.67	0.03428	2.005
3180	7678.2	117.75	0.03466	2.024
3170	7738.6	119.85	0.03505	2.043
3160	7799.1	121.98	0.03544	2.062
3150	7859.6	124.14	0.03583	2.081
3140	7920.1	126.32	0.03622	2.101
3130	7980.7	128.53	0.03662	2.120
3120	8041.4	130.76	0.03702	2.139
3110	8102.0	133.02	0.03742	2.159
3100	8162.8	135.30	0.03782	2.178
3090	8223.5	137.61	0.03823	2.198
3080	8284.3	139.95	0.03864	2.218
3070	8345.2	142.31	0.03906	2.237
3060	8406.1	144.71	0.03947	2.257
3050	8467.0	147.12	0.03989	2.277
3040	8528.0	149.57	0.04032	2.297
3030	8589.0	152.04	0.04074	2.317
3020	8650.1	154.54	0.04117	2.338

V	S(V)	A(V)	I(V)	T(V)
3010	8711.2	157.07	0.04160	2.358
3000	8772.4	159.63	0.04204	2.378
2990	8833.6	162.22	0.04248	2.399
2980	8894.9	164.84	0.04292	2.419
2970	8956.2	167.48	0.04337	2.440
2960	9017.6	170.16	0.04382	2.460
2950	9079.0	172.86	0.04427	2.481
2940	9140.4	175.60	0.04472	2.502
2930	9201.9	178.36	0.04518	2.523
2920	9263.5	181.16	0.04565	2.544
2910	9325.1	183.98	0.04611	2.565
2900	9386.7	186.84	0.04658	2.586
2890	9448.4	189.73	0.04706	2.608
2880	9510.2	192.65	0.04753	2.629
2870	9572.0	195.60	0.04801	2.651
2860	9633.9	198.59	0.04850	2.672
2850	9695.8	201.60	0.04899	2.694
2840	9757.7	204.65	0.04948	2.716
2830	9819.7	207.74	0.04998	2.738
2820	9881.8	210.86	0.05048	2.760
2810	9943.9	214.01	0.05098	2.782
2800	10006.1	217.19	0.05149	2.804
2790	10068.3	220.41	0.05200	2.826
2780	10130.6	223.67	0.05252	2.848
2770	10192.9	226.96	0.05304	2.871
2760	10255.3	230.28	0.05356	2.893
2750	10317.8	233.64	0.05409	2.916
2740	10380.3	237.04	0.05463	2.939
2730	10442.8	240.47	0.05516	2.962
2720	10505.4	243.94	0.05571	2.985
2710	10568.1	247.45	0.05625	3.008
2700	10630.8	251.00	0.05680	3.031
2690	10693.6	254.58	0.05736	3.054
2680	10756.4	258.20	0.05792	3.078
2670	10819.3	261.86	0.05849	3.101
2660	10882.2	265.56	0.05906	3.125
2650	10945.2	269.30	0.05963	3.149
2640	11008.3	273.08	0.06021	3.172
2630	11071.4	276.90	0.06079	3.196
2620	11134.6	280.76	0.06138	3.220
2610	11197.8	284.66	0.06198	3.245
2600	11261.1	288.60	0.06258	3.269
2590	11324.5	292.58	0.06318	3.293
2580	11388.0	296.61	0.06380	3.318
2570	11451.5	300.68	0.06441	3.343
2560	11515.0	304.80	0.06503	3.367

V	S(V)	A(V)	I(V)	T(V)
2550	11578.7	308.96	0.06566	3.392
2540	11642.4	313.16	0.06629	3.417
2530	11706.1	317.41	0.06693	3.442
2520	11770.0	321.70	0.06758	3.468
2510	11833.9	326.04	0.06822	3.493
2500	11897.9	330.43	0.06888	3.519
2490	11961.9	334.86	0.06954	3.544
2480	12026.1	339.34	0.07021	3.570
2470	12090.3	343.87	0.07088	3.596
2460	12154.6	348.45	0.07157	3.622
2450	12218.9	353.08	0.07225	3.648
2440	12283.4	357.76	0.07295	3.675
2430	12347.9	362.49	0.07365	3.701
2420	12412.5	367.27	0.07435	3.728
2410	12477.2	372.10	0.07507	3.755
2400	12541.9	376.98	0.07579	3.782
2390	12606.8	381.92	0.07651	3.809
2380	12671.7	386.91	0.07725	3.836
2370	12736.7	391.96	0.07799	3.863
2360	12801.8	397.06	0.07874	3.891
2350	12867.0	402.21	0.07949	3.918
2340	12932.2	407.43	0.08026	3.946
2330	12997.6	412.70	0.08103	3.974
2320	13063.0	418.03	0.08181	4.002
2310	13128.6	423.41	0.08259	4.031
2300	13194.2	428.86	0.08339	4.059
2290	13259.9	434.37	0.08419	4.088
2280	13325.8	439.93	0.08500	4.117
2270	13391.7	445.56	0.08582	4.146
2260	13457.7	451.26	0.08665	4.175
2250	13523.8	457.01	0.08748	4.204
2240	13590.0	462.83	0.08833	4.234
2230	13656.3	468.72	0.08918	4.263
2220	13722.7	474.67	0.09004	4.293
2210	13789.2	480.69	0.09092	4.323
2200	13855.8	486.77	0.09180	4.353
2190	13922.6	492.93	0.09269	4.384
2180	13989.4	499.15	0.09359	4.414
2170	14056.3	505.45	0.09450	4.445
2160	14123.4	511.81	0.09542	4.476
2150	14190.5	518.25	0.09635	4.507
2140	14257.8	524.76	0.09729	4.539
2130	14325.1	531.35	0.09824	4.570
2120	14392.6	538.01	0.09920	4.602
2110	14460.2	544.75	0.10017	4.634
2100	14527.9	551.57	0.10116	4.666

V	S(V)	A(V)	I(V)	T(V)
2090	14595.8	558.46	0.10215	4.698
2080	14663.7	565.44	0.10316	4.731
2070	14731.8	572.49	0.10417	4.764
2060	14800.0	579.63	0.10520	4.797
2050	14868.3	586.85	0.10624	4.830
2040	14936.7	594.16	0.10729	4.864
2030	15005.3	601.55	0.10836	4.897
2020	15074.0	609.03	0.10944	4.931
2010	15142.8	616.60	0.11053	4.965
2000	15211.7	624.26	0.11163	5.000
1990	15280.8	632.01	0.11275	5.034
1980	15350.0	639.85	0.11388	5.069
1970	15419.3	647.78	0.11502	5.104
1960	15488.8	655.81	0.11618	5.140
1950	15558.4	663.94	0.11735	5.175
1940	15628.1	672.16	0.11853	5.211
1930	15698.0	680.49	0.11973	5.247
1920	15768.0	688.91	0.12095	5.284
1910	15838.2	697.44	0.12218	5.320
1900	15908.5	706.08	0.12343	5.357
1890	15979.0	714.82	0.12469	5.394
1880	16049.6	723.67	0.12597	5.432
1870	16120.3	732.63	0.12726	5.469
1860	16191.2	741.70	0.12857	5.508
1850	16262.3	750.88	0.12990	5.546
1840	16333.5	760.18	0.13125	5.584
1830	16404.9	769.60	0.13261	5.623
1820	16476.5	779.14	0.13399	5.663
1810	16548.2	788.80	0.13539	5.702
1800	16620.1	798.58	0.13681	5.742
1790	16692.2	808.49	0.13825	5.782
1780	16764.4	818.53	0.13971	5.822
1770	16836.8	828.70	0.14119	5.863
1760	16909.4	839.00	0.14268	5.904
1750	16982.1	849.44	0.14420	5.946
1740	17055.1	860.01	0.14574	5.988
1730	17128.2	870.73	0.14731	6.030
1720	17201.5	881.59	0.14889	6.072
1710	17275.0	892.59	0.15050	6.115
1700	17348.7	903.74	0.15213	6.158
1690	17422.6	915.04	0.15378	6.202
1680	17496.7	926.50	0.15546	6.246
1670	17571.0	938.11	0.15717	6.290
1660	17645.5	949.89	0.15889	6.335
1650	17720.2	961.83	0.16065	6.380
1640	17795.2	973.93	0.16243	6.426

V	S(V)	A(V)	I(V)	T(V)
1630	17870.3	986.20	0.16424	6.472
1620	17945.7	998.65	0.16607	6.518
1610	18021.3	1011.27	0.16794	6.565
1600	18097.1	1024.08	0.16983	6.612
1590	18173.1	1037.07	0.17175	6.660
1580	18249.4	1050.24	0.17371	6.708
1570	18325.9	1063.61	0.17569	6.757
1560	18402.7	1077.17	0.17771	6.806
1550	18479.7	1090.94	0.17976	6.855
1540	18556.9	1104.90	0.18184	6.905
1530	18634.4	1119.08	0.18395	6.956
1520	18712.2	1133.47	0.18610	7.007
1510	18790.2	1148.07	0.18829	7.058
1500	18868.5	1162.90	0.19051	7.110
1490	18947.1	1177.95	0.19277	7.163
1480	19025.9	1193.24	0.19507	7.216
1470	19105.0	1208.76	0.19741	7.269
1460	19184.4	1224.53	0.19979	7.324
1450	19264.1	1240.55	0.20221	7.378
1440	19344.1	1256.82	0.20468	7.434
1430	19424.3	1273.35	0.20718	7.490
1420	19504.9	1290.15	0.20974	7.546
1410	19585.8	1307.23	0.21234	7.603
1400	19667.1	1324.58	0.21498	7.661
1390	19748.7	1342.23	0.21768	7.720
1380	19830.6	1360.17	0.22043	7.779
1370	19912.8	1378.42	0.22322	7.839
1360	19995.5	1396.98	0.22608	7.899
1350	20078.4	1415.86	0.22898	7.960
1340	20161.8	1435.08	0.23195	8.022
1330	20245.6	1454.63	0.23497	8.085
1320	20329.8	1474.54	0.23806	8.149
1310	20414.3	1494.81	0.24120	8.213
1300	20499.3	1515.44	0.24441	8.278
1290	20584.8	1536.46	0.24769	8.344
1280	20670.6	1557.88	0.25103	8.411
1270	20757.0	1579.70	0.25445	8.479
1260	20843.8	1601.94	0.25794	8.547
1250	20931.1	1624.61	0.26150	8.617
1240	21018.9	1647.73	0.26515	8.687
1230	21107.2	1671.31	0.26887	8.759
1220	21196.1	1695.38	0.27268	8.831
1210	21285.6	1719.95	0.27658	8.905
1200	21375.7	1745.07	0.28057	8.980
1190	21466.6	1770.76	0.28467	9.056
1180	21558.4	1797.09	0.28887	9.133

V	S(V)	A(V)	I(V)	T(V)
1170	21651.3	1824.11	0.29320	9.212
1160	21745.4	1851.92	0.29766	9.293
1150	21841.2	1880.64	0.30228	9.376
1140	21939.1	1910.47	0.30708	9.462
1130	22039.9	1941.70	0.31212	9.551
1120	22144.7	1974.68	0.31744	9.644
1110	22255.2	2010.06	0.32316	9.743
1100	22373.8	2048.78	0.32941	9.850
1090	22503.5	2091.94	0.33637	9.969
1080	22647.1	2140.80	0.34421	10.101
1070	22806.9	2196.52	0.35311	10.250
1060	22984.0	2259.92	0.36315	10.416
1050	23177.3	2331.21	0.37433	10.599
1040	23384.1	2409.88	0.38651	10.797
1030	23600.8	2495.04	0.39952	11.006
1020	23824.1	2585.77	0.41319	11.224
1010	24051.6	2681.36	0.42739	11.448
1000	24281.9	2781.50	0.44206	11.678
990	24514.8	2886.19	0.45719	11.912
980	24750.0	2995.59	0.47279	12.150
970	24987.8	3109.91	0.48888	12.394
960	25228.1	3229.36	0.50548	12.643
950	25470.9	3354.18	0.52260	12.898
940	25716.4	3484.61	0.54028	13.157
930	25964.4	3620.91	0.55854	13.423
920	26215.2	3763.34	0.57739	13.694
910	26468.8	3912.20	0.59687	13.971
900	26725.2	4067.79	0.61700	14.254
890	26984.4	4230.44	0.63782	14.544
880	27246.6	4400.49	0.65936	14.840
870	27511.8	4578.31	0.68164	15.143
860	27780.1	4764.26	0.70470	15.453
850	28051.6	4958.78	0.72859	15.771
840	28326.2	5162.28	0.75333	16.096
830	28604.2	5375.22	0.77897	16.429
820	28885.5	5598.11	0.80556	16.770
810	29170.3	5831.44	0.83314	17.119
800	29458.7	6075.79	0.86177	17.478
790	29750.7	6331.73	0.89148	17.845
780	30046.4	6599.90	0.92235	18.222
770	30345.9	6880.96	0.95443	18.608
760	30649.4	7175.62	0.98778	19.005
750	30956.9	7484.66	1.02248	19.412
740	31268.5	7808.88	1.05860	19.830
730	31584.3	8149.16	1.09620	20.260
720	31904.5	8506.43	1.13539	20.702
710	32229.3	8881.70	1.17625	21.156
700	32558.6	9276.04	1.21887	21.623
690	32892.6	9690.60	1.26336	22.104
680	33231.6	10126.63	1.30982	22.599
670	33575.5	10585.46	1.35838	23.108
660	33924.6	11068.54	1.40916	23.633
650	34279.1	11577.41	1.46231	24.174
640	34639.1	12113.75	1.5179-7	24.732
630	35004.7	12679.38	1.57630	25.308
620	35376.2	13276.25	1.63747	25.903
610	35753.7	13906.49	1.70168	26.517
600	36137.5	14572.40	1.76913	27.151
590	36527.7	15276.50	1.84003	27.807
580	36924.6	16021.50	1.91463	28.485
570	37328.4	16810.37	1.99319	29.188
560	37739.3	17646.35	2.07600	29.915
550	38157.6	18532.98	2.16337	30.669
540	38583.6	19474.13	2.25563	31.450
530	39017.6	20474.04	2.35317	32.262
520	39459.8	21537.37	2.45638	33.104
510	39910.7	22669.24	2.56573	33.979
500	40370.4	23875.30	2.68170	34.890
490	40839.4	25161.78	2.80484	35.837
480	41318.1	26535.56	2.93576	36.825
470	41806.9	28004.29	3.07512	37.854
460	42306.2	29576.44	3.22367	38.927
450	42816.4	31261.46	3.38223	40.049
440	43338.1	33069.86	3.55172	41.221
430	43871.8	35013.44	3.73317	42.448
420	44418.1	37105.39	3.92773	43.734
410	44977.5	39360.55	4.13670	45.082
400	45550.7	41795.65	4.36153	46.497
390	46138.4	44429.59	4.60387	47.985
380	46741.4	47283.81	4.86560	49.552
370	47360.4	50382.70	5.14882	51.203
360	47996.4	53754.10	5.45597	52.945
350	48650.3	57429.88	5.78982	54.788
340	49323.1	61446.71	6.15354	56.738
330	50016.1	65846.89	6.55082	58.807
320	50730.3	70679.48	6.98592	61.005
310	51467.2	76001.57	7.46380	63.345
300	52228.2	81879.97	7.99024	65.840
290	53015.0	88393.24	8.57206	68.508
280	53829.5	95634.24	9.21732	71.366
270	54673.5	103713.38	9.93557	74.436
260	55549.4	112762.74	10.73827	77.742

V	S(V)	A(V)	I(V)	T(V)
250	56459.6	122941.40	11.63918	81.312
240	57406.9	134442.33	12.65501	85.180
230	58394.6	147501.37	13.80618	89.384
220	59426.1	162409.29	15.11783	93.970
210	60505.6	179527.76	16.62125	98.993
200	61637.7	199311.22	18.35573	104.518
190	62827.9	222336.90	20.37117	110.624
180	64082.4	249346.88	22.73169	117.408
170	65408.6	281307.97	25.52083	124.991
160	66815.2	319498.55	28.84903	133.521
150	68312.6	365637.21	32.86469	143.188
140	69913.2	422078.00	37.77110	154.235
130	71632.4	492114.55	43.85259	166.982
120	73489.3	580468.73	51.51676	181.853
110	75507.8	694103.45	61.36454	199.427
100	77718.6	843631.36	74.31176	220.515

Tables of the Primary Siacci Functions

G_{SP} (Sphere) Drag Function

Quantity	Units
V	ft./sec.
S(V)	ft.-in.^{2}/lb.
A(V)	ft.-in.^{4}/lb.^{2}
I(V)	in.^{2}/lb.
T(V)	sec.-in.^{2}/lb.

V	S(V)	A(V)	~~T(V)~~ I(V)	T(V)
4500	0.0	0.00	0.00000	0.000
4490	11.7	0.00	0.00004	0.003
4480	23.4	0.00	0.00007	0.005
4470	35.2	0.00	0.00011	0.008
4460	47.0	0.00	0.00015	0.010
4450	58.8	0.01	0.00019	0.013
4440	70.6	0.01	0.00023	0.016
4430	82.4	0.01	0.00027	0.018
4420	94.3	0.01	0.00030	0.021
4410	106.2	0.02	0.00034	0.024
4400	118.1	0.02	0.00038	0.027
4390	130.0	0.03	0.00042	0.029
4380	142.0	0.03	0.00046	0.032
4370	154.0	0.04	0.00050	0.035
4360	166.0	0.04	0.00054	0.037
4350	178.0	0.05	0.00059	0.040
4340	190.1	0.06	0.00063	0.043
4330	202.2	0.07	0.00067	0.046
4320	214.3	0.07	0.00071	0.049
4310	226.4	0.08	0.00075	0.051
4300	238.6	0.09	0.00079	0.054
4290	250.7	0.10	0.00084	0.057
4280	262.9	0.11	0.00088	0.060
4270	275.2	0.12	0.00092	0.063
4260	287.4	0.14	0.00096	0.066
4250	299.7	0.15	0.00101	0.069
4240	312.0	0.16	0.00105	0.071
4230	324.3	0.17	0.00110	0.074
4220	336.7	0.19	0.00114	0.077
4210	349.1	0.20	0.00119	0.080
4200	361.5	0.22	0.00123	0.083
4190	373.9	0.23	0.00128	0.086
4180	386.4	0.25	0.00132	0.089
4170	398.9	0.27	0.00137	0.092
4160	411.4	0.28	0.00141	0.095
4150	423.9	0.30	0.00146	0.098
4140	436.5	0.32	0.00151	0.101
4130	449.1	0.34	0.00156	0.104
4120	461.7	0.36	0.00160	0.107
4110	474.4	0.38	0.00165	0.110
4100	487.0	0.40	0.00170	0.113
4090	499.7	0.42	0.00175	0.117
4080	512.5	0.45	0.00180	0.120
4070	525.2	0.47	0.00185	0.123
4060	538.0	0.49	0.00190	0.126
4050	550.8	0.52	0.00195	0.129
4040	563.7	0.54	0.00200	0.132
4030	576.5	0.57	0.00205	0.135
4020	589.4	0.60	0.00210	0.139
4010	602.4	0.62	0.00215	0.142
4000	615.3	0.65	0.00220	0.145
3990	628.3	0.68	0.00226	0.148

V	S(V)	A(V)	I(v) ~~T(V)~~	T(V)
3980	641.3	0.71	0.00231	0.152
3970	654.4	0.74	0.00236	0.155
3960	667.4	0.77	0.00241	0.158
3950	680.5	0.80	0.00247	0.162
3940	693.7	0.84	0.00252	0.165
3930	706.8	0.87	0.00258	0.168
3920	720.0	0.90	0.00263	0.172
3910	733.2	0.94	0.00269	0.175
3900	746.5	0.98	0.00274	0.178
3890	759.8	1.01	0.00280	0.182
3880	773.1	1.05	0.00286	0.185
3870	786.4	1.09	0.00291	0.189
3860	799.8	1.13	0.00297	0.192
3850	813.2	1.17	0.00303	0.196
3840	826.6	1.21	0.00309	0.199
3830	840.0	1.25	0.00315	0.203
3820	853.5	1.29	0.00321	0.206
3810	867.0	1.34	0.00327	0.210
3800	880.6	1.38	0.00333	0.213
3790	894.1	1.43	0.00339	0.217
3780	907.8	1.47	0.00345	0.220
3770	921.4	1.52	0.00351	0.224
3760	935.1	1.57	0.00357	0.228
3750	948.8	1.62	0.00363	0.231
3740	962.5	1.67	0.00370	0.235
3730	976.3	1.72	0.00376	0.239
3720	990.1	1.77	0.00382	0.242
3710	1003.9	1.83	0.00389	0.246
3700	1017.8	1.88	0.00395	0.250
3690	1031.7	1.94	0.00402	0.253
3680	1045.6	1.99	0.00409	0.257
3670	1059.6	2.05	0.00415	0.261
3660	1073.6	2.11	0.00422	0.265
3650	1087.6	2.17	0.00429	0.269
3640	1101.7	2.23	0.00435	0.273
3630	1115.8	2.29	0.00442	0.276
3620	1129.9	2.35	0.00449	0.280
3610	1144.1	2.42	0.00456	0.284
3600	1158.3	2.48	0.00463	0.288
3590	1172.6	2.55	0.00470	0.292
3580	1186.8	2.62	0.00477	0.296
3570	1201.1	2.69	0.00485	0.300
3560	1215.5	2.76	0.00492	0.304
3550	1229.9	2.83	0.00499	0.308
3540	1244.3	2.90	0.00507	0.312
3530	1258.7	2.97	0.00514	0.316

V	S(V)	A(V)	I(v) ~~T(V)~~	T(V)
3520	1273.2	3.05	0.00522	0.321
3510	1287.7	3.13	0.00529	0.325
3500	1302.3	3.20	0.00537	0.329
3490	1316.9	3.28	0.00544	0.333
3480	1331.6	3.36	0.00552	0.337
3470	1346.2	3.44	0.00560	0.341
3460	1360.9	3.53	0.00568	0.346
3450	1375.7	3.61	0.00576	0.350
3440	1390.5	3.70	0.00584	0.354
3430	1405.3	3.78	0.00592	0.359
3420	1420.2	3.87	0.00600	0.363
3410	1435.1	3.96	0.00608	0.367
3400	1450.0	4.05	0.00617	0.372
3390	1465.0	4.15	0.00625	0.376
3380	1480.0	4.24	0.00633	0.380
3370	1495.1	4.34	0.00642	0.385
3360	1510.2	4.44	0.00650	0.389
3350	1525.3	4.53	0.00659	0.394
3340	1540.5	4.64	0.00668	0.398
3330	1555.7	4.74	0.00677	0.403
3320	1571.0	4.84	0.00686	0.408
3310	1586.3	4.95	0.00694	0.412
3300	1601.6	5.05	0.00704	0.417
3290	1617.0	5.16	0.00713	0.422
3280	1632.4	5.27	0.00722	0.426
3270	1647.9	5.39	0.00731	0.431
3260	1663.4	5.50	0.00740	0.436
3250	1678.9	5.62	0.00750	0.440
3240	1694.5	5.73	0.00759	0.445
3230	1710.1	5.85	0.00769	0.450
3220	1725.8	5.97	0.00779	0.455
3210	1741.5	6.10	0.00788	0.460
3200	1757.2	6.22	0.00798	0.465
3190	1773.0	6.35	0.00808	0.470
3180	1788.9	6.48	0.00818	0.475
3170	1804.8	6.61	0.00828	0.480
3160	1820.7	6.74	0.00839	0.485
3150	1836.7	6.88	0.00849	0.490
3140	1852.7	7.01	0.00859	0.495
3130	1868.8	7.15	0.00870	0.500
3120	1884.9	7.29	0.00881	0.505
3110	1901.0	7.44	0.00891	0.510
3100	1917.2	7.58	0.00902	0.516
3090	1933.5	7.73	0.00913	0.521
3080	1949.8	7.88	0.00924	0.526
3070	1966.1	8.03	0.00935	0.531

V	S(V)	A(V)	I(V)	T(V)
3060	1982.5	8.19	0.00946	0.537
3050	1999.0	8.34	0.00958	0.542
3040	2015.5	8.50	0.00969	0.548
3030	2032.0	8.66	0.00981	0.553
3020	2048.6	8.83	0.00992	0.558
3010	2065.2	8.99	0.01004	0.564
3000	2081.9	9.16	0.01016	0.570
2990	2098.6	9.33	0.01028	0.575
2980	2115.4	9.50	0.01040	0.581
2970	2132.2	9.68	0.01052	0.586
2960	2149.1	9.86	0.01065	0.592
2950	2166.0	10.04	0.01077	0.598
2940	2183.0	10.22	0.01090	0.604
2930	2200.1	10.41	0.01102	0.609
2920	2217.2	10.60	0.01115	0.615
2910	2234.3	10.79	0.01128	0.621
2900	2251.5	10.99	0.01141	0.627
2890	2268.7	11.19	0.01155	0.633
2880	2286.0	11.39	0.01168	0.639
2870	2303.4	11.59	0.01181	0.645
2860	2320.8	11.80	0.01195	0.651
2850	2338.3	12.01	0.01209	0.657
2840	2355.8	12.22	0.01223	0.663
2830	2373.3	12.44	0.01237	0.670
2820	2391.0	12.66	0.01251	0.676
2810	2408.7	12.88	0.01265	0.682
2800	2426.4	13.10	0.01280	0.688
2790	2444.2	13.33	0.01295	0.695
2780	2462.0	13.57	0.01309	0.701
2770	2480.0	13.80	0.01324	0.708
2760	2497.9	14.04	0.01340	0.714
2750	2516.0	14.28	0.01355	0.721
2740	2534.1	14.53	0.01370	0.727
2730	2552.2	14.78	0.01386	0.734
2720	2570.4	15.03	0.01402	0.741
2710	2588.7	15.29	0.01418	0.747
2700	2607.0	15.55	0.01434	0.754
2690	2625.4	15.82	0.01450	0.761
2680	2643.9	16.09	0.01466	0.768
2670	2662.4	16.36	0.01483	0.775
2660	2680.9	16.64	0.01500	0.782
2650	2699.6	16.92	0.01517	0.789
2640	2718.3	17.20	0.01534	0.796
2630	2737.1	17.49	0.01551	0.803
2620	2755.9	17.79	0.01569	0.810
2610	2774.8	18.09	0.01587	0.817

V	S(V)	A(V)	I(V)	T(V)
2600	2793.8	18.39	0.01605	0.825
2590	2812.8	18.70	0.01623	0.832
2580	2831.9	19.01	0.01641	0.839
2570	2851.1	19.32	0.01660	0.847
2560	2870.3	19.64	0.01679	0.854
2550	2889.6	19.97	0.01698	0.862
2540	2909.0	20.30	0.01717	0.869
2530	2928.4	20.64	0.01736	0.877
2520	2947.9	20.98	0.01756	0.885
2510	2967.5	21.32	0.01776	0.893
2500	2987.1	21.67	0.01796	0.900
2490	3006.8	22.03	0.01817	0.908
2480	3026.6	22.39	0.01837	0.916
2470	3046.4	22.76	0.01858	0.924
2460	3066.3	23.13	0.01879	0.932
2450	3086.3	23.51	0.01900	0.941
2440	3106.4	23.89	0.01922	0.949
2430	3126.6	24.28	0.01944	0.957
2420	3146.8	24.68	0.01966	0.965
2410	3167.1	25.08	0.01988	0.974
2400	3187.5	25.49	0.02011	0.982
2390	3207.9	25.90	0.02034	0.991
2380	3228.5	26.32	0.02057	0.999
2370	3249.1	26.75	0.02081	1.008
2360	3269.8	27.18	0.02105	1.017
2350	3290.6	27.62	0.02129	1.026
2340	3311.5	28.07	0.02153	1.035
2330	3332.4	28.52	0.02178	1.044
2320	3353.5	28.98	0.02203	1.053
2310	3374.6	29.45	0.02228	1.062
2300	3395.8	29.92	0.02254	1.071
2290	3417.1	30.41	0.02280	1.080
2280	3438.5	30.90	0.02306	1.090
2270	3459.9	31.39	0.02333	1.099
2260	3481.5	31.90	0.02360	1.109
2250	3503.1	32.41	0.02387	1.118
2240	3524.8	32.93	0.02415	1.128
2230	3546.6	33.46	0.02443	1.138
2220	3568.5	34.00	0.02471	1.147
2210	3590.5	34.55	0.02500	1.157
2200	3612.6	35.11	0.02530	1.167
2190	3634.8	35.67	0.02559	1.177
2180	3657.1	36.24	0.02589	1.188
2170	3679.5	36.83	0.02620	1.198
2160	3702.0	37.42	0.02650	1.208
2150	3724.5	38.02	0.02682	1.219

V	S(V)	A(V)	~~T(V)~~ I(V)	T(V)
2140	3747.2	38.63	0.02713	1.229
2130	3770.0	39.25	0.02746	1.240
2120	3792.9	39.89	0.02778	1.251
2110	3815.8	40.53	0.02811	1.262
2100	3838.9	41.18	0.02845	1.273
2090	3862.1	41.84	0.02879	1.284
2080	3885.4	42.52	0.02913	1.295
2070	3908.8	43.20	0.02948	1.306
2060	3932.2	43.90	0.02983	1.318
2050	3955.9	44.61	0.03019	1.329
2040	3979.6	45.33	0.03056	1.341
2030	4003.4	46.06	0.03093	1.352
2020	4027.3	46.81	0.03130	1.364
2010	4051.4	47.56	0.03169	1.376
2000	4075.6	48.33	0.03207	1.388
1990	4099.8	49.12	0.03246	1.400
1980	4124.2	49.91	0.03286	1.413
1970	4148.8	50.73	0.03327	1.425
1960	4173.4	51.55	0.03368	1.438
1950	4198.2	52.39	0.03409	1.450
1940	4223.1	53.24	0.03452	1.463
1930	4248.1	54.11	0.03495	1.476
1920	4273.2	55.00	0.03538	1.489
1910	4298.5	55.90	0.03583	1.502
1900	4323.9	56.81	0.03628	1.516
1890	4349.4	57.74	0.03673	1.529
1880	4375.1	58.69	0.03720	1.543
1870	4400.9	59.66	0.03767	1.556
1860	4426.8	60.64	0.03815	1.570
1850	4452.9	61.64	0.03864	1.584
1840	4479.1	62.66	0.03913	1.599
1830	4505.5	63.70	0.03964	1.613
1820	4532.0	64.76	0.04015	1.627
1810	4558.6	65.83	0.04067	1.642
1800	4585.4	66.93	0.04120	1.657
1790	4612.4	68.05	0.04174	1.672
1780	4639.5	69.19	0.04228	1.687
1770	4666.7	70.35	0.04284	1.703
1760	4694.1	71.53	0.04341	1.718
1750	4721.7	72.73	0.04398	1.734
1740	4749.4	73.96	0.04457	1.750
1730	4777.3	75.21	0.04516	1.766
1720	4805.3	76.49	0.04577	1.782
1710	4833.6	77.79	0.04639	1.798
1700	4861.9	79.11	0.04701	1.815
1690	4890.5	80.46	0.04765	1.832

V	S(V)	A(V)	~~T(V)~~ I(V)	T(V)
1680	4919.2	81.84	0.04830	1.849
1670	4948.1	83.25	0.04897	1.866
1660	4977.2	84.68	0.04964	1.884
1650	5006.5	86.15	0.05033	1.901
1640	5036.0	87.64	0.05103	1.919
1630	5065.6	89.16	0.05174	1.937
1620	5095.5	90.72	0.05247	1.956
1610	5125.6	92.31	0.05321	1.974
1600	5155.8	93.93	0.05397	1.993
1590	5186.3	95.59	0.05474	2.012
1580	5217.0	97.28	0.05552	2.032
1570	5247.8	99.00	0.05632	2.051
1560	5278.9	100.77	0.05714	2.071
1550	5310.3	102.57	0.05797	2.091
1540	5341.8	104.41	0.05882	2.112
1530	5373.6	106.30	0.05969	2.132
1520	5405.6	108.22	0.06058	2.153
1510	5437.8	110.19	0.06148	2.175
1500	5470.3	112.20	0.06240	2.196
1490	5503.0	114.26	0.06334	2.218
1480	5536.1	116.36	0.06431	2.240
1470	5569.3	118.52	0.06529	2.263
1460	5602.9	120.73	0.06630	2.286
1450	5636.8	122.99	0.06733	2.309
1440	5670.9	125.31	0.06838	2.333
1430	5705.5	127.69	0.06946	2.357
1420	5740.3	130.13	0.07056	2.381
1410	5775.6	132.64	0.07169	2.406
1400	5811.2	135.21	0.07285	2.432
1390	5847.2	137.85	0.07404	2.457
1380	5883.5	140.57	0.07526	2.484
1370	5920.4	143.36	0.07652	2.510
1360	5957.6	146.24	0.07780	2.538
1350	5995.3	149.19	0.07912	2.566
1340	6033.4	152.24	0.08048	2.594
1330	6072.1	155.37	0.08187	2.623
1320	6111.2	158.61	0.08331	2.652
1310	6150.9	161.94	0.08478	2.683
1300	6191.1	165.38	0.08630	2.713
1290	6231.8	168.93	0.08786	2.745
1280	6273. 1	172.59	0.08947	2.777
1270	6315.1	176.38	0.09113	2.810
1260	6357.6	180.29	0.09284	2.843
1250	6400.7	184.33	0.09460	2.878
1240	6444.6	188.52	0.09642	2.913
1230	6489.0	192.85	0.09830	2.949

V	S(V)	A(V)	I(V) ~~T(V)~~	T(V)
1220	6534.2	197.33	0.10023	2.986
1210	6580.0	201.97	0.10223	3.024
1200	6626.6	206.78	0.10429	3.062
1190	6673.9	211.76	0.10642	3.102
1180	6722.0	216.93	0.10863	3.142
1170	6770.8	222.30	0.11090	3.184
1160	6820.5	227.86	0.11326	3.227
1150	6871.0	233.64	0.11569	3.270
1140	6922.3	239.64	0.11821	3.315
1130	6974.5	245.88	0.12081	3.361
1120	7027.6	252.36	0.12351	3.408
1110	7081.6	259.11	0.12631	3.457
1100	7136.6	266.13	0.12920	3.507
1090	7192.5	273.45	0.13220	3.558
1080	7249.5	281.06	0.13532	3.610
1070	7307.5	289.00	0.13854	3.664
1060	7366.5	297.28	0.14189	3.720
1050	7426.6	305.92	0.14537	3.777
1040	7487.9	314.94	0.14898	3.835
1030	7550.3	324.35	0.15272	3.896
1020	7613.9	334.19	0.15662	3.958
1010	7678.8	344.48	0.16067	4.021
1000	7744.9	355.24	0.16488	4.087
990	7812.3	366.50	0.16926	4.155
980	7881.0	378.29	0.17381	4.225
970	7951.1	390.64	0.17856	4.297
960	8022.7	403.58	0.18350	4.371
950	8095.6	417.16	0.18864	4.447
940	8170.1	431.41	0.19401	4.526
930	8246.1	446.37	0.19960	4.607
920	8323.7	462.08	0.20543	4.691
910	8402.9	478.59	0.21152	4.778
900	8483.8	495.96	0.21787	4.867
890	8566.4	514.23	0.22451	4.959
880	8650.8	533.46	0.23143	5.055
870	8736.9	553.71	0.23867	5.153
860	8824.9	575.04	0.24624	5.255
850	8914.8	597.54	0.25415	5.360
840	9006.7	621.26	0.26243	5.469
830	9100.6	646.30	0.27109	5.581
820	9196.5	672.75	0.28016	5.698
810	9294.6	700.70	0.28966	5.818
800	9395.0	730.26	0.29961	5.943
790	9497.5	761.53	0.31006	6.072
780	9602.5	794.64	0.32101	6.205
770	9709.9	829.72	0.33251	6.344

V	S(V)	A(V)	I(V) ~~T(V)~~	T(V)
760	9819.8	866.92	0.34459	6.488
750	9932.2	906.40	0.35728	6.637
740	10047.4	948.31	0.37063	6.791
730	10165.4	992.85	0.38468	6.952
720	10286.3	1040.24	0.39947	7.118
710	10410.2	1090.73	0.41507	7.292
700	10537.4	1144.55	0.43153	7.472
690	10667.8	1201.96	0.44890	7.660
680	10801.5	1263.21	0.46723	7.855
670	10938.6	1328.59	0.48659	8.058
660	11079.0	1398.30	0.50700	8.269
650	11222.5	1472.59	0.52852	8.488
640	11369.2	1551.77	0.55120	8.716
630	11519.0	1636.17	0.57511	8.952
620	11672.1	1726.12	0.60032	9.197
610	11828.4	1822.04	0.62691	9.451
600	11988.1	1924.36	0.65497	9.715
590	12151.2	2033.57	0.68460	9.989
580	12317.7	2150.15	0.71590	10.274
570	12487.7	2274.66	0.74898	10.569
560	12661.3	2407.69	0.78396	10.877
550	12838.5	2549.85	0.82096	11.196
540	13019.3	2701.83	0.86013	11.528
530	13203.9	2864.39	0.90161	11.873
520	13392.3	3038.38	0.94558	12.232
510	13584.7	3224.73	0.99224	12.605
500	13781.1	3424.48	1.04179	12.994
490	13981.8	3638.83	1.09449	13.400
480	14187.0	3869.07	1.15059	13.823
470	14396.7	4116.65	1.21040	14.264
460	14611.3	4383.16	1.27424	14.726
450	14830.8	4670.36	1.34247	15.208
440	15055.6	4980.25	1.41549	15.713
430	15285.8	5315.04	1.49376	16.243
420	15521.7	5677.23	1.57777	16.798
410	15763.5	6069.62	1.66811	17.381
400	16011.6	6495.38	1.765A1	17.993
390	16266.2	6958.10	1.87040	18.638
380	16527.6	7461.86	1.98389	19.317
370	16796.3	8011.29	2.10682	20.034
360	17072.7	8611.72	2.24027	20.791
350	17357.0	9269.23	2.38545	21.592
340	17649.9	9990.84	2.54378	22.441
330	17951.8	10784.69	2.71688	23.342
320	18263.3	11660.28	2.90664	24.301
310	18585.1	12628.63	3.11528	25.322

V	S(V)	A(V)	~~T(V)~~ I(V)	T(V)
300	18917.7	13702.68	3.34537	26.413
290	19261.9	14897.63	3.59993	27.580
280	19618.6	16231.51	3.88253	28.832
270	19988.7	17725.77	4.19743	30.178
260	20373.1	19406.14	4.54972	31.629
250	20773.0	21303.65	4.94554	33.198
240	21189.6	23456.00	5.39231	34.899
230	21624.4	25909.36	5.89913	36.750
220	22079.1	28720.73	6.47723	38.771
210	22555.3	31961.15	7.14054	40.987

V	S(V)	A(V)	~~T(V)~~ I(V)	T(V)
200	23055.4	35720.03	7.90661	43.427
190	23581.6	40111.13	8.79771	46.127
180	24136.8	45280.93	9.84250	49.130
170	24724.4	51420.63	11.07831	52.489
160	25348.3	58783.43	12.55454	56.273
150	26013.2	67710.34	14.33760	60.565
140	26724.7	78669.22	16.51851	65.476
130	27489.7	92315.79	19.22465	71.148
120	28316.8	109591.67	22.63872	77.772
110	29216.9	131887.76	27.03024	85.609
100	30203.9	161327.55	32.81016	95.023

REFERENCES

1a. Siacci, F., Giornale di artiglieria e genio, parte 2ᵉ (non ufficiale), 1° volume, Gennaio-Giugno, 376-411 (1880); also Revue d'Artillerie 17, 45-77 (1880-1881); and the key portions are in Ordnance Notes No. 152 (1881).

1b. Siacci, F., Rivista di artiglieria e genio, Volume III, 31-45 (1886); Revue d'Artillerie 27, 315-322 (1886).

2a. Ingalls, J. M., *Ingalls' Ballistic Tables*, Artillery Circular M, Revised 1917, Govt. Printing Office, Washington, D. C., 1918. This 1917 revision of Ref. 2b has the primary tables (S, T, I, A) at closer intervals. The major revision was some different secondary function tables. The title page is misleading. The 1893 date actually refers to the *series* of Artillery Circulars which began in 1893, not the publication date of the original Artillery Circular M (Ref. 2b), which was 1900.

2b. Ingalls, J. M., Artillery Circular M (Series of 1893), Govt. Printing Office, Washington, D. C., 1900.

2c. Zaboudski, N. A., Artilleriiskii Zhurnal #4, 299 (1894); also Revue d'Artillerie 45, 119 (1894-1895); and Journal of the U. S. Artillery 5, 369-375 (1896).

3. McShane, E. J., J. L. Kelley, and F. V. Reno, *Exterior Ballistics*, University of Denver Press, 1953. ~~1953.~~

4. Kent, R. H., and H. P. Hitchcock, "Applications of Siacci's Method to Flat Trajectories," Ballistic Research Laboratories Report No. 114, 1938.

5a. Cranz, C., and K. Becker, *Handbook of Ballistics, Vol. I, Exterior Ballistics*, translated from the 2nd German Edition, HMSO, London, 1921.

5b. Miller, D. G., "Ballistics Tables for Spheres 7.5 to 25mm (.3 to 1 in.) in Diameter," UCRL-52755, Lawrence Livermore National Laboratory, 1979.

5c. Hermann, E. E., *Exterior Ballistics*, U. S. Naval Institute, Annapolis, 1926; also 1930 and 1935 editions.

6. Hatcher, J. S., *Hatcher's Notebook*, Second Edition, The Stackpole Company, 1957.

7. Hitchcock, H. P., "Resistance Functions of Various Types of Projectiles," Ballistic Research Laboratories Report No. 27, 1935.

8. Hitchcock, H. P., "Bibliography of Tables of Drag and Related Functions," Ballistic Research Laboratories Technical Note No. 745, 1952.

9. Braun, W. F., "Aerodynamic Data for Small Arms Projectiles," Ballistic Research Laboratory Report No. 1630, 1973.

10. Hitchcock, H. P., "A Study of Form Factors of Spinning Projectiles," Ballistic Research Laboratories Report No. 166, 1939.

11. Hitchcock, H. P., "Form Factors of Projectiles," Ballistic Research Laboratories Report No. 284, 1942.

12. Hitchcock, H. P., "Table of Form Factors of Projectiles," Ballistic Research Laboratories Memorandum Report No. 564, 1951.

13. Hitchcock, H. P., "Aerodynamic Data for Spinning Projectiles," Ballistic Research Laboratories Report No. 620, 1947 (Revised 1952).

14. McCoy, R. L., "Estimation of the Static Aerodynamic Characteristics of Ordnance Projectiles at Supersonic Speeds," Ballistic Research Laboratories Report No. 1682, 1973.

15. McCoy, R. L., "MCDRAG - A Computer Program for Estimating the Drag Coefficients of Projectiles," Ballistic Research Laboratory Technical Report No. ARBRL-TR-02293, 1981.

16. McCoy, R. L., "The Aerodynamic Characteristics of .50 Ball, M33, API, M8, and APIT, M20 Ammunition," Ballistic Research Laboratory Memorandum Report No. BRL-MR-3810, 1990.

17. United States Committee on Extension to the Standard Atmosphere, *U. S. Standard Atmosphere, 1962,* U. S. Government Printing Office, Washington 25, D. C., 1962.

18. International Civil Aviation Organization, "Standard Atmosphere - Tables and Data for Altitudes to 65,800 Feet," Langley Aeronautical Laboratory, NACA Report No. 1235, 1955.

7

The Effect of Wind on Flat-Fire Trajectories

7.1 INTRODUCTION

The effect of wind on flat-fire trajectories is a logical extension of the results derived in Chapter 5. The same coordinate system is used in this chapter, with the additional definition of the wind components, illustrated in Figure 7.1.

A vector wind component is considered positive when it blows in the positive direction of one of the coordinate axes. Thus a tailwind, blowing from the gun toward the target will be taken as a positive W_x. A wind blowing vertically upward is a positive W_y, and a wind from 9:00 toward 3:00, or left to right across the line of fire, will be taken as a positive crosswind, W_z.

7.2 EQUATIONS OF MOTION

The vector differential equation of motion is similar to equation (5.3) of Chapter 5. However, the vector velocity, $\vec{V}$, in the expression for the drag force must be replaced with $(\vec{V} - \vec{W})$, because the aerodynamic drag depends on the velocity relative to the air stream, not the velocity relative to the ground.

$$\frac{d\vec{V}}{dt} = -\hat{C}_D^* \tilde{V}(\vec{V} - \vec{W}) + \vec{g} \quad (7.1)$$

where
$\vec{V}$ = vector velocity
$\frac{d\vec{V}}{dt}$ = vector acceleration
$\vec{W}$ = vector wind velocity
$\vec{g}$ = vector acceleration due to gravity
$\hat{C}_D^* = \frac{\rho S C_D}{2m}$
ρ = air density
S = projectile reference area
m = projectile mass
C_D = dimensionless drag coefficient

The quantity $\tilde{V}$ is the scalar magnitude of the velocity relative to the air stream:

$$\tilde{V} = \left|\vec{V} - \vec{W}\right| \quad (7.2)$$

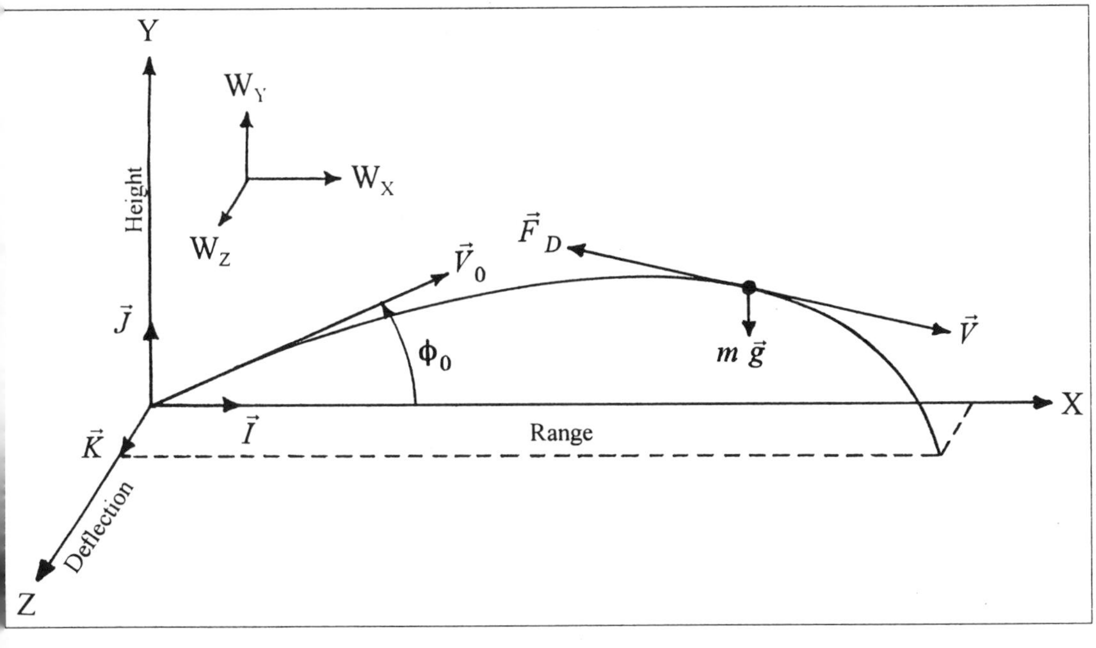

Figure 7.1 Coordinate System for a Point-Mass Trajectory with Wind.

The vectors $\vec{V}$ and $\vec{W}$ are now resolved into components along the coordinate axes:

$$\vec{V} = V_x\vec{I} + V_y\vec{J} + V_z\vec{K} \quad (7.3)$$

$$\vec{W} = W_x\vec{I} + W_y\vec{J} + W_z\vec{K} \quad (7.4)$$

where $\vec{I}$ is a unit vector along the X-axis

$\vec{J}$ is a unit vector along the Y-axis

$\vec{K}$ is a unit vector along the Z-axis

V_x, V_y, V_z are the velocity components

W_x, W_y, W_z are the wind components

Then,
$$\tilde{V}^2 = (\vec{V} - \vec{W}) \bullet (\vec{V} - \vec{W}) \quad (7.5)$$

Substituting the velocity and wind components into equation (7.5) and taking the square root of both sides:

$$\tilde{V} = \sqrt{(V_x - W_x)^2 + (V_y - W_y)^2 + (V_z - W_z)^2} \quad (7.6)$$

The differential equations of motion for a point-mass trajectory with wind are:

$$\dot{V}_x = -\hat{C}_D^*\tilde{V}(V_x - W_x) \quad (7.7)$$

$$\dot{V}_y = -\hat{C}_D^*\tilde{V}(V_y - W_y) - g \quad (7.8)$$

$$\dot{V}_z = -\hat{C}_D^*\tilde{V}(V_z - W_z) \quad (7.9)$$

Equations (7.7) through (7.9), together with equation (7.6) are an exact statement of Newton's second law of motion for a projectile acted on by aerodynamic drag, gravity, and wind. As in Chapter 5, the equations are non-linearly coupled to each other through equation (7.6), and an exact solution is possible only by numerical methods. The numerical solution of equations (7.6) through (7.9) will be addressed in the next chapter.

7.3 THE FLAT-FIRE APPROXIMATION

Equation (7.6) may be written in the equivalent form:

$$\tilde{V} = (V_x - W_x)\sqrt{1 + \varepsilon_y^2 + \varepsilon_z^2} \quad (7.10)$$

where
$$\varepsilon_y = (V_y - W_y)/(V_x - W_x) \quad (7.11)$$

$$\varepsilon_z = (V_z - W_z)/(V_x - W_x) \quad (7.12)$$

The square root in equation (7.10) is now expanded in series, using the binomial theorem:

$$\tilde{V} = (V_x - W_x)\left[1 + \frac{1}{2}(\varepsilon_y^2 + \varepsilon_z^2) - \frac{1}{8}(\varepsilon_y^2 + \varepsilon_z^2)^2 + \cdots\right] \quad (7.13)$$

It is evident that $\tilde{V}$ and $(V_x - W_x)$ will differ by a very small amount if the following inequalities are satisfied:

$$|W_x| << V_x;\ |W_y| << V_x;\quad and\ |W_z| << V_x \quad (7.14)$$

$$\varepsilon_y^2 << 1;\quad and\ \varepsilon_z^2 << 1 \quad (7.15)$$

Since all wind components are small compared with V_x, the first inequality of equation (7.15) reduces to the classical flat-fire restriction for the no-wind trajectory. It will be shown later that W_z is an upper bound for V_z, so that for small wind components the second inequality of equation (7.15) is also everywhere satisfied. Thus $\tilde{V}$ and $(V_x\text{-}W_x)$ differ by less than one percent for flat-fire trajectories if all wind components are small in comparison with the projectile velocity. Equations (7.7) through (7.9) may therefore be approximated as:

$$\dot{V}_x = -\hat{C}_D^*(V_x - W_x)^2 \quad (7.16)$$

$$\dot{V}_y = -\hat{C}_D^*(V_x - W_x)(V_y - W_y) - g \quad (7.17)$$

$$\dot{V}_z = -\hat{C}_D^*(V_x - W_x)(V_z - W_z) \quad (7.18)$$

Equations (7.16) through (7.18) are the differential equations of motion for flat-fire trajectories, acted on by winds that are two orders of magnitude smaller than the downrange velocity.

A general analytical solution of the flat-fire, small-wind equations is possible by means of quadratures. However, a more useful approach is to determine the effect of one wind component at a time on the trajectory.

Anemometer measurements of winds near the earth's surface show that vertical wind components are usually much smaller than winds parallel to the ground. In addition, the effect of a vertical wind on a flat-fire trajectory is analagous to the crosswind effect, except that it acts in the vertical plane instead of the horizontal. The vertical wind component, W_y, will therefore be neglected in the remainder of this chapter.

7.4 THE EFFECT OF A CONSTANT CROSSWIND ON THE FLAT-FIRE TRAJECTORY

For the crosswind case, $W_x = W_y = 0$, and equations (7.16) through (7.18) reduce to:

$$\dot{V}_x = -\hat{C}_D^* V_x^2 \quad (7.19)$$

$$\dot{V}_y = -\hat{C}_D^* V_x V_y - g \quad (7.20)$$

$$\dot{V}_z = -\hat{C}_D^* V_x(V_z - W_z) \quad (7.21)$$

Equations (7.19) and (7.20) are identical to equations (5.16) and (5.17) of Chapter 5, for the no-wind case. Thus the vertical plane of the flat-fire point-mass trajectory is unaffected by crosswind. (Note: This is not strictly true. The presence of crosswind causes a small aerodynamic jump effect in the vertical plane, which will be illustrated later in Chapter 12).

Equations (7.19) and (7.21) are now transformed to new equations with downrange distance, X, as the independent variable (see section 5.3 of Chapter 5):

$$V_x' = -\hat{C}_D^* V_x \tag{7.22}$$

$$V_z' = -\hat{C}_D^*(V_z - W_z) \tag{7.23}$$

where the superscript prime (') indicates differentiation with respect to X.

Since the initial line of fire lies in the X-Y plane, the initial value of V_z is zero. The general solution of equations (7.22) and (7.23) is:

$$V_x = V_{x_o} e^{-\int_0^x \hat{C}_D^* ds_1} \tag{7.24}$$

$$V_z = e^{-\int_0^x \hat{C}_D^* ds_1}\left[\int_0^x W_z \hat{C}_D^* e^{\int_0^{s_2} \hat{C}_D^* ds_1} ds_2\right] \tag{7.25}$$

If W_z is constant, the integral inside the brackets of equation (7.25) may be directly evaluated, and we obtain:

$$V_z = \frac{V_x}{V_{x_o}} W_z \left[e^{\int_0^x \hat{C}_D^* ds_1} - 1\right] = W_z\left(1 - \frac{V_x}{V_{x_o}}\right) \tag{7.26}$$

Since $0 < V_x < V_{x_o}$ for all X, $|V_z|$ is everywhere less than $|W_z|$, which verifies the earlier statement that W_z is an upper bound for V_z.

The deflection due to a constant crosswind, W_z, is:

$$\boxed{Z = \int_0^t V_z ds_1 = W_z\left(t - \frac{X}{V_{x_o}}\right)} \tag{7.27}$$

Equation (7.27) is the classical formula for crosswind deflection, and we note that it is an exact solution for a constant crosswind acting everywhere along a flat-fire point-mass trajectory. The quantity $\left(t - X/V_{x_o}\right)$ is often referred to as "lag time," since it is the time difference, or lag, between the actual flight time and the time to the same range in a vacuum. Equation (7.27) is often referred to as the "lag rule" for predicting the crosswind effect.

The classical crosswind deflection formula was first obtained in the middle of the nineteenth century by the French ballistician, Didion. In his "Cours Elémentaire de Balistique," published in 1859, Didion correctly defined the "lag time," and stated that the crosswind deflection was equal to the space passed over by the crosswind in the time represented by the lag.

Equation (7.27) also shows that if a sustainer rocket, whose thrust precisely equals the drag force were added to the base of the projectile, the lag time would vanish and there would be no deflection due to crosswind. This concept is referred to as "automet," and has been used for ordnance projectile designs that required absolute minimum sensitivity to crosswind. If the rocket thrust exceeds the drag force, the lag time will be negative, and we note that equation (7.27) correctly predicts the upwind deflection observed for high thrust rockets in crosswinds.

Example 7.1

In Table 6.6 of the previous chapter, the downrange striking velocity and time of flight of the caliber .30 Ball M2 projectile were listed, for ranges out to 600 yards. The muzzle velocity is 2800 feet per second (fps). Use equation (7.27) and the values from Table 6.6 to determine the effect of a 10 mile per hour (MPH) crosswind on the trajectory of the Ball M2 bullet, at ranges out to 600 yards.

We first convert 10 MPH to feet per second.

W_z = [(5280)/(3600)](10) = 14.67 fps

The required computations are shown in Table 7.1:

Table 7.1
(Caliber .30 Ball M2)
(10 MPH Crosswind)

Range (Yards)	X (Feet)	t (seconds)	$\left(X/V_{x_o}\right)$ (sec.)	Z (Feet)	Z (Inches)
0	0	0	0	0	0
100	300	.112	.107	.07	0.9
200	600	.234	.214	.29	3.5
300	900	.368	.321	.69	8.3
400	1200	.516	.429	1.28	15.3
500	1500	.680	.536	2.11	25.3
600	1800	.863	.643	3.23	38.7

The effect of a constant 10 MPH crosswind is obviously enough to cause a miss on the target at the longer ranges.

7.5 THE EFFECT OF A VARIABLE CROSSWIND ON THE FLAT-FIRE TRAJECTORY

The approximate effect of a variable crosswind on the flat-fire trajectory is readily obtained, using a variation of the method of section 7.4. The technique involves the linear superposition of a series of constant crosswind solutions, each of which starts at a different downrange distance from the gun muzzle.

Consider a constant crosswind, W_z, commencing at $X = X_i$, and continuing downrange. Such a crosswind is illustrated in Figure 7.2(a). The solution of equations (7.22) and (7.23) with the crosswind of Figure 7.2(a), for all ranges where $R > X_i$, is given by:

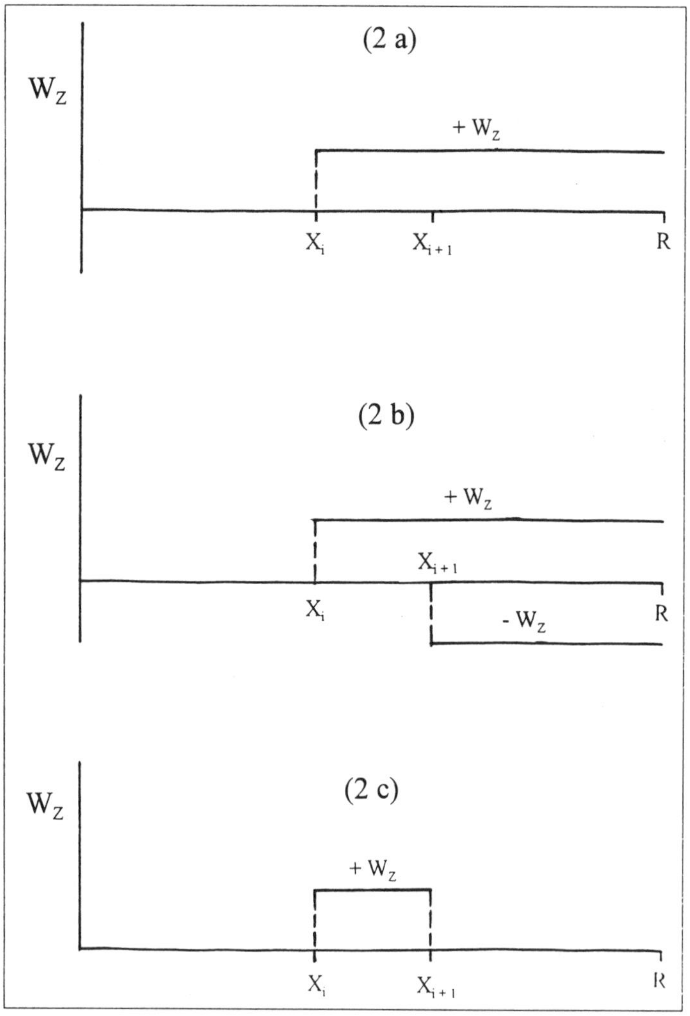

Figure 7.2 Constant Crosswind over a Short Segment of the Trajectory.

$$Z(R) = W_{zi}\,[t(R) - t(X_i) - (R - X_i)/V_{xi}] \qquad (7.28)$$

A second constant crosswind, $-W_z$, starting at a larger downrange distance, X_{i+1}, is now added to the first crosswind, as shown in Figure 7.2(b). The net crosswind acting on the trajectory is illustrated in Figure 7.2(c). For all ranges where $R > X_{i+1}$, the solution of equations (7.22) and (7.23), with the crosswind of Figure 7.2(c), is given by:

$$Z(R) = W_{zi}\,\{[t(R) - t(X_i) - (R - X_i)/V_{xi}] - [t(R) - t(X_{i+1}) - (R - X_{i+1})/V_{x(i+1)}]\} \qquad \mathbf{(7.29)}$$

Since any downrange variation of the wind can be approximated by a series of constant winds acting over short intervals, equation (7.29) provides a general method for calculating the effect of variable crosswinds on flat-fire trajectories.

We will define the crosswind weighting factor, f_{WZi}, as:

$$f_{WZi} = [t(R) - t(X_i) - (R - X_i)/V_{Xi}] - [t(R) - t(X_{i+1}) - (R - X_{i+1})/VX_{(i+1)}] \qquad \mathbf{(7.30)}$$

In practice, the crosswind weighting factors at various ranges are obtained from the first differences of a table of values for the function $[t(R) - t(X_i) - (R - X_i)/V_{xi}]$. Example 7.2 illustrates the technique, for the calber .30 Ball M2 bullet out to 600 yards range.

Example 7.2

Use equation (7.30) to construct a table of crosswind weighting factors for the caliber .30 Ball M2 bullet. The velocity and time of flight data are taken from Table 6.6 of the previous chapter, and the range to the target, R, is 600 yards. Table 7.2 shows the calculations.

The fifth column is computed using the tabulated values of X_i, V_{xi}, and $t(_{xi})$, together with the values R = 1800 feet and t(R) = 0.863 second. The crosswind weighting factors listed in the sixth column of the table are obtained by successive differences of the values in column five.

Table 7.2
(Caliber .30 Ball M2)
(Range to Target = 600 Yards)

X_i (Yards)	X_i (Feet)	V_{Xi} (fps)	$t(X_i)$ (sec.)	$[t(R) - t(X_i) - (R - X_i)/V_{xi}]$ (seconds)	f_{WZi} (seconds)
0	0	2800	0	.220	----
100	300	2571	.112	.168	.052
200	600	2349	.234	.118	.050
300	900	2135	.368	.073	.045
400	1200	1930	.516	.036	.037
500	1500	1733	.680	.010	.026
600	1800	1547	.863	0	.010

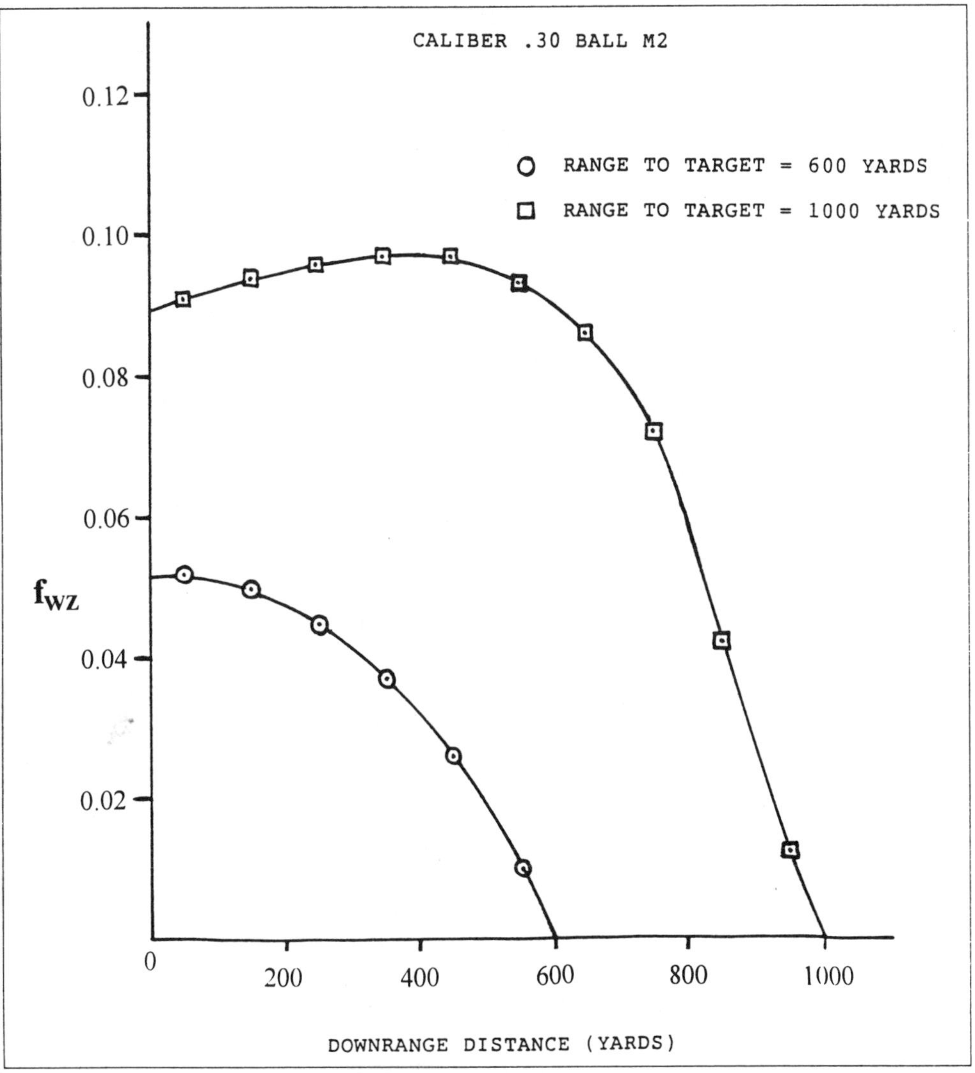

Figure 7.3 Crosswind Weighting Factors for Two Target Ranges.

The utility of the crosswind weighting factor method is based on the fact that the weighting factor represents the local sensitivity of the trajectory to crosswind. The effect of any variable crosswind on the trajectory is determined by summing the products of the average crosswind speeds over each interval and the weighting factors over the same intervals. The technique will now be illustrated for a few hypothetical variable crosswinds.

For the first hypothetical case, we will assume a constant crosswind of 10 MPH over the first half of the 600 yard Ball M2 trajectory, and no wind for the second half. Thus W_z is 14.67 fps over the first three intervals of Table 7.2. The effect of this crosswind on the deflection at 600 yards range is:

$$Z = (14.67)(.052) + (14.67)(.050) + (14.67)(.045) = 2.16 \text{ feet}$$

In the second hypothetical case, we will assume no wind over the first half of the trajectory, and a 10 MPH crosswind over the second half. Using the crosswind weighting factors in Table 7.2 for the last three intervals, we find:

$$Z = (14.67)(.037) + (14.67)(.026) + (14.67)(.010) = 1.07 \text{ feet}$$

In Example 7.1, we observed that a constant crosswind of 10 MPH acting over the entire 600 yard range would deflect the caliber .30 Ball M2 bullet by 3.23 feet. Our two hypothetical examples thus indicate that about 2/3 of the observed crosswind deflection at 600 yards range occurs in the first one-half of the trajectory, and the remaining 1/3 of the deflection occurs in the last half of the flight.

An even more striking comparison is provided by the ratio of the crosswind weighting factor over the first 100 yard interval to that over the last (500-600 yard) interval. The caliber .30 Ball M2 bullet is more than five times as sensitive to a crosswind acting over the first 100 yards, than to the same crosswind acting over the interval from 500 to 600 yards range!

Figure 7.3 illustrates the variation of the caliber .30 Ball M2 crosswind weighting factor with downrange distance from the gun, for target ranges of 600 and 1000 yards. For the 600 yard target, the bullet is most sensitive to crosswind near the gun muzzle, and the sensitivity decays ever more rapidly with increasing downrange distance. For the 1000 yard target, the point of maximum wind sensitivity occurs at around 400 yards downrange, with a very rapid decay beyond 600 yards. In both cases, the sensitivity of the trajectory to crosswind at the target is zero. This is, in fact, a general result, which can be demonstrated by choosing X_i and X_{i+1} very close to the target range, R; the crosswind at the target has absolutely no effect on any flat-fire point-mass trajectory!

7.6 THE EFFECT OF RANGEWIND ON THE FLAT-FIRE TRAJECTORY

For the rangewind case, $W_y = W_z = 0$, and equations (7.16) through (7.18) reduce to:

$$\dot{V}_x = -\hat{C}_D^*\left(V_x - W_x\right)^2 \quad \textbf{(7.31)}$$

$$\dot{V}_y = -\hat{C}_D^*\left(V_x - W_x\right)V_y - g \quad \textbf{(7.32)}$$

$$\dot{V}_z = -\hat{C}_D^*\left(V_x - W_x\right)V_z \quad \textbf{(7.33)}$$

Since there is no crosswind, we will neglect equation (7.33). Equations (7.31) and (7.32) are now transformed into new equations with downrange distance, X, as the independent variable. After some simplification we obtain:

$$V_x' + \hat{C}_D^* V_x = \hat{C}_D^* W_x\left(2 - \frac{W_x}{V_x}\right) \quad \textbf{(7.34)}$$

$$V_y' + \hat{C}_D^*\left(1 - \frac{W_x}{V_x}\right)V_y = -\left(\frac{g}{V_x}\right) \quad \textbf{(7.35)}$$

From the first inequality of (7.14), we know that the largest value of W_X must be at least two orders of magnitude smaller than V_X, at every point along the trajectory. Thus equations (7.34) and (7.35) reduce to:

$$V_x' + \hat{C}_D^* V_x = 2\hat{C}_D^* W_x \quad \textbf{(7.36)}$$

$$V_y' = \hat{C}_D^* V_y = -\frac{g}{V_x} \quad \textbf{(7.37)}$$

For a constant rangewind, the general solution of equation (7.36) is:

$$V_x = V_{x_o} e^{-\int_0^X \hat{C}_D^* ds_1} + 2W_x\left[1 - e^{-\int_0^X \hat{C}_D^* ds_1}\right] \quad \textbf{(7.38)}$$

The first term on the right hand side of equation (7.38) is the drag-induced velocity decay experienced by the projectile in the absence of rangewind. The second term on the right hand side of (7.38) gives the change in downrange velocity, caused by the presence of rangewind.

At a fixed range, R, we will denote values of the velocity components, time of flight and trajectory height, for a trajectory with rangewind, as $[V_x]$, $[V_y]$, [t], and [Y]. The same symbol without the bracket refers to the equivalent quantity along a no-wind trajectory.

Substituting equation (7.24) into equation (7.38), and denoting the left hand side of (7.38) as $[V_x]$:

$$[V_x] = V_x + 2\,W_x\,(1 - V_x / V_{x0}) \quad \textbf{(7.39)}$$

The second term in equation (7.39) shows that a constant tailwind adds an increment of downrange velocity, whose magnitude is zero at the gun muzzle, but gradually increases with increasing range. A constant headwind (negative W_x) would subtract an equivalent downrange velocity increment.

If a table of V_x versus range is available for the no-wind case, equation (7.39) provides a good approximation to the effect of rangewind on the downrange striking velocity. Equation (7.39) is valid for any flat-fire trajectory with constant rangewind, as long as the downrange velocity exceeds the constant rangewind speed by at least two orders of magnitude.

The general solution of equation (7.37) for the rangewind case is:

$$\left[V_y\right] = V_{y_o} e^{-\int_0^X \hat{C}_D^* ds_1} - g e^{-\int_0^X \hat{C}_D^* ds_1}\left(\int_0^X \frac{1}{\left[V_x\right]} e^{\int_0^X \hat{C}_D^* ds_1} ds_1\right) \quad \textbf{(7.40)}$$

With the help of equation (7.24), equation (7.40) reduces to:

$$\left[V_y\right] = V_x \tan\phi_o - gV_x \int_0^X \frac{ds_1}{V_x\left[V_x\right]} \quad \textbf{(7.41)}$$

Now, $V_x\,[V_x] = V_x^2\,(1 + 2\,W_x/V_x - 2\,W_x/V_{x0})$ **(7.42)**

Since terms of order (W_x/V_x) may be neglected in comparison with unity:

$$V_x\,[V_x] \approx V_x^2 \quad \textbf{(7.43)}$$

$$\left[V_y\right] = V_x \tan\phi_o - gV_x \int_0^X \frac{ds_1}{V_x^2} \quad \textbf{(7.44)}$$

But equation (5.29) in Chapter 5, with the help of equations (5.30) and (5.23), gives an identical result to equation (7.44), for the no-wind case.

Thus, $[V_y] \approx V_y$ **(7.45)**

Equation (7.45) tells us that for flat-fire and small ratio of rangewind speed to projectile downrange velocity, a rangewind does not significantly alter the vertical component of velocity, at any reasonable range.

To determine the effect of a constant rangewind on the time of flight, we need to find an expression for the average downrange velocity:

$$\left[V_x\right]_{(AVE)} = \frac{1}{X}\int_0^X \left[V_x\right] ds_1 = \frac{1}{X}\left(\int_0^X V_x ds_1 + 2W_x X - \frac{2W_x}{V_{x_o}}\int_0^X V_x ds_1\right) \quad (7.46)$$

But, $$\frac{1}{X}\int_0^X V_x ds_1 = V_{x(AVE)} \quad (7.47)$$

$$\left[V_x\right]_{(AVE)} = V_{x(AVE)} + 2W_x\left(1 - \frac{V_{x(AVE)}}{V_{x_o}}\right) \quad (7.48)$$

Now, $$t = \frac{R}{V_{x(AVE)}}, \text{ and } [t] = \frac{R}{\left[V_x\right]_{(AVE)}}, \quad (7.49)$$

where R = range to impact.

$$1/[t] = (1/t)(1 - 2 W_x/V_{x0}) + 2 W_x/R \quad (7.50)$$

Inverting equation (7.50) yields:

$$[t] = t/\{1 + 2 W_x(t/R - 1/V_{x0})\} \quad (7.51)$$

Equation (7.51) shows that a constant tailwind results in a shorter time of flight to a fixed range, as we would expect.

The final quantity we need to determine, for a flat-fire trajectory with rangewind, is the impact height on a vertical target. Equation (7.45) provides the result that a rangewind does not significantly affect the vertical component of velocity. Thus at a fixed range R to the target, the impact height for the rangewind case is equivalent to the impact height for the no-wind case at time [t].

$$[Y]_{(R)} = Y_{[t]} \quad (7.52)$$

For small {[t] - t}, a good approximation to equation (7.52) is the leading term in a Taylor's series expansion:

$$[Y]_{(R)} = Y_{(R)} + V_{Y(R)}\{[t] - t\} \quad (7.53)$$

The vertical component of velocity, V_y, is readily obtained from the downrange velocity and the tangent of the flight-path angle (trajectory inclination angle), for any flat-fire trajectory:

$$V_y = V_x \tan\phi \approx V \tan\phi \quad (7.54)$$

The utility of equations (7.39), (7.51), (7.53) and (7.54) will now be demonstrated by means of a numerical example.

Example 7.3

In Table 6.6 of the previous chapter, the downrange striking velocity, time of flight and vertical target impact height were tabulated for the caliber .30 Ball M2 bullet, fired at an angle of departure of 19 minutes, and with a muzzle velocity of 2800 fps. Determine the effect of a 10 MPH (14.67 fps) tailwind on this trajectory, at ranges out to 600 yards.

The ratio of the rangewind speed to the downrange velocity at 600 yards range is:

14.67/1547 = 0.0095

The first of equations (7.14) is satisfied for the Ball M2 bullet with a 10 MPH rangewind, and we may therefore proceed with the calculations. Equations (7.39) and (7.51) are used to generate the data in Table 7.3:

Table 7.3
(Caliber .30 Ball M2)
(10 MPH Tailwind)
(V_x and t From Numerical Integration)

Range (Yards)	V_x (fps)	$[V_x]$ (fps)	t (seconds)	[t] (seconds)
0	2800	2800	0	0
100	2571	2573	0.112	0.112
200	2349	2354	0.234	0.234
300	2135	2142	0.368	0.367
400	1930	1939	0.516	0.515
500	1733	1744	0.680	0.678
600	1547	1560	0.863	0.860

The effect of the constant 10 MPH rangewind on the vertical target impact height is now determined. In Table 6.4 of the previous chapter, approximate values of the downrange velocities were obtained for the caliber .30 Ball M2 bullet, using the G_8 ballistic tables. The first two columns of Table 7.4, below, are extracted from Table 6.4, and the third column of Table 7.4 is obtained from the I(V) table for the G_8 drag function. The fourth column in Table 7.4 is then found using equation (6.41) of Chapter 6, and the fact that the tangent of 19 minutes is 0.00553. The vertical component of the velocity, and the vertical target impact height at each range, are obtained from equations (7.54) and (7.53), and are tabulated in columns five and six, respectively, of Table 7.4.

Table 7.4 (Caliber .30 Ball M2 - G_8 Ballistic Tables) (10 MPH Tailwind)						
Range (Yards)	V_x (fps)	I(V)	$\tan\phi$	$[V_y]$ (fps)	[Y] (Ft.)	[Y] (In.)
0	2800	.05149	.00553	15.5	0	0
100	2573	.06441	.00417	10.7	1.47	17.6
200	2351	.07949	.00259	6.1	2.48	29.8
300	2135	.09729	.00072	1.5	2.98	35.8
400	1927	.11973	-.00164	-3.2	2.84	34.1
500	1727	.14731	-.00453	-7.8	1.93	23.2
600	1537	.18184	-.00816	-12.5	0.07	0.8

The results of modern numerical integration for the same 10 MPH tailwind are shown in Table 7.5:

Table 7.5 (Caliber .30 Ball M2) (10 MPH Tailwind) (Numerical Integration)				
Range (Yards)	$[V_x]$ (fps)	[t] (seconds)	$[V_y]$ (fps)	[Y] (Inches)
0	2800	0	15.5	0
100	2573	0.112	10.8	17.6
200	2352	0.234	6.1	29.8
300	2140	0.367	1.4	35.8
400	1937	0.515	-3.2	34.1
500	1742	0.678	-7.9	23.2
600	1558	0.860	-12.6	0.7

Comparison of Tables 7.3 and 7.4 with Table 7.5 shows that the largest error in downrange velocity is 2 feet/second; the times of flight agree to three significant figures; the vertical velocity components agree to within 0.1 foot/second; and the impact heights agree to within 0.1 inch. The flat-fire trajectory approximation for the effect of a constant rangewind thus agrees quite well with the results of modern numerical methods.

Note the nearly negligible effect of a 10 MPH rangewind on the caliber .30 Ball M2 trajectory, compared with the effect of a 10 MPH crosswind, illustrated in Example 7.1. A constant 10 MPH crosswind blows the 150 grain bullet off course nearly 39 inches at 600 yards range; a constant 10 MPH tailwind or headwind raises or lowers the vertical target impact height by less than 0.50 inch at the same range. The modern rifleman who shoots a high velocity, flat trajectory projectile at moderate ranges, is certainly justified in neglecting the range component of any wind that is blowing, and concentrating his attention on the crosswind component.

The effect of a variable rangewind on the flat-fire trajectory could be approximated by a method similar to that used in section 7.5 for variable crosswinds. In view of the generally negligible effect of rangewind on flat-fire trajectories, the rather complicated treatment of a variable rangewind is not worth the effort expended, and will not be pursued in this chapter.

7.7 SUMMARY

The effect of wind on flat-fire trajectories has been thoroughly explored in this chapter. The classical crosswind deflection formula, often referred to as the "lag rule," is shown to be an exact solution of the differential equations of motion for a flat-fire trajectory with constant crosswind. A simple and straightforward extension of the classical result is shown to accurately account for the effect of variable crosswinds along the trajectory, by means of a crosswind weighting factor technique. The effect of a constant rangewind (tailwind or headwind) is investigated, and the rangewind effect for flat-fire trajectories is shown to be negligible in comparison with the crosswind effect. Several practical computational examples are presented, to illustrate the application of the methods presented in this chapter.

8

The Point-Mass Trajectory

8.1 INTRODUCTION

In Chapter 3 we noted that the vacuum trajectory, which includes only the force of gravity, is seldom useful in modern exterior ballistics. On the other hand, the point-mass trajectory, which includes the aerodynamic drag force in addition to gravity, is a very practical and accurate approximation to the actual trajectory of any projectile that flies with predominantly small yaw. In fact, the point-mass trajectory approximation is so generally useful, it may well be considered to be the backbone of modern exterior ballistics.

8.2 EQUATIONS OF MOTION

The vector differential equation of motion for a point-mass trajectory with wind was stated as equation (7.1) in the previous chapter. The vector velocity, $\vec{V}$, must be replaced with $(\vec{V} - \vec{W})$ in the expression for the aerodynamic drag force, because the drag depends on the velocity relative to the air stream, not the velocity relative to the ground.

$$\frac{d\vec{V}}{dt} = -\hat{C}_D^* \tilde{V}\left(\vec{V} - \vec{W}\right) + \vec{g} \quad \textbf{(8.1)}$$

where $\vec{V}$ = vector velocity (relative to the ground)

$\frac{d\vec{V}}{dt}$ = vector acceleration (relative to the ground)

$\vec{W}$ = vector wind velocity (relative to the ground)

$\vec{g}$ = vector acceleration due to gravity

$\hat{C}_D^* = \frac{\rho S C_D}{2m}$

ρ = air density

S = projectile reference area

m = projectile mass

C_D = dimensionless drag coefficient

The quantity $\tilde{V}$ is the scalar magnitude of the projectile's velocity relative to the air stream:

$$\tilde{V} = \left|\vec{V} - \vec{W}\right| \quad \textbf{(8.2)}$$

Substituting the velocity and wind components into equation (8.1), and following the procedure of Chapter 7, we obtain the three scalar differential equations of motion:

$$\dot{V}_x = -\hat{C}_D^* \tilde{V}\left(V_x - W_x\right) \quad \textbf{(8.3)}$$

$$\dot{V}_y = -\hat{C}_D^* \tilde{V}\left(V_y - W_y\right) - g \quad \textbf{(8.4)}$$

$$\dot{V}_z = -\hat{C}_D^* \tilde{V}\left(V_z - W_z\right) \quad \textbf{(8.5)}$$

The scalar is given by:

$$\tilde{V} = \sqrt{\left(V_x - W_x\right)^2 + \left(V_y - W_y\right)^2 + \left(V_z - W_z\right)^2} \quad \textbf{(8.6)}$$

A vector wind component is considered positive when it blows in the positive direction of one of the coordinate axes. Thus a tailwind, blowing from the gun toward the target will be taken as a positive rangewind, W_x. A wind blowing vertically upward is a positive W_y, and a wind from 9:00 toward 3:00, or left to right across the line of fire, will be taken as a positive crosswind, W_z.

Equations (8.3) through (8.5), together with equation (8.6) are an exact statement of Newton's second law of motion for a projectile acted on by aerodynamic drag, gravity, and wind. As noted in several previous chapters, equations (8.3), (8.4) and (8.5) are nonlinearly coupled to each other through equation (8.6), and an exact (more precisely, a nearly exact) solution is possible only by numerical methods. Such methods are the subject of this chapter.

8.3 CHANGE OF INDEPENDENT VARIABLE FROM TIME TO DISTANCE

In several previous chapters, the approximate analytical solutions of flat-fire point-mass trajectories were greatly facilitated by transforming the independent variable in the differential equations from time to downrange distance. No change of independent variable is required for numerical solution of the exact differential equations of motion; either time or distance could be used, and the accuracy of the solution would not be affected. However, for most point-mass trajectories, downrange distance turns out to be a more convenient choice of independent variable. Trajectory outputs printed at fixed range intervals are generally more useful than those printed in fixed time increments, and if distance is used as the independent variable, the need for numerical interpolation in the results is avoided.

Equations (8.3) through (8.5) are now transformed to new equations with downrange distance, X, as the independent variable (see section 5.3 of Chapter 5 for the details of the transformation):

$$V_x' = -\hat{C}_D^*\left(\frac{\tilde{V}}{V_x}\right)\left(V_x - W_x\right) \quad \textbf{(8.7)}$$

$$V_y' = -\hat{C}_D^*\left(\frac{\tilde{V}}{V_x}\right)\left(V_y - W_y\right) - \left(\frac{g}{V_x}\right) \quad \textbf{(8.8)}$$

$$V_z' = -\hat{C}_D^*\left(\frac{\tilde{V}}{V_x}\right)\left(V_z - W_z\right) \quad \textbf{(8.9)}$$

where the superscript prime (') indicates differentiation with respect to X.

Equations (8.7) through (8.9) are also an exact statement of Newton's second law of motion for the point-mass trajectory. Equation (8.6) is unchanged by the transformation to a new independent variable. We note that in general, observed values of the vertical wind component, W_y, are very small near the earth's surface, and the vertical wind component is therefore neglected in the remainder of this chapter.

8.4 NUMERICAL SOLUTION OF THE EQUATIONS OF MOTION

Since the late 1940s, the widespread availability of digital computers has led to a veritable explosion in the development and use of numerical methods. At first, this growth was limited by the high cost of access to the few available large mainframe computers, and most exterior ballisticians continued to use the approximate methods discussed in previous chapters of this book. Today, the proliferation of relatively inexpensive microcomputers ("PCs") has given both amateur and professional ballisticians ready access to powerful modern computational capabilities.

A number of numerical methods are available for solving ordinary differential equations. Although a comparative treatment of these various techniques is beyond the scope of this book, a brief discussion of several commonly used numerical methods may be of interest. The most basic approach is known as Euler's method, which solves a differential equation by a stepwise procedure, in which a new value is found from the sum of the present value plus the product of the local derivative and the integration step size. Euler's method is conceptually simple, but it is not very accurate, unless extremely small values of the step size are used. A modification of Euler's method, known as Heun's method, uses the derivatives at both the beginning and the end of the integration step, to calculate an average value over the step. Heun's method can also include an iteration loop to further refine the average value of the derivative. Euler's method is called a "first order" integration scheme, and Heun's method is a "second order" method.

Some of the most powerful and generally useful numerical methods for ordinary differential equations fall into the category known as Runge-Kutta (R-K) methods. There are second, third and fourth order R-K systems, plus a number of variants of each, and all of them work very well for particular problems. The second order R-K method is equivalent to Heun's method, with a single corrector step (no iteration). There is even a fifth order R-K system, known as "Butcher's method," which has been used extensively in the calculation of high precision orbital trajectories. The numerical accuracy increases, and the computational efficiency decreases, with increasing order of the Runge-Kutta methods.

Other multi-step predictor-corrector methods, such as the Newton-Cotes method, Milne's method, and the Adams method have been used to calculate exterior ballistic trajectories. Reference 1 contains a discussion of the numerical methods commonly used in modern engineering practice, and points out some of the strong points and the weaknesses of each.

All the above methods (and others not mentioned), are highly satisfactory for the numerical solution of most ordinary differential equations. If a specific system of differential equations must be solved repeatedly, over a limited range of values for both the equation parameters and the initial conditions, there often exists an optimum numerical method that gives the shortest possible computation time, yet gives sufficient accuracy for the problem. Such is indeed the case for the numerical solution of point-mass trajectories. The cumulative experience of the Ballistic Research Laboratory has shown that the one-step, second-order methods are, in the practical sense, optimum solutions of the point-mass trajectory problem. The higher order methods give no significant improvement in practical accuracy, but require more computation time. The author's favorite method for the point-mass trajectory problem is the Heun method, with an iteratively applied corrector formula.

8.5 STANDARD ATMOSPHERES FOR POINT-MASS TRAJECTORIES

Two slightly different standard atmospheres have traditionally been used by U. S. Army Ordnance over the years, and these atmospheres have become standardized throughout the military and sporting arms and ammunition industries. The older U. S. standard atmosphere (Ref. 2) is known today as Army Standard Metro; this atmosphere was used by Army Ordnance from 1905 until the early 1960s, and is still in common use in the commercial U. S. sporting ammunition industry. The newer atmosphere is the International Civil Aviation Organization (ICAO) atmosphere (Ref. 3), up to 20 kilometers (approximately 65,800 feet) altitude, with its extension (Ref. 4) to 32 kilometers (105,000 feet) in 1962.

The decrease in air temperature with increasing altitude is accurately described, for moderate altitudes, by the following equation:

$$T(Y) = [T_0\,(°F) + 459.67]\, e^{-KY} - 459.67 \quad \textbf{(8.10)}$$

where T_0 (°F) = air temperature at the firing site (°F)

Y = altitude above firing site (feet)

T(Y) = air temperature at altitude Y (°F)

K = temperature-altitude decay factor (1/feet)

The standard sea-level air temperature for both atmospheres is 59 degrees Fahrenheit. Appropriate values of the temperature-altitude decay factor, K, are given by:

For Army Standard Metro: $K = 6.015 \times 10^{-6}$ (1/feet) **(8.11)**

For the ICAO Atmosphere:

$K = 6.858 \times 10^{-6} + (2.776 \times 10^{-11})\, Y$ (1/feet) **(8.12)**

The speed of sound in air is given by the following equations:

For Army Standard Metro:

$$a_o = 49.19\sqrt{T(Y) + 459.67} \quad \text{(fps)} \qquad \textbf{(8.13)}$$

For the ICAO Atmosphere:

$$a_o = 49.0223\sqrt{T(Y) + 459.67} \quad \text{(fps)} \qquad \textbf{(8.14)}$$

The decrease in air density with increasing altitude is accurately described, for moderate altitudes, by the following equation:

$$\rho(Y) = \rho_0 e^{-hY} \qquad \textbf{(8.15)}$$

where ρ_0 = air density at the firing site (pounds/cubic foot)

Y = altitude above firing site (feet)

$\rho(Y)$ = air density at altitude Y (pounds/cubic foot)

h = air density-altitude decay factor (1/feet)

At sea level, the standard values of air density are given in Equations (8.16) and (8.18) below:

For Army Standard Metro: ρ_0 = 0.0751265 lbs./cubic foot **(8.16)**

$h = 3.158 \times 10^{-5}$ (1/feet) **(8.17)**

For the ICAO Atmosphere:

ρ_0 = 0.0764742 lbs./cubic foot **(8.18)**

$h = 2.926 \times 10^{-5} + (1.0 \times 10^{-10})\, Y$ (1/feet) **(8.19)**

For altitudes up to 20,000 feet above sea level, the above equations give essentially exact results for the variation of air temperature and air density with increasing altitude. At 35,000 feet altitude, the errors have increased to about one percent. At altitudes above 40,000 feet the errors grow rapidly with increasing height, and the above equations should not be used where the summit of the trajectory exceeds 40,000 feet in altitude.

The air density ratio is obtained from the equation of state of an ideal gas:

$$(\rho/\rho_0) = (P/P_0)\{518.67/[T_0(°F) + 459.67]\} \qquad \textbf{(8.20)}$$

where (ρ/ρ_0) = ratio of air density at firing site to standard air density

P = barometric pressure at firing site

P_0 = standard barometric pressure

T_0(°F) = air temperature at firing site

Values of the standard air density (at sea level) were given by equations (8.16) and (8.18) for Army Standard Metro, and the ICAO Standard Atmosphere, respectively. Standard sea-level values of the barometric pressure are given below:

Army Std. Metro:

P_0 = 29.53 inches of Hg = 750 mm of Hg **(8.21)**

ICAO Atmosphere:

P_0 = 29.92 inches of Hg = 760 mm of Hg **(8.22)**

Most riflemen do not carry a thermometer and a barometer when shooting at high altitude above sea level. Table 8.1 lists nominal values of air temperature, pressure and density ratio at a number of altitudes above mean sea level, for both the Army Standard Metro and the ICAO Standard Atmosphere. These year-round average values may be used if no better local information is available.

The altitude in the first column of Table 8.1 (*top p. 168*) is the height above mean sea level.

The humidity has a small effect on both the air density and the speed of sound in air. The humidity correction (Ref. 5) to the air density ratio at sea level [equation (8.20)] is given by:

Army Std. Metro:

$$f_{\rho(R_H)} = 1 - .00378(R_H - 78)\left(\frac{P_{WV}}{29.53}\right) \qquad \textbf{(8.23)}$$

ICAO Atmosphere:

$$f_{\rho(R_H)} = 1 - .00378(R_H - 78)\left(\frac{P_{WV}}{29.92}\right) \qquad \textbf{(8.24)}$$

where $f_{\rho(R_H)}$ = humidity correction factor to the air density ratio

Table 8.1

	ARMY STANDARD METRO			ICAO STANDARD ATMOSPHERE		
Altitude (Feet)	Temp. (Deg. F)	Bar. Press. (In., Hg)	Density Ratio	Temp. (Deg. F)	Bar. Press. (In., Hg)	Density Ratio
0	59.0	29.53	1.000	59.0	29.92	1.000
500	57.4	28.97	.984	57.2	29.38	.985
1000	55.9	28.44	.969	55.4	28.86	.971
1500	54.3	27.92	.954	53.7	28.33	.957
2000	52.8	27.40	.939	51.9	27.82	.943
3000	49.7	26.39	.910	48.3	26.82	.915
4000	46.7	25.40	.881	44.7	25.84	.888
5000	43.6	24.47	.854	41.2	24.90	.862
6000	40.6	23.55	.827	37.6	23.98	.836
7000	37.6	22.71	.802	34.0	23.09	.811
8000	34.6	21.87	.777	30.5	22.23	.786
9000	31.7	21.07	.753	26.9	21.39	.761
10000	28.7	20.27	.729	23.4	20.58	.739
15000	14.3	16.81	.623	5.5	16.89	.629
20000	0.2	13.93	.532	-12.3	13.76	.533
25000	-13.4	11.54	.454	-30.0	11.12	.449
30000	-26.6	9.57	.388	-47.8	8.90	.375
35000	-39.5	7.92	.331	-65.6	7.06	.310

R_H = relative humidity (percent)

P_{WV} = water vapor pressure at the local temperature (Inches of Mercury)

The effect of humidity on the air density is accounted for by multiplying the air density ratio of Equation (8.20) by the appropriate correction factor, from Equation (8.23) or (8.24).

The humidity correction to the speed of sound in air at sea level is given (Ref. 5) by the following equations:

Army Std. Metro:

$$f_{a_o(R_H)} = 1 + .0014(R_H - 78)\left(\frac{P_{WV}}{29.53}\right) \qquad \textbf{(8.25)}$$

ICAO Atmosphere:

$$f_{a_o(R_H)} = 1 + .0014(R_H - 78)\left(\frac{P_{WV}}{29.92}\right) \qquad \textbf{(8.26)}$$

where $f_{a_o(R_H)}$ = humidity correction factor to the speed of sound in air

The effect of humidity on the speed of sound in air is now obtained by multiplying the value from Equation (8.13) or (8.14) by the correction factor from Equation (8.25) or (8.26), respectively.

For temperatures above freezing, the water vapor pressure increases rapidly with increasing air temperature, as Table 8.2 shows:

Table 8.2

Air Temperature (Deg. F)	Water Vapor Pressure, P_{WV} (In., Hg)
-40	0.006
0	0.045
32	0.18
59	0.50
70	0.74
100	1.93
130	4.53

Table 8.3 illustrates the effect of humidity on the air density ratio and the speed of sound, at various sea level temperatures, for both the Army Standard Metro and the ICAO Standard Atmosphere, at standard barometric pressures:

In general, increasing humidity causes a slight decrease in air density, because the density of water vapor is less than that of dry air. On the other hand, increasing humidity causes a slight increase in the speed of sound. For air temperatures below 70 degrees Fahrenheit, the changes in both air density and speed of sound for a 100 percent change in humidity, are less than 1 percent, and may therefore be neglected for all practical purposes. At 100 degrees Fahrenheit, the air density for saturated air is 2.5 percent below that of dry air; the difference has increased to 6.1 percent at 130 degrees Fahrenheit. Thus for air temperatures above 70 degrees Fahrenheit, the

Table 8.3

T (°F)	R_H (%)	ARMY STD. METRO ρ/ρ_o	ARMY STD. METRO a_0 (fps)	ICAO STD. ATMOS. ρ/ρ_o	ICAO STD. ATMOS. a_0 (fps)
0	0	1.134	1054.5	1.128	1051.0
0	50	1.134	1054.6	1.128	1051.2
0	78	1.134	1054.6	1.128	1051.2
0	100	1.133	1054.7	1.128	1051.3
32	0	1.060	1090.0	1.055	1087.0
32	50	1.059	1090.5	1.054	1087.5
32	78	1.058	1090.7	1.053	1087.7
32	100	1.058	1090.9	1.053	1087.9
59	0	1.005	1118.2	1.000*	1116.45**
59	50	1.002	1119.5	.997	1117.8
59	78	1.000*	1120.27**	.995	1118.5
59	100	.999	1120.9	.994	1119.1
70	0	.984	1129.0	.979	1128.2
70	50	.979	1131.0	.975	1130.2
70	78	.977	1132.1	.972	1131.3
70	100	.975	1133.0	.970	1132.1
100	0	.931	1155.4	.927	1159.7
100	50	.920	1160.7	.915	1165.0
100	78	.913	1163.7	.909	1167.9
100	100	.908	1166.1	.904	1170.2
130	0	.884	1174.5	.880	1190.4
130	50	.858	1187.3	.854	1203.0
130	78	.844	1194.5	.840	1210.1
130	100	.833	1200.1	.829	1215.7

* Sea level standard air density for this specific atmosphere
** Sea level standard speed of sound for this specific atmosphere

humidity correction to the air density is small, but not negligible. The small correction for the humidity effect on the speed of sound should also be made at temperatures above 70 degrees Fahrenheit, but it is actually important only when the projectile flight velocity is near the speed of sound, where a small change in the Mach number causes a relatively large change in the drag coefficient.

8.6 EXAMPLES OF POINT-MASS TRAJECTORIES

The examples in this section were run using the author's "MCTRAJ" computer program, which is a point-mass trajectory calculation program, using the Heun method for numerical integration. The "MCTRAJ" program has been checked against the BRL "G-TRAJ" point-mass trajectory program, and the results obtained are essentially identical out to ranges of 120 kilometers. A listing of the Q-BASIC version of the MCTRAJ computer program is given at the end of this chapter.

Example 8.1

The MCTRAJ computer program was used to solve the vacuum trajectory mortar problem of Example 3.3 in Chapter 3. The easiest way to run a vacuum trajectory with a point-mass computer program is to input zeroes for the drag coefficient values at all Mach numbers. For use with the MCTRAJ program, we enter the value $C_D = 0$, for the drag coefficient at Mach zero, and the same value again, for some suitably high Mach number that will never be exceeded, such as 10. It makes no difference which atmosphere is selected for the vacuum trajectory, since there is no drag.

The muzzle velocity is 80 meters per second (262.467 feet per second), and the range to the target is 600 meters. It is suggested that the value C = 1.0 be used for the ballistic coefficient, because it will immediately be recognized as a fictitious value. The initial height of the line-of-sight is zero for our mortar problem. Starting values of 30 degrees (1800 minutes) for the low angle solution, and 60 degrees (3600 minutes) for the high angle solution are suggested for the initial gun elevation angles.

It does not matter what values of the air density ratio and the air temperature are used, so standard values are as good as any. There can be no wind in a vacuum trajectory, so both the rangewind and crosswind values are set to zero. The trajectory match range is 600 yards, and the match height is zero, for both the low and the high angle solutions.

The two MCTRAJ output trajectories are shown in Figures 8.1 and 8.2. Inspection of these outputs shows that the low and high angle solutions give gun elevation angles of 2005.03 minutes (33.42 degrees), and 3394.97 minutes (56.58 degrees) respectively; these values agree with those found analytically in Example 3.3 of Chapter 3. The maximum ordinate of both trajectories occurs at a range of 300 meters; the low angle solution gives a peak trajectory height of 3896.5 inches (approximately 99.0 meters), and the high angle

```
DRAG FUNCTION:  VACUUM

MACH NO.       CD

 0             0
 10            0

ICAO STANDARD ATMOSPHERE

PROJECTILE IDENTIFICATION:  LOW-ANGLE VACUUM MORTAR TRAJECTORY

MUZ VEL         C             HO            ELEV          DENSITY
(FT/SEC)     (LB/IN2)      (INCHES)      (MINUTES)        RATIO

 262.467       1             0             2005.03         1

 TEMP        RANGEWIND     CROSSWIND     RMATCH         HMATCH
(DEG,F)        (MPH)         (MPH)       (METERS)       (INCHES)

 59            0             0             600             0


 RANGE      HEIGHT       DEFL.     VEL      TIME      VX        VY       VZ
(METERS)     (IN)        (IN)     (FPS)    (SEC)     (FPS)     (FPS)    (FPS)

     0        0.0        0.0      262.5    0.000     219.1     144.5    0.0
    50     1190.6        0.0      250.0    0.749     219.1     120.5    0.0
   100     2164.7        0.0      239.3    1.498     219.1      96.4    0.0
   150     2922.4        0.0      230.7    2.246     219.1      72.3    0.0
   200     3463.6        0.0      224.3    2.995     219.1      48.2    0.0
   250     3788.3        0.0      220.4    3.744     219.1      24.1    0.0
   300     3896.5        0.0      219.1    4.493     219.1       0.0    0.0
   350     3788.3        0.0      220.4    5.242     219.1     -24.1    0.0
   400     3463.6        0.0      224.3    5.990     219.1     -48.2    0.0
   450     2922.4        0.0      230.7    6.739     219.1     -72.3    0.0
   500     2164.7        0.0      239.3    7.488     219.1     -96.4    0.0
   550     1190.6        0.0      250.0    8.237     219.1    -120.5    0.0
   600        0.0        0.0      262.5    8.985     219.1    -144.5    0.0
```

Figure 8.1 Low-Angle Vacuum Mortar Trajectory.

DRAG FUNCTION: VACUUM

MACH NO.	CD
0	0
10	0

ICAO STANDARD ATMOSPHERE

PROJECTILE IDENTIFICATION: HIGH-ANGLE VACUUM MORTAR TRAJECTORY

MUZ VEL (FT/SEC)	C (LB/IN2)	HO (INCHES)	ELEV (MINUTES)	DENSITY RATIO
262.467	1	0	3394.97	1

TEMP (DEG,F)	RANGEWIND (MPH)	CROSSWIND (MPH)	RMATCH (METERS)	HMATCH (INCHES)
59	0	0	600	0

RANGE (METERS)	HEIGHT (IN)	DEFL. (IN)	VEL (FPS)	TIME (SEC)	VX (FPS)	VY (FPS)	VZ (FPS)
0	0.0	0.0	262.5	0.000	144.5	219.1	0.0
50	2734.8	0.0	232.9	1.135	144.5	182.6	0.0
100	4972.4	0.0	205.5	2.270	144.5	146.1	0.0
150	6712.7	0.0	181.4	3.405	144.5	109.5	0.0
200	7955.8	0.0	161.9	4.539	144.5	73.0	0.0
250	8701.7	0.0	149.1	5.674	144.5	36.5	0.0
300	8950.3	0.0	144.5	6.809	144.5	0.0	0.0
350	8701.7	0.0	149.1	7.944	144.5	-36.5	0.0
400	7955.8	0.0	161.9	9.079	144.5	-73.0	0.0
450	6712.7	0.0	181.4	10.214	144.5	-109.5	0.0
500	4972.4	0.0	205.5	11.349	144.5	-146.1	0.0
550	2734.8	0.0	232.9	12.483	144.5	-182.6	0.0
600	0.0	0.0	262.5	13.618	144.5	-219.1	0.0

Figure 8.2 High-Angle Vacuum Mortar Trajectory.

DRAG FUNCTION: M1911A1 - 230 GRAIN HARDBALL

MACH NO.	CD
0	.205
.85	.205

ICAO STANDARD ATMOSPHERE

PROJECTILE IDENTIFICATION: M1911A1 PISTOL - 50 YARD ZERO

MUZ VEL (FT/SEC)	C (LB/IN2)	HO (INCHES)	ELEV (MINUTES)	DENSITY RATIO
860	.161	.56	12.59	1

TEMP (DEG,F)	RANGEWIND (MPH)	CROSSWIND (MPH)	RMATCH (YARDS)	HMATCH (INCHES)
59	0	0	50	0

RANGE (YARDS)	HEIGHT (IN)	DEFL. (IN)	VEL (FPS)	TIME (SEC)	VX (FPS)	VY (FPS)	VZ (FPS)
0	-0.6	0.0	860.0	0.000	860.0	3.1	0.0
25	1.2	0.0	843.0	0.088	843.0	0.3	0.0
50	0.0	0.0	826.4	0.178	826.4	-2.6	0.0
75	-4.4	0.0	810.1	0.270	810.1	-5.5	0.0
100	-12.2	0.0	794.2	0.363	794.1	-8.3	0.0
125	-23.3	0.0	778.6	0.458	778.5	-11.2	0.0
150	-38.1	0.0	763.3	0.556	763.1	-14.1	0.0
175	-56.6	0.0	748.3	0.655	748.1	-17.0	0.0
200	-79.0	0.0	733.6	0.756	733.3	-19.9	0.0

Figure 8.3 M1911 Pistol Trajectory, for 50 Yard Zero.

solution gives a maximum trajectory height of 8950.3 inches (227.3 meters). The MCTRAJ solution again agrees with the exact analytical result from Chapter 3. Note the symmetry of the ascending and descending branches of the vacuum trajectory, and the fact that the downrange component of velocity is always constant throughout the flight.

Example 8.2

The MCTRAJ computer program was used to run the caliber .45, Ball, M1911 trajectory of Examples 5.1 and 5.2, Chapter 5. The drag coefficient is constant, at 0.205, for Mach numbers below 0.85; the muzzle velocity is taken to be 860 feet per second, and the sectional density of the 0.452" diameter, 230 grain round-nose hardball bullet is 0.161 pounds per square inch. Since the actual measured drag coefficient for this bullet is being used, the form factor is 1.000 at all speeds, and the ballistic coefficient is therefore equal to the sectional density. The height of the front sight above the bore centerline is 0.56 inch. The problem is to find the gun elevation angle required to zero the pistol at 50 yards range, in an ICAO standard, sea-level atmosphere, and print out the trajectory in 25 yard intervals out to 200 yards.

The MCTRAJ output for this case is shown as Figure 8.3. The results show essentially exact agreement with the flat-fire analytical method illustrated in Examples 5.1 and 5.2 of Chapter 5.

Example 8.3

A trajectory for the caliber .30 Ball M2 bullet, at a muzzle velocity of 2800 fps, was calculated in examples 6.1 and 6.2, using the Siacci methods of Chapter 6. Using the MCTRAJ computer program, we will compare the two trajectories obtained by: (1) the spark-range drag coefficient curve, with the ballistic coefficient equal to the sectional density (0.226 pounds per square inch), and (2) the G_8 drag coefficient curve, with a ballistic coefficient, relative to G_8 of 0.210 pounds per square inch. The gun elevation angle used for both problems is 19 minutes, and Army Standard Metro is used for both cases. The trajectory is printed out every 100 yards, out to 600 yards range.

A plot of the zero-yaw drag coefficient versus Mach number, from firings done in the BRL Aerodynamics Range, is shown as Figure 8.4 The two MCTRAJ outputs are illustrated in Figures 8.5 and 8.6. The results are insignificantly different in practice, out to 600 yards range.

Example 8.4

The caliber .30, Ball M2 projectile is again used in this example, and the next, to illustrate additional properties of point-mass trajectories. Figure 8.7 (*p. 172*) shows the envelope of trajectories for the .30, Ball M2 bullet. The reader should compare this plot with Figure 3.2 of Chapter 3. Although the maximum ranges and the maximum ordinates are both much less for point-mass trajectories than for the same bullet in a vacuum, the similarities in the two graphs are striking.

Example 8.5

Figures 8.8 and 8.9 (*p. 173*) are plots of the ratio of slant range to level ground range, versus superelevation angle, for the caliber .30, Ball M2 projectile. These two figures illustrate the effects of firing uphill and downhill, respectively, on small arms point-mass trajectories. The reader should compare these two plots with Figures 3.4 and 3.5 of Chapter 3, for vacuum trajectories. The behavior of the quantity (R_s /R) at small superelevation angles is distinctly different for the point-mass and the vacuum cases. How-

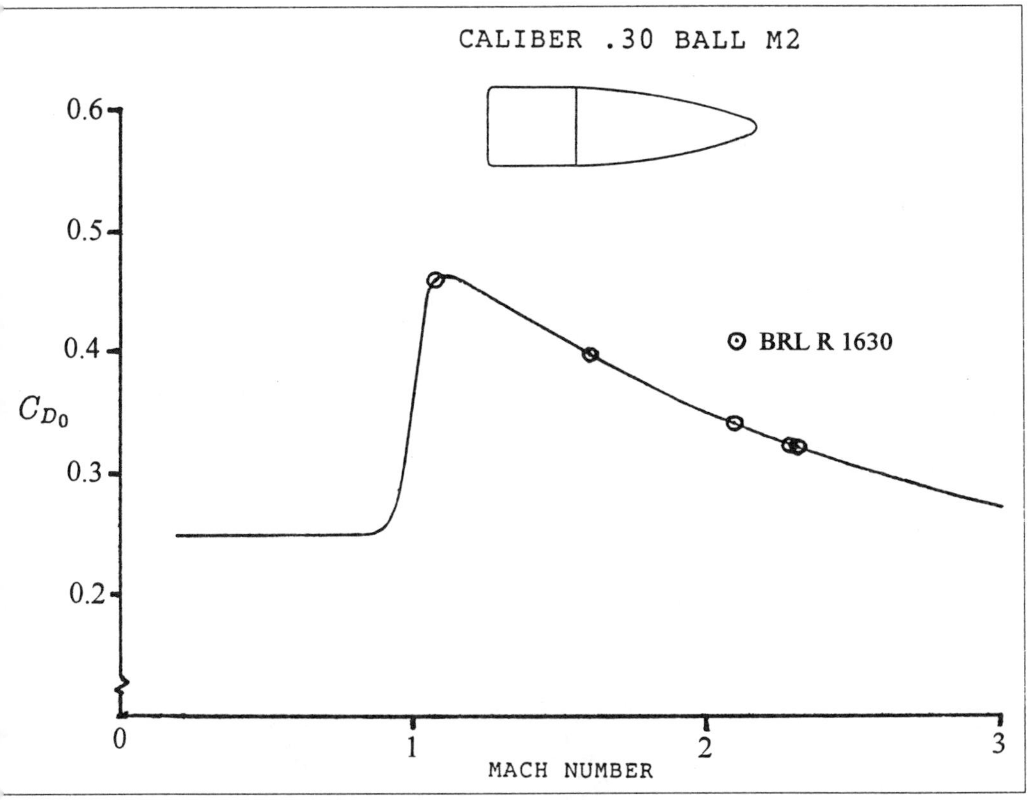

Figure 8.4 Zero-Yaw Drag Coefficient versus Mach Number.

DRAG FUNCTION: .30 BALL M2

MACH NO.	CD
0	.25
.8	.25
.9	.252
.95	.288
1	.362
1.05	.443
1.1	.464
1.2	.456
1.4	.427
1.6	.399
1.8	.373
2	.351
2.2	.331
2.5	.305
3	.271

ARMY STANDARD METRO

PROJECTILE IDENTIFICATION: .30 BALL M2

MUZ VEL (FT/SEC)	C (LB/IN2)	HO (INCHES)	ELEV (MINUTES)	DENSITY RATIO
2800	.226	0	19	1

TEMP (DEG,F)	RANGEWIND (MPH)	CROSSWIND (MPH)	RMATCH (YARDS)	HMATCH (INCHES)
59	0	0	0	0

RANGE (YARDS)	HEIGHT (IN)	DEFL. (IN)	VEL (FPS)	TIME (SEC)	VX (FPS)	VY (FPS)	VZ (FPS)
0	0.0	0.0	2800.0	0.000	2800.0	15.5	0.0
100	17.6	0.0	2570.8	0.112	2570.8	10.8	0.0
200	29.8	0.0	2349.0	0.234	2349.0	6.1	0.0
300	35.8	0.0	2135.1	0.368	2135.1	1.4	0.0
400	34.1	0.0	1929.8	0.516	1929.8	-3.2	0.0
500	23.0	0.0	1733.4	0.680	1733.4	-7.9	0.0
600	0.3	0.0	1547.1	0.863	1547.1	-12.6	0.0

Figure 8.5 Point-Mass Trajectory for the .30 Ball M2 Bullet.

DRAG FUNCTION: G8 DRAG FUNCTION

MACH NO.	CD
0	.211
.8	.21
.9	.211
.95	.257
1	.407
1.05	.448
1.1	.448
1.2	.435
1.4	.406
1.6	.378
1.8	.352
2	.329
2.2	.308
2.5	.28
3	.243

ARMY STANDARD METRO

PROJECTILE IDENTIFICATION: .30 BALL M2 - RUN WITH G8 DRAG FUNCTION

MUZ VEL (FT/SEC)	C (LB/IN2)	HO (INCHES)	ELEV (MINUTES)	DENSITY RATIO
2800	.21	0	19	1

TEMP (DEG,F)	RANGEWIND (MPH)	CROSSWIND (MPH)	RMATCH (YARDS)	HMATCH (INCHES)
59	0	0	0	0

RANGE (YARDS)	HEIGHT (IN)	DEFL. (IN)	VEL (FPS)	TIME (SEC)	VX (FPS)	VY (FPS)	VZ (FPS)
0	0.0	0.0	2800.0	0.000	2800.0	15.5	0.0
100	17.6	0.0	2572.5	0.112	2572.4	10.8	0.0
200	29.8	0.0	2350.3	0.234	2350.3	6.1	0.0
300	35.8	0.0	2134.5	0.368	2134.5	1.4	0.0
400	34.1	0.0	1926.2	0.516	1926.1	-3.2	0.0
500	23.0	0.0	1726.3	0.680	1726.3	-7.9	0.0
600	0.2	0.0	1536.4	0.864	1536.4	-12.6	0.0

Figure 8.6 Trajectory for the .30 Ball M2 Bullet, Run with G_8 Drag Function.

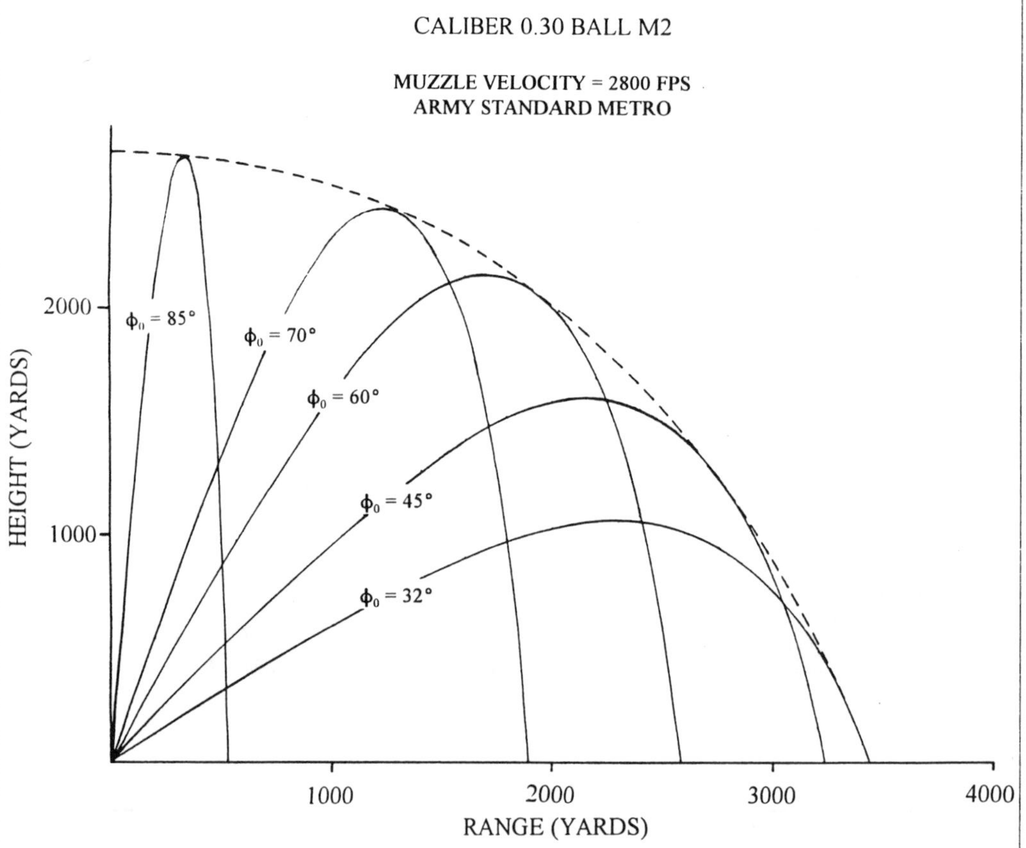

Figure 8.7 Envelope of Trajectories for the Caliber .30 Ball M2 Bullet.

ever, at larger superelevation angles (ϕ_o > 2°), the behavior of point-mass trajectories for uphill and downhill firing shows a striking resemblance to that of vacuum trajectories for the same uphill and downhill angles. The numerical values are significantly different, of course, but the general characteristics of the point-mass and vacuum curves are quite similar. Note that all the curves for uphill firing cross in the neighborhood of 10 degrees superelevation for the point-mass trajectories, compared with a crossing point of approximately 16 to 17 degrees superelevation for uphill vacuum trajectories.

Example 8.6

For the final example of this section, we will illustrate the behavior of several point-mass trajectories for a cannon artillery projectile, the 105mm, M1 Shell. Figure 8.10 (*p. 173*) is a plot of the zero-yaw drag coefficient versus Mach number, from firings conducted in the BRL Transonic Range. A sketch of the projectile contour is included in Figure 8.10.

The ranges and maximum ordinates of the M1 Shell, at a gun elevation angle of 45 degrees, using three different propelling charges, is shown in Figure 8.11 (*p. 174*). The impact ranges on level ground, with the gun located at sea-level, and using standard ICAO atmospheric conditions, vary from approximately 3,760 meters for Charge 1 (muzzle velocity = 205 meters/second), up to approximately 11,370 meters for Charge 7 (muzzle velocity = 493 meters/second). The maximum ordinates range from about 1000 meters for Charge 1, up to approximately 3500 meters for Charge 7. Since the 105mm M1 Shell is both gyroscopically and dynamically stable at nearly all flight Mach numbers, the point-mass model gives a very accurate trajectory for this projectile.

8.7 COMPARISON OF POINT-MASS AND SIACCI TRAJECTORIES

The derivation of the Siacci trajectory equations, and several applications of the method, were presented in Chapter 6. The Siacci method was generally used for ordnance trajectory calculations from

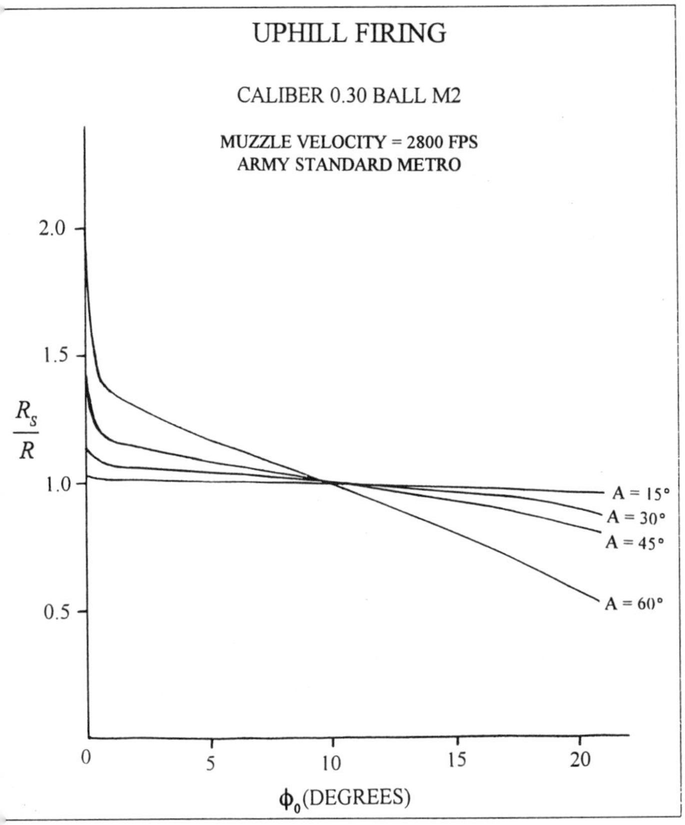

Figure 8.8 Ratio of Slant Range to Ground Range versus Gun Elevation Angle (Uphill).

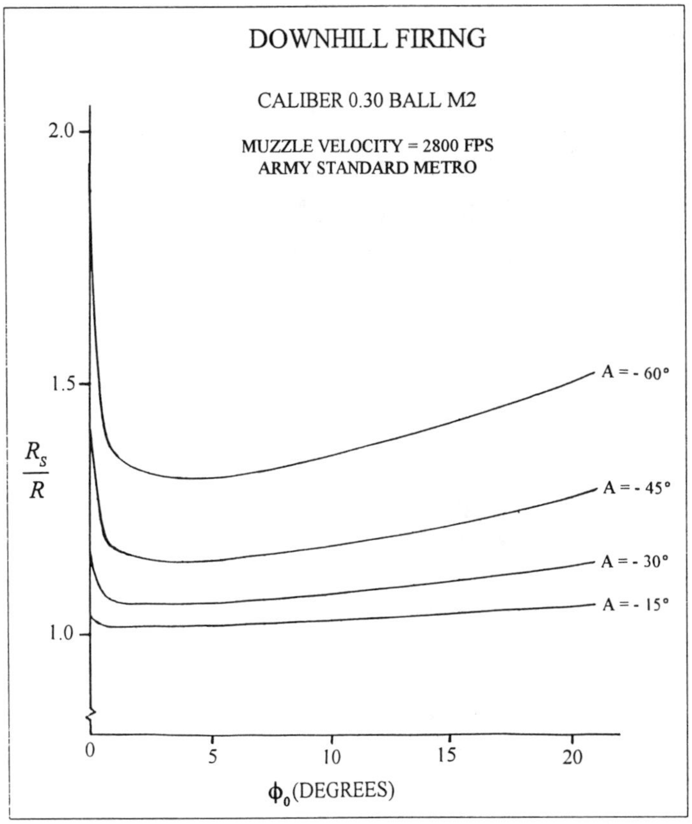

Figure 8.9 Ratio of Slant Range to Ground Range versus Gun Elevation Angle (Downhill).

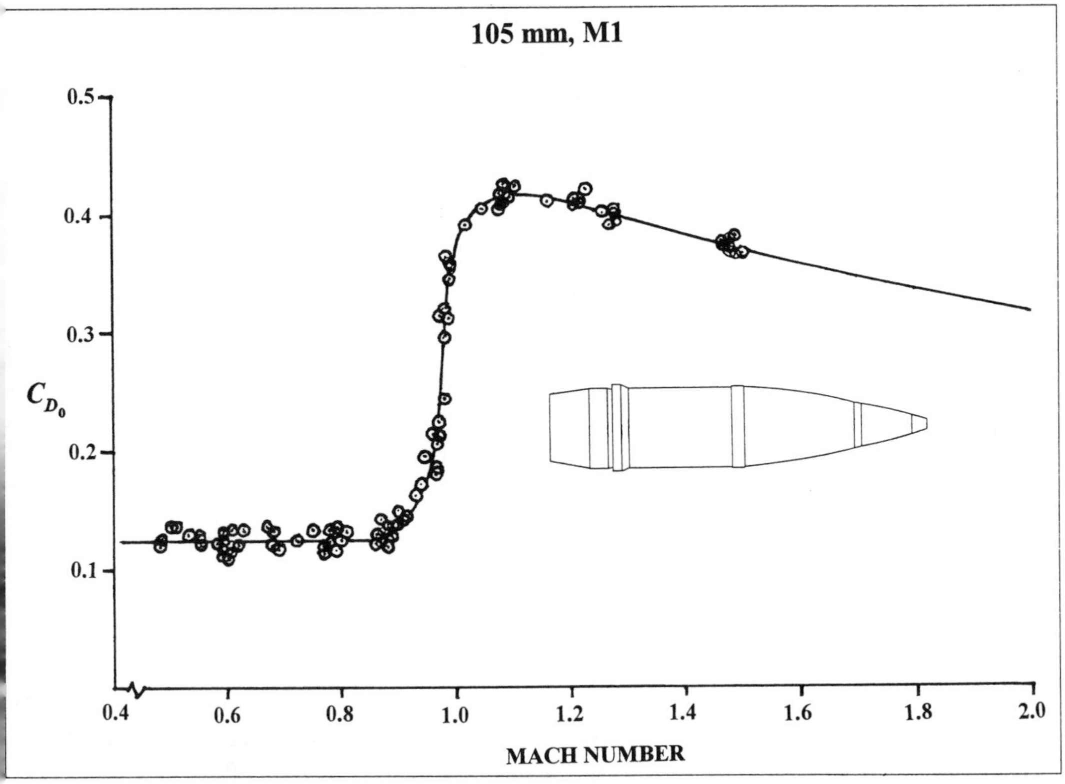

Figure 8.10 Zero-Yaw Drag Coefficient versus Mach Number, 105 mm M1 Shell.

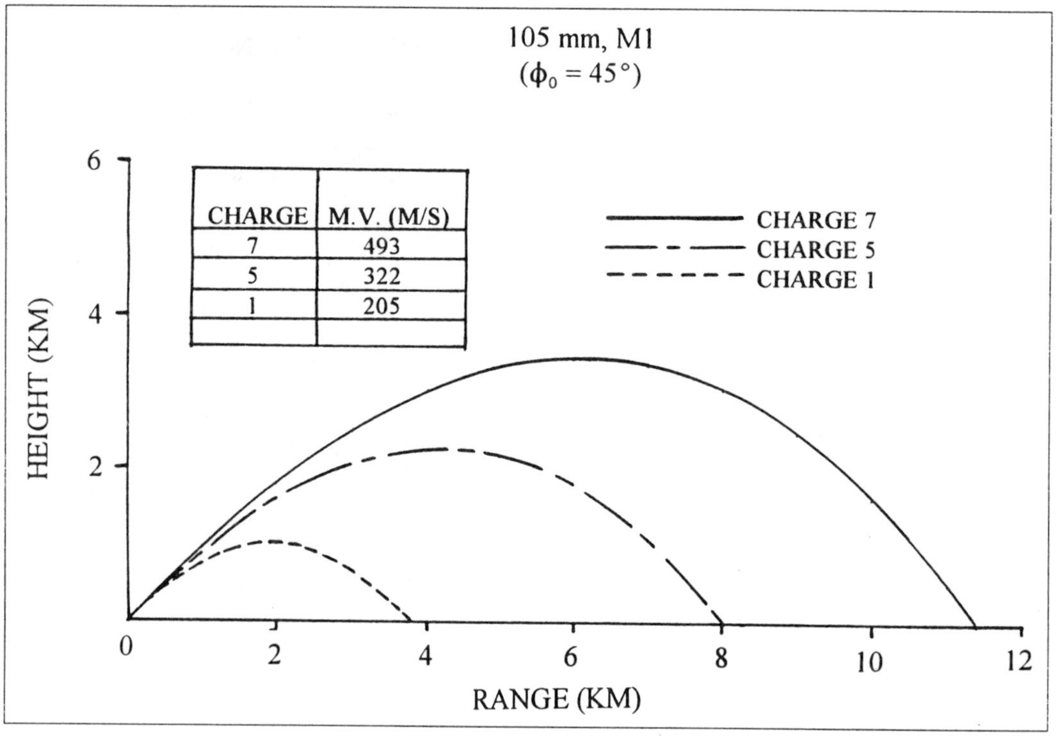

Figure 8.11 Height versus Range for the 105 mm, M1, Artillery Projectile.

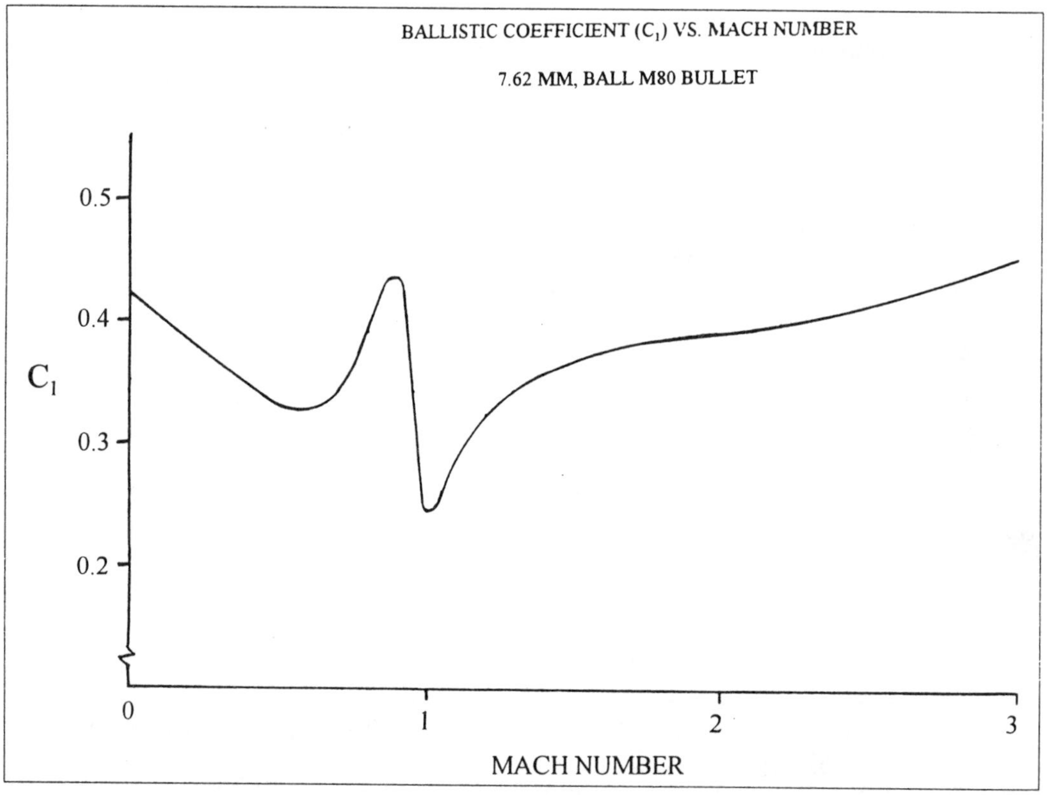

Figure 8.12 Ballistic Coefficient (C_1) versus Mach Number for the 7.62 mm Ball M80 Bullet.

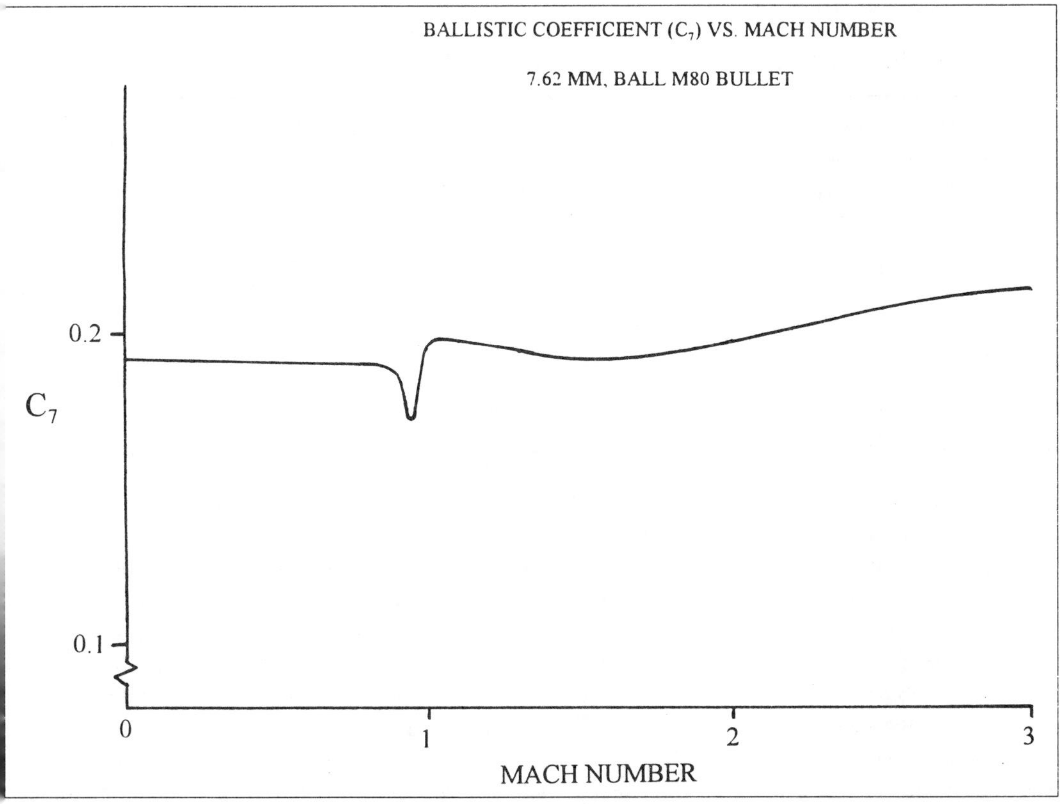

Figure 8.13 Ballistic Coefficient (C_7) versus Mach Number for the 7.62 mm Ball M80 Bullet.

about the 1880s to the early 1960s, a span of 80 years. Cannon artillery had abandoned the Siacci method by the end of World War I, due to the fact that large cannon are often fired at gun elevation angles as high as sixty-five to seventy degrees. U.S. Ordnance small arms retained the Siacci method much longer, because useful small arms trajectories generally fall into the flat-fire category (gun elevation angles less than five degrees), and the Siacci method usually works rather well for such cases, as illustrated in Chapter 6. Although U.S. Ordnance no longer uses the Siacci method , it has become the de-facto standard for the commercial small arms industry in this country, and therefore a comparison of the Siacci method with modern numerical integration of the point-mass differential equations needs to be examined.

Modern U.S. ordnance must always be concerned with the maximum range of projectiles. This requirement is not restricted to large cannon artillery and small cannon projectiles. Today, due to a rash of product liability lawsuits, such quantities as maximum range, maximum ordinate, and striking velocity at impact must be accurately determined for all projectiles, including small arms fire on test and training ranges. Since maximum ranges of most small arms projectiles occur for gun elevation angles in the neighborhood of twenty-five to thirty-five degrees, we must examine the behavior of Siacci trajectories up to these modern limits.

The first concern in running long range Siacci trajectories, at high gun elevation angles, is the behavior of the ballistic coefficient over a large velocity (Mach number) range. For a typical maximum range small arms trajectory, the projectile starts at moderate to high supersonic speed, coasts down through the transonic region, and ends up at relatively low subsonic speed. The rules laid down in Chapter 6 for choosing a standard drag function must be re-examined, for long range trajectories.

Figures 6.2 (see Chapter 6), 8.12 and 8.13 illustrate the effect of the choice of drag function on the Siacci ballistic coefficients for the 7.62mm Ball M80 boattailed bullet (Ref. 6). The form factor is the ratio of the C_D from Figure 6.2 to those tabulated in Table 6.1, at various Mach numbers. The ballistic coefficient values for the M80 bullet are then found by dividing the sectional density (0.221 pounds per square inch) by the appropriate form factors. Figure 8.12 shows the variation of the M80 ballistic coefficient C_1 with Mach number, relative to the G_1 drag coefficient; the variation of C_7 with Mach number, relative to the G_7 drag function, is illustrated in Figure 8.13. Since the accuracy of the Siacci method depends on having the ballistic coefficient be nearly constant for the entire trajectory, it is obvious that the G_7 drag function is much superior to G_1 for this boattailed .30 caliber bullet. (Some commercial software allows the ballistic coefficient to vary with velocity along the trajectory, which could partially alleviate this problem. However, the large variation of C_1 with Mach number, as illustrated in Figure 8.12, indicates that many values of the ballistic coefficient would have to be tabulated, to achieve an accurate representation for long range Siacci trajectories).

We will use the G_7 drag function, with appropriate average ballistic coefficients, to do our comparison of the Siacci method with modern numerical integration methods, for the 7.62mm Ball M80 bullet. Three cases will be considered; the first case is a flat-fire trajectory, out to 1000 yards range. The second case assumes a

Table 8.4 Comparison of Point-Mass and Siacci Trajectories for the 7.62mm Ball M80 Bullet				
	POINT-MASS TRAJECTORY		SIACCI (G_7) TRAJECTORY	
Range (Yards)	Height (Inches)	Velocity (fps)	Height (Inches)	Velocity (fps)
0	0.0	2810	0.0	2810
200	83.2	2371	83.2	2361
400	141.3	1959	141.2	1956
600	162.6	1580	162.2	1589
800	127.0	1244	126.7	1256
1000	0.0	1024	2.7	1035

gun elevation angle of 15 degrees above the horizontal, which is generally considered as the upper limit for the Siacci method. The third case is for a gun elevation of 30 degrees, which is essentially a maximum range case for this bullet, and which clearly violates the Siacci method's assumptions.

A good average value for the ballistic coefficient (C_7) of the M80 bullet, out to 1000 yards range, is 0.198 lb./in^2. The point-mass trajectory uses Army Standard Metro, and the sectional density, 0.221 lb./in^2 as its ballistic coefficient value, since the actual measured M80 drag coefficient versus Mach number curve is used. The results of the two trajectory calculations, both of which were run for a gun elevation angle of 44.4 minutes, are shown in Table 8.4, above.

The results illustrated in Table 8.4 show that at 1000 yards, which most riflemen regard as long range, the agreement between the modern point-mass method and the Siacci method is quite good. Note that for the 1000 yard case, the required gun elevation angle is less than one degree, and the flat-fire Siacci equations [equations (6.38) and (6.40) from Chapter 6] thus give very good results.

We now consider the second and third cases, as described above. For these higher gun elevation angles, the terminal (striking) velocity of the M80 bullet at ground impact is down around 400 fps, and the average ballistic coefficients (C_7) used for the Siacci trajectories were 0.191 lb./in^2 for the 15 degree elevation case, and 0.190 lb./in^2 for the 30 degree elevation case. A comparison of the results of the modern point-mass method with the Siacci method is illustrated in Figures 8.14 and 8.15, and in Table 8.5.

For gun elevation angles above 5 degrees, equations (6.34)-(6.37) from Chapter 6, which contain β, and $\cos\phi_o$ terms, should give more accurate answers than equations (6.38)-(6.41), which drop the trigonometric terms in the flat-fire approximation. To provide the most accurate comparison of the older method with modern point-mass trajectories, the Siacci method was run three ways; e.g., using equations (6.34) and (6.36) with $\beta = \sec\phi_o$, and with $\beta = \sqrt{\sec\phi_o}$, and a third run using the flat- fire equations (6.38) and (6.40). [See Chapter 6 for the details of Siacci trajectory calculation]. The numerical results are presented in Table 8.5, below.

Figure 8.14 graphically illustrates the 15 degree gun elevation case. Compared with the modern point-mass method (numerical integration), the Siacci method using equations (6.34) and (6.36) both underpredict the level-ground impact range. If β is set equal to $\sec\phi_o$ [equivalent to using equations (6.30) and (6.32)], the range error is -110 yards; if β is set equal to Col. Ingalls' value, $\sqrt{\sec\phi_o}$, the range error is -60 yards. The flat-fire Siacci equations [(6.38)-(6.40)], (equivalent to setting $\beta = 1$ and $\cos\phi_o = 1$) overestimate the level-ground range by +55 yards, for the 15 degree gun elevation case.

The Siacci solutions deteriorate significantly at 30 degrees gun elevation angle, as we would expect. The results are shown in Figure 8.15. Equations (6.34)-(6.36) again underpredict the range: for

Table 8.5 Comparison of Point-Mass and the Siacci Method for the 7.62mm Ball M80 Bullet				
		Eqns. 6.38-6.40 $(\cos\phi_o = 1)$ $(\beta = 1)$	Eqns. 6.34-6.36 $(\beta = \sec\phi_o)$	Eqns. 6.34-6.36 $(\beta = \sqrt{\sec\phi_o})$
Gun Elev. Angle (Degrees)	Point-Mass Range (Yards)	Siacci Range (Yards)	Siacci Range (Yards)	Siacci Range (Yards)
15	3735	3790	3625	3675
30	4430	4900	4085	4295

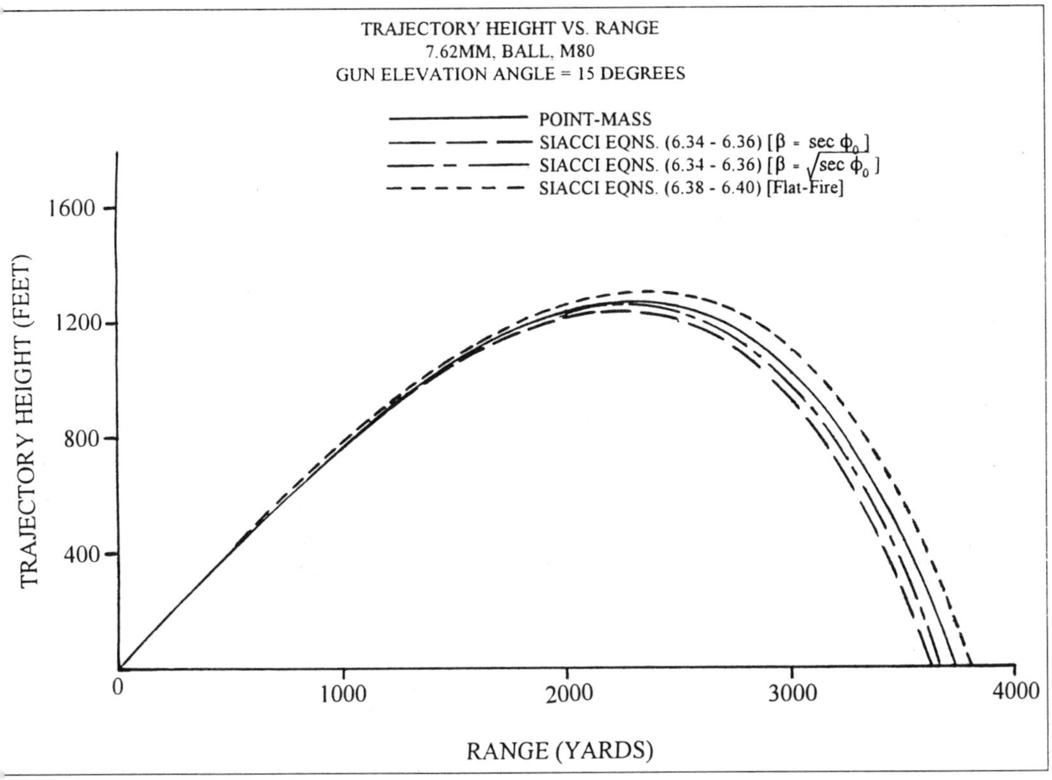

Figure 8.14 Trajectory Height versus Range, 7.62 mm Ball M80 Bullet $(\phi_o = 15°)$.

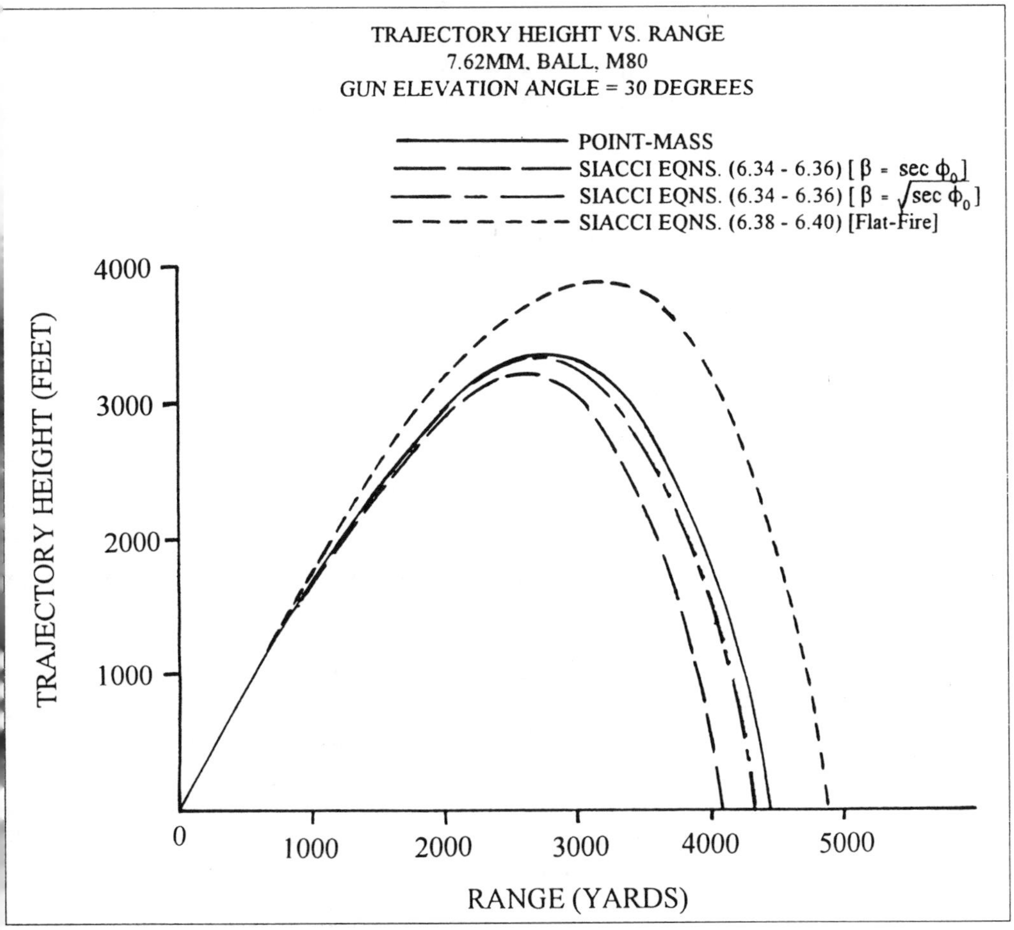

Figure 8.15 Trajectory Height versus Range, 7.62 mm Ball M80 Bullet $(\phi_o = 30°)$.

$\beta = \sec\phi_o$, the range error is -345 yards; if $\beta = \sqrt{\sec\phi_o}$, the level-ground range error is -135 yards. The flat-fire Siacci approximation [equations (6.38) and (6.40)] overpredict the range by 470 yards. Of the three different Siacci approximations considered, Ingalls's value, $\beta = \sqrt{\sec\phi_o}$, appears to be better than the other two choices, at 30 degrees gun elevation angle.

The above calculation compares numerical integration for the spark-range measured M80 drag coefficient curve with a Siacci calculation using a close (G_7) but not exact drag function. This corresponds to what would be done in practice. However, as D. G. Miller has noted, a more exact comparison of the two methods should use the same drag function for both calculations. If G_7 is used for both calculations, with $\beta = \sqrt{\sec\phi_o}$, at 15 degrees gun elevation angle, the Siacci range error is -47 yards. At 30 degrees elevation, the Siacci range error is -129 yards. The differences between the more exact comparison are smaller as expected, but are still unacceptably large.

To summarize the comparisons of modern point-mass trajectories with the Siacci method, the general conclusion is that the Siacci method is still useful for flat-fire trajectories (gun elevation angles below 5 degrees), provided a drag function is available such that the ballistic coefficient remains nearly constant over the velocity range of the intended trajectory. For higher gun elevation angles, the errors in the Siacci method grow rapidly with increasing range, and a modern point-mass trajectory will generally prove to be much more satisfactory.

8.8 THE CORIOLIS EFFECT ON POINT-MASS TRAJECTORIES

In the second section of Chapter 3 (Section 3.2), the Coriolis effect was introduced, then deferred to a later chapter. The present chapter on point-mass trajectories is an appropriate place to consider the Coriolis effect and its effect on the trajectory.

Galileo was apparently the first to describe the fundamental nature of the Coriolis effect, and it was treated in more detail by Isaac Newton. Pierre S. Laplace (1749-1827), who became Examiner of the French Royal Artillery in 1784, studied the Coriolis effect on the flight of projectiles in air, and published his results in the fourth volume of the Mechanique Celeste. In 1835, a French civil engineer, Gaspard G. de Coriolis (1792-1842), described the complete Coriolis effect as we know it today, and the effect is named in his honor.

The acceleration produced by the Coriolis effect is the quantity we will discuss in this chapter. The vector Coriolis acceleration is described by the following equation:

$$\vec{\Lambda} = 2\Omega \begin{bmatrix} -V_y \cos L \sin AZ - V_z \sin L \\ V_x \cos L \sin AZ + V_z \cos L \cos AZ \\ V_x \sin L - V_y \cos L \cos AZ \end{bmatrix} \qquad \textbf{(8.27)}$$

where $\vec{\Lambda}$ = vector Coriolis acceleration

Ω = 0.00007292 radians/second; [angular velocity of the earth, about its polar axis]

L = latitude of the firing site, positive for Northern hemisphere, negative for Southern hemisphere

AZ = azimuth of fire, measured clockwise from North

V_x = component of velocity in the X (downrange) direction [downrange is positive]

V_y = component of velocity in the Y (vertical) direction [upward is positive]

V_z = component of velocity in the Z (azimuthal) direction [to the right is positive]

For those readers unfamiliar with the vector matrix notation, the top row on the right hand side of equation (8.27) is the X-component of Coriolis acceleration; the middle row is the Y-component, and the bottom row is the Z-component of acceleration.

Equation (8.27) tells us that the Coriolis acceleration is independent of projectile weight, but varies with the projectile velocity, latitude of the firing site, and the azimuth of fire, relative to North. We will now investigate the effect of the Coriolis acceleration on the trajectory. The first case we will examine is the Coriolis effect on the vacuum trajectory. This case is conceptually simple, and gives some physical insight into the nature of the Coriolis effect.

If we substitute equation (8.27) into equation (3.1) of Chapter 3, drop the aerodynamic force terms, and divide through by the projectile mass, m, we obtain the differential equations of a vacuum trajectory with the Coriolis acceleration added:

$$\dot{V}_x = 2\Omega\left(-V_y \cos L \sin AZ - V_z \sin L\right) \qquad \textbf{(8.28)}$$

$$\dot{V}_y = -g + 2\Omega\left(+V_x \cos L \sin AZ + V_z \cos L \cos AZ\right) \qquad \textbf{(8.29)}$$

$$\dot{V}_z = 2\Omega\left(V_x \sin L - V_y \cos L \cos AZ\right) \qquad \textbf{(8.30)}$$

where $\dot{V}_x$ = X-component of acceleration

$\dot{V}_y$ = Y-component of acceleration

$\dot{V}_z$ = Z-component of acceleration

g = acceleration due to gravity

The remaining terms were defined after equation (8.27), above.

The Coriolis Effect for Vertical Fire in a Vacuum

The first problem we will consider is vertical firing, either vertically upward or downward. This turns out to be a useful case, because it illustrates the interesting nature of the Coriolis effect. For vertical (or nearly vertical) fire, V_x and V_z are practically zero, and terms in equations (8.28) through (8.30) containing these velocity components may be dropped. For convenience, we choose East as the positive X-direction; then AZ = 90 degrees, and equations (8.28)-(8.30) reduce to:

$$\dot{V}_x = -2\Omega V_y \cos L \quad \textbf{(8.31)}$$

$$\dot{V}_y = -g \quad \textbf{(8.32)}$$

Integrating the first of these equations:

$$\dot{V}_x = -2\Omega \cos L\left(Y - Y_0\right) \quad \textbf{(8.33)}$$

Vx

A positive V_x means the projectile is drifting Eastward, and a negative V_x denotes a Westward drift. Thus a projectile in nearly vertical motion, acted on only by gravity and Coriolis forces, will drift Westward whenever its altitude is above the initial altitude; whenever the projectile is below its initial altitude, its Coriolis drift will be Eastward. The reversed direction of Coriolis drift for upward vertical firing, and downward free-fall from an initial altitude, is a good illustration of the interesting properties of the Coriolis effect.

Completing the integration of equations of (8.31) and (8.32), we find:

$$V_Y = V_{Y0} - gt \quad \textbf{(8.34)}$$

$$Y = Y_0 + V_{Y0}t - \tfrac{1}{2}gt^2 \quad \textbf{(8.35)}$$

$$V_X = -2\Omega \cos L\left(V_{Y0}t - \tfrac{1}{2}gt^2\right) \quad \textbf{(8.36)}$$

$$X = -\Omega \cos L\left(V_{Y0}t^2 - 1/3\,gt^3\right) \quad \textbf{(8.37)}$$

For the downward free-fall case, we now set $V_{Y0} = 0$, and $Y = 0$ in equation (8.35), and solve for the time of flight, which is then substituted into equation (8.37):

$$Y_0 = -\tfrac{1}{2}gt^2, \text{ or } t = \sqrt{2Y_0/g} \quad \textbf{(8.38)}$$

$$X = \frac{1}{3}g\Omega \cos L\left(2Y_0/g\right)^{3/2} \quad \textbf{(8.39)}$$

For $g = 32.174$ ft/sec², $\Omega = 0.00007292$ radians/ second, and $L = 45$ degrees (North), the following Table 8.6 illustrates the Coriolis effect for different free-fall release altitudes:

Table 8.6
Coriolis Effect for Freely Falling Bodies in a Vacuum

Initial Release Altitude, Y_0 (Feet)	Eastward Coriolis Drift at Impact, X (Inches)
100	0.1
1000	3.3
2000	9.2
5000	36.4
10000	102.8

Note: the Eastward drift would be about 41% greater at the equator, and would be zero at either the North or the South pole.

We next consider the Coriolis effect for firing vertically upward from the earth's surface, again assuming a vacuum case. If we choose an upward muzzle velocity just sufficient to reach a given summital altitude, Y_s, with only gravity and Coriolis accelerations acting on the body, it can be shown that the Coriolis effect causes a Westward drift, whose magnitude is precisely four times that of the Eastward drift of a body dropped in free-fall from the summital altitude. The Westward Coriolis drift is given by the following equation:

$$X = -\frac{8}{3}\sqrt{2}\,\Omega \cos L\sqrt{Y_s^3/g} \quad \textbf{(8.40)}$$

Note: As an exercise for the student, derive equation (8.40). [Hint: First show that the time to ground impact is ($2\,V_{Y0}/g$); then the required muzzle velocity is $V_{y_0} = \sqrt{2gY_0}$, and substitute these results into equation (8.37)].

The results of firing vertically upward from the earth's surface, with only gravity and Coriolis accelerations acting on the body, gives the results shown in Table 8.7, for various summital altitudes:

Table 8.7
Coriolis Effect for Upward Vertical Firing in a Vacuum

Summital Altitude (Feet)	V_{Y0} (fps)	Westward Coriolis Drift (In.)
100	80.2	-0.4
1000	253.7	-13.0
2000	358.7	-36.8
5000	567.2	-145.4
10000	802.2	-411.4

The Coriolis Effect on Flat-Fire Vacuum Trajectories

We now return to equations (8.28)-(8.30), and make the usual flat-fire approximations:

$$V_y \ll V_x, \text{ and } V_z \ll V_x \quad \textbf{(8.41)}$$

If the flat-fire definitions of equation (8.41) are substituted into equations (8.28)-(8.30), the differential equations of motion for a flat-fire vacuum trajectory with Coriolis effects included are:

$$\dot{V}_x \approx 0 \quad \textbf{(8.42)}$$

$$\dot{V}_y \approx -g + 2\Omega V_x \cos L \sin AZ \quad \textbf{(8.43)}$$

$$\dot{V}_z \approx 2\Omega V_x \sin L \quad \textbf{(8.44)}$$

The solution of equations (8.42)-(8.44) is:

$$V_x = V_{x0} \quad \textbf{(8.45)}$$

Vx = Vxo

$$V_Y = V_{Y0} - gt\left[1 - \left(2\Omega V_{X0}/g\right)\cos L \sin AZ\right] \quad \textbf{(8.46)}$$

$$V_Z = 2\Omega V_{X0} t \sin L \quad \textbf{(8.47)}$$

A second integration gives:

$$X = V_{x0}\, t \quad \textbf{(8.48)}$$

$$Y = Y_0 + V_{Y0}t - \tfrac{1}{2}gt^2\left[1 - \left(2\Omega V_{X0}/g\right)\cos L \sin AZ\right] \quad \textbf{(8.49)}$$

$$Z = \Omega V_{X0} t^2 \sin L \quad \textbf{(8.50)}$$

We now substitute $t = X/V_{x0}$, and the definition $\tan\phi_o = V_{Y0}/V_{X0}$, into (8.49)-(8.50):

$$Y = Y_0 + X\tan\phi_o - \left(gX^2/2V_{X0}^2\right)\left[1 - \left(2\Omega V_{X0}/g\right)\cos L \sin AZ\right] \quad \textbf{(8.51)}$$

$$Z = \left(\Omega X^2 \sin L\right)/V_{X0} \quad \textbf{(8.52)}$$

Comparison of equation (8.51) with equation (3.31) of Chapter 3, shows that the effect of Coriolis acceleration on flat-fire vacuum trajectories is to multiply the value of g by the correction factor:

$$f_C = \left[1 - 2\left(\Omega V_{xo}/g\right)\cos L \sin AZ\right] \quad \textbf{(8.53)}$$

Now, $\cos L > 0$, for all possible latitudes. Therefore, if the azimuth of fire is due North (AZ = 0), or due South (AZ = 180 degrees), then $f_c = 1$, and Coriolis has no effect on the vertical plane. If the azimuth of fire is due East (AZ = 90 degrees), the effect of Coriolis acceleration is to slightly weaken the effect of gravity, and make the bullet strike slightly higher on the target. For firing due West (AZ = 270 degrees), the Coriolis effect adds a slight reinforcement to gravity, and causes the bullet to strike slightly low.

For 45 degrees North (or South) latitude, firing due East at a muzzle velocity of 4000 fps, we find the maximum effect of the Coriolis acceleration on the vertical plane to be:

$$f_c = [\, 1 - \{2\,(.00007292)(4000)\,/\,(32.174)\}(.707)\,] = 0.987$$

This is equivalent to a 1.3% decrease in the effect of gravity. At the equator, the effect would be an apparent 1.8% decrease in the effective value of gravity.

The Coriolis effect in the horizontal plane of a flat-fire vacuum trajectory is even easier to calculate. Equation (8.52) [or equation (8.50)] shows that Coriolis acceleration produces a small drift to the right of the initial line of fire for all Northern latitudes, and an equivalent drift to the left for all Southern latitudes. Since the latitude is zero at the equator, there is no Coriolis drift there.

Higher muzzle velocities cause an increase in the vertical-plane Coriolis effect; however, the reverse is true for the horizontal plane, where high velocities reduce the horizontal Coriolis drift. A few flat-fire vacuum trajectory results, using equation (8.52), are illustrated in Table 8.8, for 45 degrees North latitude:

Table 8.8
Coriolis Effect on the Horizontal Plane
of a Flat-Fire Vacuum Trajectory

X (Yards)	X (Feet)	VX0 = 2000 fps Z (Inches)	VX0 = 4000 fps Z (Inches)
100	300	0.03	0.01
500	1500	0.70	0.35
1000	3000	2.78	1.39
2000	6000	11.14	5.57

Note that for a flat-fire vacuum trajectory, the azimuth of fire has no effect on the horizontal Coriolis drift; the drift is affected only by the latitude. Firing in any direction at a fixed latitude gives the same horizontal-plane Coriolis drift.

The Coriolis Effect on Point-Mass Trajectories

The effect of Coriolis acceleration on point-mass trajectories will be illustrated by three cases: (1) the 7.62mm Ball M80 bullet, at ranges out to 2000 yards, (2) the 155mm M107 Howitzer Shell, fired at Charge 8, to a range of 18 kilometers, and (3) the Paris Gun, which the Germans used to bombard Paris in 1918, from a distance of 120 kilometers.

For the 7.62mm M80 bullet, a point-mass trajectory without Coriolis acceleration was run first, using Army Standard Metro,

Table 8.9
Coriolis Effect on 7.62mm Ball M80 Bullet,
at 45 Degrees North Latitude

Range (Yards)	AZ (Degrees)	Impact Height (In.)	Impact Defl. (In.)
500	0 (North)	0	0.6
500	90 (East)	0.6	0.6
500	180 (South)	0	0.6
500	270 (West)	-0.6	0.6
1000	0	0	2.8
1000	90	2.8	2.8
1000	180	0	2.8
1000	270	-2.8	2.8
1500	0	0	7.6
1500	90	7.6	7.6
1500	180	0	7.6
1500	270	-7.6	7.6
2000	0	0	15.6
2000	90	15.9	15.9
2000	180	0	16.1
2000	270	-15.9	15.9

with the proper gun elevation angles to zero the rifle at ranges of 500, 1000, 1500, and 2000 yards. The muzzle velocity used was 2810 fps, and the ballistic coefficient was equal to the sectional density, 0.221 lb./in². Then trajectories were run with the same initial conditions, with the Coriolis acceleration included. The results are shown in Table 8.9 (*p. 180*).

Table 8.9 shows that if a rifleman fired a 7.62mm M80 bullet due East at a 1000 yard target, then turned around and fired due West at another 1000 yard target, the easterly target should show an impact approximately 2 (2.8") = 5.6" higher than that on the westerly target. (This assumes, of course, that there is no dispersion, wind, etc., which could mask the rather small Coriolis effect). Both targets would show the same horizontal Coriolis deflection, e.g., 2.8" to the right.

The flat-fire, vacuum, horizontal Coriolis effect, given by equation (8.52), always underpredicts the observed point-mass Coriolis deflection. However, if an "ad-hoc" correction is made to equation (8.52), to account for the loss in velocity along the trajectory, the predicted results are much closer to the observed point-mass values. If we calculate the average velocity, $[V_X]_{AVE}$, over the whole trajectory, and use it to replace V_{X0} in equation (8.52), we find:

$$Z = \left(\Omega X^2 \sin L\right) / \left[V_X\right]_{AVE} \qquad \textbf{(8.54)}$$

The results of equations (8.52) and (8.54) are illustrated in Table 8.10 (*p. 182*), for the 7.62mm Ball M80 bullet, at 45 degrees North latitude, and at ranges out to 2000 yards:

Table 8.10 shows that equation (8.54) slightly overpredicts the Coriolis horizontal drift, for flat-fire small arms trajectories. However, it is still a useful approximation, for an order-of-magnitude estimate.

The second point-mass Coriolis case we will consider is that of the 155mm, M107 Howitzer Artillery Shell, fired at Charge 8 (Muzzle Velocity = 692 meters/second), and a gun elevation angle of 46 degrees above the horizontal, which gives the maximum range (approximately 18 kilometers) for this charge. A contour sketch of the M107 shell is shown in Figure 8.16, and the drag coefficient, C_D, from measurements taken in the BRL Transonic Range, are plotted against Mach number in Figure 8.17. The ballistic coefficient (equal to the sectional density) is 2.56 lb./in2. The Coriolis effect at maximum range for this shell is well illustrated in Table 8.11 (*p. 182*).

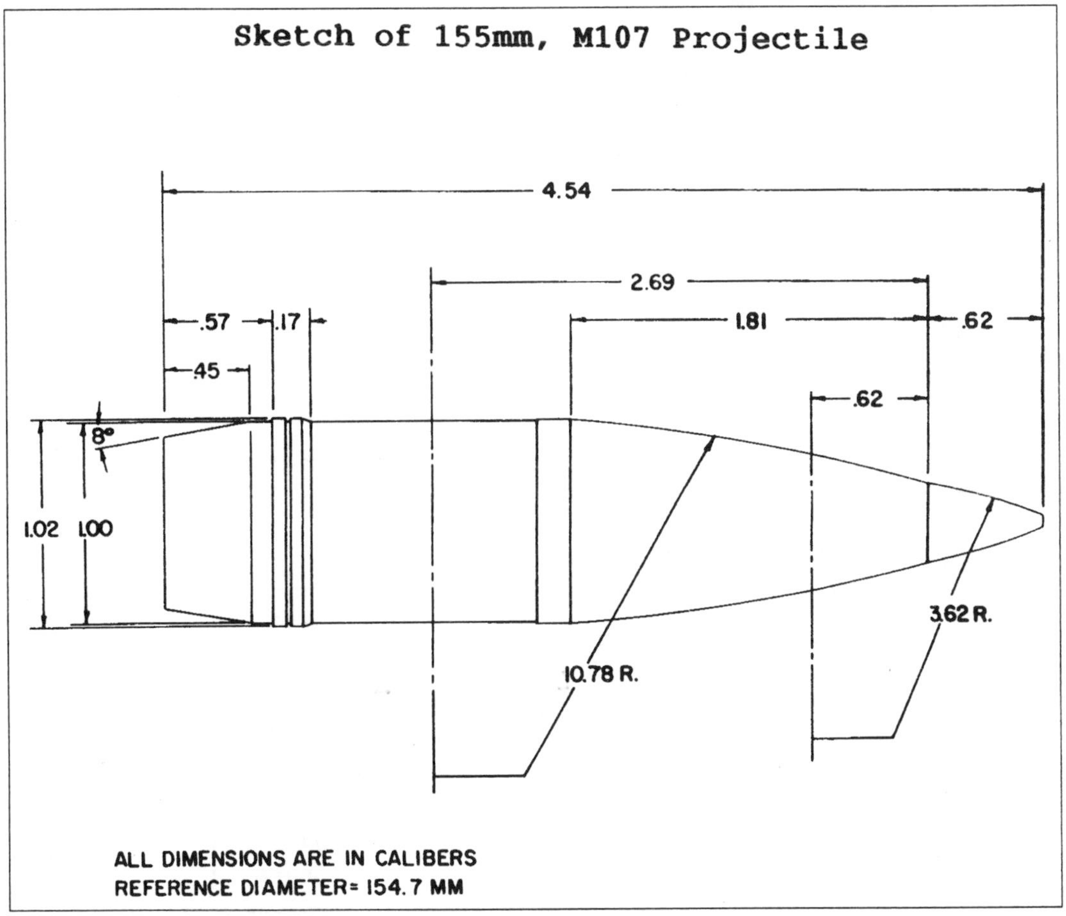

Figure 8.16 Sketch of 155 mm, M107 Projectile.

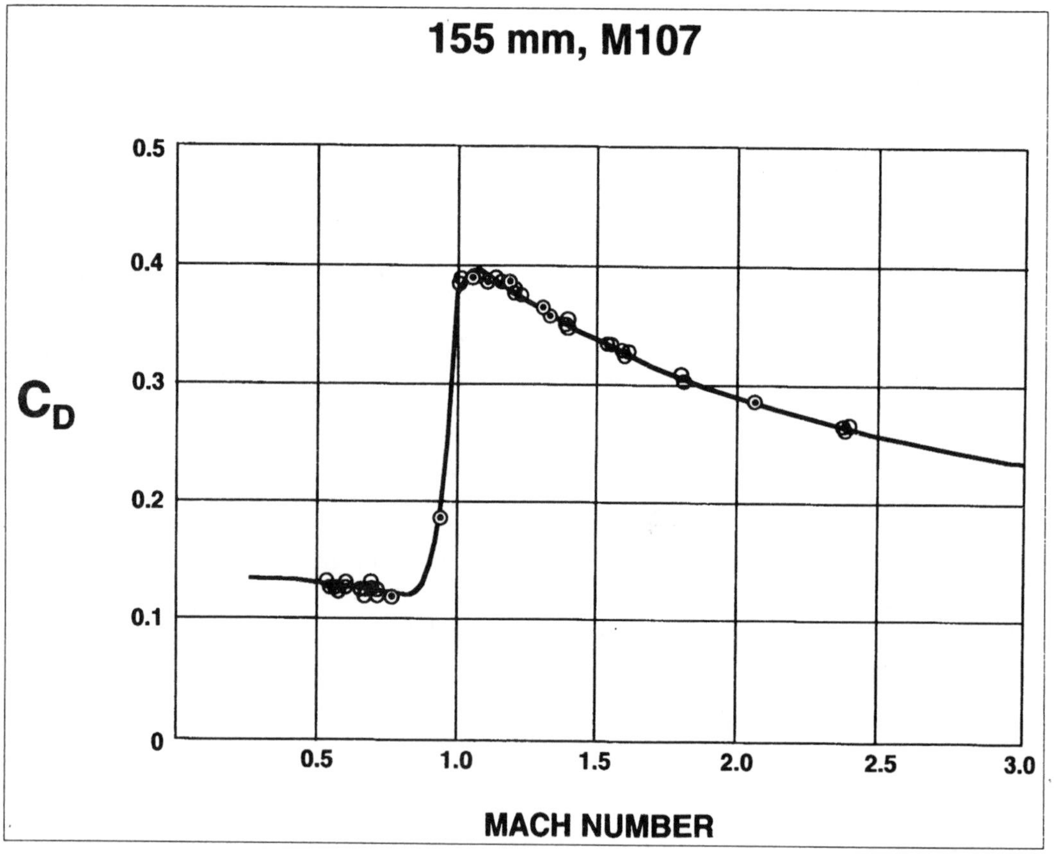

Figure 8.17 Zero-Yaw Drag Coefficient versus Mach Number, 155 mm M107 Shell.

Table 8.10
Flat-Fire Vacuum Approximations for Horizontal Coriolis Drift
7.62mm Ball M80 - Muzzle Velocity = 2810 FPS

		[Point-Mass]	[Equation 8.52]	[Equation 8.54]
Range (Yards)	$[V_x]_{AVE}$ (FPS)	Defl. (In.)	Defl. (In.)	Defl. (In.)
500	2276	0.6	0.5	0.6
1000	1819	2.8	2.0	3.1
1500	1532	7.6	4.5	8.2
2000	1364	15.9	7.9	16.3

Table 8.11
(Latitude of Firing Site = 45 Degrees, North)

				[Coriolis Effect]
Azimuth of Fire (Degrees)	Impact Range (Meters)	Impact Defl. (Meters)	Δ-Range (Meters)	Δ-Deflection (Meters)
0 (North)	17970	37	0	37
90 (East)	17995	56	25	56
180 (South)	17970	74	0	74
270 (West)	17945	56	-25	56

Table 8.11 illustrates the size of the Coriolis effect on the range and deflection of the 95-pound M107 Howitzer shell, when fired to its maximum range. (The Δ's are the differences between a trajectory with Coriolis acceleration, and the same trajectory without Coriolis). The largest range effect is only ± 25 meters, but the deflection effect (always to the right in the Northern hemisphere) can be as large as 74 meters, which is not an insignificant amount. All modern artillery firing tables contain a number of pages of information on the Coriolis effect at different latitudes, azimuths of fire, charges, and gun elevation angles.

The final Coriolis example we will do is the Paris Gun (Ref. 7). This enormous 210mm (8.27-inch) gun, firing a 106 kilogram (233.7-pound), long-ogive shell, was emplaced near Crépy-en-Laon, France, by the German Army in 1918, and was used to bombard the city of Paris from a range of approximately 120 kilometers (75 miles). The muzzle velocity of this cannon was 5400 feet/second, and the ballistic coefficient of the projectile (equal to the sectional density) was 3.42 lb./in^2. The latitude of Crépy-en-Laon is 49.5 degrees, North, and the azimuth of fire toward Paris was 232 degrees, measured clockwise from North. The Paris Gun achieved its maximum range of more than 120 kilometers, at a gun elevation angle of 50 degrees above the horizontal.

At a range of 120 kilometers, the Coriolis effect was as follows: Δ-Range = -393 meters; and the Δ-Deflection = 1343 meters. The shell hit nearly 400 meters short, and over 1340 meters (over 8/10 of a mile) to the right of where it would have landed if there were no Coriolis acceleration. It is readily apparent that the Coriolis effect is an important consideration, when firing at very long ranges.

8.9 SUMMARY

In this chapter, we have derived the differential equations of motion for a point-mass trajectory, with both time and downrange distance as independent variables. Several methods for the numerical solution were discussed, and suggestions were made as to the all-around best methods. Two standard atmospheres were described, and pertinent variables were tabulated up to 35,000 feet altitude above mean sea level. Several examples of point-mass trajectories were calculated using the MCTRAJ Basic computer program. A comparison of point-mass and Siacci trajectories was done; the results illustrated the fact that the Siacci method is still useful for flat-fire, but its accuracy deteriorates when it is used at high gun elevation angles. The Coriolis effect was introduced; its effect on vertical vacuum trajectories, and on flat-fire vacuum trajectories was treated in detail. Finally, the Coriolis effect on point-mass trajectories was explored, using three cases: (1) a flat-fire small arms trajectory, out to long range, (2) a 155mm Howitzer Artillery Shell, and (3) the very long range Paris Gun (Wilhelmgeschütze), used by the German Army to bombard the city of Paris in 1918, from a range of 120 kilometers (75 miles). The results of these three cases illustrate the interesting properties of the Coriolis acceleration, and its effect on point-mass trajectories.

MCTRAJ COMPUTER PROGRAM

```
10 REM PROGRAM [MCTRAJ.BAS], MAR 1987. [REVISED 07/90; 02/93; 05/94]
15 REM [Q-BASIC VERSION-- OCTOBER 1994]
20 CLS
30 KEY OFF
40 COLOR 7,1,8: CLS
50 KEY ON
60 DEFDBL A-H,M,O-Z
70 REM POINT MASS TRAJECTORIES FOR SMALL ARMS.
80 REM THE PROGRAM REQUIRES AN INPUT TABLE OF
90 REM DRAG COEFFICIENT (CD) VERSUS MACH NUMBER (M).
100 REM ADDITIONAL REQUIRED INPUTS ARE:
110 REM MUZZLE VELOCITY (FT/SEC); BALLISTIC COEFFICIENT (LB/IN2);
120 REM HEIGHT OF SIGHT LINE ABOVE BORE CENTERLINE (INCHES);
130 REM GUN ELEVATION ANGLE (MINUTES); RATIO OF AIR DENSITY TO
140 REM STANDARD DENSITY; AIR TEMPERATURE (DEG F); RANGE PRINT
150 REM INTERVAL (YARDS/METERS); RANGE TO TERMINATE TRAJECTORY (YARDS/METERS);
160 REM RANGE WIND SPEED (MPH--POSITIVE IF WIND BLOWS FROM GUN TO
170 REM TARGET); AND CROSSWIND SPEED (MPH--POSITIVE IF WIND BLOWS
180 REM FROM LEFT TO RIGHT ACROSS FIRING LINE).
190 REM THE PROGRAM ALSO PROVIDES AN OPTION TO ADJUST THE TRAJECTORY
200 REM TO PASS THROUGH A SPECIFIED POINT IN SPACE, DENOTED BY
210 REM RMATCH (YARDS/METERS), AND HMATCH (INCHES). THE GUN ELEVATION ANGLE
220 REM IS ADJUSTED UNTIL THE TRAJECTORY PASSES THROUGH THE POINT
230 REM (RMATCH,HMATCH). IF NO ADJUSTMENT IS DESIRED, INPUT ZEROS
240 REM FOR RMATCH AND HMATCH, AND THE TRAJECTORY WILL BE RUN WITH
250 REM THE INPUT ELEVATION ANGLE.
260 REM THE PROGRAM SOLVES THE TRAJECTORY BY NUMERICAL INTEGRATION
270 REM USING THE HEUN METHOD, WHICH IS AN ITERATIVELY APPLIED
280 REM SECOND ORDER PREDICTOR-CORRECTOR TECHNIQUE.
290 REM
300 REM THE TRAJECTORY OUTPUT IS RANGE (YARDS/METERS); HEIGHT RELATIVE TO
310 REM LINE OF SIGHT (INCHES); DEFLECTION (INCHES); TOTAL VELOCITY
320 REM (FT/SEC); TIME OF FLIGHT (SECONDS); RANGE COMPONENT OF
330 REM VELOCITY (VX--FT/SEC); VERTICAL COMPONENT OF VELOCITY
340 REM (VY--FT/SEC); AND HORIZONTAL COMPONENT OF VELOCITY (VZ--FT/SEC).
350 REM
360 REM DEFINE PROGRAM CONSTANTS.
370 REM
380 G=32.174#
390 E1=.00001#
400 U1$="###### #######.# #####.# #####.# ###.### #####.# #####.# ####.#"
410 REM INPUT DRAG COEFFICIENT TABLE.
420 REM
430 DIM M(50),D(50),E(21),H(21)
440 DIM Q(201),R(201),T(201),V(201)
450 DIM W(201),X(201),Y(201),Z(201)
460 PRINT
470 PRINT "ENTER DRAG FUNCTION TO BE USED:";
480 INPUT K$
```

```
490 PRINT
500 PRINT "THE DRAG COEFFICIENT IS ENTERED AS A"
510 PRINT "TABLE OF MACH NUMBER (M) VERSUS"
520 PRINT "DRAG COE"ICIENT (CD). ENTER THE DATA"  COEFFICIENT
530 PRINT "AS -- M, CD [RETURN] -- BEGINN1NG"
540 PRINT "WITH THE LOWEST MACH NUMBER"
550 PRINT
560 PRINT "THE LAST (HIGHEST) MACH NUMBER 1N THE TABLE"
570 PRINT "MUST BE ENTERED AS A NEGATIVE VALUE,"
580 PRINT "WHICH SIGNALS THE FINAL DRAG INPUT TO THE
PROGRAM."
590 PRINT
600 PRINT
610 I=l
620 PRINT "ENTER M, CD: ";
630 INPUT M(I),D(I)
640 IF M(I)<0 THEN 670
650 I=I+1
660 GOTO 620
670 J=I
680 M(J'ABS(M(J))   M(J)=ABS(M(J))
690 MMI=J
700 LPDC=0
710 CLS
720 PRINT
730 PRINT "DRAG FUNCTION: ";K$
740 PRINT
750 PRINT
760 PRINT "MACH NO."," CD"
770 REM ECHO INPUT DRAG COEFFICIENT TABLE.
780 FOR I=1 TO J
790 PRINT M(I),D(I)
800 NEXT I
810 JJ=J
820 PRINT
830 PRINT
840 PRINT "IS THE ABOVE DRAG TABLE CORRECT?"
850 PRINT "ENTER Y FOR YES, N FOR NO:";
860 INPUT K1$
870 IF K1$="N" THEN 460
880 PRINT
890 PRINT
900 PRINT "RANGE IN YARDS OR METERS? (ENTER Y FOR YARDS, M
FOR METERS):";
910 INPUT YM$
920 PRINT
930 PRINT
940 PRINT "ARMY STANDARD METRO OR ICAO? (ENTER S FOR
STANDARD, I FOR ICAO):";
950 INPUT SI$
960 PRINT
970 PRINT
980 IF YM$="Y" THEN 1020
990 UC=1#/.3048#
1000 UR$="(METERS)"
1010 GOTO 1040
1020 UC=3#
1030 UR$="(YARDS)"
1040 DINT=l#
1050 REM DINT IS THE DISTANCE INTEGRATION STEP (YARDS/
METERS)
1060 D3=DINT*UC
1070 IF SI$="I" THEN 1150
1080 RH1=-.00003158#
1090 RH2=0#
1100 TKIC.000006015#   TK1=0.000006015#
1110 TK2=0#
1120 PIR=-.0002048757#
1130 W1=49.19#   VV1=49.19#
1140 GOTO 1230
1150 RH1=-.00002926#
1160 RH2=-.0000000001#
1170 TK1=-.000006858#
1180 TK2=-.00000000002776#
1190 PIR=-.000208551#
1200 W1=49.0223#   VV1=49.0223#
1210 REM NOTE: PIR=-(PL8)*(RHO0/144)
1220 REM
1230 PRINT "ENTER PROJECTILE IDENTIFICATION:";
1240 INPUT K2$
1250 PRINT
1260 PRINT "ENTER MUZZLE VELOCITY (FEET/SECOND):";
1270 INPUT V0
1280 PRINT
1290 PRINT "ENTER BALLISTIC COEFFICIENT (LB0N-2):";   LB/IN2
1300 INPUT C
1310 PRINT
1320 PRINT "ENTER HEIGHT OF SIGHT LINE ABOVE BORE LINE
(INCHES):";
1330 INPUT H0
1340 PRINT
1350 PRINT "ENTER GUN ELEVATION ANGLE (MINUTES):";
1360 INPUT P0
1370 PRINT
1380 PRINT "ENTER RATIO OF AIR DENSITY TO SEA LEVEL STAN-
DARD:";
1390 INPUT R0
1400 PRINT
1410 PRINT "ENTER AIR TEMPERATURE (DEGREES, FAHRENHEIT):";
1420 INPUT TDF
1430 PT0=INT(10*TDF)/10
1440 PRINT
1450 PRINT "ENTER RANGE PRINT INTERVAL ";UR$;":";
1460 INPUT P2
1470 PRINT
1480 PRINT "ENTER RANGE TO TERMINATE TRAIECTORY ";UR$;": ";
1490 INPUT R3
1500 PRINT
1510 N1=INT(R3/P2+1.5)
1520 IFN1<=101THEN 1580   IF N1<=101 THEN 1580
1530 PRINT "THIS PRINT INTERVAL GIVES OVER 100 LINES OF
OUTPUT!"
1540 PRINT "INCREASE PRINT STEP? (ENTER Y FOR YES, N FOR NO:)";
1550 INPUT PPI$
1560 PRINT
1570 IF PPI$="Y" THEN 1450
1580 PRINT "ENTER RANGE WIND SPEED (MILES/HOUR):";
1590 INPUT W1
1600 PRINT
1610 PRINT "ENTER CROSS WIND SPEED (MILES/HOUR):";
1620 INPUT W3
1630 PRINT
1640 PRINT "THE FOLLOWING TWO INPUTS SPECIFY THE COORDI-
NATES"
1650 PRINT "OF A POINT THROUGH WHICH THE TRAJECTORY MUST
PASS."
1660 PRINT "IF IHIS OPTION IS NOT DESIRED, INPUT ZERO FOR BOTH"   THIS
1670 PRINT "THE MATCH RANGE AND THE MATCH HEIGHT."
1680 PRINT
1690 PRINT "ENTER THE TRAJECTORY MATCH RANGE, RMATCH
";UR$;":";
1700 INPUT R8
1710 PRINT
1720 PRINT "ENTER THE TRA-TECTORY MATCH HEIGHT, HMATCH   TRAJECTORY
(INCHES):";
1730 INPUT H8
1740 PRINT
1750 PRINT
1760 REM INITIALT7:R INPUT VALUES FOR TRAJECTORY CALCULA-
TION.   INITIALIZE
1770 N=2
1780 J=0
1790 P1=W1
1800 P3=W3
```

```
1810 P4=H0
1820 H0=(-H0)
1830 R4=D3*P2
1840 R5=D3*R3
1850 R6=D3*R8
1860 PR4=P2
1870 PR5=R3
1880 PR6=R8
1890 H3=H8/12
1900 W1=(2*W1)/15
1910 W3=(2*W3)/15
1920 V3=V0*COS(P0/3437.74677#)
1930 V4=V0*SIN(P0/3437.74677#)
1940 V5=0
1950 R1=0
1960 PR1=0
1970 H1=H0/12
1980 D1=0
1990 T1=0
2000 PX3=PR4
2010 REM CHECK FOR TRAJECTORY MATCH VALUES.
2020 IF PR6<>0 THEN 2060
2030 L=0
2040 PR7=PR5
2050 GOTO 2080
2060 L=1
2070 PR7=PR6          PR=PR6
2080 IF L=1 THEN 2480
2090 REM PRINT HEADERS AND FIRST LINE OUTPUT.
2100 CLS
2110 PRINT
2120 IF SI$="S" THEN PRINT "ARMY STANDARD METRO"
2130 IF SI$="I" THEN PRINT "ICAO STANDARD ATMOSPHERE"
2140 PRINT
2150 PRINT "DRAG FUNCTION: ";K$ 2160 PRINT
2170 PRINT "PROJECTILE IDENTIFICATION: ";K2$ 2180 PRINT
2190 PRINT "MUZ VEL"," C","H0"," ELEV","DENSITY"
2200 PRINT "(FT/SEC)","(LB/IN2)","(INCHES)","(MINUTES)"," RATIO"
2210 PRINT          LB/IN2
2220 PP0=INT(1000*P0+.5)/1000
2230 PRINT V0,C,P4,PP0,R0
2240 PRINT
2250 PRINT
2260 PRINT
"TEMP","RANGEWIND","CROSSWIND","RMATCH","HMATCH"
2270 PRINT "(DEG,F)"," (MPH)"," (MPH)",UR$,"(INCHES)"
2280 PRINT
2290 PRINT PT0,P1,P3,R8,H8
2300 PRINT
2310 PRINT
2320 PRINT
2330 PRINT
TAB(1);"RANGE";TAB(11);"HEIGHT";TAB(23);"DEFL";TAB(33);"VEL";TAB(41);"TIME";
TAB(51);"VX" ;TAB(60);"VY";TAB(68);"VZ"
2340 PRINT
UR$;TAB(12);"(IN)";TAB(24);"(IN)";TAB(32);"(FPS)";TAB(40);"(SEC)";TAB(50);"(FPS)";T
AB(59);"(FPS)" ;TAB(67);"(FPS)"
2350 PRINT
2360 Q(1)=R1
2370 R(1)=H0
2380 T(1)=D1
2390 V(1)=V0
2400 W(1)=T1
2410 X(1)=V3
2420 Y(1)=V4
2430 Z(1)=V5          U1$ Q(1)
2440 PRINT USING U1$;Q(1);R(1);T(1);V(1);W(1);X(1);Y(1);Z(1)
2450 REM
2460 REM BEGIN TRAJECTORY CALCULATION.
2470 REM
2480 C3=(PIR*R0)/C
2490 B1=SQR((V3-W1)^2+V4^2+(V5-W3)^2)
```

```
2500 T0=(TDF+459.67#)*EXP((TK1+TK2*H1)*H1-459.67#
2510 V1=W1*SQR(T0+459.67#)        V1= VV1* SQR(T0+459.67-#)
2520 X1=B1/V1
2530 GOSUB 4010
2540 C1=X2
2550 C4=(C3*C1*B1*EXP((RH1+RH2*H1)*H1))/V3
2560 A1=C4*(V3-W1)
2570 A2=C4*V4-G/V3
2580 A3=C4*(V5-W3)
2590 REM APPLY EULER PREDICTOR FORMULA
2600 R2=R1+D3
2610 PR2=PR1+DINT
2620 V6=V3+A1*D3
2630 V7=V4+A2*D3
2640 V8=V5+A3*D3
2650 B2=SQR((V6-W1)^2+V7^2+(V8-W3)^2)
2660 REM APPLY ITERATIVE HEUN CORRECTOR FORMULA
2670 U=B2
2680 T0=(TDF+459.67#)*EXP((TK1+TK2*H1)*H1-459.67#
2690 V1=W1*SQR(T0+459.67#)        V1= VV1* SQR(T0 + 459.67 #)
2700 X1=B2/V1
2710 GOSUB 4010
2720 C2=X2
2730 C5=(C3*C2*B2*EXP((RH1+RH2*H1)*H1))/V6
2740 A4=C5*(V6-W1)
2750 A5=C5*V7-G/V6
2760 A6=C5*(V8-W3)
2770 V6=V3+.5*(A1+A4)*D3
2780 V7=V4+.5*(A2+A5)*D3
2790 V8=V5+.5*(A3+A6)*D3
2800 B2=SQR((V6-W1)^2+V7^2+(V8-W3)^2)
2810 E2=ABS((B2-U)/B2)
2820 IF E2>E1 THEN 2670
2830 REM COMPUTE VALUES AT R2.
2840 H2=H1+((V4+V7)/(V3+V6))*D3
2850 D2=D1+((V5+V8)/(V3+V6))*D3
2860 T2=T1+(2*D3)/(V3+V6)
2870 V2=SQR(V6^2+V7^2+V8^2)
2880 REM RESET CONDITIONS AT R1 TO NEW CONDITIONS AT R2.
2890 R1=R2
2900 PR1=PR2
2910 H1=H2
2920 D1=D2
2930 T1=T2
2940 V3=V6
2950 V4=V7
2960 V5=V8
2970 A1=A4
2980 A2=A5
2990 A3=A6
3000 P5=PR2
3010 P6=12*H2
3020 P7=12*D2
3030 REM CHECK STATUS OF PRINT CONDITIONS.
3040 IF L=1 THEN 3190
3050 IF PR2<PX3 THEN 3190
3060 Q(N)=P5
3070 R(N)=P6
3080 T(N)=P7
3090 V(N)=V2
3100 W(N)=T2
3110 X(N)=V6
3120 Y(N)=V7
3130 Z(N)=V8
3140 PRINT USING U1$;Q(N);R(N);T(N);V(N);W(N);X(N);Y(N);Z(N)
3150 N=N+1
3160 REM INCREMENT PRINT RANGE.
3170 PX3=PX3+PR4
3180 REM CHECK FOR CONDITIONS TO STOP TRAJECTORY CALCULA-
TION.
3190 IF PR2>=PR7 THEN 3210
3200 GOTO 2600
```

```
3210 IF L=0 THEN 3420
3220 REM ITERATION TO ADJUST ELEVATION FOR MATCH RANGE
AND HEIGHT.
3230 E3=ABS(H2-H3)
3240 IF E3<.00001# THEN 3370
3250 J=J+1
3260 E(J)=P0
3270 H(J)=H2
3280 IF P=2 THEN 3330   IF J≥2 THEN 3330
3290 E(J+1)=P0+2#
3300 P0=E(J+1)
3310 GOTO 1920
3320 REM ALGORITHM TO ADJUST ELEVATION ANGLE.
3330 IF H(J-1)=H(J) THEN 4100
3340 E(J+ 1)=E(J)+(H3-H(J))*(E(J-1)-E(J)/(H(J-1)-H(J))   H3+H(J)+
3350 IF J<20 THEN 3300
                                    WITH
3360 REM RUN FINAL TRAJECTORY WIIH PRINTS.
3370 PR6=0
3380 GOTO 1920
3390 REM [CHECK FOR HARD COPY OF OUTPUT]
3400 REM [SAVE OUTPUT FOR HARD COPY, IF DESIRED]
3410 REM (N2=NO. OF TRAJECTORY LINES IN OUTPUT)
3420 N2=N- 1
3430 PRINT
3440 PRINT
3450 PRINT "DO YOU WANT HARD COPY OF THIS OUTPUT?"
3460 PRINT "ENTER Y FOR YES, N FOR NO:";
3470 INPUT K1$
3480 IF K1$="N" THEN 3900
3490 IF K1$="Y" THEN 3510
3500 GOTO 3440
3510 REM ECHO INPUT DRAG COEFFICIENT TABLE.
3520 LPRINT
3530 LPRINT "DRAG FUNCTION: ";K$
3540 LPRINT
3550 IF LPDC=1 THEN 3610
3560 LPRINT "MACH NO."," CD"
3570 FOR I=1 TO JJ
3580 LPRINT M(I),D(I)
3590NEXTI          3590 NEXT I
3600 LPDC=1
3610 LPRINT
3620 IF SI$="S" THEN LPRINT "ARMY STANDARD METRO"
3630 IF SI$="I" THEN LPR1NT "ICAO STANDARD ATMOSPHERE"
3640 LPRINT
3650 LPRINT "PROJECTILE IDENTIFICATION: ";K2$
3660 LPRINT
3670 LPRINT "MUZ VEL"," C"," H0"," ELEV","DENSITY"
3680 LPRINT "(FT/SEC)","(LB/IN2)","(1NCHES)","(MINUTES)"," RATIO"
3690 LPRINT
3700 PP0=INT(1000*P0+.5)/1000
3710 LPRINT V0,C,P4,PP0,R0
3720 LPRINT
3730 LPRINT
3740 LPRINT "
TEMP","RANGEWIND","CROSSWIND","RMATCH","HMATCH"
3750 LPRINT "(DEG,F)"," (MPH)"," (MPH)",UR$,"(INCHES)"
3760 LPRINT
3770 LPRINT PT0,P1,P3,R8,H8
3780 LPRINT
3790 LPRINT
3800 LPRINT
TAB( l);"RANGE";TAB( 1 l);"HEIGHT";TAB(23);"DEFL."
;TAB(33);"VEL";TAB(41);"TIME";
TAB(51);"VX" ;TAB(60);"VY";TAB(68);"VZ"
3810 LPRINT
UR$;TAB(12);"(IN)" ;TAB(24);"(IN)" ;TAB(32);"(FPS)"
;TAB(40);"(SEC)";TAB(50);"(FPS)" ;T
AB(59);"(FPS)" ;TAB(67);"(FPS)"
3820 LPRINT
3830 FOR N=1 TO N2
3840 LPRINT USING U1$;Q(N);R(N);T(N);V(N);W(N);X(N);Y(N);Z(N)
3850 NEXT N
3860 REM CHECK FOR ADDITIONAL CASES.
3870 LPRINT
3880 LPRINT
3890 LPRINT
3900 PRINT
3910 PRINT
3920 PRINT "RUN ANOTHER CASE? (ENTER Y FOR YES, N FOR NO:)";
3930 INPUT K1$
3940 IF K1$="N" THEN 4170
3950 PRINT
3960 PRINT "USE SAME DRAG COEFFICIENT TABLE?"
3970 PRINT "ENTER Y FOR YES, N FORNO:";
3980 INPUT K1$
3990 IF K1$="N" THEN 460
4000 GOTO 880
4010 REM SUBROUTINE FOR INTERPOLATION IN DRAG TABLE
4020 I=1
4030 IF (I+1)>MMI THEN 4130
4040 IF X1<M(I+l) THEN 4070
4050 I=I+1
4060 GOTO 4030
4070 S=(D(I+1)-D(I))/(M(I+1)-M(I))
4080 X2=D(I)+S*(X1-M(I))
4090 RETURN
4100 PRINT: PRINT
4110 PRINT "ELEVATION ANGLE ITERATION DID NOT CONVERGE. "
4120 GOTO 3880
4130 PRINT: PRINT
4140 PRINT "TRAJECTORY CANNOT REACH THE SPECIFIED MAXIMUM
RANGE."
4150 PRINT "TRY A SHORTER MAXIMUM RANGE."
4160 GOTO 3880
4170 END
```

REFERENCES

1. Carnahan, B, H. A. Luther, and J. O. Wilkes, *Applied Numerical Methods*, Wiley, New York, 1969.

2. *Exterior Ballistic Tables Based on Numerical Integration*, Ordnance Department, U.S. Army, 1924.

3. International Civil Aviation Organization, *Standard Atmosphere - Tables and Data for Altitudes to 65,800 Feet*, Langley Aeronautical Laboratory, NACA Report No. 1235, 1955.

4. United States Committee on Extension to the Standard Atmosphere, *U.S. Standard Atmosphere, 1962*, U.S. Government Printing Office, Washington 25, D.C., 1962.

5. Murphy, C. H., "Data Reduction for the Free Flight Spark Ranges," Ballistic Research Laboratories Report No. 900, 1954.

6. Braun, W. F., "Aerodynamic Data for Small Arms Projectiles," Ballistic Research Laboratories Report No. 1630, 1973.

7. Bull, G. V., and C. H. Murphy, *Paris Kanonen - the Paris Guns (Wilhelmgeschütze) and Project HARP*, Verlag E. S. Mittler & Sohn GmbH, Herford, Germany, 1988.

9

Six-Degrees-Of-Freedom (6-DOF) and Modified Point-Mass Trajectories

9.1 INTRODUCTION

Six-degrees-of-freedom (6-DOF) trajectory calculations are a rather recent advance in the state-of- the-art of exterior ballistics. The foundations of modern 6-DOF trajectory models for rotationally symmetric, spinning projectiles were laid in the early part of the twentieth century, with the classical work of the English scientists Fowler, Gallop, Lock and Richmond (Ref. 1), published in 1920. The vector notation introduced by Fowler et al. was further refined in the early 1950s by R. H. Kent (Ref. 2) at the Ballistic Research Laboratory (BRL), and in unpublished work by A. S. Galbraith, also of the BRL. Kent and Galbraith incorporated the complete aerodynamic force-moment system first advanced by Nielsen and Synge of Canada (Ref. 3) in 1943, and further refined by J. L. Kelley and E. J. McShane (Ref. 4) at the BRL. The modern 6-DOF differential equations of motion presented in this chapter are simply an updated version of those formulated by Kent and Galbraith in the early 1950s.

Many exterior ballisticians who worked at Aberdeen Proving Ground, and other ballistic research organizations, were very familiar with the basic 6-DOF differential equations as early as the 1930s. However, no numerical (nearly exact) solution of these formidable equations was possible, in the practical sense, until the advent of modern high-speed digital computers, and this did not occur until the late 1940s. Practical 6-DOF computer programs did not appear until the late 1950s and early 1960s, when the memory size and computational speed of mainframe computers had advanced to the point that solutions could be obtained in a reasonable length of time. The largest and fastest modern computers can solve long-range 6-DOF trajectories in milliseconds, and such solutions are routinely done today in the larger ballistic research and development laboratories.

The vector 6-DOF differential equations of motion presented in this chapter are an updated edition of those published at the BRL in 1964 (Ref. 5), and are formulated to solve the projectile pitching and yawing motion in terms of direction cosines of the projectile's axis of symmetry, rather than the Euler-angle method used in several other 6-DOF computer programs (see References 6 and 7 for two examples). One advantage of direction cosines is that no alternate coordinate system is required for large-angle-of-attack flight; the direction cosines method is valid at all angles of attack. In addition, the development of the linearized equations of pitching and yawing motion, which will be covered in the next chapter, seems to flow more naturally from a 6-DOF model specified in terms of the direction cosines of the projectile's axis of rotational symmetry. However, the two methods are, in principle, equivalent and modern 6-DOF computer programs using either approach should give essentially identical answers.

Modern numerical integration of the 6-DOF differential equations of motion gives the most accurate solution possible, for the trajectory and flight dynamic behavior of a rotationally symmetric, spinning or non-spinning projectile, provided that all the aerodynamic forces and moments, and the initial conditions, are known to a high degree of accuracy. Scientists and engineers who routinely use 6-DOF methods are often heard to say, "GI-GO" (Garbage In - Garbage Out!). No computed trajectory or flight dynamic analysis can be any better than the quality of its input data.

9.2 EQUATIONS OF MOTION FOR SIX-DEGREES-OF-FREEDOM TRAJECTORIES

We will adopt a right-handed, rectangular coordinate system, with the origin of coordinates located at the gun muzzle. The 6-DOF coordinate axis labels are changed to [1,2,3] instead of the [X,Y,Z] labels we have used in previous chapters. The reason is that the letter symbols will be used to represent other quantities in the 6-DOF differential equations, and numbered axis labels are therefore used to avoid confusion. In our earth-fixed coordinate system the 1-3 plane is tangent to the earth's surface at the launch point, the 1-axis points downrange, the 2-axis points vertically upward through the launch point, and the 3-axis points to the right, when looking downrange. Figure 9.1 illustrates the trajectory and the 6-DOF coordinate system used.

Newton's laws of motion (Ref. 8) state that the rate of change of linear momentum must equal the sum of all the externally applied forces, and that the rate of change of angular momentum must equal the sum of all the externally applied moments. Our 6-DOF equations of motion include a provision for rockets as well as conventional projectiles; thus forces and moments due to rocket thrust and jet damping terms must be included as well. Newton's laws for a projectile are:

$$m\frac{d\vec{V}}{dt} = \sum \vec{F} + m\vec{g} + m\vec{\Lambda} + \textit{Rocket Thrust Forces} \quad \textbf{(9.1)}$$

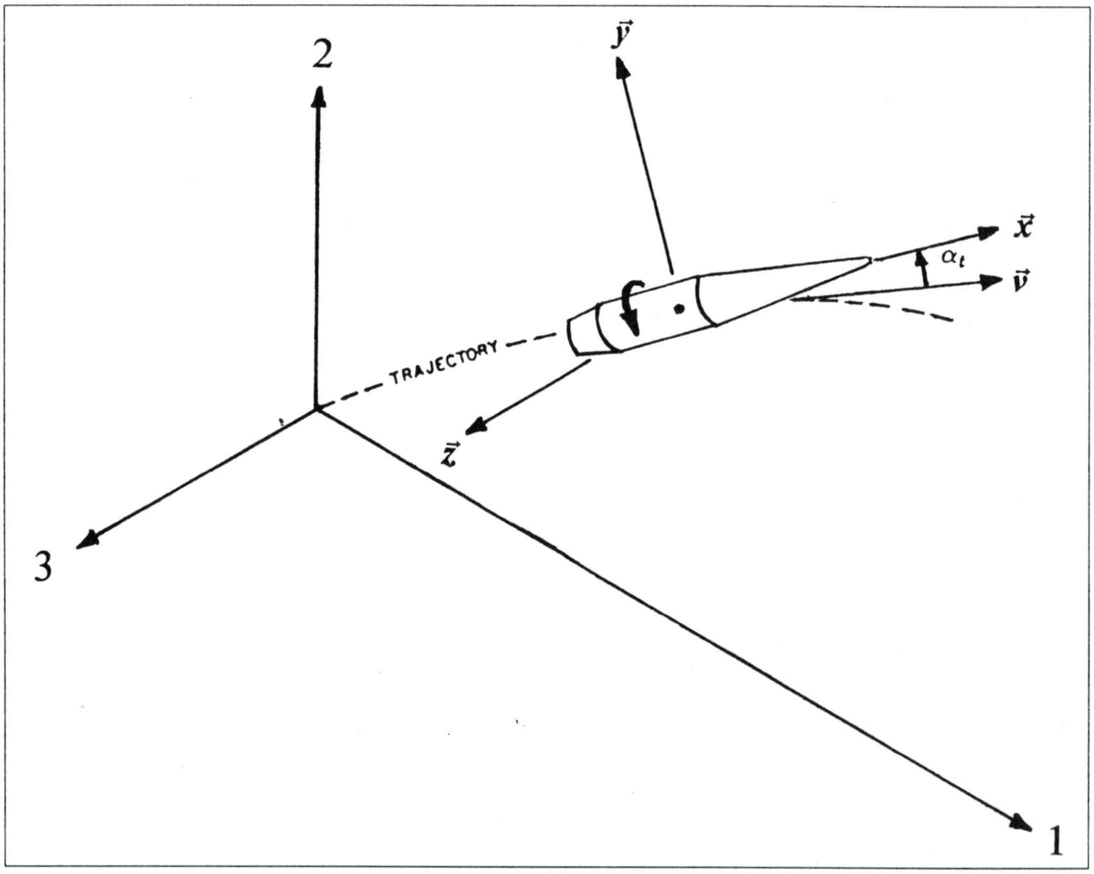

Figure 9.1 Coordinate System for Six-Degrees-Of-Freedom Trajectories.

$$\frac{d\vec{H}}{dt} = \sum \vec{M} + \textit{Rocket Thrust Moments} \tag{9.2}$$

where,

m = projectile mass

$\vec{V}$ = vector velocity with respect to the ground-fixed coordinate axes

t = time

$\Sigma\vec{F}$ = vector sum of all the aerodynamic forces

$\vec{g}$ = acceleration due to gravity

$\vec{\Lambda}$ = Coriolis acceleration due to the earth's rotation

$\vec{H}$ = total vector angular momentum of the projectile

$\Sigma\vec{M}$ = vector sum of all the aerodynamic moments (referenced to the center of mass)

We will choose a unit vector, $\vec{x}$, along the projectile's axis of rotational symmetry, directed positive from tail to nose (illustrated in Figure 9.1). The projectile is assumed to be both rigid (non-flexible), and rotationally symmetric about its spin axis; therefore every transverse axis that passes through the center of mass, and is perpendicular to the axis of symmetry, is a principal axis of inertia. Given these assumptions, the total projectile vector angular momentum may be expressed as the sum of two vectors: (1) the angular momentum about $\vec{x}$, and (2) the angular momentum about any axis perpendicular to $\vec{x}$, and passing through the projectile's center of mass.

The angular momentum about $\vec{x}$ has the magnitude $I_x p$, where I_x is the projectile's axial moment of inertia (moment of inertia about the spin axis), and p is the axial spin, in radians per second. Thus the first component of the angular momentum is $I_x p\vec{x}$, where a positive axial spin, p, would cause a right-hand screw to advance in the direction of $\vec{x}$.

The total vector angular velocity about any perpendicular axis is given by the vector cross product (A). Thus the second component of the angular momentum is (B) where I_y is the projectile's transverse moment of inertia, about any axis through the center of mass. The total projectile vector angular momentum is therefore given by the sum of the two parts:

$$A = \left(\vec{x} \times \frac{d\vec{x}}{dt}\right) \qquad B = I_y\left(\vec{x} \times \frac{d\vec{x}}{dt}\right)$$

$$\vec{H} = I_x p\vec{x} + I_y\left(\vec{x} \times \frac{d\vec{x}}{dt}\right) \tag{9.3}$$

Note that the transverse angular velocities q and r are contained n the vector $\frac{d\vec{x}}{dt}$. We now set $\vec{h} = \frac{\vec{H}}{I_y}$, and divide both sides of quation (9.3) by I_y:

$$\vec{h} = \frac{I_x p}{I_y}\vec{x} + \left(\vec{x} \times \frac{d\vec{x}}{dt}\right) \qquad \textbf{(9.4)}$$

The rate of change of the vector angular momentum divided y I_y, is now given by:

$$\frac{d\vec{h}}{dt} = \frac{I_x \dot{p}}{I_y}\vec{x} + \frac{I_x p}{I_y}\frac{d\vec{x}}{dt} + \left(\vec{x} \times \frac{d^2\vec{x}}{dt^2}\right) \qquad \textbf{(9.5)}$$

In addition to equations (9.4) and (9.5), we will need both the ector dot product, and the cross product of $\vec{h}$ with $\vec{x}$. Performing he two vector operations, we find:

$$\left(\vec{h} \bullet \vec{x}\right) = \frac{I_x p}{I_y} \qquad \textbf{(9.6)}$$

$$\left(\vec{h} \times \vec{x}\right) = \frac{d\vec{x}}{dt} \qquad \textbf{(9.7)}$$

The six-degrees-of-freedom vector differential equations of notion, for a rigid, rotationally symmetric projectile, acted on by ll significant aerodynamic forces and moments, in addition to wind, ravity and Coriolis forces, rocket thrust and spin torque, and jet lamping forces and moments, are now summarized in equations 9.8) and (9.9)

$$\begin{aligned}\frac{d\vec{V}}{dt} = &-\frac{\rho v S C_D}{2m}\vec{v} + \frac{\rho S C_{L_\alpha}}{2m}\left[v^2\vec{x} - (\vec{v}\bullet\vec{x})\vec{v}\right]\\ &-\frac{\rho S d C_{N_{p\alpha}}}{2m}\left(\frac{I_y}{I_x}\right)\left(\vec{h}\bullet\vec{x}\right)\left(\vec{x}\times\vec{v}\right) + \frac{\rho v S d\left(C_{N_q} + C_{N_{\dot\alpha}}\right)}{2m}\left(\vec{h}\times\vec{x}\right)\\ &+\vec{g} + \vec{\Lambda} + \frac{gT}{m}\vec{x} + \left(\frac{I_y}{m r_t} - \frac{\dot m r_e}{m}\right)\left(\vec{h}\times\vec{x}\right)\end{aligned} \qquad \textbf{(9.8)}$$

Equation (9.8) is the vector differential equation of motion of the projectile's center of mass. The differential equation describing the projectile's angular motion (spin, pitch, and yaw) about its cen- er of mass is stated as equation (9.9):

$$\begin{aligned}\frac{d\vec{h}}{dt} = &\frac{\rho v S d^2 C_{l_p}}{2I_x}\left(\vec{h}\bullet\vec{x}\right)\vec{x} + \frac{\rho v^2 S d \delta_F C_{l_\delta}}{2I_y}\vec{x}\\ &+\frac{\rho v S d C_{M_\alpha}}{2I_y}\left(\vec{v}\times\vec{x}\right) + \frac{\rho S d^2 C_{M_{p\alpha}}}{2I_x}\left(\vec{h}\bullet\vec{x}\right)\left[\vec{v} - (\vec{v}\bullet\vec{x})\vec{x}\right]\\ &+\frac{\rho v S d^2\left(C_{M_q} + C_{M_{\dot\alpha}}\right)}{2I_y}\left[\vec{h} - \left(\vec{h}\bullet\vec{x}\right)\vec{x}\right] + \frac{gT_S}{I_y}\vec{x}\\ &-\left(\frac{\dot I_y - \dot m r_e r_t}{I_y}\right)\left[\vec{h} - \left(\vec{h}\bullet\vec{x}\right)\vec{x}\right]\end{aligned} \qquad \textbf{(9.9)}$$

where,

$\vec{V}$ = vector velocity of the projectile with respect to the earth fixed coordinate system

$\vec{W}$ = vector wind velocity, relative to the earth fixed coordinates

$\vec{v}$ = vector velocity of the projectile with respect to the air $\left(\vec{v} = \vec{V} - \vec{W}\right)$

$\vec{x}$ = unit vector along the projectile's rotational axis of symmetry

$\vec{h}$ = vector angular momentum divided by the transverse moment of inertia, I_Y

t = time

ρ = air density

d = projectile reference diameter

S = projectile reference area (usually taken as S = $\pi d^2/4$)

m = projectile mass

I_x = projectile axial moment of inertia

I_y = projectile transverse moment of inertia, about any axis through the center of mass

C_D = drag force coefficient

C_{L_α} = lift force coefficient

$C_{N_{p\alpha}}$ = Magnus force coefficient

$\left(C_{N_q} + C_{N_{\dot\alpha}}\right)$ = pitch damping force coefficient

C_{l_p} = spin damping moment coefficient

C_{l_δ} = rolling moment due to fin cant

δ_F = fin cant angle (radians)

C_{M_α} = pitching (or overturning) moment coefficient

$C_{M_{p\alpha}}$ = Magnus moment coefficient

$\left(C_{M_q} + C_{M_{\dot\alpha}}\right)$ = pitch damping moment coefficient

$\vec{g}$ = vector acceleration due to gravity

$\vec{\Lambda}$ = vector Coriolis acceleration (see section 8.8 of Chapter 8)

T = rocket thrust force

T_S = rolling moment due to rocket spin torque

r_t = distance from projectile center of mass to the throat of the rocket nozzle (positive if the throat is *aft* of the center of mass).

r_e = distance from projectile center of mass to the rocket nozzle exit (positive if the throat is *aft* of the center of mass)

$\dot{m} = \frac{dm}{dt}$ = rate of change of the rocket projectile's mass

$\dot{I}_y = \frac{dI_y}{dt}$ = rate of change of the rocket projectile's transverse moment of inertia

Note that the last two terms in both equations (9.8) and (9.9) are rocket thrust and jet damping terms, all of which are to be set equal to zero for conventional (non-rocket) projectiles.

It is also noted that equations (9.8) and (9.9) are intimately coupled to each other. The differential equation for the vector velocity contains many terms involving the vector angular momentum, and conversely. Therefore the 6-DOF differential equations of motion must always be solved simultaneously.

We now expand the two vector differential equations into their respective [1,2,3] components along the coordinate axes of Figure 9.1, and the result, written in a "shorthand" notation, is the following six ordinary differential equations, one for each degree of freedom:

$$\dot{V}_1 = -\left[\tilde{C}_D\right]v_1 + \left[\tilde{C}_{L_\alpha}\right]\left(v^2 x_1 - v v_1 \cos\alpha_t\right) - \left[\tilde{C}_{N_{p\alpha}}\right]\left(x_2 v_3 - x_3 v_2\right) + \left[\tilde{C}_{N_q}\right]\left(h_2 x_3 - h_3 x_2\right) + g_1 + \Lambda_1 + \frac{gT}{m}x_1 + \left[\tilde{J}_{DF}\right]\left(h_2 x_3 - h_3 x_2\right) \quad (9.10)$$

$$\dot{V}_2 = -\left[\tilde{C}_D\right]v_2 + \left[\tilde{C}_{L_\alpha}\right]\left(v^2 x_2 - v v_2 \cos\alpha_t\right) - \left[\tilde{C}_{N_{p\alpha}}\right]\left(x_3 v_1 - x_1 v_3\right) + \left[\tilde{C}_{N_q}\right]\left(h_3 x_1 - h_1 x_3\right) + g_2 + \Lambda_2 + \frac{gT}{m}x_2 + \left[\tilde{J}_{DF}\right]\left(h_3 x_1 - h_1 x_3\right) \quad (9.11)$$

$$\dot{V}_3 = -\left[\tilde{C}_D\right]v_3 + \left[\tilde{C}_{L_\alpha}\right]\left(v^2 x_3 - v v_3 \cos\alpha_t\right) - \left[\tilde{C}_{N_{p\alpha}}\right]\left(x_1 v_2 - x_2 v_1\right) + \left[\tilde{C}_{N_q}\right]\left(h_1 x_2 - h_2 x_1\right) + g_3 + \Lambda_3 + \frac{gT}{m}x_3 + \left[\tilde{J}_{DF}\right]\left(h_1 x_2 - h_2 x_1\right) \quad (9.12)$$

$$\dot{h}_1 = \left(\left[\tilde{C}_{l_p}\right] + \left[\tilde{C}_{l_\delta}\right]\right)x_1 + \left[\tilde{C}_{M_\alpha}\right]\left(v_2 x_3 - v_3 x_2\right) + \left[\tilde{C}_{M_{p\alpha}}\right]\left(v_1 - v x_1 \cos\alpha_t\right) + \left[\tilde{C}_{M_q}\right]\left(h_1 - \frac{I_x p}{I_y}x_1\right) + \frac{gT_S}{I_y}x_1 - \left[\tilde{J}_{DM}\right]\left(h_1 - \frac{I_x p}{I_y}x_1\right) \quad (9.13)$$

$$\dot{h}_2 = \left(\left[\tilde{C}_{l_p}\right] + \left[\tilde{C}_{l_\delta}\right]\right)x_2 + \left[\tilde{C}_{M_\alpha}\right]\left(v_3 x_1 - v_1 x_3\right) + \left[\tilde{C}_{M_{p\alpha}}\right]\left(v_2 - v x_2 \cos\alpha_t\right) + \left[\tilde{C}_{M_q}\right]\left(h_2 - \frac{I_x p}{I_y}x_2\right) + \frac{gT_S}{I_y}x_2 - \left[\tilde{J}_{DM}\right]\left(h_2 - \frac{I_x p}{I_y}x_2\right) \quad (9.14)$$

$$\dot{h}_3 = \left(\left[\tilde{C}_{l_p}\right] + \left[\tilde{C}_{l_\delta}\right]\right)x_3 + \left[\tilde{C}_{M_\alpha}\right]\left(v_1 x_2 - v_2 x_1\right) + \left[\tilde{C}_{M_{p\alpha}}\right]\left(v_3 - v x_3 \cos\alpha_t\right) + \left[\tilde{C}_{M_q}\right]\left(h_3 - \frac{I_x p}{I_y}x_3\right) + \frac{gT_S}{I_y}x_3 - \left[\tilde{J}_{DM}\right]\left(h_3 - \frac{I_x p}{I_y}x_3\right) \quad (9.15)$$

where, $v_1 = V_1 - W_1 : v_2 = V_2 - W_2 : v_3 = V_3 - W_3$

$$v^2 = \vec{v} \bullet \vec{v} = v_1^2 + v_2^2 + v_3^2 : v = \sqrt{v_1^2 + v_2^2 + v_3^2}$$

$\cos\alpha_t = \frac{v_1 x_1 + v_2 x_2 + v_3 x_3}{v}$, the cosine of the total angle of attack

$$\frac{I_x p}{I_y} = \vec{h} \bullet \vec{x} = h_1 x_1 + h_2 x_2 + h_3 x_3$$

$p = \frac{I_y}{I_x}\left(\vec{h} \bullet \vec{x}\right)$ [Note: p = projectile axial spin rate (radians/second)]

$$\left[\tilde{C}_D\right] = \frac{\rho v S C_D}{2m} \qquad \left[\tilde{C}_{l_\delta}\right] = \frac{\rho v^2 S d \delta_F C_{l_\delta}}{2I_y}$$

$$\left[\tilde{C}_{L_\alpha}\right] = \frac{\rho v S C_{L_\alpha}}{2m} \qquad \left[\tilde{C}_{M_\alpha}\right] = \frac{\rho v S d C_{M_\alpha}}{2I_y}$$

$$\left[\tilde{C}_{N_{p\alpha}}\right] = \frac{\rho S d C_{N_{p\alpha}} p}{2m} \qquad \left[\tilde{C}_{M_{p\alpha}}\right] = \frac{\rho S d^2 C_{M_{p\alpha}} p}{2I_y}$$

$$\left[\tilde{C}_{N_q}\right] = \frac{\rho v S d\left(C_{N_q} + C_{N_{\dot{\alpha}}}\right)}{2m} \qquad \left[\tilde{C}_{M_q}\right] = \frac{\rho v S d^2\left(C_{M_q} + C_{M_{\dot{\alpha}}}\right)}{2I_y}$$

$$\left[\tilde{J}_{DF}\right] = \left(\frac{\dot{I}_y}{m r_t} - \frac{\dot{m} r_e}{m}\right) \qquad \left[\tilde{J}_{DM}\right] = \left(\frac{\dot{I}_y - \dot{m} r_e r_t}{I_y}\right)$$

$$\left[\tilde{C}_{l_p}\right] = \frac{\rho v S d^2 C_{l_p} p}{2I_y}$$

The position of the projectile's center of mass, relative to the ground-fixed [1,2,3] coordinate system, is given by the vector $\vec{X}$, whose components are:

$$X_1 = X_{1_0} + \int_0^t V_1 dt \quad : \quad X_2 = X_{2_0} + \int_0^t V_2 dt \quad : \quad X_3 = X_{3_0} + \int_0^t V_3 dt \quad (9.16)$$

For very long range trajectories, the trajectory relative to the spherical earth's surface is usually preferred over the ground-fixed $[X_1, X_2, X_3]$ coordinates, that are measured relative to a flat, horizontal plane, tangent to the earth's surface at the firing site. The trajectory coordinates $[E_1, E_2, E_3]$ relative to the spherical earth, are given by the following approximations:

$$\vec{E} \approx \begin{bmatrix} E_1 = X_1 \\ E_2 = X_2 + X_1^2/(2R) \\ E_3 = X_3 \end{bmatrix} \qquad \textbf{(9.17)}$$

where R = Average radius of the earth = 6,951,844 yards (6,356,766 meters)

The difference between E_2 and X_2 height coordinates (the 1 and 3 coordinates are unchanged) is illustrated in Table 9.1, below, at various ranges to level ground impact:

Table 9.1
Effect of a Spherical Earth on the Impact Height of the Trajectory

X_1(Yards)	$[E_2-X_2]$ (Inches)
100	0.03
500	0.65
1000	2.59
2000	10.36
5000	64.73
10000	258.92

Table 9.1 shows that at short to moderate ranges, the effect of curvature in the earth's surface is insignificant. However, at long ranges (e.g., 2000 yards and beyond), the differences between spherical and flat-earth coordinates become appreciable.

The 6-DOF approximation used for the vector acceleration due to gravity is given by the following equations:

$$\vec{g} \approx -g \begin{bmatrix} X_1/R \\ 1 - 2X_2/R \\ 0 \end{bmatrix} \qquad \textbf{(9.18)}$$

where $g = 32.174\,[\,1 - 0.0026 \cos(2L)]$ (feet/second^2) **(9.19)**

R = Average radius of the earth

L = latitude of the firing site (+ for Northern hemisphere, - for Southern)

Note that the gravitational constant in equation (9.19) contains a correction for the centripetal acceleration due to the earth's rotation. The small centripetal correction depends on the latitude, as equation (9.19) illustrates. Note also that the value of g = 32.174 ft/sec^2 occurs at ±45 degrees latitude. At the equator (L = 0), g = 32.090 ft/sec^2, and at either the North or South pole (L = ± 90°), g = 32.258 ft/sec^2.

The Coriolis effect was discussed rather extensively in the eighth section of Chapter 8, and the reader is referred back to that section for a review. A restatement of equation (8.27) is given below, with conversion to the [1,2,3] coordinate system of the present chapter:

$$\vec{\Lambda} = \begin{bmatrix} \Lambda_1 = 2\Omega(-V_2 \cos L \sin AZ - V_3 \sin L) \\ \Lambda_2 = 2\Omega(V_1 \cos L \sin AZ + V_3 \cos L \cos AZ) \\ \Lambda_3 = 2\Omega(V_1 \sin L - V_2 \cos L \cos AZ) \end{bmatrix} \qquad \textbf{(9.20)}$$

[See Chapter 8 for the definitions of symbols in equation (9.20)].

Before we can discuss the numerical solution of the above differential equations of motion, we must address the problem of initial conditions. The next section of this chapter covers the topic of 6-DOF initial conditions, in some detail.

9.3 INITIAL CONDITIONS FOR SIX-DEGREES-OF-FREEDOM TRAJECTORIES

The previous two sections of this chapter covered the six-degrees-of-freedom differential equations of motion, and the physical characteristics of the projectile. The proper specification of the initial conditions is equally important for the accurate calculation of 6-DOF trajectories. The initial conditions are the initial values, at the muzzle of the gun (or at the end of the launcher, for rockets), of all the quantities on the right hand sides of equations (9.10) through (9.15). The various motion variables, and their initial conditions, are listed below.

$$\vec{V}_0 = \begin{bmatrix} V_{1_0} \\ V_{2_0} \\ V_{3_0} \end{bmatrix} = V_0 \begin{bmatrix} \cos\phi_0 \cos\theta_0 \\ \sin\phi_0 \cos\theta_0 \\ \sin\theta_0 \end{bmatrix} \qquad \textbf{(9.21)}$$

$$\vec{v}_0 = \begin{bmatrix} v_{1_0} \\ v_{2_0} \\ v_{3_0} \end{bmatrix} = \begin{bmatrix} V_{1_0} - W_{1_0} \\ V_{2_0} - W_{2_0} \\ V_{3_0} - W_{3_0} \end{bmatrix} \qquad \textbf{(9.22)}$$

where $\vec{V}_0$ = Muzzle velocity vector

$V_0 = \sqrt{V_{1_0}^{\,2} + V_{2_0}^{\,2} + V_{3_0}^{\,2}}$, the scalar magnitude of the muzzle velocity

$\vec{v}_0$ = Initial velocity vector with respect to air $\left[\vec{v}_0 = \vec{V}_0 - \vec{W}_0\right]$

$v_0 = \sqrt{v_{1_0}^{\,2} + v_{2_0}^{\,2} + v_{3_0}^{\,2}}$, the scalar magnitude of initial velocity with respect to air

ϕ_0 = vertical angle of departure, positive upward

θ_0 = horizontal angle of departure relative to the 1-2 plane, positive to the right when looking downrange

In addition to the unit vector $\vec{x}$, we will also need two other unit vectors, $\vec{y}$ and $\vec{z}$, both of which originate at the projectile's center of mass, and are perpendicular to $\vec{x}$. The [x,y,z] unit vectors form a triad, with the unit z-vector perpendicular to the x-vector, and lying in the horizontal plane. The y-vector is then defined as the vector cross product, $\vec{y} = (\vec{z} \times \vec{x})$. Figure 9.1 illustrates the [x,y,z] triad, and shows the direction of the three orthogonal unit vectors. The initial components of the three unit vectors are listed below.

$$\vec{x}_0 = \begin{bmatrix} x_{1_0} \\ x_{2_0} \\ x_{3_0} \end{bmatrix} = \begin{bmatrix} \cos(\phi_0 + \alpha_0)\cos(\theta_0 + \beta_0) \\ \sin(\phi_0 + \alpha_0)\cos(\theta_0 + \beta_0) \\ \sin(\theta_0 + \beta_0) \end{bmatrix} \qquad \textbf{(9.23)}$$

$$\vec{y}_0 = \begin{bmatrix} y_{1_0} \\ y_{2_0} \\ y_{3_0} \end{bmatrix} = \frac{1}{\sqrt{Q}} \begin{bmatrix} -\cos^2(\theta_0 + \beta_0)\sin(\phi_0 + \alpha_0)\cos(\phi_0 + \alpha_0) \\ \cos^2(\theta_0 + \beta_0)\cos^2(\phi_0 + \alpha_0) + \sin^2(\theta_0 + \beta_0) \\ -\sin(\theta_0 + \beta_0)\cos(\theta_0 + \beta_0)\sin(\phi_0 + \alpha_0) \end{bmatrix} \qquad \textbf{(9.24)}$$

$$\vec{z}_0 = \begin{bmatrix} z_{1_0} \\ z_{2_0} \\ z_{3_0} \end{bmatrix} = \frac{1}{\sqrt{Q}} \begin{bmatrix} -\sin(\theta_0 + \beta_0) \\ O \\ \cos(\theta_0 + \beta_0)\cos(\phi_0 + \alpha_0) \end{bmatrix} \qquad \textbf{(9.25)}$$

where α_0 = initial pitch angle at the gun muzzle

β_0 = initial yaw angle at the gun muzzle

and, $$Q = \sin^2(\theta_0 + \beta_0) + \cos^2(\theta_0 + \beta_0)\cos^2(\phi_0 + \alpha_0) \qquad \textbf{(9.26)}$$

The vector $\frac{d\vec{x}_0}{dt}$ is given by: $d\vec{x}_0/dt = \vec{\omega}_0 \times \vec{x}_0 = (\vec{\omega}_0 \cdot \vec{z}_0)\vec{y}_0 - (\vec{\omega}_0 \cdot \vec{y}_0)\vec{z}_0$

$\vec{\omega}_0$ in earth-fixed system $\quad \omega_{z0} \quad \omega_{y0}$

$$\frac{d\vec{x}_0}{dt} = \left[\omega_{z_0}\vec{y}_0 - \omega_{y_0}\vec{z}_0\right] = \begin{bmatrix} \dot{x}_{1_0} \\ \dot{x}_{2_0} \\ \dot{x}_{3_0} \end{bmatrix} = \begin{bmatrix} \omega_{z_0}y_{1_0} - \omega_{y_0}z_{1_0} \\ \omega_{z_0}y_{2_0} - \omega_{y_0}z_{2_0} \\ \omega_{z_0}y_{3_0} - \omega_{y_0}z_{3_0} \end{bmatrix} \qquad \textbf{(9.27)}$$

where ω_{y_0} and ω_{z_0} are the scalar initial components of the projectile's transverse angular velocity, about the $\vec{y}$ and $\vec{z}$ unit vectors, respectively.

Substituting the y-vector and z-vector components [equations (9.24) and (9.25)] into equation (9.27) yields the components of the $\frac{d\vec{x}_0}{dt}$ vector:

$$\dot{x}_{1_0} = \frac{1}{\sqrt{Q}} \begin{bmatrix} -\omega_{z_0}\cos^2(\theta_0 + \beta_0)\sin(\phi_0 + \alpha_0)\cos(\phi_0 + \alpha_0) \\ +\omega_{y_0}\sin(\theta_0 + \beta_0) \end{bmatrix} \qquad \textbf{(9.28)}$$

$$\dot{x}_{2_0} = \frac{1}{\sqrt{Q}}\left[\omega_{z_0}\cos^2(\theta_0 + \beta_0)\cos^2(\phi_0 + \alpha_0) + \omega_{z_0}\sin^2(\theta_0 + \beta_0)\right] \qquad \textbf{(9.29)}$$

$$\dot{x}_{3_0} = \frac{1}{\sqrt{Q}} \begin{bmatrix} -\omega_{z_0}\sin(\theta_0 + \beta_0)\cos(\theta_0 + \beta_0)\sin(\phi_0 + \alpha_0) \\ -\omega_{y_0}\cos(\theta_0 + \beta_0)\cos(\phi_0 + \alpha_0) \end{bmatrix} \qquad \textbf{(9.30)}$$

It should be noted that a positive ω_{y_0} (radians/second) is an initial transverse angular velocity that causes the nose of the projectile to rotate (yaw) to the left, when looking downrange. A positive vertical angular velocity ω_{z_0}, (also radians/second), causes the nose of the projectile to rotate (pitch) upward. In practice, values of the initial transverse angular velocities are usually chosen so that the correct values of pitch and yaw are obtained at the first maximum yaw location along the trajectory.

The initial, or muzzle value of the h-vector is denoted by $\vec{h}_0$, and is given by:

$$\vec{h}_0 = \begin{bmatrix} h_{1_0} \\ h_{2_0} \\ h_{3_0} \end{bmatrix} = \begin{bmatrix} \frac{I_x p_0}{I_y}x_{1_0} + x_{2_0}\dot{x}_{3_0} - x_{3_0}\dot{x}_{2_0} \\ \frac{I_x p_0}{I_y}x_{2_0} - x_{1_0}\dot{x}_{3_0} + x_{3_0}\dot{x}_{1_0} \\ \frac{I_x p_0}{I_y}x_{3_0} + x_{1_0}\dot{x}_{2_0} - x_{2_0}\dot{x}_{1_0} \end{bmatrix} \qquad \textbf{(9.31)}$$

where $p_0 = \frac{2\pi V_0}{nd}$ = axial spin rate (radians/second) at the gun muzzle

n = rifling twist rate at the gun muzzle (calibers/turn)

Equations (9.23) and (9.28) through (9.30) can now be substituted into equations (9.31), to define the initial h_0-vector, and this completes our specification of the initial conditions for a six-degrees-of- freedom trajectory.

Note that equations (9.28) through (9.30) specify *only* the initial values of $\frac{d\vec{x}}{dt}$. Along the trajectory, the time rate of change of $\vec{x}$ is found by expanding equation (9.7) into its [1,2,3] components:

$$\frac{d\vec{x}}{dt} = (\vec{h} \times \vec{x}) = \begin{bmatrix} \dot{x}_1 \\ \dot{x}_2 \\ \dot{x}_3 \end{bmatrix} = \begin{bmatrix} h_2x_3 - h_3x_2 \\ h_3x_1 - h_1x_3 \\ h_1x_2 - h_2x_1 \end{bmatrix} \qquad \textbf{(9.32)}$$

9.4 NUMERICAL SOLUTION OF SIX-DEGREES-OF-FREEDOM TRAJECTORIES

The numerical solution of six-degrees-of-freedom trajectories is a significantly more complicated problem than the solution of point-mass trajectories, discussed in Chapter 8. We have six ordinary differential equations to solve, instead of three, and the specification of initial conditions for the 6-DOF problem is considerably more complicated, as the previous section indicates. Higher order methods of numerical integration are usually required, and the central-processing-unit (CPU) time on the computer can be two orders of magnitude longer than that required for the solution of a similar point-mass trajectory.

The numerical algorithms ordinarily used for solving a single first-order differential equation, with a single initial condition, are based on one of two approaches: (1) direct or indirect use of Taylor's expansion of the solution function, or (2) the use of open or closed integration formulas. There are also one-step and multistep methods for the implementation of the above procedures. One-step methods are self-starting; i.e., they do not require pre-existing information that lies outside the current integration step. On the other hand, the one-step methods require more computation than multistep methods, to produce results of comparable accuracy. Both methods thus have advantages and disadvantages, and practical experience provides the only useful guidance in making the best decision.

The cumulative experience of six-degrees-of-freedom computer program users over the past thirty years suggests that the various one-step, fourth-order *Runge-Kutta* methods (Ref. 9) are essentially optimum for this particular problem. Two popular variations of this method will be presented in this section.

Any first-order, ordinary differential equation may be expressed in the form:

$$\frac{dy}{dx} = f(x,y) \qquad \textbf{(9.33)}$$

where x = the independent variable
y = the dependent variable

Rocket forces and moments (which vary with time) are often included in 6-DOF trajectories, thus 6-DOF computer programs use time as the independent variable, rather than distance. The three linear velocities plus the three angular velocities are the six dependent variables.

All the Runge-Kutta methods use algorithms of the general form:

$$y_{i+1} = y_i + h\Phi(x_i, y_i, h) \qquad \textbf{(9.34)}$$

where x_i = value of the independent variable at the ith integration step
x_{i+1} = value of the independent variable at the $(i+1)^{th}$ integration step
y_i = value of the dependent variable at $x = x_i$
y_{i+1} = value of the dependent variable at $x = x_{i+1}$
h = integration step size
Φ = the increment function

The "increment function" is nothing more than a suitably chosen approximation to f(x,y) over the interval $x_i \le x \le x_{i+1}$. For Runge-Kutta (R-K) methods up to and including the fourth-order, the system of R-K equations is always underdetermined (Ref. 9), and one of the R-K constants may therefore be chosen arbitrarily. Depending on this choice, various R-K algorithms are possible, and two of the most commonly used fourth-order equation sets are illustrated below.

The first fourth-order R-K form we will discuss is attributed (Ref. 9) to Kutta:

$$y_{i+1} = y_i + \frac{h}{6}\left(k_1 + 2k_2 + 2k_3 + k_4\right) \qquad \textbf{(9.35)}$$

where

$$k_1 = f(x_i, y_i)$$
$$k_2 = f\left(x_i + \tfrac{1}{2}h, y_i + \tfrac{1}{2}hk_1\right)$$
$$k_3 = f\left(x_i + \tfrac{1}{2}h, y_i + \tfrac{1}{2}hk_2\right)$$
$$k_4 = f\left(x_i + h, y_i + hk_3\right)$$

Note that (9.35) reduces to Simpson's rule if f (x,y) is a function of x only.

Perhaps the most widely used fourth-order R-K method is the one advanced by Gill (Ref. 10):

$$y_{i+1} = y_i + \frac{h}{6}\left[k_1 + 2\left(1 - \frac{1}{\sqrt{2}}\right)k_2 + 2\left(1 + \frac{1}{\sqrt{2}}\right)k_3 + k_4\right] \qquad \textbf{(9.36)}$$

where

$$k_1 = f(x_i, y_i)$$
$$k_2 = f\left(x_i + \tfrac{1}{2}h, y_i + \tfrac{1}{2}hk_1\right)$$
$$k_3 = f\left(x_i + \frac{1}{2}h, y_i + \left[-\frac{1}{2} + \frac{1}{\sqrt{2}}\right]hk_1 + \left[1 - \frac{1}{\sqrt{2}}\right]hk_2\right)$$
$$k_4 = f\left(x_i + h, y_i - \frac{1}{\sqrt{2}}hk_2 + \left[1 + \frac{1}{\sqrt{2}}\right]hk_3\right)$$

Equations (9.36) are referred to as the Runge-Kutta-Gill (RKG) method. The RKG constants were originally chosen to reduce the amount of temporary computer storage required in the solution of large systems of simultaneous first-order differential equations. With the advent of computers having large memories, the need for the RKG algorithm has largely disappeared, but the Runge-Kutta subroutines found in most computer-program libraries still employ the Gill constants. The Ballistic Research Laboratory (BRL) six-degrees-of-freedom computer program (Ref. 5) has used the RKG method since its inception, and it is still in use today.

The final topic of this section involves the integration step. Thirty years experience with the fourth-order Runge-Kutta methods, applied to the 6-DOF trajectory problem, suggests that roughly fifty integrations per yaw cycle are required, in order to achieve a numerical solution that is accurate to four or five significant figures. A larger time step gives less accuracy, while a smaller step gives good results, but requires excessive amounts of CPU time on the computer. The method currently in use at the BRL is a variable time-step approach, in which the time period of the yaw cycle is constantly evaluated during the solution, and the integration time step is adjusted accordingly. This approach allows an optimum time step to be maintained throughout the trajectory solution.

It is helpful, when running 6-DOF trajectories, to have a quick way to check the accuracy of the numerical integration as the solution proceeds. One such method has been used for many years at the BRL, with excellent results. It consists of integrating equations (9.32) at each time step, then calculating the vector dot product of $\vec{x}$ with itself:

$$\vec{x} \bullet \vec{x} = x_1^2 + x_2^2 + x_3^2 \qquad \textbf{(9.37)}$$

We recall that the vector $\vec{x}$ is defined as a unit vector, and the above dot product should therefore be identically equal to unity. The initial value, $\vec{x}_0$, was stated earlier in this section, in equation (9.23), and it is easily shown that the components of equation (9.23) do indeed exactly satisfy equation (9.37), and that $\vec{x}_0$ is therefore a unit vector.

If the integration time step selected is too large, the calculated components of along the trajectory will not be able to "keep up" with the rapidly changing pitching and yawing motion, and the vector dot product in equation (9.37) will gradually start to deviate from a magnitude of one. Many years experience has shown that if this deviation from unity in the dot product, $\vec{x} \bullet \vec{x}$, exceeds ±0.00001 at any point along the calculated flight path, the integration time step is too large, and should be reduced.

9.5 EXAMPLES OF SIX-DEGREES-OF-FREEDOM TRAJECTORIES

Example 9.1

The first example we will discuss is the flight dynamic performance of the .30 caliber (.308" diameter), 168 grain Sierra International bullet, that is loaded into 7.62mm M852 match ammunition for highpower rifle competition shooting. This bullet has been extensively tested (Ref. 11) in the BRL Aerodynamics Range; a contour sketch of the projectile and its aerodynamic properties are given in Appendix A of this chapter. We will investigate the gyroscopic stability, and the pitching and yawing motion of this bullet, out to a range of 1000 yards. The physical characteristics of the .308," 168 grain Sierra match bullet are listed in Table 9.2.

Table 9.2

Physical Characteristics of the .308," 168 Grain Sierra International Bullet

Reference Diameter = 0.308"
Bullet Total Length = 1.226"
Bullet Weight = 168 Grains (0.024008 lb.)
Axial Moment of Inertia = 0.000247 lb.-in^2
Transverse Moment of Inertia = 0.001838 lb.-in^2
Center of Gravity = 0.474" from Base

The initial conditions used for the six-degrees-of-freedom trajectory were: a muzzle velocity of 2600 feet per second; a right-

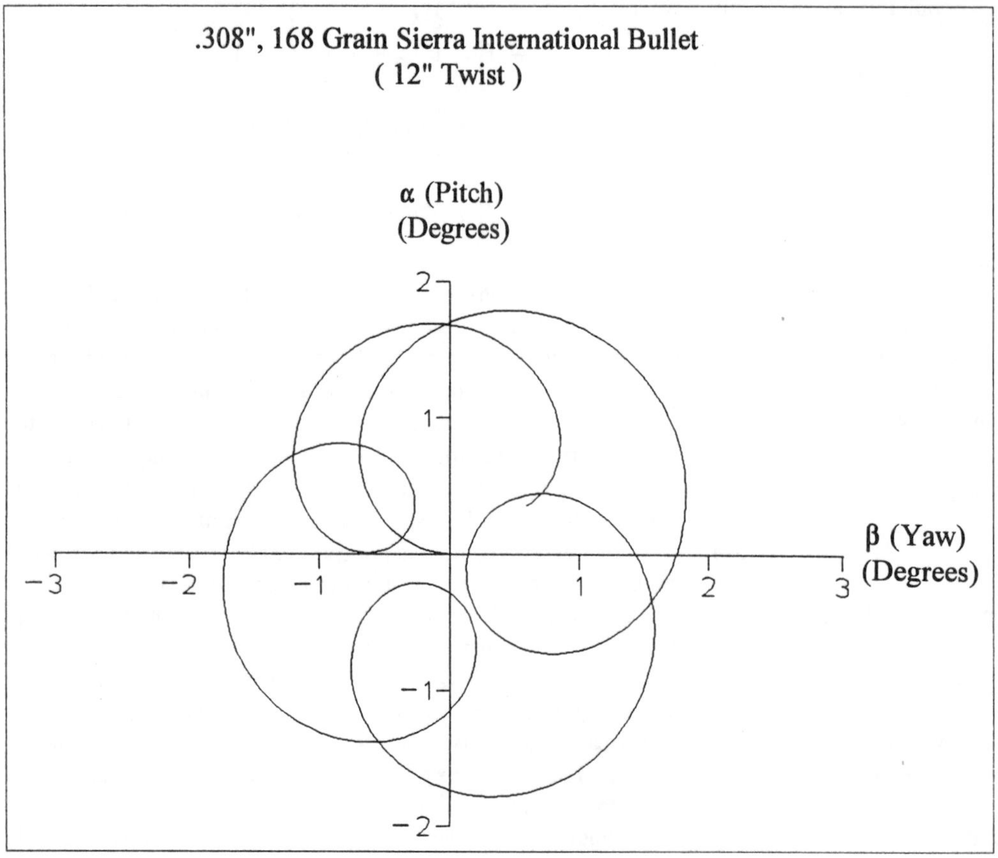

Figure 9.2 Pitch versus Yaw, Muzzle to 15 Yards Range.

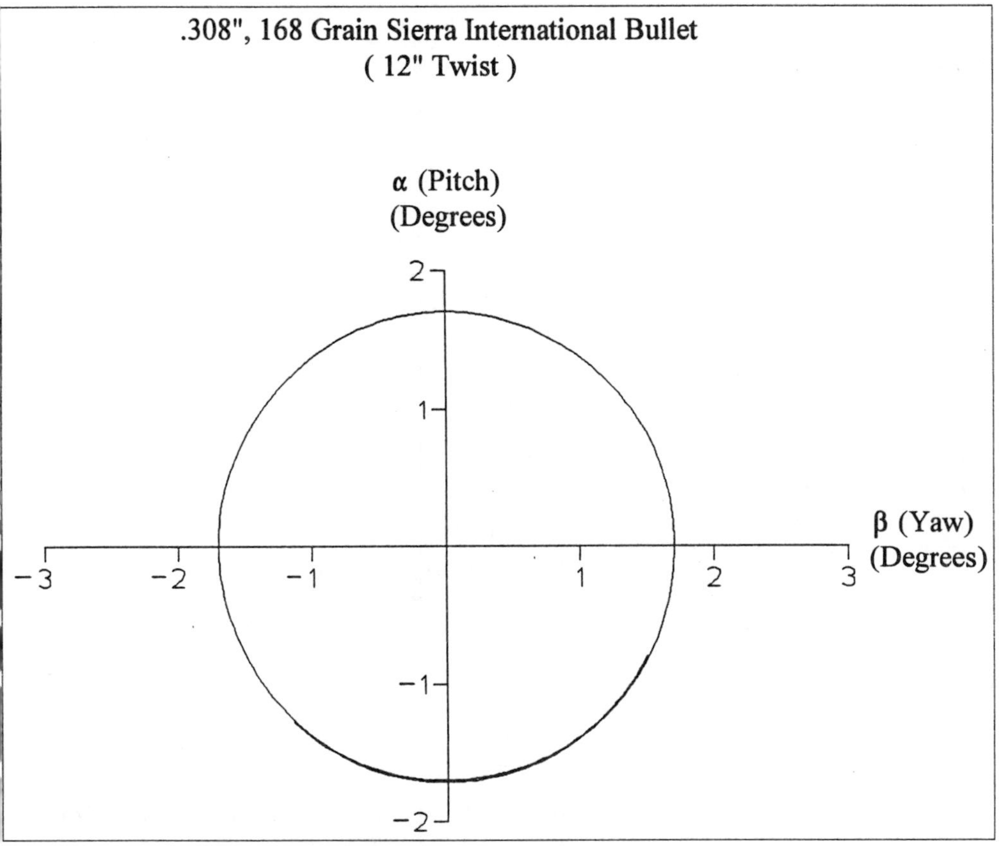

Figure 9.3 Pitch versus Yaw, 180 Yards to 200 Yards Range.

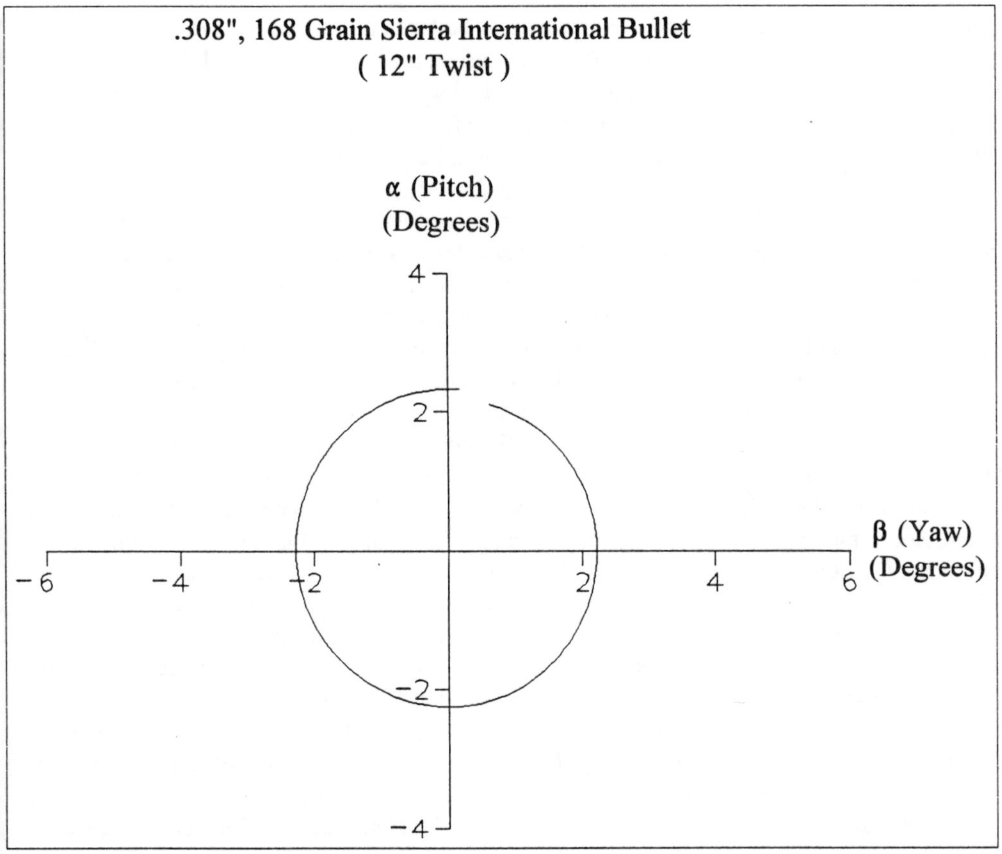

Figure 9.4 Pitch versus Yaw, 580 Yards to 600 Yards Range.

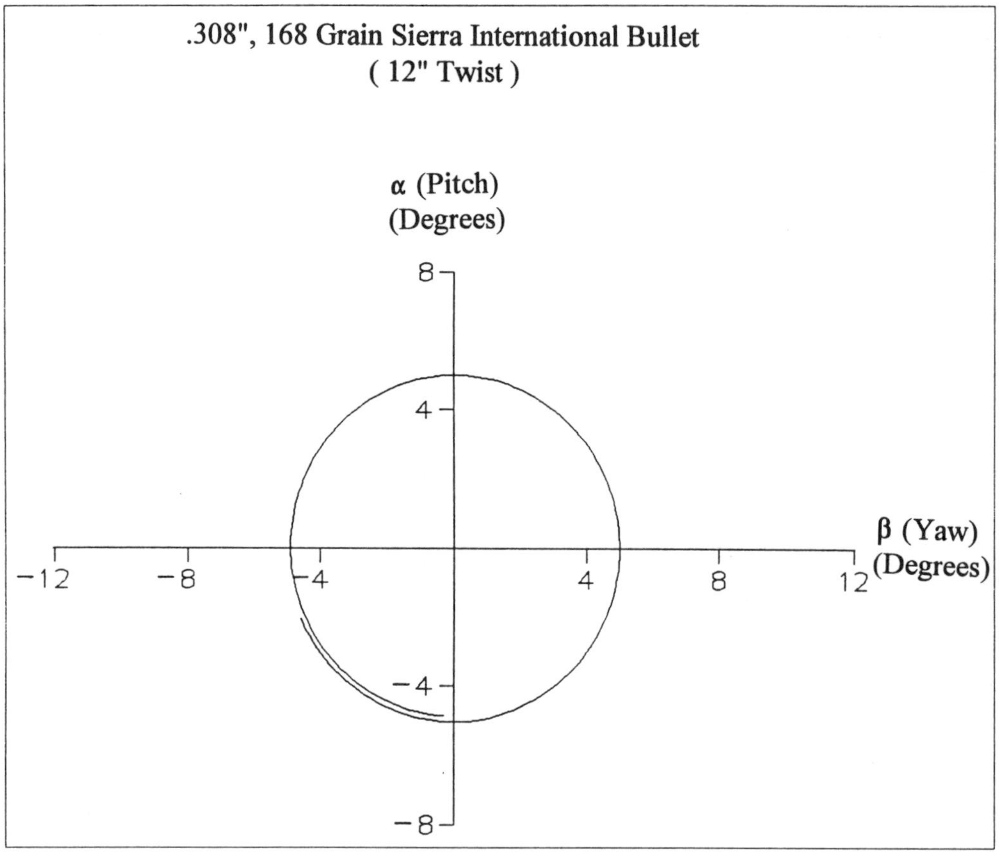

Figure 9.5 Pitch versus Yaw, 870 Yards to 900 Yards Range.

hand rifling twist rate of 12" (38.96 calibers) per turn; a muzzle yaw rate, γ, equal to 25 radians per second, which produced a first maximum yaw of 2.0 degrees; and a gun elevation angle of 14.95 mils (50.46 minutes), which zeroed the trajectory at 1000 yards range. The muzzle gyroscopic stability factor (S_g), for the 12" twist of rifling at sea-level, standard ICAO atmospheric conditions, was 1.70. (Additional 6-DOF trajectories were run for rifling twist rates of 10" per turn, and 14" per turn, but the plots of pitching and yawing motion are qualitatively similar to those of the 12" twist, and are therefore not shown).

Figures 9.2 through 9.5 illustrate the pitching and yawing motion of the .308," 168 grain Sierra match bullet, at four downrange locations, on the way to the 1000 yard target. The graphs show the pitch angle, α , plotted against the yaw angle, β, both in degrees. The intersection of the (β, α) coordinate axes represents the local position of the velocity vector (flight path), from the viewpoint of someone standing directly behind the gun. The plotted pitching and yawing motion is a trace of the changing angular difference (in degrees) between the bullet's axis of symmetry and the trajectory, but it may also be thought of as the path traced out by the nose of the bullet, as it travels away from the observer.

Figure 9.2 shows the epicyclic pitching and yawing motion, from the rifle's muzzle, out to 15 yards range. The motion was started by an initial yaw rate, or tip-off rate, of 25 radians per second, that started the bullet's nose moving to the left of the line of fire at the instant it was released from the muzzle. The result is an initial leftward movement of the bullet's axis of symmetry. However, the axial spin imparted to the projectile by the right-hand rifling causes the motion to proceed clockwise, in a pattern described as epicyclic, with two characteristic frequencies. (A discussion of the geometry of epicyclic motion will be deferred until the next chapter, where we will go into it in some detail).

Note that each successive loop in the pitching and yawing motion is slightly smaller in amplitude than the previous loop, as the motion proceeds clockwise around the origin of the coordinate system. This means the yawing motion is damping as the bullet travels downrange. There are two frequencies, or "modes," in the motion, and they do not necessarily damp at the same rate. This fact is apparent in Figure 9.3, which is a plot of the pitching and yawing motion as the bullet approaches 200 yards range. The motion appears circular in this figure, which tells us that one of the two modes (in this case, the higher frequency one) has damped out entirely, and only a circular coning motion remains (in this case, at the slow-mode frequency). Note that the amplitude of the remaining slow-mode motion is approximately 1.7 degrees, at a range of 200 yards. At this point in the flight, it takes approximately 47 feet of downrange distance (from the 12" twist), for the slow-mode coning motion to make one complete revolution.

Figure 9.4 illustrates the pitching and yawing motion as the Sierra match bullet approaches 600 yards range. The slow-mode circular coning motion still persists, but has now grown to an amplitude of approximately 2.3 degrees. As the bullet approaches 900

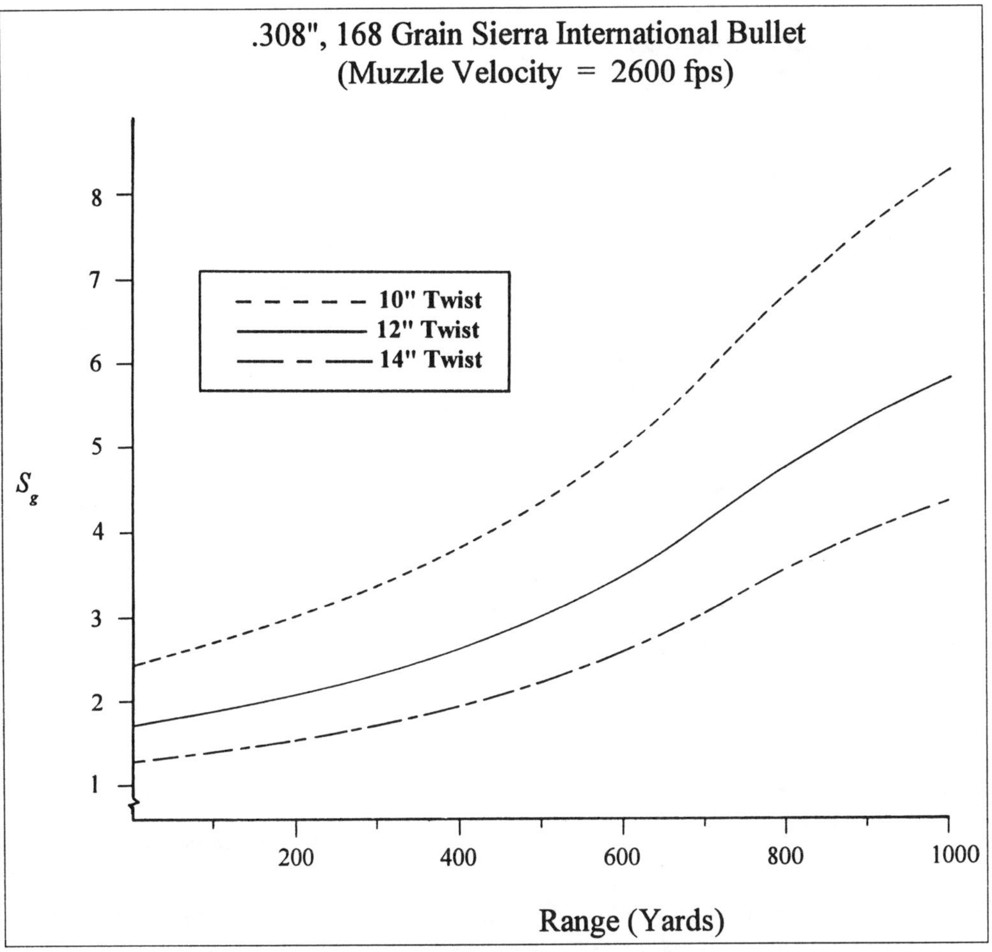

Figure 9.6 Gyroscopic Stablility Factor versus Range.

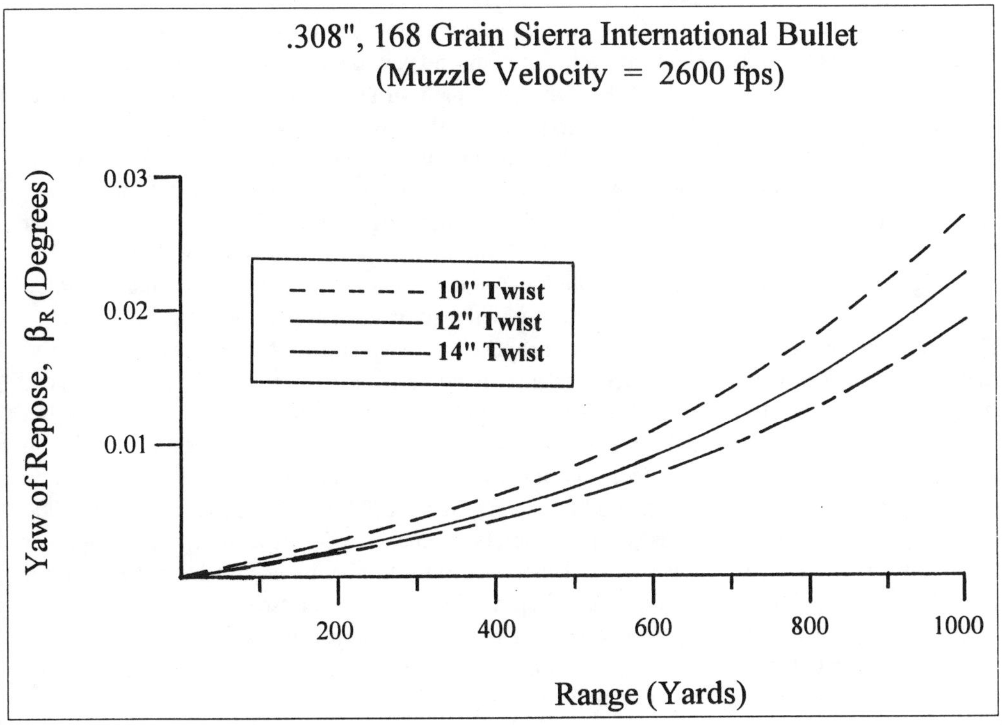

Figure 9.7 Yaw of Repose versus Range.

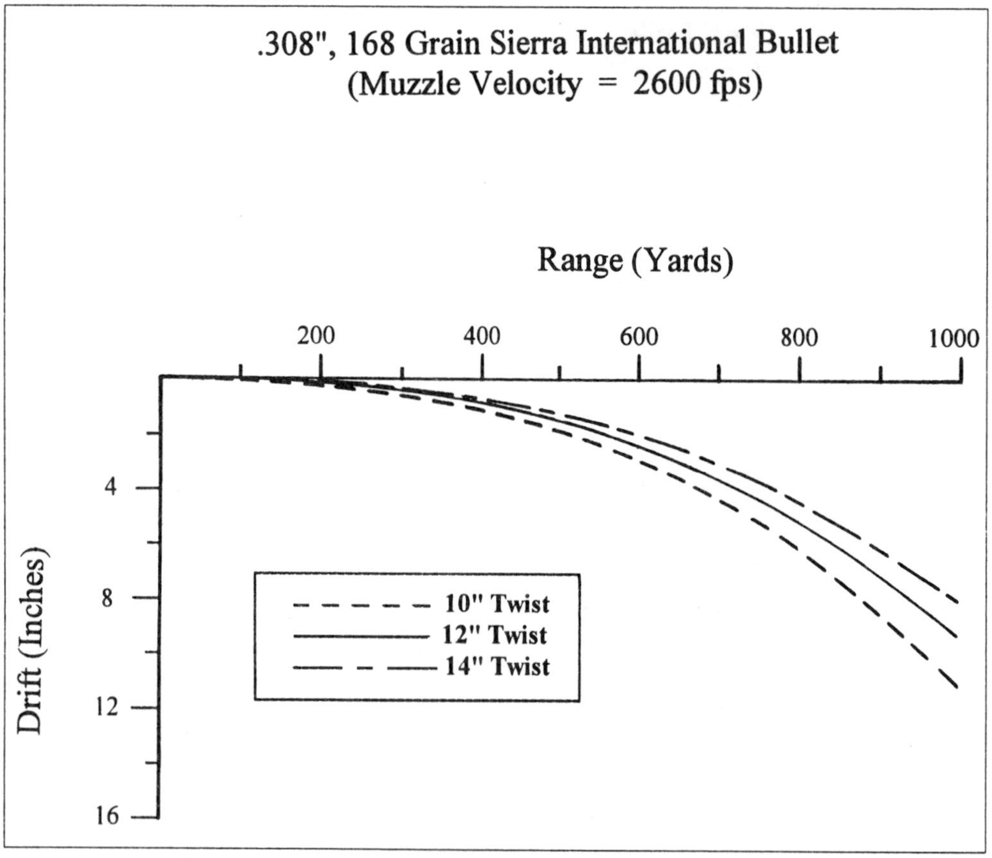

Figure 9.8 Drift versus Range.

yards range, Figure 9.5 shows that the slow-mode coning amplitude has grown to 5.0 degrees. At 900 yards, the size of the coning motion has levelled off, and it remains at about 5 degrees on out to 1000 yards range. The distance required for the coning motion to complete one revolution (again, from the 12" rifling twist rate) is approximately 62 feet at 600 yards, and about 77 feet at 900 yards range.

For flat-fire trajectories, the gyroscopic stability factor of non-finned, spin-stabilized projectiles always increases as the projectile travels downrange, due to the fact that S_g is proportional to the square of the spin-to-velocity ratio, and the forward velocity slows down much faster than the axial spin. This effect is illustrated for the .308," 168 grain Sierra International bullet in Figure 9.6, for three rifling twist rates. For the 12" twist, the gyroscopic stability factor at the muzzle is 1.7, but it increases significantly as the bullet travels downrange, and at 1000 yards, S_g is equal to 5.8. The increasing gyroscopic stability factor with range is similar, for the 10" and 14" rifling twists, as Figure 9.6 shows.

The reader may wonder why the slow-mode coning motion of the bullet's axis of symmetry around the flight path is increasing (Figures 9.3 through 9.5), at the same time the gyroscopic stability factor is already greater than 2, and is rapidly growing. The answer is, the growth in the slow-mode amplitude, illustrated in Figures 9.3 through 9.5, is *not a gyroscopic instability*; it is a *small-yaw dynamic instability* caused by a nonlinear Magnus moment, that leads to *limit-cycle yawing motion.* These phenomena will be discussed at some length in later chapters of this book.

Figure 9.7 is a plot of the "yaw of repose" versus range, for the .308," 168 grain Sierra match bullet, when fired from 10," 12" and 14" rifling twist rates. For a right-hand twist, in addition to the transient, epicyclic pitching and yawing motion, the bullet's nose points to the right of the flight path, in a small, steady-state yaw of repose. For flat-fire trajectories, the yaw of repose lies almost entirely in the horizontal plane, and is denoted by β_R. The yaw of repose is present in Figures 9.2 through 9.6, but it is very small for flat-fire, and is masked by the much larger epicyclic pitching and yawing motion. Figure 9.7 shows that β_R is only a few *hundredths* of a degree for the flat-fire trajectory of the .308" Sierra match bullet. The yaw of repose will also be discussed in the next chapter.

The yaw of repose has one significant effect on the trajectory; it produces the right-hand deflection referred to by ballisticians as *drift.* Drift is illustrated for the .308," 168 grain Sierra match bullet in Figure 9.8. For short ranges the drift is very small, but it can grow to a significant value at long range. For our .308" Sierra match bullet, fired from a rifle with 12" twist of rifling, the drift at 1000 yards is approximately 9.3 inches. (Corresponding values for other twists are 11.1 inches drift for the 10" twist, and 8.0 inches drift for the 14" twist). In practice, the small right-hand drift due to yaw of repose is usually masked by the trajectory deflection due to cross-wind, which is often between one and two orders of magnitude larger than the drift.

Example 9.2

As a second example of six-degrees-of-freedom trajectory calculations, we will look at the flight dynamic behavior of the 105mm, High Explosive (HE), M1 spin-stabilized artillery projectile, at both low and high muzzle velocities, and at two quadrant elevation (QE) angles, 45 degrees (800 mils) and 70 degrees (1244.5 mils). Two rifling twist rates were also included in the 6-DOF study. The first twist was the standard 1 turn in 18 calibers (1/18) of the M103 Howitzer, and the second was a slower twist, 1 turn in 25 calibers (1/25).

The aerodynamic characteristics of the 105mm, HE, M1 shell have probably been studied more intensely than those of any other spin-stabilized artillery shell. Data at small angles of attack were published (Ref. 12) in 1955. Free-flight measurements of the aerodynamic forces and moments were made in 1971-72, at angles of attack up to 35 degrees at subsonic speeds, and up to 25 degrees at supersonic speeds. Also, wind tunnel measurements of the aerodynamic forces and moments at subsonic speeds have been made (Ref. 13), at various ratios of axial spin to forward velocity, for all angles of attack up to 180 degrees. A contour sketch of the 105mm M1 shell, and the aerodynamic properties used in the present study, are given in Appendix B at the end of this chapter.

The physical characteristics of the 105mm M1 projectile used in the 6-DOF calculations are summarized in Table 9.3. The values listed in this table are averages of several lots of projectiles, fitted with different fuzes, and are used only as nominal values for the present study.

Table 9.3

Physical Characteristics of the 105mm, HE, M1 Projectile

Reference Diameter = 104.8 mm
Projectile Total Length = 49.47 cm
Projectile Weight = 14.97 kg.
Axial Moment of Inertia = 0.02326 kg.-m.^{2}
Transverse Moment of Inertia = 0.23118 kg.-m.^{2}
Center of Gravity = 18.34 cm. from Base

The two muzzle velocities selected for the 6-DOF study of the 105mm M1 projectile correspond to Charge 1 (M.V. = 205 meters/second), and Charge 7 (M.V. = 493 meters/second). Coincidentally, the values of the overturning moment coefficients, C_{M_α}, at the two selected muzzle velocities, are virtually identical. For Charge 1, the muzzle Mach number at standard conditions is 0.602, and the corresponding value of C_{M_α} is 3.75. At Charge 7, the muzzle Mach number is 1.449, and the overturning moment coefficient has the value 3.76. For both charges, at sea-level standard ICAO atmospheric conditions, the muzzle gyroscopic stability factor of the 105mm M1 projectile, fired from the 1/18 twist of the M103 howitzer, has the value S_g = 3.1.

A lower muzzle gyroscopic stability factor for the 6-DOF computer runs was obtained by assuming a theoretical rifling twist rate of 1 turn in 25 calibers. At both Charge 1 and Charge 7, a value of muzzle S_g equal to 1.6 is obtained from a 1/25 twist of rifling, again at sea-level, standard ICAO atmospheric conditions. A muzzle gy-

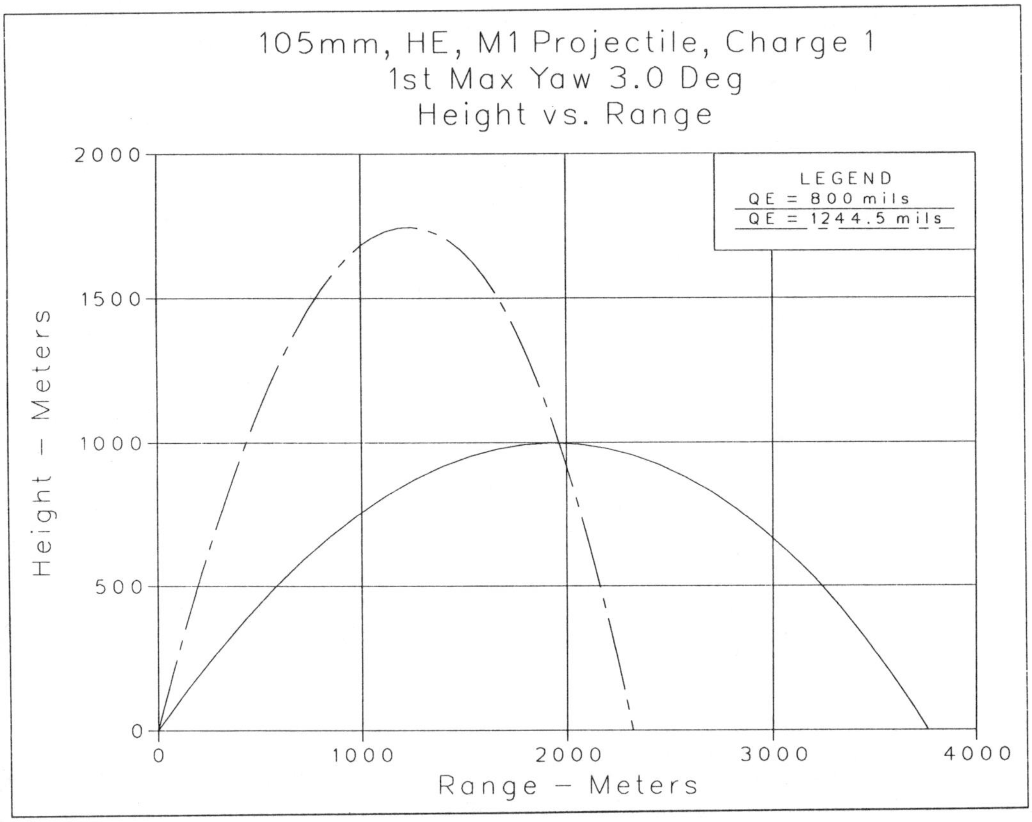

Figure 9.9 Height versus Range, for Charge 1.

Table 9.4.
Initial Conditions for the 105mm, M1 Six-Degrees-of-Freedom Trajectories

Run Number	Twist, Calibers	Charge	M.V. (m/s)	QE (deg.)	ω_{y_0} (rad/sec)	1st Max Yaw, deg	Muzzle S_g
1	1/18	1	205	45	1.44	3.0	3.1
2	1/18	1	205	70	1.47	3.0	3.1
3	1/18	7	493	45	3.61	3.0	3.1
4	1/18	7	493	70	3.64	3.0	3.1
5	1/25	1	205	45	0.76	3.0	1.6
6	1/25	1	205	70	0.79	3.0	1.6
7	1/25	7	493	45	1.97	3.0	1.6
8	1/25	7	493	70	1.98	3.0	1.6

roscopic stability factor of 1.5 to 1.6 is essentially an optimum value, because it is the lowest value that provides sufficient safety margin to permit cold weather firing at sea-level. (Incidentally, the lowest muzzle S_g for the 105mm M1 projectile occurs for firing at Charge 5, which gives a muzzle velocity of 322 meters/second. The muzzle value of C_{M_α} is 4.45 at Mach 0.946 and the value of S_g at the muzzle is 1.4, from a 1/25 twist at sea-level standard atmospheric conditions. If the M1 were the *only* projectile in the 105mm inventory, a 1/25 twist would be a satisfactory choice for the M103 Howitzer.)

A total of eight 6-DOF trajectory runs were made, using the Fortran "HTRAJ" computer program (Ref. 5), developed many years ago by the Firing Tables Branch of BRL, at Aberdeen Proving Ground, Maryland. Four trajectories were computed for each rifling twist rate, using Charges 1 and 7, at 45 degrees and 70 degrees quadrant elevation angles. All trajectories used an initial (muzzle) yaw rate ω_{y_0}, sufficient to produce a first maximum yaw of three degrees, which is a typical value observed in field firings of the M103 Howitzer. The initial conditions for the eight 6-DOF trajectories are summarized in Table 9.4.

The reason for selecting the 45 degree (800 mil) quadrant elevation angle for the 6-DOF study of the 105mm M1 shell is that it represents essentially a maximum range case, yet the yaw of repose near apogee (trajectory summit) is not large. The 70 degree (1244.5 mil) quadrant elevation angle is only a few degrees below the maximum trail angle of this shell, when fired from the M103 Howitzer. At quadrant elevation angles of 75 degrees (1333 mils), the first

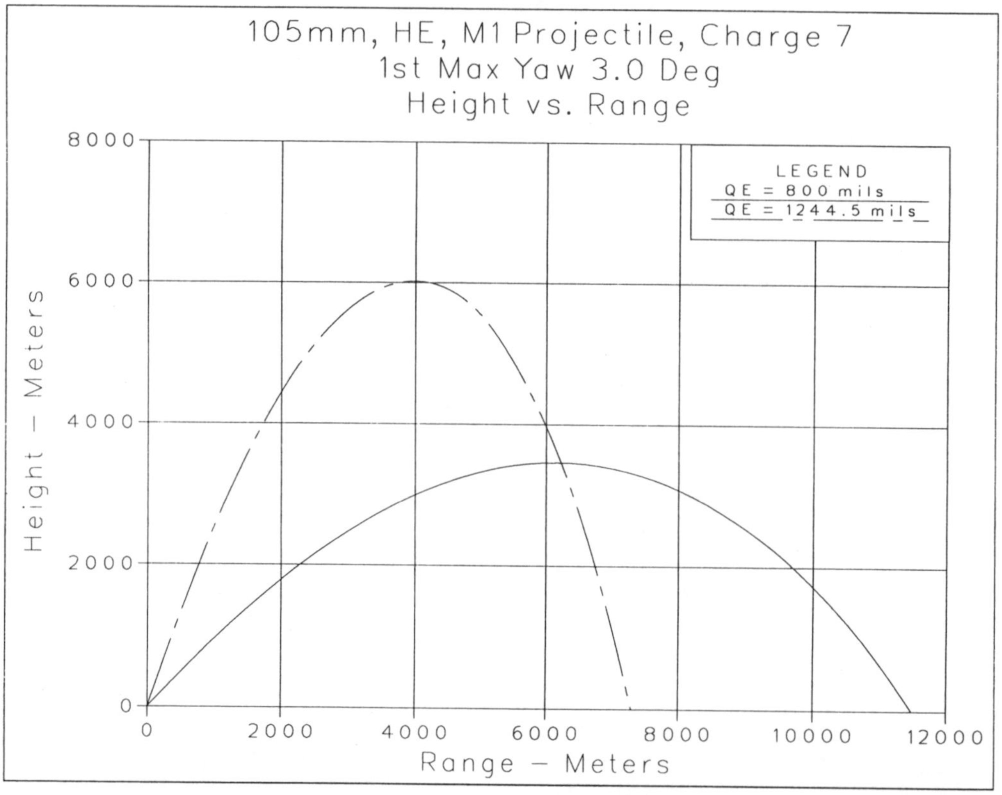

Figure 9.10 Height versus Range, for Charge 7.

observations of *left-drift* begin to occur in field firings (Ref. 13), which means an occasional shell is *failing to trail* at this elevation, and is descending *base-forward* on the downleg of the trajectory. Thus the 70 degree quadrant elevation angle is essentially a "worst case" for the present study.

Figures 9.9 (*p. 199*) and 9.10 show the 6-DOF predicted variation in trajectory height with range, for the two propelling charges, and the two quadrant elevation angles. All the trajectories shown in Figures 9.9 and 9.10 are for the 1/18 twist of the M103 Howitzer, and they were all started with a first maximum yaw of three degrees (see Run numbers 1 through 4 in Table 9.4). Similar plots for the 1/25 twist cannon are insignificantly different in appearance, and are therefore not shown.

Figure 9.9 illustrates the 6-DOF predicted trajectory height versus range for Charge 1. It shows that at 45 degrees (800 mils) QE, the 105mm M1 projectile, fired at sea-level into a standard ICAO atmosphere with no wind, will achieve a level-ground impact range of 3760 meters. The time of flight of this trajectory is slightly over 28.5 seconds, and the maximum height is about 1000 meters. At 70 degrees (1244.5 mils) QE for the same charge, the predicted level-ground range is about 2320 meters; the time of flight to impact is approximately 38.5 seconds, and the maximum height is about 1750 meters above the altitude of the firing site.

Figure 9.10 illustrates the same information for Charge 7. At 45 degrees (800 mils) QE, the predicted range to impact is approximately 11,500 meters; the time of flight is slightly greater than 52.5 seconds, and the maximum height is 3460 meters. At 70 degrees (1244.5 mils) QE, the predicted level-ground range is 7300 meters; the time of flight to impact is about 70.5 seconds, and the maximum height is slightly over 6000 meters.

Figures 9.11 through 9.14 show the detailed pitching and yawing motion of the 105mm M1 projectile, when fired from the 1/18 twist of the M103 Howitzer. Figure 9.11 is a plot of the total angle of attack, α_t , in degrees, versus the range in meters, for Charge 1, and a quadrant elevation angle of 45 degrees. (Note that for small angle of attack, $\alpha_t \approx \sqrt{\alpha^2 + \beta^2}$, where α is the pitch angle, and β is the yaw angle). The high frequency fast-mode pitching and yawing motion (often called "nutation"), damps out along the flight path, and has virtually disappeared by impact. The slow-mode motion (often called "precession") persists at a 2 to 3 degree amplitude throughout much of the flight, with the maximum value of the yaw of repose (β_R), contributing approximately 2.1 degrees to the total motion at apogee. The dashed curve in Figure 9.11 illustrates the variation of the yaw of repose with range. At apogee, the slow-mode coning motion with amplitude K_s and the yaw of repose combine, as shown in the inset sketch of Figure 9.11, to produce the observed variation of the total angle of attack, α_t, with range. On the final part of the trajectory downleg, a slow-mode limit-cycle yaw of about three degrees amplitude is observed. This slow-mode limit-cycle yaw, observed on the final downleg portion of all the 105mm M1 trajectories, is caused by the behavior of the nonlinear Magnus moment at subsonic speeds (see Reference 14, and the Magnus

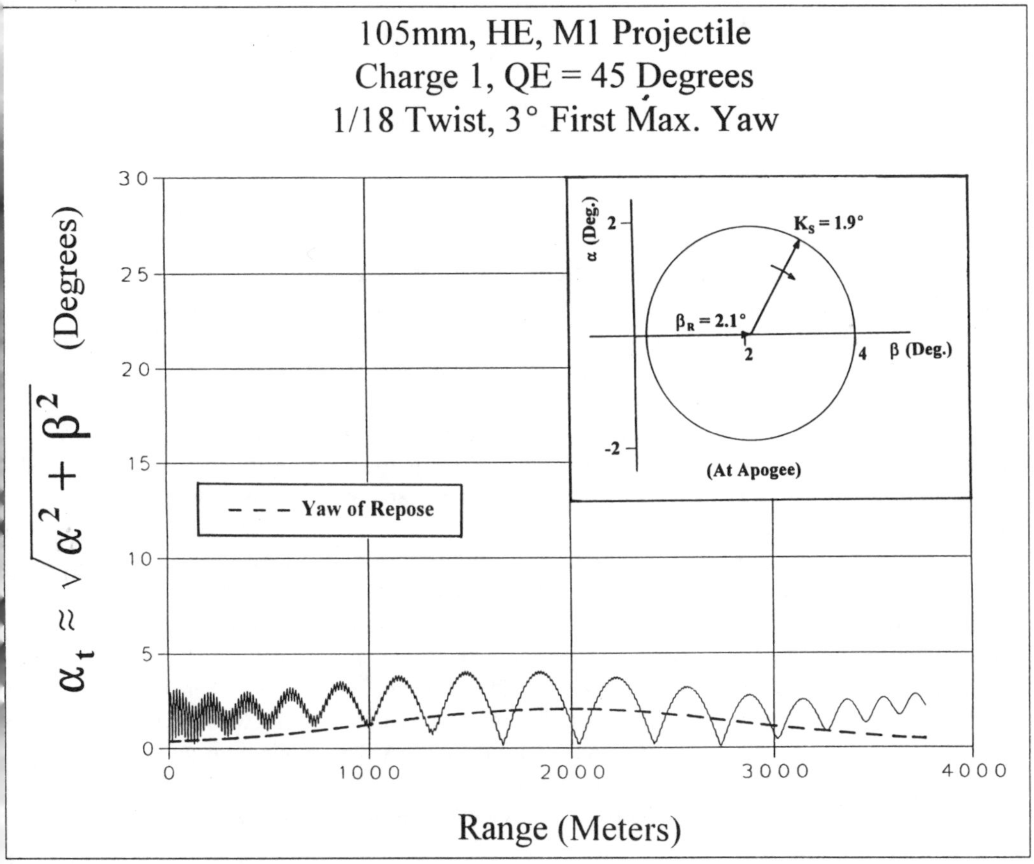

Figure 9.11 Total Angle of Attack verus Range, Charge 1, 45 Degrees QE.

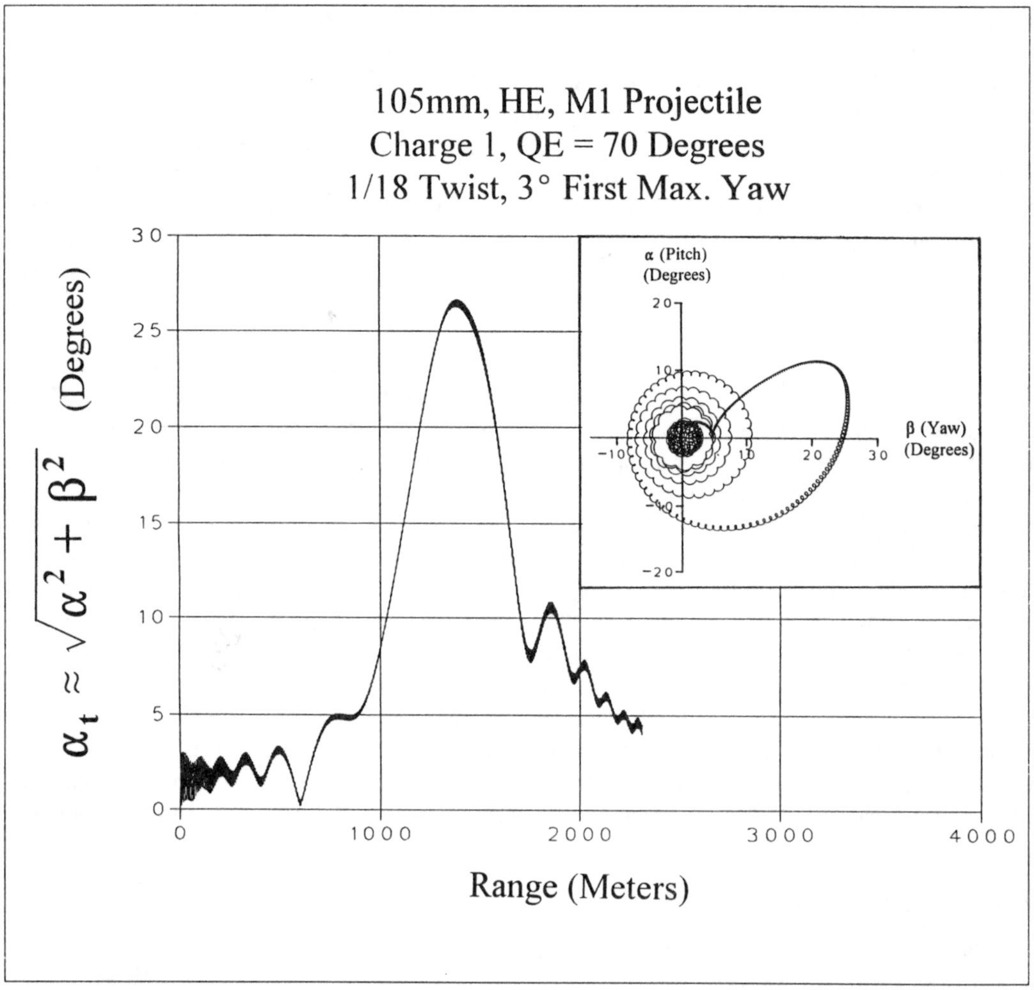

Figure 9.12 Total Angle of Attack verus Range, Charge 1, 70 Degrees QE.

moment coefficient data listed in Appendix B of this chapter). The gyroscopic stability factor, which was 3.1 at the muzzle, grows to a value of 7.6 at apogee, then decreases back to the original muzzle value of 3.1 at impact.

Figure 9.12 is a plot of the total angle of attack, α_t , against range, for the 105mm M1 shell, fired at Charge 1 and a quadrant elevation angle of 70 degrees. After the damping of the initial transient epicyclic pitching and yawing motion, a small-amplitude fast-mode motion persists throughout most of this flight. The large summital yaw of repose, caused by the high quadrant elevation angle, is dramatically illustrated in this graph. Near apogee, the yaw of repose grows to approximately 26 degrees, then decreases rapidly along the downleg of the trajectory! Another view of this large amplitude motion is shown in the inset pitch-versus-yaw plot of Figure 9.12. Note that for high QE, the total yaw of repose near the trajectory summit has a significant vertical "pitch of repose" (α_R) component, in addition to the horizontal (β_R) yaw component. Also note, on the final portion of the downleg, the persistence of a slow-mode limit-cycle yaw of about 4 degrees amplitude, with a small fast-mode motion of approximately 1 degree amplitude superimposed. The gyroscopic stability factor grows from 3.1 at the muzzle, to a value of 43 at apogee, then decreases to a value of 3.0 at impact!

The decrease in air density at high altitude is part of the reason for the large yaw of repose and the huge value of S_g , observed at the summit of a high QE trajectory. (At 1750 meters altitude, the air is 84% as dense as at sea level, and at an altitude of 6000 meters, the air density is only 54% of the sea level value). The other major contribution comes from the fact that the projectile's forward velocity slows down much faster on the trajectory upleg than the axial spin does, and the result is a large value of the spin-to-velocity ratio at apogee.

Figure 9.13 shows the variation of total angle of attack, with range, for the 105mm M1 shell, fired from a 1/18 twist cannon at Charge 7, and at a quadrant elevation angle of 45 degrees. After the damping of the initial transient motion, small yaw flight is observed for the remainder of the trajectory. At apogee, where the gyroscopic stability factor has increased from 3.1 to 16, the largest value of the yaw of repose is 1.2 degrees. A slow-mode limit-cycle yaw of 2 to 3 degrees is present on the downleg of the trajectory. At impact, the gyroscopic stability factor has decreased to a value of 4.1.

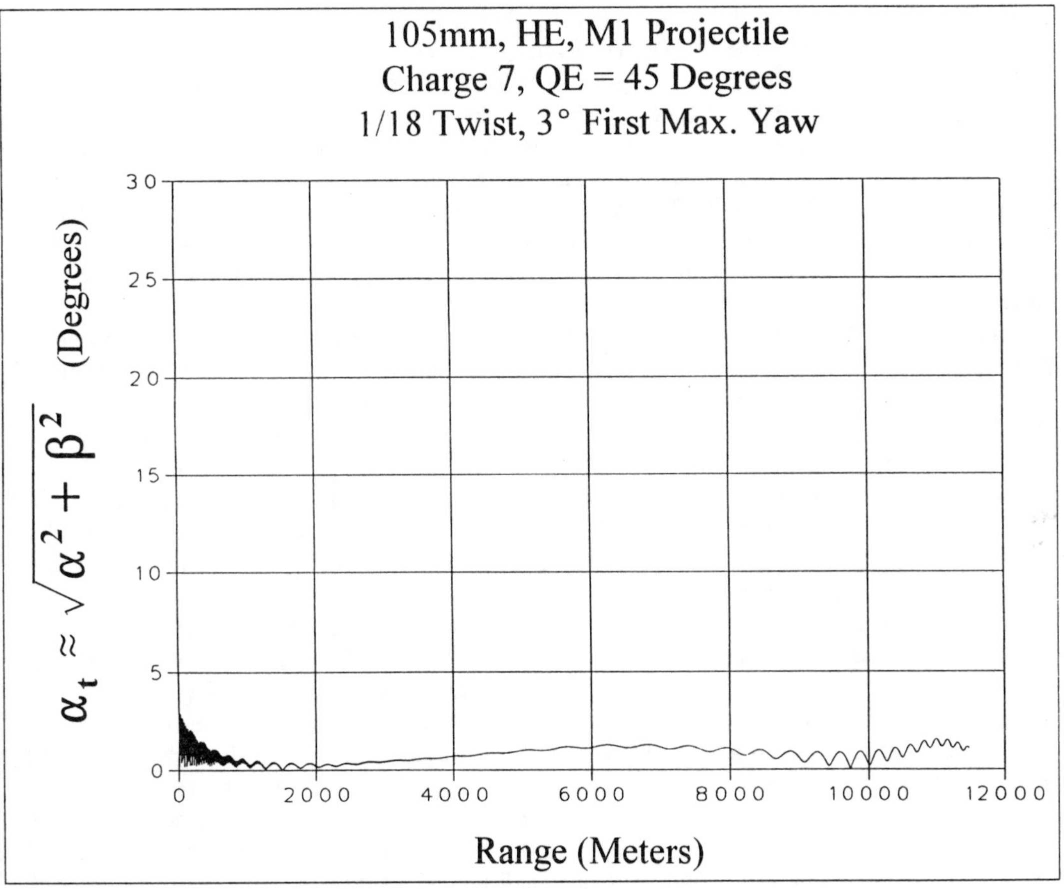

Figure 9.13 Total Angle of Attack verus Range, Charge 7, 45 Degrees QE.

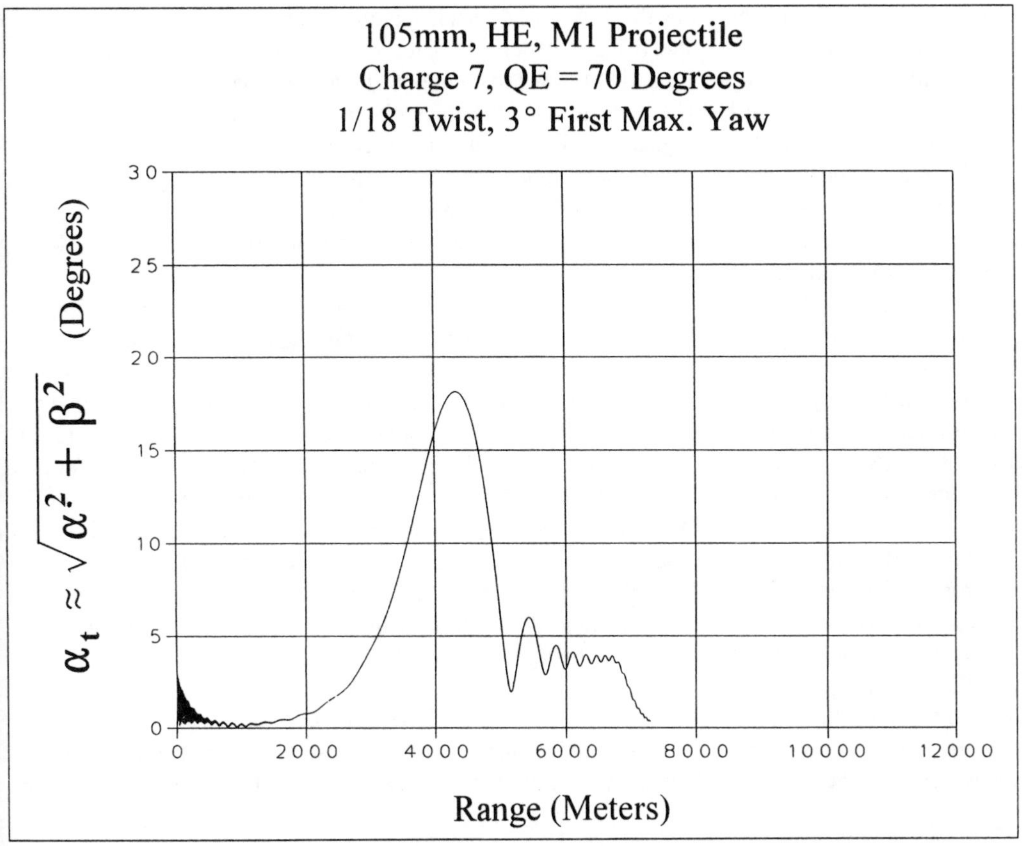

Figure 9.14 Total Angle of Attack verus Range, Charge 7, 70 Degrees QE.

Figure 9.14 illustrates the behavior of the total angle of attack for Charge 7, and a quadrant elevation angle of 70 degrees. The initial transient motion damps out quickly, and the yaw of repose grows to nearly 18 degrees at apogee, where the gyroscopic stability factor has increased from 3.1 to 102! A slow-mode limit-cycle yaw of 3 to 4 degrees amplitude again persists for much of the trajectory downleg. Note the apparent damping of the limit-cycle yaw on the final portion of the downleg. The reason is the increasing velocity as the projectile approaches impact. For the 105mm M1 shell fired at Charge 7 and 70 degrees QE, the terminal velocity just before impact has increased to Mach 0.92, where the nonlinear Magnus moment characteristics allow the slow-mode limit-cycle yaw to take on a smaller value. The gyroscopic stability factor at impact has decreased to a value of 3.0.

The next set of plots, Figures 9.15 through 9.18, show the effect of changing the rifling twist rate from 1/18 to 1/25. Figure 9.15 is a plot of the total angle of attack, in degrees, versus the range in meters, for Charge 1, and a quadrant elevation angle of 45 degrees. The in-flight pitching and yawing motion is qualitatively similar to that observed in Figure 9.11. The slow-mode limit-cycle again persists throughout much of the trajectory, at a 2 to 3 degree amplitude, and the maximum value of the yaw of repose (β_R), contributes about 1.5 degrees to the total angle of attack at apogee. The gyroscopic stability factor, which was 1.6 at the muzzle, grows to a value of 3.9 at the summit of the trajectory, then decreases to the muzzle value of 1.6 at impact.

Figure 9.16 is a plot of the total angle of attack, α_t , against range, for the 105mm M1 shell, fired from a 1/25 twist at Charge 1, and a quadrant elevation angle of 70 degrees. The free-flight pitching and yawing motion is similar to that illustrated in Figure 9.12, but the peak value of the yaw of repose is smaller, because of the lower axial spin rate. Near apogee, the yaw of repose grows to approximately 18 degrees, then decreases rapidly along the downleg of the trajectory. Another view of the same large-amplitude motion is shown in the inset pitch-versus-yaw plot of Figure 9.16. Note the persistence of a one-degree amplitude fast-mode motion (two degrees peak-to-peak), throughout the flight. Again, the total yaw of repose near the trajectory summit has a significant vertical "pitch of repose" (α_R) component, in addition to the horizontal (β_R) yaw component. On the final portion of the trajectory downleg, the total pitching and yawing motion damps to a slow-mode limit-cycle yaw value of about 4 degrees amplitude, with the small, persistent fast-mode motion superimposed. The gyroscopic stability factor grows from 1.6 at the muzzle, to a value of 20 at apogee, then decreases to a value of 1.5 at impact.

Figure 9.17 shows the variation of total angle of attack, α_t , with range, for the 105mm M1 shell, fired from a 1/25 twist cannon at Charge 7, and at a quadrant elevation angle of 45 degrees. After the damping of the initial transient motion, the remainder of the trajectory shows predominantly small yaw flight. At apogee, where the gyroscopic stability factor has increased from 1.6 to 8.2, the largest value of the yaw of repose is about 1.0 degree. A slow-mode limit-cycle yaw of 2 to 3 degrees amplitude is present on the downleg of the trajectory. At impact, the gyroscopic stability factor has decreased to a value of 2.1.

Figure 9.18 illustrates the behavior of the total angle of attack for the 105mm M1 shell, fired from a 1/25 twist at Charge 7, and a quadrant elevation angle of 70 degrees. The initial transient motion damps out rapidly, and the yaw of repose grows to a peak value of 12 degrees at apogee, where the gyroscopic stability factor has increased from 1.6 to 50. A slow-mode limit-cycle yaw of 3 to 4 degrees amplitude again persists for much of the trajectory downleg. The decreasing amplitude of the slow-mode limit-cycle yaw, on the final portion of the downleg, is again due to increasing velocity as the projectile approaches impact. The gyroscopic stability factor at impact has decreased to a value of 1.5.

Figures 9.19 and 9.20 are the last two figures for this projectile, and they show the effect of the yaw of repose on the right-hand drift of the 105mm M1 shell, for the various charges, rifling twist rates, and quadrant elevation angles. (Note that the drift would be to the left, if the guns were rifled using a left-hand twist). The rifling twist rate affects the drift in approximately inverse proportion to the twist, in accordance with linearized exterior ballistic theory (Ref. 14). At a fixed charge, quadrant elevation angle, and range, the drift from a 1/25 twist cannon is about 72 percent (18/25 = 0.720) of the drift observed from a similar cannon with a 1/18 twist.

Figure 9.19 illustrates the variation of drift with range, for firing at Charge 1, and Figure 9.20 presents the same results for Charge 7. The effect of rifling twist rate has already been noted in the previous paragraph. Both figures show the dramatic effect of high quadrant elevation angles on the drift of spin-stabilized artillery shell. For the 105mm M1 shell, given a fixed charge and rifling twist rate, firing at 70 degrees quadrant elevation angle produces between 1.8 and 2.4 times the amount of drift observed at 45 degrees QE! The enormous drift values observed at high quadrant elevation angles are a direct result of the aerodynamic lift force, acting on the large yaw of repose that the shell experiences at high QE angles. The drift predicted by the 6-DOF model for the 1/18 twist agrees closely with the observed drift from field firings of the M103 Howitzer.

The six-degrees-of-freedom calculations done for this chapter indicate that for quadrant elevation angles up to 70 degrees, the 105mm M1 projectile "trails properly" from the 1/18 twist of the M103 Howitzer, which launches this shell at sea-level standard atmospheric conditions, with a muzzle gyroscopic stability factor of 3.1. A comparison of the plots for the 1/18 twist with those for the 1/25 twist, shows that the 105mm M1 shell does not fly significantly, if any, better from the slower twist of rifling, that gives essentially an optimum muzzle gyroscopic stability factor (S_g = 1.6). The only notable effect of the slower twist is to give a smaller yaw of repose near the summit of the trajectory, and a consequent reduction in the right-hand drift.

Example 9.3

As a final example of six-degrees-of-freedom trajectory calculations, we will look at the flight dynamic behavior of a family of

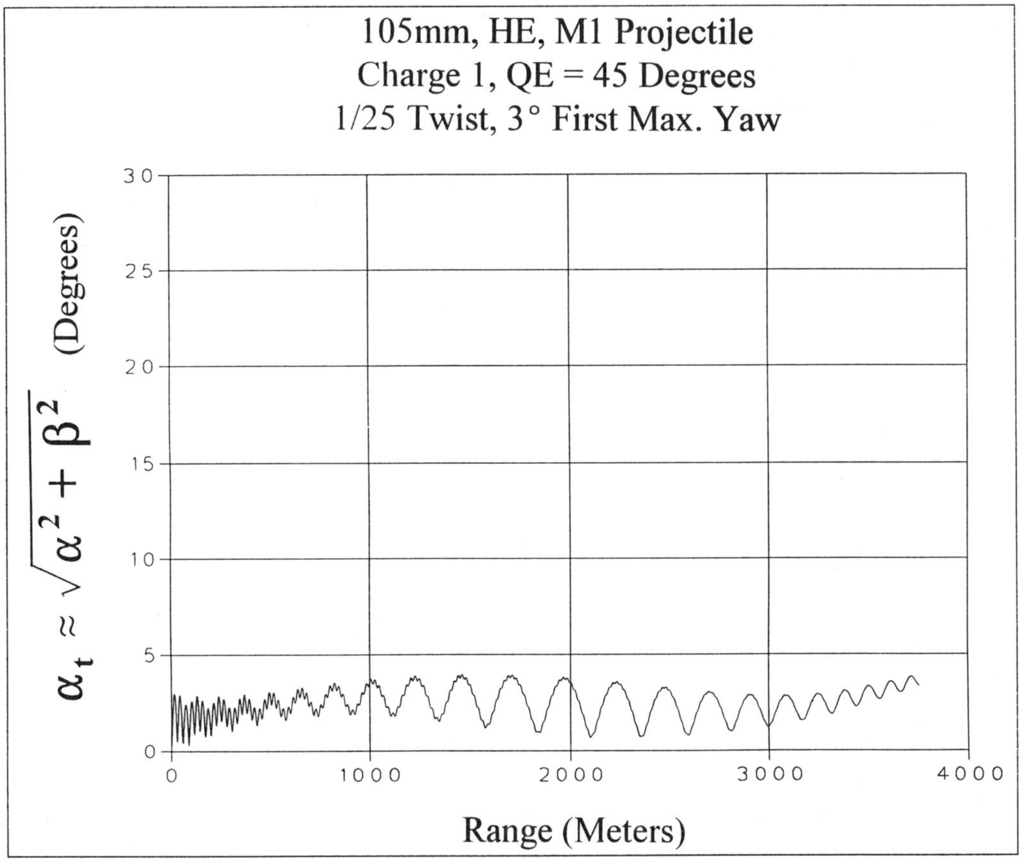

Figure 9.15 Total Angle of Attack verus Range, Charge 1, 45 Degrees QE.

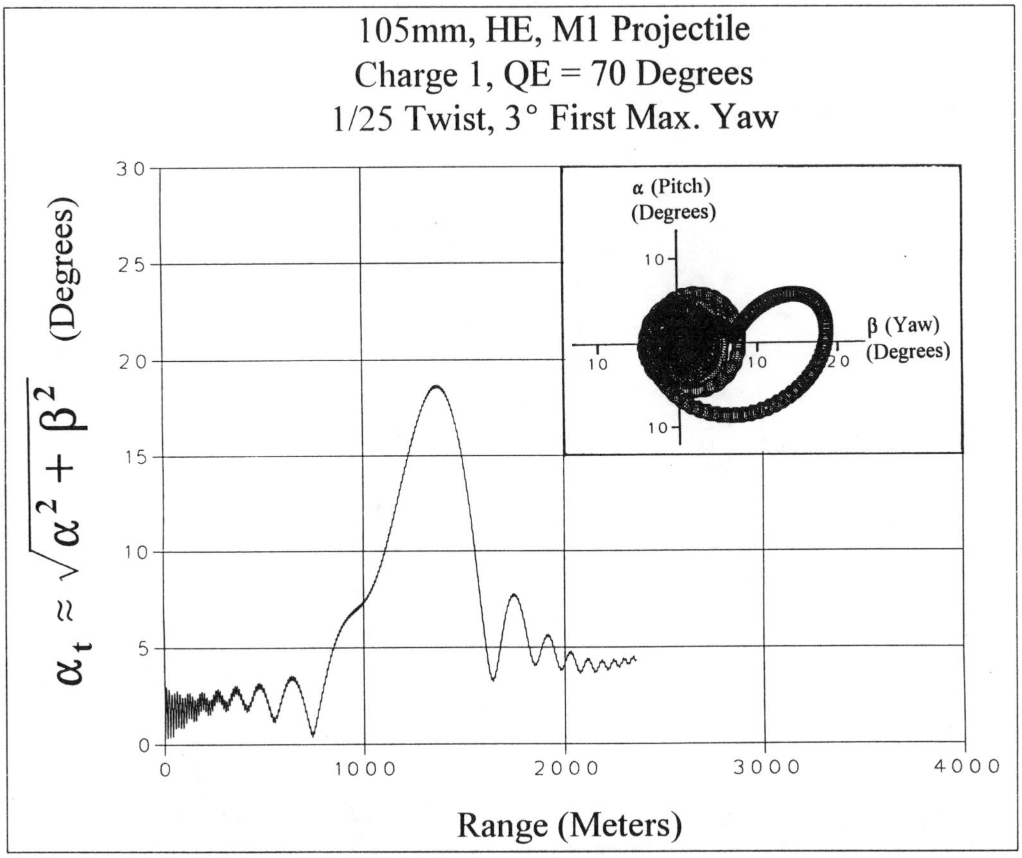

Figure 9.16 Total Angle of Attack verus Range, Charge 1, 70 Degrees QE.

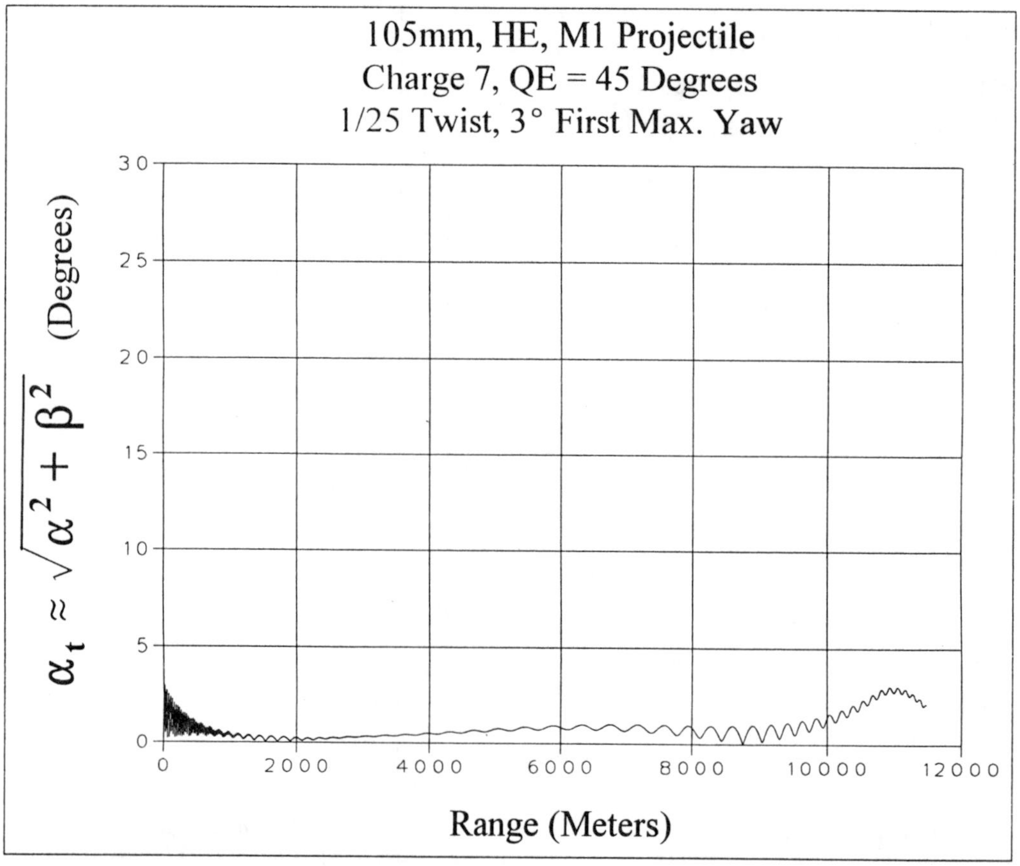

Figure 9.17 Total Angle of Attack verus Range, Charge 7, 45 Degrees QE.

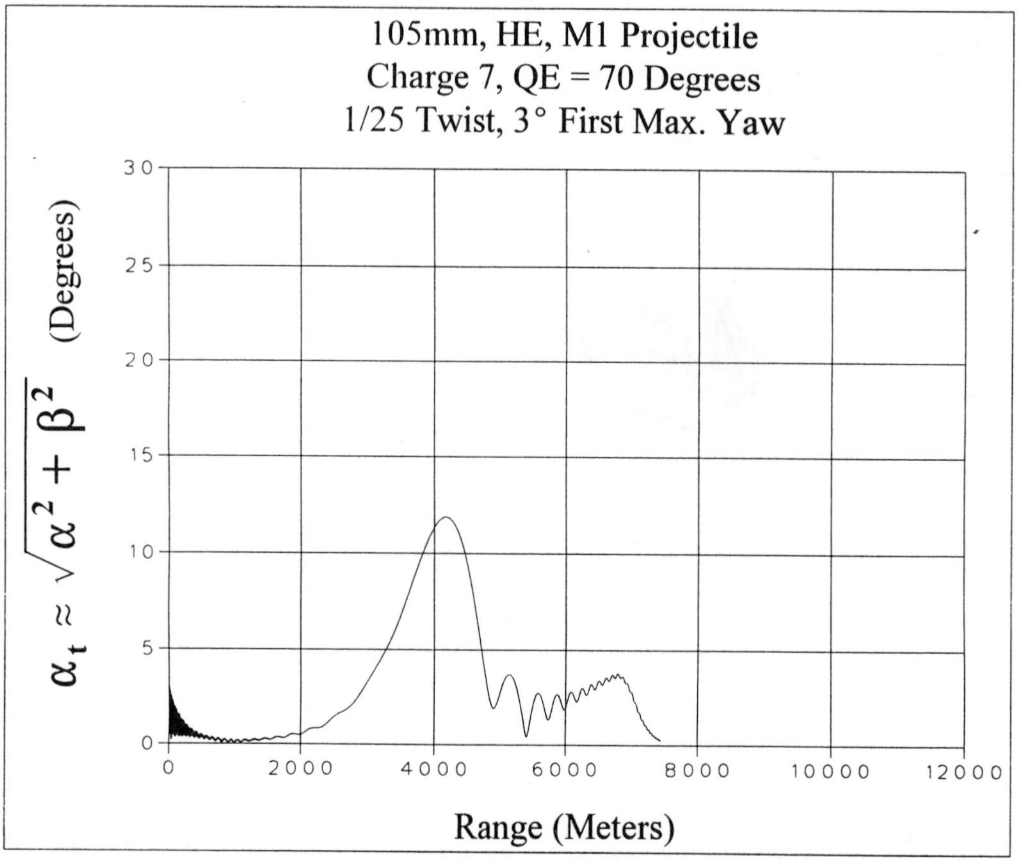

Figure 9.18 Total Angle of Attack verus Range, Charge 7, 70 Degrees QE.

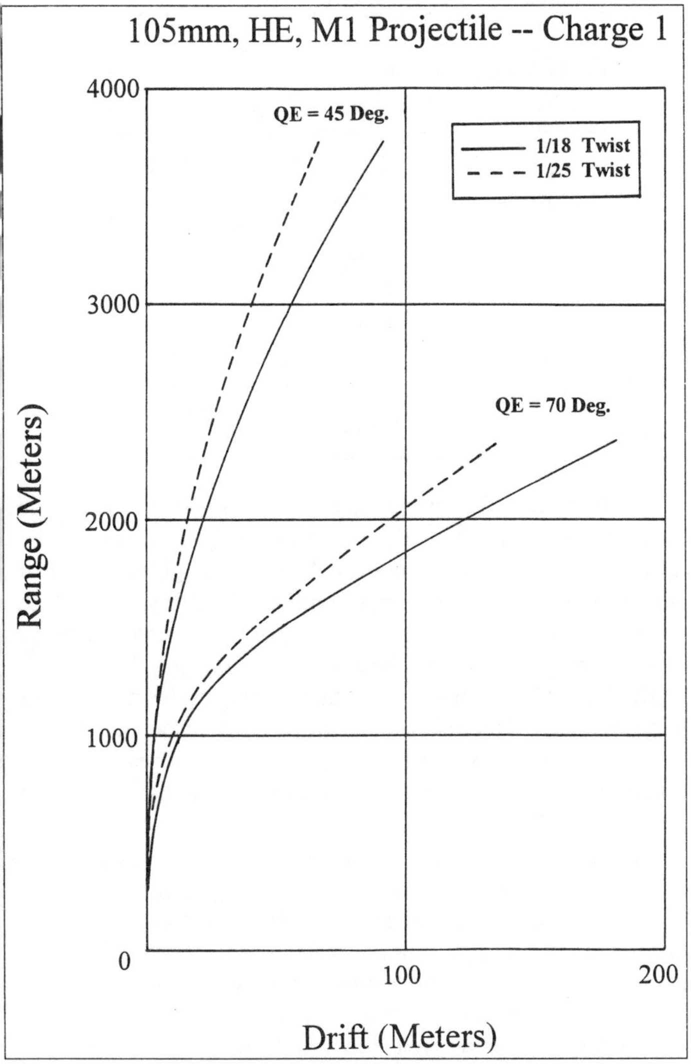

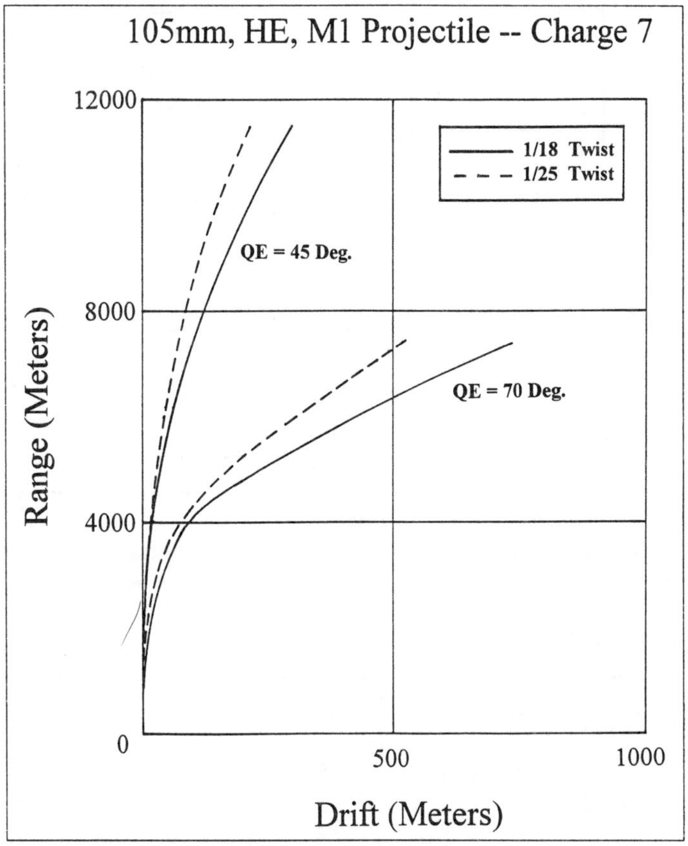

Figure 9.20 Drift versus Range, for Charge 7.

(Left) *Figure 9.19 Drift versus Range, for Charge 1.*

120mm mortar projectiles, consisting of the HE, M934, the Illuminating, M930, and the Smoke, M929 rounds. Three quadrant elevation angles, at both low and high muzzle velocities, were included in the 6-DOF study for this chapter.

The aerodynamic characteristics of the non-rolling, finned 120mm mortar shell were obtained from firings in the BRL Transonic Range, and were reported in Reference 15. A contour sketch of a typical 120mm finned mortar shell, and the average aerodynamic properties used in the present study, are given in Appendix C of this chapter. The physical characteristics listed in Table 9.5 are averages for the three types of mortar projectiles, and are used only as nominal values for the present study.

Table 9.5

Average Physical Characteristics of 120mm Mortar Projectiles

Reference Diameter = 119.56 mm
Projectile Total Length = 70.49 cm
Projectile Weight = 13.585 kg
Axial Moment of Inertia = 0.02335 kg-m^2
Transverse Moment of Inertia = 0.23187 kg-m^2
Center of Gravity = 42.29 cm from Base

The two muzzle velocities selected for the 6-DOF study of the 120mm mortar rounds correspond to Charge 0 (M.V. = 102 meters/second), and Charge 4 (M.V. = 318 meters/second). Trajectories were run at three quadrant elevation angles: 45, 65, and 85 degrees. A total of six trajectories were calculated, using initial (muzzle) pitch rates (ω_{z_0}) sufficient to produce first maximum yaw (actually 1st maximum "pitch," in this case) values of 8 degrees at Charge 0, and 3 degrees at Charge 4. The above values of first maximum yaw were average values, measured in the field by means of yaw card firings. Initial conditions for the six 120mm mortar trajectories are listed in Table 9.6.

Table 9.7
Time of Flight to Impact, Impact Range, and Maximum Ordinate
(Six-Degrees-of-Freedom, 120mm Mortar Trajectories)

Run Number	Charge	M.V. (m/s)	QE (deg)	t_I (seconds)	R_I (meters)	Max. Ord. (meters)
1	0	102	45	14.6	1010	260
2	0	102	65	18.6	770	420
3	0	102	85	20.5	165	510
4	4	318	45	41.4	7315	2100
5	4	318	65	52.6	5570	3380
6	4	318	85	57.7	1275	4070

Table 9.6
Initial Conditions for 120mm Mortar 6-DOF Trajectories

Run Number	Charge	M.V. (m/s)	QE (deg.)	ω_{z_0} (rad/sec)	1st Max Yaw (deg)
1	0	102	45	0.913	8.0
2	0	102	65	0.913	8.0
3	0	102	85	0.913	8.0
4	4	318	45	1.795	3.0
5	4	318	65	1.795	3.0
6	4	318	85	1.795	3.0

The time of flight to level-ground impact, the impact range, and the maximum altitude predicted by the 6-DOF trajectory model are listed in Table 9.7 for the 120mm mortar shell fired at sea-level into an ICAO standard atmosphere with no wind.

Figures 9.21 through 9.23 show the planar pitching motion of the 120mm mortar rounds, when fired at three quadrant elevation angles, and with a muzzle velocity corresponding to Charge 0. (Recall that the 120mm mortar projectiles have uncanted fins, and do not roll or spin at any point along the trajectory. Since the angular motion was started at the muzzle by an upward pitch rate, and there is no axial spin, the observed motion starts and remains as purely planar pitching for the entire trajectory. There is no horizontal, or yawing, motion at any point in the flight).

Figure 9.21 is a plot of the pitch angle versus time, for a QE angle of 45 degrees. Note the relatively slow damping of the sinusoidal pitching motion, due to the low velocity flight, and the correspondingly low dynamic pressure $\left(1/2\,\rho V^2\right)$. Near the summit of the trajectory (around 7.5 seconds), a small "pitch of repose" (α_R), of about 0.6 degree in magnitude, appears. It dies out, along with the transient planar pitching, on the downleg of the flight.

Figure 9.22 is a similar plot, for the same propelling charge, but at 65 degrees quadrant elevation angle. Note the slightly larger (approximately 2.5 degrees) pitch of repose at apogee, which occurs at about 9 seconds time of flight. Even at 65 degrees QE, the mortar shell is flying very well.

The flight dynamic performance of the 120mm mortar at Charge 0, and 85 degrees quadrant elevation angle, is illustrated in Figure 9.23. Note the dramatic effect of high QE on the observed planar pitching motion, near the maximum ordinate of the trajectory, which occurs at about 10.5 seconds time of flight. The pitch angle at the trajectory summit grows to a peak value of 47 degrees! The large-amplitude pitching motion then begins to damp as the mortar starts on the downleg of its trajectory. However, it takes a considerable amount of time for such a large angular motion to damp out; at ground impact (20.5 seconds time of flight), a pitch-amplitude of approximately 3 degrees still remains!

Figures 9.24 through 9.26 show the dynamic behavior of the 120mm mortar rounds, when fired at Charge 4. Figure 9.24 is a plot of the planar pitch angle against time, for Charge 4, and 45 degrees quadrant elevation angle. The initial peak amplitude of 3 degrees damps very rapidly at this high subsonic speed (high dynamic pressure). Two seconds into the flight, the initial transient motion is essentially gone, and the projectile flies the remainder of its trajectory with extremely small planar pitching motion. There is no evidence of any pitch of repose (α_R), near the maximum ordinate.

Figure 9.25 is a similar plot for Charge 4, and for a quadrant elevation angle of 65 degrees. Again, the initial transient pitching motion damps quickly, and is gone by two seconds of flight. Near apogee (25.5 seconds time of flight), the pitch of repose has grown to its maximum value of about 0.2 degree! This tiny value then damps to zero on the final part of the trajectory downleg.

The flight dynamic performance for Charge 4, at 85 degrees QE, is similar to that observed at lower muzzle velocity for the same quadrant elevation angle. Comparison of Figure 9.26 with Figure 9.23 (for Charge 0), shows that the effect of high QE on the planar pitching motion is qualitatively similar, at low and high muzzle velocities. The peak pitch angle at apogee (27.5 seconds time of flight, for Charge 4), is only 13 degrees, compared with the 47 degree peak pitch amplitude observed for Charge 0, at the same quadrant elevation angle. The higher dynamic pressure on the downleg of the Charge 4 trajectory causes the sinusoidal, planar pitching motion to damp faster than it did for the low muzzle velocity case. At impact, the amplitude of the pitching motion has essentially damped to zero.

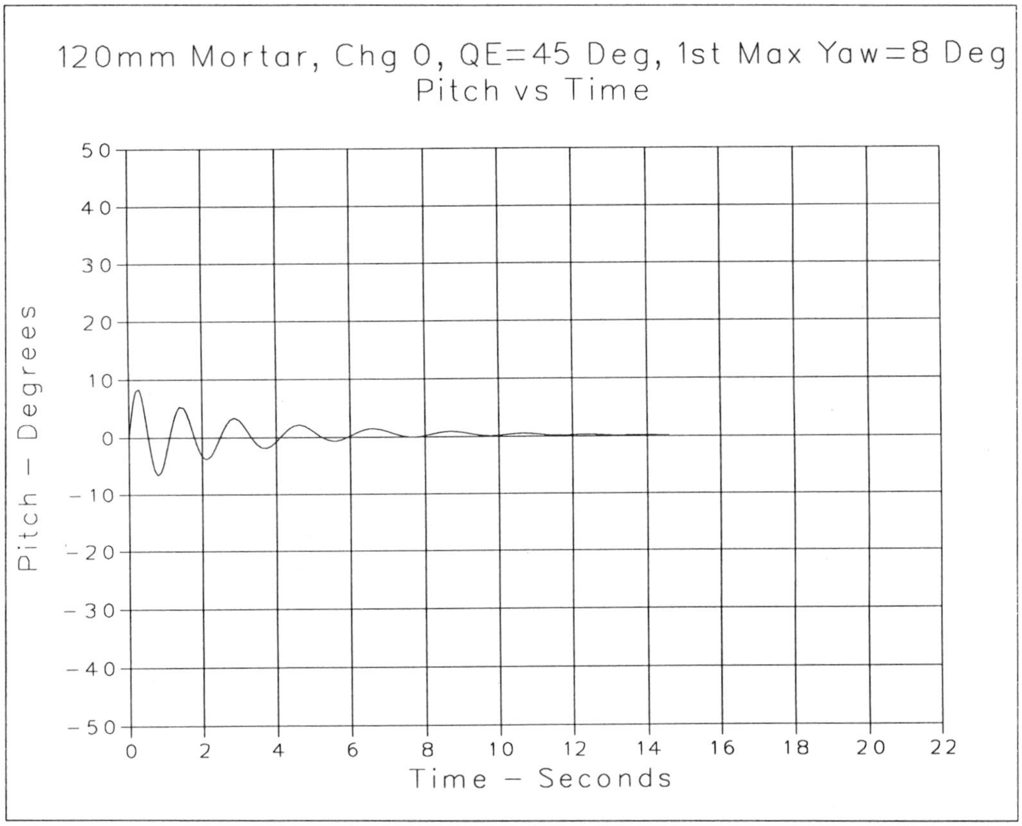

Figure 9.21 Pitch versus Time, Charge 0, 45 Degrees QE.

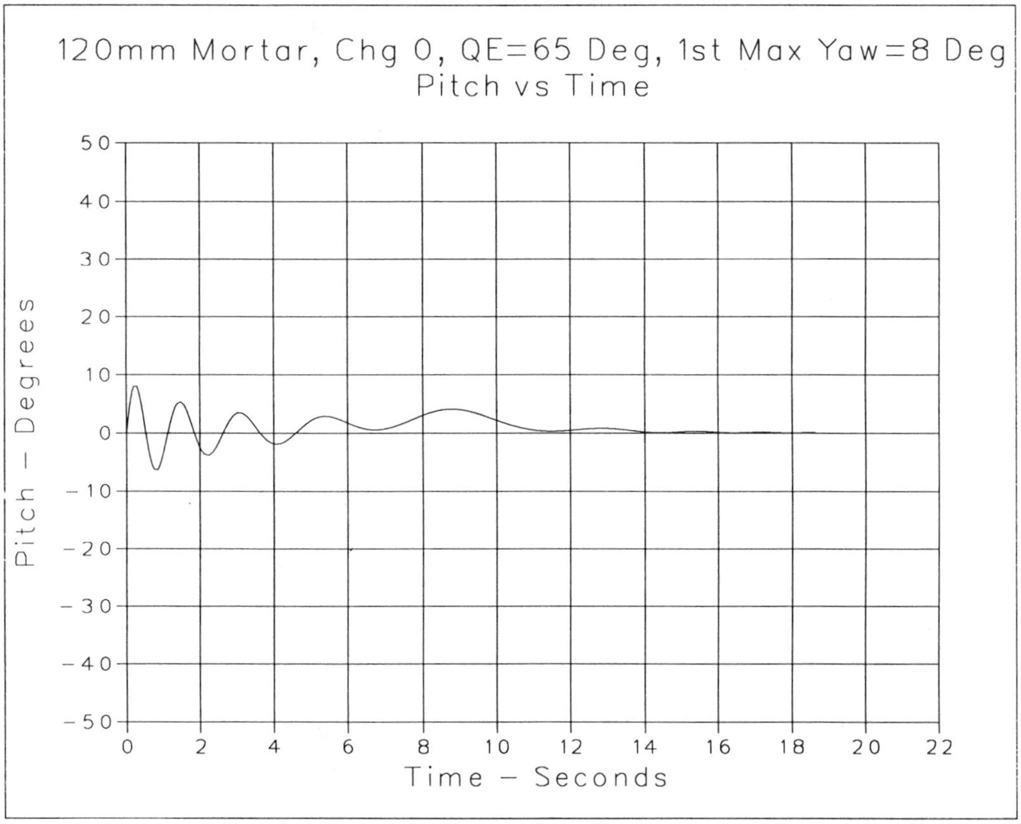

Figure 9.22 Pitch versus Time, Charge 0, 65 Degrees QE.

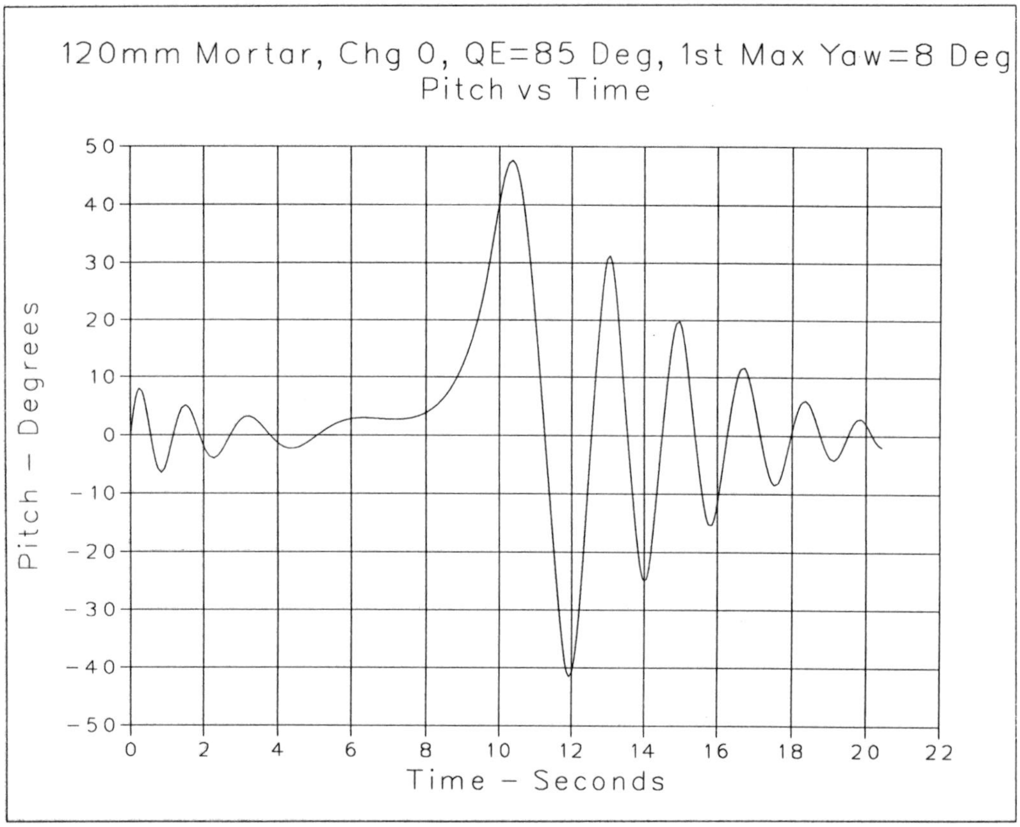

Figure 9.23 Pitch versus Time, Charge 0, 85 Degrees QE.

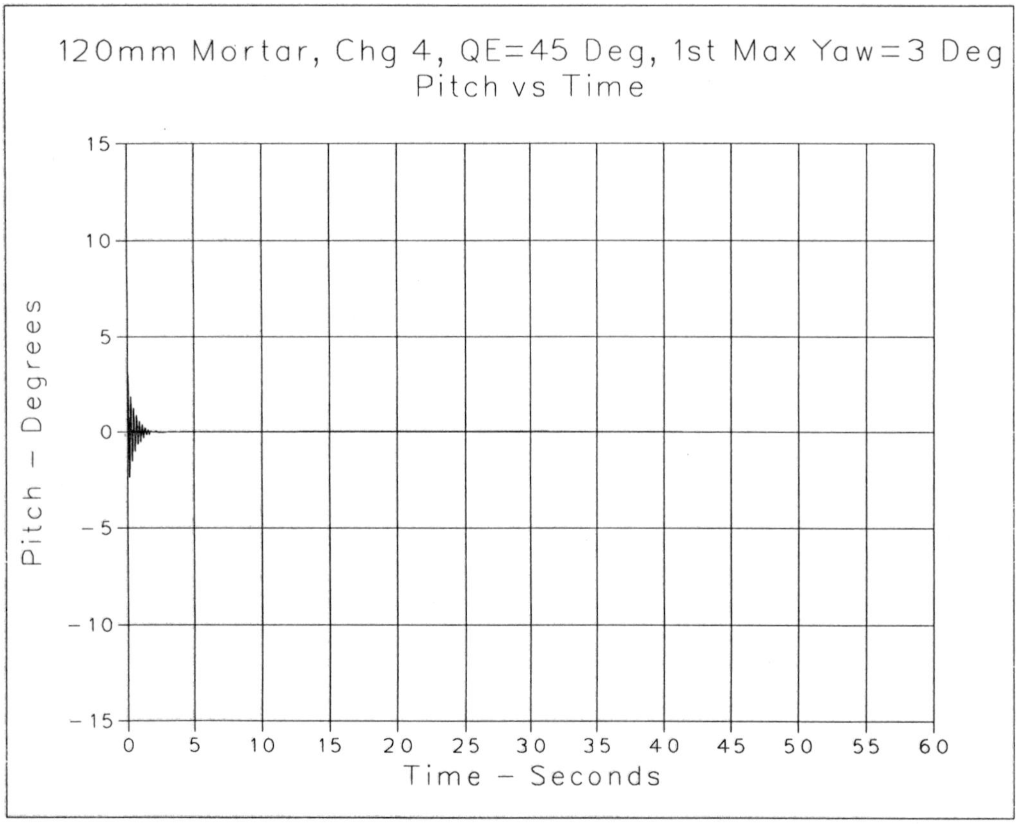

Figure 9.24 Pitch versus Time, Charge 4, 45 Degrees QE.

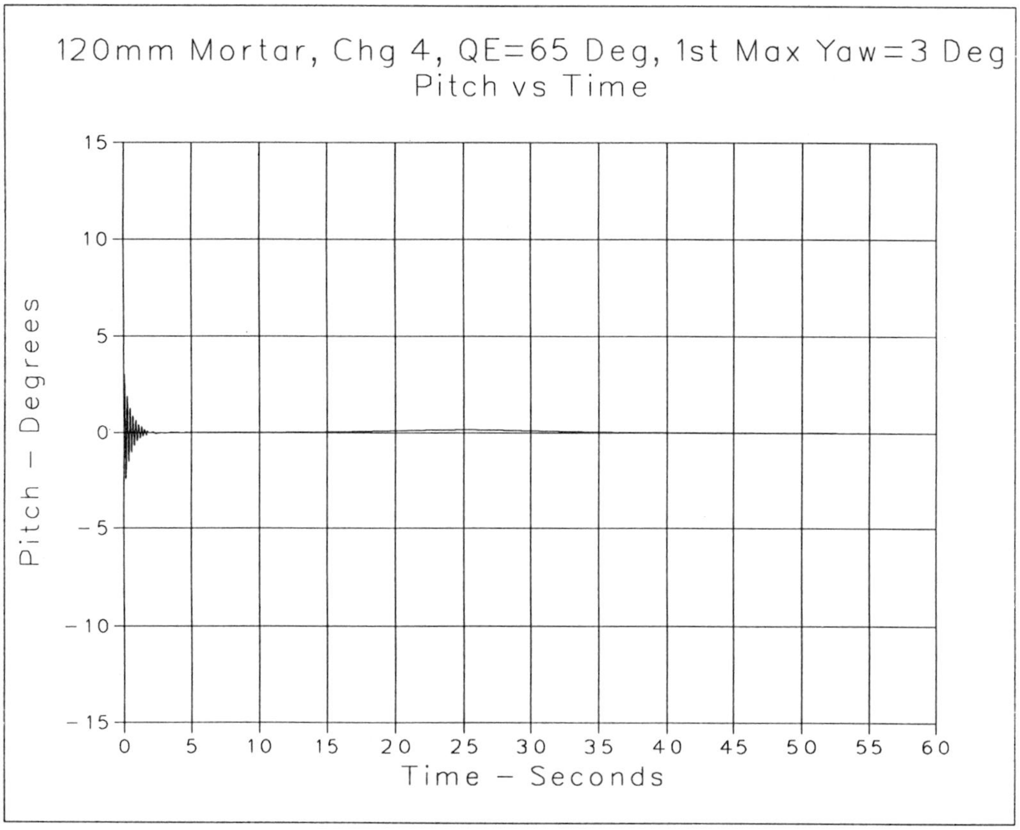

Figure 9.25 Pitch versus Time, Charge 4, 65 Degrees QE.

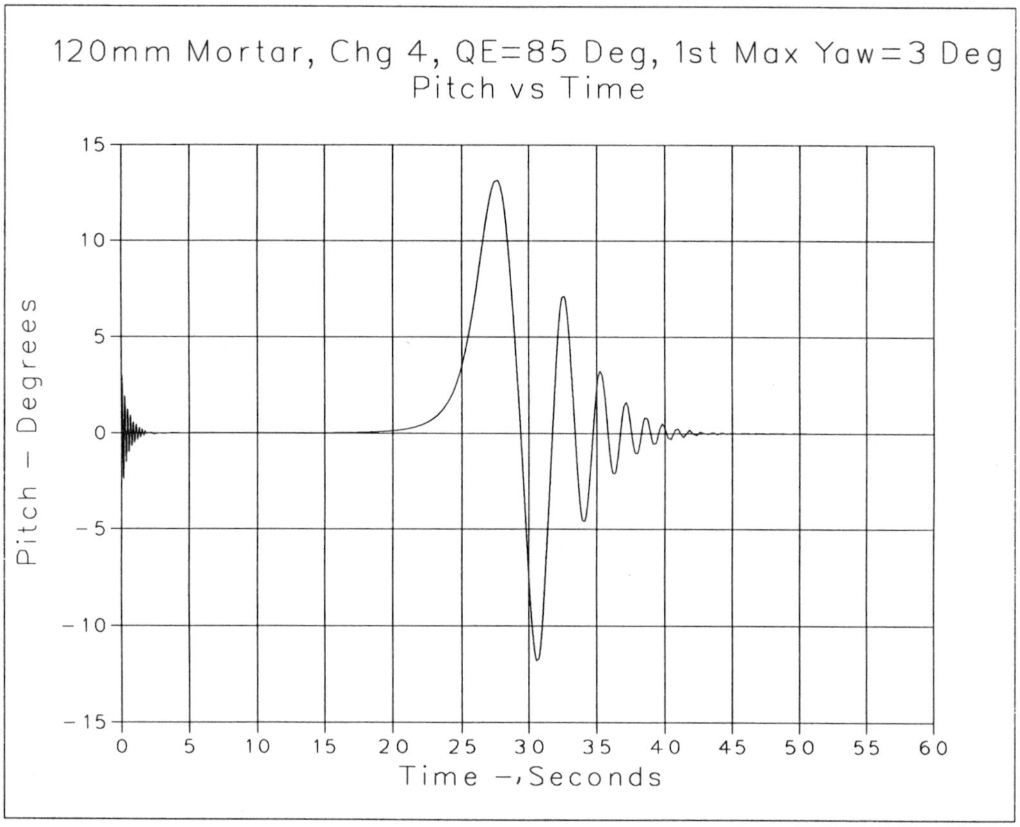

Figure 9.26 Pitch versus Time, Charge 4, 85 Degrees QE.

9.6 SUMMARY AND COMMENTS ON SIX-DEGREES-OF-FREEDOM TRAJECTORIES

It was noted in the first chapter of this book, that 6-DOF trajectories are not required for routine work in exterior ballistics. If the total angle of attack is small everywhere along a projectile's flight path, a point-mass trajectory is often sufficiently accurate for all practical purposes. If a drift solution is required, in addition to the height versus range profile, the modified point-mass method, discussed in the next section, gives a very accurate trajectory for all but the highest quadrant elevation angles.

In general, six-degrees-of-freedom methods are required any time a projectile experiences large-yaw flight. The three examples used in section 9.5 of this chapter illustrate this fact very well. The flight dynamic analysis for the .308," 168 grain Sierra International match bullet, along a flat-fire trajectory, can actually be done by simpler methods, as we will demonstrate in later chapters of this book. Figures 9.2 through 9.5 show that the amplitude of the pitching and yawing motion never exceeds 5 degrees, which is certainly not large-yaw flight. (If the .308" Sierra match bullet were fired at a gun elevation angle of 70 degrees, it would also fly at large yaw near the apogee of its trajectory, and would require a 6-DOF analysis. Likewise, if the 168 grain .308" match bullet were fired sidewise from a high-speed aircraft, a six-degrees-of-freedom calculation would be needed to handle the large-yaw flight induced by a "several hundred mile per hour" crosswind).

The second two examples considered in section 9.5 show that the 105mm M1, and the 120mm mortar projectiles, when fired at the highest quadrant elevation angles, do experience large pitching and yawing motion for a substantial portion of their flight, and therefore they require a 6-DOF analysis for best results. The modified point-mass trajectory model has often been used to predict the flight of spin-stabilized artillery shell, even at very high quadrant elevation angles, where the model itself is no longer valid, and has started to break down. The only correct way to determine a proper upper bound on quadrant elevation angle for the modified point-mass model, is to first do a six-degrees-of-freedom study for the artillery or mortar shell in question, then use the 6-DOF results to guide the modified point-mass trajectory model.

9.7 THE MODIFIED POINT-MASS TRAJECTORY MODEL

The six-degrees-of-freedom equations, (9.8) and (9.9), are the starting point for the modified point-mass equations of motion. We begin by restating these two vector differential equations, using the "shorthand" notation for the aerodynamic forces and moments introduced in equations (9.10) through (9.15). All rocket motor forces and moments have been dropped, and the very small pitch damping *force* is neglected.

$$\frac{d\vec{V}}{dt} = -\left[\tilde{C}_D\right]\vec{v} + \left[\tilde{C}_{L_\alpha}\right]\left[\vec{v}\times(\vec{x}\times\vec{v})\right] + \left[\tilde{C}_{N_{p\alpha}}\right](\vec{v}\times\vec{x}) + \vec{g} + \vec{\Lambda} \quad \textbf{(9.38)}$$

$$\frac{d\vec{h}}{dt} = \frac{I_x\dot{p}}{I_y}\vec{x} + \frac{I_x p}{I_y}\frac{d\vec{x}}{dt} + \left(\vec{x}\times\frac{d^2\vec{x}}{dt^2}\right) = \left(\left[\tilde{C}_{l_p}\right]+\left[\tilde{C}_{l_\delta}\right]\right)\vec{x} + \left[\tilde{C}_{M_\alpha}\right](\vec{v}\times\vec{x})$$
$$+\left[\tilde{C}_{M_{p\alpha}}\right]\left[\vec{x}\times(\vec{v}\times\vec{x})\right] + \left[\tilde{C}_{M_q}\right]\left(\vec{x}\times\frac{d\vec{x}}{dt}\right) \quad \textbf{(9.39)}$$

The unit vector $\vec{x}$ is always perpendicular to its derivative with respect to time; therefore the dot product of $\vec{x}$ and $d\vec{x}/dt$ is identically zero. We now take the vector dot product of $\vec{x}$ with equation (9.39), and multiply both sides by the ratio (I_y/I_x):

$$\frac{dp}{dt} = \left(\frac{I_y}{I_x}\right)\left(\left[\tilde{C}_{l_p}\right]+\left[\tilde{C}_{l_\delta}\right]\right) \quad \textbf{(9.40)}$$

For a rotationally symmetric projectile, equation (9.40) illustrates one of the most important consequences of that symmetry; the spinning, or rolling motion is *uncoupled* from the pitching and yawing motion. The spin history is readily obtained from the numerical solution of the scalar differential equation (9.40).

Substituting equation (9.40) into equation (9.39) yields the 6-DOF differential equation for the pitching and yawing motion:

$$\frac{I_x p}{I_y}\left(\frac{d\vec{x}}{dt}\right) + \left(\vec{x}\times\frac{d^2\vec{x}}{dt^2}\right) = \left[\tilde{C}_{M_\alpha}\right](\vec{v}\times\vec{x})$$
$$+\left[\tilde{C}_{M_{p\alpha}}\right]\left[\vec{x}\times(\vec{v}\times\vec{x})\right] + \left[\tilde{C}_{M_q}\right]\left(\vec{x}\times\frac{d\vec{x}}{dt}\right) \quad \textbf{(9.41)}$$

where, $\left[\tilde{C}_D\right] = \dfrac{\rho v S C_D}{2m}$ $\quad\left[\tilde{C}_{l_\delta}\right] = \dfrac{\rho v^2 S d \delta_F C_{l_\delta}}{2I_y}$

$$\left[\tilde{C}_{L_\alpha}\right] = \frac{\rho S C_{L_\alpha}}{2m} \qquad \left[\tilde{C}_{M_\alpha}\right] = \frac{\rho v S d C_{M_\alpha}}{2I_y}$$

$$\left[\tilde{C}_{N_{p\alpha}}\right] = \frac{\rho S d C_{N_{p\alpha}} p}{2m} \qquad \left[\tilde{C}_{M_{p\alpha}}\right] = \frac{\rho S d^2 C_{M_{p\alpha}} p}{2I_y}$$

$$\left[\tilde{C}_{l_p}\right] = \frac{\rho v S d^2 C_{l_p} p}{2I_y} \qquad \left[\tilde{C}_{M_q}\right] = \frac{\rho v S d^2\left(C_{M_q} + C_{M_{\dot{\alpha}}}\right)}{2I_y}$$

Equations (9.38), (9.40) and (9.41) are an exact restatement of equations (9.8) and (9.9), with all rocket forces and moments dropped, and the pitch damping *force* neglected.

The general solution of these 6-DOF differential equations yields the high-frequency, epicyclic pitching and yawing motion illustrated in section 9.5 of this chapter. The small integration time step required for numerical solution of these equations, translates into long computer run times for six-degrees-of-freedom trajectories. In the early 1960s, the long run times required for 6-DOF calculations led to the development and use of the modified point-mass trajectory model (Ref. 16).

For small yaw, and short segments of the trajectory, Murphy (Ref. 14) gives an approximate analytical solution of the six-degrees-of-freedom differential equations, that describes the pitching and yawing motion of any rigid, rotationally symmetric projectile. The solution of the approximate second order differential equation consists of a complimentary function (epicyclic motion) plus a particular solution (the quasi steady-state yaw of repose). The modified point-mass approach is to extract the particular solution, and neglect the transient epicyclic solution, thus preserving the yaw of repose, the drift, and at least part of the yaw-drag effect. Therefore, the primary assumption of the modified point-mass model is that the epicyclic pitching and yawing motion is small, everywhere along the trajectory.

Six-degrees-of-freedom calculations have repeatedly demonstrated that the yaw of repose of a rotationally symmetric projectile is usually a slowly varying quantity along the trajectory. The only known exception to this rule is the region near apogee, for a projectile fired at a very high quadrant elevation angle. We will define a vector yaw of repose, $\vec{\alpha}_R$, and will assume that $\left(d\vec{\alpha}_R/dt\right)$ is everywhere negligible in comparison with $\vec{\alpha}_R$. Our definition of the vector yaw of repose is:

$$\vec{\alpha}_R = \vec{i} \times \left(\vec{x} \times \vec{i}\right) = \vec{x} - \left(\cos\alpha_t\right)\vec{i} \qquad \textbf{(9.42)}$$

where $\vec{i} = \dfrac{\vec{v}}{|v|}$, a unit vector in the direction of the velocity, $\vec{v}$. **(9.43)**

The reader will recall the definition, $\vec{v} = \vec{V} - \vec{W}$, where $\vec{W}$ is the vector wind. If $\vec{W}$ is very small in comparison with $\vec{V}$, then the vector velocity relative to the ground is also well approximated by $\vec{V} \approx V\vec{i}$.

The vector yaw, $\vec{\alpha}_R$, has the magnitude ($\sin\alpha_t$), where α_t is the total angle of attack; $\vec{\alpha}_R$ is perpendicular to the trajectory, and is directed from the flight path toward the projectile's axis of rotational symmetry. We now differentiate equation (9.42) with respect to time:

$$\frac{d\vec{\alpha}_R}{dt} = \frac{d\vec{x}}{dt} - \left(\cos\alpha_t\right)\left(\frac{d\vec{i}}{dt}\right) + \left(\sin\alpha_t\right)\vec{i} \qquad \textbf{(9.44)}$$

For small yaw, $\sin\alpha_t << \cos\alpha_t$, and the reader will recall our assumption that the time rate of change of the yaw of repose, $\left(d\vec{\alpha}_R/dt\right)$, is everywhere negligible in comparison with $\vec{\alpha}_R$. If these approximations are substituted into equation (9.44):

$$\frac{d\vec{x}}{dt} \approx \left(\cos\alpha_t\right)\frac{d\vec{i}}{dt} \qquad \textbf{(9.45)}$$

Differentiating equation (9.45), we find:

$$\frac{d^2\vec{x}}{dt^2} \approx \left(\cos\alpha_t\right)\frac{d^2\vec{i}}{dt^2} \qquad \textbf{(9.46)}$$

If equation (9.42) is solved for $\vec{x}$:

$$\vec{x} = \vec{\alpha}_R + \left(\cos\alpha_t\right)\vec{i} \qquad \textbf{(9.47)}$$

Equations (9.45) through (9.47) are now used to eliminate the unit vector $\vec{x}$ and its time derivatives from equations (9.38) and (9.41):

$$\frac{d\vec{V}}{dt} = -\left[\bar{C}_D\right]v\vec{i} + \left[\bar{C}_{L_\alpha}\right]v^2\vec{\alpha}_R + \left[\bar{C}_{N_{p\alpha}}\right]v\left(\vec{i} \times \vec{\alpha}_R\right) \qquad \textbf{(9.48)}$$

$$+\vec{g} + \vec{\Lambda} \approx \dot{V}\vec{i} + V\frac{d\vec{i}}{dt}$$

$$\gamma\frac{I_xP}{I_y}\left(\frac{d\vec{i}}{dt}\right) + \gamma\left(\vec{\alpha}_R \times \frac{d^2\vec{i}}{dt^2}\right) + \gamma^2\left(\vec{i} \times \frac{d^2\vec{i}}{dt^2}\right) = \left[\bar{C}_{M_\alpha}\right]v\left(\vec{i} \times \vec{\alpha}_R\right) \qquad \textbf{(9.49)}$$

← α as subscript

$$-\left[\bar{C}_{M_{p\alpha}}\right]v\left[\gamma\vec{\alpha}_R - \left(\sin^2\alpha\right)\vec{i}\right] + \gamma\left[\bar{C}_{M_q}\right]\left[\left(\vec{\alpha}_R + \gamma\vec{i}\right) \times \left(\frac{d\vec{i}}{dt}\right)\right]$$

where $\gamma = \left(\vec{i} \bullet \vec{x}\right) = \cos\alpha_t$

We will neglect the very small Coriolis term in comparison with $\vec{g}$, and we also neglect the small $\left(\sin^2\alpha_t\right)$ term on the right hand side of (9.49), in comparison with γ . The vector cross product of $\vec{i}$ with equations (9.48) and (9.49) yields two linear equations in the vector unknowns, $\vec{\alpha}_R$ and $\left(\vec{i} \times \vec{\alpha}_R\right)$. Solving the linear system for $\vec{\alpha}_R$ and converting back from our shorthand notation, we obtain the solution for the quasi steady-state yaw of repose:

$$\vec{\alpha}_R = \frac{G_1 + G_2 + G_3 + G_4}{F_1 \bullet F_2 + F_3 + F_4}, \qquad \textbf{(9.50)}$$

where $F_1 = \dfrac{1}{2}\rho S v^2\left(\dfrac{pd}{v}\right)C_{N_{p\alpha}}$

$$F_2 = \frac{1}{2}\rho S d v^2\left(\frac{pd}{v}\right)\gamma C_{M_{p\alpha}}$$

$$F_3 = \left[\frac{1}{2}\rho S v^2 C_{L_\alpha}\right]\left[\frac{1}{2}\rho S d v^2 C_{M_\alpha}\right]$$

$$F_4 = \left[\frac{1}{2}\rho S v^2 C_{L_\alpha}\right]\left[\gamma I_y\left(\vec{i} \bullet \frac{d^2\vec{i}}{dt^2}\right)\right]$$

$$G_1 = -\frac{1}{2}m\rho S d^2 v^2\left(\frac{pd}{v}\right)\gamma C_{M_{p\alpha}}\left[\left(\vec{i} \times \frac{d\vec{V}}{dt}\right) - \left(\vec{i} \times \vec{g}\right)\right]$$

$$G_2 = \gamma^2 I_y\left[\frac{1}{2}\rho S v^2 C_{L_\alpha}\right]\left[\frac{d\vec{i}}{dt^2} - \left(\vec{i} \bullet \frac{d^2\vec{i}}{dt^2}\right)\vec{i}\right]$$

$$G_3 = -\left[\frac{1}{2}\rho S v^2 C_{L_\alpha}\right]\left[\gamma I_x p\left(\vec{i} \times \frac{d\vec{i}}{dt}\right)\right]$$

$$G_4 = -\gamma^2\left[\frac{1}{2}\rho S v^2 C_{L_\alpha}\right]\left[\frac{1}{2}\rho S d^2 v\left(C_{M_q} + C_{M_{\dot{\alpha}}}\right)\frac{d\vec{i}}{dt}\right]$$

Taking the vector dot product of $\vec{i}$ with equation (9.48), and neglecting the small Coriolis term:

$$\dot{V} = -\frac{\rho S C_D v^2}{2m} + \left(\vec{i} \bullet \vec{g}\right) \qquad \textbf{(9.51)}$$

Substituting into equation (9.48) and simplifying:

$$\frac{d\vec{i}}{dt} = \frac{\rho S C_{L_\alpha} v^2}{2m}\vec{\alpha}_R + \left[\vec{i}\times\left(\vec{g}\times\vec{i}\right)\right] \tag{9.52}$$

$$\frac{d^2\vec{i}}{dt^2} \approx \left[2\left(\vec{i}\cdot\vec{g}\right)^2 - g^2\right]\vec{i} - \left(\vec{i}\cdot\vec{g}\right)\vec{g} \tag{9.53}$$

Substituting equation (9.43) into equations (9.52) and (9.53):

$$\frac{d\vec{i}}{dt} = \frac{\rho S C_{L_\alpha} v^2}{2m}\vec{\alpha}_R + \left[\vec{v}\times\left(\vec{g}\times\vec{v}\right)\right]/v^2 \tag{9.54}$$

$$\frac{d^2\vec{i}}{dt^2} \approx \left[2\left(\vec{v}\cdot\vec{g}\right)^2/v^2 - g^2\right]\left(\vec{v}/v\right) - \left(\vec{v}\cdot\vec{g}\right)\left(\vec{g}/v\right) \tag{9.55}$$

We now substitute equations (9.43), (9.54) and (9.55) into equation (9.50). With the help of the classical size assumptions, and after considerable simplification, we find:

$$\vec{\alpha}_R = \frac{-2I_x C_{L_\alpha} p\left(\vec{v}\times\frac{d\vec{V}}{dt}\right) - 2md^2 p C_{M_{p\alpha}}\left[\vec{v}\times\left(\frac{d\vec{V}}{dt}-\vec{g}\right)\right]}{\rho S d v^2\left[v^2 C_{L_\alpha} C_{M_\alpha} + p^2 d^2 C_{N_{p\alpha}} C_{M_{p\alpha}}\right]} \tag{9.56}$$

Equation (9.56) is the yaw of repose for spin-stabilized projectiles. The classical form is found by neglecting Magnus forces and moments in (9.56) in comparison with the much larger lift force and pitching moment terms. The classical form of the yaw of repose is:

$$\vec{\alpha}_R = \frac{-2I_x p\left(\vec{v}\times\frac{d\vec{V}}{dt}\right)}{\rho S d v^4 C_{M_\alpha}} \tag{9.57}$$

For a positive overturning moment (statically unstable projectile), the yaw of repose points to the right of the trajectory, for right-hand spin.

For a non-spinning, statically stable (finned) missile, a good approximation to equation (9.50) is:

$$\vec{\alpha}_R = \left(\frac{C_{M_q} d}{C_{M_\alpha} v^4}\right)\left[\vec{v}\times\left(\vec{v}\times\vec{g}\right)\right] \tag{9.58}$$

If the missile is non-spinning, or very slowly rolling, then the overturning moment coefficient, C_{M_α}, must be negative for static stability. The value of the pitch damping moment coefficient, C_{M_q}, must also be negative for dynamically stable flight. If the overturning moment coefficient and the pitch damping moment coefficient are both negative, the yaw of repose of a non-spinning, statically stable missile points slightly above its trajectory.

An appropriate estimate of the yaw of repose, from equations (9.56), (9.57) or (9.58) is now substituted into equation (9.48). Equation (9.48) is then numerically integrated, along with the differential equation (9.40) for axial spin. The final modified point-mass equations are:

$$\frac{d\vec{V}}{dt} = -\frac{\rho S C_D}{2m} v\vec{v} + \frac{\rho S C_{L_\alpha}}{2m} v^2\vec{\alpha}_R + \frac{\rho S d C_{N_{p\alpha}}}{2m} p\left(\vec{v}\times\vec{\alpha}_R\right) + \vec{g} + \vec{\Lambda} \tag{9.59}$$

$$\frac{dp}{dt} = -\frac{\rho S d^2 v}{2I_x} p C_{l_p} + \frac{\rho S d v^2}{2I_x}\delta_F C_{l_\delta} \tag{9.60}$$

Bradley (Ref. 17) has derived an expression for the vector yaw of repose that does not contain the acceleration $\left(d\vec{V}/dt\right)$ on the right hand side of the equation. Reference 17 contains a complete derivation of Bradley's equation, and only his final results are presented in this chapter.

Bradley's equation for the yaw of repose of a spin-stabilized artillery shell is:

$$\vec{\alpha}_R = B\left(\vec{G}_A \times \vec{v}\right) \tag{9.61}$$

where $B = \frac{2I_x}{\rho S d^3 C_{M_\alpha}}\left(\frac{pd}{v}\right)\left(\frac{d}{v^3}\right)$

$$\vec{G}_A = \frac{1}{1+h_a}\left[\vec{g} + \vec{\Lambda} + \frac{h_L\left(\vec{g}\times\vec{v} + \vec{\Lambda}\times\vec{v}\right)}{\left(1-h_M\right)v}\right]$$

$$h_L = \left(\frac{I_x}{md^2}\right)\left(\frac{C_{L_\alpha}}{C_{M_\alpha}}\right)\left(\frac{pd}{v}\right)$$

$$h_M = \left(\frac{I_x}{md^2}\right)\left(\frac{C_{N_{p\alpha}}}{C_{M_\alpha}}\right)\left(\frac{pd}{v}\right)^2$$

$$h_a = \frac{h_L^2}{1-h_M} - h_M$$

Order of magnitude estimates show that and in Bradley's approximation, and the yaw of repose predicted by equation (9.61) therefore reduces to the simple result:

$$\vec{\alpha}_R = \frac{2I_x p\left(\vec{g}\times\vec{v}\right)}{\rho S d v^4 C_{M_\alpha}} \tag{9.62}$$

Equations (9.61) and (9.57) are essentially equivalent. Equation (9.61) is a better choice than (9.57), if it is desired to fit the model to known trajectory data, and thereby determine the parametric values that give a best fit. In fact, equation (9.62) is a sufficiently good approximation for nearly all practical purposes.

9.8 EXAMPLES OF MODIFIED POINT-MASS TRAJECTORIES

For the combination of spin-stabilized projectiles, flat-fire trajectories, and small transient epicyclic pitching and yawing motion, the

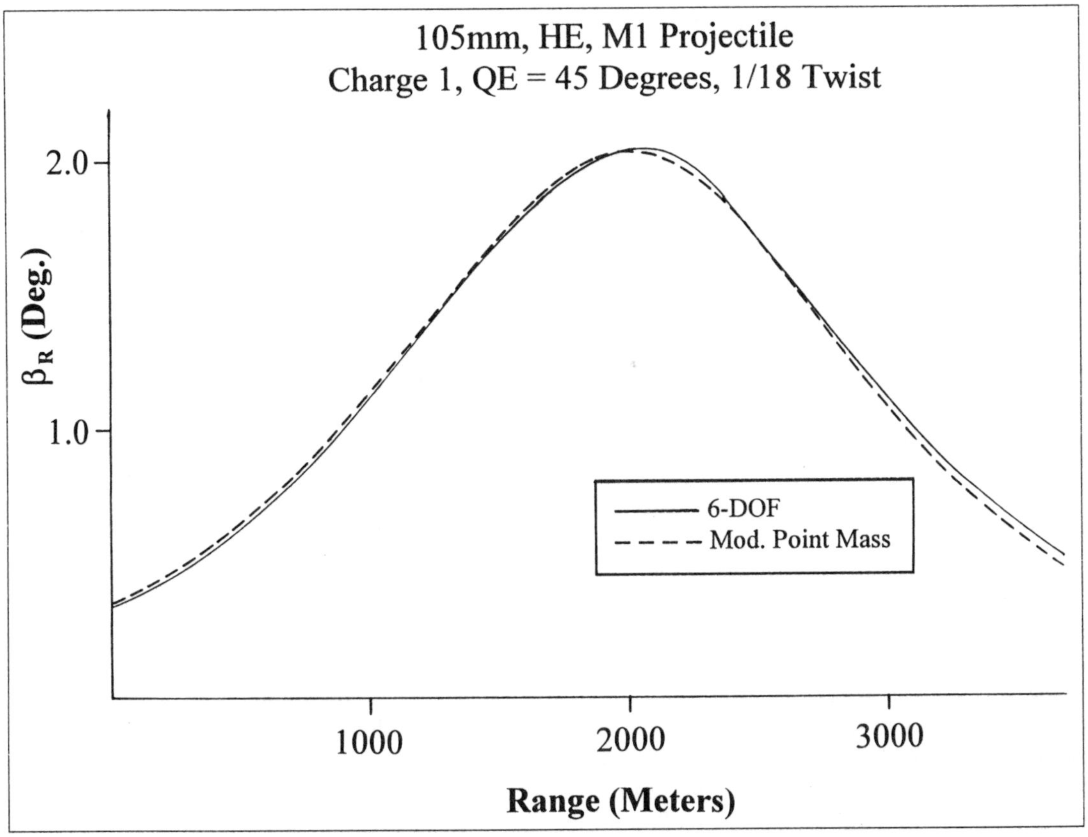

Figure 9.27 Yaw of Repose versus Range, Charge 1, 45 Degrees QE.

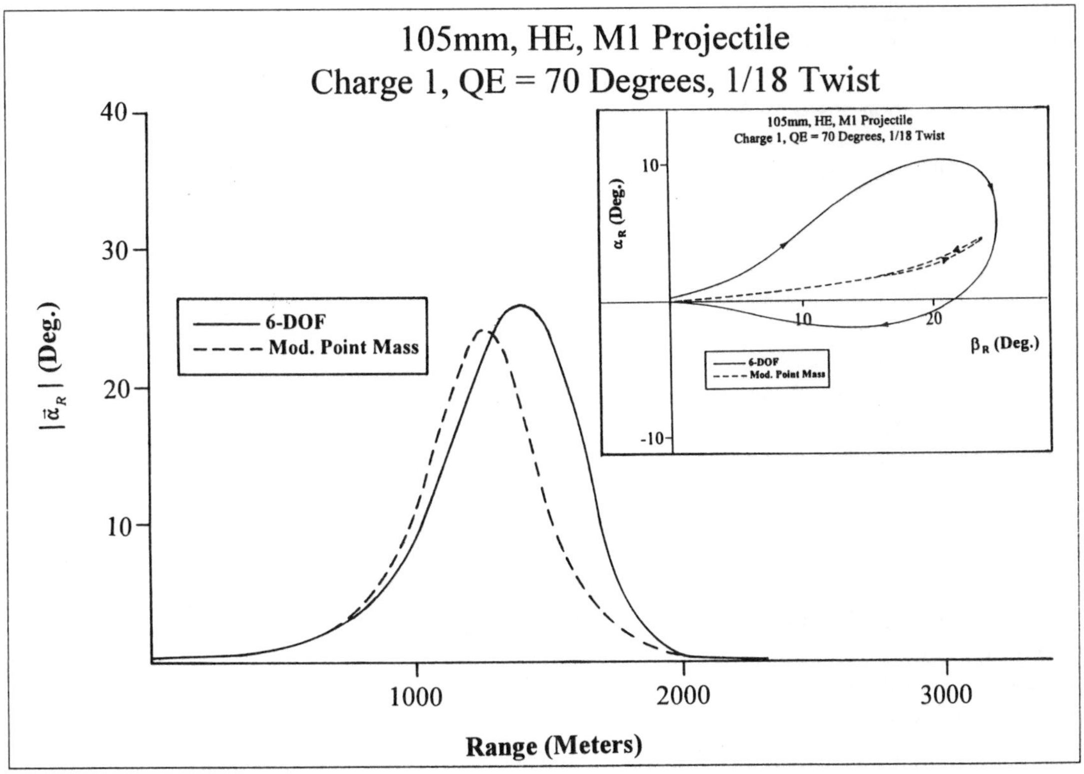

Figure 9.28 Yaw of Repose versus Range, Charge 1, 70 Degrees QE.

modified point-mass method provides an essentially exact solution. Earlier in this chapter, Figures 9.7 and 9.8 illustrated the 6-DOF predicted yaw of repose and the right-hand drift, respectively, for the .308," 168 grain Sierra International match bullet. Modified point-mass trajectories were also run for the same three rifling twist rates, and the results were compared against the six-degrees-of-freedom solutions. The modified point-mass values and the 6-DOF values agreed so closely that the plots showed no significant difference.

At higher quadrant elevation angles, typical of cannon artillery firing, the modified point-mass method gives excellent results, up to gun elevation angles near the maximum trail angle. The next example shows comparisons of modified point-mass and six-degrees-of-freedom calculations, for the 105mm, HE, M1 shell, fired at Charge 1, from the 1/18 twist of the M103 Howitzer.

Example 9.4

Figure 9.27 compares the 6-DOF and modified point-mass predicted yaw of repose, for the 105mm M1 projectile, fired at Charge 1, and at 45 degrees quadrant elevation angle, from the 1/18 twist howitzer. The six-degrees-of-freedom trajectory was run with no initial pitch or yaw rate at the muzzle, so there was no initial transient pitching and yawing motion. Note the excellent agreement of the two methods in the prediction of the yaw of repose, which is essentially a pure β_R; the largest "pitch of repose" at any point along this trajectory is of order of 0.04 degree. The only significant difference between the modified point-mass and the 6-DOF predictions is a small phase shift; the modified point-mass estimate of β_R "leads" the six-degrees-of-freedom yaw of repose, by about 100 meters in range. The peak value of the yaw of repose occurs at about 2000 meters range for the modified point-mass estimate, compared with a peak value at approximately 2100 meters for the more nearly exact 6-DOF calculation.

The same comparison, for a quadrant elevation angle of 70 degrees, is shown in Figure 9.28. The peak amplitude of the total yaw of repose, $|\vec{\alpha}_R|$, predicted by the modified point-mass method is about 24 degrees, which occurs at a range of 1250 meters; the 6-DOF predicted peak value of $|\vec{\alpha}_R|$ is 26 degrees, at a range of 1400 meters. The phase shift is more pronounced at 70 degrees QE than it was at 45 degrees, and the amount of shift varies with the range.

The inset in Figure 9.28 shows that at 70 degrees QE, the 6-DOF calculation for the 105mm M1 shell predicts a significant α_R, or "pitch of repose," in addition to the larger yaw of repose, β_R. The modified point-mass estimate shows a smaller α_R at any point along the flight path. The projectile nose moves slightly up and mostly to the right, according to the modified point-mass model, until the shell reaches apogee. The yaw of repose then re-traces essentially the same path back to the origin on the trajectory downleg. The 6-DOF calculation shows that the total yaw of repose traces out distinctly different paths, on the upleg and the downleg portions of the trajectory. Nevertheless, the range, time of flight, and the right-hand drift estimated by the modified point-mass model agree very closely with the values calculated by the 6-DOF method. This fact confirms the validity and usefulness of the modified point-mass method, for calculation of spin-stabilized cannon artillery projectiles fired at high quadrant elevation angles.

Example 9.5

The final modified point-mass trajectories we will do for this chapter are for the 120mm mortar shell, fired at Charge 0, and quadrant elevation angles of 45 degrees, 65 degrees, and 85 degrees. The results of 6-DOF calculations for the same cases were shown earlier in this chapter, as Figures 9.21, 9.22, and 9.23, respectively. For the non-spinning 120mm mortar projectile, the total yaw of repose, $|\vec{\alpha}_R|$, is actually equivalent to α_R, since the shell's angular motion is totally confined to the vertical plane, hence is a pure pitching motion.

Figure 9.29 illustrates the modified point-mass estimate of the "pitch of repose" for the 120mm mortar shell, at quadrant elevation angles of 65 degrees and 85 degrees. (No plot of the 45 degree elevation case is included, because the peak value of $|\vec{\alpha}_R|$ at the apogee of this trajectory is less than 0.6 degree). At 65 degrees QE, the peak $|\vec{\alpha}_R|$ at the summit is approximately 2.4 degrees, which compares very well with the 6-DOF result, plotted in Figure 9.22.

The situation changes dramatically for the 85 degree quadrant elevation case, as the solid curve of Figure 9.29 shows. The peak value of $|\vec{\alpha}_R|$, which occurs at the summit (about 10.4 seconds into the flight) of this extremely high angle trajectory, is approximately 47 degrees! It is instructive to compare this plot with the 6-DOF motion for the same case, shown earlier as Figure 9.23. The first large up-swing in the 6-DOF plot, which begins at about 8 seconds

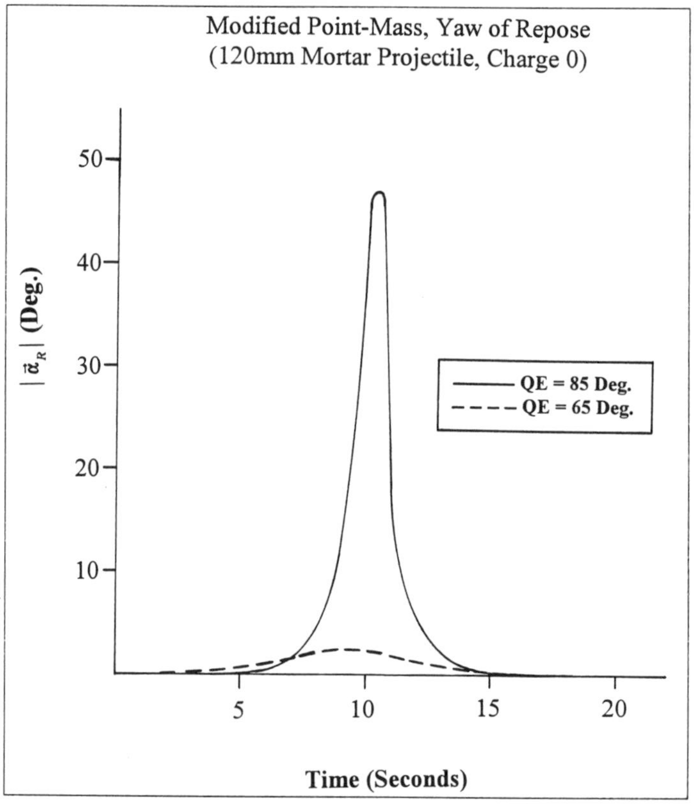

Figure 9.29 Yaw of Repose versus Time, for Charge 0.

of flight and ends at apogee, is due to the rapid growth of the yaw of repose. The yaw (actually pitch) of repose grows to its peak value, then falls off very quickly; it has virtually disappeared after 14 seconds of flight.

The 6-DOF calculation for the 85 degree QE case, plotted in Figure 9.23, shows a large amplitude pitching motion that is initially induced by the rapid upward surge in the yaw of repose near apogee, then damps slowly as the finned mortar shell begins the downleg of its trajectory. This oscillatory motion cannot be predicted by the modified point-mass model, because it *assumes* a steady-state solution in the first place. However, the modified point-mass method (Figure 9.29) *does* correctly capture the large value of $|\vec{\alpha}_R|$ at the apogee of the 85 degree QE trajectory, which permits it to calculate part of the induced drag due to the summital angle of attack. The range and time of flight to impact agree very closely between the two methods, which verifies that the modified point-mass model is also useful for the calculation of trajectories for non-spinning, or slowly rolling, finned mortar shell.

APPENDIX A

Tabulated Aerodynamic Characteristics of the .308," 168 Grain Sierra International Bullet
(BRL Aeroballistic Nomenclature)

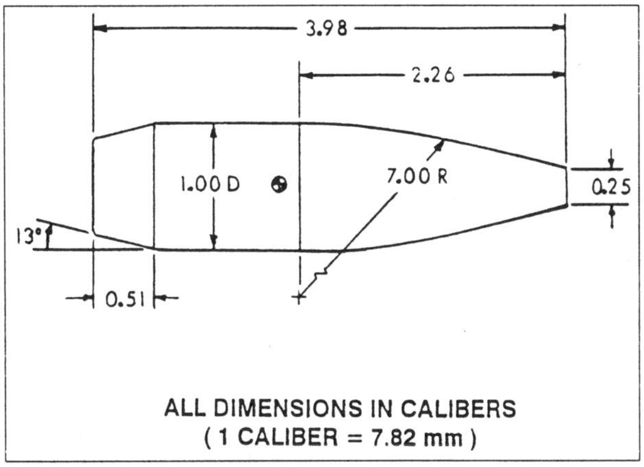

Contour Sketch of the .308," 168 Grain Sierra International Bullet

Mach No.	C_{D_0}	Mach No.	$C_{D_{\delta^2}}$	Mach No.	C_{l_p}	Mach No.	C_{L_α}	Mach No.	$C_{M_{\alpha_0}}$
0	.140	0	2.9	0	-.0150	0	1.75	0	3.05
.8	.140	.95	2.9	.5	-.0125	.5	1.63	.5	3.26
.85	.142	1.0	3.0	.8	-.0108	.8	1.45	.8	3.38
.90	.160	1.05	3.1	.85	-.0107	.85	1.40	.85	3.40
.95	.240	1.1	3.6	.90	-.0105	.90	1.35	.90	3.43
1.00	.430	1.2	6.5	.95	-.0103	.95	1.30	.95	3.45
1.05	.449	1.4	7.6	1.00	-.0100	1.0	1.35	1.0	3.24
1.1	.447	1.6	7.3	1.05	-.0099	1.05	1.55	1.05	3.17
1.2	.434	1.8	6.8	1.1	-.0098	1.1	1.70	1.1	3.15
1.4	.410	2.0	6.1	1.2	-.0095	1.2	1.90	1.2	3.12
1.6	.385	2.2	5.4	1.4	-.0088	1.4	2.15	1.4	3.06
1.8	.365	2.5	4.4	1.6	-.0083	1.6	2.32	1.6	2.98
2.0	.350			1.8	-.0080	1.8	2.45	1.8	2.88
2.2	.339			2.0	-.0075	2.0	2.58	2.0	2.79
2.5	.320			2.2	-.0073	2.2	2.68	2.2	2.69
				2.5	-.0068	2.5	2.85	2.5	2.56

Mach No.	$C_{M_{\alpha_2}}$	Mach No.	$\left(C_{M_q} + C_{M_{\dot{\alpha}}}\right)$
0	-4.3	0	1.2
.95	-4.3	1.05	1.2
1.0	-4.35	1.1	0.5
1.05	-4.4	1.2	-3.6
2.5	-4.4	1.4	-7.3
		1.6	-8.2
		2.5	-8.2

Mach No.	$\alpha_t^2(Deg.^2)$	$C_{M_{p\alpha}}$
0	0	-2.6
0	29.2	.06
0	400	.06
.90	0	-2.6
.90	29.2	.06
.90	400	.06
1.1	0	-1.35
1.1	18.4	.05
1.1	400	.05
1.4	0	-.51
1.4	9.9	.24
1.4	400	.24
1.7	0	-.33
1.7	5.6	.10
1.7	400	.10
2.5	0	-.33
2.5	5.6	.10
2.5	400	.10

Notes:
For small values of pitch and yaw, $\alpha_t \approx \sqrt{\alpha^2 + \beta^2}$, the total angle of attack.
The drag force and pitching moment coefficients vary with the total angle of attack, according to the following equations:

$$C_D = C_{D_0} + C_{D_{\delta^2}} \sin^2 \alpha_t$$

$$C_{M_\alpha} = C_{M_{\alpha 0}} + C_{M_{\alpha 2}} \sin^2 \alpha_t$$

For the .308," 168 Grain Sierra International bullet, note that the spin damping moment coefficient, C_{l_p}, the lift force coefficient, C_{L_α} , and the pitch damping moment coefficient, $\left(C_{M_q} + C_{M_{\dot\alpha}}\right)$, do not vary with total angle of attack.

APPENDIX B

Tabulated Aerodynamic Characteristics of the 105mm, M1 Projectile
(BRL Aeroballistic Nomenclature)

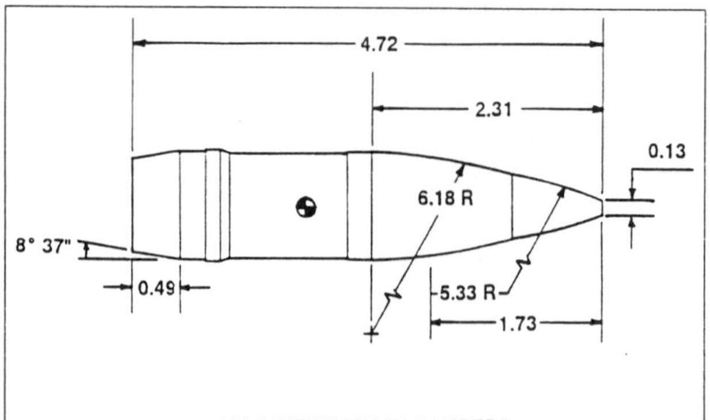

Contour Sketch of the 105mm, HE, M1 Projectile

Mach No.	C_{D_0}	Mach No.	$C_{D_{\delta^2}}$	Mach No.	C_{l_p}	Mach No.	$C_{L_{\alpha 0}}$	Mach No.	$C_{L_{\alpha 2}}$
0	.124	0	3.2	0	-.0178	0	1.63	0	0.1
.875	.124	.88	3.2	.43	-.0149	.4	1.63	.2	0.1
.925	.150	.97	6.3	.70	-.0135	.7	1.41	.6	3.5
.965	.200	.99	4.0	.91	-.0126	.89	1.22	.8	6.6
.990	.350	1.15	5.0	1.4	-.0110	.99	1.73	.985	9.2
1.025	.375	1.25	5.4	1.75	-.0101	1.09	1.57	1.09	8.8
1.085	.415	1.3	5.5	2.1	-.0094	1.5	1.97	1.3	12.0
1.19	.415	2.5	5.5	2.5	-.0087	2.0	2.25	1.5	13.7
1.35	.385					2.5	2.50	2.0	16.0
1.80	.335							2.5	17.0
2.0	.318								
2.5	.276								

Mach No.	$C_{M_{\alpha 0}}$
0	3.55
.46	3.55
.61	3.76
.78	3.92
.87	3.96
.925	4.85
.97	4.0
1.09	3.83
1.5	3.75
2.5	3.75

Mach No.	$C_{M_{\alpha 2}}$
0	-2.9
.4	-2.9
.45	-3.1
.65	-4.4
.78	-3.45
.885	-1.78
.98	-3.0
1.075	-2.1
1.25	-3.325
1.5	-4.45
2.0	-4.6
2.5	-4.6

Mach No.	$\left(C_{M_q} + C_{M_{\dot{\alpha}}}\right)$
0	-3.15
.79	-3.15
1.15	-9.1
1.55	-9.5

Mach No.	$\alpha_t^2\left(Deg.^2\right)$	$C_{N_{p\alpha}}$
0	0	-.34
0	632	-.91
0	908	-1.42
0	1316	-2.63
.22	0	-.34
.22	632	-.91
.22	908	-1.42
.22	1316	-2.63
.31	0	-.125
.31	21.4	-.465
.31	364.5	-.503
.31	638	-1.015
.31	1316	-2.92
.48	0	-.34
.48	348.5	-.591
.48	1316	-2.45
.999	0	-.34
.999	348.5	-.591
.999	1316	-2.45
1.001	0	-.36
1.001	706	-1.68
1.55	0	-.36
1.55	706	-1.68

Mach No.	$\alpha_t^2\left(Deg.^2\right)$	$C_{M_{p\alpha}}$
0	0	.10
0	403.6	.173
0	630.2	.345
0	1316	2.35
.22	0	.10
.22	403.6	.173
.22	630.2	.345
.22	1316	2.35
.31	0	.10
.31	410.8	.133
.31	637.7	.471
.31	915.9	1.276
.31	1316	2.35
.48	0	-.46
.48	27.5	.08
.48	375.2	.022
.48	1316	.94
.81	0	-.46
.81	27.5	.08
.81	375.2	.022
.81	1316	.94
.87	0	.4175
.87	315.3	.053
.87	743.9	.285
.92	0	.4175
.92	315.3	.053
.92	743.9	.285
.96	0	.3747
.96	322.2	.05
.96	1316	.665
.995	0	.3747
.995	322.2	.05
.995	1316	.665
1.02	0	.20
1.02	375.2	.301
1.1	0	.20
1.1	375.2	.301
1.21	0	.193
1.21	403.6	.50
1.21	705.7	.445
1.28	0	.193
1.28	403.6	.50
1.28	705.7	.445
1.46	0	.215
1.46	410.8	.495
1.55	0	.215
1.55	410.8	.495

Notes:
For small values of pitch and yaw, $\alpha_t \approx \sqrt{\alpha^2 + \beta^2}$, the total angle of attack

The drag force, lift force, and pitching moment coefficients vary with the total angle of attack according to the following equations:

$$C_D = C_{D_0} + C_{D_{\delta^2}} \sin^2 \alpha_t$$

$$C_{L_\alpha} = C_{L_{\alpha 0}} + C_{L_{\alpha 2}} \sin^2 \alpha_t$$

$$C_{M_\alpha} = C_{M_{\alpha 0}} + C_{M_{\alpha 2}} \sin^2 \alpha_t$$

For the 105mm, HE, M1 projectile, note that the spin damping moment coefficient, C_{l_p}, and the pitch damping moment coefficient, $\left(C_{M_q} + C_{M_{\dot{\alpha}}}\right)$, do not vary with total angle of attack.

APPENDIX C

Tabulated Aerodynamic Characteristics of the 120mm Mortar Projectile (BRL Aeroballistic Nomenclature)

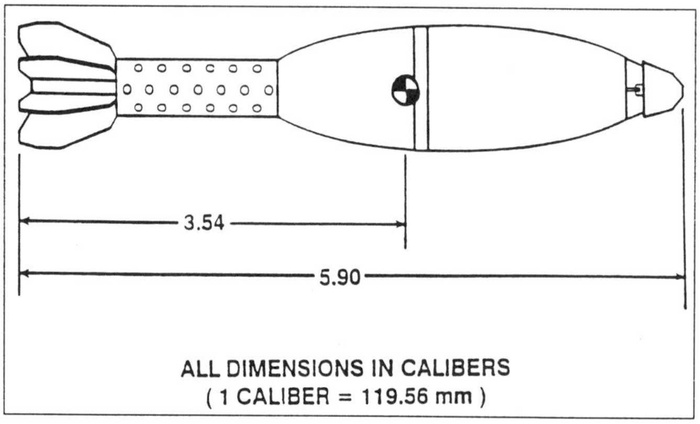

Contour Sketch of the 120mm Mortar Projectile

Mach No.	C_{D_0}
0	.119
.7	.119
.85	.120
.87	.122
.90	.126
.93	.148
.95	.182

Mach No.	$C_{D_{\delta^2}}$
0	2.32
.4	2.44
.6	2.66
.7	2.87
.75	3.01
.85	3.55
.90	4.03
.95	5.20

Mach No.	$C_{L_{\alpha_0}}$
0	1.75
.6	1.95
.8	2.02
.9	2.06
.95	2.08

Mach No.	$C_{L_{\alpha_2}}$
0	14.8
.5	14.8
.6	4.5
.63	1.4
.7	0.4
.8	8.8
.9	28.3
.95	40.0

Mach No.	$C_{M_{\alpha_0}}$
0	-.02
.4	-1.02
.6	-1.62
.8	-2.41
.9	-2.72
.92	-2.75
.95	-2.71

Mach No.	$C_{M_{\alpha_2}}$
0	-15.1
.45	-15.1
.6	-12.7
.7	-8.5
.75	-4.5
.8	1.5
.85	13.9
.90	30.2
.95	59.9

Mach No.	$\left(C_{M_q} + C_{M_{\dot\alpha}}\right)_0$
0	-22.0
.8	-21.1
.85	-21.9
.9	-24.2
.92	-26.8
.95	-31.5
~~.9~~	~~-468~~
~~.95~~	

Mach No.	$\left(C_{M_q} + C_{M_{\dot\alpha}}\right)_2$
0	+48
.5	-46
.6	-86
.7	-144
.8	-259
.85	-357
.9	-468
~~-745~~	
.95	-745

Notes:
For small values of pitch and yaw, $\alpha_t \approx \sqrt{\alpha^2 + \beta^2}$, the total angle of attack

The drag force, lift force, pitching moment, and pitch damping moment coefficients vary with the total angle of attack according to the following equations:

$$C_D = C_{D_0} + C_{D_{\delta^2}} \sin^2 \alpha_t$$
$$C_{L_\alpha} = C_{L_{\alpha_0}} + C_{L_{\alpha_2}} \sin^2 \alpha_t$$
$$C_{M_\alpha} = C_{M_{\alpha_0}} + C_{M_{\alpha_2}} \sin^2 \alpha_t$$
$$C_{M_q} + C_{M_{\dot\alpha}} = \left(C_{M_q} + C_{M_{\dot\alpha}}\right)_0 + \left(C_{M_q} + C_{M_{\dot\alpha}}\right)_2 \sin^2 \alpha_t$$

For the non-rolling 120mm Mortar projectile, all the aerodynamic coefficients vary with total angle of attack.

REFERENCES (Chapter 10 actually)

1. Synge, J., and B. Griffith, *Principles of Mechanics*, McGraw-Hill, New York, NY, 1959.

2. Murphy, C. H., "Free Flight Motion of Symmetric Missiles," Ballistic Research Laboratories Report No. 1216, 1963.

3. Kent, R. H., "Notes on a Theory of Spinning Shell," Ballistic Research Laboratories Report No. 898, 1954.

4. Kelley, J. L., and E. J. McShane, "On the Motion of a Projectile With Small or Slowly Changing Yaw," Ballistic Research Laboratories Report No. 446, 1944.

5. Mann, F. W., *The Bullet's Flight from Powder to Target*, Munn & Company, New York, New York, 1909.

6. Murphy, C. H., "On Stability Criteria of the Kelley-McShane Linearized Theory of Yawing Motion," Ballistic Research Laboratories Report No. 853, 1953.

7. McShane, E. J., J. L. Kelley and F. V. Reno, *Exterior Ballistics*, University of Denver Press, 1953.

8. Nicolaides, J. D., "On the Free Flight Motion of Missiles Having Slight Configurational Asymmetries," Ballistic Research Laboratories Report No. 858, 1953.

9. Nicolaides, J. D., "Two Nonlinear Problems in the Flight Dynamics of Modern Ballistic Missiles," IAS Report 59-17, 1959.

10. Maple, C. G., and J. L. Synge, "Aerodynamic Symmetry of Projectiles," *Quarterly of Applied Mathematics*, Volume 4, 1949.

REFERENCES - CHAPTER 9

1. Fowler, R. H., E. G. Gallop, C. N. H. Lock and H. W. Richmond, "The Aerodynamics of a Spinning Shell," *Philosophical Transactions of the Royal Society of London*, Series A, Volume 221, 1920.

2. Kent, R. H., "Notes on a Theory of Spinning Shell," Ballistic Research Laboratories Report No. 898, 1954.

3. Nielsen, K. L., and J. L. Synge, "On the Motion of a Spinning Shell," Ballistic Research Laboratories Report No. X-116, 1943.

4. Kelley, J. L., and E. J. McShane, "On the Motion of a Projectile With Small or Slowly Changing Yaw," Ballistic Research Laboratories Report No. 446, 1944.

5. Lieske, R. F., and R. L. McCoy, "Equations of Motion of a Rigid Projectile," Ballistic Research Laboratories Report No. 1244, 1964.

6. DeGrafft, W. E., "An IBM 7090 Six-Degree-of-Freedom Trajectory Program, Naval Ordnance Laboratory Technical Report No. 64-225, White Oak, Maryland, 1965.

7. Friedman, E. M., "PANOL Six-Degrees-of-Freedom System Analysis and Usage," U.S. Army Armament Research and Development Command Technical Report ARLCD-TR-77025, 1977.

8. Synge, J., and B. Griffith, *Principles of Mechanics*, McGraw-Hill, New York, NY, 1959.

9. Carnahan, B., H. A. Luther, and J. O. Wilkes, *Applied Numerical Methods*, John Wiley & Sons, New York, NY, 1969.

10. Gill, S., "A Process for the Step-by-Step Integration of Differential Equations in an Automatic Computing Machine," *Proceedings of the Cambridge Philosophical Society*, No. 46, 1951.

11. McCoy, R. L., "The Aerodynamic Characteristics of 7.62mm Match Bullets," Ballistic Research Laboratory Memorandum Report No. BRL-MR-3733, 1988.

12. Roecker, E. T., "The Aerodynamic Properties of the 105mm HE Shell, M1, in Subsonic and Transonic Flight," Ballistic Research Laboratories Memorandum Report No. 929, 1955.

13. McCoy, R. L., "The Subsonic Aerodynamic Characteristics of the 105mm HE Shell, M1, at Angles of Attack From Zero to 180 Degrees," Ballistic Research Laboratories Memorandum Report No. 2353, 1974.

14. Murphy, C. H., "Free Flight Motion of Symmetric Missiles," Ballistic Research Laboratories Report No. 1216, 1963.

15. Brown, T. G., Jr., and R. L. McCoy, "Free-Flight Aerodynamic Characteristics of Three 120mm Mortar Projectiles: XM934-HE, XM930-Illuminating, XM929-Smoke," Ballistic Research Laboratory Memorandum Report No. BRL-MR-3884, 1991.

16. Lieske, R. F., and M. L. Reiter, "Equations of Motion for a Modified Point Mass Trajectory," Ballistic Research Laboratories Report No. 1314, 1966.

17. Bradley, J. W., "An Alternative Form of the Modified Point-Mass Equation of Motion," Ballistic Research Laboratory Memorandum Report No. BRL-MR-3875, 1990.

There is NO index!!!

Chapter 9 references are appended below.

10

Linearized Pitching and Yawing Motion of Rotationally Symmetric Projectiles

10.1 INTRODUCTION

In Chapter 9, the six-degrees-of-freedom trajectory model was presented and discussed. It was noted there that if the aerodynamic forces and moments and the initial conditions are accurately known, an essentially exact calculation of the projectile's pitching and yawing motion is readily obtained by numerical methods. A linearized analysis of the same problem implies an approximate solution, and the reader might well ask why anyone would want an approximate result when a nearly exact numerical solution is available.

The great value of a linearized solution lies in the fact that it gives an *analytical* result, as opposed to a table of numbers. Suppose you ran a 6-DOF trajectory for a new artillery shell, using accurately known aerodynamic and initial condition data, and discovered that the pitching and yawing motion grew to enormous size at long range. (Of course, you would want to fire the shell in the field, and verify that the calculations are correct!). Given only the table of numbers produced by the six-degrees-of-freedom calculations, could you identify the particular aerodynamic forces or moments that would be the most likely cause of the problem? Without an analytical solution that tells you which physical and aerodynamic parameters affect the gyroscopic and dynamic stability, you would have no idea where to start.

In this chapter, the projectile is assumed to be a rigid (nonflexible) body. It is further assumed to be either a body of revolution whose spin axis coincides with a principal axis of inertia, or a finned missile with three or more identical fins, spaced symmetrically around the circumference of a body of revolution. The aeroballistician describes such a missile as having "at least trigonal symmetry." The projectile may be either spin-or fin-stabilized, but it is assumed to fly at small yaw along a flat-fire trajectory, with no wind.

10.2 EQUATIONS OF MOTION FOR THE LINEARIZED PROBLEM

The vector differential equations of motion we will use are abbreviated versions of equations (9.1) and (9.2) from the previous chapter. We will drop all rocket forces and moments from consideration, and will neglect the small Coriolis effect, in comparison with the acceleration due to gravity. Our simplified vector differential equations of motion are:

$$m\frac{d\vec{V}}{dt} = \Sigma\vec{F} + m\vec{g} \qquad \textbf{(10.1)}$$

$$\frac{d\vec{H}}{dt} = \Sigma\vec{M} \qquad \textbf{(10.2)}$$

where m = projectile mass

$\vec{V}$ = vector velocity with respect to the ground-fixed coordinate axes

t = time

$\Sigma\vec{F}$ = vector sum of all the significant aerodynamic forces

$\vec{g}$ = acceleration due to gravity

$\vec{H}$ = total vector angular momentum of the projectile

$\Sigma\vec{M}$ = vector sum of all the significant aerodynamic moments (referenced to the center of mass)

In addition to the ground-fixed [X,Y,Z] coordinate system, with its $\left[\vec{I},\vec{J},\vec{K}\right]$ triad of unit vectors (see Figure 10.1), we will also need a *non-rolling* coordinate system that is attached to, and moving with, the projectile's center of mass. This new coordinate system is a triad of orthogonal unit vectors, $\left[\vec{i},\vec{j},\vec{k}\right]$, where the unit vector $\vec{i}$ moves so that it is always tangent to the trajectory. The perpendicular unit vector $\vec{k}$ *initially* lies in the horizontal plane, and points to the right, if the observer is standing behind the gun, and looking downrange. (Later in this chapter, we will verify that the $\left[\vec{i},\vec{j},\vec{k}\right]$ coordinate system is non-rolling, and show that the departure of the vector $\vec{k}$ from the horizontal plane is very small). The third orthogonal unit vector is defined as $\vec{j} = \vec{k} \times \vec{i}$. For a flat-fire trajectory, $\vec{j}$ is a unit vector directed essentially upward.

Since $\vec{i}$ is a unit vector in the direction of $\vec{V}$, we may write:

$$\vec{V} = V\vec{i} \qquad \textbf{(10.3)}$$

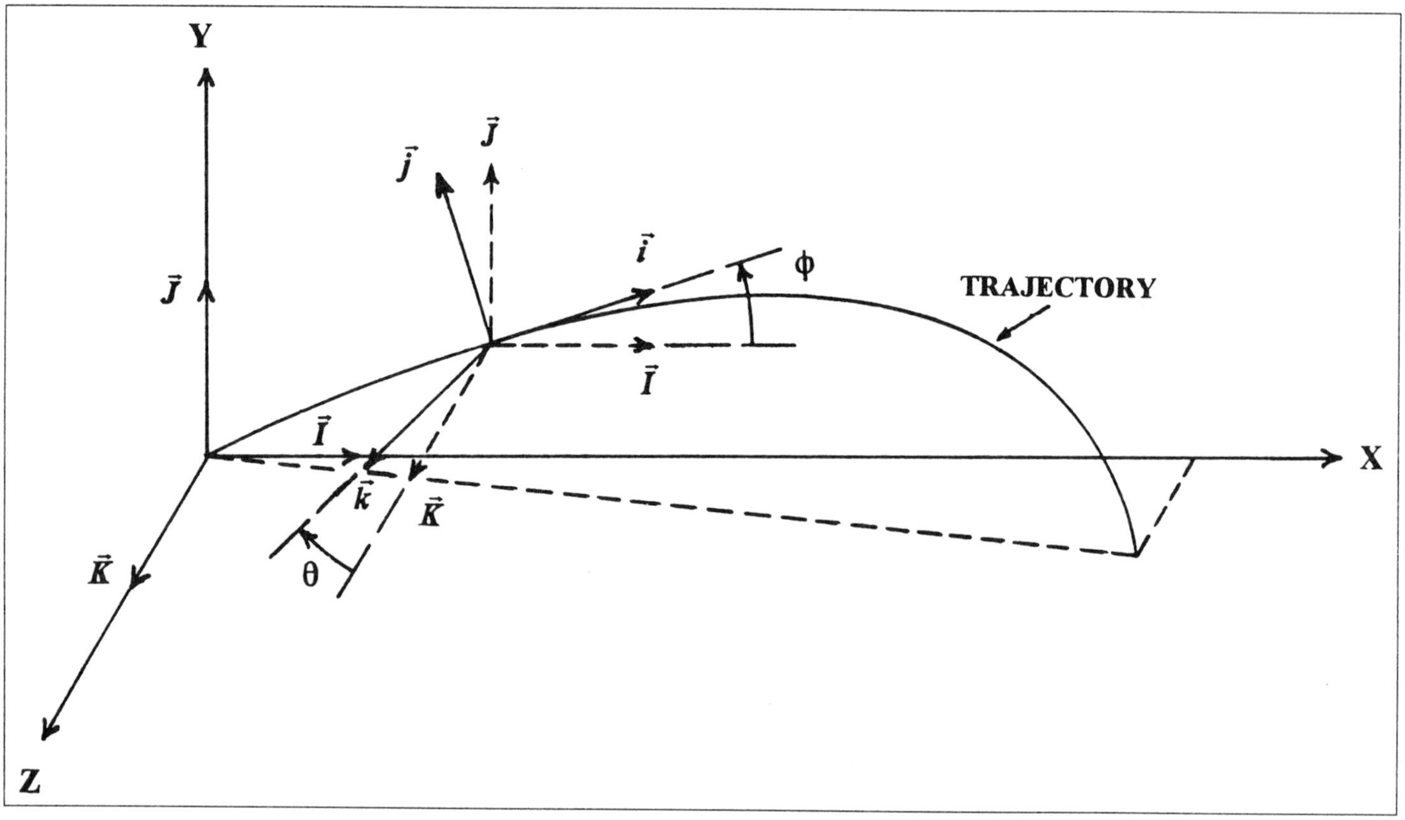

Figure 10.1 Ground-Fixed and Non-Rolling Coordinate System.

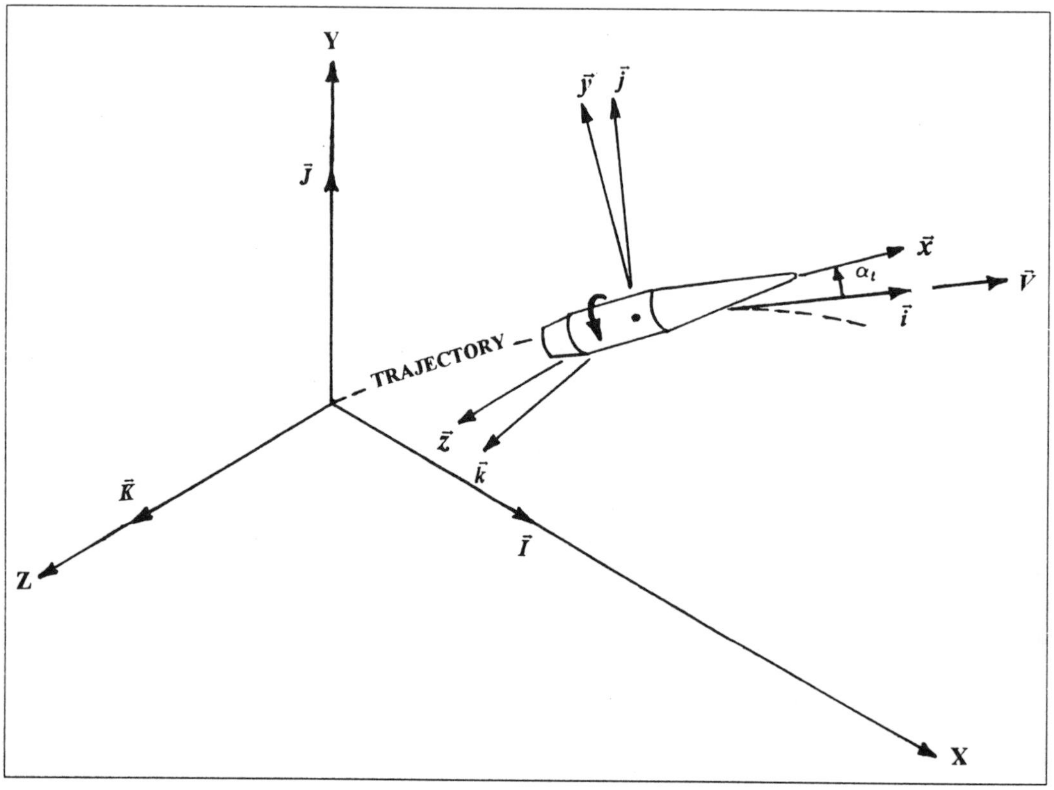

Figure 10.2 Non-Rolling and Body-Fixed Coordinate Systems.

We next define the unit vector $\vec{x}$ along the projectile's axis of rotational symmetry (see Figure 10.2). By definition, the axis of rotational symmetry is a principal axis of inertia. Since we have assumed both rigidity and rotational symmetry, every transverse axis that passes through the center of mass, and is perpendicular to the axis of symmetry, is a principal axis of inertia. Given these assumptions, the total projectile vector angular momentum may be expressed as the sum of two vectors: (1) the angular momentum about $\vec{x}$, and (2) the angular momentum about any axis perpendicular to $\vec{x}$, and passing through the projectile's center of mass.

The angular momentum about $\vec{x}$ has the magnitude $I_x p$, where I_x is the projectile's axial moment of inertia (moment of inertia about the spin axis), and p is the axial spin, in radians per second. Thus the first component of the angular momentum is $I_x p\vec{x}$, where a positive axial spin, p, is clockwise, to an observer behind the gun, and looking downrange.

The total vector angular velocity about any perpendicular axis is given by the vector cross product $(\vec{x} \times d\vec{x}/dt)$. Thus the second component of the angular momentum is $I_y(\vec{x} \times d\vec{x}/dt)$, where I_y is the projectile's transverse moment of inertia about any axis perpendicular to $\vec{x}$, and passing through the center of mass. The total projectile vector angular momentum is therefore given by the sum of the two parts:

$$\vec{H} = I_x p\vec{x} + I_y\left(\vec{x} \times \frac{d\vec{x}}{dt}\right) \quad \textbf{(10.4)}$$

In this chapter, we will retain only the most significant aerodynamic forces and moments that act on spin-stabilized and fin-stabilized projectiles. A significant force or moment is defined as one that produces a measurable effect on the flight. Fifty years of aeroballistic research in wind tunnels and spark photography ranges has taught us that certain aerodynamic forces and moments have significant effects on the flight of projectiles, and others do not. The aerodynamic forces and moments that are important for projectiles are listed below (see chapter 2 for a more detailed discussion of the forces and moments):

Drag Force = $-\frac{1}{2}\rho S C_D V\vec{V} = -\frac{1}{2}\rho S C_D V^2\vec{i}$ **(10.5)**

Lift Force = $\frac{1}{2}\rho S C_{L_\alpha}\left[\vec{V} \times (\vec{x} \times \vec{V})\right] = \frac{1}{2}\rho S C_{L_\alpha} V^2\left[\vec{i} \times (\vec{x} \times \vec{i})\right]$ **(10.6)**

Spin Damping Moment = $\frac{1}{2}\rho S d V^2\left(\frac{pd}{V}\right)C_{l_p}\vec{x}$ **(10.7)**

Rolling Moment = $\frac{1}{2}\rho S d V^2 \delta_F C_{l_\delta}\vec{x}$ (for a finned missile with canted fins) **(10.8)**

Overturning Moment =

$$\frac{1}{2}\rho S d C_{M_\alpha} V(\vec{V} \times \vec{x}) = \frac{1}{2}\rho S d C_{M_\alpha} V^2(\vec{i} \times \vec{x}) \quad \textbf{(10.9)}$$

Magnus Moment = $\frac{1}{2}\rho S d V\left(\frac{pd}{V}\right)C_{M_{p\alpha}}\left[\vec{x} \times (\vec{V} \times \vec{x})\right]$

$$= \frac{1}{2}\rho S d V^2\left(\frac{pd}{V}\right)C_{M_{p\alpha}}\left[\vec{x} \times (\vec{i} \times \vec{x})\right] \quad \textbf{(10.10)}$$

Pitch Damping Moment =

$$\frac{1}{2}\rho S d^2 C_{M_q} V\left(\vec{x} \times \frac{d\vec{x}}{dt}\right) + \frac{1}{2}\rho S d^2 C_{M_{\dot\alpha}} V\left[\left(\vec{x} \times \frac{d\vec{x}}{dt}\right) - \left(\vec{x} \times \frac{d\vec{i}}{dt}\right)\right] \quad \textbf{(10.11)}$$

where $\vec{V}$ = vector velocity of the projectile with respect to the earth-fixed coordinate system (also the vector velocity with respect to air, since we have assumed there is no wind)

$\vec{i} = \vec{V}/|V|$, a unit vector in the direction of $\vec{V}$

$\vec{x}$ = a unit vector along the projectile's rotational axis of symmetry

t = time

p = projectile axial spin (radians/second)

ρ = air density

d = projectile reference diameter

S = projectile reference area (usually taken as ~~S=d²/4)~~ $S = \pi d^2/4$)

m = projectile mass

I_x = projectile axial moment of inertia

I_y = projectile transverse moment of inertia, about any axis through the center of mass

C_D = drag force coefficient

C_{L_α} = lift force coefficient

C_{l_p} = spin damping moment coefficient

C_{l_δ} = rolling moment due to fin cant

δ_F = fin cant angle (radians)

C_{M_α} = pitching (or overturning) moment coefficient

$C_{M_{p\alpha}}$ = Magnus moment coefficient

C_{M_q} = pitch damping moment coefficient due to transverse angular velocity, q

$C_{M_{\dot\alpha}}$ = pitch damping moment coefficient due to rate of change of angle of attack, $\dot\alpha$

Referring to Figure 10.1, the angle ϕ between the unit vector $\vec{i}$, which is always tangent to the trajectory, and the unit vector $\vec{I}$, is the local inclination of the trajectory, relative to the horizontal plane tangent to the earth's surface at the firing point. The vector $\vec{K}$ is defined to lie in the horizontal plane, and we will show later in this chapter that the departure of $\vec{k}$ from the horizontal is very small. Thus the angle θ between the unit vectors $\vec{k}$ and $\vec{K}$, is the local azimuth of the trajectory relative to the $\vec{I}$, or downrange direction. We will need the Eulerian angular, or rotational relationships between the $[\vec{i},\vec{j},\vec{k}]$ and the $[\vec{I},\vec{J},\vec{K}]$ coordinate systems several times in this chapter:

$$\vec{i} = \cos\phi\cos\theta\vec{I} + \sin\phi\cos\theta\vec{J} + \sin\theta\vec{K} \quad \textbf{(10.12)}$$

$$\vec{j} = -\sin\phi\vec{I} + \cos\phi\vec{J} \quad \textbf{(10.13)}$$

$$\vec{k} = -\cos\phi\sin\theta\vec{I} - \sin\phi\sin\theta\vec{J} + \cos\theta\vec{K} \quad \textbf{(10.14)}$$

The inverse transformations are:

$$\vec{I} = \cos\phi\cos\theta\vec{i} - \sin\phi\vec{j} - \cos\phi\sin\theta\vec{k} \quad \textbf{(10.15)}$$

$$\vec{J} = \sin\phi\cos\theta\vec{i} + \cos\phi\vec{j} - \sin\phi\sin\theta\vec{k} \quad \textbf{(10.16)}$$

$$\vec{K} = \sin\theta\vec{i} + \cos\theta\vec{k} \quad \textbf{(10.17)}$$

At this point, a subtle distinction must be made between the capital $[\vec{I},\vec{J},\vec{K}]$ and the lower-case $[\vec{i},\vec{j},\vec{k}]$ coordinate systems. We note that the $[\vec{I},\vec{J},\vec{K}]$ coordinate system is attached to the surface of the earth at the firing site, and if the proper Coriolis and centripetal terms are added to the vector differential equations of motion [see equations (9.8), (9.9) and (9.18) of the previous chapter], the $[\vec{I},\vec{J},\vec{K}]$ system becomes close enough to a Newtonian (inertial) frame of reference for all practical purposes. For the numerical solution of the six-degrees-of-freedom equations, the vectors $\vec{V}$ and $\vec{x}$ were both specified in this inertial reference frame. However, in this chapter, we will specify the vector $\vec{x}$ relative to the $[\vec{i},\vec{j},\vec{k}]$ coordinate system, which moves with the projectile center of mass, so that the vector $\vec{i}$ is always tangent to the local flight path. Thus $[\vec{i},\vec{j},\vec{k}]$ the coordinate system is rotating with respect to a Newtonian frame of reference, and when we differentiate either $\vec{x}$ or $\vec{H}$ in a rotating coordinate system, we must use the rule (Ref. 1) from classical mechanics:

$$\left[\frac{d\vec{Q}}{dt}\right]_{(N/S)} = \frac{d\vec{Q}}{dt} + \vec{\omega}\times\vec{Q} \quad \textbf{(10.18)}$$

where $\vec{Q}$ can be any vector quantity, and $\vec{\omega}$ is the vector angular velocity of the rotating coordinate system relative to inertial space. The time derivative on the right-hand side of equation (10.18) is the value relative to moving coordinates, and the left-hand side [(N/S) subscript], is the time derivative with respect to a fixed, or Newtonian Space.

The vectors $\vec{V}$, $\vec{i}$, and $\vec{g}$ have all been specified in the earth-fixed coordinate system, and they must now be expressed in the body-fixed, *nonrolling* $[\vec{i},\vec{j},\vec{k}]$ coordinates. With the help of equation (10.16), the vector acceleration due to gravity becomes:

$$\vec{g} = -g\vec{J} = -g\left(\sin\phi\cos\theta\vec{i} + \cos\phi\vec{j} - \sin\phi\sin\theta\vec{k}\right) \quad \textbf{(10.19)}$$

But the elevation angle and the azimuth angle are both very small for flat-fire trajectories, and equation (10.19) reduces to:

$$\vec{g} \approx -g\cos\phi\vec{j} \quad \textbf{(10.20)}$$

Substituting equations (10.3), (10.5), (10.6) and (10.20) into equation (10.1), and dividing both sides by the projectile mass, m:

$$\frac{d\vec{V}}{dt} = \dot{V}\vec{i} + V\frac{d\vec{i}}{dt} = \frac{-\rho SC_D V^2}{2m}\vec{i} + \frac{\rho SC_{L_\alpha} V^2}{2m}\left[\vec{i}\times(\vec{x}\times\vec{i})\right] - g\cos\phi\vec{j} \quad \textbf{(10.21)}$$

We now take the dot product of the unit vector with $\vec{i}$ both sides of equation (10.21):

$$\dot{V} = \frac{-\rho SC_D}{2m}V^2 \quad \textbf{(10.22)}$$

Substituting equation (10.22) into equation (10.21), and dividing both sides by V:

$$\frac{d\vec{i}}{dt} = \frac{\rho SC_{L_\alpha}}{2m}V\left[\vec{i}\times(\vec{x}\times\vec{i})\right] - \frac{g\cos\phi}{V}\vec{j} \quad \textbf{(10.23)}$$

Following C. H. Murphy (Ref. 2), we will adopt the "starred convention" for aerodynamic coefficients for the remainder of this chapter. [Note: the star (an asterisk) is appended as a superscript to the symbol for each coefficient. Some of the stars appear quite small, and unfortunately the word processor used to type this text does not allow the use of a larger star].

The definition of a starred coefficient is the product of the coefficient and the dimensionless quantity, $(\rho Sd/2m)$. The starred coefficients for drag and lift become:

$$C_D^* = \frac{\rho Sd}{2m}C_D\text{, and } C_{L_\alpha}{}^* = \frac{\rho Sd}{2m}C_{L_\alpha} \quad \textbf{(10.24)}$$

Equations (10.22) and (10.23) may now be written in the form:

$$\dot{V} = -C_D^*\left(\frac{V}{d}\right)V \quad \textbf{(10.25)}$$

$$\frac{d\vec{i}}{dt} = C_{L_\alpha}{}^*\left(\frac{V}{d}\right)\left[\vec{x} - (\vec{i}\bullet\vec{x})\vec{i}\right] - \frac{g\cos\phi}{V}\vec{j} \quad \textbf{(10.26)}$$

If the independent variable is changed from time to dimensionless arclength, the equations that determine the pitching and yawing motion become independent of the size of the projectile, which turns out to be very convenient in the analysis of free-flight range data. A large artillery shell will then have the same period of yaw, measured in calibers of travel, as a smaller scale model. We now change the independent variable from time to dimensionless arclength, s, measured in calibers of travel:

$$s = \frac{1}{d}\int_o^t V dt \tag{10.27}$$

$$\dot{V} = \frac{dV}{ds}\cdot\frac{ds}{dt} = \left(\frac{V}{d}\right)V' \tag{10.28}$$

where

$$V' = \left(\frac{dV}{ds}\right) \tag{10.29}$$

For the remainder of this chapter, a prime ($'$) or double prime ($''$) superscript will denote a first or second derivative with respect to dimensionless arclength, s. (Note that for a flat-fire trajectory, arclength s is insignificantly different from downrange distance, in calibers, along the X-axis).

We now substitute equation (10.28) into equation (10.25):

$$V' = -C_D^* V \tag{10.30}$$

Let

$$G = \frac{gd\cos\phi}{V^2} \tag{10.31}$$

Equation (10.31) is now substituted into equation (10.26), and (V/d) is factored out:

$$\frac{d\vec{i}}{dt} = \left(\frac{V}{p}\right)\left\{C_{L_\alpha}{}^*\left[\vec{x} - (\vec{i}\bullet\vec{x})\vec{i}\right] - G\vec{j}\right\} \tag{10.32}$$

The vector angular velocity of the moving $\left[\vec{i},\vec{j},\vec{k}\right]$ coordinate system, relative to the Newtonian $\left[\vec{I},\vec{J},\vec{K}\right]$ frame of reference, is given by:

$$\vec{\omega} = \vec{i} \times \frac{d\vec{i}}{dt} = \left(\frac{V}{d}\right)\left[C_{L_\alpha}{}^*(\vec{i}\times\vec{x}) - G\vec{k}\right] \tag{10.33}$$

The vectors $\vec{x}$ and $\vec{H}$ may now be differentiated, using equation (10.18):

$$\left[\frac{d\vec{x}}{dt}\right]_{(N/S)} = \frac{d\vec{x}}{dt} + \vec{\omega}\times\vec{x} \tag{10.34}$$

$$\left[\frac{d\vec{H}}{dt}\right]_{(N/S)} = \frac{d\vec{H}}{dt} + \vec{\omega}\times\vec{H} \tag{10.35}$$

Substituting equation (10.34) into equation (10.4), we find:

$$\vec{H} = I_x p\vec{x} + I_y\left(\vec{x}\times\frac{d\vec{x}}{dt}\right) + I_y\left[\vec{\omega} - (\vec{\omega}\bullet\vec{x})\vec{x}\right] \tag{10.36}$$

We now use equation (10.35) to differentiate equation (10.36):

$$\left[\frac{d\vec{H}}{dt}\right]_{(N/S)} = \frac{d\vec{H}}{dt} + \vec{\omega}\times\vec{H} = I_x\dot{p}\vec{x} + I_x p\frac{d\vec{x}}{dt} + I_y\left(\vec{x}\times\frac{d^2\vec{x}}{dt^2}\right) + I_y\frac{d\vec{\omega}}{dt}$$
$$- I_y\left(\frac{d\vec{\omega}}{dt}\bullet\vec{x}\right)\vec{x} - 2I_y(\vec{\omega}\bullet\vec{x})\frac{d\vec{x}}{dt} + I_x p(\vec{\omega}\times\vec{x}) - I_y(\vec{\omega}\bullet\vec{x})(\vec{\omega}\times\vec{x}) \tag{10.37}$$

The vector differential equation describing the projectile's angular momentum is now obtained by setting equation (10.37) equal to the sum of all the significant aerodynamic moments:

$$I_x\dot{p}\vec{x} + I_x p\frac{d\vec{x}}{dt} + I_y\left(\vec{x}\times\frac{d^2\vec{x}}{dt^2}\right) + I_y\frac{d\vec{\omega}}{dt} - I_y\left(\frac{d\vec{\omega}}{dt}\bullet\vec{x}\right)\vec{x} - 2I_y(\vec{\omega}\bullet\vec{x})\frac{d\vec{x}}{dt}$$
$$+ I_x p(\vec{\omega}\times\vec{x}) - I_y(\vec{\omega}\bullet\vec{x})(\vec{\omega}\times\vec{x}) = \frac{1}{2}\rho SdV^2\left(\frac{pd}{V}\right)C_{l_p}\vec{x} + \frac{1}{2}\rho SdV^2\delta_F C_{l_\delta}$$
$$+ \frac{1}{2}\rho SdC_{M_\alpha}V^2(\vec{i}\times\vec{x}) + \frac{1}{2}\rho SdV^2\left(\frac{pd}{V}\right)C_{M_{p\alpha}}\left[\vec{i} - (\vec{i}\bullet\vec{x})\vec{x}\right]$$
$$+ \frac{1}{2}\rho Sd^2C_{M_q}V\left(\vec{x}\times\frac{d\vec{x}}{dt}\right) + \frac{1}{2}\rho Sd^2C_{M_{\dot\alpha}}V\left[\vec{x}\times\left(\frac{d\vec{x}}{dt} - \frac{d\vec{i}}{dt}\right)\right] \tag{10.38}$$

We now take the vector dot product of $\vec{x}$ with both sides of equation (10.38), which allows us to uncouple the roll equation from the equations for the pitching and yawing motion:

$$I_x\dot{p} = \frac{1}{2}\rho SdV^2\left(\frac{pd}{V}\right)C_{l_p} + \frac{1}{2}\rho SdV^2\delta_F C_{l_\delta} \tag{10.39}$$

Dividing both sides of equation (10.39) by the axial moment of inertia, we obtain:

$$\dot{p} = \frac{dp}{dt} = k_x^{-2}\left(\frac{V}{d}\right)^2\left[\left(\frac{pd}{V}\right)C_{l_p}{}^* + \delta_F C_{l_\delta}{}^*\right] \tag{10.40}$$

where, $k_x^{-2} = \dfrac{md^2}{I_x}$, $C_{l_p}^* = \dfrac{\rho Sd}{2m}C_{l_p}$, *and* $C_{l_\delta}{}^* = \dfrac{\rho Sd}{2m}C_{l_\delta}$

Equation (10.40) is the differential equation of rolling motion. We will proceed with the derivation of the differential equation of pitching and yawing motion, and will return to the spin, or roll equation, later in this chapter.

We now substitute equation (10.40) into equation (10.38), divide both sides by I_y and collect terms:

$$\left(\frac{d^2\vec{x}}{dt^2}\right) + \left[\frac{I_x p}{I_y} - 2(\vec{\omega}\bullet\vec{x})\right]\frac{d\vec{x}}{dt} + \left[\frac{I_x p}{I_y} - (\vec{\omega}\bullet\vec{x})\right](\vec{\omega}\times\vec{x}) + \frac{d\vec{\omega}}{dt}$$
$$-\left(\frac{d\vec{\omega}}{dt}\bullet\vec{x}\right)\vec{x} = \left(\frac{V}{d}\right)^2 k_y^{-2}C_{M_\alpha}{}^*(\vec{i}\times\vec{x}) + \left(\frac{V}{d}\right)^2 k_x^{-2}pC_{M_{p\alpha}}{}^*\left[\vec{i} - (\vec{i}\bullet\vec{x})\vec{x}\right]$$
$$+\left(\frac{V}{d}\right)k_y^{-2}C_{M_q}{}^*\left(\vec{x}\times\frac{d\vec{x}}{dt}\right) + \left(\frac{V}{d}\right)k_y^{-2}C_{M_{\dot\alpha}}{}^*\left[\vec{x}\times\left(\frac{d\vec{x}}{dt} - \frac{d\vec{i}}{dt}\right)\right] \tag{10.41}$$

where, $C_{M_\alpha}{}^* = \dfrac{\rho Sd}{2m}C_{M_\alpha}$, $C_{M_{p\alpha}}{}^* = \dfrac{\rho Sd}{2m}C_{M_{p\alpha}}$, $C_{M_q}{}^* = \dfrac{\rho Sd}{2m}C_{M_q}$,

$C_{M_{\dot\alpha}}{}^* = \dfrac{\rho Sd}{2m}C_{M_{\dot\alpha}}$, $k_x^{-2} = \dfrac{md^2}{I_x}$, $k_y^{-2} = \dfrac{md^2}{I_y}$

$$P = \left(\frac{I_x}{I_y}\right)\left(\frac{pd}{V}\right) \tag{10.42}$$

We will now define the components of the vector $\vec{x}$, in the rotating $\left[\vec{i},\vec{j},\vec{k}\right]$ coordinate system:

$$\vec{x} = \cos\alpha\cos\beta\vec{i} + \sin\alpha\cos\beta\vec{j} + \sin\beta\vec{k} \quad (10.43)$$

Note that the above definition does not assume small yaw; equation (10.43) is valid for large as well as small pitch and yaw angles. However, this chapter *does* assume small yaw, and we will therefore adopt the following small angle approximations to equation (10.43):

$$\vec{x} = \gamma\vec{i} + \alpha\vec{j} + \beta\vec{k}\ , \quad (10.44)$$

where $\gamma = \cos\alpha\cos\beta \approx 1 : \alpha \approx \sin\alpha\cos\beta \approx \sin\alpha : \beta \approx \sin\beta$

We will also need the following definitions and approximations:

$$\frac{d\vec{x}}{dt} = \dot{\gamma}\vec{i} + \dot{\alpha}\vec{j} + \dot{\beta}\vec{k} \quad (10.45)$$

$$\frac{d^2\vec{x}}{dt^2} = \frac{d^2\gamma}{dt^2}\vec{i} + \frac{d^2\alpha}{dt^2}\vec{j} + \frac{d^2\beta}{dt^2}\vec{k} \quad (10.46)$$

$$\vec{x} \times \frac{d\vec{x}}{dt} = \left(\alpha\dot{\beta} - \beta\dot{\alpha}\right)\vec{i} + \left(\beta\dot{\gamma} - \gamma\dot{\beta}\right)\vec{j} + \left(\gamma\dot{\alpha} - \alpha\dot{\gamma}\right)\vec{k} \quad (10.47)$$

$$\vec{x} \times \frac{d^2\vec{x}}{dt^2} = \left(\alpha\frac{d^2\beta}{dt^2} - \beta\frac{d^2\alpha}{dt^2}\right)\vec{i} + \beta\left(\frac{d^2\gamma}{dt^2} - \gamma\frac{d^2\beta}{dt^2}\right)\vec{j} \quad (10.48)$$

$$+\left(\gamma\frac{d^2\alpha}{dt^2} - \alpha\frac{d^2\gamma}{dt^2}\right)\vec{k}$$

$$\vec{i} \times \vec{x} = -\beta\vec{j} + \alpha\vec{k} \quad (10.49)$$

$$\vec{\omega} = \left(\frac{V}{d}\right)\left[-C_{L_\alpha}{}^{*}\beta\vec{j} + \left(C_{L_\alpha}{}^{*}\alpha - G\right)\vec{k}\right] \quad (10.50)$$

$$\vec{\omega} \bullet \vec{x} = -\left(\frac{V}{d}\right)G\beta \quad (10.51)$$

$$\vec{\omega} \times \vec{x} = \left(\frac{V}{d}\right)\left(-\left[C_{L_\alpha}{}^{*}\beta^2 + C_{L_\alpha}{}^{*}\alpha^2 - G\alpha\right]\vec{i} + \gamma\left[C_{L_\alpha}{}^{*}\alpha - G\right]\vec{j} + \gamma C_{L_\alpha}{}^{*}\beta\vec{k}\right)$$

$$(10.52)$$

We will neglect terms involving the products of starred coefficients with the squares of pitch and yaw angles, in comparison with first order terms. [Note: this will be discussed in more detail later in this section]. Dropping the small second order terms, equation (10.52) becomes:

$$\vec{\omega} \times \vec{x} = \left(\frac{V}{d}\right)\left[G\alpha\vec{i} + \gamma\left(C_{L_\alpha}{}^{*}\alpha - G\right)\vec{j} + \gamma C_{L_\alpha}{}^{*}\beta\vec{k}\right] \quad (10.53)$$

In obtaining the time derivative of $\vec{\omega}$, we will also neglect the term $\dot{G}$ in comparison with G:

$$\frac{d\vec{\omega}}{dt} = \left(\frac{V}{d}\right)C_{L_\alpha}{}^{*}\left[-\dot{\beta}\vec{j} + \dot{\alpha}\vec{k}\right] \quad (10.54)$$

The scalar quantity $\left({}^{d\vec{\omega}}\!/_{dt} \bullet \vec{x}\right)$ also vanishes under the same size assumptions used in obtaining equation (10.53).

The final quantity we need to calculate is:

$$\vec{x} \times \frac{d\vec{i}}{dt} = \left(\frac{V}{d}\right)\left[-G\alpha\vec{i} - \gamma\left(C_{L_\alpha}{}^{*}\beta - G\right)\vec{j} + \gamma C_{L_\alpha}{}^{*}\alpha\vec{k}\right] \quad (10.55)$$

Substituting equation (10.42), and equations (10.44) through (10.55) into equation (10.41), we obtain three scalar ordinary second-order differential equations (one equation for each of the three unit vectors). These equations are transformed into new equations with non-dimensional distance, s, as the independent variable, instead of time. The transformation equations are:

$$\dot{\alpha} = \left(\frac{V}{d}\right)\alpha' : \dot{\beta} = \left(\frac{V}{d}\right)\beta' : \dot{\gamma} = \left(\frac{V}{d}\right)\gamma' \quad (10.56)$$

$$\frac{d^2\alpha}{dt^2} = \left(\frac{V}{d}\right)^2\left[\alpha'' - C_D^{*}\alpha'\right] : \frac{d^2\beta}{dt^2} = \left(\frac{V}{d}\right)^2\left[\beta'' - C_D^{*}\beta'\right] :$$

$$\frac{d^2\gamma}{dt^2} = \left(\frac{V}{d}\right)^2\left[\gamma'' - C_D^{*}\gamma'\right] \quad (10.57)$$

The three ordinary, second-order differential equations that describe the linearized pitching and yawing motion of the projectile are given below:

For the i-component:

$$\left(\beta'' - C_D^{*}\beta'\right)\alpha - \left(\alpha'' - C_D^{*}\alpha'\right)\beta + \left(P + 2G\beta\right)\gamma' + \left(P + G\beta\right)G\alpha =$$

$$k_x^{-2}PC_{M_{p\alpha}}{}^{*}\left(1 - \gamma^2\right) + k_y^{-2}C_{M_q}{}^{*}\left(\alpha\beta' - \beta\alpha'\right) + k_y^{-2}C_{M_{\dot{\alpha}}}\left(\alpha\beta' - \beta\alpha' + G\alpha\right)$$

$$(10.58)$$

For the j-component:

$$\left(\gamma'' - C_D{}^{*}\gamma'\right)\beta - \left(\beta'' - C_D{}^{*}\beta'\right)\gamma + \left(P + 2G\beta\right)\alpha'$$

$$+\gamma\left(P + G\beta\right)\left(C_{L_\alpha}{}^{*}\alpha - G\right) - C_{L_\alpha}{}^{*}\beta' = -k_y^{-2}C_{M_\alpha}{}^{*}\beta - k_x^{-2}PC_{M_{p\alpha}}{}^{*}\gamma\alpha$$

$$+k_y^{-2}C_{M_q}{}^{*}\left(\beta\gamma' - \gamma\beta'\right) + k_y^{-2}C_{M_{\dot{\alpha}}}{}^{*}\left[\beta\gamma' - \gamma\beta' + \gamma\left(C_{L_\alpha}\beta - G\right)\right]$$

$$(10.59)$$

For the k-component:

$$\left(\alpha'' - C_D^{*}\alpha'\right)\gamma - \left(\gamma'' - C_D^{*}\gamma'\right)\alpha + \left(P + 2G\beta\right)\beta'$$

$$+\gamma\left(P + G\beta\right)C_{L_\alpha}{}^{*}\beta + C_{L_\alpha}{}^{*}\alpha' = k_y^{-2}C_{M_\alpha}{}^{*}\alpha - k_x^{-2}PC_{M_{p\alpha}}{}^{*}\gamma\beta$$

$$+k_y^{-2}C_{M_q}{}^{*}\left(\gamma\alpha' - \alpha\gamma'\right) + k_y^{-2}C_{M_{\dot{\alpha}}}\left(\gamma\alpha' - \alpha\gamma' - \gamma C_{L_\alpha}{}^{*}\alpha\right)$$

$$(10.60)$$

The above three formidable differential equations will now be considerably simplified, by means of the small yaw assumption and the classical size assumptions of exterior ballistics. The small yaw assumption will be discussed first.

The term γ is of order of $\cos\delta$, where δ is defined here as $\sqrt{\alpha^2+\beta^2}$, and α, β and δ are all of the order of [10⁻¹] for small yaw. Expanding $\cos\delta$ in series gives $\gamma \approx 1-\frac{1}{2}\delta^2$; then $\gamma' \approx \delta\delta'$, and $\gamma'' \approx \delta'^2 - \delta\delta''$. Thus when we write $\gamma = 1$ we are neglecting a term of order of δ^2 in comparison with unity. We will now make the small yaw approximation, $\gamma = 1$. Products of α or β with γ' and γ'' are of order of $\delta'\delta^2$ and $(\delta\delta'^2 - \delta''\delta^2)$ respectively, and are negligible in comparison with terms of order of δ. Following the above argument we will also neglect products and squares of α and β, and products with their derivatives, in comparison with α or β.

The classical size assumptions are based on the fact that the relative density factor, $(\rho Sd/2m)$ is of order of $[10^{-5}]$, and since the largest aerodynamic coefficients themselves are of order of $[10^{2}]$, all starred coefficients are of order of $[10^{-3}]$, and may therefore be neglected in comparison with unity. Products and squares of starred coefficients may also be neglected in comparison with a starred coefficient alone. Note that the term G in equations (10.58) through (10.60) is of the order of a starred coefficient. However, the term P can be of order of $[10^{-1}]$ for very high axial spin rates, thus the product of *P* with a starred coefficient will be retained. (We also note that the above classical size assumptions do not apply to torpedoes in water, or dirigibles in air).

Application of the small yaw assumption and the classical size assumptions to the above three differential equations show that equation (10.58), for the i-component of the motion, vanishes entirely. Many small terms vanish in equations (10.59) and (10.60), and we are left with two differential equations that are considerably simpler:

$$-\beta'' - C_D^*\beta' + P\alpha' - PG + PC_{L_\alpha}{}^*\alpha - C_{L_\alpha}{}^*\beta' = -k_y^{-2}C_{M_\alpha}{}^*\beta$$
$$-k_x^{-2}PC_{M_{p\alpha}}{}^*\alpha - k_y^{-2}\left(C_{M_q}{}^* + C_{M_{\dot\alpha}}{}^*\right)\beta' \qquad \textbf{(10.61)}$$

$$\alpha'' - C_D^*\alpha' + P\beta' + PC_{L_\alpha}{}^*\beta + C_{L_\alpha}{}^*\alpha' = k_y^{-2}C_{M_\alpha}{}^*\alpha$$
$$-k_x^{-2}PC_{M_{p\alpha}}{}^*\beta + k_y^{-2}\left(C_{M_q}{}^* + C_{M_{\dot\alpha}}{}^*\right)\alpha' \qquad \textbf{(10.62)}$$

Note that the pitch damping moment due to angular velocity, *q*, and the pitch damping moment due to rate of change of angle of attack, $\dot\alpha$, which started out as two independent quantities, end up in combination for small yaw and flat-fire trajectories. This means that the two coefficients are inseparable in free flight ballistic ranges, and are therefore usually expressed as the pitch damping moment coefficient sum, $\left(C_{M_q} + C_{M_{\dot\alpha}}\right)$. [See section 2.10 of Chapter 2].

We now introduce complex variables into our linearized equations of pitching and yawing motion. Complex notation is not only mathematically convenient; it also takes advantage of the rotational symmetry we have assumed for the projectile. We will now multiply both sides of equation (10.61) by the quantity $-i = -\sqrt{-1}$. [Note that the complex number $i = \sqrt{-1}$ is unrelated to the unit vector $\vec{i}$ we have used throughout this chapter]. The product of *-i* and equation (10.61) is:

$$i\beta'' - iC_D^*\beta' - iP\alpha' + iPG - iPC_{L_\alpha}{}^*\alpha + iC_{L_\alpha}{}^*\beta' = ik_y^{-2}C_{M_\alpha}{}^*\beta$$
$$+ik_x^{-2}PC_{M_{p\alpha}}{}^*\alpha + ik_y^{-2}\left(C_{M_q}{}^* + C_{M_{\dot\alpha}}{}^*\right)\beta' \qquad \textbf{(10.63)}$$

Equations (10.62) and (10.63) are now added:

$$(\alpha'' + i\beta'') - C_D^*(\alpha' + i\beta') + P(\beta' - i\alpha') + PC_{L_\alpha}{}^*(\beta - i\alpha)$$
$$+C_{L_\alpha}{}^*(\alpha' + i\beta') + iPG = k_y^{-2}C_{M_\alpha}{}^*(\alpha + i\beta) - k_x^{-2}PC_{M_{p\alpha}}{}^*(\beta - i\alpha)$$
$$+k_y^{-2}\left(C_{M_q}{}^* + C_{M_{\dot\alpha}}{}^*\right)(\alpha' + i\beta') \qquad \textbf{(10.64)}$$

The lower case Greek symbol, ξ, [written in English as (xi)], is now introduced to denote the complex yaw. Our definition of ξ and its derivatives are given below:

Let $\xi = \alpha + i\beta$: then $\xi' = \alpha' + i\beta'$, and $\xi'' = \alpha'' + i\beta''$

Also, $-i\xi = \beta - i\alpha$, and $-i\xi' = \beta' - i\alpha'$

Substituting the above definitions into equation (10.64), we obtain:

$$\xi'' - C_D^*\xi' - iP\xi' - iPC_{L_\alpha}{}^*\xi + C_{L_\alpha}{}^*\xi' + iPG = k_y^{-2}C_{M_\alpha}{}^*\xi$$
$$+ik_x^{-2}PC_{M_{p\alpha}}{}^*\xi + k_y^{-2}\left(C_{M_q}{}^* + C_{M_{\dot\alpha}}{}^*\right)\xi' \qquad \textbf{(10.65)}$$

Collecting coefficients of ξ and its derivatives, we find:

$$\boxed{\xi'' + (H - iP)\xi' - (M + iPT)\xi = -iPG} \qquad \textbf{(10.66)}$$

where $H = C_{L_\alpha}{}^* - C_D{}^* - k_y^{-2}\left(C_{M_q}{}^* + C_{M_{\dot\alpha}}{}^*\right)$

$$P = \left(\frac{I_x}{I_y}\right)\left(\frac{pd}{V}\right)$$

$$M = k_y^{-2}C_{M_\alpha}{}^*$$

$$T = C_{L_\alpha}{}^* + k_x^{-2}C_{M_{p\alpha}}{}^*$$

$$G = \frac{gd\cos\phi}{V^2}$$

and $\xi = \alpha + i\beta$

Note that the author's definition of $\xi = \alpha + i\beta$ differs from Murphy's (Ref. 2) definition, $\xi = \beta + i\alpha$. Both definitions are classical, but the reasons for the difference need to be explained.

Murphy's definition follows Kelley and McShane (Ref. 4 and 7) and is usually preferred by mathematicians. If the observer is initially positioned behind the gun and is looking downrange, the α axis is positive *upwards*, the β axis is positive when pointing to the *left*, and the two epicyclic pitch and yaw arms rotate *clockwise* for standard right-hand twist of rifling.

The observer now moves downrange, and looks back toward the gun. From this new viewpoint the projectile is flying straight at the observer; the α axis remains positive upwards, but the β axis is now positive when pointing to the *right*, and the two epicyclic arms rotate *counterclockwise* for right-hand twist. If we define the β axis (now pointing to the right) as the real axis, and the upward-directed α axis as the imaginary axis, the representation of any complex number follows the classical mathematical definition found in any textbook on complex variable. In addition, multiplication of any vector (complex number) by $e^{i\theta}$ rotates the vector by an angle θ, and the direction of rotation is from the real axis toward the imaginary axis, which is *counterclockwise* for Murphy's coordinate system.

The author's definition of $\xi = \alpha + i\beta$ was first chosen by Fowler et al., and was adopted by R. H. Kent (Ref. 3). This definition is usually preferred by gunners and engineers. The gunner-observer looks downrange from a position located just behind the gun. Upward and *to the right* are *always considered as the positive directions*. Thus it is natural for the gunner to define the α axis as positive upward; the β axis as positive *to the right*; and the *clockwise* direction of all rotations as positive, for right-hand twist of rifling. But the last definition requires that the upward-pointing α axis be chosen as the real axis, and the β axis (pointing to the right) be designated as the imaginary axis, so the axial spin and the two clockwise epicyclic turning rates will all have positive values for right-hand twist.

Except for the definition of ξ, equation (10.66) is equivalent to Murphy's equation (6.12), in Reference 2. The only other difference is the inhomogeneous term on the right hand side. Murphy's inhomogeneous term is real, whereas the author's corresponding term is imaginary. Also, Murphy includes the axial spin term, *P*, in his definition of the gravity term, *G*. The author prefers to keep the *P* and the *G* terms separate [as in equation (10.66)], to highlight the effect of spin on the yaw of repose.

In general, the term *P* changes slowly along the trajectory. This means that equation (10.66) is a linear, second order differential equation, with "almost constant" complex coefficients. It describes the pitching and yawing motion of spinning and non-spinning projectiles, flying at small yaw along flat-fire trajectories. Later in this chapter, we will demonstrate the fact that equation (10.66) is, in fact, a very good approximation to the actual flight of symmetric projectiles.

Before we solve equation (10.66), and discuss its solution, we will briefly return to the differential equations describing the downrange velocity and axial spin. After solving these two equations, we will return to the pitching and yawing motion described by equation (10.66).

10.3 SOLUTION OF THE DIFFERENTIAL EQUATIONS FOR VELOCITY AND SPIN

The solution of the first order differential equation (10.30) may be found in any textbook on ordinary differential equations:

$$V = V_0 e^{\int_0^s -C_D^* ds} \quad \textbf{(10.67)}$$

where V_0 is the muzzle velocity.

For relatively short segments of flat-fire trajectories, the variation of the drag coefficient over the flight is small, and we may write equation (10.67) in a simpler form with sufficient accuracy:

$$\boxed{V = V_0 e^{-C_D^* s}} \quad \textbf{(10.68)}$$

Equation (10.68) tells us that the velocity decays exponentially with increasing downrange distance.

The solution of the differential equation (10.40) for spin, or roll, is somewhat more difficult. We first define the roll angle, ϕ, and its derivatives, noting that the roll rate or axial spin, *p*, is the time derivative of the roll angle. (The symbol ϕ has previously been used to denote the local vertical inclination of the trajectory, but since these equations are never used together, no confusion should result).

$$p = \frac{d\phi}{dt}, \text{ and } \dot{p} = \frac{d^2\phi}{dt^2} \quad \textbf{(10.69)}$$

$$\dot{\phi} = \frac{d\phi}{ds} \bullet \frac{ds}{dt} = \left(\frac{V}{d}\right)\phi', \text{ and } \frac{d^2\phi}{dt^2} = \left(\frac{V}{d}\right)\left[\left(\frac{V}{d}\right)\phi'' + \left(\frac{V'}{d}\right)\phi'\right] \quad \textbf{(10.70)}$$

Substituting equations (10.30), (10.69) and (10.70) into equation (10.40), and dividing both sides by $(V/d)^2$:

$$\boxed{\phi'' + K_p\phi' - K_\delta = 0} \quad \textbf{(10.71)}$$

where

$$K_p = -\left[k_x^{-2} C_{l_p}^* + C_D^*\right] \quad \textbf{(10.72)}$$

$$K_\delta = k_x^{-2} \delta_F C_{l_\delta}^* \quad \textbf{(10.73)}$$

The solution of this linear, second-order differential equation, with "almost constant" coefficients, is also found in elementary textbooks:

$$\boxed{\phi = \phi_0 + \phi'_{(s/s)} s + A\left(e^{-K_p s} - 1\right)} \quad \textbf{(10.74)}$$

where $\phi'_{(s/s)}$ is the steady-state spin, or rolling velocity, measured in radians per caliber of travel:

$$\phi'_{(s/s)} = K_\delta / K_p \quad \textbf{(10.75)}$$

and

$$A = \frac{K_\delta - \phi'_0 K_p}{K_p^2} = \frac{\phi'_{s/s} - \phi'_0}{K_p} \quad \textbf{(10.76)}$$

For a spin-stabilized body of revolution, or a finned missile with uncanted fins, there is no rolling moment, and K_δ is therefore zero. For this case, equation (10.74) reduces to:

$$\boxed{\phi = \phi_0 - \frac{\phi'_0}{K_p}\left(e^{-K_p s} - 1\right)} \quad \textbf{(10.77)}$$

If equation (10.77) is differentiated with respect to non-dimensional distance, s:

$$\left(\frac{pd}{V}\right) = \left(\frac{pd}{V}\right)_0 e^{-K_p s}$$ **(10.78)**

For a body of revolution with no fins, K_p is usually negative, and pd/V (measured in radians per caliber of travel) *increases* exponentially as the projectile travels downrange. However, the exponent K_p is usually of order -[10^{-4}], and the actual increase in pd/V is not significant over a short segment of the flat-fire trajectory. For a finned projectile with uncanted fins, C_{l_p} can be of order of -[10], and K_p may then be of order of +[10^{-3}]. The axial spin of a finned missile with uncanted fins will damp exponentially (and rapidly), with increasing downrange distance.

10.4 SIMPLIFIED PITCHING AND YAWING MOTION OF A SPINNING PROJECTILE

The best way to introduce the reader to epicyclic pitching and yawing motion is to start with a simplified version of equation (10.66). We will neglect *all* aerodynamic *forces*, and retain only the largest aerodynamic *moment* (the pitching, or overturning moment) in our simplified analysis. Under these assumptions, equation (10.66) reduces to:

$$\xi'' - iP\xi' - M\xi = -iPG$$ **(10.79)**

The solution of this simplified differential equation of motion will be used to demonstrate the fundamental nature of epicyclic pitching and yawing motion, to study the concept of *gyroscopic stability*, and to examine the yaw of repose for flat-fire trajectories, without the added complication caused by the presence of other aerodynamic forces and moments. Later in this chapter, we will return to the solution of the complete differential equation (10.66), and will investigate the damping (or undamping) of the epicyclic motion, and the related topic of *dynamic stability*.

Equation (10.79) is a linear, second-order differential equation with complex coefficients, and its solution may be found in standard textbooks on ordinary differential equations. The solution of equation (10.79) is:

$$\xi = K_F e^{i\phi_F} + K_S e^{i\phi_S} + i\beta_R$$ **(10.80)**

where $\xi = \alpha + i\beta$

K_F = amplitude of the fast epicyclic yaw mode (or arm)

K_S = amplitude of the slow epicyclic yaw mode (or arm)

$\phi_F = \phi_{F_0} + \phi'_F s$

$\phi_S = \phi_{S_0} + \phi'_S s$

ϕ_{F_0} = initial phase angle of the fast epicyclic yaw arm

ϕ_{S_0} = initial phase angle of the slow epicyclic yaw arm

$\phi'_F = \frac{1}{2}\left[P + \sqrt{P^2 - 4M}\right]$, the fast arm turning rate (radians/caliber) **(10.81)**

$\phi'_S = \frac{1}{2}\left[P - \sqrt{P^2 - 4M}\right]$, the slow arm turning rate (radians/caliber) **(10.82)**

$\beta_R = \frac{PG}{M}$, the steady-state yaw of repose (the particular solution) **(10.83)**

Equation (10.80) shows that the pitching and yawing motion of a symmetric projectile consists of two modes, or arms, that rotate at different angular velocities, or frequencies. Some authors refer to the fast mode as "nutation," and the slow mode as "precession." As an historical note, Dr. F. W. Mann, in his classical textbook *The Bullet's Flight from Powder to Target* (Ref. 5), refers to the fast-arm motion as "oscillation," and to the slow-arm motion as "gyration."

If (P^2 - $4M$) > 0, the exponents $i\phi_F$ and $i\phi_S$ in equation (10.80) are pure imaginary, and the fast and slow epicyclic arms therefore rotate with angular velocities ϕ'_F and ϕ'_S, respectively. Since the exponents contain no real parts, the *lengths* of the fast and slow arms, K_F and K_S, remain fixed; they neither damp nor grow as the projectile flies downrange. Equation (10.80) thus provides an excellent example of *undamped* epicyclic pitching and yawing motion, illustrated in Figure 10.3 for a rotationally symmetric projectile with right-hand spin.

The flight path, or direction of the velocity vector, is represented by the intersection of the coordinate axes. The slow arm rotates clockwise, tracing out a circular motion whose center lies at

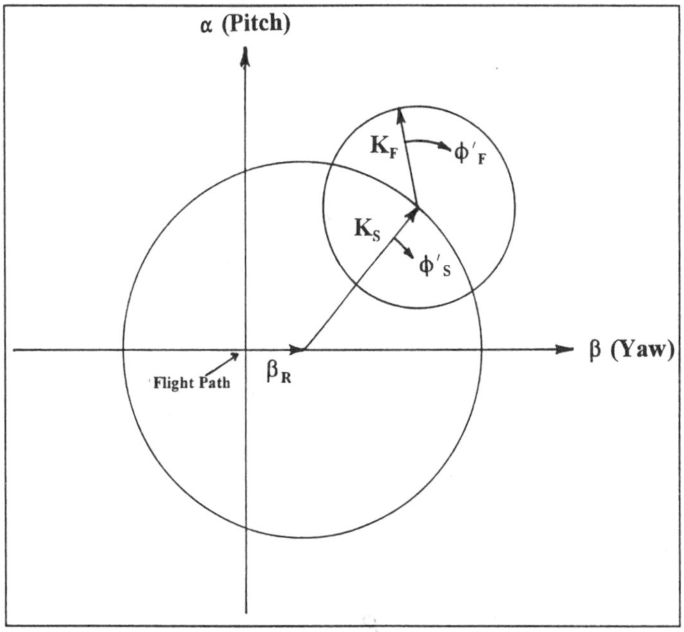

Figure 10.3 Geometry of Undamped Epicyclic Pitching and Yawing Motion.

the right end of the yaw of repose, β_R. The fast arm also rotates clockwise, and it also traces out a circular motion, whose center lies at the moving outer end of the rotating K_S arm. The motion of a point on a circle, whose center moves along the circumference of another circle, is geometrically described as an *epicycle*, hence the name "epicyclic motion" for the pitching and yawing motion of spinning projectiles. (Note that for a left-hand twist of rifling, P would be *negative*; the fast and slow epicyclic arms would both rotate *counterclockwise*, and the yaw of repose would point to the *left* of the trajectory).

The geometry of undamped epicyclic pitching and yawing motion for a spin-stabilized projectile is further illustrated in Figure 10.4, for right-hand twist of rifling. This figure shows that the complex yaw, $\xi = \alpha + i\beta$, traces out a series of loops, as the projectile travels along the trajectory. The initial phase angles, and the lengths of the fast and slow epicyclic yaw arms depend on the initial conditions, as we will see presently. Either arm can be the larger of the two, or they may be the same size. The center of the epicyclic pitching and yawing motion lies at the right end of the yaw of repose, so that the "average" of the total motion is displaced by an amount β_R, to the right of the flight path. The yaw of repose will be discussed in more detail in section 10.6 of this chapter.

Equations (10.80) through (10.83) show that for a spinning finned missile ($M < 0$), the two epicyclic pitch and yaw arms rotate in *opposite* directions. The *fast* arm rotates in the direction of spin, just as it does for a spin-stabilized projectile. However, the *slow* arm for a finned missile rotates in the opposite direction to that of the spin and the fast epicyclic pitch and yaw arm. In addition, the yaw of repose for a finner points to the *left* for right-hand spin. These observed flight characteristics highlight some of the interesting differences between fin-stabilized and spin-stabilized projectiles.

10.5 THE CLASSICAL GYROSCOPIC STABILITY CRITERION

It was noted in the previous section that the quantity (P^2 - 4M) in equations (10.81) and (10.82) must be greater than zero. Consider what would occur if this were not true. If (P^2 - 4M) < 0, its square root will be imaginary, and both epicyclic turning rates will have imaginary components. If complex values for ϕ_F and ϕ_S are substituted into equation (10.80), the exponents will have *real* parts, one of which will cause the slow epicyclic yaw arm (K_S) to grow exponentially, without bound. This is the *definition* of an *unstable motion*, and we are thus led naturally to the concept of gyroscopic stability:

$$\left(P^2 - 4M\right) > 0 \qquad \textbf{(10.84)}$$

Classical exterior ballistics defines the gyroscopic stability factor, S_g, as:

$$S_g = \frac{P^2}{4M} = \frac{I_x^2 p^2}{2 p I_y S d V^2 C_{M_\alpha}} \qquad \textbf{(10.85)}$$

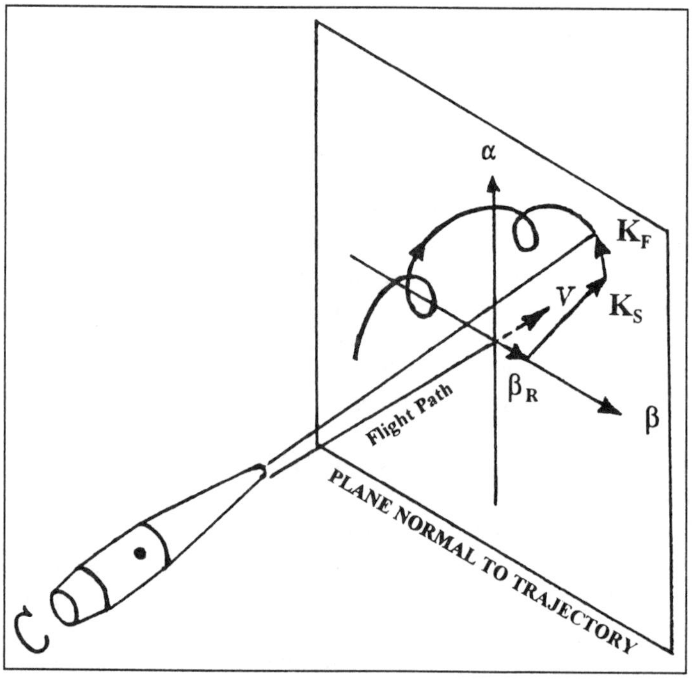

Figure 10.4 Pitch versus Yaw for a Typical Spin-Stabilized Projectile.

Equation (10.85) may be written in another way, by noting [see equations (10.81) and (10.82)] that the sum of the epicyclic turning rates is equal to P, and the product of the rates is equal to M. We may therefore write equation (10.85) in the equivalent form:

$$S_g = \frac{P^2}{4M} = \frac{\left(\phi_F' + \phi_S'\right)^2}{4\phi_F'\phi_S'} \qquad \textbf{(10.86)}$$

Spark photography range or yaw card firings provide measurements of the fast and slow arm turning rates, and equation (10.86) illustrates the method used to measure the gyroscopic stability factor, from free-flight range firing data. Data reduction techniques will be discussed in a later chapter of this book.

Eliminating P^2 between equation (10.84) and equation (10.85):

$$4M\left(S_g - 1\right) > 0 \qquad \textbf{(10.87)}$$

For a statically unstable (spin stabilized) projectile, $M > 0$, and equation (10.87) reduces to the classical gyroscopic stability criterion:

$$S_g > 1 \qquad \textbf{(10.88)}$$

Equation (10.84) is a more general result than equation (10.88), because equation (10.84) shows that a statically stable missile ($M < 0$), is gyroscopically stable without spin! We state the two generalized gyroscopic stability criteria in Table 10.1:

Table 10.1
Generalized Gyroscopic Stability Criteria

Projectile Type	Gyroscopic Stability Criterion
Spin Stabilized (M>0)	$S_g > 1$
Fin-, Flare-, or Mass-Stabilized (M<0)	Gyroscopically Stable Regardless of Spin

It is also noted here, with some emphasis, that *gyroscopic stability does not guarantee that a projectile will fly with small yaw.* For a linear pitching moment, the criterion for gyroscopic stability *does not* depend in any way on the *amplitude* of the epicyclic motion, and conversely. Thus a projectile can fly with an enormous pitch and yaw amplitude, and still be gyroscopically stable. Gyroscopic stability merely insures that the projectile will not immediately tumble in front of the gun, and that it will exhibit periodic pitching and yawing motion as it travels downrange.

10.6 THE YAW OF REPOSE FOR SPIN-STABILIZED PROJECTILES

The yaw of repose for spin-stabilized projectiles is given by the particular solution of equation (10.79), and it is caused by the interaction of axial spin and the acceleration due to gravity. Gravity constantly pulls the trajectory downward, and the projectile's spin axis always lags very slightly behind. The result is a tiny overturning torque, caused by the pitching moment, that tries to rotate the shell's nose upward. But the spin-axis of a gyroscope rotates in the direction of the vector applied torque (Ref. 1), thus the nose moves slightly to the right for right-hand spin, and conversely. [Note that for spinning, *statically stable* projectiles, such as fin, flare, or mass stabilized shell ($M < 0$), the yaw of repose would point to the left of the flight path, for right-hand spin!].

Equation (10.83) defined the yaw of repose, β_R, for a spin-stabilized projectile flying along a flat-fire trajectory. For flat-fire, both P and G increase slowly, and therefore the yaw of repose increases, as the projectile travels downrange. A good illustration of the very small yaw of repose for a modern match-grade rifle bullet was shown in Figure 9.7 of the previous chapter. As an example problem using the linearized equations, we will calculate the gyroscopic stability factor and the yaw of repose for the .308," 168 Grain Sierra International bullet, fired at a muzzle velocity of 2600 feet/second, from a right-hand, 12" twist of rifling, at ranges of 600 yards and 1000 yards. The standard air density used for the 6-DOF calculations was 0.076474 lb./ft³. Values of the moments of inertia were given in section 9.5 of the previous chapter, and are re-stated here for completeness: I_X = 0.000247 lb.-in²; and I_Y = 0.001838 lb.-in². The remaining values we will need are listed in the first four columns of Table 10.2 (*below*), and values of P, M, and G are calculated, using the definitions following equation (10.66).

We may now compare the values from the linearized theory with the results from 6-DOF calculations. The values obtained for the gyroscopic stability factors and the yaw of repose are listed in Table 10.3:

Table 10.3
Comparisons of Linearized Theory with 6-DOF Calculations

Range (Yards)	Method	S_g	β_R (Degrees)
600	Eqs. (10.85), (10.83)	3.5	0.009
600	6-DOF	3.5	0.009
1000	Eqs. (10.85), (10.83)	5.7	0.023
1000	6-DOF	5.7	0.022

The agreement between the linearized equations and the six-degrees-of-freedom calculations is excellent, for a spin-stabilized small arms bullet, along a flat-fire trajectory.

10.7 INITIAL CONDITIONS FOR SIMPLIFIED EPICYCLIC MOTION

The amplitudes and the initial orientations of the fast and slow epicyclic yaw arms depend on the initial conditions, i.e., the initial yaw and initial yaw rate that exist at the instant the projectile leaves the muzzle of the gun. The first step in obtaining the initial conditions is to neglect the very small yaw of repose in equation (10.80), then differentiate the remainder with respect to s:

$$\xi' = i\phi_F' K_F e^{i\phi_F} + i\phi_S' K_S e^{i\phi_S} \qquad \textbf{(10.89)}$$

At the muzzle of the gun, $s = 0$, and we have:

$$\boxed{\xi_0 = K_F e^{i\phi_{F0}} + K_S e^{i\phi_{S0}}} \qquad \textbf{(10.90)}$$

$$\boxed{\xi_0' = i\phi_F' K_F e^{i\phi_{F0}} + i\phi_S' K_S e^{i\phi_{S0}}} \qquad \textbf{(10.91)}$$

The values ξ_0 and ξ_0' are the initial yaw and the initial yaw rate (radians/caliber), respectively, at the gun muzzle. The quantities ξ_0 and ξ_0' are physically introduced by projectile dynamic unbalance, in-bore yaw, balloting in the gun, sabot discard effects, and crosswinds at the muzzle. The causes of initial yaw and yaw rate will be discussed in more detail, in a later chapter of this book.

Table 10.2
Gyroscopic Stability and Yaw of Repose for 168 Grain Sierra Match Bullet

Range (Yards)	Velocity (Ft./Sec.)	(pd/V) (rad./cal.)	C_{M_α}	P (rad./cal.)	M	G
600	1503	.2500	3.07	.0336	.00008046	$3.66\text{x}10^{-7}$
1000	1019	.3373	3.42	.0453	.00008963	$7.95\text{x}10^{-7}$

Equations (10.90) and (10.91) may be solved for the initial amplitudes and phase angles of the fast and slow arms, in terms of the initial yaw and yaw rate:

$$K_F e^{i\phi_{F0}} = \frac{-(i\xi_0' + \phi_S'\xi_0)}{\phi_F' - \phi_S'} \quad \textbf{(10.92)}$$

$$K_S e^{i\phi_{S0}} = \frac{(i\xi_0' + \phi_F'\xi_0)}{\phi_F' - \phi_S'} \quad \textbf{(10.93)}$$

Most projectiles are launched with very small initial yaw (ξ_0), and the initial yaw rate, ξ_0', is usually the major cause of the observed epicyclic pitching and yawing motion. Equations (10.92) and (10.93) show that for very small initial yaw, ξ_0, the fast and slow arms are nearly equal in magnitude, and are almost oppositely directed. On the other hand, if the projectile is fired sidewise from a high speed aircraft, then ξ_0' would be very small in comparison with the large initial yaw, ξ_0, due to crosswind. For this case, the ratio (K_s/K_F) is proportional to (ϕ_F'/ϕ_S'). If the projectile happens to be gyroscopically overstable, so that $(\phi_F' >> \phi_S')$, the result is one-arm, slow-mode coning motion around the flight path.

10.8 COMPLETE LINEARIZED PITCHING AND YAWING MOTION OF PROJECTILES

We now return to the solution of equation (10.66), for the complete linearized pitching and yawing motion of symmetric projectiles. Equation (10.66) is re-stated here for convenience:

$$\xi'' + (H - iP)\xi' - (M + iPT)\xi = -iPG \quad \textbf{(10.66)}$$

where $H = C_{L_\alpha}{}^* - C_D{}^* - k_y^{-2}\left(C_{M_q}{}^* + C_{M_{\dot\alpha}}{}^*\right)$

$$P = \left(\frac{I_x}{I_y}\right)\left(\frac{pd}{V}\right)$$

$$M = k_y^{-2} C_{M_\alpha}{}^*$$

$$T = C_{L_\alpha}{}^* + k_x^{-2} C_{M_{p\alpha}}{}^*$$

$$G = \frac{gd\cos\phi}{V^2}$$

and $\xi = \alpha + i\beta$

This differential equation contains all the significant aerodynamic forces and moments that affect the pitching and yawing motion of a spinning or non-spinning symmetric projectile, and we should therefore expect its solution to give a good approximation to the complete six-degrees-of-freedom motion, for small yaw amplitudes and flat-fire trajectories. Such is indeed the case, as we will demonstrate later in this chapter.

The solution of equation (10.66) is basically the same as the solution of the reduced equation (10.79), but with modified coefficients:

$$\xi = K_F e^{i\phi_F} + K_S e^{i\phi_S} + i\beta_R \quad \textbf{(10.94)}$$

where $\xi = \alpha + i\beta$

$K_F = K_{F_0} e^{\lambda_F s}$, the amplitude of the fast epicyclic yaw mode (or arm)

$K_S = K_{S_0} e^{\lambda_S s}$, the amplitude of the slow epicyclic yaw mode (or arm)

$\phi_F = \phi_{F_0} + \phi_F' s$

$\phi_S = \phi_{S_0} + \phi_S' s$

ϕ_{F_0} = initial phase angle of the fast epicyclic yaw arm

ϕ_{S_0} = initial phase angle of the slow epicyclic yaw arm

$$\beta_R = \frac{PG}{M + iPT} \quad \textbf{(10.95)}$$

$$\lambda_F + i\phi_F' = \frac{1}{2}\left[-H + iP + \sqrt{4M + H^2 - P^2 + 2iP(2T - H)}\right] \quad \textbf{(10.96)}$$

$$\lambda_S + i\phi_S' = \frac{1}{2}\left[-H + iP - \sqrt{4M + H^2 - P^2 + 2iP(2T - H)}\right] \quad \textbf{(10.97)}$$

In general, $|PT| << |M|$, and we observe that the more general expression for the yaw of repose [equation (10.95)] is insignificantly different from the earlier estimate, stated in equation (10.83). The first two terms in equation (10.94) describe the epicyclic pitching and yawing motion of the projectile, which is qualitatively similar to the motion discussed in section 10.4. Note that the amplitudes, or lengths, of the fast and slow arms are now multiplied by *real* exponential terms, which tells us that either arm can damp or grow exponentially, with increasing distance along the trajectory. The resulting motion is called "damped epicyclic motion," if both λ_F and λ_S are negative, and "undamped epicyclic motion," if *either* damping exponent, λ_F *or* λ_S, is positive.

Murphy (Ref. 6) has solved equations (10.96) and (10.97) for *P*, *M*, *H*, and *PT*. We will omit the lengthy algebra involved, and will merely state the results:

$$P = \phi_F' + \phi_S' \quad \textbf{(10.98)}$$

$$M = \phi_F'\phi_S' - \lambda_F\lambda_S \quad \textbf{(10.99)}$$

$$H = -[\lambda_F + \lambda_S] \quad \textbf{(10.100)}$$

$$PT = -[\phi_F'\lambda_S + \phi_S'\lambda_F] \quad \textbf{(10.101)}$$

Equations (10.98) through (10.101) may be inverted, and solved for the epicyclic turning rates, and the damping exponents. The product of the damping exponents in equation (10.99) is neglected, because it is two orders of magnitude smaller than the product of the turning rates.

$$\phi'_F = \frac{1}{2}\left[P + \sqrt{P^2 - 4M}\right] \tag{10.102}$$

$$\phi'_S = \frac{1}{2}\left[P - \sqrt{P^2 - 4M}\right] \tag{10.103}$$

$$\lambda_F = -\frac{1}{2}\left[H - \frac{P(2T - H)}{\sqrt{P^2 - 4M}}\right] \tag{10.104}$$

$$\lambda_S = -\frac{1}{2}\left[H + \frac{P(2T - H)}{\sqrt{P^2 - 4M}}\right] \tag{10.105}$$

10.9 GYROSCOPIC AND DYNAMIC STABILITY OF SYMMETRIC PROJECTILES

Note that equations (10.102) and (10.103) are identical to equations (10.81) and (10.82), in section 10.4. This result tells us that the epicyclic frequencies, or turning rates, depend only on P and M, and are unaffected by any of the other aerodynamic forces and moments. The gyroscopic stability criteria for the complete linearized solution are therefore the same criteria we derived earlier, in section 10.5. Equations (10.84) through (10.88), and Table 10.1, of section 10.5, accurately describe the gyroscopic stability criteria for any spinning or non-spinning symmetric projectile.

Dynamic stability requires that both damping exponents, λ_F and λ_S, be negative throughout the projectile's flight. If either damping exponent becomes (and remains) positive, that yaw mode will begin to grow, which is the *definition* of instability. In practice, one of the λ' s can become slightly positive for a short time, then return to a negative value, with no significant adverse affect on the flight. [Note that it is *always* undesirable to *launch* a projectile at a Mach number where it is dynamically unstable, because the initial pitching and yawing motion can then quickly grow to a large amplitude].

For a non-spinning (or very slowly rolling) statically stable missile, $M < 0$, and P is either zero, or is small enough to be neglected. Equations (10.104) and (10.105) show that for this case, the only requirement for dynamic stability is that $H > 0$. For finned or flare-stabilized missiles, the pitch damping moment coefficient sum, $\left(C_{M_q} + C_{M_{\dot\alpha}}\right)$, is usually negative. The lift and drag force coefficients are both positive, and $C_{L_\alpha} > C_D$; therefore H is nearly always greater than zero, and the dynamic stability is assured.

For spin-stabilized projectiles, equations (10.104) and (10.105) tell us that both damping exponents will be negative *if and only if*:

$$\left[H \mp \frac{P(2T - H)}{\sqrt{P^2 - 4M}}\right] > 0 \tag{10.106}$$

The dynamic stability factor, S_d, is now defined (Ref. 2) and introduced:

$$\boxed{S_d = \frac{2T}{H} = \frac{2\left(C_{L_\alpha} + k_x^{-2} C_{M_{p\alpha}}\right)}{C_{L_\alpha} - C_D - k_y^{-2}\left(C_{M_q} + C_{M_{\dot\alpha}}\right)}} \tag{10.107}$$

Substituting equation (10.107) into equation (10.106) leads to two inequalities, *both* of which must be satisfied for dynamic stability:

$$\boxed{H > 0} \tag{10.108}$$

$$\left[\frac{P^2(S_d - 1)^2}{P^2 - 4M}\right] < 1 \tag{10.109}$$

Solving equation (10.109) for ($4M/P^2$):

$$\frac{4M}{P^2} < S_d(2 - S_d) \tag{10.110}$$

Substituting equation (10.85) into equation (10.110):

$$\boxed{\frac{1}{S_g} < S_d(2 - S_d)} \tag{10.111}$$

Equations (10.108) and (10.111) are the generalized dynamic stability criteria for any spinning or non-spinning symmetric projectile. Nearly all projectiles fall into one of two distinct classes; (a) statically stable, non-spinning or slowly rolling missiles, or (b) statically unstable projectiles, which must be spin-stabilized. The detailed criteria for both classes are listed below.

Statically Stable Missiles ($M < 0$)

(1) A statically stable missile is *always* gyroscopically stable, regardless of spin.

(2) If the dynamic stability factor, S_d, lies within the interval ($0 < S_d < 2$), a statically stable missile is *always* dynamically stable, regardless of spin.

(3) If the dynamic stability factor, S_d, is greater than two, or less than zero, *too much spin* will make a statically stable missile become dynamically *unstable*! The upper bound on axial spin, for dynamic stability, is:

$$P^2 < \left[\frac{4M}{S_d(2 - S_d)}\right] \tag{10.112}$$

Statically Unstable Projectiles (M > 0)

(1) For a statically unstable projectile, *gyroscopic stability is a necessary, but not a sufficient condition for dynamic stability*! Stated another way, a gyroscopically stable projectile may or may not be dynamically stable, but a *gyroscopically unstable projectile is always dynamically unstable*!

(2) If the dynamic stability factor, S_d, lies within the interval ($0 < S_d < 2$), a statically unstable projectile may *always* be spin-stabilized. The amount of axial spin required for dynamic stability is:

$$P^2 > \left[\frac{4M}{S_d(2 - S_d)}\right] \qquad \textbf{(10.113)}$$

(3) If the dynamic stability factor, S_d, is greater than two, or less than zero, *a statically unstable projectile cannot be made dynamically stable, with any amount of axial spin*!

(4) For a statically unstable projectile, a more useful form of equation (10.111) is:

$$\boxed{S_g > \frac{1}{S_d(2 - S_d)}} \qquad \textbf{(10.114)}$$

Figure 10.5 is a plot of equation (10.114), and it illustrates the interaction between the gyroscopic and dynamic stability factors, for statically unstable, spin-stabilized projectiles. If the dynamic stability factor, S_d, happens to have a value near unity, e.g. ($0.8 < S_d < 1.2$), then $S_g > 1$ is sufficient for dynamic stability, as well as gyroscopic stability. However, if the dynamic stability factor, as defined in equation (10.107), is equal to 0.5 (or 1.5), the value of S_g would have to be greater than 1.33, to insure dynamic stability. If S_d equals 0.1 (or 1.9), the projectile would not be dynamically stable unless $S_g > 5.26$! As McShane, Kelley, and Reno point out in *Exterior Ballistics* (Ref. 7), equation (10.114) may be considered as a "sharpening" of the classical gyroscopic stability criterion. Instead of requiring only that $S_g > 1$, we require that S_g be greater than the right hand side of equation (10.114), which is, by reason of its form, always greater than unity.

Figure 10.5 shows that it is dangerous to select a rifling twist rate for a particular projectile, based solely on the classical requirement that $S_g > 1$. For a given projectile design, intended for use over a wide velocity region, the probability is very low that the dynamic stability factor, S_d, will always be close to one. In particular, if the dynamic stability factor is unknown, and the projectile must be launched at a transonic or subsonic speed, a value of the gyroscopic stability factor in the range ($1.5 < S_g < 2.0$) should be selected, to provide an adequate flight dynamic safety factor.

10.10 INITIAL CONDITIONS FOR DAMPED EPICYCLIC MOTION

The damping exponents in equation (10.94) have a small effect on the initial conditions. In section 10.6 of this chapter, equations (10.90) through (10.93) defined the relationships between the initial complex yaw and yaw rate, and the amplitudes of the fast and slow epicyclic yaw arms. We will again neglect the very small yaw of repose, and differentiate the remainder of equation (10.94) with respect to s:

$$\xi' = (\lambda_F + i\phi'_F)K_F e^{i\phi_F} + (\lambda_S + i\phi'_S)K_S e^{i\phi_S} \qquad \textbf{(10.115)}$$

At the muzzle of the gun, $S = 0$, and the initial complex yaw and yaw rate become:

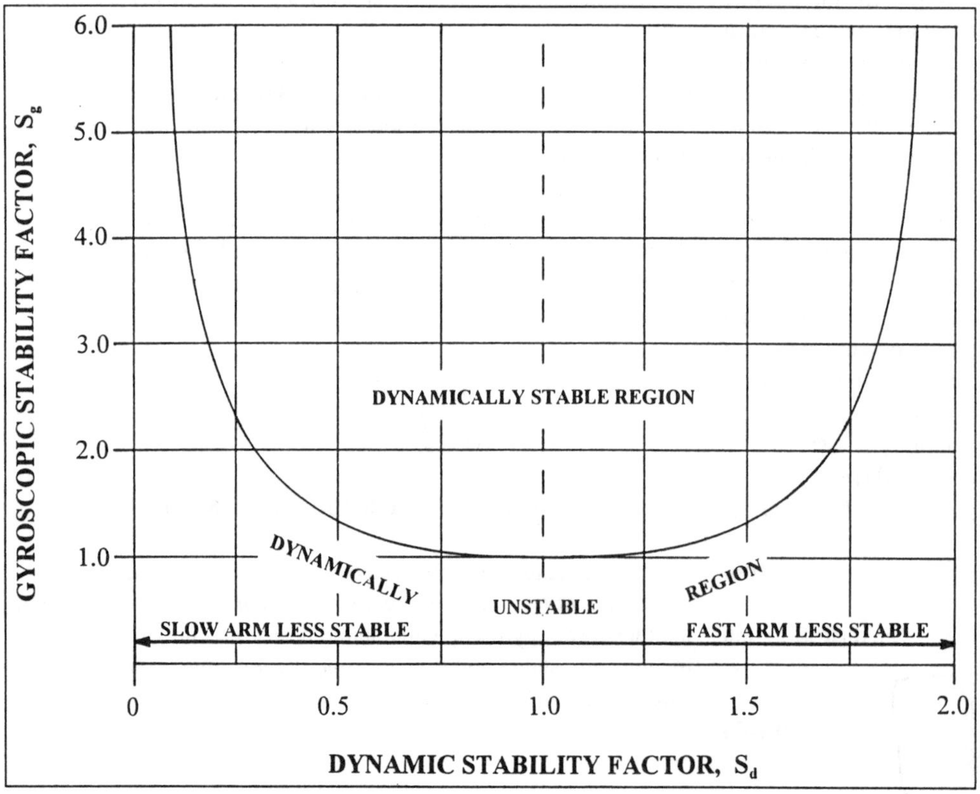

Figure 10.5 Gyroscopic Stability Factor versus Dynamic Stability Factor.

$$\boxed{\xi_0 = K_{F_0} e^{i\phi_{F0}} + K_{S_0} e^{i\phi_{S0}}} \quad \textbf{(10.116)}$$

$$\boxed{\xi_0' = (\lambda_F + i\phi_F')K_{F_0} e^{i\phi_{F0}} + (\lambda_S + i\phi_S')K_{S_0} e^{i\phi_{S0}}} \quad \textbf{(10.117)}$$

Equations (10.116) and (10.117) may be solved for the initial amplitudes and phase angles of the fast and slow arms, in terms of the initial yaw and yaw rate:

$$\boxed{K_{F_0} e^{i\phi_{F0}} = \frac{\xi_0' - (\lambda_S + i\phi_S')\xi_0}{\lambda_F - \lambda_S + i(\phi_F' - \phi_S')}} \quad \textbf{(10.118)}$$

$$\boxed{K_{S_0} e^{i\phi_{S0}} = \frac{\xi_0' - (\lambda_F + i\phi_F')\xi_0}{\lambda_S - \lambda_F + i(\phi_S' - \phi_F')}} \quad \textbf{(10.119)}$$

In general, the damping exponents are between one and two orders of magnitude smaller than the turning rates, and very good approximations to equations (10.118) and (10.119) are given by:

$$\boxed{K_{F_0} e^{i\phi_{F0}} = \left(\frac{i\xi_0' + \phi_S'\xi_0}{\phi_F' - \phi_S'}\right)} \quad \textbf{(10.120)}$$

$$\boxed{K_{S_0} e^{i\phi_{S0}} = \left(\frac{i\xi_0' + \phi_F'\xi_0}{\phi_F' - \phi_S'}\right)} \quad \textbf{(10.121)}$$

Note that the only difference between equations (10.120) and (10.121), and those derived previously as equations (10.92) and (10.93), is the zero-subscript on the amplitudes of the fast and slow epicyclic yaw arms.

10.11 AN EXAMPLE OF THE LINEARIZED PITCHING AND YAWING MOTION

In Example 9.1 of Chapter 9, a six-degrees-of-freedom trajectory for the .308," 168 Grain Sierra International Bullet was illustrated. The muzzle velocity was 2600 feet/second, and the rifling twist rate used was 12 inches/turn. An initial yaw rate of 25 radians/second (which produced the experimentally observed average first maximum yaw of 2 degrees) was used. Using the physical properties listed in Table 9.2, and the aerodynamic characteristics listed in Appendix A of Chapter 9, we will calculate the gyroscopic and dynamic stability factors of the Sierra match bullet at the instant the bullet separates from the gun muzzle. Finally, we will plot the pitching and yawing motion predicted by the linearized equations over the first fifteen yards of flight, and compare the result against the 6-DOF calculation that was shown as Figure 9.2 in the previous chapter.

At a muzzle velocity of 2600 feet/second, the ICAO (see Chapter 8 for the definition of this atmosphere) sea-level launch Mach number is 2.33, and the air density is 0.076474 pounds per cubic foot. The maximum yaw amplitude over the first fifteen yards of flight is 2.0 degrees, and only the Magnus moment coefficient shows significant nonlinear behavior at this small angle of attack. Values of the physical and aerodynamic characteristics we will need are:

$$k_x^{-2} = 9.224; k_y^{-2} = 1.238; C_{D_0} = 0.331; C_{M_\alpha} = 2.63; C_{L_\alpha} = 2.75;$$

$$\left(C_{M_q} + C_{M_{\dot\alpha}}\right) = -8.2; \left[Average C_{M_{p\alpha}} = -0.22\right]; \left(\frac{pd}{V}\right)_0 = 0.16127 rad./cal.$$

$$P = 0.021645; \frac{\rho S d}{2m} = 0.000021158; \xi_0' = -i\beta_0' = -i\frac{d}{V}\dot\beta = -0.000246795i$$

Values of M, H, T, and S_g are now readily obtained:

$$M = 0.000068889; H = 0.00026597; T = 0.000015249; S_g = 1.70$$

The dynamic stability factor, S_d, is now calculated, using equation (10.107), and we find that $S_d = 0.1147$. Substituting this value into equation (10.114) shows that S_g must be greater than 4.6, for dynamic stability! (Note that the launch gyroscopic stability factor is only 1.7). Furthermore, Figure 10.5 indicates that the dynamic instability will occur in the slow mode. Calculating the required epicyclic parameters, we obtain:

$$K_{F_0} e^{i\phi_{F0}} = -0.017767; K_{S_0} e^{i\phi_{S0}} = 0.017767$$

$$\phi_{F_0} = 180°; \phi_{S_0} = 0°$$

$$\phi_F' = 0.017768 radians/caliber; \phi_S' = 0.003877 radians/caliber$$

$$\lambda_F = -0.00031645 per caliber; \lambda_S = +0.00005048 per caliber$$

The slow arm shows a mild small-yaw dynamic instability, as predicted. This case is an excellent example of the dynamic stability criteria of this chapter. The value of S_g at launch is 1.7; yet the bullet is dynamically unstable, and the slow epicyclic yaw arm is undamped! At first glance, it might appear desirable to increase the rifling twist rate, from 12 inches/turn to perhaps 7 inches/turn, which would increase the muzzle gyroscopic stability factor to 5.0, and force the match bullet to be dynamically stable. However, benchrest and match shooters know from long experience that a faster-than-necessary twist of rifling usually has an adverse effect on the accuracy of fire. (In fact, benchrest shooters generally prefer a 14-inch twist, that gives a muzzle S_g of 1.25, for the .308," 168 Grain Sierra International bullet). It turns out that it is better for accuracy, in this case, to live with the mild small-yaw dynamic instability. Note: the slow arm *does not* actually continue to grow without bound, as equation (10.94) predicts for this case. The nonlinear Magnus moment coefficient for this Sierra match bullet becomes less negative at larger yaw levels (see Appendix A of Chapter 9), which leads to limit-cycle yaw behavior. [A discussion of the limit-cycle yaw is deferred until a later chapter, on nonlinear aerodynamic forces and moments].

With the above values for the epicyclic parameters, the pitching and yawing motion over the first fifteen yards of flight was calculated, using equation (10.94). The result is plotted in Figure 10.6. In chapter 9, Figure 9.2 showed the epicyclic pitching and yawing motion for the same case, calculated by a modern six-degrees-of-freedom computer program. An overlay of the two figures shows no discernable difference between the 6-DOF results and the linearized method. Many years experience in modern exterior ballistics has confirmed that, in general, the linearized equations provide very accurate results, for flat-fire trajectories and small-yaw flight.

10.12 THE MOTION OF THE ROTATING $\left[\vec{i},\vec{j},\vec{k}\right]$ COORDINATE SYSTEM

The vector angular velocity of the moving $\left[\vec{i},\vec{j},\vec{k}\right]$ coordinate system, relative to the inertial $\left[\vec{I},\vec{J},\vec{K}\right]$ frame of reference, was given in section 10.2 of this chapter as equation (10.33), and is re-stated here for convenience:

$$\vec{\omega} = \vec{i} \times \frac{d\vec{i}}{dt} = \left(\frac{V}{d}\right)\left[C_{L_\alpha}{}^{*}\left(\vec{i} \times \vec{x}\right) - G\vec{k}\right] \qquad \textbf{(10.33)}$$

If we take the vector dot product of $\vec{i}$ with both sides of equation (10.33):

$$\vec{\omega} \bullet \vec{i} = 0 \qquad \textbf{(10.122)}$$

Equation (10.122) tells us that the $\left[\vec{i},\vec{j},\vec{k}\right]$ coordinate system has no component of vector angular velocity in the direction of the unit vector $\vec{i}$ (tangent to the trajectory); therefore the $\left[\vec{i},\vec{j},\vec{k}\right]$ system is a *non-rolling coordinate system*, relative to earth-fixed coordinates. With the help of equation (10.50):

$$\frac{d\vec{j}}{dt} = \vec{\omega} \times \vec{j} = -\left(\frac{V}{d}\right)\left[C_{L_\alpha}{}^{*}\alpha - G\right]\vec{i} \qquad \textbf{(10.123)}$$

$$\frac{d\vec{k}}{dt} = \vec{\omega} \times \vec{k} = -\left(\frac{V}{d}\right)C_{L_\alpha}{}^{*}\beta\vec{i} \qquad \textbf{(10.124)}$$

If the departure of $\vec{k}$ from the earth-fixed horizontal (X-Z) plane is small, then $\vec{j}$ will also remain close to the earth-fixed vertical (X-Y) plane, because we have restricted the problem to small yaw and flat-fire trajectories. If the independent variable in equation (10.124) is changed from time to dimensionless arc length, s:

$$\vec{k}' = -C_{L_\alpha}{}^{*}\beta\vec{i} \qquad \textbf{(10.125)}$$

Our only concern is the departure of the vector $\vec{k}$ from the earth-fixed horizontal plane; therefore we need the component of equation (10.125) in the earth-fixed $\vec{J}$, or vertical direction. Equation (10.16) is re-stated here for convenience:

$$\vec{J} = \sin\phi\cos\theta\vec{i} + \cos\theta\vec{j} - \sin\phi\sin\theta\vec{k} \qquad \textbf{(10.16)}$$

The vector dot product of equation (10.125) and equation (10.16) yields:

$$\vec{k}' \bullet \vec{J} = -C_{L_\alpha}{}^{*}\beta\sin\phi\cos\theta \qquad \textbf{(10.126)}$$

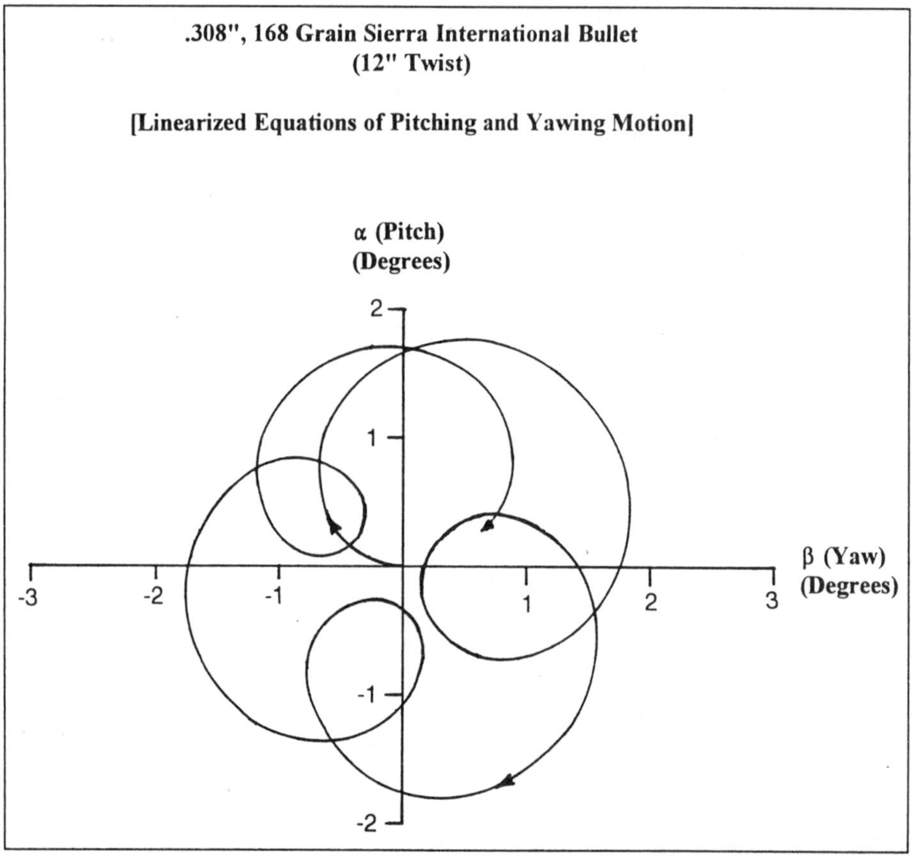

Figure 10.6 Pitch versus Yaw (Linearized Theory), Muzzle to 15 Yards Range.

Finally, from equation (10.94), we have:

$$\sin\beta \approx \beta = K_{F_0} e^{\lambda_F s} \sin\left(\phi_{F_0} + \phi'_F s\right) + K_{S_0} e^{\lambda_S s} \sin\left(\phi_{S_0} + \phi'_S s\right) + \beta_R \qquad \textbf{(10.127)}$$

Now, the vertical and horizontal flight path angles, ϕ and θ, are very small angles for flat-fire trajectories that lie in close proximity to the earth-fixed X-axis. Therefore the quantity $(\beta \sin\phi)$ is of order of a starred coefficient, and the right hand side of equation (10.126) is of the same order as the product of two starred coefficients, or $[10^{-6}]$.

Integrating the above expression for $\vec{k}\cdot\vec{J}$ over the length (say, 10^3 calibers) of a typical aeroballistic firing range, we find that the departure of the unit vector $\vec{k}$ from the earth-fixed horizontal plane is of the order of $\sin^{-1}(10^{-3})$, or about 0.06 degree. This a negligible value, and our non-rolling $\left[\vec{i},\vec{j},\vec{k}\right]$ coordinate system is therefore essentially equivalent to fixed-plane coordinates, for small yaw and flat-fire trajectories over moderate ranges.

10.13 PITCHING AND YAWING MOTION OF A SLIGHTLY ASYMMETRIC MISSILE

No actual projectile is ever *exactly* rotationally symmetric, although many are close enough for all practical purposes. The missile may have a small control surface deflection, or a small wing and/or tail incidence. Structural damage due to rough handling may result in a bent fin, or a slightly bent projectile body. In addition to configurational asymmetries, the projectile may be slightly mass-asymmetric, due to such factors as runout in the shell wall thickness, or voids in the shell casing or the payload. Regardless of the physical cause, any of the above mass or configurational asymmetries will cause the missile to fly with a small trim angle of attack. Both fin- and spin-stabilized projectiles can exhibit tricyclic yawing motion, but spin lock-in and catastrophic yaw (to be discussed later in this section) have only been observed for finned missiles.

J. D. Nicolaides introduced the tricyclic theory in 1953 (Ref. 8) to account for several flight-dynamic phenomena that had been observed for statically stable finned projectiles. For example: (1) non-rolling finned projectiles usually have large dispersion, and adding even a slow roll reduces the dispersion; (2) even for generally well-performing finned missiles, occasionally one goes berserk, and is observed to tumble in flight, and (3) peculiar pitching and yawing motion is often observed when the roll frequency and the pitch frequency approach coincidence.

We will make the fundamental assumption that the contribution of the asymmetry is sufficiently "slight" that it may be added linearly to our differential equations of motion, without significantly violating the previously-made assumptions of trigonal or greater rotational symmetry. In practice, it turns out that most mass and configurational asymmetries that have been observed in spark photography range firings over the past forty years do indeed fall within the "slight" asymmetry requirement.

In this chapter, the derivation and solution of tricyclic motion parallels that of Nicolaides (Ref. 8) and Murphy (Ref. 2). Nicolaides and Murphy show that the general effect of a small asymmetry is to add a "trim normal force and side force," and a "trim pitching moment and yawing moment" into the aerodynamic force-moment system. Neglecting the very small yaw of repose, the differential equation for the pitching and yawing motion of an "almost symmetric" missile is given by a modified form of equation (10.66):

$$\xi'' + (H - iP)\xi' - (M + iPT)\xi = iAe^{i\phi} \qquad \textbf{(10.128)}$$

where $A = \dfrac{\rho S d}{2m}\left[k_y^{-2}\left(C_{m_0} + iC_{n_0}\right) + (\phi' - 1)\left(C_{Y_0} + iC_{Z_0}\right)\right]$

$C_{m_0} + iC_{n_0}$ is the complex sum of the trim pitching moment and the trim yawing moment coefficients

$C_{Y_0} + iC_{Z_0}$ is the complex sum of the trim normal force and the trim side force coefficients

$\phi' = \dfrac{pd}{V}$, and $\phi = \int_0^{s} \phi' ds_1$, the roll angle

The remaining symbols were defined below equation (10.66).

For a constant roll rate, the aerodynamic asymmetry introduces an exponential forcing function. A particular solution to this inhomogeneous equation is readily obtained by assuming a solution of the same form (see any textbook on ordinary differential equations):

$\xi = K_T e^{i(\phi_0 + \phi)}$, where ϕ_0 is the initial roll angle at $s = 0$. **(10.129)**

The general solution of equation (10.128), for constant roll rate is:

$$\boxed{\xi = K_F e^{i\phi_F} + K_S e^{i\phi_S} + K_T e^{i(\phi_0 + \phi)}} \qquad \textbf{(10.130)}$$

where $$K_T e^{i\phi_0} = \frac{-iA}{\phi'^2 - P\phi' + M - i(\phi' H - PT)} \qquad \textbf{(10.131)}$$

The denominator of the right hand side of equation (10.131) is usually dominated by the real part, which is the same quadratic expression we observed earlier for the epicyclic pitch and yaw frequencies. Thus, if the spin rate is equal to one of the two characteristic pitching frequencies, the amplitude of the trim arm, K_T, can grow to a large value. For most rolling missiles, this *spin-pitch resonance phenomenon* occurs when the spin rate equals the fast epicyclic turning rate.

Note that if the roll rate is zero throughout the flight, the tricyclic arm will maintain a fixed orientation in space. The aerodynamic lift force, acting on this constant-direction trim angle of attack, will then produce a lateral trajectory deflection that increases quadratically with increasing downrange distance. Thus, finned missiles should always be given at least a slow roll rate, to average out the effect of small asymmetries, and thereby reduce the dispersion.

Most missiles do not, in general, have constant roll rates. If the roll rate happens to be rapidly passing through resonance, equation (10.130) turns out to be a very poor approximation. Murphy has studied the case of a varying roll rate, using the method of variation of parameters. The interested reader is encouraged to study the details of this derivation in Reference 2.

Spin-Pitch Lock-In and Catastrophic Yaw

Nicolaides first introduced the concept of aerodynamic moments that depend on the roll orientation angle (Ref. 9), and he demonstrated the possibility of spin-pitch lock-in, and large amplification factors for the trim angle. In this section, we will follow Murphy's treatment (Ref. 2) of the catastrophic yaw phenomenon.

The complex angle of attack, ξ, may be described in polar coordinates by an amplitude, δ, and an orientation angle, Ψ, which is the angle between the plane of the angle of attack, and a fixed plane on the missile, such as one containing a fin. Nicolaides' model assumed that there is both a roll moment and a side moment, depending on δ and Ψ. The revised form of the rolling moment coefficient becomes:

$$C_l = \delta_F C_{l_\delta} + \left(\frac{pd}{V}\right) C_{l_p} + \delta C_{l_\alpha}(\Psi, \delta) \qquad \textbf{(10.132)}$$

If the missile has an angle of rotational symmetry, Ψ_S, then C_{l_α} is periodic with period Ψ_S. If there is a differential fin cant, δ_F, used to generate roll, then no plane of mirror symmetry can exist. If none of the fins are differentially canted $(\delta_F = 0)$, and the missile has a plane of mirror symmetry, then the rolling moment due to orientation must be zero when the angle of attack plane lies in the plane of symmetry. (This follows from the fact that if we measure Ψ from a plane of mirror symmetry, and transform coordinates by a mirror reflection, the missile maps onto itself. The rolling moments are reversed, but otherwise unchanged).

Application of the Maple-Synge analysis (Ref. 10) to a missile with n identical, equally-spaced fins, leads (see Ref. 2) to the simplest expression for C_{l_α}:

$$C_{l_\alpha} = b_{10}\delta^{n-1}\sin n\Psi \qquad \textbf{(10.133)}$$

Substituting equation (10.133) into the expression for the general rolling moment [equation (10.132)], the differential equation for the rolling motion [equation 10.71)] assumes the revised form:

$$\phi'' + K_P\phi' - K_\delta - K_\alpha\left(\tilde{\Psi} - \phi, \delta\right) = 0 \qquad \textbf{(10.134)}$$

where $K_\alpha = \dfrac{\rho S d^3}{2 I_x}\delta C_{l_\alpha}$

$\tilde{\Psi} = \Psi + \phi$ is the orientation of the angle of attack plane with respect to a fixed plane

During conventional spin-pitch resonance, a missile performs a circular yawing motion at the constant frequency, $\tilde{\Psi}'$. For a missile in circular constant frequency motion, equation (10.134) predicts a constant rolling motion when $\tilde{\Psi} - \phi = \Psi^*$, a constant, and:

$$\tilde{\Psi}' = \phi' = \frac{K_\delta + K_\alpha\left(\Psi^*, \delta\right)}{K_P} \qquad \textbf{(10.135)}$$

When this occurs, the rolling motion is "locked" to the circular pitching motion, and the missile performs "lunar motion" (the moon rotates about the earth in such a way that it always presents the same face to our view). For many pitching and yawing motions that are nearly circular, lock-in can occur and a resonance situation can exist. The occurrence of lock-in depends on the roll frequency and the pitch frequency being close to each other at some point of the flight, because widely different frequencies will make C_{l_α} vary rapidly with a nearly-zero average, and it will then have little effect on the pitching and yawing motion.

If we now consider the possibility of a side moment dependent on roll orientation, a Magnus-like moment could exist for very small roll rates. If we add this term and an asymmetric moment term (see Ref. 2) to our differential equation of pitching and yawing motion, we find:

$$\xi'' + (H - iP)\xi' - \left[M + i\left(PT + M_S\right)\right]\xi = iAe^{i\phi} \qquad \textbf{(10.136)}$$

where $M_S = \dfrac{\rho S d}{2m} k_y^{-2} C_{SM_\alpha}$

For circular pitching and yawing motion that is "locked-in" with the rolling motion:

$$K_T e^{i\phi_0} = \frac{A}{\phi' H - PT - M_S\left(\Psi^*, K_T\right)} \qquad \textbf{(10.137)}$$

If we have an unfortunate value of M_S that makes the denominator of equation (10.137) nearly zero, a very large amplification factor is possible. This can cause the situation that Nicolaides described as "catastrophic yaw."

10.14 SUMMARY

The linearized differential equations of pitching and yawing motion for spinning and non-spinning symmetric projectiles, flying at small yaw along flat-fire trajectories, have been derived and solved in this chapter. The solution shows that the pitching and yawing motion of symmetric projectiles is epicyclic in nature. Criteria for gyroscopic and dynamic stability are derived. If the projectile is dynamically stable, the epicyclic motion is damped, and eventually the transient pitching and yawing motion will disappear. For a dynamically unstable shell, the epicyclic motion will grow, sometimes without bound, or in other cases, to a limit-cycle yaw value. The solution shows that there is also a small, steady-state yaw of repose, in addition to the epicyclic motion.

The differential equation for roll, or axial spin was derived and solved, for bodies of revolution and for finned missiles, with canted or uncanted fins. The solution shows that there are three distinct cases of rolling or spinning motion. For unfinned, spin-stabilized bodies of revolution, the spin per caliber of travel always increases as the projectile travels downrange, along a flat-fire trajectory. For finned missiles with uncanted fins, the spin per caliber of travel usually damps rapidly along the flight path. For finned missiles with *canted* fins, the spin per caliber of travel approaches a steady-state value along the trajectory.

The pitching, yawing, and rolling motions of slightly asymmetric projectiles were studied. The phenomena of spin-pitch resonance, spin lock-in, and catastrophic yaw were also analyzed, and were shown to explain some occurrences of poor flight characteristics that have occasionally been observed for rolling, finned missile configurations.

REFERENCES

1. Synge, J., and B. Griffith, *Principles of Mechanics*, McGraw-Hill, New York, NY, 1959.

2. Murphy, C. H., "Free Flight Motion of Symmetric Missiles," Ballistic Research Laboratories Report No. 1216, 1963.

3. Kent, R. H., "Notes on a Theory of Spinning Shell," Ballistic Research Laboratories Report No. 898, 1954.

4. Kelley, J. L., and E. J. McShane, "On the Motion of a Projectile With Small or Slowly Changing Yaw," Ballistic Research Laboratories Report No. 446, 1944.

5. Mann, F. W., *The Bullet's Flight from Powder to Target*, Munn & Company, New York, New York, 1909.

6. Murphy, C. H., "On Stability Criteria of the Kelley-McShane Linearized Theory of Yawing Motion," Ballistic Research Laboratories Report No. 853, 1953.

7. McShane, E. J., J. L. Kelley and F. V. Reno, *Exterior Ballistics*, University of Denver Press, 1953.

8. Nicolaides, J. D., "On the Free Flight Motion of Missiles Having Slight Configurational Asymmetries," Ballistic Research Laboratories Report No. 858, 1953.

9. Nicolaides, J. D., "Two Nonlinear Problems in the Flight Dynamics of Modern Ballistic Missiles," IAS Report 59-17, 1959.

10. Maple, C. G., and J. L. Synge, "Aerodynamic Symmetry of Projectiles," *Quarterly of Applied Mathematics*, Volume 4, 1949.

11

Linearized Swerving Motion of Rotationally Symmetric Projectiles

11.1 INTRODUCTION

In the introduction to Chapter 8, we noted that the point-mass trajectory is a practical and accurate approximation to the flight of any projectile whose pitching and yawing motion is very small at all points along the flight path. In the present chapter, the point-mass trajectory (with aerodynamic drag and gravity as the only significant forces), is regarded as a "first approximation" to the actual trajectory. If the projectile is pitching and yawing, the aerodynamic lift force "pulls" the center-of-mass in a direction perpendicular to the flight path. The motion of the projectile's center-of-mass, perpendicular to the point-mass trajectory, is called the *swerving motion*.

11.2 THE DIFFERENTIAL EQUATION OF SWERVING MOTION

The vector differential equation that describes the projectile's center-of-mass motion, along a flat-fire trajectory with no wind, was derived as equation (10.21) in Chapter 10. We re-state that equation here, in slightly different form, as equation (11.1):

$$\frac{d\vec{V}}{dt} = \frac{-\rho S C_D V}{2m}\vec{V} + \frac{\rho S C_{L_\alpha} V^2}{2m}\left[\vec{i} \times \left(\vec{x} \times \vec{i}\right)\right] - g\vec{J} \qquad \textbf{(11.1)}$$

where, $\vec{V}$ = vector velocity of the projectile with respect to earth-fixed $\left[\vec{I},\vec{J},\vec{K}\right]$ coordinates

$\vec{i} = \vec{V}/|V|$, a unit vector in the direction of $\vec{V}$; $\vec{i}$ is always tangent to the flight path

$\vec{x}$ = a unit vector along the projectile's rotational axis of symmetry

V = scalar magnitude of the vector velocity

g = acceleration due to gravity

t = time

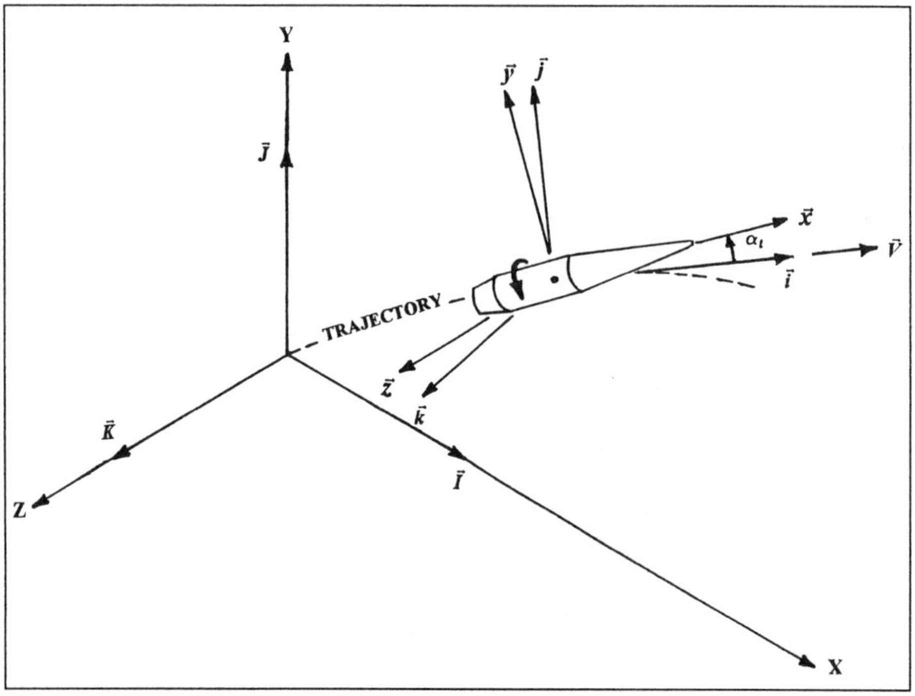

Figure 11.1 Non-Rolling and Body-Fixed Coordinate System.

ρ = air density

d = projectile reference diameter

S = projectile reference area (usually taken as S = $\pi d^2/4$) $\pi d^2/4$

m = projectile mass

C_D = drag force coefficient

C_{L_α} = lift force coefficient

Figure 11.1 illustrates the $\left[\vec{I},\vec{J},\vec{K}\right]$ and $\left[\vec{i},\vec{j},\vec{k}\right]$ coordinate systems used in this chapter.

The unit vector $\vec{x}$, in the rotating $\left[\vec{i},\vec{j},\vec{k}\right]$ coordinate system, was defined as equation (10.43) in Chapter 10. We re-state that equation for this chapter, as equation (11.2):

$$\vec{x} = \cos\alpha\cos\beta\vec{i} + \sin\alpha\cos\beta\vec{j} + \sin\beta\vec{k} \tag{11.2}$$

Equation (11.2) does not assume small yaw; it is valid for large as well as small pitch and yaw angles. However, our linearized flat-fire equations *do* assume small yaw, and we will therefore adopt the same small angle approximations that were used in Chapter 10:

$$\vec{x} = \gamma\vec{i} + \alpha\vec{j} + \beta\vec{k} \tag{11.3}$$

where $\gamma = \cos\alpha\cos\beta \approx 1 : \alpha \approx \sin\alpha\cos\beta \approx \sin\alpha : \beta \approx \sin\beta$

Then $\vec{i}\bullet\vec{x} = \gamma$, and the vector triple product in equation (11.1) reduces to:

$$\vec{i}\times\left(\vec{x}\times\vec{i}\right) = \vec{x} - \left(\vec{i}\bullet\vec{x}\right)\vec{i} = \alpha\vec{j} + \beta\vec{k} \tag{11.4}$$

We will again adopt the "starred convention" (Ref. 1) for aerodynamic coefficients, for the remainder of this chapter. The definition of a starred coefficient is the product of the coefficient and the dimensionless quantity, $\left(\rho Sd/2m\right)$. The starred coefficients for drag and lift become:

$$C_D^* = \frac{\rho Sd}{2m}C_D \text{ , and } C_{L_\alpha}{}^* = \frac{\rho Sd}{2m}C_{L_\alpha} \tag{11.5}$$

For flat-fire trajectories that remain everywhere close to the earth-fixed X-axis, the flight path elevation and azimuth angles, ϕ and θ, respectively, are very small. Substituting the small angle approximations into equations (10.13) and (10.14) of Chapter 10, we find that $\vec{j} \approx \vec{J}$, and $\vec{k} \approx \vec{K}$. The vector triple product in equation (11.4) may therefore be written as:

$$\vec{i}\times\left(\vec{x}\times\vec{i}\right) \approx \alpha\vec{J} + \beta\vec{K} \tag{11.6}$$

In equations (5.4) and (5.5) of Chapter 5, the vector velocity and acceleration were expanded into components:

$$\vec{V} = V_x\vec{I} + V_y\vec{J} + V_z\vec{K} \tag{11.7}$$

$$\frac{d\vec{V}}{dt} = \dot{V}_x\vec{I} + \dot{V}_y\vec{J} + \dot{V}_z\vec{K} \tag{11.8}$$

With the help of the small angle approximations, and the definitions of equations (11.5) through (11.8), equation (11.1) may be written in vector component form, in the earth-fixed $\left[\vec{I},\vec{J},\vec{K}\right]$ coordinate system:

$$\frac{d\vec{V}}{dt} = \dot{V}_x\vec{I} + \dot{V}_y\vec{J} + \dot{V}_z\vec{K} = -C_D^*\frac{V}{d}\left[V_x\vec{I} + V_y\vec{J} + V_z\vec{K}\right] \tag{11.9}$$

$$+C_{L_\alpha}{}^*\frac{V^2}{d}\left[\alpha\vec{J} + \beta\vec{K}\right] - g\vec{J}$$

Equating coefficients of the unit vectors on both sides of equation (11.9):

$$\dot{V}_x = -C_D^*\frac{V}{d}V_x \tag{11.10}$$

$$\dot{V}_y = -C_D^*\frac{V}{d}V_y + C_{L_\alpha}{}^*\frac{V^2}{d}\alpha - g \tag{11.11}$$

$$\dot{V}_z = -C_D^*\frac{V}{d}V_z + C_{L_\alpha}{}^*\frac{V^2}{d}\beta \tag{11.12}$$

The independent variable is now changed from time to dimensionless arclength along the trajectory, *s*, measured in calibers of travel:

$$s = \frac{1}{d}\int_0^t Vdt \tag{11.13}$$

For the remainder of this chapter, a prime (′) or double prime (″) superscript will denote a first or second derivative with respect to dimensionless arclength, s. (Note that for a flat-fire trajectory, arclength s is insignificantly different from downrange distance, in calibers, along the X-axis).

The components of velocity and acceleration, with arclength, s, as the independent variable, are:

$$V_y = \frac{V_x}{d}Y' \text{, and } V_z = \frac{V_x}{d}Z' \tag{11.14}$$

$$\dot{V}_x = \frac{V_x}{d}V_x' \tag{11.15}$$

$$\dot{V}_y = \frac{d^2Y}{dt^2} = \left(\frac{V_x}{d}\right)^2\left[Y'' + \left(\frac{V_x'}{V_x}\right)Y'\right] \tag{11.16}$$

$$\dot{V}_z = \frac{d^2Z}{dt^2} = \left(\frac{V_x}{d}\right)^2 \left[Z'' + \left(\frac{V_x'}{V_x}\right) Z'\right] \quad \textbf{(11.17)}$$

For flat-fire trajectories, whose departure at any point from the earth-fixed X-axis is small, we may replace V_x with V, without significant error. Equations (11.14) through (11.17) are now substituted into equations (11.10) through (11.12), and we obtain:

$$\dot{V}_x = \frac{V}{d}V' = -C_D^* \frac{V}{d}V, \quad or\ V' = -C_D^* V \quad \textbf{(11.18)}$$

$$\dot{V}_y = \left(\frac{V}{d}\right)^2 \left[Y'' + \left(\frac{V'}{V}\right)Y'\right] = -C_D^*\left(\frac{V}{d}\right)^2 Y' + C_{L_\alpha}{}^*\left(\frac{V^2}{d}\right)\alpha - g \quad \textbf{(11.19)}$$

$$\dot{V}_z = \left(\frac{V}{d}\right)^2 \left[Z'' + \left(\frac{V'}{V}\right)Z'\right] = -C_D^*\left(\frac{V}{d}\right)^2 Z' + C_{L_\alpha}{}^*\left(\frac{V^2}{d}\right)\beta \quad \textbf{(11.20)}$$

The solution of equation (11.18) for constant C_D was given as equation (10.68) in Chapter 10, and is re-stated here as equation (11.21):

$$\boxed{V = V_0 e^{-C_D^* s}} \quad \textbf{(11.21)}$$

We now substitute the definition into equations (11.19) and (11.20), and divide both sides of these equations by $(V/d)^2$:

$$Y'' = C_{L_\alpha}{}^* \alpha d - \frac{gd^2}{V^2} \quad \textbf{(11.22)}$$

$$Z'' = C_{L_\alpha}{}^* \beta d \quad \textbf{(11.23)}$$

Let $\quad Y = y\,d$, and $Z = z\,d$, $\quad$ **(11.24)**

where $\quad y$ = vertical component of swerve (sometimes called "heave"), measured in calibers

z = horizontal component of swerve, measured in calibers

Note that the vertical and horizontal components of swerve, y and z, are unrelated to the $\vec{y}$ and $\vec{z}$ unit vectors used in the nonrolling coordinate system attached to the projectile.

Substituting equations (11.24) into equations (11.22) and (11.23):

$$y'' = C_{L_\alpha}{}^* \alpha - \frac{gd}{V^2} \quad \textbf{(11.25)}$$

$$z'' = C_{L_\alpha}{}^* \beta \quad \textbf{(11.26)}$$

We now multiply equation (11.26) by $i = \sqrt{-1}$, add it to equation (11.25) and define $\xi = \alpha + i\beta$, as was done in the previous chapter:

$$y'' + iz'' = C_{L_\alpha}{}^* \xi - \frac{gd}{V^2} \quad \textbf{(11.27)}$$

Equation (11.21) is now substituted into equation (11.27):

$$\boxed{y'' + iz'' = C_{L_\alpha}{}^* \xi - \frac{gd}{V_0^2} e^{2C_D^* s}} \quad \textbf{(11.28)}$$

Equation (11.28) is the complex, second-order differential equation that describes the point-mass motion plus the swerving motion due to lift, for a spinning or non-spinning symmetric projectile, flying at small yaw along a flat-fire trajectory. Integrating equation (11.28) twice, we obtain:

$$\boxed{y + iz = (y_0 + iz_0) + (y_0' + iz_0')s - \frac{gds^2}{2V_0^2}\left[\frac{e^{2C_D^* s} - 2C_D^* s - 1}{2(C_D^* s)^2}\right] + C_{L_\alpha}{}^* \int_0^s \int_0^{r_2} \xi\, dr_1 dr_2} \quad \textbf{(11.29)}$$

where $\quad y_0$ = initial value of y (calibers)

z_0 = initial value of z (calibers)

$y_0' = \tan\phi_0$, the tangent of the trajectory's vertical angle of departure (positive upward)

$z_0' = \tan\theta_0$, the tangent of the trajectory's horizontal angle of departure (positive to the right, when looking downrange)

The first three terms on the right-hand side of equation (11.29) describe the flat-fire, point-mass trajectory, which accounts for the forces of aerodynamic drag and gravity. The last term (with the double integral) in equation (11.29) is the center-of-mass *swerving motion*, caused by the aerodynamic lift force acting on the pitching and yawing motion.

11.3 SOLUTION OF THE DIFFERENTIAL EQUATION FOR SWERVE

The solution of the differential equation of pitching and yawing motion was given as equation (10.94) in the previous chapter. We re-state that equation, in slightly different form, as equation (11.30):

$$\xi = K_{F_0} e^{i\phi_{F_0}} e^{(\lambda_F + i\phi_F')s} + K_{S_0} e^{i\phi_{S_0}} e^{(\lambda_S + i\phi_S')s} + i\frac{PG}{M} \quad \textbf{(11.30)}$$

where $\quad \xi = \alpha + i\beta$

K_{F_0} = the initial amplitude of the fast epicyclic yaw arm

K_{S_0} = the initial amplitude of the slow epicyclic yaw arm

ϕ_{F_0} = initial phase angle of the fast epicyclic yaw arm

ϕ_{S_0} = initial phase angle of the slow epicyclic yaw arm

λ_F = damping rate of the fast epicyclic yaw arm

λ_S = damping rate of the slow epicyclic yaw arm

ϕ'_F = turning rate of the fast epicyclic yaw arm

ϕ'_S = turning rate of the slow epicyclic yaw arm

$$P = \left(\frac{I_x}{I_y}\right)\left(\frac{pd}{V}\right) = \phi'_F + \phi'_S$$

$$M = k_y^{-2} C_{M_\alpha}{}^* \approx \phi'_F \phi'_S$$

$$G = \frac{gd\cos\phi}{V^2} = \frac{gd}{V_0^2} e^{2C_D^* s}$$

Equation (11.30) is now substituted into equation (11.29). The evaluation of the double integral in equation (11.29) is straightforward, and may be found in any textbook on integral calculus.

Let
$$I_L = \int_0^s \int_0^{r^2} \xi \, dr_1 dr_2 \qquad \textbf{(11.31)}$$

Performing the indicated double integration, we find:

$$I_L = -\left[\left(\frac{\lambda_F - i\phi'_F}{\lambda_F^2 + \phi_F'^2}\right)K_{F_0} e^{i\phi_{F0}} + \left(\frac{\lambda_S - i\phi'_S}{\lambda_S^2 + \phi_S'^2}\right)K_{S_0} e^{i\phi_{S0}}\right]s \qquad \textbf{(11.32)}$$

$$+\left(R_{F_1} - iR_{F_2}\right)K_{F_0} e^{i\phi_{F0}}\left[e^{(\lambda_F + i\phi'_F)s} - 1\right]$$

$$+\left(R_{S_1} - iR_{S_2}\right)K_{S_0} e^{i\phi_{S0}}\left[e^{(\lambda_S + i\phi'_S)s} - 1\right] + i\left(\frac{PG_0}{M}\right)s^2\left[\frac{e^{2C_D^* s} - 2C_D^* s - 1}{\left(2C_D^* s\right)^2}\right]$$

where
$$R_{F_1} = \frac{\lambda_F^2 - \phi_F'^2}{\left(\lambda_F^2 + \phi_F'^2\right)^2} \approx -\frac{1}{\phi_F'^2} \text{ for } \lambda_F^2 << \phi_F^2 \qquad \textbf{(11.33)}$$

$$R_{F_2} = \frac{2\lambda_F \phi'_F}{\left(\lambda_F^2 + \phi_F'^2\right)^2} \approx 0 \qquad \textbf{(11.34)}$$

$$R_{S_1} = \frac{\lambda_S^2 - \phi_S'^2}{\left(\lambda_S^2 + \phi_S'^2\right)^2} \approx -\frac{1}{\phi_S'^2}, \text{ for } \lambda_S^2 << \phi_S^2 \qquad \textbf{(11.35)}$$

$$R_{S_2} = \frac{2\lambda_S \phi'_S}{\left(\lambda_S^2 + \phi_S'^2\right)^2} \approx 0 \qquad \textbf{(11.36)}$$

$$G_0 = \frac{gd}{V_0^2} \qquad \textbf{(11.37)}$$

In general, the damping exponents are between one and two orders of magnitude smaller than the epicyclic turning rates, and a very accurate approximation to equation (11.32) is given by:

$$I_L = i\left[\frac{1}{\phi'_F}K_{F_0} e^{i\phi_{F0}} + \frac{1}{\phi'_S}K_{S_0} e^{i\phi_{S0}}\right]s - \frac{1}{\phi_F'^2}K_{F_0} e^{i\phi_{F0}}\left[e^{(\lambda_F + i\phi'_F)s} - 1\right]$$
$$-\frac{1}{\phi_S'^2}K_{S_0} e^{i\phi_{S0}}\left[e^{(\lambda_S + i\phi'_S)s} - 1\right] + i\left(\frac{PG_0}{M}\right)s^2\left[\frac{e^{2C_D^* s} - 2C_D^* s - 1}{\left(2C_D^* s\right)^2}\right]$$

(11.38)

The product of the starred lift force coefficient, $C_{L_\alpha}{}^*$, and equation (11.38), is the complete swerving motion, caused by the aerodynamic lift force acting on the pitching and yawing motion. The first term on the right-hand side of equation (11.38) is a linear term; e.g., the quantity in brackets in the first term is a "slope." The second and third terms on the right-hand side of (11.38) are swerve components that resemble the epicyclic pitching and yawing motion, but with modified amplitudes. The last term in the above equation grows slightly faster than a quadratic dependence on *s*, as a Maclaurin series expansion of the final bracketed term in (11.38) shows:

$$\left[\frac{e^{2C_D^* s} - 2C_D^* s - 1}{\left(2C_D^* s\right)^2}\right] = \frac{1}{2}\left[1 + \frac{2}{3}\left(C_D^* s\right) + \frac{1}{3}\left(C_D^* s\right)^2 + \frac{2}{15}\left(C_D^* s\right)^3 + \cdots\right]$$

(11.39)

We observe that the product $\left[C_{L_\alpha}{}^* I_L\right]$ is composed of three separate parts, and these parts have been given special names in classical exterior ballistics. The first part is called "Aerodynamic Jump," and it is given by the expression:

$$J_A = iC_{L_\alpha}{}^*\left[\frac{K_{F_0}}{\phi'_F} e^{i\phi_{F0}} + \frac{K_{S_0}}{\phi'_S} e^{i\phi_{S0}}\right] \qquad \textbf{(11.40)}$$

The second part is called "Epicyclic Swerve," and its equation is:

$$S_E = -C_{L_\alpha}{}^*\left(\frac{K_{F_0}}{\phi_F'^2} e^{i\phi_{F0}}\left[e^{(\lambda_F + i\phi'_F)s} - 1\right] + \frac{K_{S_0}}{\phi_S'^2} e^{i\phi_{S0}}\left[e^{(\lambda_S + i\phi'_S)s} - 1\right]\right)$$

(11.41)

The third part of the total swerving motion is called "Drift," and it is given by:

$$D_R = iC_{L_\alpha}{}^*\left(\frac{PG_0}{2M}\right)s^2\left[1 + \frac{2}{3}\left(C_D^* s\right) + \frac{1}{3}\left(C_D^* s\right)^2 + \cdots\right] \qquad \textbf{(11.42)}$$

where J_A = *Aerodynamic Jump* (J_A is the tangent of an angle)

S_E = *Epicyclic Swerve* (S_E is an oscillatory motion about the mean flight path)

D_R = *Drift* (a deflection to the right or left of the flight path, for spinning projectiles)

11.4 DISCUSSION OF THE LINEARIZED SWERVING MOTION

If a projectile is statically unbalanced, e.g., its center-of-mass lies laterally off the axis of rotational symmetry, an additional component of swerve, called *"Lateral Throwoff"* is also present. (Note that a saboted projectile may also have a *"Sabot-Discard Jump."* However, the sabot-discard jump can usually be treated as an additional lateral throwoff effect. Lateral throwoff will be discussed in the next chapter). Including the lateral throwoff, the complete flat-fire trajectory consists of five separate and distinct parts:

The Complete Flat-Fire Trajectory = The Flat-Fire Point-Mass Trajectory + Lateral Throwoff + Aerodynamic Jump + Epicyclic Swerve + Drift **(11.43)**

Equation (11.43) states a *general* result, that is actually true for *all* symmetric projectile trajectories, regardless of the gun elevation angle, or the amplitude of the pitching and yawing motion. However, our *linearized equations*, presented in Chapters 10 and 11, are only valid for flat-fire, and small amplitude pitching and yawing motion. For high quadrant elevation angles, and/or large yaw flight, a numerical six-degrees-of-freedom trajectory caclulation is required.

Discussion of Aerodynamic Jump

The aerodynamic jump is readily expressed in terms of the initial conditions of the pitching and yawing motion. Equations (10.120) and (10.121) of the previous chapter provide the relationships between the initial yaw and initial yaw rate, and the initial amplitudes and phase angles of the epicyclic solution. Those equations are restated here for the reader's convenience:

$$K_{F_0} e^{i\phi_{F0}} = -\frac{\left(i\xi_0' + \phi_S' \xi_0\right)}{\phi_F' - \phi_S'} \qquad \textbf{(10.120)}$$

$$K_{S_0} e^{i\phi_{S0}} = -\frac{\left(i\xi_0' + \phi_F' \xi_0\right)}{\phi_F' - \phi_S'} \qquad \textbf{(10.121)}$$

Substituting equations (10.120) and (10.121) into equation (11.40), we obtain:

$$J_A = iC_{L_\alpha}{}^* \left[\frac{-i\xi_0' - \phi_S' \xi_0}{\phi_F'\left(\phi_F' - \phi_S'\right)} + \frac{i\xi_0' + \phi_F' \xi_0}{\phi_S'\left(\phi_F' - \phi_S'\right)} \right] \qquad \textbf{(11.44)}$$

$$\text{But } \phi_F' \phi_S' = M = k_y^{-2} C_{M_\alpha}{}^* \qquad \textbf{(11.45)}$$

$$\text{and } P = \phi_F' + \phi_S' \qquad \textbf{(11.46)}$$

Substituting equations (11.45) and (11.46) into equation (11.44), and simplifying:

$$J_A = k_y^2 \left(\frac{C_{L_\alpha}}{C_{M_\alpha}} \right) \left[iP\xi_0 - \xi_0' \right] \qquad \textbf{(11.47)}$$

$$\text{where } \quad k_y^2 = \frac{I_y}{md^2} \qquad \textbf{(11.48)}$$

The causes of aerodynamic jump will be studied in some detail in the next chapter. However, before we move on to a discussion of epicyclic swerve, a geometric interpretation of aerodynamic jump may be helpful to the reader. We will use the non-rolling "Basic Finner" model as an illustrative example.

Example 11.1

The aerodynamic properties of the 20mm Basic Finner were reported by L. C. MacAllister (Ref. 2) in 1955. One of the model types tested in the BRL Free Flight Aerodynamics Range (Ref. 3) was a symmetric, cruciform-finned, homogeneous aluminum alloy projectile, launched at Mach 1.8, from a special "rail gun" with a cruciform-shaped bore. Yaw induction was accomplished by embedding a small, high strength magnet in the projectile, and firing it through an 18,000 Gauss electromagnetic field, located just downrange of the gun muzzle. First maximum yaws up to 10 degrees were obtained, using the electromagnetic yaw-induction technique.

The Basic Finner configuration was 10 calibers long, with a 20-degree included angle conical nose. The cruciform tail fin section was located at the base of the body, and it consisted of four uncanted wedge-airfoil sections, each with 8% thickness. Each fin panel had a 1 caliber chord, and the overall span of the model was 3 calibers. Figure 11.2 is a contour sketch of the Basic Finner model, showing the relevant dimensions. The physical and aerodynamic characteristics we will need are listed in Table 11.1, below.

Table 11.1

Reference diameter = 0.786"
Projectile weight = 0.3256 lb.
Axial moment of inertia = 0.0299 lb.-in.^{2}
Transverse moment of inertia = 1.217 lb.-in.^{2}
Center of gravity = 3.96 calibers from base

At Mach 1.8, the following average aerodynamic coefficients were obtained:

C_D=0.61; C_{M_α} =-23.0; C_{L_α} =11.6; $\left(C_{M_q} + C_{M_{\dot\alpha}}\right)$=-155; $C_{M_{p\alpha}}$ =0

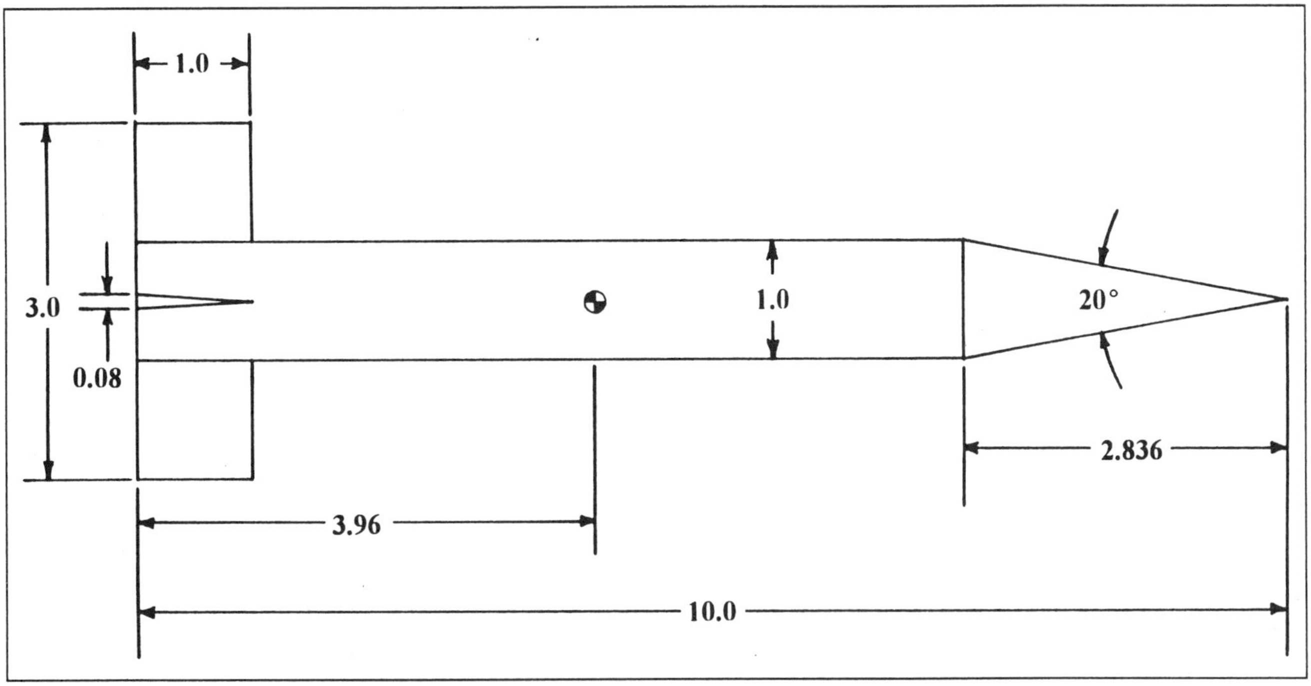

Figure 11.2 Sketch of the 20 mm Non-Rolling Basic Finner Configuration.

Using the methods of the previous chapter, we can now calculate the flight motion parameters, and check the dynamic stability. The quantities we will need are listed below:

$$P = \phi_F' + \phi_S' \equiv 0; \;\; \therefore \phi_S' = -\phi_F'$$

$$M = k_y^{-2} C_{M_\alpha}{}^* = -0.00009854$$

$$\phi_F' = -\phi_S' = 0.009927 \text{ radians/caliber}$$

$$H = C_{L_\alpha}{}^* - C_D^* - k_y^{-2}\left(C_{M_q}{}^* + C_{M_{\dot\alpha}}{}^*\right) = 0.0009489 \, ;$$

$$T = C_{L_\alpha}{}^* = 0.0003007 \;\; \lambda_F = \lambda_S = -0.000474 \text{ per caliber}$$

We will assume that the initial yaw, ξ_0, is zero, and that the yaw inducer "kicks" the model in the horizontal plane (to the right when looking downrange). For a first maximum yaw of 10 degrees, the following values are obtained for the initial amplitudes and phase angles of the two epicyclic yaw arms:

$$K_{F_0} = K_{S_0} = 0.093594; \;\; \phi_{F_0} = 0; \;\; \phi_{S_0} = 180°$$

Since the Basic Finner is statically stable ($M < 0$) at Mach 1.8, it is also gyroscopically stable (see Chapter 10). The dynamic stability factor turns out to be 0.63 [see equation (10.107) of Chapter 10], therefore the projectile is also dynamically stable. (Note that both damping exponents are negative, which also confirms the dynamic stability).

With the help of equations (10.120) and (10.121), and the fact that $\xi_0 = 0$, we find:

$\xi_0' = 0.0018582i; \;\; J_A = 0.0056694i$ (remember that $|J_A|$ is the tangent of an angle)

The tip-off rate (or yaw rate, in this case), is in the horizontal plane, and points to the right. The aerodynamic jump is calculated using equation (11.47), and it is also to the right, in the horizontal plane.

Figure 11.3(a) illustrates the planar yawing motion (the motion is all β for this case; $\alpha \equiv 0$) for the demonstration example. The yawing starts off to the right just after launch, and the amplitude damps from 10 degrees at the gun, to about 2.5 degrees, at a point 200 feet downrange. At Mach 1.8, this aluminum Basic Finner model completes one cycle of the yawing motion in about 42 feet of travel.

Figure 11.3(b) is a plot of the *swerving motion* versus downrange distance, and it illustrates both the aerodynamic jump and the epicyclic swerve very well. In fact, the epicyclic swerve and the aerodynamic jump are closely interrelated. The Basic Finner's initial direction of flight is along the X-axis, which is taken to be the true line of departure. However, the yawing motion shown in Figure 11.3(a) causes the projectile's center-of-mass to fly in the damped sinusoidal planar path (epicyclic swerve), shown as the solid curve in Figure 11.3(b). The *dashed curve* in Figure 11.3(b) is the *aerodynamic jump*, and it is seen to be the mean, or the *average direction* of the damped sinusoidal motion.

The *initial amplitude* of the sinusoidal center-of-mass swerving motion is only 0.45 inch, or 0.57 caliber. This very small initial harmonic motion is further attenuated as the flight continues, and at 200 feet (3053 calibers) downrange distance, the swerve amplitude has damped to 0.11 inch, or 0.13 caliber. At the same range, the *aerodynamic jump* (dashed curve) has deflected the Basic

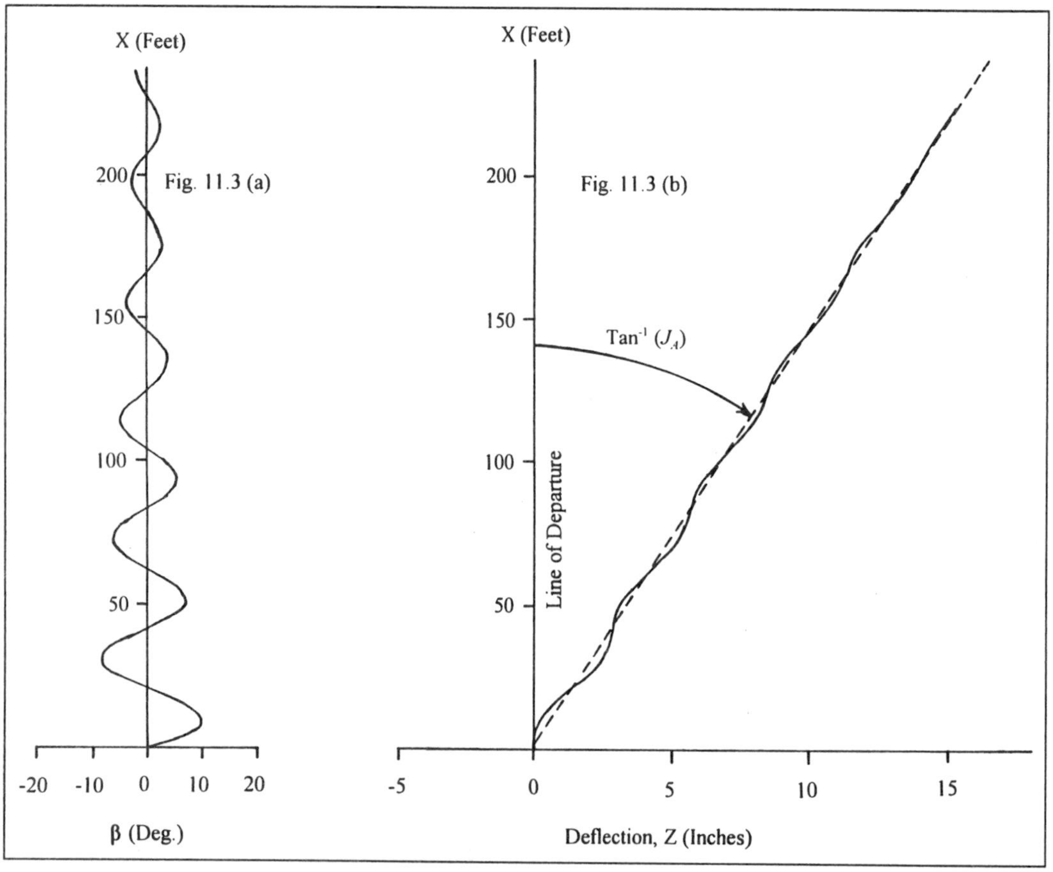

Figure 11.3 Yaw and Deflection versus Range for the 20 mm Non-Rolling Basic Finner.

Finner's center-of-mass J_A s calibers [(0.0056694)(3053) = 17.31 calibers], or 13.61 inches to the right of where it would have impacted, had it followed its initial line of departure! Figure 11.3(b) is an excellent illustration of the fact that the *aerodynamic jump* generally has a *much more significant* effect on the flight of projectiles, than does the epicyclic swerve!

The geometric interpretation of Aerodynamic Jump may be stated as follows. When a projectile is forced into epicyclic swerving motion by the action of aerodynamic lift, the average of the sinusoidal (or helical) center-of-mass motion must literally "go off on a tangent" to the initial direction of departure, at the muzzle of the gun. Aerodynamic Jump effectively changes the line of departure of the trajectory, so that it coincides with the mean, or average, of the epicyclic center-of-mass swerving motion.

An examination of equation (11.47) shows that for a statically stable missile ($M < 0$), such as the Basic Finner, the aerodynamic jump takes the same direction as the initial complex tip-off rate. However, the direction of aerodynamic jump for a statically *unstable* ($M > 0$), spin-stabilized projectile, is reversed! If the initial yawing motion of a spin-stabilized shell starts out to the *right*, the aerodynamic jump will deflect it 180 degrees out of phase, or to the *left* of the initial line of departure! This effect will be demonstrated in the next section, and will be further discussed in Chapter 12.

Equation (11.47) also shows that for spinning projectiles, a second component of aerodynamic jump can exist, proportional to the product of the non-dimensional axial spin, and an initial complex *yaw* (as opposed to an initial *yaw rate*). This part of aerodynamic jump acts in a direction perpendicular to the initial complex yaw, and it gives rise to such phenomena as the port/starboard jump effect, when firing into a crosswind. The effect of initial yaw on aerodynamic jump will also be discused in Chapter 12.

Discussion of Epicyclic Swerve

The epicyclic component of swerve was stated earlier as equation (11.41). An alternate form of this equation, which is often more useful, is found by making a simple substitution for $C_{L_\alpha}{}^*$. With the help of equation (11.45) we may write:

$$C_{L_\alpha}{}^* = \left(\frac{C_{L_\alpha}{}^*}{M}\right) M = k_y^2 \left(\frac{C_{L_\alpha}}{C_{M_\alpha}}\right) \phi'_F \phi'_S \qquad \textbf{(11.48)}$$

Equation (11.48) is now sutstituted into equation (11.41), and we obtain:

$$\boxed{S_E = -k_y^2 \left(\frac{C_{L_\alpha}}{C_{M_\alpha}}\right) \left(\frac{\phi'_S}{\phi'_F} K_{F_0} e^{i\phi_{F0}} \left[e^{(\lambda_F + i\phi'_F)s} - 1\right] + \frac{\phi'_F}{\phi'_S} K_{S_0} e^{i\phi_{S0}} \left[e^{(\lambda_S + i\phi'_S)s} - 1\right]\right)} \qquad \textbf{(11.49)}$$

Equation (11.49) is the most generally useful form for the epicyclic swerve. However, there are two special cases that frequently occur in practice, in which even simpler swerve equations exist.

These two special cases are: (A) Non-rolling, statically stable missiles; and (B) Spin-stabilized projectiles, whose launch gyroscopic stability factors exceed 1.5. We will now examine these two special cases of epicyclic swerving motion.

Case A. Non-Rolling, Statically Stable Missile

$$\{M < 0;\ P \equiv 0;\quad \therefore \phi'_S = -\phi'_F\}$$

Since the turning rates of the two epicyclic pitch and yaw arms are equal in magnitude and opposite in sign, both the yawing and swerving motions are always coplanar. Equation (11.49) reduces to:

$$S_E = k_y^2\left(\frac{C_{L_\alpha}}{C_{M_\alpha}}\right)\left(K_{F_0}e^{i\phi_{F0}}\left[e^{(\lambda_F + i\phi'_F)s} - 1\right] + K_{S_0}e^{i\phi_{S0}}\left[e^{(\lambda_S + i\phi'_S)s} - 1\right]\right) \quad \textbf{(11.50)}$$

Since $P \equiv 0$, equation (11.30) reduces to:

$$\xi = K_{F_0}e^{i\phi_{F0}}e^{(\lambda_F + i\phi'_F)s} + K_{S_0}e^{i\phi_{S0}}e^{(\lambda_S + i\phi'_S)s} \quad \textbf{(11.51)}$$

At $s = 0$, $$\xi(0) = \xi_0 = K_{F_0}e^{i\phi_{F0}} + K_{S_0}e^{i\phi_{S0}} \quad \textbf{(11.52)}$$

Substituting equations (11.51) and (11.52) into equation (11.50) leads to the very simple, but highly useful, result for *non-spinning, statically stable missiles*:

$$S_E = k_y^2\left(\frac{C_{L_\alpha}}{C_{M_\alpha}}\right)(\xi - \xi_0) \quad \textbf{(11.53)}$$

An example of *epicyclic swerve* for a non-spinning, statically missile has already been introduced [see Figure 11.3(b)], which illustrated the planar sinusoidal swerving motion for the Basic Finner configuration. It was noted that the planar yawing, with a 10-degree first maximum yaw, produced a coplanar epicyclic swerving motion, whose initial amplitude was 0.57 caliber (or 0.45 inch). Two-hundred feet downrange, the swerve amplitude has damped to 0.13 caliber (0.11 inch). [Note: Equation (11.53) shows that for a non-spinning, statically stable missile, the amplitude of the swerving motion is directly proportional to the amplitude of the yawing motion; therefore the swerve and the yaw amplitudes always damp at the same rate].

Case B. Spinning, Gyroscopically Stable Projectile

$$\{M > 0;\ S_g > 1.5;\ and\ (\phi'_F)^2 >> (\phi'_S)^2\}$$

The following inequality can be shown:

$$\text{If} \quad S_g > \frac{3}{2} \quad \text{, then} \quad \left(\frac{\phi'_F}{\phi'_S}\right)^2 > \left(2 + \sqrt{3}\right)^2 \quad \textbf{(11.54)}$$

The lengthy algebra required in the derivation of equation (11.54) is omitted for the sake of brevity.

We recall from equation (11.41) that the lengths of the two epicyclic swerve radii are inversely proportional to the squares of their respective frequencies. Inequality (11.54) thus tells us that if the amplitudes of the two epicyclic pitch and yaw arms are comparable in size, then for $S_g > 1.5$, the ratio of the fast epicyclic swerve radius to the slow mode swerve radius is less than 0.07. Thus for a spin-stabilized projectile, whose gyroscopic stability factor exceeds 1.5, we may neglect the fast component of the swerving motion without incurring significant error. For a spin-stabilized projectile, whose $S_g > 1.5$, an excellent approximation to equation (11.49) is given by the simpler expression:

$$S_E = -k_y^2\left(\frac{C_{L_\alpha}}{C_{M_\alpha}}\right)\left(\frac{\phi'_F}{\phi'_S}\right)K_{S_0}e^{i\phi_{S0}}\left[e^{(\lambda_S + i\phi'_S)s} - 1\right] \quad \textbf{(11.55)}$$

Comparison of equation (11.53) with equation (11.55) shows that there is a fundamental difference between the epicyclic swerving motions of non-rolling, statically stable missiles, and statically unstable, spin-stabilized projectiles. For the non-rolling missile, both the complex yawing and swerving motions are coplanar. The spin-stabilized projectile demonstrates epicyclic pitching and yawing motion, and equation (11.55) shows that its swerving motion is *helical*; e.g., the projectile's center-of-mass describes a *spiral*, or *helix*, about the mean flight path.

For a projectile whose swerving motion is accurately described by equation (11.55), we observe that the swerve amplitude, or *radius of the helix*, is given by:

$$R_L = k_y^2\left(\frac{C_{L_\alpha}}{C_{M_\alpha}}\right)\left(\frac{\phi'_F}{\phi'_S}\right)K_{S_0}e^{\lambda_S s} \quad \textbf{(11.56)}$$

where R_L = swerve radius (measured in calibers), due to the aerodynamic lift force

The swerving motion is "in phase" with the slow arm of the pitching and yawing motion, and the swerve amplitude damps (for negative λ_S), or grows (for positive λ_S) at the same rate as the slow frequency epicyclic yaw arm.

Example 11.2

In Chapter 9, six-degrees-of-freedom trajectory results were presented, that illustrated typical epicyclic pitching and yawing motion of the .308," 168 grain Sierra International bullet (Ref. 4), at several downrange distances. The angular motion near the gun was shown as Figure 9.2, reproduced in this chapter as Figure 11.4 (*p. 248*). The 6-DOF calculated deflection-plane (X-Z plane) component of the *epicyclic swerve* is plotted for this bullet in Figure 11.5 (*p. 249*), which illustrates the combined effects of aerodynamic jump, epicyclic swerve, and a small drift contribution.

The first maximum yaw of the .308," 168 grain Sierra match bullet is 2.0 degrees, when fired at a muzzle velocity of 2600 feet/second, from a 12" twist of rifling, with an initial yaw rate of 25

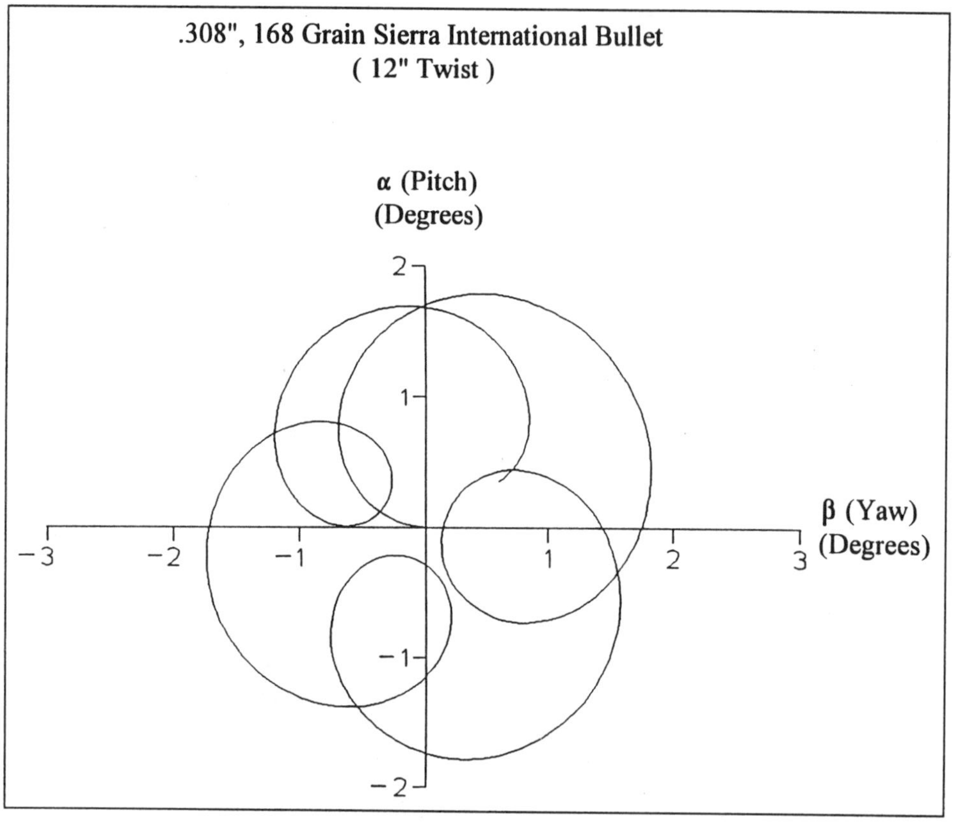

Figure 11.4 Pitch versus Yaw (6-DOF), Muzzle to 15 Yards Range.

radians/second. The initial swerve amplitude (initial radius of the helix) produced by this pitching and yawing motion is 0.07 caliber (0.02 inch). The 168 grain Sierra International bullet has a very mild small-yaw, slow-arm dynamic instability (α_S is a very small positive quantity), that causes a slow growth in K_s along the flight path. The result [see equation (11.56)] is a slowly increasing swerve amplitude, illustrated in Figure 11.5. At a range of 300 feet, the swerve radius has increased to 0.10 caliber (0.03 inch). Note that for the *left-directed* initial yaw rate shown in Figure 11.4, the aerodynamic jump produces a deflection of 0.75 inch to the *right* at the same range, and the drift carries the bullet an additional 0.05" to the right, giving a total deflection to the right of 0.80 inch, at 300 feet range. Again we observe that the contribution of epicyclic swerve is very small, in comparison with the effect of aerodynamic jump.

If a second shot was fired with the same initial yaw rate, but directed to the *right* instead of the left, the pitching and yawing motion would be the mirror image of Figure 11.4. This shot would strike -0.75" + 0.05" = -0.70," to the *left* of the initial flight line, and the two bullet holes in the 100 yard target would be 1.50" apart! We see that the aerodynamic jump can cause significant spreading of groups at the target, even for relatively small pitching and yawing motion. **If a small group at the target (small dispersion) is required, either the amplitude of the pitching and yawing motion for all shots must be very small, or both the direction and magnitude of the initial yaw rates must be very consistent, from one shot to the next.**

Inspection of equations (11.47) and (11.56), with consideration given to the relative magnitudes of their various component parts, leads to a general conclusion regarding the epicyclic swerving motion and the aerodynamic jump, for statically unstable, spin-stabilized projectiles:

If a spin-stabilized projectile has an $S_g > 1.5$, is dynamically stable, and is launched at small yaw along a flat-fire trajectory, the contribution of epicyclic swerve to the total center-of-mass motion will be of second order, and may usually be neglected. At long range, the effect of aerodynamic jump on the trajectory is much larger than the effect of epicyclic swerve, and in general, the aerodynamic jump must always be retained.

The small epicyclic swerving motion is routinely measured today, in modern high-precision ballistic test ranges, and this measurement is used to determine C_{L_α} from free-flight spark range firings. The determination of C_{L_α} from a swerve reduction will be discussed in the last chapter of this book.

Large yaw flight will generally produce an epicyclic swerving motion that is too large to neglect. The aerodynamic jump effect is also large, for spin-stabilized projectiles with high-amplitude pitching and yawing motion. The large pitching and yawing motion leads to high aerodynamic drag, and the large aerodynamic jump leads to high dispersion. The usual result is unsatisfactory flight performance, and the projectile must be redesigned so it flies with small yaw.

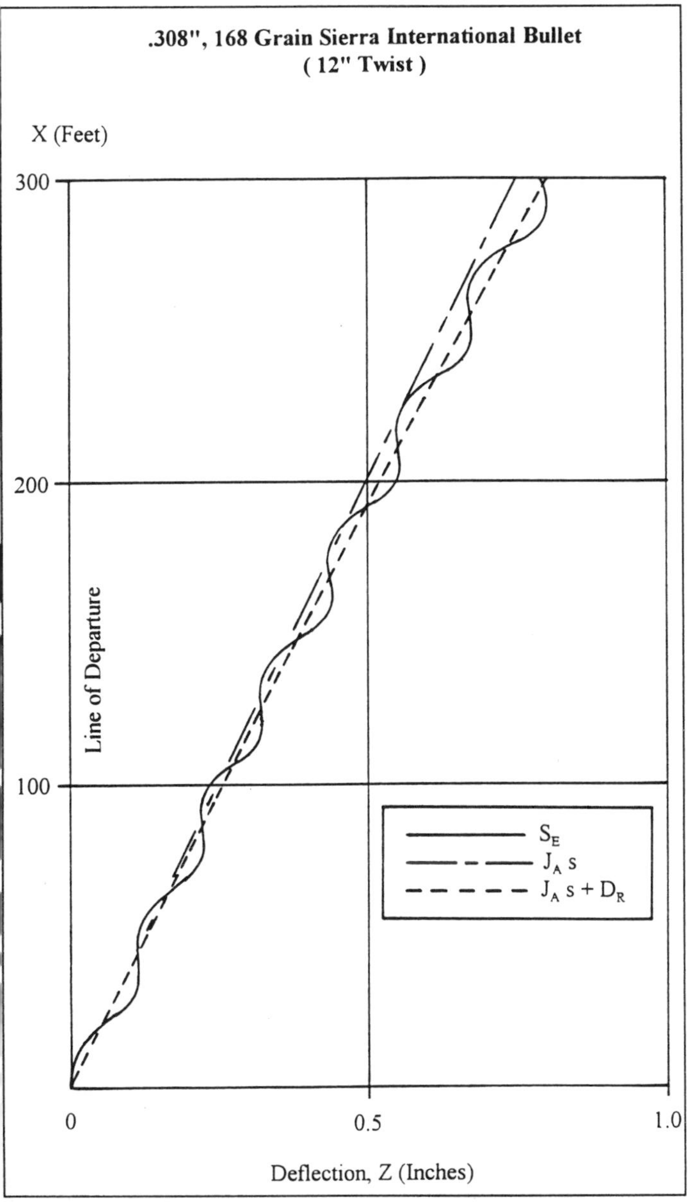

Figure 11.5 Deflection versus Range, Showing Aerodynamic Jump, Epicyclic Swerve and Drift.

Discussion of Drift

If the definition, $M = k_y^{-2} C_{M_\alpha}{}^*$ is substituted into equation (11.42), an alternate form of the drift equation is obtained:

$$D_R = i k_y^2 \left(\frac{PG_0}{2} \right) \left(\frac{C_{L_\alpha}}{C_{M_\alpha}} \right) s^2 \left[1 + \frac{2}{3}(C_D^* s) + \frac{1}{3}(C_D^* s)^2 + \cdots \right] \quad \textbf{(11.57)}$$

Equation (11.57) shows that there are five distinctly different possibilities for the drift; these five cases are listed in Table 11.2. Note that R. H. means "Right Hand" and L. H. means "Left Hand" in the table. Cases 1 and 2 are statically unstable, spin-stabilized projectiles, with right and left hand spin, respectively. Cases 3 and 4 are statically stable configurations, which may be fin, flare, or mass stabilized, with right and left hand spin. Case 5 is a non-rolling, statically stable missile, which has no drift.

Table 11.2
Direction of Drift for Different Types of Projectiles

Case	Sign of M	Sign of P	Direction of Drift
1	M>0	P>0 (R.H. Spin)	To the Right
2	M>0	P<0 (L.H. Spin)	To the Left
3	M<0	P>0 (R.H. Spin)	To the Left
4	M<0	P<0 (L.H. Spin)	To the Right
5	Either Sign of M	P=0 (Zero Spin)	Zero Drift

For short ranges, where $(C_D^* s) << 1$, equation (11.57) shows that the drift of a spinning projectile, along a flat-fire trajectory, increases approximately in proportion to the square of the distance travelled. We say "approximately" because the quantity P may also vary with s. Equation (10.78) of Chapter 10 tells us that for a body of revolution, with no two-dimensional lifting surfaces (such as fins), the spin per caliber of travel usually *increases* slowly along a flat-fire trajectory. The same equation, with order estimates for finned missiles, shows that the spin per caliber of travel, for a finned projectile with *uncanted* fins, usually *decays rapidly* along the flight path. (See section 10.3 of Chapter 10).

The roll behavior of a finned missile with canted fins depends on the magnitude of the initial spin, relative to the steady-state rolling velocity. We will differentiate equation (10.74) of Chapter 10, set $\phi' = (pd/V)$, and multiply both sides of the result by the ratio (I_x/I_y):

$$P = P_{s/s} - (P_{s/s} - P_0) e^{-K_p s} \quad \textbf{(11.58)}$$

where $P = \frac{I_x}{I_y}\left(\frac{pd}{V}\right)$

$$P_0 = \frac{I_x}{I_y}\left(\frac{pd}{V}\right)_0$$

$$P_{s/s} = \frac{I_x}{I_y}\left(\frac{K_\delta}{K_p}\right)$$

$$K_p = -\left[k_x^{-2} C_{l_p}{}^* + C_D^*\right]$$

$$K_\delta = k_x^{-2} \delta_F C_{l_\delta}{}^*$$

$$k_x^{-2} = \frac{md^2}{I_x}$$

Since K_p is usually of order of +[10^{-3}] for a finned missile, we observe that if $P_0 < P_{S/S}$, the spin per caliber of travel will *increase* until it reaches the steady-state value. If $P_0 > P_{S/S}$, the nondimensional spin rate will *decrease* until it reaches the steady-state value. If, by chance, the initial value of P happens to coincide with the steady-state rolling velocity, then P will be *constant* along the trajectory, for a finned missile with *canted* fins.

At long range, equation (11.57) shows that the drift increases faster than a simple quadratic dependence on the distance travelled. However, no simple, analytical equation gives a truly accurate prediction of drift at long range. We have already noted that, in general, the nondimensional spin term, P, varies slowly with increasing range. In addition, the three aerodynamic coefficients that appear in equation (11.57) also vary with Mach number along the trajectory.

Equation (11.57) is sufficiently accurate for spark photography range data reduction, because the trajectory is flat, and the distance travelled is relatively short. For a long-range drift calculation, a much better method, even for flat-fire trajectories, is to numerically integrate the modified point-mass differential equations (9.59), (9.60), and (9.62) of Chapter 9. Examples of six-degrees-of-freedom drift predictions were shown in figures 9.8, 9.19, and 9.20, and the modified point-mass method was found to agree very closely with the 6-DOF calculations, for all quadrant elevation angles below the maximum trail angle.

Several examples of modified point-mass drift calculations for modern small arms bullets are illustrated in Figures 11.6 and 11.7. The calculations have been done for ranges out to 2 kilometers, for several 5.56mm, 7.62mm, and .50 caliber military projectiles [good quality aeroballistic data are available for these bullets; (see References 4 through 8, at the end of this chapter)]. Figure 11.6 is a plot of the right-hand drift versus range to the target, for two boattailed 5.56mm (.22 caliber) bullets. The solid curve in Figure 11.6 is for the 62-grain, M855 NATO Ball projectile, fired from an M16A2 rifle, with a rifling twist rate of 1 turn in 7 inches. The dashed curve is the calculated drift for the older 55-grain, Ball, M193 bullet, fired from the M16A1 rifle, with a twist of 1 turn in 12 inches. The curves are coincidentally similar, which indicates that the effect of the rifling twist rate difference is offset by differences in the physical and aerodynamic properties of the two bullets.

Figure 11.7 compares the drift characteristics of two 7.62mm (.30 caliber) bullets, with the drift of a .50 caliber machine gun bullet. The solid and dashed curves are for the 147-grain, 7.62mm Ball, M80 and the 174-grain, 7.62mm Match, M118 bullet, respectively, fired from an M14 rifle, with a rifling twist rate of 1 turn in 12 inches. The longer, heavier M118 bullet drifts less than the shorter and lighter M80 projectile. The primary reasons are: (1) the ratio of the axial to the transverse moment of inertia is smaller for the longer bullet, thus the nondimensional spin, P, is lower for the M118; (2) the overturning moment coefficient, C_{M_α}, is significantly larger for the longer M118 bullet.

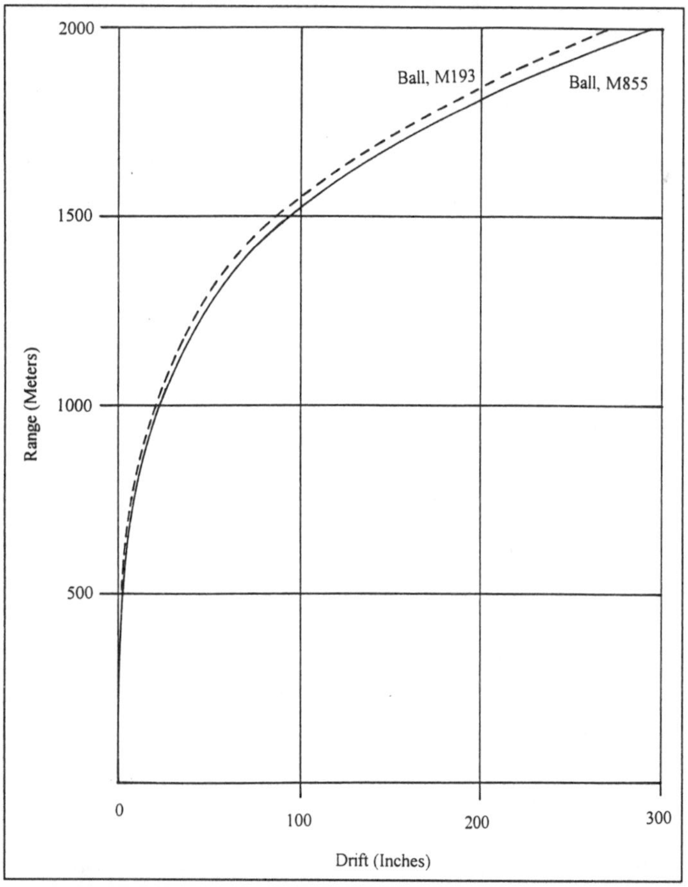

Figure 11.6 Drift versus Range for Two 5.6 mm Projectiles.

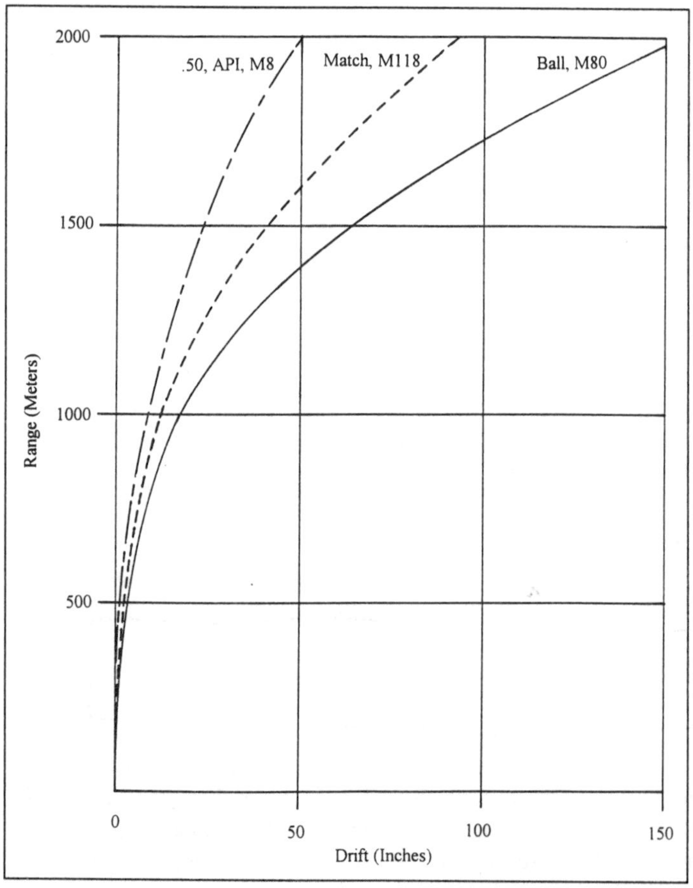

Figure 11.7 Drift versus Range for Three Spin-Stabilized Small Arms Projectiles.

The .50 caliber, API (Armor Piercing Incendiary), M8 projectile is fired from the Browning, M2 machine gun, with a right-hand rifling twist rate of 15 inches per turn, and it is seen to have significantly less drift than either of the .30 caliber bullets. The general trend observed in Figures 11.6 and 11.7, is that the drift tends to be smaller for larger caliber guns. This is because the drift is proportional to a power series [see equation (11.57)] in nondimensional distance, s, along the trajectory, and at a fixed dimensional range (e.g., 1500 meters), the distance s, in calibers, is greater for a small caliber projectile than for a larger one.

Note that at short and moderate ranges (less than 1000 meters), the drift is usually very small for modern, high velocity, boattailed small arms bullets. The G_0 term in equation (11.57) contains the square of the muzzle velocity in the denominator, which tells us that the drift will be significantly larger for low velocity projectiles, such as pistol bullets, or infantry grenades.

If high quality physical measurements and aerodynamic data are available for a spin-stabilized projectile, the *calculated drift*, from a modified point-mass or six-degrees-of-freedom trajectory program, will usually be *more accurate* than a measured drift curve! The reason is that at long ranges, where the drift is large enough to measure, the effect of *crosswind* on the trajectory deflection is many times larger than the effect of *drift*. Thus the *very small drift* must be found by subtracting out the *much larger crosswind deflection*, which can lead to large errors in the values obtained for the drift. (Note that the Coriolis effect is often the same order of magnitude as the drift; therefore, the Coriolis deflection must also be calculated, and subtracted from the measured total deflection).

Before the advent of modern high-speed wind tunnels, spark photography ranges, and digital computers, exterior ballisticians had recognized the fundamental difficulty in attempting to measure drift, and had devised a novel method to circumvent the crosswind problem (see Reference 9, Chapter XII, Section 3). The old "drift firing" technique took advantage of the fact that reversing the direction of the rifling also reverses the direction of drift. Guns with right and left-twist barrels were mounted parallel to each other, and fired simultaneously. Both projectiles experienced the same crosswind and Coriolis deflections, thus the drift could be directly determined from each pair of rounds fired. Drift firings are seldom done today, because high quality aeroballistic data are routinely obtained during the course of development of a new projectile, and the drift can be accurately calculated using modified point-mass or six-degrees-of-freedom methods.

Summary

The linearized swerving motion of rotationally symmetric projectiles has been illustrated in this chapter. We have observed that for small yaw and flat-fire trajectories, the effect of epicyclic swerve is usually very small, in comparison with the effect of aerodynamic jump. At short and moderate ranges, the drift has also been shown to be very small. A general conclusion may be drawn at this point; *aerodynamic jump is the most important effect* caused by the pitching and yawing motion, on the small-yaw, flat-fire trajectory.

For large yaw flight, increased aerodynamic drag can significantly degrade the range of a projectile, and the epicyclic swerving motion may become too large to neglect. For high quadrant elevation angles, the yaw of repose and the drift of spin-stabilized shell can increase dramatically. However, neither of these problems can be accurately calculated using linearized methods. If the projectile is fired at high gun elevation angles, and/or flies with large pitching and yawing motion, only a modern six-degrees-of-freedom trajectory calculation will give an accurate trajectory.

REFERENCES

1. Murphy, C. H., "Free Flight Motion of Symmetric Missiles," Ballistic Research Laboratories Report No. 1216, 1963.

2. MacAllister, L. C., "The Aerodynamic Properties of a Simple Non Rolling Finned Cone-Cylinder Configuration Between Mach Numbers 1.0 and 2.5," Ballistic Research Laboratories Report No. 934, 1955.

3. Braun, W. F., "The Free Flight Aerodynamics Range," Ballistic Research Laboratories Report No. 1048, 1958.

4. McCoy, R. L., "The Aerodynamic Characteristics of 7.62mm Match Bullets," Ballistic Research Laboratory Memorandum Report No. BRL-MR-3733, 1988.

5. Piddington, M. J., "The Aerodynamic Properties of a Caliber .223 Remington Bullet Used in M16 (AR-15) Rifle," Ballistic Research Laboratories Memorandum Report No. 1758, 1966.

6. McCoy, R. L., "Aerodynamic and Flight Dynamic Characteristics of the New Family of 5.56mm NATO Ammunition," Ballistic Research Laboratory Memorandum Report No. BRL-MR-3476, 1985.

7. Piddington, M. J., "Aerodynamic Characteristics of the 7.62mm NATO Ammunition M-59, M-80, M-61, M-62," Ballistic Research Laboratories Memorandum Report No. 1833, 1967.

8. McCoy, R. L., "The Aerodynamic Characteristics of .50 Ball, M33, API, M8, and APIT, M20 Ammunition," Ballistic Research Laboratory Memorandum Report No. BRL-MR-3810, 1990.

9. McShane, E. J., J. L. Kelley and F. V. Reno, *Exterior Ballistics*, University of Denver Press, 1953.

12

Lateral Throwoff and Aerodynamic Jump

12.1 INTRODUCTION

Figure 12.1 illustrates a *statically unbalanced* projectile, whose center of mass lies laterally off its axis of rotational symmetry. As the unbalanced projectile travels down a rifled gun barrel, it is mechanically constrained to rotate about its geometric center of form, and the center of mass therefore traces out a helical, or spiral path about the bore centerline. At the muzzle, the barrel's mechanical constraint is abruptly removed, and the projectile's center of mass literally "flies off on a tangent" to the in-bore helix. The trajectory deflection caused by this effect was first identified by F. W. Mann (Ref. 1), who called it the "X-Error." Mann went on to show that by drilling holes in rifle bullets, and deliberately unbalancing them, he could produce any desired trajectory deflection at will.

Lateral Throwoff is the modern term for Mann's "X-Error." The static unbalance that produces lateral throwoff may be due to either a mass asymmetry, or to in-bore yawing, which causes the projectile to be "tilted" in the gun barrel. The trajectory deflections caused by mass asymmetry and in-bore yaw will be investigated later in this chapter.

For a saboted projectile, an additional trajectory deflection due to asymmetric sabot discard has recently been identified (Ref. 2). Most sabots are either the pusher-cup type, or are composed of several "petals" that surround the projectile body in the gun. Sabot/projectile separation usually begins shortly after the assembly clears the gun muzzle. If the sabot separation is not perfectly axisymmetric, some transverse linear and angular momentum is usually transferred to the projectile, which causes a *lateral throwoff* effect on the trajectory. In addition, an imperfect sabot discard may cause a temporary *asymmetric aerodynamic disturbance*, which makes an additional contribution to the total lateral throwoff.

The trajectory deflection caused by *Aerodynamic Jump* was also first identified by Mann (Ref. 1), who referred to it as the "Y-Error." Mann conducted numerous experimental firings in the early years of the twentieth century, with .32 caliber, cast lead bullets, at velocities around 1400 feet per second. He discovered that he could drill two holes on opposite sides of a rifle bullet, one ahead of the center of gravity, and the other behind, to produce a bullet that was *statically balanced*, but *dynamically unbalanced*. Such a bullet has no lateral throwoff, but has an exaggerated initial yaw rate and aerodynamic jump. Mann also found that by firing his .32 caliber lead bullets close to a 12-feet long, flat surface (he referred to this as "plank shooting"), he could induce a fairly large (approximately 10 degrees) *initial yaw*, with almost no *initial yaw rate*, at the end of the flat surface. He used yaw cards to make the first reasonably accurate measurements of the epicyclic swerve and the aerodynamic jump produced by initial yaw, and by an initial yaw rate.

Mann thought of the epicyclic swerve and the aerodynamic jump as *geometric* properties of the trajectory. He did not have an aeronautical engineering background, and therefore he could not have anticipated the results presented in Chapter 11 of this book. The first correct analytical treatment of epicyclic swerve, aerodynamic jump and drift was given in 1920, by Fowler, Gallop, Lock and Richmond (Ref. 3). However, these pioneering English investigators regarded the epicyclic swerve and the aerodynamic jump as very small quantities, and they neglected both effects in comparison with the drift. For spin-stabilized field artillery projectiles, fired at high quadrant elevation angles, the drift can indeed be very large (see section 9.5 of Chapter 9), compared with the aerodynamic jump effect. However, for modern high-velocity, spin-stabilized, flat-fire munitions, the lateral throwoff and the aerodynamic jump are often much larger than the drift, at moderate ranges.

Aerodynamic Jump was discussed and illustrated in the previous chapter for a non-rolling finned missile configuration, and for a typical modern spin-stabilized small arms bullet. In general, a mass asymmetry in the projectile causes an initial yaw *and* an initial yaw rate, at the instant of separation from the gun muzzle, and equation (11.47) of the previous chapter tells us that the result will be an *aerodynamic jump*. In-bore yaw, or "bullet tilt" in the barrel, is one significant cause of muzzle tip- off rates and aerodynamic jump; a dynamically unbalanced bullet is another. A crosswind blowing across the muzzle of the gun also produces an *aerodynamic jump*. All these effects will be derived and discussed in later sections of this chapter.

The importance of the *lateral throwoff* effect and the *aerodynamic jump* effect on the trajectories of spin-stabilized, flat-fire munitions, is sufficient to justify an entire chapter devoted to their study. In particular, the reader whose primary concern is the *precision* of fire (often incorrectly referred to as "accuracy"), should study this chapter in detail, and become thoroughly familiar with it. [In ballistics, the terms "precision" and "accuracy" have different meanings. *Precision* refers to the ability to tightly cluster all shots into a small group on the target, regardless of where the center of

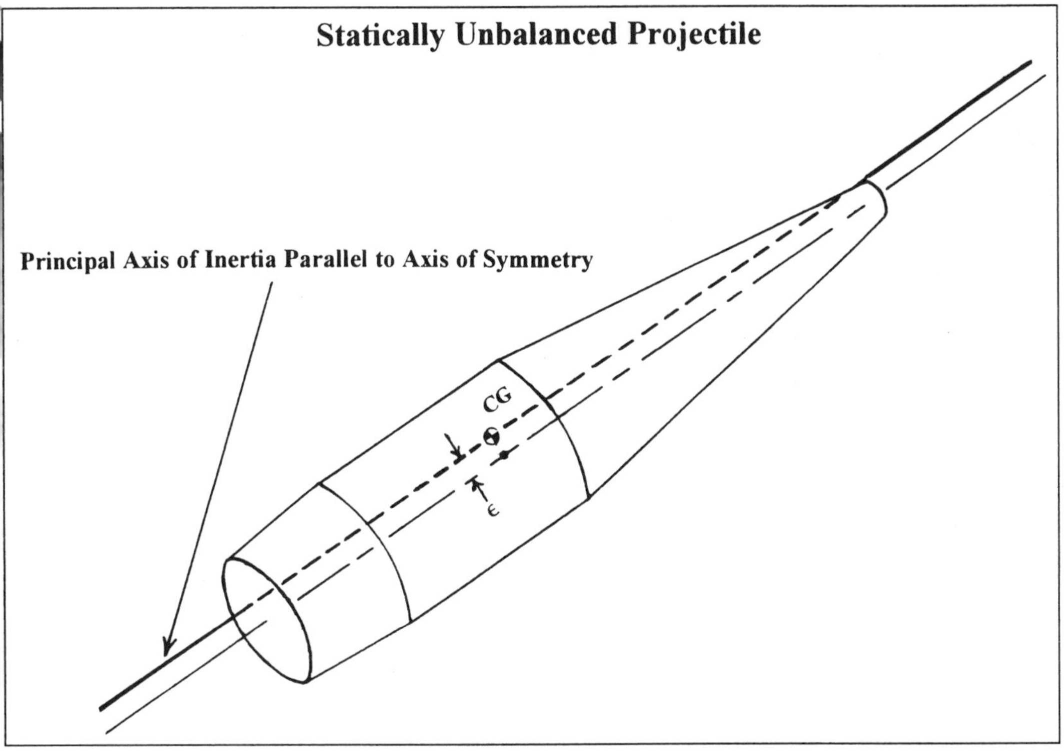

Figure 12.1 Sketch of a Statically Unbalanced Projectile.

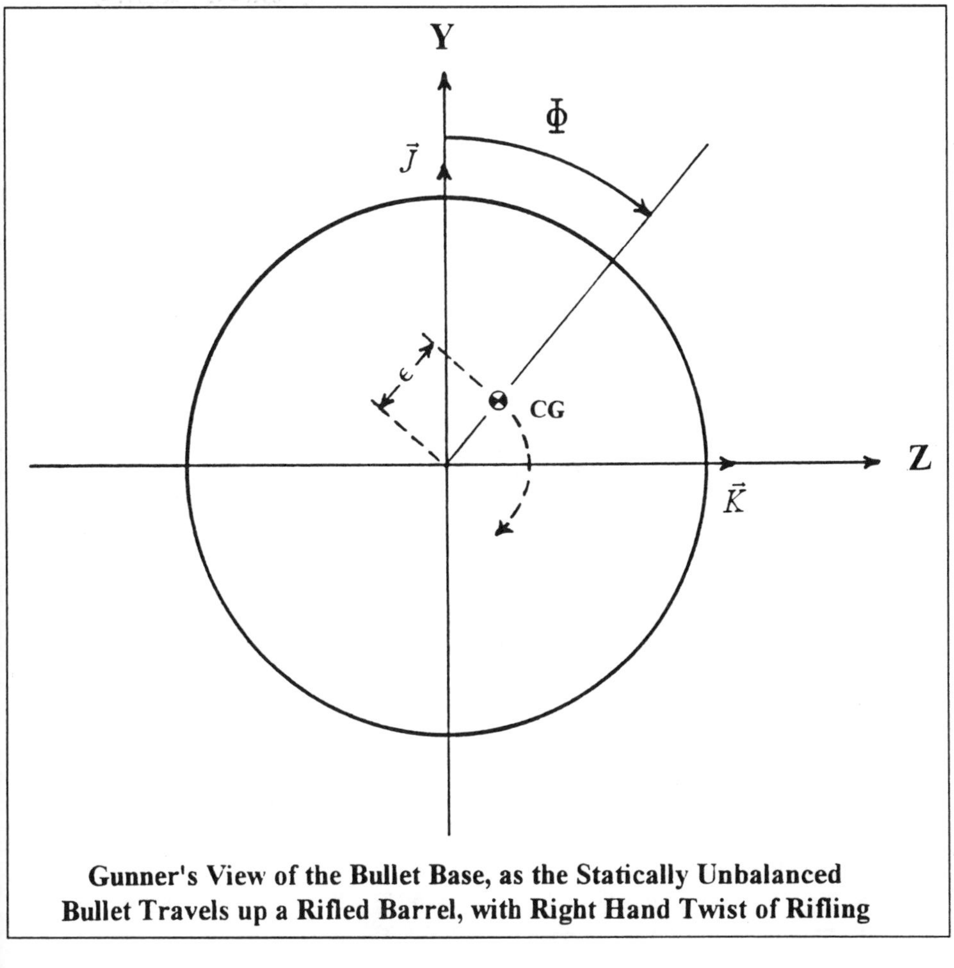

Figure 12.2 In-Bore Motion of a Statically Unbalanced Projectile.

impact of the group falls. *Accuracy* is the ability to hit a given mark, or aiming point on the target. A very small group in the 7-ring of the target illustrates good precision, but poor accuracy].

12.2 DERIVATION OF THE LATERAL THROWOFF EFFECT

During its travel down a rifled gun barrel, a rotationally symmetric, *statically unbalanced* projectile (illustrated in Figure 12.1), is mechanically constrained to rotate about its geometric center of form. As long as the projectile is in the barrel, the center of gravity (CG) is forced to trace out a spiral, or helical path about the bore centerline. (Note that we use the terms *center of mass* and *center of gravity* interchangeably in this book). We may assume, without loss in generality, that the gun is pointed along the X-axis, in our earth-fixed coordinate system (see Figure 10.1 of Chapter 10). Figure 12.2 shows the component of the CG-motion in the Y-Z plane, at an arbitrary instant of time.

The radius of the center-of-mass helix is denoted by the Greek letter $\hat{\varepsilon}$ (epsilon), and it is equal to the static unbalance, or the lateral CG-offset. The pitch of the spiral is governed by the rifling twist rate. We denote the roll orientation angle at any instant of time as the Greek letter Φ (Phi). The angle Φ is the angle between the vertical plane (X-Y plane) and the plane containing both the offset CG and the projectile's axis of symmetry. The angle Φ is measured clockwise from the vertical plane.

The earth-fixed coordinate system is specified by the triad of unit vectors $[\vec{I},\vec{J},\vec{K}]$ (see Figure 10.1 of Chapter 10). The vector velocity of the projectile's center of gravity is the sum of two parts; the forward velocity in the $\vec{I}$ direction, and a component normal to $\vec{I}$, which is the tangential velocity component in the Y-Z plane.

$$\text{Forward Velocity} = V\vec{I} \qquad \textbf{(12.1)}$$

For circular motion, classical mechanics gives us the relationship between the projectile's rotational angular velocity, and the instantaneous tangential velocity of the center of gravity (see Figure 12.3):

$$\text{Tangential Velocity} = \vec{v}_T = \hat{\varepsilon}\left(\frac{d\Phi}{dt}\right)\vec{e}_\phi \qquad \textbf{(12.2)}$$

where $\hat{\varepsilon} = |\vec{r}|$

$\vec{r}$ = instantaneous vector position of the CG, relative to the projectile's spin axis

$\vec{e}_\phi$ = a unit vector perpendicular to $\vec{r}$, and in the direction of increasing Φ

$\frac{d\Phi}{dt} = p$ = instantaneous projectile axial spin rate (radi ans/second) (radians/second)

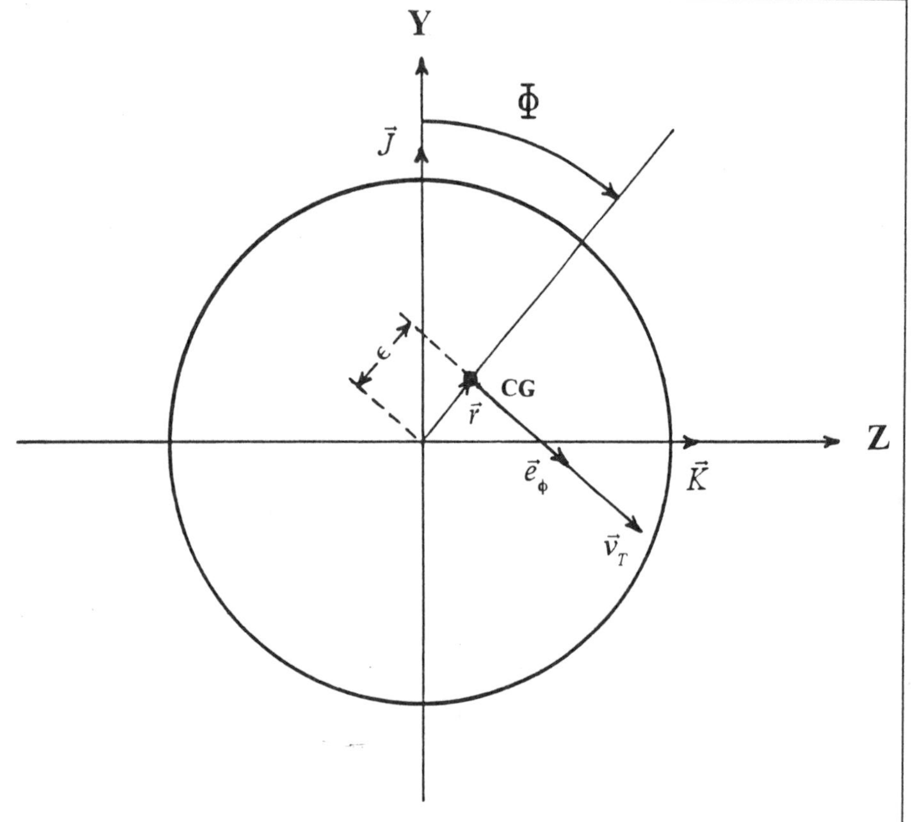

Gunner's View of the Bullet Base, as the Statically Unbalanced Bullet Travels up a Rifled Barrel, with Right Hand Twist of Rifling

Figure 12.3 Vector Geometry for a Statically Unbalanced Projectile.

Figure 12.3 shows that a correct representation of the unit vector $\vec{e}_\phi$ is:

$$\vec{e}_\phi = \cos\Phi\vec{K} - \sin\Phi\vec{J} \tag{12.3}$$

The total vector velocity of the projectile's center-of-mass is now given by:

$$\vec{V} = V\vec{I} + p\hat{\varepsilon}\left(\cos\Phi\vec{K} - \sin\Phi\vec{J}\right) \tag{12.4}$$

At the muzzle of the gun, the mechanical constraint provided by the barrel is suddenly removed, and the initial conditions of the free-flight trajectory are found by evaluating equation (12.4) at s = 0. We will denote values at the muzzle by a zero-subscript.

$$V_{x_0} = V_0 \tag{12.5}$$

$$V_{y_0} = -p_0\hat{\varepsilon}\sin\Phi_0 \tag{12.6}$$

$$V_{z_0} = p_0\hat{\varepsilon}\sin\Phi_0 \tag{12.7}$$

We observe that the effect of a lateral center-of-mass offset, or *static unbalance*, is to change the initial direction of the trajectory at the gun muzzle. The angular displacement is given by:

$$\frac{V_{y_0} + iV_{z_0}}{V_{x_0}} = \left(\frac{p_o\hat{\varepsilon}}{V_0}\right)\left[-\sin\Phi_0 + i\cos\Phi_0\right] \tag{12.8}$$

But, $ie^{i\Phi_0} = -\sin\Phi_0 + i\cos\Phi_0$, and we find:

$$T_L = \frac{V_{y_0} + iV_{z_0}}{V_{x_0}} = i\left[\left(\frac{p_0 d}{V_0}\right)\left(\frac{\hat{\varepsilon}}{d}\right)e^{i\phi_0}\right] \tag{12.9}$$

where T_L is the lateral throwoff. (Note that T_L is the tangent of an angle)

Since the quantity (p_0 d/V_0) is precisely (2π/n), where n is the rifling twist rate at the muzzle, in calibers/turn, equation 12.9 may be written as:

$$\text{Lateral Throwoff} = T_L = i\left[\left(\frac{2\pi}{n}\right)\left(\frac{\hat{\varepsilon}}{d}\right)e^{i\Phi_0}\right] \tag{12.10}$$

where
n = Twist of rifling (calibers/turn)

$\hat{\varepsilon}$ = Static unbalance, or lateral offset of the center-of-mass

d = Projectile reference diameter

Φ_0 = Roll orientation angle of the CG, at emergence from the muzzle

T_L = Lateral throwoff (the tangent of the deflection angle)

Equation (12.10) shows that the effect of lateral throwoff due to mass unbalance is to deflect the trajectory at right angles to the orientation at which the center of mass emerges from the muzzle. For a right-hand twist of rifling, if the CG emerges at the 12:00 o'clock position (upward, or $\Phi_0 = 0$), the direction of deflection due to lateral throwoff will be toward 3:00 o'clock (to the right), on the target. [Note that a left-twist gun (negative n) would deflect the same projectile to the left, or toward 9:00 o'clock]. We will discuss the lateral throwoff, and illustrate the use of equation (12.10) later in this chapter.

12.3 THE EFFECT OF A SLIGHT MASS ASYMMETRY ON THE INITIAL PITCHING AND YAWING MOTION OF A SPINNING PROJECTILE

The spinning projectile is initially assumed to possess both configurational and mass symmetry about the longitudinal, or spin axis. A small amount of mass is then removed from an arbitrary point located off the axis of symmetry, thereby introducing a slight dynamic unbalance (and a slight *static* unbalance as well) in the projectile. The amount of mass removed is assumed to be very small, and the original principal moments of inertia are assumed to be essentially unchanged. If the original mass is denoted by the letter *m*, and the very small mass removed is denoted by m_E :

$$m_E << m \tag{12.11}$$

We must also specify the location of the point within the projectile, from which the mass, m_E, is removed. Figure 12.4 (*p. 256*) illustrates the geometry.

The mass is removed at an arbitrary axial distance, l_E, from the projectile's center of gravity (CG), and at an arbitrary distance, r_E, off the axis of symmetry. The distance l_E will be defined as positive if the mass is removed ahead of the CG, and negative if m_E is removed aft of the CG location.

We will need two orthogonal coordinate systems to investigate the pitching and yawing motion of a projectile with a slight dynamic unbalance. The first coordinate system is the non-rolling triad of unit vectors $\left(\vec{i},\vec{j},\vec{k}\right)$, as defined in Chapter 10 (see Figure 10.2). The unit vector $\vec{i}$ is tangent to the trajectory; the unit vector $\vec{k}$ lies in the horizontal plane, and points to the right when looking downrange, and $\vec{j} = \vec{k} \times \vec{i}$. For a flat-fire trajectory, $\vec{j}$ is a unit vector pointing essentially *upward.*

The second coordinate system we will need is a non-rolling triad of unit vectors $(\vec{x},\vec{y},\vec{z})$ attached to the projectile, with the unit vector $\vec{x}$ directed along the rotational axis of symmetry. The unit vector $\vec{z}$ lies in the horizontal plane, and points to the right when looking downrange. The unit vector $\vec{y} = \vec{z} \times \vec{x}$. The origins of both the $\left(\vec{i},\vec{j},\vec{k}\right)$ and the $(\vec{x},\vec{y},\vec{z})$ coordinate systems lie at the projectile center of gravity.

The vector $\vec{r}$ is constructed, directed from the CG to the point at which the small mass was removed. Note that $\vec{r}$ *is not a unit*

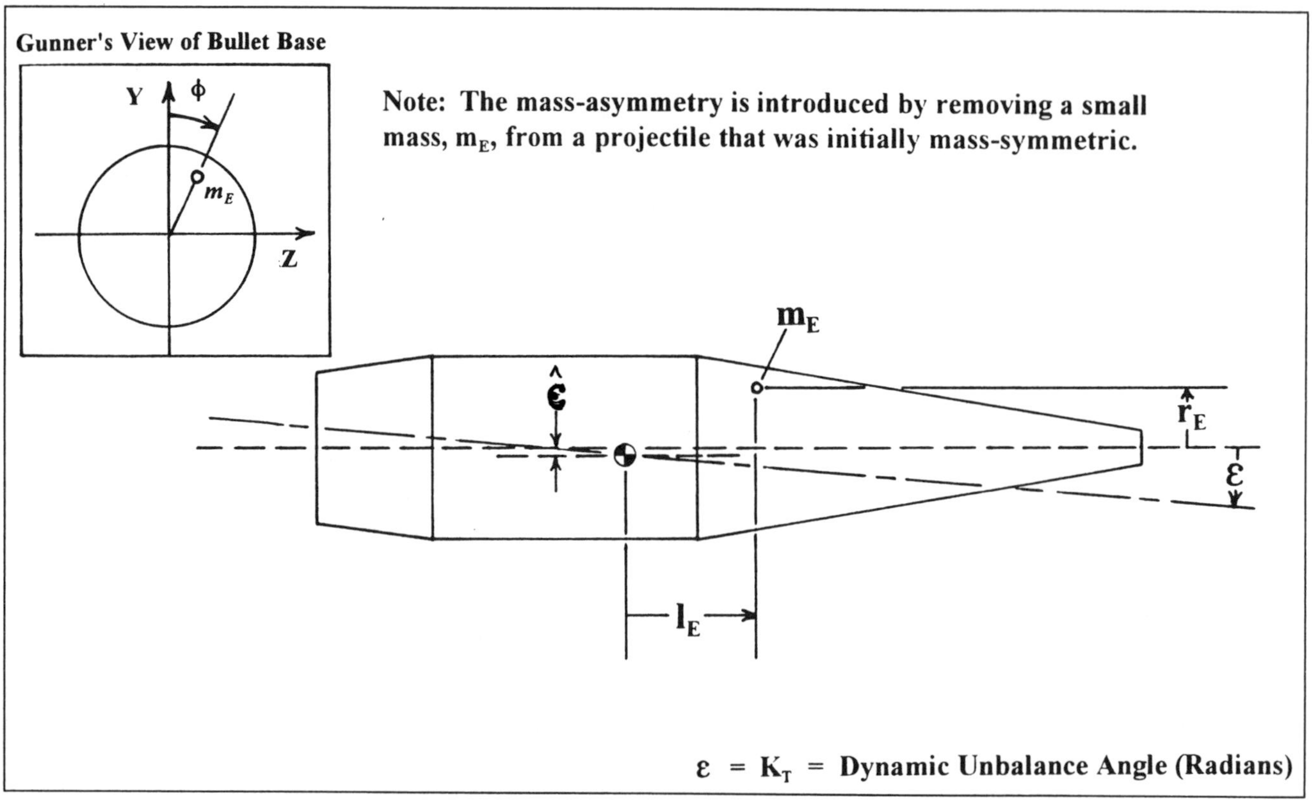

Figure 12.4 Sketch of a Mass-Asymmetric Projectile, with Both Static and Dynamic Unbalance.

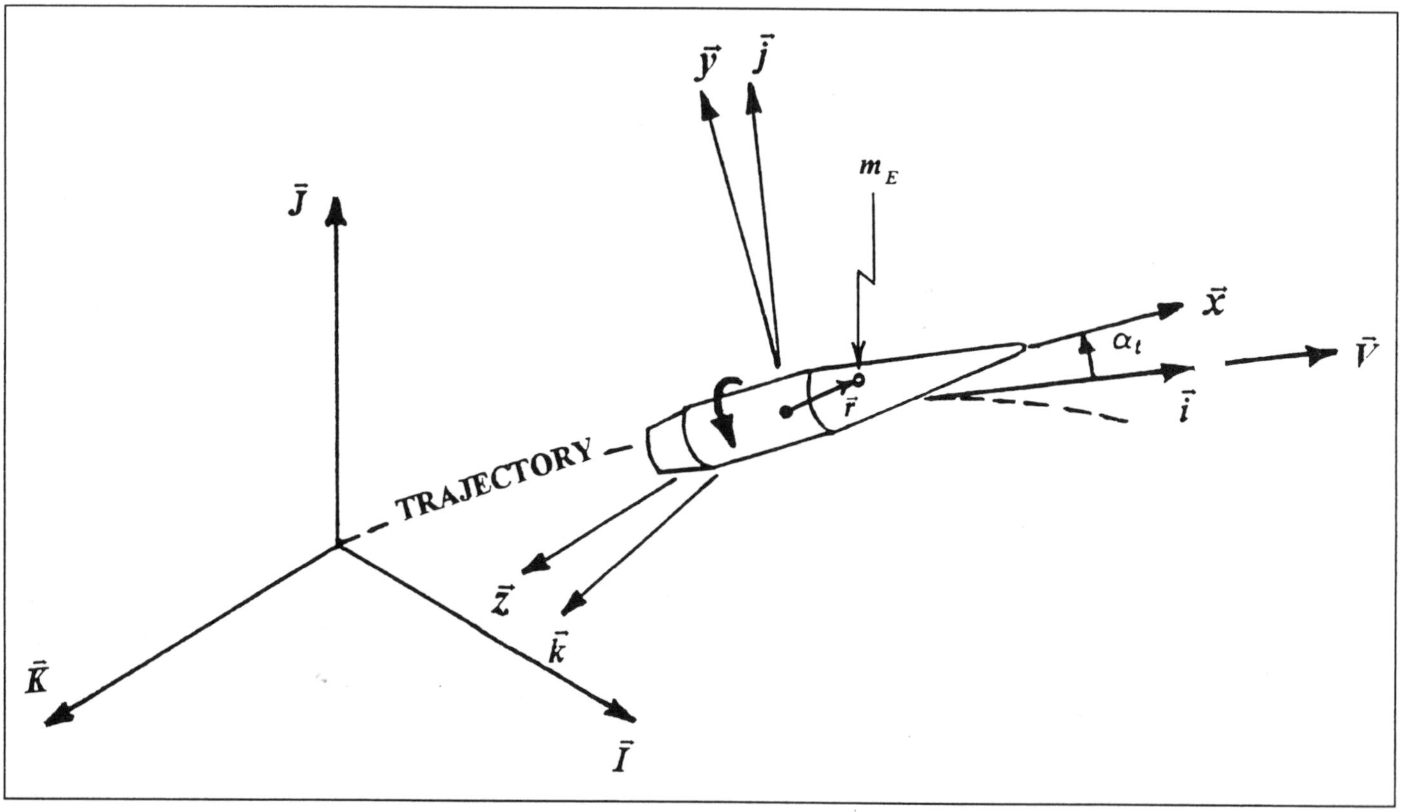

Figure 12.5 Coordinate Systems for a Projectile with Mass Asymmetry.

vector. (Also note that it is not the same vector $\vec{r}$ we used in the previous section of this chapter). Figure 12.5 illustrates the geometry of the two coordinate systems, for a projectile with a small dynamic unbalance, at an angle of attack, a_t. The relationships between the $(\vec{i},\vec{j},\vec{k})$ and the $(\vec{x},\vec{y},\vec{z})$ coordinate systems are given by the angular transformations:

$$\vec{x} = \cos\alpha\cos\beta\vec{i} + \sin\alpha\cos\beta\vec{j} + \sin\beta\vec{k} \qquad \textbf{(12.12)}$$

$$\vec{y} = -\sin\alpha\vec{i} + \cos\alpha\vec{j} \qquad \textbf{(12.13)}$$

$$\vec{z} = -\cos\alpha\sin\beta\vec{i} - \sin\alpha\sin\beta\vec{j} + \cos\beta\vec{k} \qquad \textbf{(12.14)}$$

We now make the small yaw approximation (see section 10.2 of Chapter 10), and equations (12.12) through (12.14) reduce to:

$$\vec{x} = \gamma\vec{i} + \alpha\vec{j} + \beta\vec{k} \qquad \textbf{(12.15)}$$

$$\vec{y} = -\alpha\vec{i} + \vec{j} \qquad \textbf{(12.16)}$$

$$\vec{z} = -\beta\vec{i} + \vec{k} \qquad \textbf{(12.17)}$$

where $\gamma = \cos\alpha\cos\beta \approx 1$

The total vector angular momentum of the spinning, rotationally symmetric projectile, containing a slight dynamic unbalance, is well approximated by the expression:

$$\vec{H} = I_x p\vec{x} + I_y\left(\vec{x} \times \frac{d\vec{x}}{dt}\right) - m_E(\vec{r} \times \vec{v}) \qquad \textbf{(12.18)}$$

where $\vec{H}$ = total vector angular momentum of the spinning projectile

$\vec{x}$ = a unit vector along the projectile's rotational axis of symmetry

t = time

p = projectile axial spin (radians/second)

I_x = projectile axial moment of inertia

I_y = projectile transverse moment of inertia, about any axis through the center of mass

m_E = small amount of mass removed from projectile

$\vec{r}$ = vector position at which the small mass was removed

$\vec{v}$ = vector velocity of the point at which the small mass was removed

The vector velocity, $\vec{v}$, is given by:

$$\vec{v} = p(\vec{x} \times \vec{r}) + \left[\left(\vec{x} \times \frac{d\vec{x}}{dt}\right) \times \vec{r}\right] \qquad \textbf{(12.19)}$$

Forming the vector cross product $(\vec{r} \times \vec{v})$, and expanding the vector triple product:

$$\vec{r} \times \vec{v} = -p(\vec{r} \bullet \vec{x})\vec{r} - \left(\vec{r} \bullet \frac{d\vec{x}}{dt}\right)(\vec{r} \times \vec{x}) + (\vec{r} \bullet \vec{x})\left(\vec{r} \times \frac{d\vec{x}}{dt}\right) \qquad \textbf{(12.20)}$$

The total vector angular momentum of the projectile, with a slight dynamic unbalance, is:

$$\vec{H} = \left(I_x p - m_E p r_E^2\right)\vec{x} + I_y\left(\vec{x} \times \frac{d\vec{x}}{dt}\right) - m_E(\vec{r} \times \vec{v}) \qquad \textbf{(12.21)}$$

But $(\vec{r} \bullet \vec{x} = l_E)$. For a spin-stabilized projectile, $\left|\frac{d\vec{x}}{dt}\right| << p$, and from equation (12.1), we have $m_E << m$. Thus, terms of order $\left[m_E \frac{d\vec{x}}{dt}\right]$ are neglected, and (12.21) reduces to:

$$\vec{H} \approx I_x p\vec{x} + I_y\left(\vec{x} \times \frac{d\vec{x}}{dt}\right) - m_E l_E p\vec{r} \qquad \textbf{(12.22)}$$

We define the roll angle, ϕ, as:

$$\phi = \int_0^t p\,dt \qquad \textbf{(12.23)}$$

The vector $\vec{r}$ may now be written as:

$$\vec{r} = l_E\vec{x} + r_E\cos\phi\vec{y} + \vec{r}_E\sin\phi\vec{z} \qquad \textbf{(12.24)}$$

Substituting equations (12.15) through (12.17) into equation (12.24), and collecting terms:

$$\vec{r} = \left(l_E\gamma - r_E\alpha\cos\phi - r_E\beta\sin\phi\right)\vec{i} + \left(i_E\alpha + r_E\cos\phi\right)\vec{j}$$
$$+\left(l_E\beta + r_E\sin\phi\right)\vec{k} \qquad \textbf{(12.25)}$$

But l_E and r_E are of the same order of magnitude, and both α and β are much smaller than γ. Thus the first term on the right-hand side of equation (12.25) reduces to $l_E\gamma\vec{i}$, and the vector $\vec{r}$ is well approximated by:

$$\vec{r} = l_E\gamma\vec{i} + \left(l_E\alpha + r_E\cos\phi\right)\vec{j} + \left(l_E\beta + r_E\sin\phi\right)\vec{k} \qquad \textbf{(12.26)}$$

We now differentiate equation (12.26) with respect to time, using $\dot{\phi} = \frac{d\phi}{dt} = p$, from equation (12.23).

$$\frac{d\vec{r}}{dt} = l_E\dot{\gamma}\vec{i} + \left(l_E\dot{\alpha} - r_E p\sin\phi\right)\vec{j} + \left(l_E\dot{\beta} + r_E p\cos\phi\right)\vec{k} \qquad \textbf{(12.27)}$$

In this section, we will consider only the first period of the epicyclic pitching and yawing motion, when the projectile has just cleared the muzzle of the gun. For the short distances we are concerned with, all aerodynamic *forces* and the acceleration due to gravity may be neglected. We will also neglect all aerodynamic moments *except the pitching (overturning) moment.* Making the above assumptions, we may differentiate equation (12.22), and set the derivative equal to the aerodyamic overturning moment, as defined by equation (10.9) of Chapter 10:

$$\frac{d\vec{H}}{dt} = I_x p \frac{d\vec{x}}{dt} + I_y\left(x \times \frac{d^2\vec{x}}{dt^2}\right) - m_E l_E p \frac{d\vec{r}}{dt} = \frac{1}{2}\rho S d C_{M_\alpha} V^2\left(\vec{i} \times \vec{x}\right) \quad \textbf{(12.28)}$$

We will also need the following vector derivatives and definitions:

$$\frac{d\vec{x}}{dt} = \dot{\gamma}\vec{i} + \dot{\alpha}\vec{j} + \dot{\beta}\vec{k} \quad \textbf{(12.29)}$$

$$\frac{d^2\vec{x}}{dt^2} = \frac{d^2\gamma}{dt^2}\vec{i} + \frac{d^2\alpha}{dt^2}\vec{j} + \frac{d^2\beta}{dt^2}\vec{k} \quad \textbf{(12.30)}$$

$$\vec{x} \times \frac{d^2\vec{x}}{dt^2} = \left(\alpha\frac{d^2\beta}{dt^2} - \beta\frac{d^2\alpha}{dt^2}\right)\vec{i} + \left(\beta\frac{d^2\gamma}{dt^2} - \gamma\frac{d^2\beta}{dt^2}\right)\vec{j} \quad \textbf{(12.31)}$$

$$+\left(\gamma\frac{d^2\alpha}{dt^2} - \alpha\frac{d^2\gamma}{dt^2}\right)\vec{k}$$

$$\vec{i} \times \vec{x} = -\beta\vec{j} + \alpha\vec{k} \quad \textbf{(12.32)}$$

We now substitute equation (12.27) and equations (12.29) through (12.32) into equation (12.28), and the result is three scalar ordinary differential equations, one for each of the $\left(\vec{i},\vec{j},\vec{k}\right)$ vector components.

For the i-component:

$$I_x p\dot{\gamma} + I_y\left(\alpha\frac{d^2\beta}{dt^2} - \beta\frac{d^2\alpha}{dt^2}\right) + m_E l_E^2 p\dot{\gamma} = 0 \quad \textbf{(12.33)}$$

For the j-component:

$$I_x p\dot{\alpha} + I_y\left(\beta\frac{d^2\gamma}{dt^2} - \gamma\frac{d^2\beta}{dt^2}\right) + m_E l_E p\left(l_E\dot{\alpha} - r_E p\sin\phi\right) \quad \textbf{(12.34)}$$

$$= -\frac{1}{2}\rho S d C_{M_\alpha} V^2\beta$$

For the k-component:

$$I_x p\dot{\beta} + I_y\left(\gamma\frac{d^2\alpha}{dt^2} - \alpha\frac{d^2\gamma}{dt^2}\right) + m_E l_E p\left(l_E\dot{\beta} - r_E p\cos\phi\right) \quad \textbf{(12.35)}$$

$$= \frac{1}{2}\rho S d C_{M_\alpha} V^2\alpha$$

We now transform equations (12.33) through (12.35) into new equations, with non-dimensional distance, s, as the independent variable.

$$s = \frac{1}{d}\int_0^t V dt \quad \textbf{(12.36)}$$

$$\dot{\alpha} = \left(\frac{V}{d}\right)\alpha' : \quad \dot{\beta} = \left(\frac{V}{d}\right)\beta' : \quad \dot{\gamma} = \left(\frac{V}{d}\right)\gamma' \quad \textbf{(12.37)}$$

Since no forces act on the projectile, the velocity is constant, and the second derivatives are:

$$\frac{d^2\alpha}{dt^2} = \left(\frac{V}{d}\right)^2\alpha'' : \quad \frac{d^2\beta}{dt^2} = \left(\frac{V}{d}\right)^2\beta'' : \quad \frac{d^2\gamma}{dt^2} = \left(\frac{V}{d}\right)^2\gamma'' \quad \textbf{(12.38)}$$

We now substitute equations (12.37) and (12.38) into equations (12.33) through (12.35), and divide both sides through by the quantity $I_y (V/d)^2$. After some simplification, the differential equations for the i, j, and k components reduce to:

$$P\left(1 + \frac{m_E l_E^2}{I_y}\right)\gamma' + \alpha\beta'' - \beta\alpha'' = 0 \quad \textbf{(12.39)}$$

$$P\left(1 + \frac{m_E l_E^2}{I_x}\right)\alpha' + \beta\gamma'' - \gamma\beta'' + M\beta - \left(\frac{I_E I_y}{I_x^2}\right)P^2\sin\phi = 0 \quad \textbf{(12.40)}$$

$$P\left(1 + \frac{m_E l_E^2}{I_x}\right)\beta' + \gamma\alpha'' - \alpha\gamma'' - M\alpha - \left(\frac{I_E I_y}{I_x^2}\right)P^2\cos\phi = 0 \quad \textbf{(12.41)}$$

where

$$P = \frac{I_x}{I_y}\left(\frac{pd}{V}\right) \quad \textbf{(12.42)}$$

$$M = \frac{\rho S d^3}{2I_y}C_{M_\alpha} \quad \textbf{(12.43)}$$

$$I_E = m_E r_E l_E \quad \textbf{(12.44)}$$

Note that a superscript prime (') indicates differentiation with respect to *s*.

We now make the small yaw and classical size assumptions (see Chapter 10), and neglect the small quantity $\left(m_E l_E^2/I_x\right)$ in comparison with unity. The small yaw assumption allows products of α or β and their derivatives to be neglected. For small yaw, $\gamma \approx 1$, and products of α or β with a derivative of γ are also negligible. Equation (12.39) vanishes entirely, under the small yaw assumption, and equations (12.40) and (12.41) reduce to:

$$P\alpha' - \beta'' + M\beta = \left(\frac{I_E I_y}{I_x^2}\right)P^2\sin\phi \quad \textbf{(12.45)}$$

$$P\beta' + \alpha'' - M\alpha = -\left(\frac{I_E I_y}{I_x^2}\right)P^2\cos\phi \quad \textbf{(12.46)}$$

Equation (12.45) is now multiplied by $-i = -\sqrt{-1}$, and added to equation (12.46):

$$\alpha'' + i\beta'' + P\left(\beta' - i\alpha'\right) - M\left(\alpha + i\beta\right) = -\left(\frac{I_E I_y}{I_x^2}\right)P^2\left(\cos\phi - i\sin\phi\right) \quad \textbf{(12.47)}$$

Let $\xi = \alpha + i\beta$. Then, $\xi'' = \alpha'' + i\beta''$; and $-i\xi' = \beta' - i\alpha'$.

From elementary trigonometry, $\cos\phi + i\sin\phi = e^{i\phi}$. Substituting these definitions into equation (12.47) gives the differential equation for the pitching and yawing motion of a spinning projectile, with a small dynamic unbalance, near the muzzle of the gun:

$$\boxed{\xi'' = -iP\xi' - M\xi = -\left(\frac{I_E I_y}{I_x^2}\right)P^2 e^{i\phi}} \quad \textbf{(12.48)}$$

The solution of the homogeneous part (right-hand side set equal to zero) of equation (12.48) is found in elementary textbooks on ordinary differential equations:

$$\xi = K_F e^{i\phi_F} + K_S e^{i\phi_S} \qquad \textbf{(12.49)}$$

where $\xi = \alpha + i\beta$

K_F = amplitude of the fast epicyclic yaw mode (or arm)

K_S = amplitude of the slow epicyclic yaw mode (or arm)

$\phi_F = \phi_{F_0} + \phi'_F s$

$\phi_S = \phi_{S_0} + \phi'_S s$

ϕ_{F_0} = initial phase angle of the fast epicyclic yaw arm

ϕ_{S_0} = initial phase angle of the slow epicyclic yaw arm

$\phi'_F = \frac{1}{2}\left[P + \sqrt{P^2 - 4M}\right]$, the fast arm turning rate (radians/caliber) **(12.50)**

$\phi'_S = \frac{1}{2}\left[P + \sqrt{P^2 - 4M}\right]$, the slow arm turning rate (radians/caliber) **(12.51)**

The solution to the inhomogeneous equation (12.48) is a tricycle:

$$\boxed{\xi = K_F e^{i\phi_F} + K_S e^{i\phi_S} + K_T e^{i\phi}} \qquad \textbf{(12.52)}$$

where K_T is the amplitude of the trim (tricyclic) pitch and yaw arm, and the roll angle is defined as:

$$\boxed{\phi = \phi_0 + \phi' s = \phi_0 + \left(\frac{pd}{V}\right)s} \qquad \textbf{(12.53)}$$

The particular solution (the tricyclic pitch and yaw arm) of equation (12.52) must also satisfy the differential equation (12.48). Therefore we substitute the tricyclic solution and its derivatives, plus the definition $\phi' = pd/V$, into equation (12.48), and solve for the magnitude of the trim arm:

$$K_T = \frac{I_E I_y P^2}{I_x^2\left(\phi'^2 - P\phi' + M\right)} = \frac{I_E I_y P^2}{I_y^2 P^2 - I_y I_x P^2 + I_x^2 M} \qquad \textbf{(12.54)}$$

Dividing both the numerator and the denominator of the last equation of (12.54) by $\left(I_y P^2\right)$:

$$K_T = \frac{I_E}{I_y - I_x + \left(I_x^2 M / I_y P^2\right)} \qquad \textbf{(12.55)}$$

We assume the projectile to be gyroscopically stable, thus $P^2/4M > 1$. Then, $M / P^2 < 1/4$, and in general, $I_x/I_y < 1/5$. The last term in the denominator of equation (12.55) is therefore very small, in comparison with I_x or I_y, and is neglected. An excellent approximation to equation (12.55) is:

$$\boxed{K_T \approx \frac{I_E}{I_y - I_x}} \qquad \textbf{(12.56)}$$

where $I_E = m_E r_E l_E$

This simple and useful result gives us a mathematical relationship between a slight dynamic unbalance due to mass asymmetry, and the size of the tricycle, or trim, arm that it adds to the epicyclic pitching and yawing motion. [Murphy has derived the same result in References 4 and 5]. Equations (12.52) and (12.56) show that a slight mass asymmetry adds a very small third arm, which rotates at the spin frequency, to the fast and slow epicyclic yaw arms considered in Chapter 10. Note that a *configurational asymmetry*, such as a finned missile with a bent fin, or a spinning projectile with a slightly bent nose, will also produce a *tricyclic pitch and yaw arm*. In general, the size of the K_T arm is very small, compared with the amplitude of the fast and slow epicyclic yaw arms, as will be seen presently.

12.4 THE GENERALIZED AERODYNAMIC JUMP EFFECT

In the previous chapter, we observed that the epicyclic pitching and yawing motion produces three separate and distinct effects on a flat-fire trajectory; aerodynamic jump, epicyclic swerve, and drift. For modern high-velocity, small-yaw, ground-launched flat-fire trajectories, the epicyclic swerve and the drift are generally small and insignificant compared with the aerodynamic jump. We recall equation (11.47) from the previous chapter [renumbered here as equation (12.57)]:

$$\boxed{Aerodynamic\ jump = J_A = k_y^2\left(\frac{C_{L_\alpha}}{C_{M_\alpha}}\right)\left[iP\xi_0 - \xi'_0\right]} \qquad \textbf{(12.57)}$$

where $k_y^2 = \dfrac{I_y}{md^2}$

C_{L_α} = Aerodynamic Lift Force Coefficient

C_{M_α} = Aerodynamic Overturning Moment Coefficient

$P = \dfrac{I_x}{I_y}\left(\dfrac{pd}{V}\right)$

ξ_0 = Initial complex yaw angle

ξ'_0 = Initial complex yaw rate, or tip-off rate (radians/caliber)

J_A = Aerodynamic Jump (J_A is the tangent of the deflection angle due to jump)

Two illustrative examples of aerodynamic jump were presented in Chapter 11. The first was example 11.1, that showed the effect of tip-off rate on the aerodynamic jump of a non-spinning, Basic Finner model (see Figure 11.2) launched at Mach 1.8. The calculations showed that an initial yaw rate, $\xi_0' = 0.0018582$ radians/caliber (directed to the right of the line of fire), produced a first maximum yaw of 10 degrees, and an aerodynamic jump, $J_A = 0.0056694$, also directed to the right. The yawing and swerving motions were illustrated in Figure 11.3, which showed that the aerodynamic jump deflected the trajectory 13.6 inches [Deflection = (0.0056694)(200)(12) = 13.6"] to the right, at a range of 200 feet!

The second example of aerodynamic jump presented in Chapter 11 was for the .308," 168 grain Sierra International bullet, fired at a muzzle velocity of 2600 feet per second, from a barrel with 12" twist of rifling, and an initial yaw rate of 25 radians/second [ξ_0' = (25)(0.308)/{(12)(2600)} = 0.0002468 radians/caliber (directed to the left of the line of fire)]. The epicyclic pitching and yawing motion was shown in Figure 11.4, and the trajectory deflections produced by this yawing motion were illustrated in Figure 11.5. At a range of 300 feet, the epicyclic swerve radius is 0.03," and the drift is 0.05," to the right. At the same range, the trajectory deflection due to aerodynamic jump is 0.75" to the right, which is an order of magnitude larger effect than that produced by either the epicyclic swerve or the drift.

12.5 THE EFFECT OF MASS ASYMMETRY ON LATERAL THROWOFF AND AERODYNAMIC JUMP

Let $\phi_F = \phi_{F_0} + \phi_F' s; \quad \phi_S = \phi_{S_0} + \phi_S' s; \quad \phi = \phi_0 + \phi' s;$ **(12.58)** and substitute these definitions into equation (12.52). If we then differentiate equation (12.52) with respect to s, and set s = 0 in both (12.52) and its derivative, we obtain:

$$\xi_0 = K_{F_0} e^{i\phi_{F0}} + K_{S_0} e^{i\phi_{S0}} + K_T e^{i\phi_0} \qquad \mathbf{(12.59)}$$

$$\xi_0' = i\phi_F' K_{F_0} e^{i\phi_{F0}} + i\phi_S' K_{S_0} e^{i\phi_{S0}} + i\phi' K_T e^{i\phi_0} \qquad \mathbf{(12.60)}$$

We recall the expression for the aerodynamic jump (with no mass asymmetry) from the previous chapter:

$$J_A = iC_{L_\alpha}{}^* \left[\frac{K_{F_0}}{\phi_F'} e^{i\phi_{F0}} + \frac{K_{S_0}}{\phi_S'} e^{i\phi_{S0}} \right] \qquad \mathbf{(11.40)}$$

It can be shown that for *tricyclic* pitching and yawing motion the aerodynamic jump is given by:

$$J_A = iC_{L_\alpha}{}^* \left[\frac{K_{F_0}}{\phi_F'} e^{i\phi_{F0}} + \frac{K_{S_0}}{\phi_S'} e^{i\phi_{S0}} + \frac{K_T}{\phi'} e^{i\phi_0} \right] \qquad \mathbf{(12.61)}$$

With the help of equations (10.120) and (10.121) from Chapter 10, equation (12.61) may be written in the alternate form:

$$J_A = \frac{iC_{L_\alpha}{}^*}{\phi_F' \phi_S'} \left(\left[(\phi_F' + \phi_S')\xi_0 - \xi_0' \right] + \left[K_T e^{i\phi_0} (\phi' - \phi_F' - \phi_S') \right] \right) \qquad \mathbf{(12.62)}$$

For spin-stabilized projectiles, $\phi_F' \ll \phi'$, and $\phi_S' \ll \phi'$.

Making these approximations in equation (12.62) leads to the simpler form:

$$J_A = \frac{iC_{L_\alpha}{}^*}{\phi_F' \phi_S'} \left(\left[(\phi_F' + \phi_S')\xi_0 - \xi_0' \right] + \left[\phi' K_T e^{i\phi_0} \right] \right) \qquad \mathbf{(12.63)}$$

The following definitions are needed to transform equation (12.63) into the desired final form:

$$k_y^2 = \frac{I_y}{md^2} \qquad \mathbf{(12.64)}$$

$$k_y^{-2} C_{M_\alpha} = \phi_F' \phi_S' \qquad \mathbf{(12.65)}$$

$$\phi' = \frac{pd}{V} = \frac{2\pi}{n} \qquad \mathbf{(12.66)}$$

$$P = \frac{I_x}{I_y} \frac{pd}{V} = \phi_F' + \phi_S' \qquad \mathbf{(12.67)}$$

$$K_T = \frac{I_E}{I_y - I_x} = \frac{m_E r_E l_E}{I_y - I_x} \qquad \mathbf{(12.68)}$$

Substituting the above definitions in equation (12.63) and doing the necessary algebraic manipulation, we obtain:

$$J_A = k_y^2 \frac{C_{L_\alpha}}{C_{M_\alpha}} \left[(iP\xi_0 - \xi_0') + (i\phi' K_T e^{i\phi_0}) \right]$$

$$= k_y^2 \frac{C_{L_\alpha}}{C_{M_\alpha}} \left[(iP\xi_0 - \xi_0') + \left(i \frac{2\pi}{n} \frac{m_E r_E l_E}{I_y - I_x} e^{i\phi_0} \right) \right] \qquad \mathbf{(12.69)}$$

Equation (12.69) contains the aerodynamic jump due to any initial angle or angular rate, in addition to the contribution due to mass asymmetry. If we factor out the mass-asymmetry effect so that it stands alone, we obtain our final result:

$$\boxed{J_A = i\left(\frac{2\pi}{n}\right)\left(\frac{m_E r_E l_E}{md^2}\right)\left(\frac{C_{L_\alpha}}{C_{M_\alpha}}\right) e^{i\phi_0}} \qquad \mathbf{(12.70)}$$

An example of the application of equation (12.70) will be given presently.

The lateral throwoff due to the removal of a small mass, m_E, is readily obtained. Taking first moments (mass times distance) about the projectile's axis of rotational symmetry, $m\hat{\varepsilon} = m_E r_E$, and we find that the static unbalance, due to removal of a small mass m_E, located at a distance r_E off the projectile's axis of rotational symmetry is given by:

$$\boxed{\hat{\varepsilon} = \frac{m_E r_E}{m}} \qquad \mathbf{(12.71)}$$

Substituting equation (12.71) into equation (12.10) gives the lateral throwoff for a small mass-asymmetry:

$$\boxed{T_L = i\left(\frac{2\pi}{n}\right)\left(\frac{m_E r_E}{md}\right) e^{i\phi_0}} \qquad \mathbf{(12.72)}$$

Remember that the mass m_E is removed at an arbitrary axial distance, l_E, from the projectile's center of gravity (CG), and at an arbitrary distance, r_E, laterally off the axis of symmetry. The distance l_E is defined as positive if the mass is removed ahead of the CG, and negative if m_E is removed aft of the CG location. Also note that the roll orientation angle Φ_0 used to define the lateral throwoff [equation (12.72)] is the orientation of the *projectile's CG*, at the instant of separation from the gun muzzle, not the roll orientation of the mass, m_E. Thus the two angles, Φ_0 and ϕ_0 are 180 degrees out of phase with each other.

Example 12.1

The first example we will present illustrates the effect of a mass asymmetry on the tricyclic pitching and yawing motion, the lateral throwoff, and the aerodynamic jump. The experimental firings were conducted in the Naval Ordnance Laboratory (NOL) Pressurized Aeroballistics Range, and were reported by J. E. Long, G. Parrish, and J. D. Nicolaides in Reference 6.

The NOL firings of mass-asymmetric projectiles utilized 20mm steel cone-cylinder models, whose geometry is shown in Figure 12.6. The configuration had a pointed conical nose, 2 calibers in length, followed by a 3-caliber long cylindrical afterbody. The 5-caliber long cone-cylinder projectile was deliberately unbalanced by drilling one or two off-axis holes in the base, to a depth of 1 caliber. Only the one-hole model is considered in this chapter.

The relevant physical and aeroballistic characteristics of the steel cone-cylinder projectile are summarized in the table below:

Table 12.1

Muzzle velocity = 2210 feet per second
Launch Mach number = 1.98
Rifling twist rate = 25.5 calibers/turn, right-hand twist
Reference diameter = 0.786"
Projectile length = 3.93"
Projectile weight = 0.392 lb.
Center of gravity = 1.47" from base
Axial moment of inertia = 0.0282 lb.-in.^{2}
Transverse moment of inertia = 0.3263 lb.-in.^{2}
Mass removed by drilling one hole = m_E = 0.007 lb.
Center of drilled hole, off axis of symmetry = r_E = 0.196"
Diameter of drilled hole = 0.198"
Centroid of drilled hole (aft of CG) = l_E = -1.077"

[Note that the drilled hole emerged ***down*** (6:00 position) at the muzzle, thus ϕ_0 = 180 degrees, and Φ_0 = 0 degrees]

Additional aeroballistic quantities for the 20mm steel cone-cylinder projectile, obtained from firings in the NOL Aeroballistics range, are (in BRL Aeroballistic nomenclature):

C_D =0.377; C_{M_α} =3.50; C_{L_α} =2.61; $\left(C_{M_q} + C_{M_{\dot\alpha}}\right)$=-18.8; $C_{M_{p\alpha}}$=0.60
S_g =2.03; S_d=*0.94;* ϕ'_F=0.01822rad./cal.; ϕ'_S =0.00307rad./cal.;

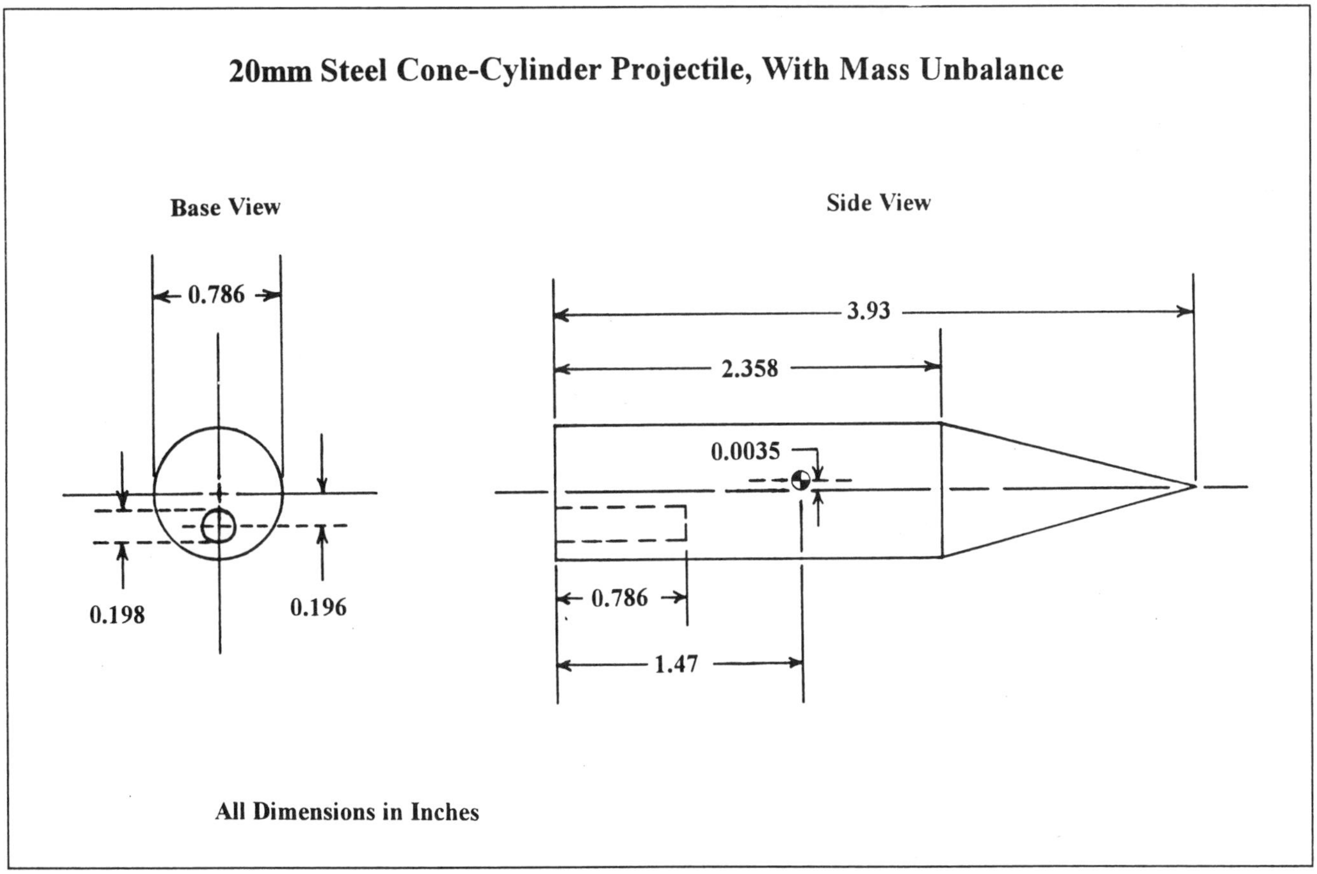

Figure 12.6 Sketch of a Mass-Unbalanced 20 mm Steel Cone-Cylinder Projectile.

$$\phi' = \left(\frac{pd}{V}\right) = 0.2464 \text{ rad./cal.}; \quad \lambda_F = -0.000195 \text{ /cal.} \quad \lambda_S = 0.000166 \text{ /cal.}$$

The quantity I_E and the dynamic unbalance angle, K_T, are:

$I_E = m_E r_E l_E =$ (.007 lb.)(.196")(-1.077") = - 0.001478 lb.-in.^{2}

$$K_T = \frac{|I_E|}{I_y - I_x} = (0\ .001478)/(.3263 - .0282) = 0.004958 \text{ radian} = 0.28 \text{ degree}$$

Note that the *theoretical value* of the dynamic unbalance angle, K_T, *calculated* from equation (12.56), is 0.004958 radian, or 0.28 degree. The amplitude of the tricyclic arm, *measured* in the NOL range was 0.30 degree. Thus the theoretical and the experimental values of K_T disagree by only 0.02 degree, for this case.

Substituting the appropriate values from Table 12.1 into equation (12.70):

$$J_A = i\left(\frac{2\pi}{25.2}\right)\left[\frac{(.007)(.196)(-1.077)}{(.392)(.786)^2}\right]\left(\frac{2.61}{3.50}\right)(-1) = 0.001121i$$

At 300 feet range, the deflection due to aerodynamic jump = (300)(12)(.001121) = 4.0 inches, to the right.

The lateral throwoff is found by substituting the appropriate values from Table 12.1 into equation (12.72):

$$T_L = i\left(\frac{2\pi}{25.2}\right)\left[\frac{(.007)(.196)}{(.392)(.786)}\right] = 0.001097i$$

At 300 feet range, the deflection due to lateral throwoff = (300)(12)(.001097) = 3.9 inches, also to the right. The total deflection due to both aerodynamic jump and lateral throwoff is 7.9 inches.

Figure 12.7 is a plot of the pitching and yawing motion of the 20mm mass-asymmetric cone-cylinder projectile, over the first 100 feet of its flight. Note that the very small tricyclic (K_T) arm is too small ($K_T \approx 0.3$ degree) to be visible in this plot, and the observed pitching and yawing motion appears to be a characteristic epicycle for a dynamically stable, spin-stabilized shell. The first maximum yaw (approximately 9 degrees) occurs about 27 feet downrange of the gun muzzle.

Figure 12.8 is a plot of the vertical and horizontal trajectory components, over 300 feet of the same flight. The top plot [Figure 12.8(a)] shows the vertical plane of the trajectory, and it illustrates the small epicyclic swerving motion, superimposed on the point-mass (dashed curve) trajectory. The bottom graph [Figure 12.8(b)] is a plot of the horizontal trajectory component, and it shows the lateral throwoff, the aerodynamic jump, and the epicyclic swerve caused by the deliberately-introduced mass-asymmetry. The epicyclic swerve radius is approximately 0.30" at the gun muzzle; this value has damped to about 0.14" at a point 300 feet downrange. The lateral throwoff deflects the trajectory 3.9 inches to the right at this distance, and the aerodynamic jump causes an additional right-deflection of 4.0 inches, so that the projectile impacts 7.9 inches to

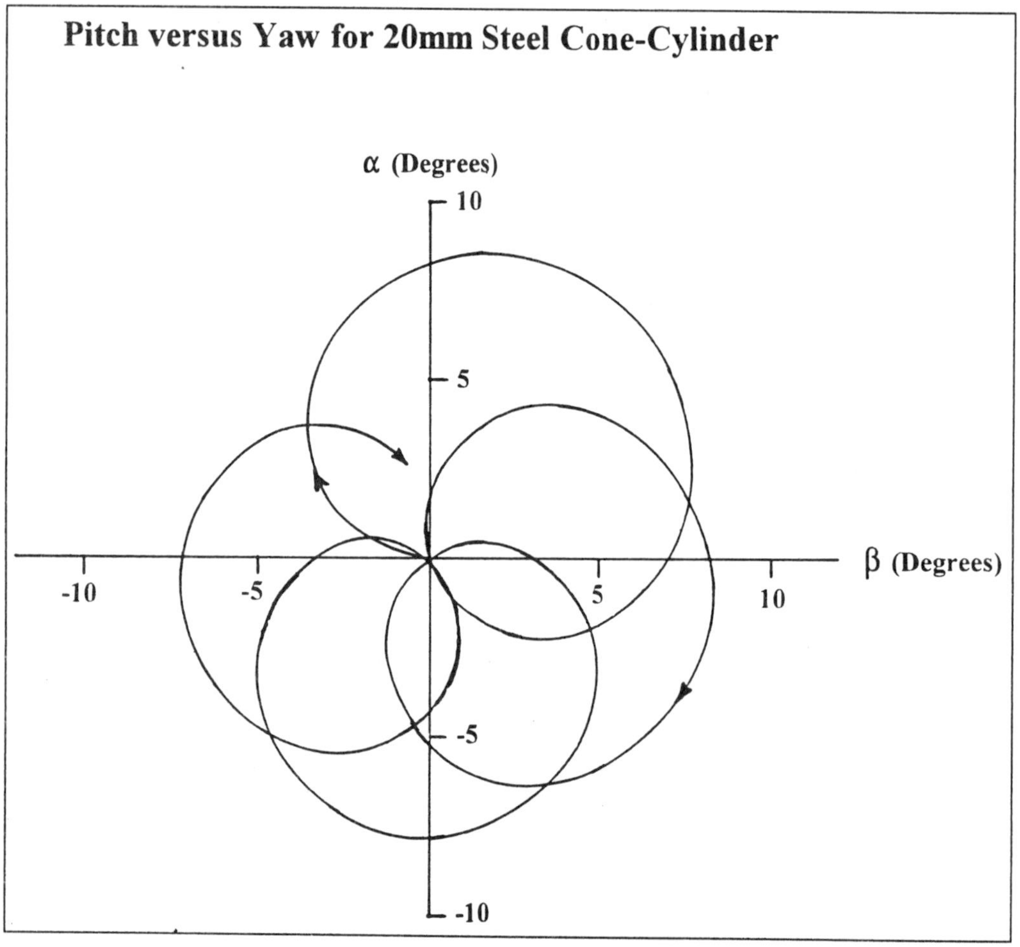

Figure 12.7 Pitch versus Yaw for a Mass-Unbalanced Projectile.

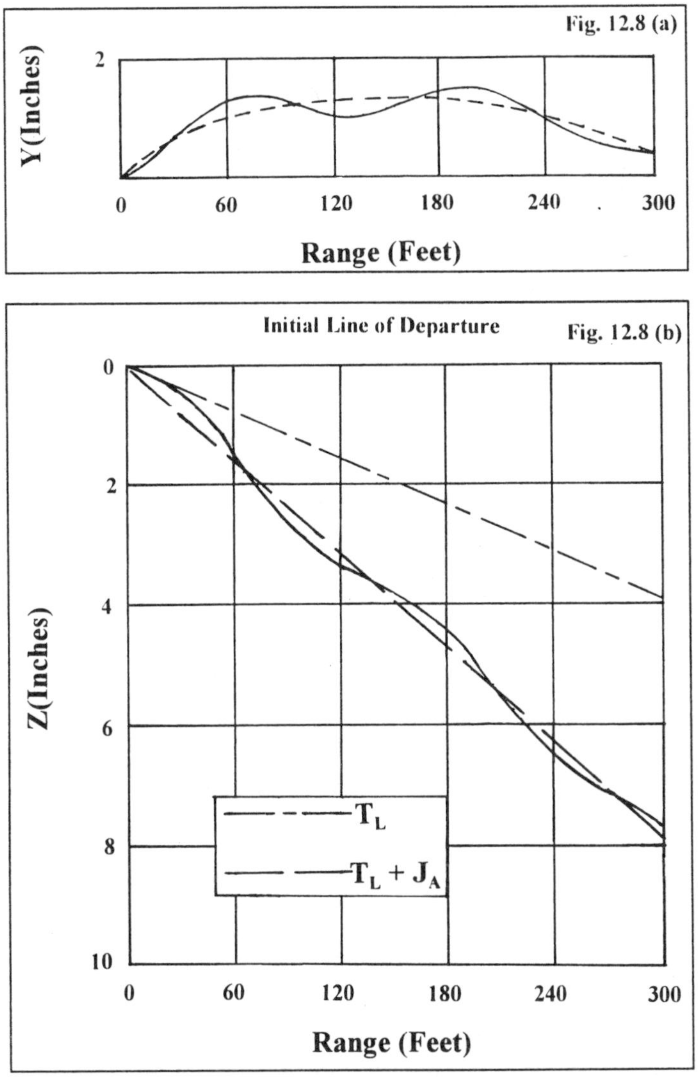

Figure 12.8 Height and Deflection versus Range for a Mass-Unbalanced 20 mm Projectile.

the right of the initial line of departure. [There is also a very small right-hand drift, D_R, but it amounts to less than 0.1 inch at 300 feet range, and therefore the drift is not visible in the horizontal deflection plot].

Note that if a gun with *left twist of rifling* had been used, and the base-drilled hole had again emerged *down* at the muzzle, the direction of initial yawing (ξ_0') would have been to the *right* of the line of fire, and both the lateral throwoff and the aerodynamic jump would have produced *left-deflections.*

Also note that if the small mass m_E had been removed *ahead* of the projectile's center-of-gravity, and the drilled hole had emerged *down* at the muzzle, from a *right-hand twist of rifling*, the lateral throwoff would still be to the *right*, but the direction of initial yawing (ξ_0') would also have been to the *right*, and the resulting aerodynamic jump would have been to the *left* of the initial line of fire. This illustrates the fact that a mass-unbalance *aft* of the projectile's CG (center of gravity) causes the lateral throwoff and aerodynamic jump effects to *reinforce* each other, whereas a mass-unbalance *forward* of the projectile's CG causes a *partial cancellation* of the two effects! Although *zero* mass-unbalance is the universally desired production goal in the manufacture of projectiles, *a small mass-unbalance at the nose is always preferable to an unbalance at the base.* This fact was first established experimentally by F. W. Mann (Ref. 1), and our modern aeroballistic analysis quantifies and confirms Mann's results.

Static and dynamic unbalance are independent properties of a projectile, although they usually occur in conjunction. Figure 12.1 illustrated a *pure static unbalance*, in which the center-of-mass is displaced laterally off the axis of rotational symmetry, but the longitudinal principal axis of inertia remains *parallel* to the axis of symmetry. In this case, there will be a *lateral throwoff* at the muzzle, but *no aerodynamic jump.* Figure 12.9 shows a *pure dynamic unbalance*, in which the center-of- mass remains on the axis, but the longitudinal principal axis of inertia is *inclined* at a small angle to the rotational axis of symmetry. For this case, there will be an *aero-*

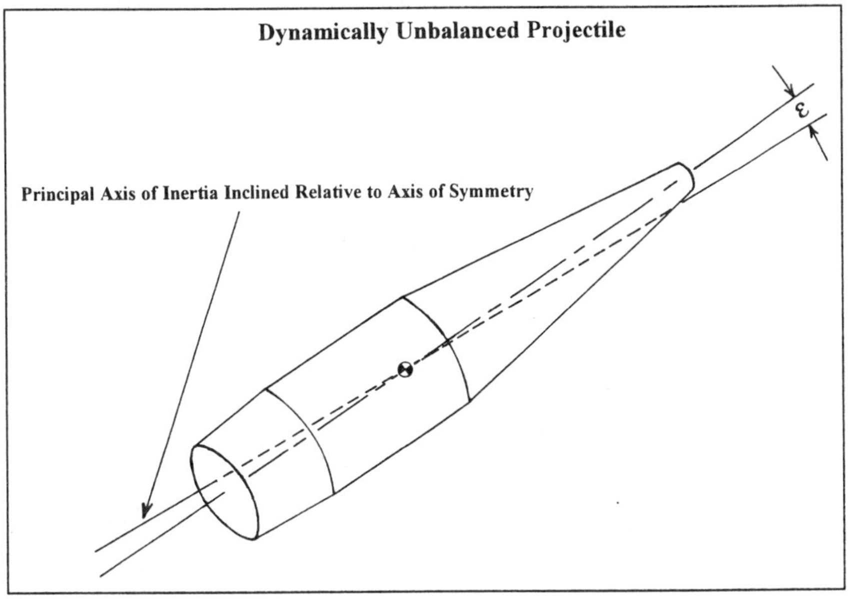

Figure 12.9 Sketch of a Statically Balanced, but Dynamically Unbalanced Projectile.

dynamic jump at launch, but *no lateral throwoff.* In practice, most projectiles will possess *both a static and a dynamic unbalance*, and will therefore exhibit both *lateral throwoff and aerodynamic jump* at the instant of separation from the muzzle.

12.6 DERIVATION OF KENT'S EQUATION FOR A SMALL MASS-ASYMMETRY

The relationship between the dynamic unbalance angle, K_T, and the first maximum yaw angle, δ_{MAX}, is referred to as "Kent's Equation." To derive it, we return to equations (12.63) and (12.65) of the previous section.

We first add equations (12.63) and (12.65), and then subtract them. Two useful equations are obtained by these operations:

$$K_{F_0} + K_{S_0} = \left(\frac{2\phi' - P}{\phi_F' - \phi_S'}\right)K_T = \frac{\left(2I_y/I_x - 1\right)PK_T}{\phi_F' - \phi_S'} \qquad \textbf{(12.73)}$$

$$K_{F_0} - K_{S_0} = K_T \qquad \textbf{(12.74)}$$

Equation (12.74) shows that for a very small amplitude dynamic unbalance angle, the fast and slow epicyclic yaw arms are nearly the same size.

In Chapter 10, the following two equations were derived:

$$\phi_F' = \frac{1}{2}\left[P + \sqrt{P^2 - 4M}\right] \qquad \textbf{(10.102)}$$

$$\phi_S' = \frac{1}{2}\left[P - \sqrt{P^2 - 4M}\right] \qquad \textbf{(10.103)}$$

where $P = \dfrac{I_x}{I_y}\left(\dfrac{pd}{V}\right)$

$$M = \frac{\rho S d^3}{2I_y}C_{M_\alpha}$$

If equations (10.102) and (10.103) are first added, then subtracted, we obtain:

$$\phi_F' + \phi_S' = P; \quad \phi_F' - \phi_S' = \sqrt{P^2 - 4M} \qquad \textbf{(12.75)}$$

$$\text{But, } \frac{P^2}{4M} = S_g; \quad \therefore 4M = \frac{P^2}{S_g}; \phi_F' - \phi_S' = P\sqrt{1 - \frac{1}{S_g}} \qquad \textbf{(12.76)}$$

Substituting these results into equation (12.73) and simplifying:

$$\sin\delta_{MAX} = K_{F_0} + K_{S_0} = \left(2\frac{I_y}{I_x} - 1\right)\left(\frac{K_T}{\sqrt{1 - 1/S_g}}\right) \qquad \textbf{(12.77)}$$

We note that C. H. Murphy has derived the same result in Reference 4.

We also note that the trim angle, K_T, of a dynamically unbalanced projectile is precisely equal to the dynamic unbalance angle, ε, where ε is the angle between the longitudinal principal axis of inertia, and the geometric axis of rotational symmetry. Figure 12.9 illustrates a *statically balanced,* but *dynamically unbalanced* projectile. Since K_T (or ε) is a *very small angle*, it is always permissible to replace the sine of the angle ε with the angle itself (in radians). Replacing K_T with ε leads to the classical form of Kent's equation:

$$\boxed{\sin\delta_{MAX} = \left(2\frac{I_y}{I_x} - 1\right)\left(\frac{\varepsilon}{\sqrt{1 - 1/S_g}}\right)} \qquad \textbf{(12.78)}$$

where ε = the dynamic unbalance angle (radians)

δ_{MAX} = the first maximum yaw angle

Note that the dynamic unbalance angle is denoted by the *script* Greek letter epsilon, ε. The Greek letter epsilon with a carat, $\hat{\varepsilon}$, is used throughout this chapter to denote the amount of *static* unbalance in a projectile. The two symbols look somewhat alike, and the reader needs to pay careful attention to which ones are used in a given equation.

Example 12.2

Use Kent's equation to calculate the first maximum yaw for the mass-asymmetric, 20mm steel cone-cylinder projectile of Example 1.

Substituting the values provided in Table 12.1 into equation (12.78), we find:

$$\sin\delta_{MAX} = \left[2\left(\frac{.3263}{.0282}\right) - 1\right]\left[\frac{.004958}{\sqrt{1 - (1/2.03)}}\right] = 0.15412$$

Thus $\delta_{MAX} = Sin^{-1}(0.15412) = 8.9$ degrees.

Comparison of this value with the plotted first maximum yaw (illustrated in Figure 12.7), shows excellent agreement.

12.7 THE EFFECT OF IN-BORE YAW ON LATERAL THROWOFF AND AERODYNAMIC JUMP

In this section, we will consider a spin-stabilized projectile that is rotationally symmetric, both in configuration and mass distribution. The projectile is assumed to be "eccentrically engraved," i.e., it is "tilted" as it enters the rifling, and it is assumed that the tilt persists throughout its passage through the rifled barrel. We further assume that the front bourrelet rides a single land or groove all the way down the gun tube and the rear bourrelet (or rotating band) rides the opposite land or groove, so there is no "balloting," or bouncing from one land or groove to another. Under these assumptions, the shell's axis of rotational symmetry "precesses" at the roll or spin rate as it travels down the rifled barrel.

The tilted bullet in the barrel is illustrated (with a greatly exaggerated tilt) in Figure 12.10. The tilt angle, (in-bore yaw angle) is denoted by the Greek letter ε. We assume that the tilt occurs about the mid-point of the bullet's cylindrical center section; thus if the center-of-gravity is either ahead of or behind this mid-point, there will also be a static unbalance, denoted by the Greek letter $\hat{\varepsilon}$. Fig-

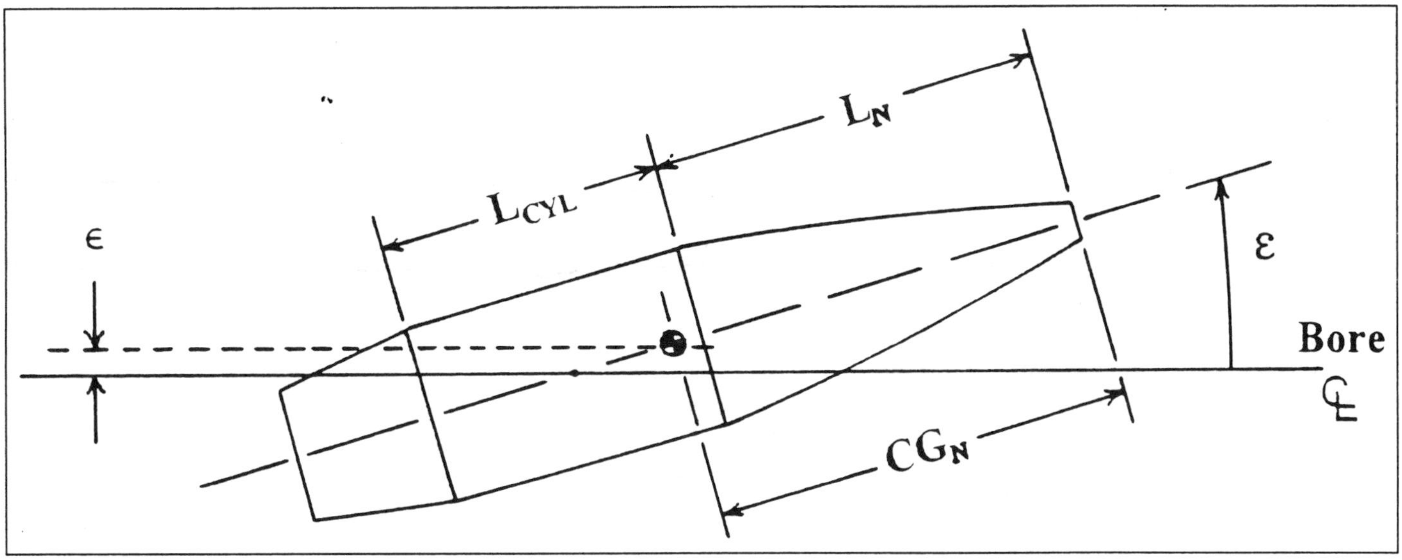

Figure 12.10 Sketch of a Projectile with In-Bore Yaw.

ure 12.10 shows that the relationship between the static unbalance and the tilt angle is given by the following equation:

$$\frac{\hat{\varepsilon}}{d} = \left(L_N + \tfrac{1}{2}L_{CYL} - CG_N\right)\tan\varepsilon \qquad \textbf{(12.79)}$$

where L_N = projectile nose length (calibers)

L_{CYL} = length of the cylindrical center section (calibers)

CG_N = the distance from the nose to the center of gravity (calibers)

d = bullet reference diameter (usually taken as the front bourrelet diameter)

$\hat{\varepsilon}$ = static unbalance due to bullet tilt (in-bore yaw)

For the very small tilt angles considered, $\tan\varepsilon \approx \sin\varepsilon$, and we may write (12.79) as:

$$\boxed{\frac{\hat{\varepsilon}}{d} = \left(L_N + \tfrac{1}{2}L_{CYL} - CG_N\right)\sin\varepsilon} \qquad \textbf{(12.80)}$$

If the center of gravity location is forward of the mid-point of the cylinder (which is usually the case), the static unbalance is in the same direction as the angle ε. For a CG located aft of the cylindrical mid-point, $\hat{\varepsilon}$ and ε are oppositely directed.

We now define the roll orientation angle at the muzzle, ϕ_0, to be the angle between the vertical (12:00 position) and the plane containing both ε and the bore centerline. Then the initial yaw at launch is given by:

$$\xi_0 = \sin\varepsilon e^{i\phi_0} \qquad \textbf{(12.81)}$$

Substitution of equation (12.81) into equations (12.66) and (12.67) yields the tip-off rate, and after some simplification, we find:

$$\xi_0' = i\left(\frac{I_y}{I_x}\right)P\sin\varepsilon e^{i\phi_0} = i\left(\frac{2\pi}{n}\right)\sin\varepsilon e^{i\phi_0} \qquad \textbf{(12.82)}$$

where n = rifling twist rate (calibers/turn, taken as positive for right-hand twist).

Equations (12.81) and (12.82) are now substituted into equation (12.57), and the aerodynamic jump for a bullet with in-bore yaw is given by:

$$\boxed{J_A = -i\left[\left(\frac{2\pi}{n}\right)\left(k_y^2 - k_x^2\right)\left(\frac{C_{L_\alpha}}{C_{M_\alpha}}\right)\sin\varepsilon\right]e^{i\phi_0}} \qquad \textbf{(12.83)}$$

where $k_y^2 = \dfrac{I_y}{md^2}$

$k_x^2 = \dfrac{I_x}{md^2}$

C_{L_α} = Aerodynamic Lift Force Coefficient

C_{M_α} = Aerodynamic Overturning Moment Coefficient

The lateral throwoff due to bullet tilt is now found by substituting equation (12.80) into equation (12.10):

$$\boxed{T_L = i\left[\left(\frac{2\pi}{n}\right)\left(L_N + \tfrac{1}{2}L_{CYL} - CG_N\right)\sin\varepsilon\right]e^{i\phi_0}} \qquad \textbf{(12.84)}$$

Equations (12.83) and (12.84) show that for a tilted bullet, with it's center-of-gravity location forward of the bullet's cylindrical mid-point, the aerodynamic jump and the lateral throwoff oppose each other, and therefore a partial cancellation effect occurs. In general, the aerodynamic jump due to in-bore yaw is larger in magnitude than the lateral throwoff, thus the trajectory is *usually* deflected to the left (toward 9:00 on the target), for a bullet that emerges *nose up*, from a *right-hand twist of rifling*.

Example 12.3

The effect of bullet tilt, or in-bore yaw, will be demonstrated using the .308," 168 Grain Sierra International bullet, fired at a muzzle velocity of 2600 fps, from a .308 Winchester rifle with a right-hand, 12" twist of rifling. The physical and aerodynamic characteristics we will need were listed in Chapter 9, and are summarized in Table 12.2:

Table 12.2

d = 0.308" = 0.025667 ft. ; m = 168 grains = 0.024008 lb. ;

n = 12 (in./turn) / 0.308 (in./cal.) = 38.96 cal./turn ; I_X = 0.000001713 lb.-ft.^{2} ;

I_Y = 0.00001277 lb.-ft.^{2} ; k_Y^2 = 0.808 ; k_X^2 = 0.108 ; (pd/V) = .16127 rad./cal. ;

P = 0.021645 rad./cal. ; Launch Mach Number = 2.33 ; C_{L_α} = 2.75 ; C_{M_α} = 2.63 ;

L_N = 2.26 calibers ; L_{CYL} = 1.21 calibers ; CG_N = 2.44 calibers from nose

We will assume an in-bore yaw angle, ε , of 0.1 degree; then, $\sin\varepsilon$ = 0.00175. We further assume that the roll-orientation of the bullet tilt is *up* (12:00 position) at the gun muzzle; then ϕ_0 = 0 degrees. The aerodynamic jump and the lateral throwoff produced by this small bullet tilt are computed below:

$$J_A = -\left(\frac{2\pi}{38.96}\right)[.808 - .108]\left(\frac{2.75}{2.63}\right)(.00175)i = -0.000207i$$

$$T_L = +\left(\frac{2\pi}{38.96}\right)[2.26 + .605 - 2.44]\left(\frac{2.75}{2.63}\right)(.00175)i = +0.000120i$$

At 300 feet range, the deflections produced by the aerodynamic jump and lateral throwoff are:

Defl. due to aero. jump = - (300) (12) (.000207) i = - 0.75" , to the left

Defl. due to lat. throwoff = (300) (12) (.000120) i = 0.45" , to the right

The total deflection at 300 feet range is seen to be - 0.30" to the left. Although this is a rather small deflection, and would not ordinarily be considered significant, it could well be of some importance in a precision shooting sport, such as benchrest shooting. The projectile designer *could* attempt to minimize the effect of bullet tilt, or in-bore yaw, by choosing bullet design parameters that minimize the algebraic sum of the lateral throwoff and the aerodynamic jump:

$$T_L + J_A = i\left(\frac{2\pi}{n}\right)\left[\left(L_N + \tfrac{1}{2}L_{CYL} - CG_N'\right) - \left(k_y^2 - k_x^2\right)\left(\frac{C_{L_\alpha}}{C_{M_\alpha}}\right)\right]\sin\varepsilon e^{i\phi_0} \quad (12.85)$$

Nearly all spin-stabilized projectiles have at least some static and dynamic unbalance, and have some in-bore yaw, however small. Note that the twist of rifling, *n*, appears in the denominators of equations (12.83), (12.84) and (12.85), and Sterne has pointed out (Ref. 9) that because of this fact, the best accuracy usually results from using the slowest possible twist rate. We state the general conclusion below:

The slowest twist of rifling (largest n) that barely gyroscopically stabilizes a statically unstable projectile will, in general, give the best accuracy at short ranges. However, the value of the gyroscopic stability factor, S_g , at the gun muzzle must be sufficiently larger than unity to insure dynamic stability under actual firing conditions.

12.8 DERIVATION OF KENT'S EQUATION FOR A SMALL IN-BORE YAW

We assume that a rotationally symmetric projectile is "tilted" relative to the bore centerline as it enters the rifling, and that this "tilt" persists throughout the interior ballistic phase of the trajectory. We further assume that the front bourrelet rides a single land or groove, all the way down the gun tube, and that the rear bourrelet (or rotating band) rides the opposite land or groove, so that there is no "balloting," or bouncing from one land or groove to another. If these assumptions are satisfied, then the projectile's axis of rotational symmetry "precesses" at the roll or spin rate as it travels down the rifled barrel.

Most modern artillery shell are mechanically or hydraulically rammed into the origin of rifling, and whatever in-bore yaw is present at the end of ramming is probably due to dimensional clearance between the shell and the gun barrel. Modern small arms bullets are usually loaded into a cartridge case, and the entire cartridge is then chambered. There may be runout in the case neck, which would cause the bullet to be initially misaligned with the bore. In addition, there is usually some "free run" before the bullet makes mechanical contact with the throat of the rifling, and during this unsupported "free run" phase, additional bullet "tilt" may occur. Modern small arms bullets tend to be constructed of materials that are much softer than barrel steel, and they usually exhibit plastic behavior under the high stresses that occur during firing. Thus, a gilding-metal jacketed bullet with a soft lead core, that enters the rifled bore with a small tilt angle, will probably retain that tilt throughout its travel up the barrel. Small cannon projectiles are also loaded into cartridge cases, but like artillery shell, the projectile outer wall is usually made of steel. There is considerable evidence of balloting in modern high-velocity, small-caliber cannon projectiles. Since the detailed nature of the balloting is, in general, difficult to measure or predict, the assumptions made in this section are less likely to be satisfied for small caliber cannon projectiles than they are for conventional small arms bullets. [Note that balloting can be calculated today, using complex multi-degrees-of-freedom dynamic structural codes on super computers].

We assume that the projectile emerges from the muzzle of a rifled barrel with a small in-bore yaw angle, ε. If the axial spin of the tilted projectile is given by p, in radians per second, then one of the principles of mechanics tells us that a transverse component of angular velocity will be introduced at the instant of separation from the muzzle. This transverse, or cross angular velocity will be perpendicular to the shell's axis of symmetry, and will be proportional to the product of the axial spin and the sine of the in-bore yaw angle. The initial yaw and yaw rate are stated below, in complex variable notation:

$$\xi_0 = \varepsilon; \qquad \dot{\xi}_0 = ip\varepsilon \qquad \textbf{(12.86)}$$

With the help of equations (12.37), the second equation of (12.86) becomes:

$$\xi_0' = i\left(\frac{pd}{V}\right)\varepsilon = i\phi'\varepsilon \qquad \textbf{(12.87)}$$

From Chapter 10, we recall the initial condition equations:

$$K_{F_0}e^{i\phi_{F0}} = -\frac{\left(i\xi_0' + \phi_S'\xi_0\right)}{\phi_F' - \phi_S'} \qquad \textbf{(10.120)}$$

$$K_{S_0}e^{i\phi_{S0}} = -\frac{\left(i\xi_0' + \phi_F'\xi_0\right)}{\phi_F' - \phi_S'} \qquad \textbf{(10.121)}$$

Substituting equation (12.87) and the first equation of (12.86) into equations (10.120) and (10.121):

$$K_{F_0}e^{i\phi_{F0}} = -\frac{\left(\phi' - \phi_S'\right)\varepsilon}{\phi_F' - \phi_S'} \qquad \textbf{(12.88)}$$

$$K_{S_0}e^{i\phi_{S0}} = -\frac{\left(\phi' - \phi_F'\right)\varepsilon}{\phi_F' - \phi_S'} \qquad \textbf{(12.89)}$$

We now add, then subtract equations (12.88) and (12.89), to get the first minimum and first maximum yaws, respectively:

$$K_{F_0}e^{i\phi_{F0}} + K_{S_0}e^{i\phi_{S0}} = \varepsilon \qquad \textbf{(12.90)}$$

$$K_{F_0}e^{i\phi_{F0}} - K_{S_0}e^{i\phi_{S0}} = \frac{\left[2\phi' - \left(\phi_F' + \phi_S'\right)\right]\varepsilon}{\phi_F' - \phi_S'} \qquad \textbf{(12.91)}$$

Equation (12.90) confirms that the initial minimum yaw is equal to the in-bore yaw, ε. If we substitute equation (12.42), plus the first equation of (12.75) and the last equation of (12.76) into equation (12.91), and divide the result through by P, we again obtain Kent's equation:

$$\sin\delta_{MAX} = \left(2\frac{I_x}{I_y} - 1\right)\left(\frac{\varepsilon}{\sqrt{1 - 1/S_g}}\right) \qquad \textbf{(12.92)}$$

where ε = the in-bore yaw angle (radians), at muzzle exit

$\sin\delta_{MAX}$ = the first maximum yaw angle

Equation (12.92) was first published (Ref. 7) in 1928, by R. H. Kent and H. P. Hitchcock. A more modern derivation is given by McShane, Kelley and Reno (Ref. 8), who refer to equation (12.92) as "Kent's formula." Note that the derivations of References 7 and 8 assumed an *in-bore yaw* of magnitude ε, not a mass asymmetry.

McShane, Kelley and Reno discussed the effect of mass eccentricity in Section 7, Chapter XII of Reference 8, although no derivation was presented. The authors noted that the effect of a dynamic unbalance angle of magnitude ε, and an in-bore yaw angle of magnitude ε, produce *almost precisely the same first maximum yaw*. Our present analysis confirms that statement.

Actually, this result is neither surprising nor coincidental. In both cases, the longitudinal principal axis of inertia forms an angle ε, relative to the bore centerline, and precesses about the centerline with angular velocity, p. Thus the same transverse angular velocity is imparted to the projectile at the instant of separation from the muzzle, regardless of whether the angular velocity is produced by a dynamic unbalance or an in-bore yaw.

Inspection of equations (12.78) and (12.92) shows how a very small in-bore yaw, or dynamic unbalance angle, is amplified into a much larger first maximum yaw, after the projectile exits the muzzle of the gun. For a typical spin-stabilized projectile, the ratio I_y/I_x is of order ten, and for gyroscopic stability, $S_g > 1$. Thus the first maximum yaw angle is of order twenty times the in-bore yaw angle, or the dynamic unbalance angle.

Equations (12.78) and (12.92) also tell us that by merely observing the amplitude of the first maximum yaw, we cannot distinguish between the two predominant causes of the epicyclic pitching and yawing motion. Unless additional physical evidence is present, we cannot tell if dynamic unbalance, or in-bore yaw, or some combination of the two, was the cause of the observed first maximum yaw. McShane, Kelley and Reno note in Reference 8 that the dynamic unbalance and the in-bore yaw are probably *not* statistically independent. This is a fertile research area for some enterprising young engineer to investigate, with modern high-precision instrumentation.

12.9 THE AERODYNAMIC JUMP DUE TO CROSSWIND

Equation (12.57) tells us that there are two possible causes of aerodynamic jump for spinning projectiles. The examples presented in several previous sections of this chapter have assumed very small initial yaw, and have highlighted the jump due to tip-off rate, ξ_0'. However, if a spinning shell has a significant initial yaw, ξ_0, equation (12.57) shows that the initial yaw will cause an additional component of aerodynamic jump, proportional in magnitude, and perpendicular in direction, to the product $P\xi_0$.

If a spinning projectile has an *initial yaw*, ξ_0, but no significant tip-off rate, equation (12.57) reduces to the simpler form:

$$J_A = ik_y^2\left(\frac{C_{L_\alpha}}{C_{M_\alpha}}\right)P\xi_0 \qquad \textbf{(12.93)}$$

As an example of aerodynamic jump due to initial yaw, we will consider the case of a flat-fire trajectory with a crosswind. The coordinate system selected is the same as Figure 7.1 of Chapter 7. The rifleman is assumed to be firing horizontally (parallel to the X-axis), and the crosswind is blowing from left to right, across the line of fire. The vector geometry, from a position above the firing line, is illustrated Figure 12.11(a).

Since the vector velocity must be specified relative to the wind axes, we see that the left-to-right crosswind, W_z, [illustrated in Figure 12.11(a)], effectively shifts the initial velocity vector, V_0, to the left (toward 9:00 on the target) of the line of fire. The directed angle from the shifted velocity vector to the projectile's spin axis is a pure initial yaw angle (zero pitch component), and we have:

$$\sin\beta_0 = \left(\frac{W_z}{V_0}\right) \qquad \textbf{(12.94)}$$

If we now move to a position directly behind the gun, looking downrange toward the target, we see the Y-Z plane, normal to the trajectory, as illustrated in Figure 12.11(b). The initial yaw, caused by the crosswind, is given by:

$$\xi_0 = i\sin\beta_0 = i\left(\frac{W_z}{V_0}\right) \qquad \textbf{(12.95)}$$

Note that we approximate with throughout this section, in accordance with the flat-fire approximation discussed in Chapter 5. We now substitute equation (12.95) into equation (12.93):

$$J_A = -k_y^2\left(\frac{C_{L_\alpha}}{C_{M_\alpha}}\right)P\left(\frac{W_z}{V_0}\right) \qquad \textbf{(12.96)}$$

At the muzzle of the gun, $P = \left(\frac{I_x}{I_y}\right)\left(\frac{pd}{V}\right)_0 = \left(\frac{I_x}{I_y}\right)\left(\frac{2\pi}{n}\right)$ **(12.97)**

Substituting equation (12.97) into (12.96), and simplifying yields the aerodynamic jump due to crosswind:

$$\boxed{J_A = -k_x^2\left(\frac{C_{L_\alpha}}{C_{M_\alpha}}\right)\left(\frac{2\pi}{n}\right)\left(\frac{W_z}{V_0}\right)} \qquad \textbf{(12.98)}$$

where $\quad k_x^2 = \dfrac{I_x}{md^2}$

n = rifling twist rate (calibers/turn)

V_0 = muzzle velocity

W_z = crosswind component of wind speed (same units as the muzzle velocity)

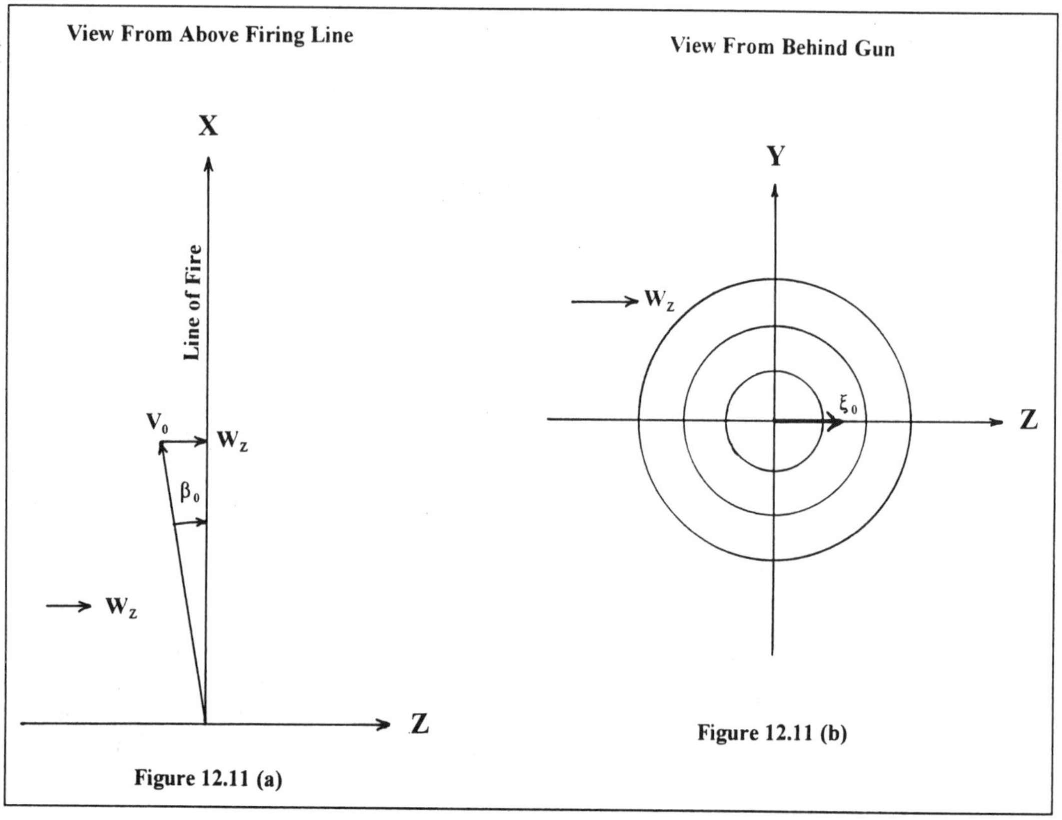

Figure 12.11 Vector Geometry of a Projectile Fired into a Crosswind.

As a first example, we will investigate the effect of aerodynamic jump due to crosswind for the .308," 168 Grain Sierra International bullet, used in the previous example of this chapter. We will take a 10 mile per hour (MPH) crosswind (W_z) as a typical value, and assume that it blows from left to right across the line of fire. Converting the crosswind speed to feet per second, we find that $W_z = (10)(1.4667) = 14.667$ fps. The remaining values we need are listed in Table 12.2, and the jump calculation is shown below:

$$J_A = -(.108)\left(\frac{2\pi}{38.96}\right)\left(\frac{2.75}{2.63}\right)\left(\frac{14.667}{2600}\right) = -0.000103$$

At 300 feet range, the downward deflection (negative *Y*-direction) due to aerodynamic jump is:

$$Y = -\,(12)(300)(.000103) = -0.37 \text{ inch, downward}$$

The 10 MPH left-to-right crosswind causes the bullet to strike 0.37" *lower* on the 100 yard target than it would have if there had been no wind.

The horizontal deflection to the right, for the same crosswind, is given by equation (7.27) from Chapter 7, restated here in slightly different form:

$$\boxed{Z = W_z\left(t - \frac{X}{V_0}\right)} \qquad \textbf{(12.99)}$$

where X = range to the target

t = time of flight to the target

V_0 = muzzle velocity

W_z = crosswind component of wind speed (same units as the muzzle velocity)

Z = horizontal deflection due to crosswind

The time of flight to 300 feet range for the 168 grain Sierra International bullet, fired at a muzzle velocity of 2600 feet/second, is known to be 0.1203 second, from six-degrees-of-freedom calculations done for Chapter 9 of this book. Substituting the appropriate values into equation (12.93), we find:

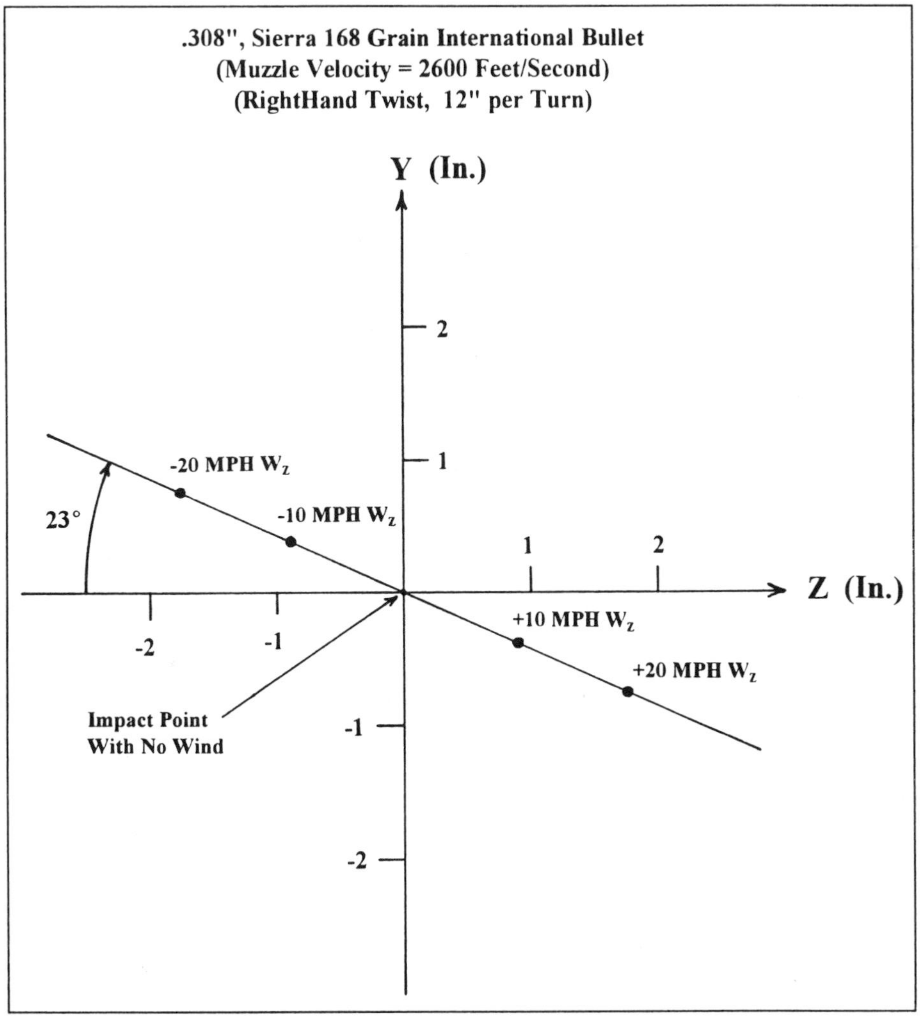

Figure 12.12 Effect of a Crosswind on the Impact Point of a Spin-Stabilized Projectile.

$$Z = (12)(14.667)\left(.1203 - \frac{300}{2600}\right) = 0.87 \text{ inch, to the right}$$

Note that both the vertical deflection due to aerodynamic jump, and the horizontal deflection, are linear in the magnitude of crosswind speed. Thus a 20 MPH left-to-right crosswind will deflect the .308," 168 Grain Sierra International bullet -0.74" (down) and 1.74" to the right, at 300 feet range. Also note that at the same range, a *right-to-left* crosswind (negative W_z) would deflect the same bullet +0.37" (*up*) and 0.87" to the *left*. Thus all shots fired in variable crosswinds will impact along the same inclined straight line, as illustrated in Figure 12.12.

The angle between the impact slant line and the Z-axis of Figure 12.12 (*p. 269*) is 23 degrees. This is the well-known 10:00/4:00 slant of groups, which many benchrest shooters have observed at 100 yards range, when firing on windy days. Note that for a *left-twist of rifling* [negative *n*], equation (12.98) predicts an *upward* Y-deflection for a *left-to-right crosswind.* Thus the slant line would be reversed, and we would see an 8:00/2:00 slant for firing into variable crosswinds with a *left-twist* barrel. Also note that a faster or slower rifling twist rate would change the angle the slant line makes relative to the Z-axis. For a 10" twist, the angle between the slant line and the Z-axis would be about 27 degrees, and for a 14" twist, the corresponding angle would be approximately 20 degrees, for the .308," 168 grain Sierra International bullet fired at a muzzle velocity of 2600 feet per second.

12.10 FIRING SIDEWISE FROM AN AIRPLANE

Another interesting case of the aerodynamic jump due to crosswind occurs for firing a gun sidewise from a high-speed aircraft. This problem was first addressed by T. E. Stern in 1943 (Ref. 10). Reference 10 was written for the BRL mathematicians who were tasked with generating firing tables for machine guns, used in sidewise fire from high speed airplanes. In 1943, the speed of combat aircraft had reached 400 miles/hour (587 feet/second), and the very large vertical crosswind (aerodynamic jump) effect on a .30 caliber machine gun bullet in sidewise fire from such an aircraft had to be accurately accounted for.

A more recent example involved firing the caliber .50 Browning M2 Machine Gun sidewise from an aircraft flying at 450 knots (760 feet/second) airspeed. The ammunition used was caliber .50, API (Armor Piercing Incendiary) M8, with a reference diameter of 0.510," a nominal bullet weight of 648 grains, and a nominal muzzle velocity of 2950 feet/second from the service machine gun.

In support of this project, firings were conducted at average yaw levels up to 14 degrees, in the BRL Aerodynamics Range. The physical characteristics of the API M8 projectile, and the aeroballistic test results are reported in Reference 11. Based on these test results, six-degrees-of-freedom (6-DOF) trajectories were run for many different aircraft flight speeds, off-axis firing azimuths, and gun quadrant elevation angles. A single 6-DOF case was selected for presentation in this chapter, to illustrate the aerodynamic jump for a very large effective crosswind.

The 6-DOF trajectory selected for this chapter assumed horizontal fire (zero degrees quadrant elevation angle), and firing 90 degrees to starboard (right-hand side), off the aircraft's flight path. For firing perpendicular to the aircraft line of flight, the initial yaw is given by:

$$\beta_0 = Tan^{-1}\left(\frac{760}{2950}\right) = 14.45 \; degrees; \quad \xi_0 = i \sin\beta_0 = 0.2495i$$

The aircraft altitude was 1000 feet above mean sea level; the ICAO air density was 0.07426 lb./ft.^{3}; the air temperature was 55.4 °F; and the speed of sound in air was 1112.57 feet/second. The projectile's muzzle velocity and the aircraft's flight speed combine to give the total muzzle velocity, V_T, and launch Mach number, relative to wind axes:

$$V_T = \sqrt{(2950)^2 + (760)^2} = 3046 \; ft./sec.; \; Launch \; Mach \; Number = 2.74$$

The rifling twist rate of the Browning M2 machine gun is 15 inches/turn, right-hand. Additional physical characteristics of the API M8 bullet are:

$$I_x = 0.00268 \; lb.\text{-}in^2; \; I_y = 0.02525 \; lb.\text{-}in^2; \; m = 0.09257 \; lb.$$
$$k_x^2 = 0.1113; \; k_y^{-2} = 0.954; \; k_x^{-2} = 8.98; \; n = (15)/(.510) = 29.41 \; cal./turn$$

For the large-yaw flight, the following aerodynamic characteristics of the API M8 bullet are obtained, at Mach 2.74:

$$C_D = 0.63; \; C_{M_\alpha} = 2.60; \; C_{L_\alpha} = 3.52; \; C_{M_{p\alpha}} = 0.27; \; C_{M_q} + C_{M_{\dot\alpha}} = -6.6$$

Using the definitions given after equation (10.66) of Chapter 10, we find:

$$P = .02268 \; rad./cal.; \; M = .00006009; \; T = .000144; \; H = .0002224$$

Equations (10.102) through (10.105) of Chapter 10 provide the following values:

$$\phi'_F = .01962 \; rad./cal.; \; \phi'_S = .00306 \; rad./cal.; \; \lambda_F = -.000066 \; /cal.;$$
$$\lambda_S = -.000156 \; /cal.$$
$$S_g = 2.14; \quad S_d = 1.29$$

In section 10.7 of Chapter 10, it was shown [see equations (10.92) and (10.93)] that for a very small tip-off rate, ξ'_0, and a large initial yaw, ξ_0, the magnitudes of the initial epicyclic pitch and yaw arms are well approximated by:

$$K_{F_0} = \left(\frac{\phi'_S}{\phi'_F - \phi'_S}\right)\xi_0; \quad K_{S_0} = \left(\frac{\phi'_F}{\phi'_F - \phi'_S}\right)\xi_0 \qquad \textbf{(12.100)}$$

For a gyroscopically overstable shell, where the fast-arm turning rate is an order of magnitude greater than the slow-arm turning rate, equations (12.100) tell us that the slow-arm amplitude will be an order of magnitude larger than the fast-arm amplitude. This condition is satisfied for the .50 API M8 bullet fired sidewise from a high speed aircraft. Substituting the values of the epicyclic turning rates and the initial yaw into equations (12.100) we find:

$K_{F_0} = 0.0462$; $K_{S_0} = 0.2957$; $\phi_{F_0} = 270\ deg.$; $\phi_{S_0} = 90\ deg.$

The epicyclic pitching and yawing motion for this trajectory is plotted in Figure 12.13, for the first 400 feet of the trajectory. The first maximum yaw is approximately 17 degrees, and it occurs about 16 feet downrange of the gun muzzle. The motion is dynamically stable ($S_d = 1.29$), and both epicyclic arms damp fairly quickly along the flight path. At 400 feet range, the slow arm amplitude has damped from an initial value of 17 degrees, to approximately 5 degrees, and it is still damping. The fast arm, whose initial value was about 2.5 degrees, has damped to about 1.5 degrees, at the same range.

Substituting the appropriate values for the .50 API M8 bullet into equation (12.98), we obtain a value for the downward aerodynamic jump due to the 450 knot (760 fps) crosswind:

$$J_A = -(.113)\left(\frac{3.52}{2.60}\right)\left(\frac{2\pi}{29.41}\right)\left(\frac{760}{2950}\right) = -0.00829$$

At 400 feet range, the downward deflection due to aerodynamic jump is:

Y = - (12) (400) (.00829) = - 39.8 inches

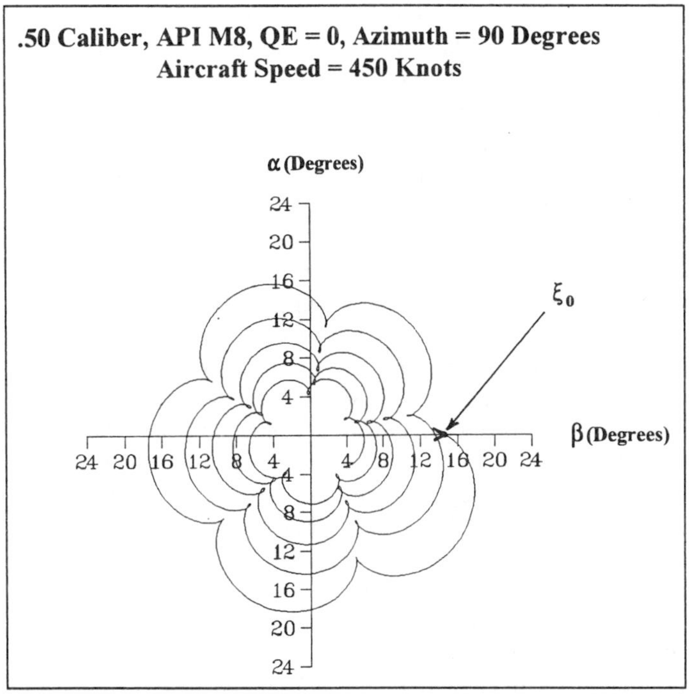

Figure 12.13 Pitch versus Yaw, for a .50 Caliber Bullet Fired Sidewise from an Aircraft.

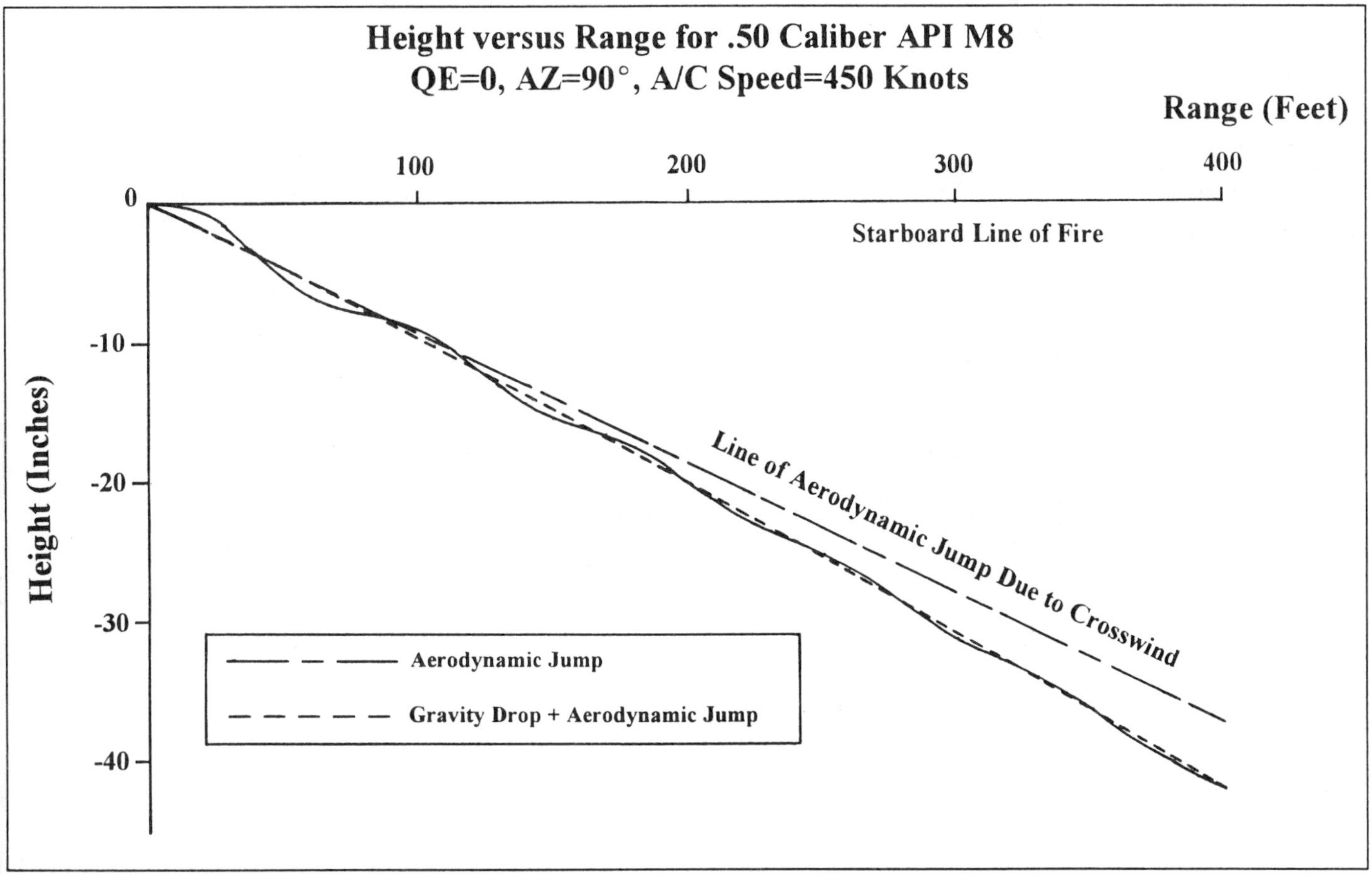

Figure 12.14 Height versus Range, for a.50 Caliber Bullet Fired Sidewise from an Aircraft.

Figure 12.14 (*p. 271*) is a plot, taken from the 6-DOF program output, that shows the downward deflection of the trajectory, from the initially horizontal line of fire, over the first 400 feet of the bullet's flight. The solid curve is the actual trajectory, and it includes everything; the epicyclic swerve, the gravity drop, and the aerodynamic jump. The initial epicyclic swerve radius, caused by the large initial pitching and yawing motion, is approximately 1.2 inches; the bullet's center-of-mass is initially flying in a 2.4-inch diameter helix about the mean trajectory. At 400 feet range, the swerve radius has damped to about 0.3 inch, and the epicyclic swerving motion has almost vanished. The gravity drop at 400 feet range is approximately 4 inches, and a graphical construction shows that the aerodynamic jump is about 38 inches, downward. [Note that equation (12.98) predicts a downward deflection due to jump of about 40 inches; the two calculations disagree by approximately 2 inches at 400 feet range]. The sum of all the downward deflections, calculated by the 6-DOF computer program, is approximately 42 inches at a range of 400 feet.

If the aircraft gunner were firing at a 90 degree starboard target 600 yards away (using caliber .50 API M8 ammunition, at an aircraft speed of 450 knots), and made no correction for the aerodynamic jump due to crosswind, *the bullet would strike between 14 and 15 feet below the intended impact point*! If the target were at the same range, but off the *port* (left) side of the aircraft, the bullet would strike the same distance *above the impact point*! Thus the vertical aerodynamic jump effect due to crosswind becomes an extremely important factor to the machine gunner who must fire sidewise at targets from a high speed aircraft.

Note that if the rifling twist were *left-hand* instead of the standard right-hand twist, the direction of aerodynamic jump would be reversed. For *left-twist barrels*, the projectile would strike *high* when firing to starboard, and *low* when firing to port. Needless to say, mixing right and left twist guns for aircraft armament would lead to an insurmountable difficulty.

12.11 SUMMARY

In Chapter 12, the lateral throwoff and aerodynamic jump of projectiles have been investigated in considerable detail. The trajectory deflections caused by static mass unbalance, dynamic mass unbalance, in-bore yaw (or bullet "tilt" in the barrel), and the initial yaw due to crosswind have been studied. Two independent derivations of Kent's equation illustrate the mechanism by which a very small dynamic unbalance, or a very small in-bore yaw, leads to a much larger first maximum yaw, after the projectile leaves the gun muzzle.

Several numerical examples are presented to highlight the application of modern aeroballistic theory to the practical problems of hitting a target. The ballistician who is primarily interested in the *precision* of fire (small groups at the target), will find the material in this chapter to be very useful.

REFERENCES

1. Mann, F. W., *The Bullet's Flight from Powder to Target*, Munn & Company, New York, New York, 1909.

2. Plostins, P., "A Method for Extracting the Sabot Discard Impulse from Transitional Ballistic Data," Ballistic Research Laboratory Technical Report No. BRL-TR-3244, 1991.

3. Fowler, R. H., E. G. Gallop, C. N. H. Lock and H. W. Richmond, "The Aerodynamics of a Spinning Shell," *Philosophical Transactions of the Royal Society of London*, Series A, Volume 221, 1920.

4. Murphy, C. H., "Yaw Induction by Means of Asymmetric Mass Distribution," Ballistic Research Laboratories Memorandum Report No. 2669, 1976.

5. Murphy, C. H., "Yaw Induction by Mass Asymmetry," *Journal of Spacecraft and Rockets*, Vol.14, No. 8, August 1977, pp. 511-512.

6. *"Proceedings of the Aerodynamics Range Symposium, January 1957, Unclassified Papers,"* Ballistic Research Laboratories Report No. 1005 (Part I), 1957.

7. Kent, R. H. and H. P. Hitchcock, "The Effect of Cross Wind on the Yaw of Projectiles," Ballistic Research Laboratory File A-IV-31, Aberdeen Proving Ground, Maryland, 1928.

8. McShane, E. J., J. L. Kelley and F. V. Reno, *Exterior Ballistics*, University of Denver Press, 1953.

9. Sterne, T. H., "On Jump Due to Bore Clearance," Ballistic Research Laboratories Report No. 491, 1944.

10. Sterne, T. H., "The Effect of Yaw Upon Aircraft Gunfire Trajectories," Ballistic Research Laboratories Report No. 345, 1943.

11. McCoy, R. L., "The Aerodynamic Characteristics of .50 Ball, M33, API, M8, and APIT, M20 Ammunition," Ballistic Research Laboratory Memorandum Report No. BRL-MR-3810, 1990.

13

Nonlinear Aerodynamic Forces and Moments

13.1 INTRODUCTION

Previous chapters of this book have assumed a linearized aerodynamic force-moment system, which implies that all the aerodynamic coefficients used are independent of the yaw amplitude. Experimental results obtained over the past forty years in wind tunnels and free flight spark photography ranges have repeatedly demonstrated that practically all projectile aerodynamic force-moment systems are, to some extent, nonlinear. In this chapter, we will explore the general nature of aerodynamic nonlinearities, and study their effects on the flight dynamic characteristics of symmetric projectiles.

The flight of projectiles with large amplitude pitching and yawing motion requires a proper treatment of both geometric and aerodynamic nonlinearities. Geometric nonlinearity arises from the large size of the pitching and yawing motion itself, and it becomes important whenever the pitch angle, α , or the yaw angle, β, is large enough that either cos α or cos β is significantly less than unity. [See equations (10.43) and (10.44) in Chapter 10]. The effect of geometric nonlinearity is therefore insignificant if the yaw is small everywhere along the trajectory. On the other hand, many projectiles show *significant nonlinear aerodynamic behavior*, even at relatively small amplitude pitching and yawing motion. In this chapter we will assume that the yaw level is small enough to neglect geometric nonlinearity, but will retain all significant nonlinear aerodynamic forces and moments in the analysis.

According to the Maple-Synge hypothesis (Ref. 1), one of the consequences of projectile rotational symmetry is that only certain types of nonlinear aerodynamic forces and moments are possible. The results of Maple-Synge analysis show that in a power series expansion of an aerodynamic force or moment coefficient, only even power terms in total angle of attack should be retained. Thus if the drag coefficient, C_D, varies with the amplitude of the pitching and yawing motion, the proper form of the coefficient power series expansion is:

$$\boxed{C_D = C_{D_0} + C_{D_{\delta^2}}\delta^2 + \cdots} \qquad \textbf{(13.1)}$$

where C_{D_o} = the drag coefficient at zero total angle of attack

$C_{D_{\delta^2}}$ = the quadratic yaw-drag coefficient

$$\delta = \sin\alpha_t$$

$\alpha_t \approx \sqrt{\alpha^2 + \beta^2}$, for small total angle of attack

α = angle of attack (pitch)

β = angle of sideslip (yaw)

The series expansion for the overturning moment coefficient would be:

$$\boxed{C_{M_\alpha} = C_{M_{\alpha 0}} + C_{M_{\alpha 2}}\delta^2 + \cdots} \qquad \textbf{(13.2)}$$

where C_{M_α} = the pitching (overturning) moment coefficient

$C_{M_{\alpha 0}}$ = the linear pitching moment coefficient at zero total angle of attack

$C_{M_{\alpha 2}}$ = the cubic pitching moment coefficient

The pitch, yaw and total angle of attack were defined above, and the extension to other aerodynamic force-moment coefficients is obvious. (Note that in the series expansion of the pitching moment coefficient, we write:

$$C_M = C_{M_{\alpha 0}}\sin\alpha + C_{M_{\alpha 2}}\sin^3\alpha + C_{M_{\alpha 4}}\sin^5\alpha + \cdots$$

The first term on the right hand side is *linear* in $\sin\alpha$, the second term is *cubic* in $\sin\alpha$, the third term is *quintic* in $\sin\alpha$, etc. Thus if the first two terms on the right hand side are required to describe a given pitching moment, we say the moment is "cubic" in angle of attack).

13.2 ANALYSIS OF NONLINEAR DRAG COEFFICIENT DATA

Figure 13.1 shows a contour sketch of the 30mm, T306E10 shell that was under consideration for use by the U.S. Air Force in the mid 1950's. The design was not adopted, but in the meantime a significant amount of high-quality aeroballistic test data had been collected. The linear and nonlinear aerodynamic forces and moments were obtained in the BRL supersonic wind tunnels and in the free-flight spark photography ranges. A sample comparison of the drag results obtained from the two facilities is shown in Figure 13.2.

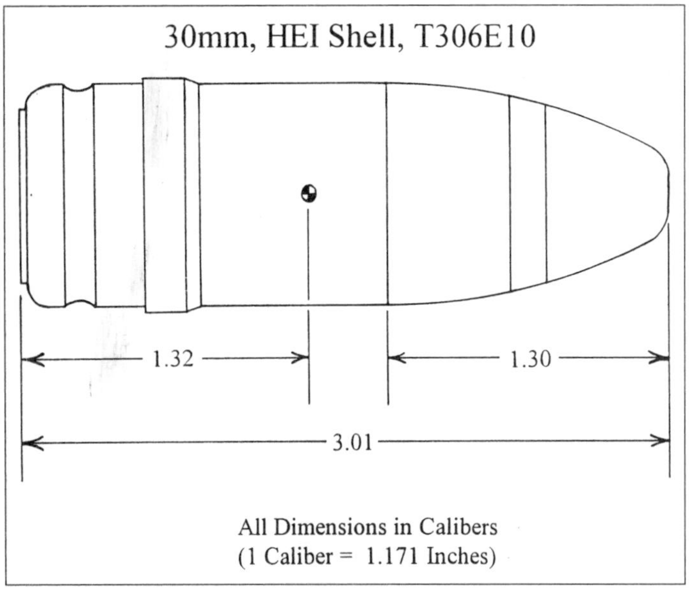

Figure 13.1 Contour Sketch of the 30 mm, HEI Shell, T306E10.

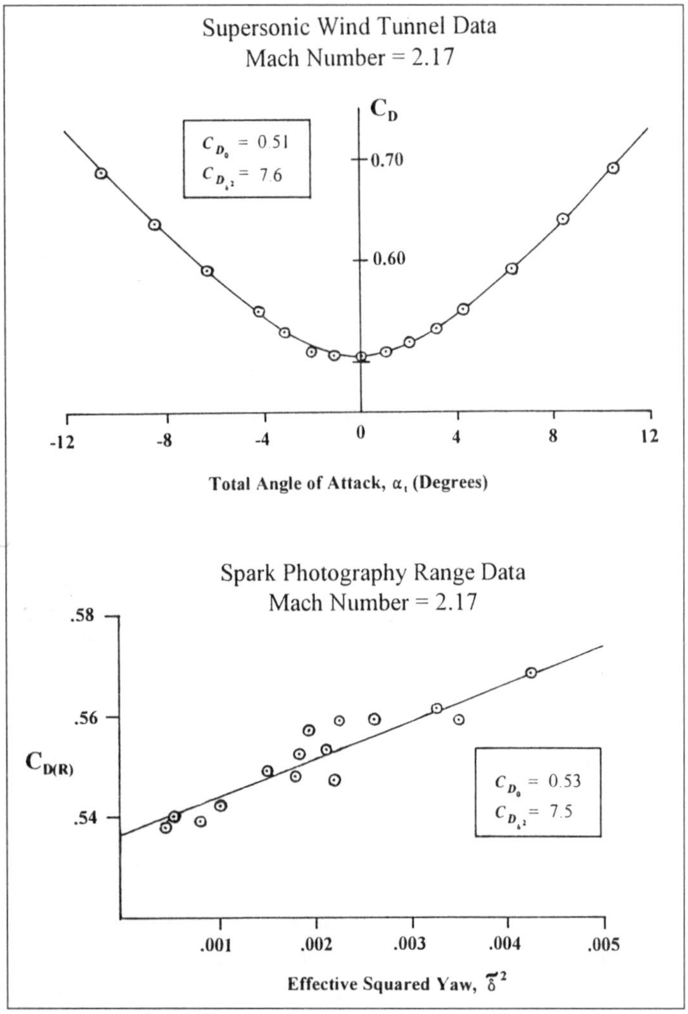

Figure 13.2 Comparison of Wind Tunnel and Spark Range Drag Coefficients, T306E10.

The top plot of Figure 13.2 shows the supersonic wind tunnel drag coefficient data (Ref. 2) obtained at Mach 2.17, for angles of attack up to ±10 degrees. Fitting the data to a parabola in the sine of the angle of attack, gives numerical values of 0.51 and 7.6, respectively, for the zero-yaw and the yaw-drag coefficients. The bottom plot of Figure 13.2 illustrates the spark photography range data (Ref. 3) collected at the same nominal Mach number. Fitting the "range" drag coefficient, $C_{D(R)}$, against the *effective squared yaw parameter* (to be defined presently), gives numerical values of 0.53 and 7.5, respectively, for the same two aerodynamic coefficients. The agreement between the spark range and the wind tunnel results for the T306E10 projectile is excellent.

The wind tunnel method *directly* measures the drag force, whereas the free flight range technique is an *indirect* measurement, that *infers* the force from the observed free-flight motion. If nonlinear force and moment coefficient expansions are substituted into the linearized differential equations of motion presented in Chapters 10 and 11, the resulting nonlinear equations cannot be solved explicitly, and we must turn to a *quasi-linear* method of analysis. The quasi-linear technique (Ref. 4) consists of finding a solution to a linear differential equation that approximately satisfies the parent nonlinear equation. As a demonstration of the quasi-linear method, we will consider the flight of a projectile acted on by a nonlinear drag coefficient whose variation with total angle of attack is accurately described by equation (13.1).

We recall from Chapter 10, that the general solution for the pitching and yawing motion of a spinning, symmetric shell is given by:

$$\xi = K_F e^{i\phi_F} + K_S e^{i\phi_S} + i\beta_R \quad \textbf{(10.94)}$$

where $\xi = \alpha + i\beta$

$K_F = K_{F_0} e^{\lambda_F s}$, the amplitude of the fast epicyclic yaw mode (or arm)

$K_S = K_{S_0} e^{\lambda_S s}$ the amplitude of the slow epicyclic yaw mode (or arm)

$$\phi_F = \phi_{F_0} + \phi_F' s$$

$$\phi_S = \phi_{S_0} + \phi_S' s$$

ϕ_{F_0} = initial phase angle of the fast epicyclic yaw arm

ϕ_{S_0} = initial phase angle of the slow epicyclic yaw arm

$\beta_R = \dfrac{PG}{M + iPT}$, the yaw of repose

$$\lambda_F + i\phi_F' = \frac{1}{2}\left[-H + iP + \sqrt{4M + H^2 - P^2 + 2iP(2T - H)}\right]$$

$$\lambda_S + i\phi_S' = \frac{1}{2}\left[-H + iP - \sqrt{4M + H^2 - P^2 + 2iP(2T - H)}\right]$$

For the flat-fire trajectories common to free-flight ballistic ranges, we will neglect the very small yaw of repose, and re-write equation (10.94) as:

$$\xi = K_F e^{i\phi_F} + K_S e^{i\phi_S} \qquad \textbf{(13.3)}$$

We next note that the complex conjugate of equation (13.3) is:

$$\bar{\xi} = K_F e^{-i\phi_F} + K_S e^{-i\phi_S} \qquad \textbf{(13.4)}$$

and that the squared amplitude of the total angle of attack is given by the product of the complex yaw, ξ, and its conjugate (Ref. 5):

$$\xi\bar{\xi} = \sin^2\alpha + \sin^2\beta = \delta^2 = K_F^2 + K_S^2 + 2K_F K_S \cos(\phi_F - \phi_S) \qquad \textbf{(13.5)}$$

Free-flight ballistic ranges measure the drag coefficient over a distance that is many times longer than the period of δ^2; thus the average value of the fluctuating cosine term in equation (13.5) is essentially zero, and may be neglected. If the effects of damping are also neglected, the average value of δ^2 over the length of a ballistic firing range may be approximated by the simple result:

$$\bar{\delta}^2 \approx K_F^2 + K_S^2 \qquad \textbf{(13.6)}$$

In Reference 6, Murphy shows that the damping (or undamping) of the epicyclic pitching and yawing motion must be properly accounted for in order to obtain the most accurate definition of the *effective squared yaw* for use in the quasi-linear analysis of free-flight drag coefficient data. Murphy (Ref. 6) obtains the higher order approximation:

$$\tilde{\delta}^2 = K_{F_C}{}^2 + K_{S_C}{}^2 + \frac{5L_R^2}{84}\left[\lambda_F^2 K_{F_C}{}^2 + \lambda_S^2 K_{S_C}{}^2\right] + \cdots \qquad \textbf{(13.7)}$$

where L_R = the length of the instrumented ballistic firing range (calibers)

K_{F_C} = the fast arm amplitude at the center (mid-point) of the range

K_{S_C} = the slow arm amplitude at the center (mid-point) of the range

$\tilde{\delta}^2$ = the correct effective squared yaw for analysis of free-flight drag coefficient data

If there is no damping $\lambda_F \equiv \lambda_S \equiv 0$, equation (13.7) reduces identically to equation (13.6). However, some damping (or undamping) is almost always present, and the proper *effective squared yaw*, as defined by equation (13.7) should be calculated for each test round fired in a free-flight aeroballistic range. In practice, several data rounds are fired at the same Mach number, but at varying amplitudes of the pitching and yawing motion. The measured "range" values of the drag coefficient, $C_{D(R)}$, are then plotted against $\tilde{\delta}^2$. The data points should fall on a straight line (see the bottom plot of Figure 13.2). The intercept of the plot is the zero-yaw drag coefficient, C_{D_0}, and the slope of the line is the yaw-drag coefficient, $C_{D_{\delta^2}}$.

The quasi-linear method of analysis has been used with complete success for more than forty years to determine C_{D_0} and $C_{D_{\delta^2}}$ for many types of symmetric projectiles. Several examples were presented in section 4.9 of Chapter 4.

Figure 13.3 (*p. 276*) shows the data obtained from a large angle of attack firing program (Ref. 7), conducted in 1955. A variable-lip yaw inducer was used to achieve total angles of attack up to 25 degrees, for the 20mm T282E1 projectile. A linear least-squares fit of the data plotted in Figure 13.3 gives values of 0.425 for C_{D_0}, and 4.6 for $C_{D_{\delta^2}}$, at Mach 2.3. The spark-range yaw-drag coefficient agreed very well with the supersonic wind tunnel value of 4.7, obtained at the same test Mach number.

If measured values of C_{D_0} and $C_{D_{\delta^2}}$ are substituted into equation (13.1), the effect of the pitching and yawing motion on the total in-flight drag coefficient may be readily calculated. For example, at Mach 2.3 and zero yaw, the total drag coefficient for the 20mm T282E1 projectile is just the zero-yaw value, 0.425. At 10 degrees yaw, the total drag coefficient has increased to 0.564, which is a 33 percent increase in drag. At 18 degrees yaw, the total drag coefficient is 0.864, which is more than double the zero-yaw value!

13.3 QUASI-LINEAR ANALYSIS OF A CUBIC PITCHING MOMENT

C. H. Murphy enunciated his well-known quasi-linear theory (Ref. 4) in 1956. A number of projectiles that possessed known nonlinearities in their aerodynamic force-moment systems had been fired in the BRL spark photography ranges, and it was found that their free-flight motions were very well fitted by solutions of the linearized equations. The flight motion parameters, and the derived "range values" of the various aerodynamic coefficients, were observed to vary with the amplitude of the pitching and yawing motion. The essence of the quasi-linear technique (Ref. 4, Ref. 6) consisted of finding the proper "effective squared yaw angle" for each aerodynamic coefficient, so that a plot of each coefficient's "range values" against the associated effective squared yaw parameters would yield a correct interpretation of the nonlinear coefficient data. The quasi-linear method for the analysis of drag coefficient data was illustrated in the previous section of this chapter. In this section, we will examine the quasi-linear technique for analysis of the pitching and yawing motion of spinning and nonspinning projectiles acted on by cubic pitching moments.

The simplest possible nonlinearity in the aerodynamic moment is a cubic pitching moment, whose coefficient expansion is described by equation (13.2), truncated at the δ^2 term. Many projectiles exhibit cubic pitching (or overturning) moments, even for small amplitude pitching and yawing motion. In section 10.4 of Chapter 10, we considered the simplified pitching and yawing motion of a spinning projectile acted on by a *linear* pitching moment. If we neglect the small effect of gravity in equation (10.79), and expand the pitch-

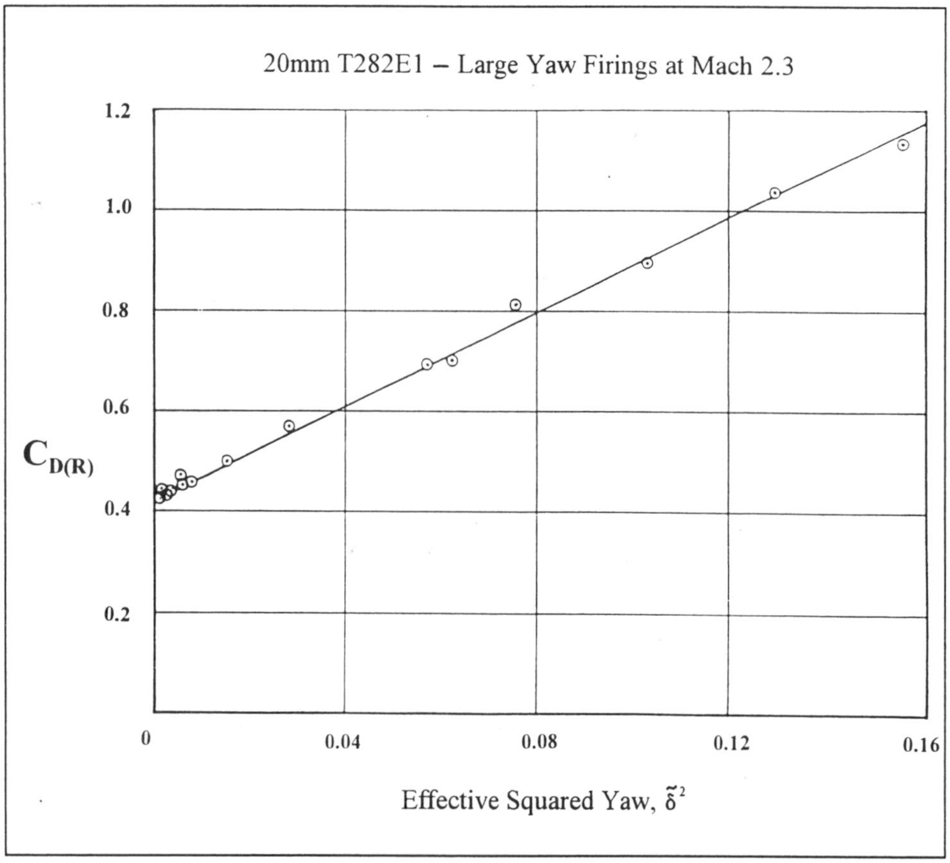

Figure 13.3 Drag Coefficient versus Effective Squared Yaw.

ing moment to include a cubic term, we obtain the nonlinear differential equation:

$$\xi'' - iP\xi' - \left(M_0 + M_2\delta^2\right)\xi = 0 \qquad \textbf{(13.8)}$$

where $\xi = \alpha + i\beta$

$\delta^2 = \xi\bar{\xi} = \sin^2 \alpha_t$

$$P = \left(\frac{I_x}{I_y}\right)\left(\frac{pd}{V}\right)$$

$M_0 = \dfrac{\rho S d}{2m} k_y^{-2} C_{M_{\alpha_0}}$, the linear pitching moment term

$M_2 = \dfrac{\rho S d}{2m} k_y^{-2} C_{M_{\alpha_2}}$, the cubic pitching moment term

p = projectile axial spin (radians/second)

V = projectile speed

ρ = air density

d = projectile reference diameter

S = projectile reference area (usually taken as $S = \pi d^2 / 4$) $\pi d^2/4$

m = projectile mass

$k_y^{-2} = \dfrac{md^2}{I_y}$

I_x = projectile axial moment of inertia

I_y = projectile transverse moment of inertia, about any axis through the center of mass

An exact solution of equation (13.8) exists in terms of elliptic functions, which Murphy presents in section 8.3 of Reference 6. Although elliptic functions are cumbersome, the exact solution is useful as a check on the quasi-linear result, and Murphy has done the comparisons in Reference 6, finding good agreement in all cases considered. The interested reader may consult this reference.

The solution to the linearized form of equation (13.8) is an epicycle without damping, previously stated as equation (13.3). If we differentiate equation (13.3) twice, and substitute the epicyclic solution into the nonlinear equation (13.8), we obtain:

$$\begin{aligned} &K_F e^{i\phi_F}\left[-\phi_F'^2 + P\phi_F' - M_0 - M_2\left(K_F^2 + 2K_S^2\right)\right] \\ &+K_S e^{i\phi_S}\left[-\phi_S'^2 + P\phi_S' - M_0 - M_2\left(K_S^2 + 2K_F^2\right)\right] \\ &-M_2\left[K_F^2 K_S e^{i(2\phi_F - \phi_S)} + K_S^2 K_F e^{i(2\phi_S - \phi_F)}\right] = 0 \qquad \textbf{(13.9)} \end{aligned}$$

We know from many observations in spark photography ranges that the epicyclic solution is an excellent description of the actual motion of projectiles possessing cubic pitching moments. Therefore, we neglect the third term in equation (13.9), which contains mixed frequencies, and the following pair of equations is obtained:

$$\phi_F'\left(P - \phi_F'\right) = M_0 + M_2\delta_{eF}^2 \tag{13.10}$$

$$\phi_S'\left(P - \phi_S'\right) = M_0 + M_2\delta_{eS}^2 \tag{13.11}$$

where

$$\delta_{eF}^2 = K_F^2 + 2K_S^2 \tag{13.12}$$

$$\delta_{eS}^2 = K_S^2 + 2K_F^2 \tag{13.13}$$

Equations (13.10) and (13.11) may be solved for the two epicyclic frequencies, retaining the larger root of equation (13.10), and the smaller root of (13.11). Equations (13.12) and (13.13) show that the effective squared yaw for each frequency is twice as sensitive to the amplitude of the other frequency as it is to its own amplitude. We now eliminate M_0, and then P, between equations (13.10) and (13.11), and we find:

$$\phi_F' + \phi_S' = P + M_2\left(\frac{K_F^2 - K_S^2}{\phi_F' - \phi_S'}\right) \tag{13.14}$$

$$\phi_F' \bullet \phi_S' = M_0 + M_2\delta_e^2 \tag{13.15}$$

$$\delta_e^2 = \frac{\phi_F'\delta_{eS}^2 - \phi_S'\delta_{eF}^2}{\phi_F' - \phi_S'} = K_F^2 + K_S^2 + \frac{\phi_F'K_F^2 - \phi_S'K_S^2}{\phi_F' - \phi_S'} \tag{13.16}$$

From equation (13.15) we obtain:

$$\boxed{C_{M_{\alpha(R)}} = C_{M_{\alpha 0}} + C_{M_{\alpha 2}}\delta_e^2} \tag{13.17}$$

Equation (13.17) tells us that observed "range" values of the pitching moment coefficient, $C_{M_{\alpha(R)}}$, obtained from free-flight ballistic range firings, should be plotted against the effective squared yaw, as defined by equation (13.16). For a cubic pitching moment, the data points should fall along a straight line, whose intercept is the zero-yaw pitching moment coefficient, $C_{M_{\alpha 0}}$, and whose slope is the cubic coefficient, $C_{M_{\alpha 2}}$. Note that the proper effective squared yaw for the pitching moment coefficient, δ_e^2, is **not** the same as $\tilde{\delta}^2$ [equation (13.7)], used for the analysis of nonlinear drag coefficient data. We also note [see equations (13.14) and (13.15)] that for a nonlinear pitching moment, the epicyclic frequencies depend on the *amplitude* of the pitching and yawing motion. This is a general characteristic of nonlinear systems, and is in contrast to the behavior of a spinning projectile with a *linear* pitching moment (see Chapter 10), in which the two epicyclic frequencies are independent of the amplitude of the motion.

In References 4 and 6, Murphy uses a more elegant quasi-linear method than the simple derivation presented above. Murphy's technique is an extension of the Kryloff-Bogoliuboff equivalent linearization method (Ref. 8), which may also be used for nonlinear damping. Since the Kryloff-Bogoliuboff method gives the same results in all cases as the direct substitution approach, but requires more than twice the algebraic effort, we will use the simpler direct substitution method throughout this chapter. The reader may consult References 4 and 6 for the more elegant Kryloff-Bogoliuboff treatment of the nonlinear problem.

A few examples of nonlinear pitching moment coefficient data will now be presented. Figure 13.4 illustrates the behavior of the cubic pitching moment for a 120mm, non-spinning, finned mortar shell, at subsonic and transonic speeds. The mortar projectiles were fired through the BRL Transonic Range, and a yaw inducer was

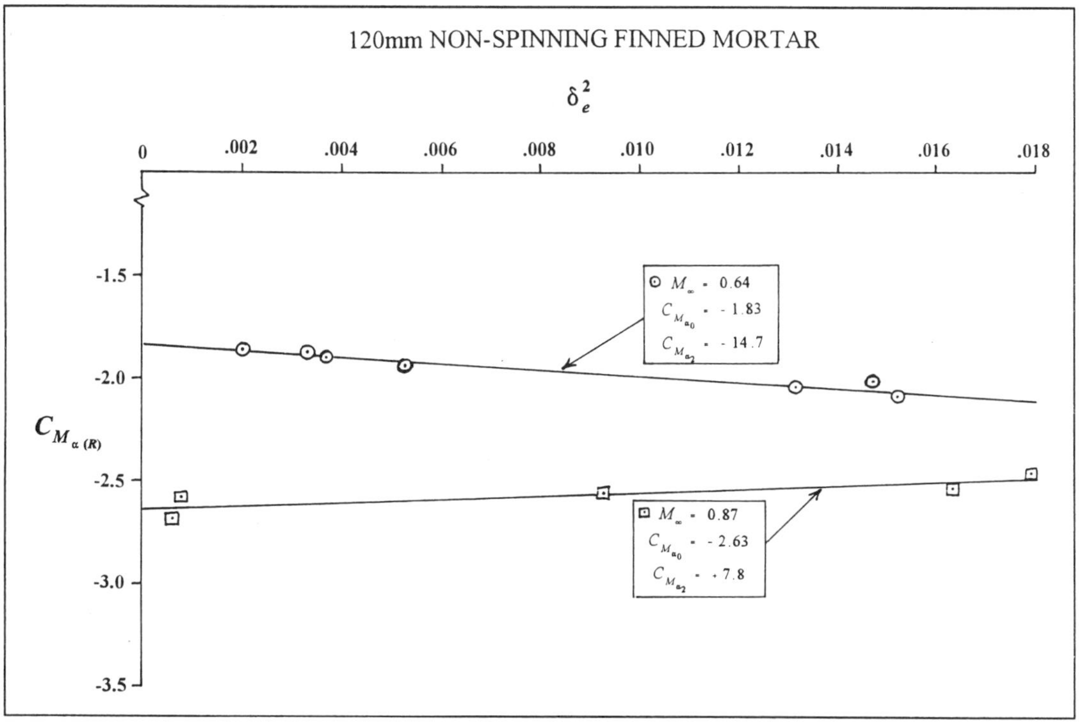

Figure 13.4 Pitching Moment Coefficient versus Effective Squared Yaw.

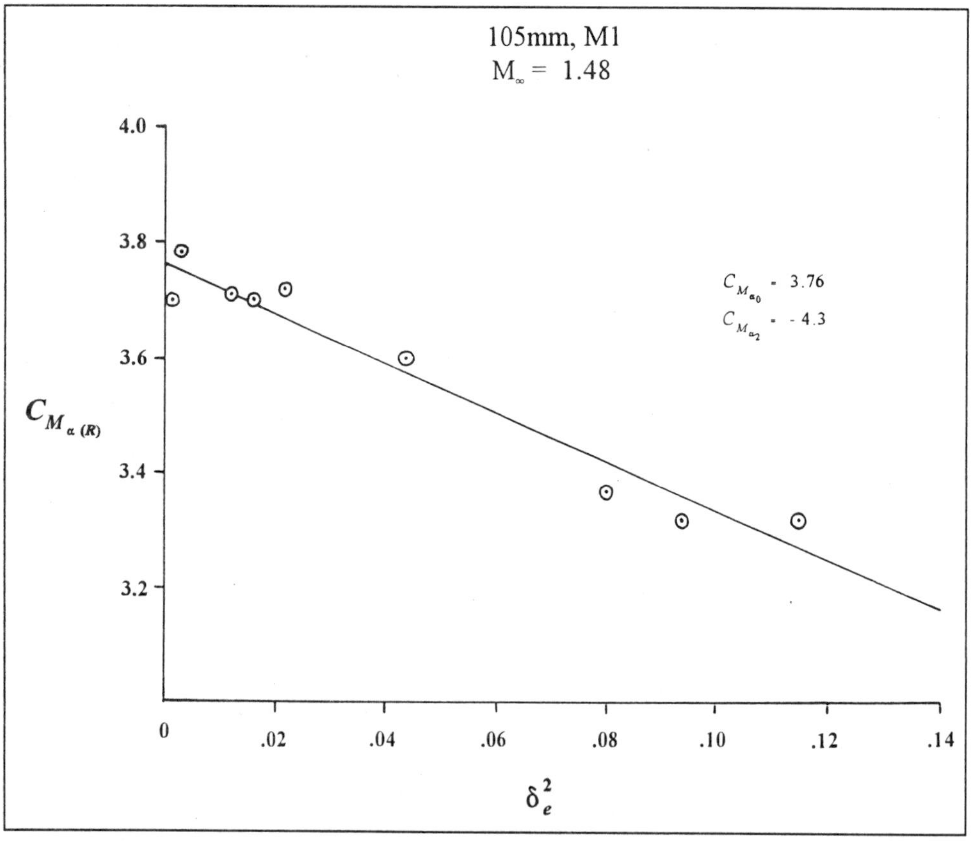

Figure 13.5 Pitching Moment Coefficient versus Effective Squared Yaw.

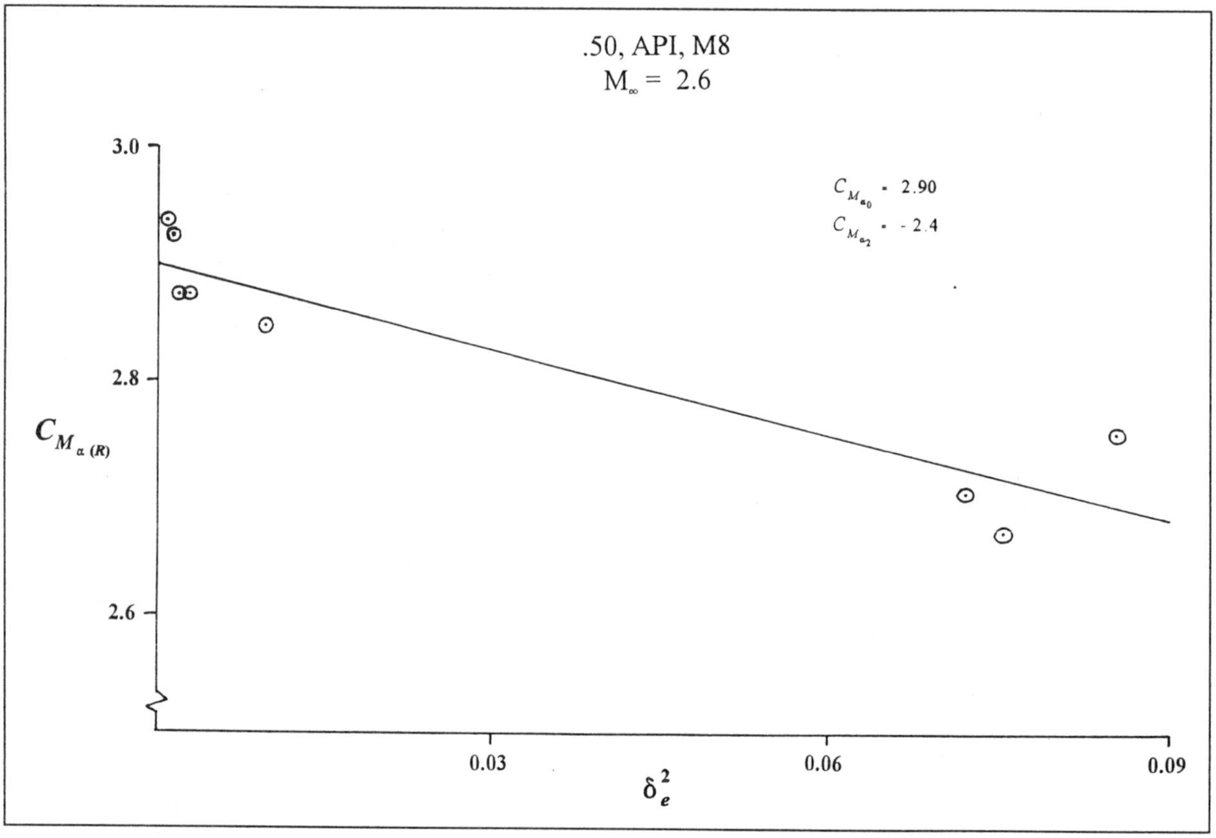

Figure 13.6 Pitching Moment Coefficient versus Effective Squared Yaw.

used to obtain first maximum yaw angles up to twenty degrees. The linear pitching moment coefficient was observed to be negative at all speeds tested.

At Mach 0.64, the 120mm mortar shell experiences subsonic flow over the entire configuration, and the cubic pitching moment coefficient is observed to be negative. Since both the linear and the cubic pitching moment coefficients are negative at this flight speed, the mortar shell is statically stable at small angles of attack, and *more statically stable* at large angles of attack.

Figure 13.4 also shows the behavior of the nonlinear pitching moment coefficient for the 120mm finned mortar shell, at Mach 0.87. At this flight speed, shock waves stand on the surface of the body, and the flowfield around the projectile is therefore transonic. Note that transonic flow causes the cubic pitching moment coefficient to be *positive* at Mach 0.87. This case illustrates another type of static stability. At Mach 0.87, the 120mm finned mortar shell is statically stable at small angles of attack, and *less statically stable* at larger angles of attack. The generalized effects of cubic pitching moments on static and gyroscopic stability will be discussed further in the next section of this chapter.

At transonic speeds, a *positive* value of the cubic pitching moment coefficient is a *general characteristic* of non-spinning or slowly rolling finned mortar projectiles. Note that if the pitch or yaw angle were equal to 35.5 degrees, the 120mm mortar shell at Mach 0.87 would become neutrally stable (this is an extrapolated value), and for even larger yaw, it would become statically *unstable*. However, such very large yaws do not occur in field firings of the 120mm mortar shell, so static instability is never observed.

Figure 13.5 illustrates the variation of $C_{M_{\alpha(R)}}$ with δ_e^2, for the spin-stabilized 105mm M1 projectile, at Mach 1.48. For this case, the linear coefficient, $C_{M_{\alpha 0}}$, is positive, and the cubic coefficient, $C_{M_{\alpha 2}}$, is found to be negative. Thus, if the 105mm M1 shell is fired at Charge 7 from the M103 Howitzer, with a rifling twist rate of 1/18 calibers, the projectile will be gyroscopically stable at small yaw, and *more gyroscopically stable* at larger yaw levels. In fact, the cubic pitching moment coefficient, $C_{M_{\alpha 2}}$, for the 105mm M1 shell is negative at all flight speeds, although the value of the coefficient varies with the Mach number.

Figure 13.6 shows a similar plot for the caliber .50, API, M8 projectile, at Mach 2.6. Again, the linear pitching moment coefficient is positive, and the cubic coefficient is negative. Thus the API M8 projectile is *more gyroscopically stable* at larger yaw levels than it is at smaller yaw. The same general behavior has been observed for many different spin-stabilized projectiles, in all speed regions. The author's conclusion is that a *negative cubic pitching moment coefficient is a general characteristic of typical spin-stabilized projectiles.*

13.4 THE EFFECT OF A CUBIC PITCHING MOMENT ON STABILITY

For spin-stabilized projectiles, we need to recall the definition of the gyroscopic stability factor, derived in Chapter 10. For a linear pitching moment ($C_{M_{\alpha 2}} \equiv 0$), the classical gyroscopic stability factor is:

$$S_{g_0} = \frac{P^2}{4M_0} = \frac{I_x^2 p^2}{2\rho I_y S d V^2 C_{M_{\alpha 0}}} \tag{13.18}$$

The generalized effects of cubic pitching moments on static and gyroscopic stability are summarized below. The first four cases are for statically unstable, spin-stabilized projectiles, and the last four cases are for statically stable, non-spinning (or slowly rolling) fin-stabilized missiles.

Statically Unstable, Spin-Stabilized Projectiles

Case (A): $C_{M_{\alpha 0}} > 0; C_{M_{\alpha 2}} < 0; S_{g_0} > 1$. Projectile is gyroscopically stable at small yaw, and is *more stable* at larger yaw. Periodic pitching and yawing motion at any amplitude is possible.

Case (B): $C_{M_{\alpha 0}} > 0; C_{M_{\alpha 2}} < 0; S_{g_0} < 1$. Projectile is gyroscopically *unstable* at small yaw, but becomes more stable at larger yaw. Periodic pitching and yawing motion is possible if the median value of δ^2 yields a gyroscopically stable condition.

Case (C): $C_{M_{\alpha 0}} > 0; C_{M_{\alpha 2}} > 0; S_{g_0} > 1$. Projectile is gyroscopically stable at small yaw, but becomes *less stable* at larger yaw. For periodic circular pitching and yawing motion, the cubic part of the total pitching moment cannot exceed two-thirds of the linear part (see Ref. 6).

Case (D): $C_{M_{\alpha 0}} > 0; C_{M_{\alpha 2}} > 0; S_{g_0} < 1$. Projectile is gyroscopically *unstable* at all yaw levels. Any initial pitching and yawing motion grows exponentially with increasing distance along the trajectory.

Statically Stable, Non-Spinning (or Slowly Rolling) Fin-Stabilized Missiles

Case (E): $C_{M_{\alpha 0}} < 0; C_{M_{\alpha 2}} < 0$. Missile is statically stable at small yaw, and is more stable at larger yaw. Periodic pitching and yawing motion of any amplitude is possible.

Case (F): $C_{M_{\alpha 0}} < 0; C_{M_{\alpha 2}} > 0$. Missile is statically stable at small yaw, but is *less stable* at larger yaw. Periodic pitching and yawing motion is possible at all amplitudes for which the total pitching moment coefficient remains negative.

Case (G): $C_{M_{\alpha 0}} > 0; C_{M_{\alpha 2}} < 0$. Missile is statically *unstable* at small yaw, but is *more stable* at larger yaw. Periodic pitching and yawing motion is possible if a median value of δ^2 yields a statically stable condition.

Case (H): $C_{M_{\alpha 0}} > 0; C_{M_{\alpha 2}} > 0$. Missile is statically *unstable* at all yaw levels. Any initial pitching and yawing motion grows exponentially with increasing distance along the trajectory.

Discussion of the Stability Conditions for Nonlinear Pitching Moments

For spin-stabilized munitions, Case (A) is the optimum condition, because the projectile will always be gyroscopically stable, regardless of the size of the pitching and yawing motion. Fortunately, most spin-stabilized projectiles, at most flight speeds, have negative cubic pitching moment coefficients, and Case (A) is therefore a commonly observed condition.

The very interesting Case (B) occurs whenever the rifling twist rate is slightly too slow, and the muzzle gyroscopic stability factor is therefore slightly *less* than unity. Since the projectile is gyroscopically *unstable* at small yaw, the yaw begins to grow. But at larger yaw, the negative cubic pitching moment causes the projectile to become *gyroscopically stable*, and the yaw begins to damp. The net result is periodic pitching and yawing motion, but at a somewhat larger amplitude than if the projectile had been gyroscopically stable everywhere, as in Case (A). Riflemen sometimes fire small arms bullets from rifling twist rates that are slightly too slow for classical gyroscopic stability, and they often find that the flight is generally satisfactory. An aeroballistician might describe such a Case (B) behavior by stating, "the projectile is *living* on its cubic pitching moment!"

Case (C) is seldom seen, because positive values of the cubic pitching moment coefficient rarely occur for statically unstable, spin-stabilized projectiles. Case (D) is another infrequently encountered condition.

For a statically stable, non-spinning, or slowly rolling fin-stabilized missile, Case (E) is the optimum condition, because the missile will always be statically stable, regardless of the size of the pitching and yawing motion. Most statically stable missiles, at supersonic and subsonic speeds, have negative cubic pitching moment coefficients, and therefore fall into Case (E).

Positive cubic pitching moments have often been observed for statically stable, fin-stabilized mortar shell at transonic flight speeds. Such a projectile falls into Case (F), in the above table. As long as the amplitude of the pitching and yawing motion does not get so large that the total pitching moment coefficient becomes positive, the pitching and yawing motion will remain periodic.

Case (G) generally requires a careful investigation. The non-spinning (or slowly rolling) projectile is statically unstable at small yaw, but becomes stable at some larger yaw level. The critical question is, how large? If the design becomes statically stable at a yaw level of only a few degrees, the flight may be satisfactory. However, if the point of neutral static stability occurs at a truly large yaw (i.e., more than ten degrees), it is highly unlikely that the flight will ever be satisfactory, and the projectile will have to be re-designed.

Case (H) is a non-spinning, or slowly rolling missile that is statically unstable at all yaw levels, and this projectile design is usually unsatisfactory.

13.5 PITCHING AND YAWING MOTION WITH ALL NONLINEAR MOMENTS

The linearized differential equation describing the pitching and yawing motion of a spinning, rotationally symmetric projectile, was derived in Chapter 10:

$$\xi'' + (H - iP)\xi' - (M + iPT)\xi = -iPG \qquad \textbf{(10.66)}$$

where $\xi = \alpha + i\beta$

$$H = C_{L_\alpha}{}^* - C_D^* - k_y^{-2}\left(C_{M_q}{}^* + C_{M_{\dot\alpha}}{}^*\right)$$

$$P = \left(\frac{I_x}{I_y}\right)\left(\frac{pd}{V}\right)$$

$$M = k_y^{-2} C_{M_\alpha}{}^*$$

$$T = C_{L_\alpha}{}^* + k_x^{-2} C_{M_{p\alpha}}{}^*$$

$$G = \frac{gd\cos\phi}{V^2}$$

We will neglect the very small effect of gravity in equation (10.66), and expand all the aerodynamic moments to include cubic terms (see Ref. 4). The resulting nonlinear differential equation is:

$$\xi'' + \left(H_0 + H_2\delta^2 - iP\right)\xi' - \left[M_0 + M_2\delta^2 + iP\left(T_0 + T_2\delta^2\right)\right]\xi = 0 \qquad \textbf{(13.19)}$$

where $\delta^2 = \sin^2\alpha_t$

$$H_0 = \frac{\rho S d}{2m}\left[C_{L_{\alpha 0}} - C_{D_0} - k_y^{-2}\left(C_{M_q} + C_{M_{\dot\alpha}}\right)_0\right] \qquad \textbf{(13.20)}$$

$$H_2 = \frac{\rho S d}{2m}\left[C_{L_{\alpha 2}} - C_{D_{\delta^2}} - k_y^{-2}\left(C_{M_q} + C_{M_{\dot\alpha}}\right)_2\right] \qquad \textbf{(13.21)}$$

$$P = \left(\frac{I_x}{I_y}\right)\left(\frac{pd}{V}\right) \qquad \textbf{(13.22)}$$

$$M_0 = \frac{\rho S d}{2m} k_y^{-2} C_{M_{\alpha 0}} \qquad \textbf{(13.23)}$$

$$M_2 = \frac{\rho S d}{2m} k_y^{-2} C_{M_{\alpha 2}} \qquad \textbf{(13.24)}$$

$$T_0 = \frac{\rho S d}{2m}\left(C_{L_{\alpha 0}} + k_x^{-2} C_{M_{p\alpha 0}}\right) \qquad \textbf{(13.25)}$$

$$T_2 = \frac{\rho S d}{2m}\left(C_{L_{\alpha 2}} + k_x^{-2} C_{M_{p\alpha 2}}\right) \qquad \textbf{(13.26)}$$

p = projectile axial spin (radians/second)

V = projectile speed

ρ = air density

d = projectile reference diameter

S = projectile reference area (usually taken as $S = \pi d^2/4$) $\pi d^2/4$

m = projectile mass

$$k_y^{-2} = \frac{md^2}{I_y} \qquad k_x^{-2} = \frac{md^2}{I_x}$$

I_x = projectile axial moment of inertia

I_y = projectile transverse moment of inertia, about any axis through the center of mass

If all the cubic terms appearing in equation (13.19) were zero, the solution of the linearized differential equation would be given by equation (13.3):

$$\xi = K_F e^{i\phi_F} + K_S e^{i\phi_S}, \tag{13.3}$$

where

$$K_F = K_{F_0} e^{\lambda_F s} \tag{13.27}$$

$$K_S = K_{S_0} e^{\lambda_S s} \tag{13.28}$$

$$\phi_F = \phi_{F_0} + \phi'_F s \tag{13.29}$$

$$\phi_S = \phi_{S_0} + \phi'_S s \tag{13.30}$$

The average squared yaw is given by:

$$\delta^2 = \xi\bar{\xi} = K_F^2 + K_S^2 + 2K_F K_S \cos(\phi_F - \phi_S) \tag{13.31}$$

Since the damped epicyclic solution given by equation (13.3) is known to accurately fit the free-flight motions of projectiles with known nonlinear pitching, Magnus and pitch damping moments, we will substitute (13.3) and its derivatives into the nonlinear equation (13.19), and again discard the mixed frequency terms. The details of this substitution and the collection of terms are left as an exercise for the interested student. After considerable algebraic simplification, the following pair of equations is obtained:

$$(\lambda_F + i\phi'_F)^2 + (H_0 - iP)(\lambda_F + i\phi'_F) - \left[M_0 + M_2\delta_{eF}^2 + iP\left(T_0 + T_2\delta_{eF}^2\right)\right]$$
$$+ H_2\left[(\lambda_F + i\phi'_F)\left(K_F^2 + K_S^2\right) + (\lambda_S + i\phi'_S)K_S^2\right] = 0 \tag{13.32}$$

$$(\lambda_S + i\phi'_S)^2 + (H_0 - iP)(\lambda_S + i\phi'_S) - \left[M_0 + M_2\delta_{eS}^2 + iP\left(T_0 + T_2\delta_{eS}^2\right)\right]$$
$$+ H_2\left[(\lambda_S + i\phi'_S)\left(K_F^2 + K_S^2\right) + (\lambda_F + i\phi'_F)K_F^2\right] = 0 \tag{13.33}$$

where

$$\delta_{eF}^2 = K_F^2 + 2K_S^2 \tag{13.34}$$

$$\delta_{eS}^2 = K_S^2 + 2K_F^2 \tag{13.35}$$

Equations (13.32) and (13.33) may now be separated into real and imaginary parts, and the following four equations are obtained:

$$\lambda_F^2 - \phi_F'^2 + \lambda_F H_0 + P\phi'_F - M_0 - M_2\delta_{eF}^2 + H_2\left[\lambda_F\left(K_F^2 + K_S^2\right) + \lambda_S K_S^2\right] = 0 \tag{13.36}$$

$$2\lambda_F - \phi'_F + H_0\phi'_F - P\lambda_F - P\left(T_0 + T_2\delta_{eF}^2\right) + H_2\left[\phi'_F\left(K_F^2 + K_S^2\right) + \phi'_S K_S^2\right] = 0 \tag{13.37}$$

$$\lambda_S^2 - \phi_S'^2 + \lambda_S H_0 + P\phi'_S - M_0 - M_2\delta_{eS}^2 + H_2\left[\lambda_S\left(K_F^2 + K_S^2\right) + \lambda_F K_F^2\right] = 0 \tag{13.38}$$

$$2\lambda_S\phi'_S + H_0\phi'_S - P\lambda_S - P\left(T_0 + T_2\delta_{eS}^2\right) + H_2\left[\phi'_S\left(K_F^2 + K_S^2\right) + \phi'_F K_F^2\right] = 0 \tag{13.39}$$

Equations (13.36) and (13.38) are now solved for the epicyclic frequencies:

$$\phi'_F(P - \phi'_F) = M_0 + M_2\delta_{eF}^2 - \lambda_F^2 - \lambda_F H_0 - H_2\left[\lambda_F\left(K_F^2 + K_S^2\right) + \lambda_S K_S^2\right] \tag{13.40}$$

$$\phi'_S(P - \phi'_S) = M_0 + M_2\delta_{eS}^2 - \lambda_S^2 - \lambda_S H_0 - H_2\left[\lambda_S\left(K_F^2 + K_S^2\right) + \lambda_F K_F^2\right] \tag{13.41}$$

If the small effect of damping on the epicyclic frequencies is neglected, equations (13.40) and (13.41) reduce to (13.10) and (13.11), respectively, and we find:

$$\phi'_F + \phi'_S = P + M_2\left(\frac{K_F^2 - K_S^2}{\phi'_F - \phi'_S}\right) \approx P \tag{13.42}$$

$$\phi'_F \bullet \phi'_S = M_0 + M_2\delta_e^2 \tag{13.43}$$

$$\delta_e^2 = \frac{\phi'_F\delta_{eS}^2 - \phi'_S\delta_{eF}^2}{\phi'_F - \phi'_S} = K_F^2 + K_S^2 + \frac{\phi'_F K_F^2 - \phi'_S K_S^2}{\phi'_F - \phi'_S} \tag{13.44}$$

Equations (13.37) and (13.39) may now be solved for the damping exponents. Substituting the ~~definition~~ approximation $P = \phi'_F + \phi'_S$ from equation (13.42) we obtain:

$$\lambda_F = \frac{-H_0\phi'_F + P\left(T_0 + T_2\delta_{eF}^2\right) - H_2\left[\phi'_F\left(K_F^2 + K_S^2\right) + \phi'_S K_S^2\right]}{\phi'_F - \phi'_S} \tag{13.45}$$

$$\lambda_S = \frac{+H_0\phi'_S - P\left(T_0 + T_2\delta_{eS}^2\right) + H_2\left[\phi'_S\left(K_F^2 + K_S^2\right) + \phi'_F K_F^2\right]}{\phi'_F - \phi'_S} \tag{13.46}$$

We recall the linearized equations (10.100) and (10.101) from Chapter 10:

$$H = -\left[\lambda_F + \lambda_S\right] \tag{10.100}$$

$$PT = -\left[\phi'_F\lambda_S + \phi'_S\lambda_F\right] \tag{10.101}$$

Substituting equations (13.45) and (13.46) into (10.100) and (10.101), and simplifying:

$$H = H_0 + PT_2\left[\frac{K_F^2 - K_S^2}{\phi'_F - \phi'_S}\right] + H_2\left[\frac{\phi'_F K_S^2 - \phi'_S K_F^2}{\phi'_F - \phi'_S}\right] \tag{13.47}$$

$$T = T_0 + T_2\delta_e^2 - H_2\left[\frac{\phi_F'^2 K_F^2 - \phi_S'^2 K_S^2}{\phi_F'^2 - \phi_S'^2}\right] \quad (13.48)$$

We now substitute equation (13.42), and the definitions of equations (13.20) through (13.26) into equations (13.47) and (13.48), and solve for the aerodynamic coefficients. The left-hand sides of these equations represent the "range" [(R)-subscript] values of the Magnus and pitch damping moment coefficients that are obtained by fitting the linearized solution for the pitching and yawing motion [see Chapter 10, equation (10.94)] to the observed nonlinear free-flight data. After some simplification, we obtain the useful results:

$$C_{M_{p\alpha(R)}} = C_{M_{p\alpha_0}} + C_{M_{p\alpha_2}}\delta_e^2 + \left(C_{M_q} + C_{M_{\dot\alpha}}\right)_2 \delta_{e_{TH}}^2 \quad (13.49)$$

$$\left(C_{M_q} + C_{M_{\dot\alpha}}\right)_{(R)} = \left(C_{M_q} + C_{M_{\dot\alpha}}\right)_0 + C_{M_{p\alpha_2}}\delta_{e_{HH}}^2 + \left(C_{M_q} + C_{M_{\dot\alpha}}\right)_2 \delta_{e_{HT}}^2 \quad (13.50)$$

where,

$$\delta_e^2 = K_F^2 + K_S^2 + \left[\frac{\phi_F' K_F^2 - \phi_S' K_S^2}{\phi_F' - \phi_S'}\right] \quad (13.51)$$

$$\delta_{e_{TH}}^2 = \left(\frac{I_x}{I_y}\right)\left[\frac{\phi_F'^2 K_F^2 - \phi_S'^2 K_S^2}{\phi_F'^2 - \phi_S'^2}\right] \quad (13.52)$$

$$\delta_{e_{HH}}^2 = \left(\frac{I_y}{I_x}\right)\left(K_S^2 - K_F^2\right)\left[\frac{\phi_F' + \phi_S'}{\phi_F' - \phi_S'}\right] \quad (13.53)$$

$$\delta_{e_{HT}}^2 = \frac{\phi_F' K_S^2 - \phi_S' K_F^2}{\phi_F' - \phi_S'} \quad (13.54)$$

The definitions of the various effective squared yaws required for the analysis of nonlinear Magnus and pitch damping moment coefficient data are given in equations (13.51) through (13.54), above. These definitions are consistent with those of Murphy (References 4 and 6), and with Bradley (Ref. 9). [Note: Bradley and Miller have observed that "effective squared yaw" (actually the squared sine of an angle) may be an awkward label for the quantities defined in equations (13.52) through (13.54), since they *could* be *negative* (particularly $\delta_{e_{HH}}^2$), depending on the size of K_F and K_S. However, except for δ_e^2 (which is never negative) one does not ever need to take the square root of the effective squared yaw, and the negative values therefore do not cause a problem].

Equations (13.49) and (13.50) illustrate the fact that the range values of the cubic Magnus and pitch damping moment coefficients are coupled through the nonlinear least-squares data reduction process. Unfortunately, this coupling means that if *either* coefficient is nonlinear, the free-flight range data for the two coefficients must be analyzed simultaneously. The proper effective squared yaw values [see equations (13.51) through (13.54)] should be calculated for each round fired, and used for the nonlinear coefficient analysis.

Murphy analyzed the free-flight spark range data from several firing programs at supersonic speeds (Ref. 4), and found no significant values of the cubic pitch damping moment coefficient. In his later treatment (Ref. 6), Murphy drops the cubic pitch damping moment from his analysis of free-flight spark range data. However, the author has obtained well-determined values of the cubic pitch damping moment coefficient for spin-stabilized projectiles flying at subsonic speeds. Two examples of this behavior are illustrated in References 10 and 11. (Note that the *definitions* of $\delta_{e_{HH}}^2$ and $\delta_{e_{HT}}^2$ were inadvertently reversed in the analysis of Reference 10). Significant cubic pitch damping moment coefficients have also been observed for a non-rolling, finned mortar shell at subsonic speeds.

If a fin-stabilized projectile has zero roll throughout its flight, all Magnus force and moment coefficients are identically zero. Equation (13.49) disappears for this case, and equation (13.50) reduces to the simple expression:

$$\left(C_{M_q} + C_{M_{\dot\alpha}}\right)_{(R)} = \left(C_{M_q} + C_{M_{\dot\alpha}}\right)_0 + \left(C_{M_q} + C_{M_{\dot\alpha}}\right)_2 \delta_{e_{HT}}^2 \quad (13.55)$$

Figure 13.7 shows the variation of $\left(C_{M_q} + C_{M_{\dot\alpha}}\right)_{(R)}$ with $\delta_{e_{HT}}^2$, for a non-rolling, 120mm finned mortar shell, at subsonic and transonic speeds. In both cases, the effect of increasing average angle of attack is to increase the magnitude of the pitch damping moment.

No significant values of the cubic pitch damping moment coefficient have ever been observed for spin-stabilized projectiles at supersonic speeds. If we set $\left(C_{M_q} + C_{M_{\dot\alpha}}\right)_2 = 0$, equations (13.49) and (13.50) reduce to the simpler forms:

$$C_{M_{p\alpha(R)}} = C_{M_{p\alpha_0}} + C_{M_{p\alpha_2}}\delta_e^2 \quad (13.56)$$

$$\left(C_{M_q} + C_{M_{\dot\alpha}}\right)_{(R)} = \left(C_{M_q} + C_{M_{\dot\alpha}}\right)_0 + C_{M_{p\alpha_2}}\delta_{e_{HH}}^2 \quad (13.57)$$

Murphy analyzed the nonlinear Magnus moment and pitch damping moment coefficients for the 9-Caliber Long Army-Navy Spinner Rocket at Mach 1.8, and presented the results in Reference 6. Models were tested with a forward and a rear center-of-gravity (CG) location. A sketch of the 20mm models is shown in Figure 13.8, and the nonlinear Magnus moment and pitch damping moment coefficient results are illustrated in Figures 13.9 (*p. 284*) and 13.10 (*p. 284*), respectively.

Plotting the range values (see Figure 13.9) of the Magnus moment coefficient against δ_e^2, and fitting straight lines to the data by least squares, yields values of 71±8 for the cubic Magnus moment coefficient of the forward center-of-gravity projectiles, and 13±1, for the rear CG models. (Note: the ± values are the standard errors in the least-squares-determined values of the coefficients). Similar plots of the range values of the pitch damping moment coefficients against $\delta_{e_{HH}}^2$ [see equation (13.57)] are shown in Figure 13.10. For the forward CG models, the slope of the least-squares fitted line (which again is the cubic Magnus moment coefficient) is 66±8.

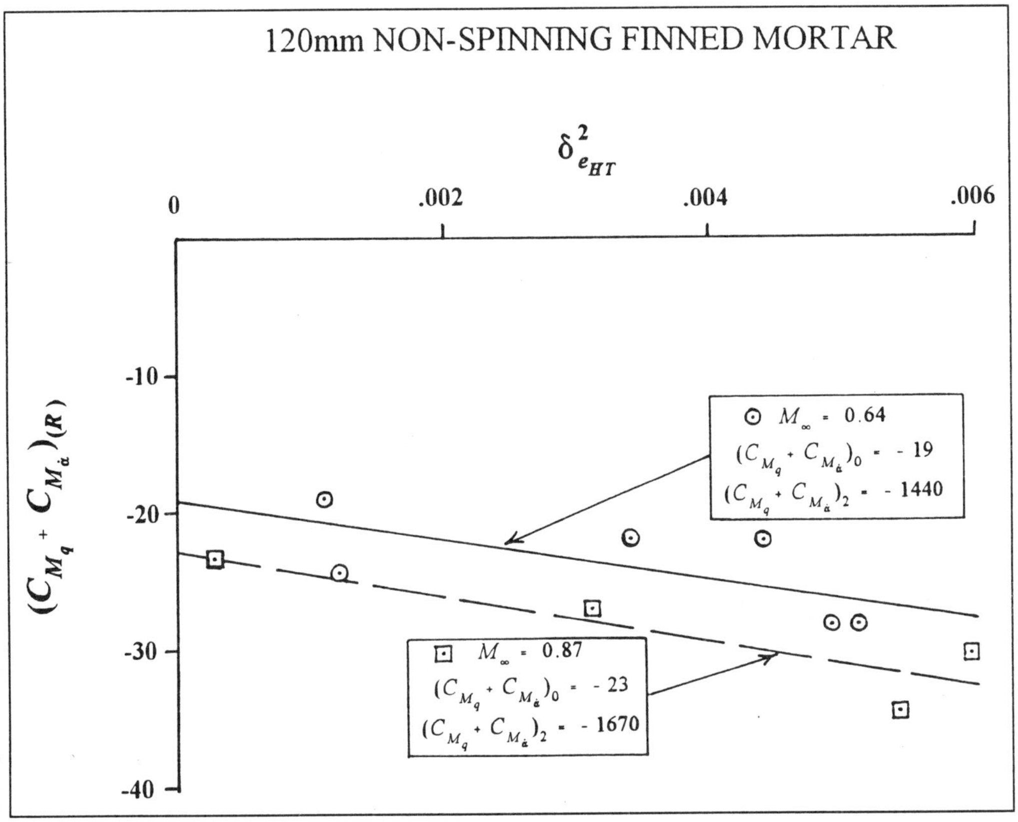

Figure 13.7 Pitch Damping Moment Coefficient versus Effective Squared Yaw.

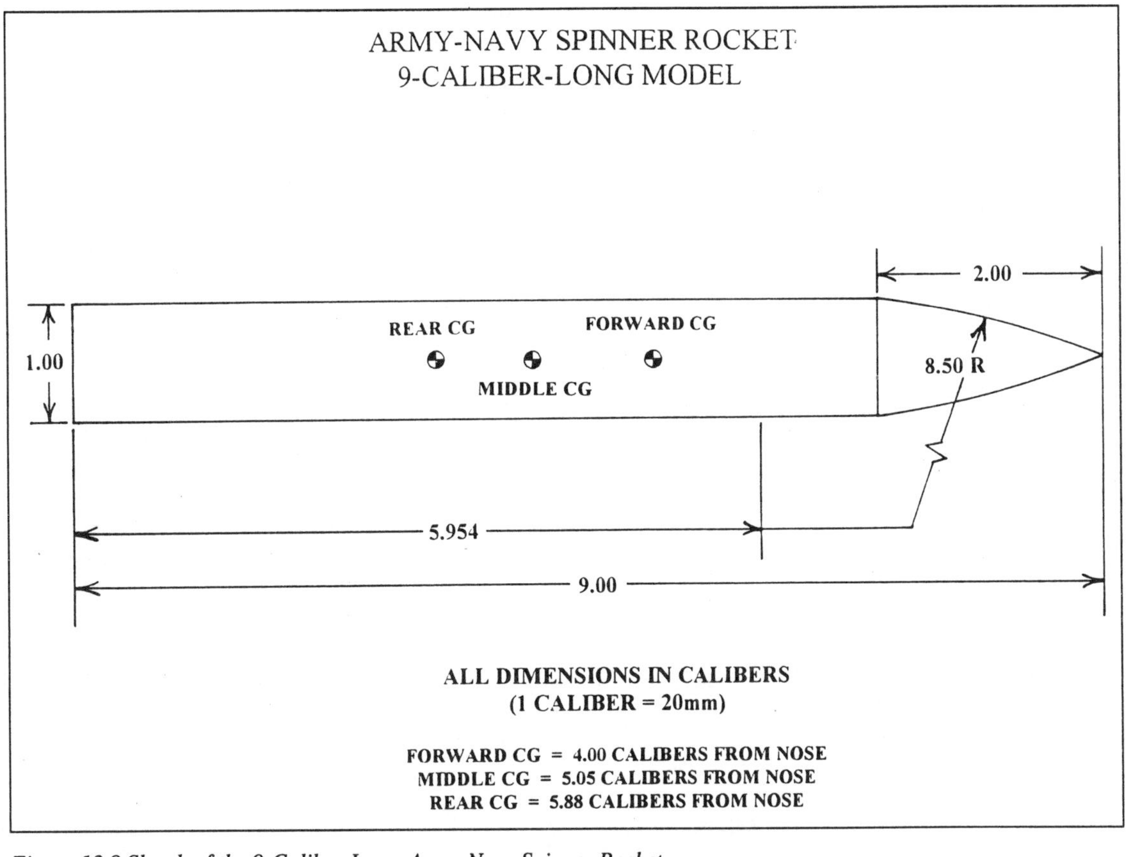

Figure 13.8 Sketch of the 9-Caliber-Long, Army-Navy Spinner Rocket.

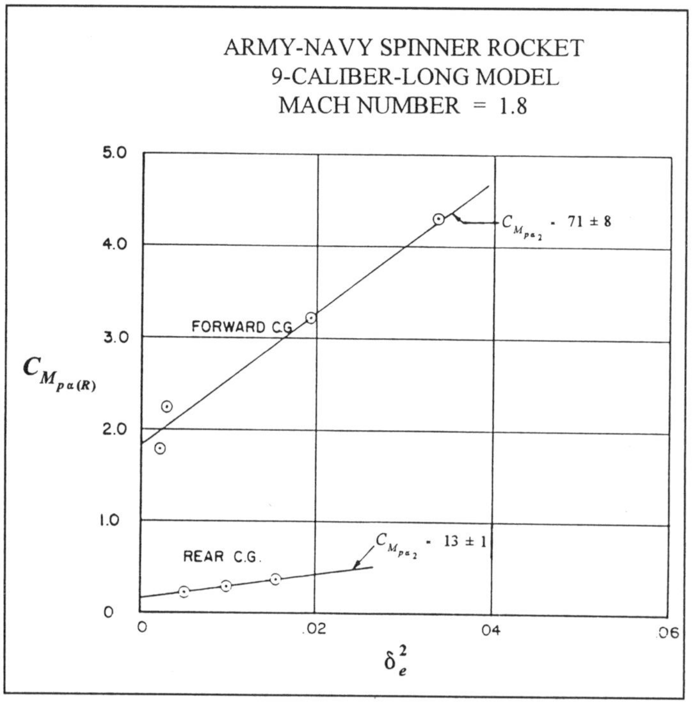

Figure 13.9 Magnus Moment Coefficient versus Effective Squared Yaw.

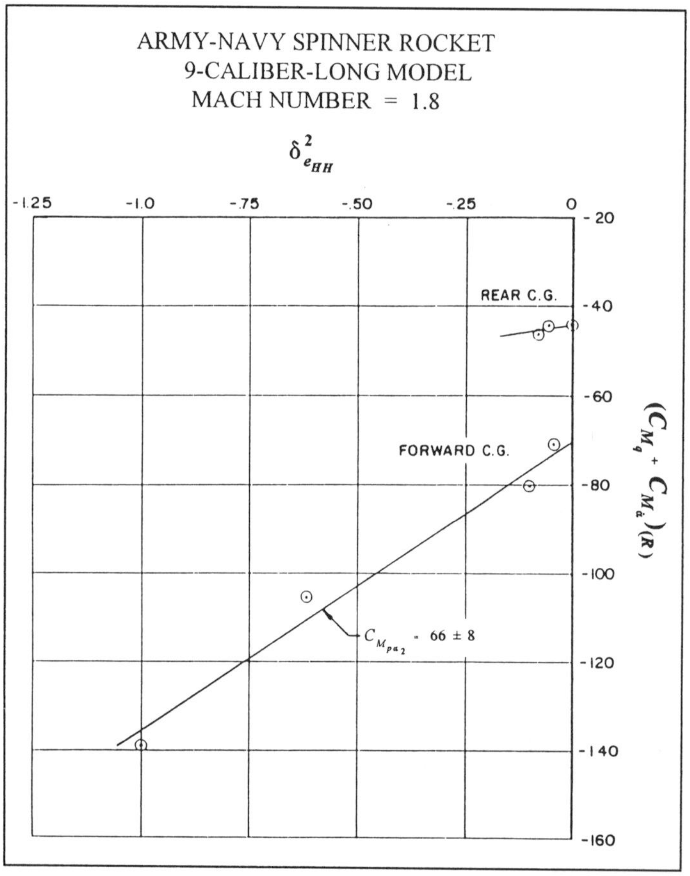

Figure 13.10 Pitch Damping Moment Coefficient versus Effective Squared Yaw.

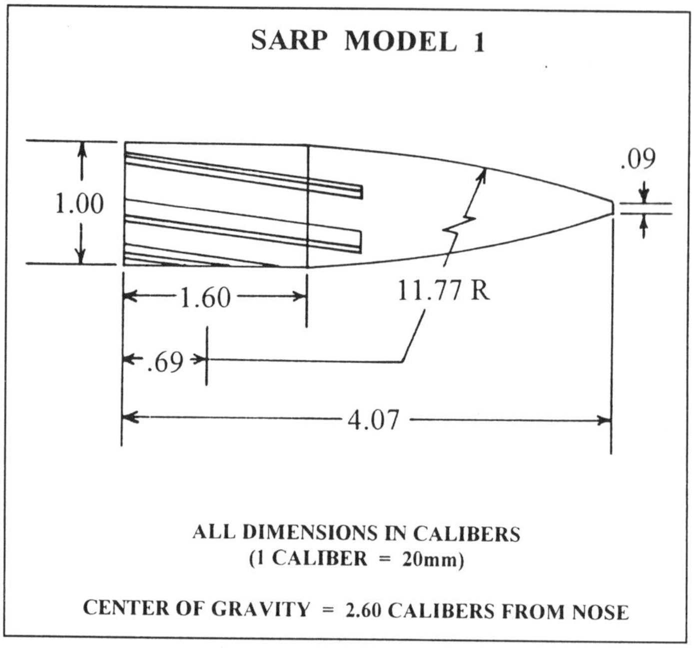

Figure 13.11 Sketch of the 20 mm, SARP Model 1 Projectile.

This result may be compared with the value 71±8, obtained from the Magnus moment coefficient analysis. Although no significant value of the cubic Magnus moment coefficient could be obtained from pitch damping moment data for the rear CG models, the slope 13±1, obtained from Figure 13.9, appears to fit the rear CG pitch damping data very well. Such good agreement between the results obtained independently from the Magnus and the pitch damping moment analysis, confirms the fact that there is no significant cubic pitch damping moment acting on these projectiles. The observed nonlinearity in both $C_{M_{p\alpha}}$ and $\left(C_{M_q} + C_{M_{\dot\alpha}}\right)$ is caused by the cubic Magnus moment coefficient.

13.6 BI-CUBIC AND TRI-CUBIC MAGNUS MOMENTS

In the spring of 1966, a Small Arms Research Program (SARP) was initiated at the Exterior Ballistic Laboratory of the BRL, at Aberdeen Proving Ground, Maryland. The first of several projectile shapes tested under the overall SARP project is illustrated in Figure 13.11. This projectile had a nose shape similar to that of the 155mm, M101 artillery shell; it was 20mm in diameter; was made of hard Tobin bronze to resist in-bore deformation, and was fully engraved in the manner of conventional flat-based small arms projectiles. Later in the SARP program, caliber .50 and caliber .30 models of the same projectile were tested to find out if varying the Reynolds number had any significant effect on the flight of typical small arms bullets. (The results showed that, in general, Reynolds number effects appeared to be very small across the above size range). The small angle-of-attack SARP data were published in Reference 12.

The subsonic values of the range-measured Magnus moment coefficients obtained for the SARP Model 1 projectiles are plotted against δ_e^2 in Figure 13.12 *(p. 285)*. Note that the data appear to fall along two distinct straight lines, which is the *definition* of bi-cubic

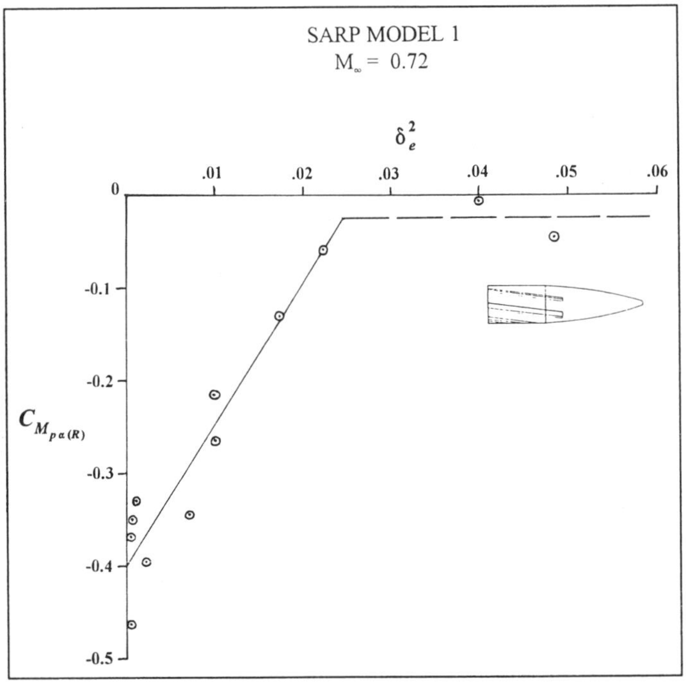

Figure 13.12 Magnus Moment Coefficient versus Effective Squared Yaw.

behavior. At small angles of attack, we observe the usual cubic variation of the Magnus moment. At larger yaw, the range-determined Magnus moment coefficient appears to level off at a constant value. (The transition point for the SARP Model 1 shape occurs at a total angle-of-attack of approximately 9.0 degrees). Analysis of the pitch damping moment coefficient data for this projectile shows that no significant cubic pitch damping moment exists. The observed dependence of the range-measured damping moment coefficients on the amplitude of motion is due to the effect of the cubic Magnus moment coefficient [see equation (13.57)].

The average value of the pitch damping moment coefficient, corrected for the cubic Magnus effect, is -5.7±1.2, at both supersonic and subsonic speeds. This is a sufficiently negative value, and it causes no flight problems. However, the behavior of the nonlinear Magnus moment coefficient at subsonic speeds has a significant impact on the flight dynamic behavior of this projectile, as we will show presently.

As a second example of *bi-cubic* Magnus moment coefficient data, we will examine the behavior of three U.S. caliber .50 bullets, which were fired in the BRL Aerodynamics Range in 1988. The aerodynamic data is published in Reference 13, and a sketch of the projectile contour is shown in Figure 13.13. The variation of the range-determined Magnus moment coefficients with δ_e^2 is shown in Figures 13.14 and 13.15 (*p. 286*), respectively, for low supersonic and subsonic speeds. Note that large-yaw firings were done only for one bullet, the .50 API, M8.

Figure 13.14 shows the bi-cubic behavior of the caliber .50 bullets at low supersonic speeds. The Magnus moment coefficient increases from -0.80 at zero yaw to +0.27 at 3.4 degrees total angle of attack, at which point the coefficient levels off and remains constant for total angles of attack at least as large as 9.0 degrees. Between zero and 3.4 degrees yaw, the value of the cubic Magnus moment coefficient is 290. The average value of the pitch damping moment coefficient at low supersonic speeds, corrected for the cubic Magnus effect, was found to be -5.7. Figure 13.15 is a plot of the caliber .50 Magnus moment coefficient data versus δ_e^2, at subsonic speeds. For subsonic flight, the Magnus moment coefficients for the caliber .50 bullets are observed to obey a simple cubic law, up to total angles of attack about 6 degrees. The slope of the line, which is the cubic Magnus moment coefficient, is 120 for flight Mach numbers between 0.6 and 0.9. The average value of the subsonic pitch damping moment coefficient, corrected for the cubic Magnus effect, is -3.0.

Figure 13.16 (*p. 286*) illustrates a *tri-cubic* Magnus moment. This plot contains the small, intermediate, and large angle-of-attack data for the 105mm, M1 Shell, obtained from firings at subsonic speeds in the BRL Transonic Range. The small-yaw data were published in Reference 14. A yaw inducer was used, and average angles of attack up to thirty degrees were obtained. Note the sharp

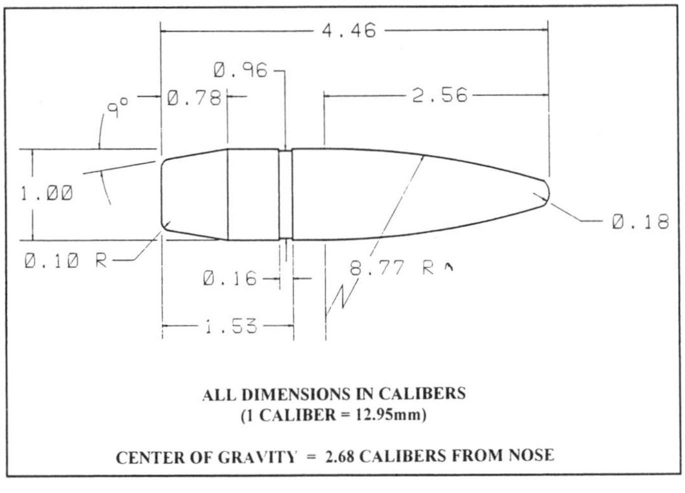

Figure 13.13 Sketch of the .50 Caliber Projectiles.

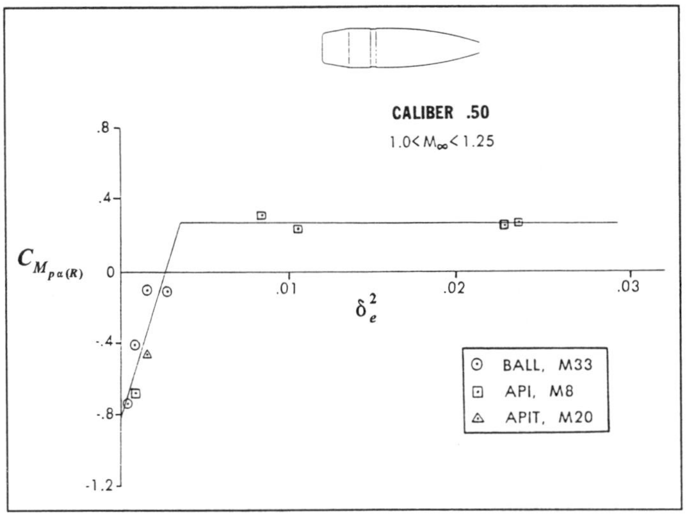

Figure 13.14 Magnus Moment Coefficient versus Effective Squared Yaw.

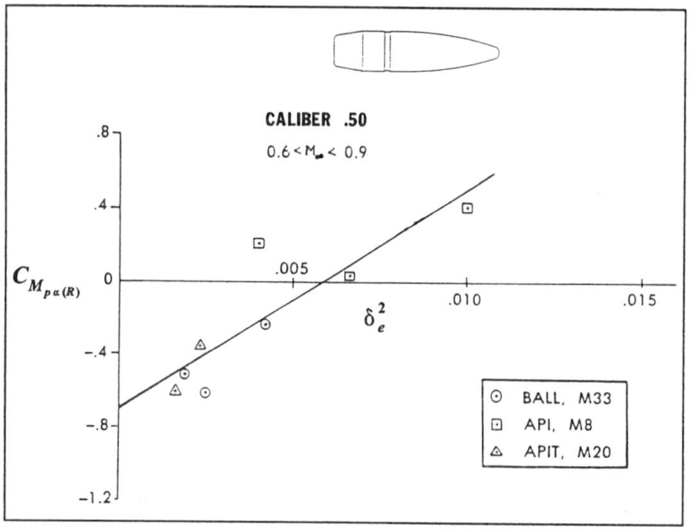

Figure 13.15 Magnus Moment Coefficient versus Effective Squared Yaw.

discontinuities in slope, for the three different angle of attack regions.

The intercept of Figure 13.16, which is the zero-yaw value of the Magnus moment coefficient, is -0.39. The small-yaw cubic Magnus moment coefficient (slope of the first cubic) is +52, and the curve crosses the horizontal axis at $\delta_e^2 = 0.00742$, which corresponds to an angle of attack of 4.9 degrees. At $\delta_e^2 = 0.00849$ (angle of attack = 5.3 degrees), the first cubic ends, and the second curve begins. The second cubic, with its slight downward slope, continues until $\delta_e^2 = 0.1081$ (angle of attack = 19.2 degrees), after which the third, large yaw region begins. The third cubic again shows a growing Magnus moment coefficient, with increasing effective squared yaw. The large-yaw curve starts at 19.2 degrees, and continues upward until the angle of attack is of order of 35 degrees. The effects of the strongly nonlinear Magnus moment on the subsonic flight dynamic characteristics of the 105mm, M1 shell will be discussed in the next section of this chapter.

Nonlinear Magnus moments are routinely observed today in wind tunnels and spark photography ranges, for nearly all spin stabilized projectiles at subsonic and transonic speeds. If the projectile flies its entire trajectory with small yaw, the subsonic and transonic Magnus moments will probably be adequately described by a simple cubic dependence on total angle of attack. In many cases, the cubic Magnus moment coefficients cause limit-cycle yaw behavior, which we will discuss in the next section. Most observed flight dynamic instabilities are caused by nonlinear Magnus moments. Occasionally, nonlinear Magnus moment behavior is observed at supersonic speeds, but it does not usually cause flight dynamic problems.

Bi-cubic or tri-cubic Magnus moment behavior has been illustrated in several of this chapter's examples, without any discussion of the fluid-dynamic mechanisms that cause such dramatic effects. In general, for spin-stabilized projectiles, the small-yaw nonlinear behavior (first cubic curve) of the Magnus moment coefficient is caused by the combined effects of the axial spin, the angle of attack, and the asymmetric boundary layer displacement thickness. If the projectile is at angle of attack, but not spinning, the boundary

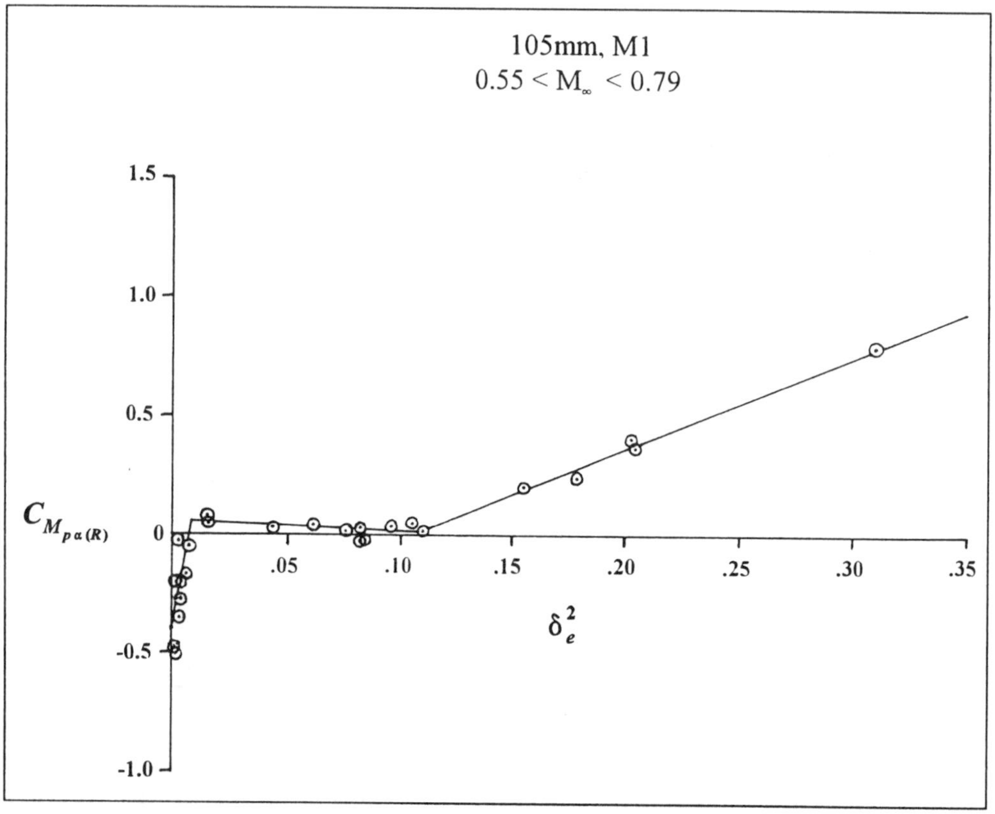

Figure 13.16 Magnus Moment Coefficient versus Effective Squared Yaw.

layer is thicker on the leeward flow side than on the windward side. In the absence of spin, the displacement thickness would be symmetric about the angle-of-attack plane, and no side force or moment would be produced. The addition of axial spin causes the asymmetric boundary layer displacement thickness to be rotated out of the plane of the angle of attack, thereby producing a side (Magnus) force and moment, in addition to a nonlinear normal force and pitching moment. This side force and moment often exhibit strongly nonlinear behavior, even at very small angles of attack.

As the angle of attack is increased from the small yaw region into the intermediate region, a critical angle is attained, above which the boundary layer first begins to separate along the leeward side of the projectile. Once lee-side boundary layer separation occurs, a pair of vortices appear, but for intermediate angles of attack they remain close to the lee side of the projectile. Again, if there were no axial spin, the two vortices would have equal circulation strengths, and would remain symmetric, relative to the plane of the angle of attack. However, the addition of axial spin causes the two vortices to have unequal circulation strengths, and to be rotated into a non-symmetric configuration, which again leads to a nonlinear side (Magnus) force and moment. In general, the size of the Magnus moment in the intermediate (second cubic curve) angle of attack region tends to be smaller than the small angle of attack (first cubic curve) values. In addition, the *cubic* Magnus moment coefficients in the intermediate region are usually smaller than those observed at small angles of attack.

At large angle of attack, complete boundary layer separation occurs on the leeward side of the projectile, and the airflow becomes similar to the two-dimensional crossflow around a spinning circular cylinder. This is the large-yaw, tri-cubic Magnus moment (third cubic curve) region. For conventional spin-stabilized projectiles, this large-yaw region begins at a nominal angle of attack of about 19 degrees. The third cubic curve for the 105mm, M1 shell at subsonic speeds begins at an angle of attack of approximately 19 degrees, as illustrated in Figure 13.16. For large yaw flight, the *cubic* Magnus moment coefficient is a significant positive value, and the size of $C_{M_{p\alpha}}$ can therefore grow quite large, at large angles of attack.

Some authors prefer to represent the tri-cubic Magnus moment curve of Figure 13.16 with a seventh-power (or higher) series expansion, stated as equation (13.58):

$$C_{M_{p\alpha}} = C_{M_{p\alpha_0}} + C_{M_{p\alpha_2}} \sin^2\alpha + C_{M_{p\alpha_4}} \sin^4\alpha + C_{M_{p\alpha_6}} \sin^6\alpha + \cdots \quad \textbf{(13.58)}$$

However, the power-series expansion of equation (13.58) does not permit the discontinuities in slope that are so readily apparent in Figure 13.16. It is the author's belief that a bi-cubic or tri-cubic representation of the nonlinear Magnus moment coefficient is usually a *better* approximation than equation (13.58), for two reasons. First, the bi-cubic or tri-cubic usually fits the experimental data better than a polynomial does. Second, the power-series approximation does not recognize the fact that the Magnus moment is caused by different fluid mechanisms, in the various angle of attack regions. Flow visualization experiments have confirmed that the fluid mechanisms change almost instantaneously at critical angles of attack. This fact implies that the changes in the Magnus moment coefficient at critical angles are probably *discontinuous* in nature, rather than smooth and continuous, as assumed in equation (13.58).

13.7 NONLINEAR MAGNUS MOMENTS AND LIMIT-CYCLE YAWING MOTION

As we have seen in the previous section, cubic or bi-cubic Magnus moment coefficients are often observed for spin-stabilized projectiles, particularly at transonic and subsonic speeds. In fact, nonlinear Magnus moments occur so frequently that modern aeroballisticians consider them to be one of the normal characteristics of spinning shell. Although occasional determinations of cubic pitch damping moment coefficients have been made, it is usually the nonlinear Magnus moment coefficient that dominates the flight dynamic behavior of spin-stabilized projectiles.

We now return to the expressions for the nonlinear damping exponents, stated as equations (13.45) and (13.46). For a linear pitch damping moment and a cubic Magnus moment, the H_2 term disappears, and the damping exponents take on the simpler form:

$$\lambda_F = \frac{-H_0\phi'_F + P\left(T_0 + T_2\delta_{eF}^2\right)}{\phi'_F - \phi'_S} \quad \textbf{(13.59)}$$

$$\lambda_S = \frac{+H_0\phi'_S - P\left(T_0 + T_2\delta_{eS}^2\right)}{\phi'_F - \phi'_S} \quad \textbf{(13.60)}$$

These two equations may be written in the equivalent form:

$$\lambda_F = \lambda_{F_0} + \lambda_{F_2}\delta_{eF}^2 \quad \textbf{(13.61)}$$

$$\lambda_S = \lambda_{S_0} + \lambda_{S_2}\delta_{eS}^2 \quad \textbf{(13.62)}$$

where $$\lambda_{F_0} = \frac{-H_0\phi'_F + PT_0}{\phi'_F - \phi'_S} \quad \textbf{(13.63)}$$

$$\lambda_{S_0} = \frac{+H_0\phi'_S - PT_0}{\phi'_F - \phi'_S} \quad \textbf{(13.64)}$$

$$\lambda_{F_2} = -\lambda_{S_2} = \frac{PT_2}{\phi'_F - \phi'_S} \quad \textbf{(13.65)}$$

In Chapter 10, we discussed the dynamic stability of spinning symmetric projectiles, and showed that both the fast and slow arm damping exponents must be negative quantities for satisfactory flight. According to the linearized theory of Chapter 10, if both damping exponents are negative quantities, the transient epicyclic pitching and yawing motion will eventually damp to zero amplitude, and disappear. However, if either λ_F or λ_S are positive, the motion will be dynamically unstable, and the modal arm associated with the positive exponent will eventually grow to a large size. Note that under a linearized theory, the damping exponents are fixed val-

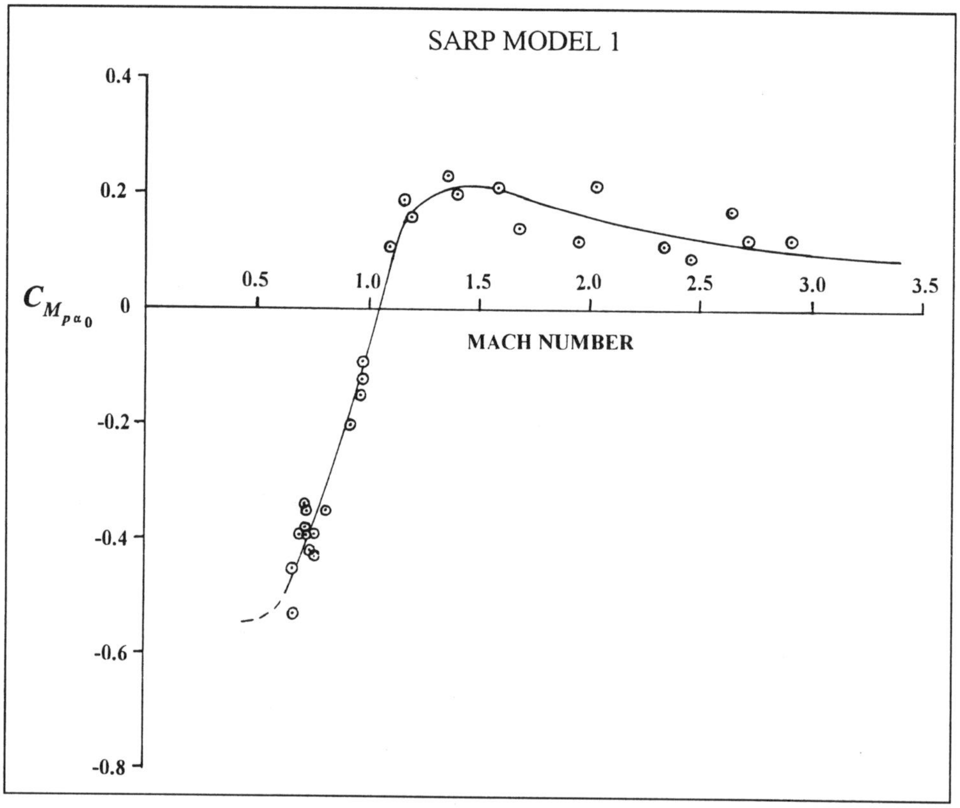

Figure 13.17 Zero-Yaw Magnus Moment Coefficient versus Mach Number.

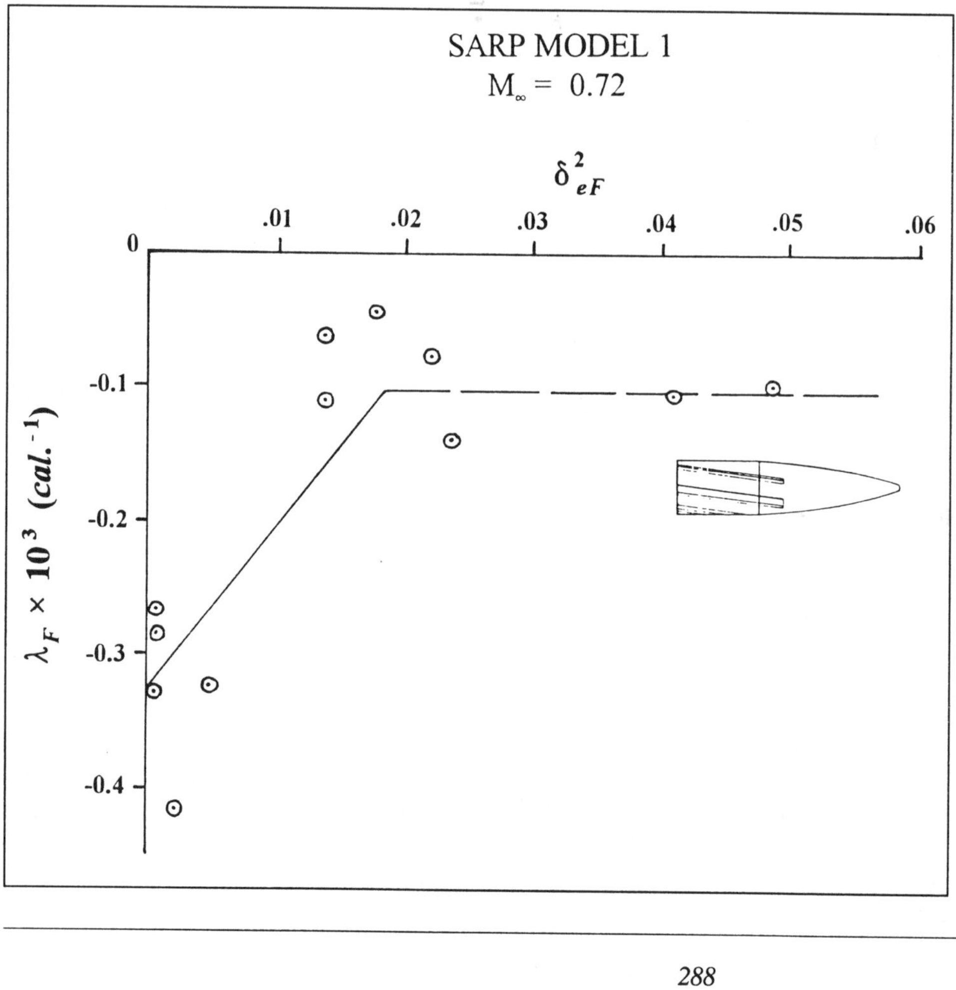

Figure 13.18 Fast-Arm Damping Exponent versus Effective Squared Yaw.

ues for a given flight Mach number, and they *cannot vary* with the amplitude of the pitching and yawing motion.

For a nonlinear system, the linearized results of Chapter 10 must be modified. Equations (13.61) through (13.65) show that if the Magnus moment is nonlinear, the damping exponents vary with the *amplitude* of the pitching and yawing motion. In particular, if one of the damping exponents is positive for small amplitude motion, but becomes negative at larger yaw levels, a *limit-cycle yawing motion* will occur. Several examples of limit-cycle yaw behavior will now be illustrated.

The first example of limit-cycle yaw we will consider is the SARP Model 1 (see Figure 13.11), flying at subsonic speed. Fired from a rifling twist rate of 29 calibers/turn, this projectile is both gyroscopically and dynamically stable at supersonic speeds, and it flies very well. However, as the flight speed falls below Mach 1, the zero-yaw Magnus moment coefficient switches from a small positive to a rapidly increasing negative quantity, as shown in Figure 13.17. (Note: the average value of the zero-yaw pitch damping moment coefficient, corrected for the cubic Magnus moment, is -5.7±1.2, at all speeds, from Mach 3.0 down to Mach 0.6). The large negative zero-yaw Magnus moment coefficient at Mach numbers below 0.8 causes the projectile to become dynamically unstable at small angles of attack. However, we observed in Figure 13.12 that increasing yaw level caused the subsonic Magnus moment coefficient to become less negative (smaller in absolute magnitude). We will now plot the spark-range observed subsonic damping exponents of the SARP Model 1 against their respective effective squared yaws, as specified by equations (13.61) and (13.62).

Figure 13.18 is a plot of the subsonic fast-arm damping exponent versus its effective squared yaw. The behavior is bi-cubic, because it follows the bi-cubic Magnus moment coefficient previously plotted as Figure 13.12. Note that the fast-arm damping exponent, λ_F, is everywhere negative at subsonic speeds. Thus the fast epicyclic pitch and yaw mode is damped, regardless of the yaw level, for subsonic as well as supersonic speeds, and we would therefore expect to observe no fast frequency pitching and yawing motion at long distances from the gun. (Another way of stating this would be that the fast epicyclic pitch and yaw arm for the SARP Model 1 projectile is everywhere dynamically stable, at all flight Mach numbers, and all reasonable yaw levels).

A plot of the slow-arm damping exponent at subsonic speed (average Mach number = 0.72) versus its proper effective squared yaw is shown in Figure 13.19. This graph illustrates the slow-arm limit cycle yaw behavior of the SARP Model 1 projectile at subsonic speeds. For small angles of attack, the damping exponent λ_S is positive; therefore if the amplitude of the pitching and yawing motion is small, the slow arm will begin to grow. However, when the average angle of attack reaches the amplitude required to reduce λ_S to zero (7.3 degrees, for the SARP Model 1 projectile), the growth in the slow mode amplitude will cease, and that amplitude will afterward remain constant, at the limit-cycle yaw value of 7.3 degrees. (Note that for a changing flight Mach number, the size of the limit-cycle yaw may also change).

The fast epicyclic yaw arm for the SARP Model 1 is damped at all flight speeds, and for all reasonable angles of attack. If the projectile is fired at a supersonic velocity, the fast arm will damp exponentially with increasing distance, and we would therefore expect a pure slow-arm limit cycle yaw at subsonic speeds. Its size is readily obtained from Figure 13.19 (*p. 290*), given that the straight line crosses the effective-squared-yaw axis at a value of $\delta_{eS}^2 = 0.0163$. The fast arm amplitude is assumed to be zero, since it is everywhere dynamically stable, thus $\delta_{eS}^2 \approx K_S^2$ [see equation (13.35)]. The slow-arm limit-cycle yaw value is therefore found from the simple calculation, $K_{S_{(L/C)}} = Sin^{-1}\left(\sqrt{0.0163}\right) = 7.3°$. If the projectile is fired at a supersonic velocity, and subsequently coasts down to subsonic speed, the observed pitching and yawing motion at long ranges will be a slow-mode coning motion about the flight path, at an amplitude of 7.3 degrees.

What would happen if the subsonic amplitude of the pitching and yawing motion somehow became larger than the limit cycle value? Figure 13.19 also provides the answer to this question. If the average amplitude of the pitching and yawing motion were to exceed the 7.3-degree limit cycle yaw value, then the damping exponent would be *negative*, and the amplitude would *damp* to the limit cycle value. *Thus, the limit-cycle yaw represents a dynamically stable situation, in the sense that the amplitude of the motion will not grow with increasing time or distance along the trajectory.* Again, we note that the limit-cycle yaw amplitude changes slowly along the trajectory, as the flight Mach number changes.

The nonlinear behavior of the Magnus moment coefficient for three U.S. caliber .50 bullets was previously illustrated, in Figures 13.14 and 13.15. Plots of the range-measured damping exponents versus their respective effective squared yaws are shown in Figures 13.20 through 13.23. Figure 13.20 (*p. 290*) shows the variation of the fast-arm damping exponent, λ_F, with δ_{eF}^2 for the .50 caliber bullets at low supersonic speeds. The behavior of the fast-arm damping exponent is bi-cubic, as expected, and λ_F is observed to be everywhere negative. The fast epicyclic yaw arm is therefore dynamically stable at low supersonic speeds, and is damped at all small and intermediate yaw levels.

Figure 13.21 is a plot of the slow-arm damping exponent, λ_S, against δ_{eS}^2 for the same .50 caliber bullets at low supersonic speeds. We again observe bi-cubic behavior, and the plot predicts a slow-arm limit-cycle yaw. At small angles of attack, λ_S is positive, but for larger yaw levels the slow-arm damping exponent crosses the δ_{eS}^2 axis and becomes negative. For $\delta_{eS}^2 = 0.0027, \lambda_S = 0$, which means that the slow-arm limit-cycle yaw amplitude will be
$K_{S_{(L/C)}} = Sin^{-1}\left(\sqrt{0.00027}\right) = 3.0°$.

Figures 13.22 and 13.23 illustrate the variation of the subsonic damping rate exponents with their effective squared yaws, for the three .50 caliber bullets. Figure 13.22 is a plot of λ_F versus δ_{eF}^2, for Mach numbers between 0.6 and 0.9. Although the two data points for the APIT M20 bullet are slightly positive, the average value of λ_F is approximately -0.0001 per caliber, and in general, the fast epicyclic pitch and yaw arm will be damped for all reasonable yaw levels at subsonic speeds.

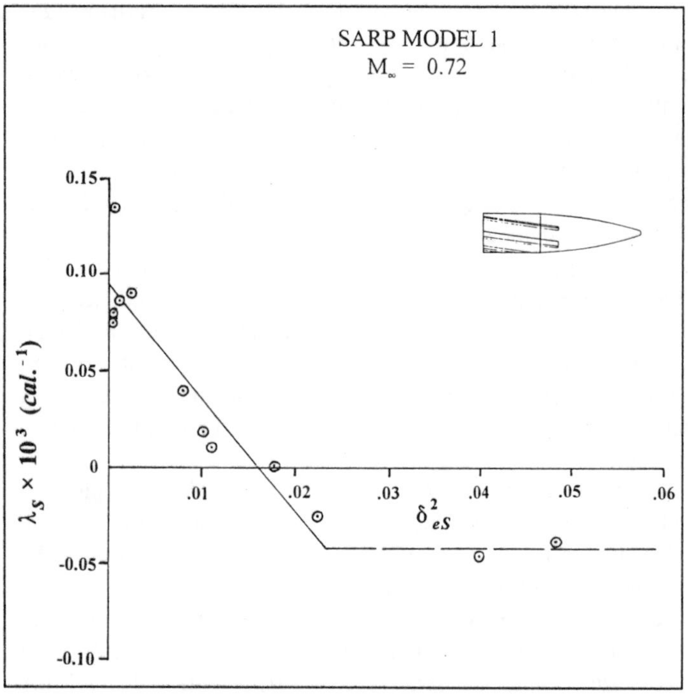

Figure 13.19 Slow-Arm Damping Exponent versus Effective Squared Yaw.

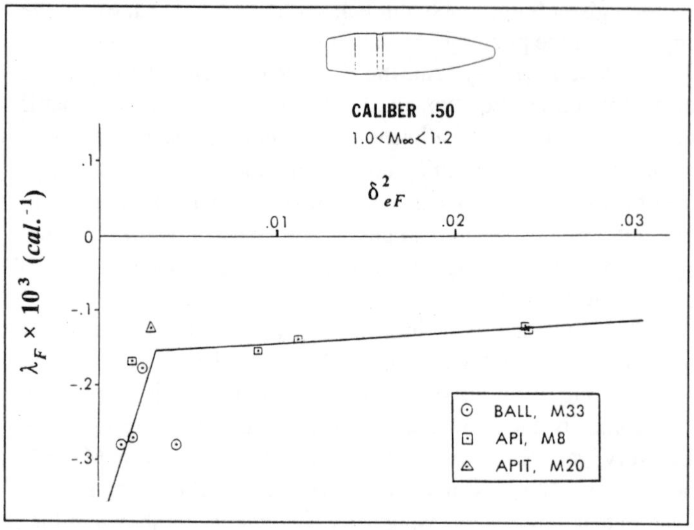

Figure 13.20 Fast-Arm Damping Exponent versus Effective Squared Yaw.

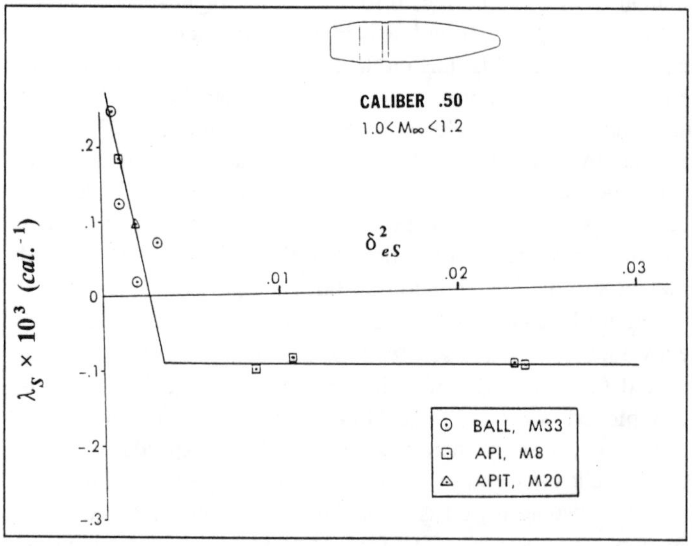

Figure 13.21 Slow-Arm Damping Exponent versus Effective Squared Yaw.

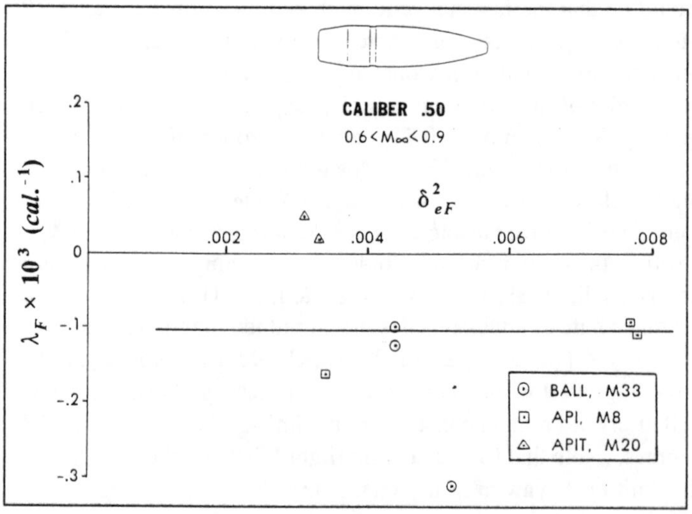

Figure 13.22 Fast-Arm Damping Exponent versus Effective Squared Yaw.

Figure 13.23 shows typical slow-arm limit-cycle yaw behavior. A straight line, fitted to the data by least squares, crosses the horizontal axis at $\delta^2_{eS} = 0.0058$. Thus, the .50 caliber bullets will fly with a 4.4 degree amplitude slow-arm limit-cycle yaw, at subsonic speeds.

The flight dynamic behavior of the 105mm, M1 shell at subsonic speeds is illustrated in Figures 13.24 and 13.25. Both curves are tri-cubic as expected, because they follow the nonlinear Magnus moment coefficient, previously plotted as Figure 13.16. Figure 13.24 is a plot of λ_F versus δ^2_{eF} for small, intermediate, and large yaw levels. Note that the fast epicyclic pitch and yaw arm is damped for all small and intermediate yaw levels at subsonic speeds. However, if the total angle of attack attained (by whatever means) a value greater than 22.6 degrees ($\sin^2 \alpha_t > 0.1471$), the fast epicyclic pitch and yaw arm would begin to grow. Furthermore, if the projectile were *launched* with a yaw exceeding the critical value at subsonic speed, the ever-increasing positive λ_F would drive the already large fast arm into exponential growth. The effect would be a *very large yaw flight*, and a catastrophic "short range" impact! (Fortunately, the conditions required to produce a very large launch yaw do not normally occur, and such a catastrophic "short round" has never been observed in field firings of the 105mm, M1 artillery shell).

Figure 13.25 (*p. 292*) is a plot of λ_S versus δ^2_{eS} for the 105mm, M1 shell at subsonic speeds. Again, we observe limit-cycle yaw behavior. For small amplitude motion, the slow arm damping exponent is positive, hence the slow epicyclic yaw arm will grow. The curve crosses the horizontal axis at $\delta^2_{eS} = 0.0044$ ($\alpha_t = 3.8$ degrees), which means the slow arm limit-cycle yaw value will be 3.8 degrees at subsonic speeds. For all larger yaw levels, the sub-

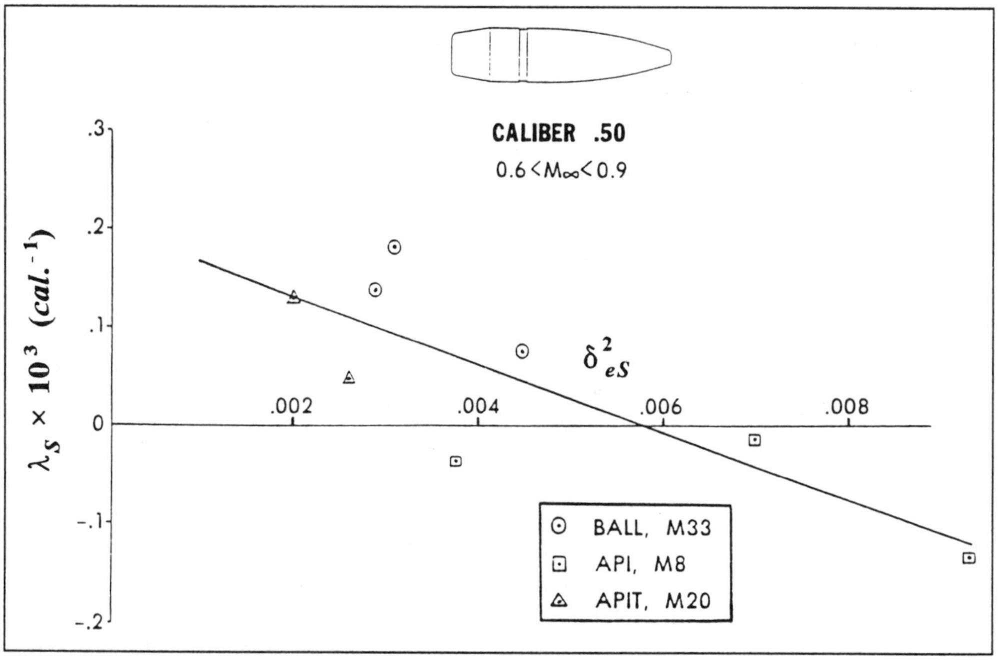

Figure 13.23 Slow-Arm Damping Exponent versus Effective Squared Yaw.

sonic slow arm damping exponent is negative, therefore the shell exhibits slow-arm dynamic stability at large yaw.

All the previous examples of limit-cycle yaw have illustrated a *slow-arm* limit cycle. At this point, the reader may be tempted to conclude that fast-arm flight dynamic instabilities are never observed in practice. However, a famous case of fast-mode flight instability occurred in the early 1970s, with the development of a new long-range artillery shell.

The 155mm, M549 low-drag artillery shell was developed in the late 1960s, to extend the range of the 155mm, M109A1 Howitzer. This new shell (designated the XM549 at that time), had a three-caliber long, low-drag secant ogive nose, and a 0.58 caliber-long boattail, with a supersonic optimum (minimum drag) boattail angle of 7.5 degrees. Figure 13.26 (*p. 292*) is a contour sketch of the XM549 shell, with pertinent measured physical characteristics.

Field firings of the XM549 were conducted (Ref. 15) in the winter of 1969-70. All propellant charges and muzzle velocities showed normal, expected behavior, except for one transonic launch speed. Large dispersion in range was observed when the shell was fired at Charge 4, with an ambient temperature of 48 degrees Fahrenheit. The nominal muzzle velocity of the XM549 shell at Charge 4 was 1027 feet per second. At 48°F, the corresponding launch Mach number is 0.93, and it is very close to a worst-case condition.

At sea-level, standard atmospheric conditions, the launch gyroscopic stability factor of the M549 shell, when fired at Charge 4 from the M109A1 Howitzer with a rifling twist rate of 1 turn in 20 calibers of travel, is 1.26 (Ref. 16). This very low value of launch S_g (see Figure 13.27, *p. 292*) provides no margin of safety for cold weather, with its attendant high air density. In addition, both the zero-yaw Magnus moment coefficient, $C_{M_{p\alpha_0}}$, and the cubic Magnus moment coefficient, $C_{M_{p\alpha_2}}$, are nearly at their highest positive values (Ref. 16) at Mach 0.93 (see Figure 13.28, *p. 293*). The result is a *fast-arm dynamic instability* ($\lambda_F > 0$) that causes any initial fast-mode pitching and yawing motion to grow rapidly. As the velocity and the flight Mach number decay to subsonic speeds, the large positive Magnus moment decreases in size, and the fast-arm damping exponent approaches zero (neutral damping). The slow-mode damping exponent, λ_S, is negative at all flight Mach numbers, and for all yaw levels. However, any initial fast-mode motion resulting from the Charge 4 launch will be greatly amplified during the transonic part of the flight, and since $\lambda_F \approx 0$ at subsonic speeds, the large- amplitude fast-mode yawing motion will persist throughout the remainder of the trajectory.

The unsatisfactory flight of the M549 shell, when fired at Charge 4 in cold weather, could have been corrected by either of

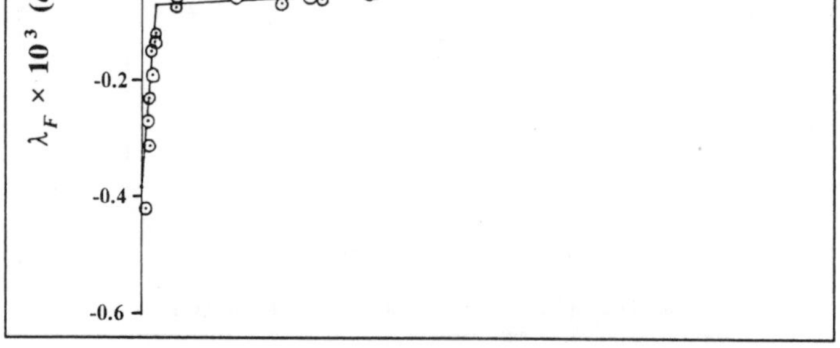

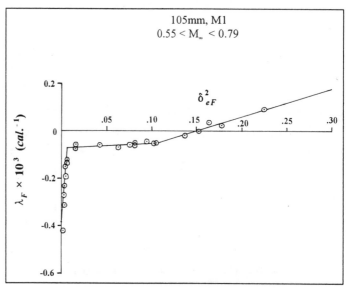

Figure 13.24 Fast-Arm Damping Exponent versus Effective Squared Yaw.

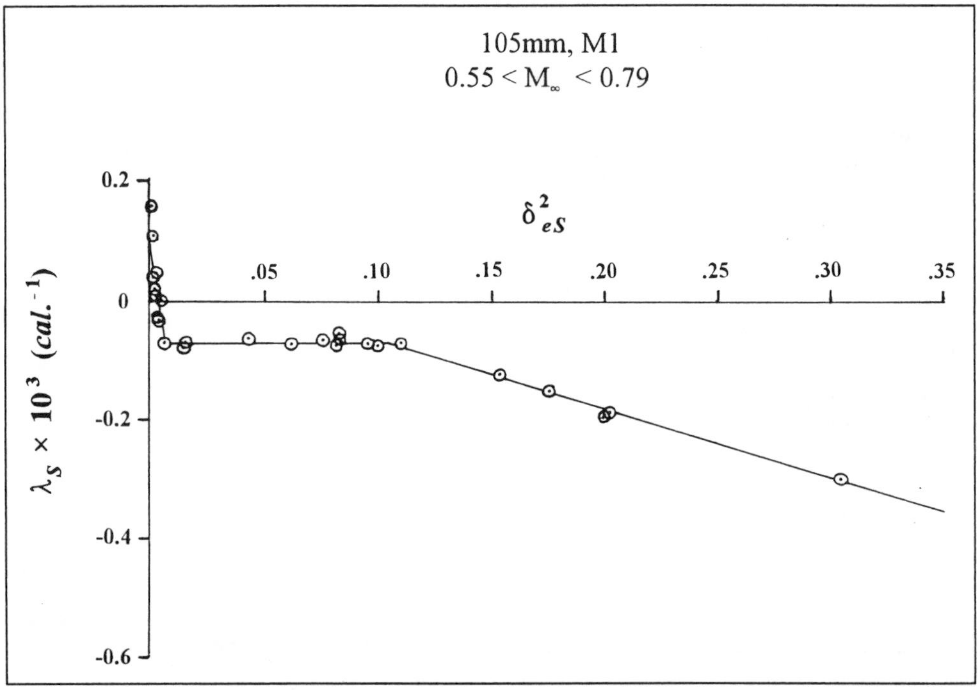

Figure 13.25 Slow-Arm Damping Exponent versus Effective Squared Yaw.

two methods: (1) redesign the shell, or (2) make sure the M549 is never fired at Charge 4. Of course, the Army elected to implement the inexpensive solution; Charge 4 was removed from the firing table, and the problem disappeared.

A number of examples of observed nonlinear Magnus moment behavior have been presented in this section. The reader may feel that too much discussion has been devoted to this subject. However, the importance of this aerodynamic moment can hardly be overemphasized. The fundamental nature of the Magnus moment acting on spinning projectiles, particularly at transonic and subsonic speeds, is usually troublesome. Most observed transonic and subsonic flight dynamic instabilities can be traced to this single cause. Limit-cycle yaw behavior is caused by the nonlinear Magnus moment, and *limit cycle yaw* is so commonly observed that it is now recognized as a *characteristic behavior* of transonic and subsonic flight. The information presented in this chapter clearly shows that no aeroballistic analysis of a spin-stabilized projectile is complete without a thorough investigation of its Magnus moment characteristics.

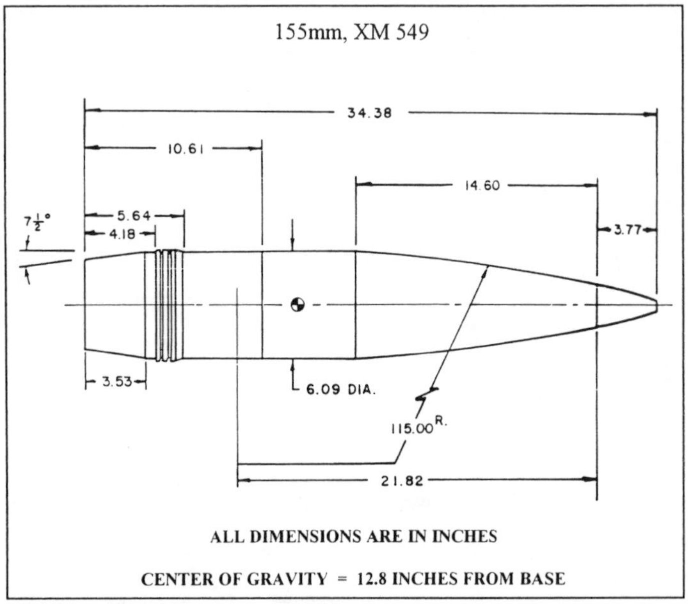

Figure 13.26 Sketch of the 155 mm, XM549 Shell.

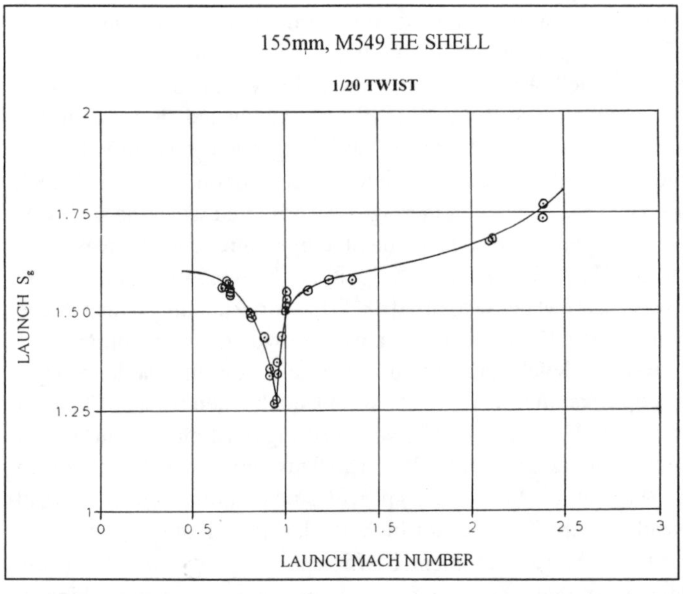

Figure 13.27 Launch Gyroscopic Stability Factor versus Launch Mach Number, M549 Shell.

13.8 QUASI-LINEAR ANALYSIS OF A CUBIC LIFT FORCE

The aerodynamic lift force coefficient, C_{L_α}, may be measured by two methods in modern aeroballistic firing ranges. The direct method of obtaining C_{M_α} is from an epicyclic swerve reduction, based on the solution obtained in Chapter 11. The indirect method consists of firing models of the projectile with different center-of-gravity (CG) locations, and plotting the pitching (overturning) moment coefficients, against the CG location. The indirect analysis actually yields the normal force coefficient, C_{N_α}, rather than the lift force coefficient. However, if the drag coefficient has also been measured, the lift force coefficient can be calculated from the normal force and the drag coefficients. We will consider the indirect problem first.

Equations (2.12) and (2.13) are restated from Chapter 2:

$$C_D = C_{N_\alpha} \sin^2 \alpha_t - C_X \cos \alpha_t \tag{2.12}$$

$$C_{L_\alpha} = C_{N_\alpha} \cos \alpha_t + C_X \tag{2.13}$$

where $\alpha_t \approx \sqrt{\alpha^2 + \beta^2}$, or total yaw angle

α = angle of attack (pitch)

β = angle of sideslip (yaw)

If the axial force coefficient, C_X, is eliminated between equations (2.12) and (2.13), we obtain the useful equation:

$$C_{N_\alpha} = C_D + C_{L_\alpha} \cos \alpha_t \tag{13.66}$$

From Table 2.1 of Chapter 2, we recall that the effect of a center-of-gravity shift on the pitching moment coefficient is described by the equation:

$$\hat{C}_{M_\alpha} = C_{M_\alpha} + \Delta_{CG} C_{N_\alpha} \tag{13.67}$$

If cubic normal and lift forces are assumed, as well as a quadratic drag force, we have:

$$C_{N_\alpha} = C_{N_{\alpha 0}} + C_{N_{\alpha 2}} \delta^2 \tag{13.68}$$

$$C_{L_\alpha} = C_{L_{\alpha 0}} + C_{L_{\alpha 2}} \delta^2 \tag{13.69}$$

$$C_D = C_{D_0} + C_{D_\delta^2} \delta^2 \tag{13.70}$$

where $\delta = \sin \alpha_t$

For small total angle of attack, $\cos \alpha_t \approx 1 - \frac{1}{2}\delta^2$. Substituting this expression, and equations (13.68) through (13.70) into equation (13.66):

$$C_{N_{\alpha 0}} + C_{N_{\alpha 2}} \delta^2 = C_{D_0} + C_{D_\delta^2} \delta^2 + C_{L_{\alpha 0}} - \frac{1}{2} C_{L_{\alpha 0}} \delta^2 + C_{L_{\alpha 2}} \delta^2 - \frac{1}{2} C_{L_{\alpha 2}} \delta^4 \tag{13.71}$$

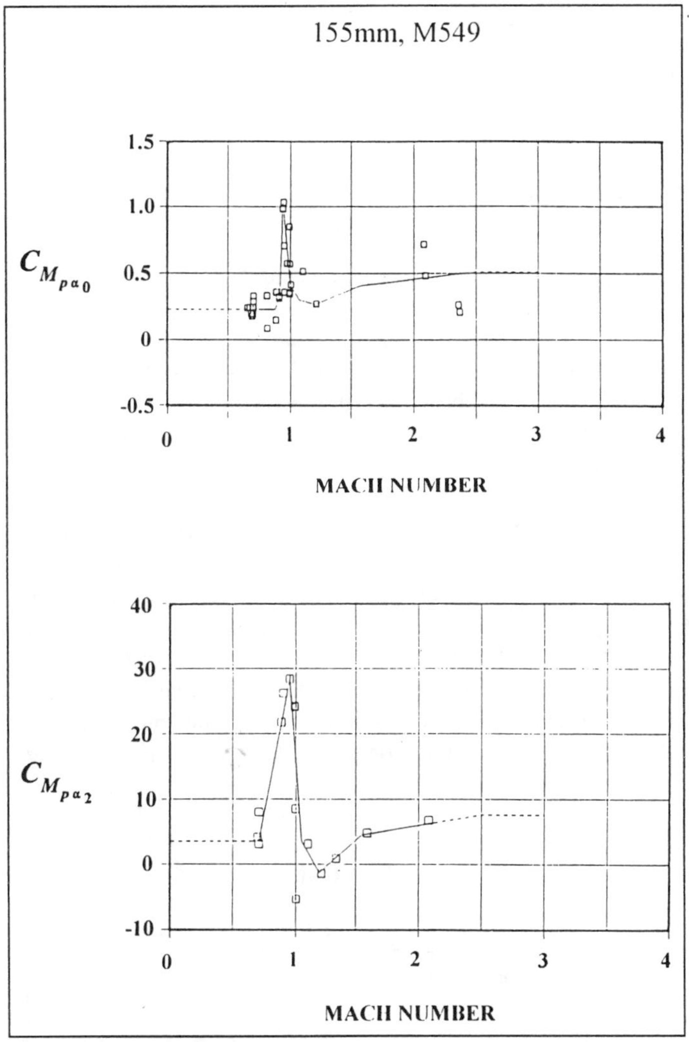

Figure 13.28 Zero-Yaw and Cubic Magnus Moment Coefficient versus Mach Number.

Neglecting the small fourth-order term in equation (13.71), and collecting terms yields:

$$C_{N_{\alpha 0}} = C_{D_0} + C_{L_{\alpha 0}} \tag{13.72}$$

$$C_{N_{\alpha 2}} = C_{D_\delta^2} + C_{L_{\alpha 2}} - \frac{1}{2} C_{L_{\alpha 0}} \tag{13.73}$$

The pitching moment coefficient with a circumflex overscript, $\hat{C}_{M_\alpha}$, is the value after a center-of-gravity shift of Δ_{CG} (in calibers), considered positive if the CG shift is toward the tail of the projectile. Substituting the zero-yaw and the cubic terms into equation (13.67):

$$\hat{C}_{M_{\alpha 0}} = C_{M_{\alpha 0}} + \Delta_{CG} C_{N_{\alpha 0}} \tag{13.74}$$

$$\hat{C}_{M_{\alpha 2}} = C_{M_{\alpha 2}} + \Delta_{CG} C_{N_{\alpha 2}} \tag{13.75}$$

Thus by firing models with forward and rear center-of-gravity locations, all at the same nominal Mach number but at various yaw levels, both $C_{N_{\alpha0}}$ and $C_{N_{\alpha2}}$ may be determined from the pitching and yawing motion alone. If C_{D_0} and $C_{D_\delta^2}$ are also known from a drag reduction, we can readily determine both $C_{L_{\alpha0}}$ and $C_{L_{\alpha2}}$:

$$C_{L_{\alpha0}} = C_{N_{\alpha0}} - C_{D_0} \tag{13.76}$$

$$C_{L_{\alpha2}} = C_{N_{\alpha2}} - C_{D_\delta^2} + \frac{1}{2} C_{L_{\alpha0}} \tag{13.77}$$

Murphy presented an excellent example (Ref. 6) of the indirect method for determining the zero-yaw and the cubic lift force coefficients. He plotted the range-determined pitching moment coefficients against δ_e^2, for forward, middle, and rear center-of-gravity models of the 9-caliber-long Army-Navy Spinner Rocket, fired at Mach 1.8. A sketch of the test models is shown in Figure 13.8. Straight lines were fitted to the nonlinear pitching moment coefficient data, by the method of least squares. The results of the cubic pitching moment coefficient analysis are illustrated in Figure 13.29.

In Figure 13.30, the zero-yaw and the cubic pitching moment coefficients, obtained from Figure 13.29, are plotted against the center of gravity location. Again, fitting straight lines to the data [see equations (13.74) and (13.75)] by the method of least squares, provides values of the zero-yaw and the cubic normal force coefficients. A drag reduction was also done for the 20mm Spinner Rocket models. The zero-yaw drag coefficient, C_{D_0}, and the yaw-drag coefficient, $C_{D_\delta^2}$, were found to be 0.40 and 5.9, respectively, for the 9-caliber Army-Navy Spinner Rocket at Mach 1.8. Equations (13.76) and (13.77) are now used to obtain the zero-yaw and the cubic lift force coefficients, from the pitching moment versus CG analysis:

$$C_{L_{\alpha0}} = 2.9 - 0.4 = 2.5$$

$$C_{L_{\alpha2}} = 35 - 5.9 + 1.25 = 30$$

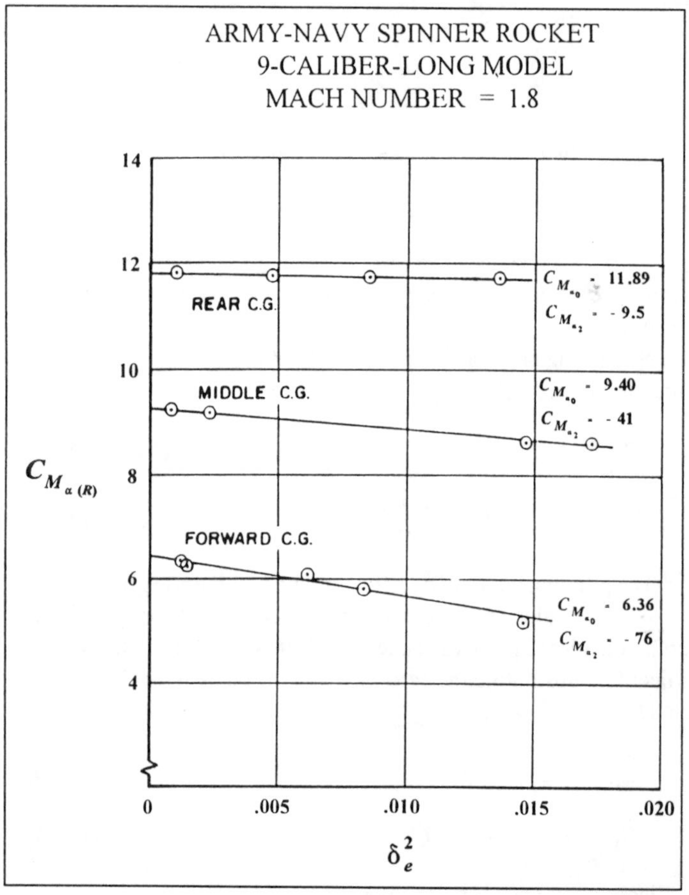

Figure 13.29 Pitching Moment Coefficient versus Effective Squared Yaw.

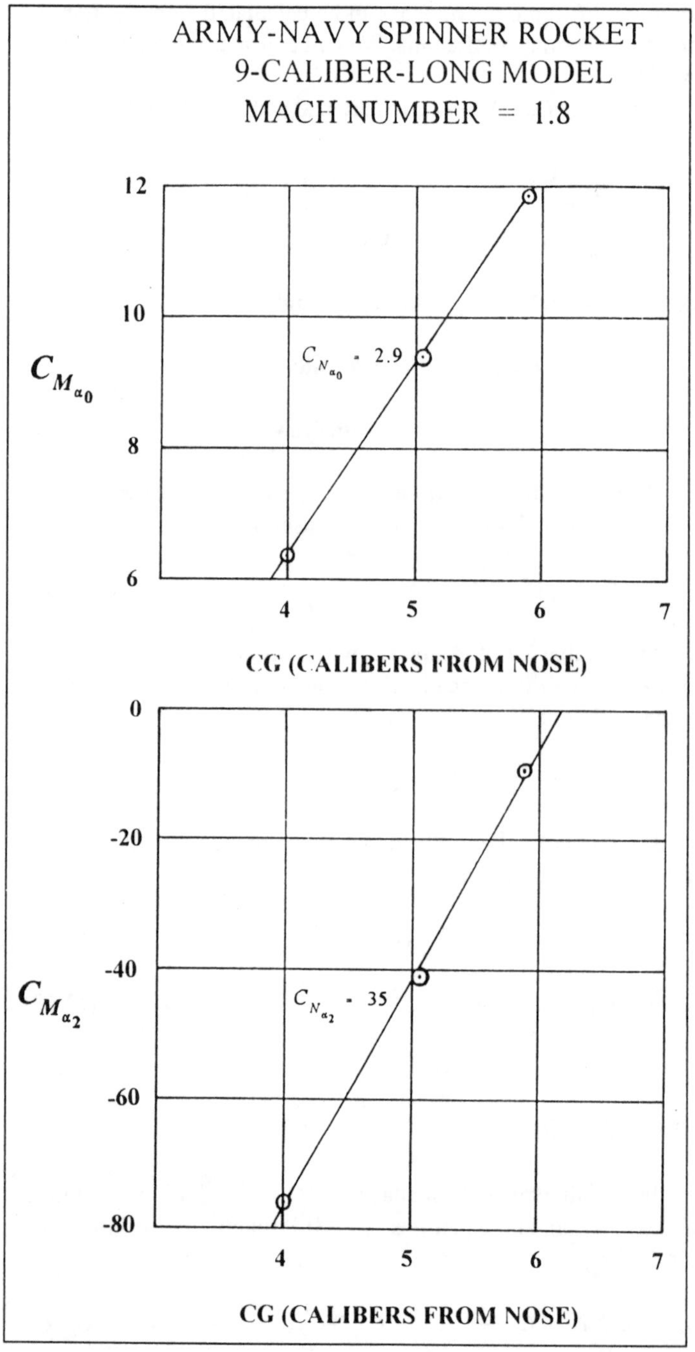

Figure 13.30 Zero-Yaw and Cubic Pitching Moment Coefficients versus CG.

The values obtained for $C_{L_{\alpha 0}}$ and $C_{L_{\alpha 2}}$ from the epicyclic swerve reduction were 2.7, and 34, respectively, for the 9-caliber Army-Navy Spinner Rocket at Mach 1.8. The good agreement between the two methods of measurement is very encouraging.

We now turn our attention to the direct method of obtaining the lift force coefficient, from the epicyclic swerve reduction. Equation (11.31) from Chapter 11 defines the double integral, I_L, as:

$$I_L = \int_0^s \int_0^{r_2} \xi \, dr_1 dr_2 \qquad \textbf{(11.31)}$$

The general solution of the linearized epicyclic pitching and yawing motion (neglecting the very small yaw of repose) is:

$$\xi = K_F e^{i\phi_F} + K_s e^{i\phi_S} \qquad \textbf{(13.78)}$$

where $\xi = \alpha + i\beta$

$K_F = K_{F_0} e^{\lambda_F s}$, the amplitude of the fast epicyclic yaw arm

$K_S = K_{S_0} e^{\lambda_S s}$, the amplitude of the slow epicyclic yaw arm

$\phi_F = \phi_{F_0} + \phi_F' s$

$\phi_S = \phi_{S_0} + \phi_S' s$

ϕ_{F_0} = initial phase angle of the fast epicyclic yaw arm

ϕ_{S_0} = initial phase angle of the slow epicyclic yaw arm

Substituting equation (13.78) into equation (11.31), and multiplying both sides by $C_{L_\alpha}^*$ gives the *linear* lift force contribution to epicyclic swerve:

$$C_{L_\alpha}^* I_L = C_{L_\alpha}^* \int_0^s \int_0^{r_2} \left[K_F e^{i\phi_F} + K_S e^{i\phi_S}\right] dr_1 dr_2 \qquad \textbf{(13.79)}$$

where $C_{L_\alpha}^* = \dfrac{\rho S C_{L_\alpha}}{2m}$

Performing the double integration, we obtain:

$$C_{L_\alpha}^* I_L = -C_{L_\alpha}^* \left[\frac{K_F e^{i\phi_F}}{\phi_F'^2} + \frac{K_S e^{i\phi_S}}{\phi_S'^2}\right] \qquad \textbf{(13.80)}$$

If the lift force is cubic in total angle of attack, then we must substitute equation (13.69) into equation (13.79). However, $C_{L_\alpha}^*$ is now a variable instead of a constant, and it must be taken inside the integral signs:

$$\left[C_{L_\alpha}^* I_L\right] = \int_0^s \int_0^{r_2} \left(C_{L_{\alpha 0}}^* + C_{L_{\alpha 2}}^* \delta^2\right)\left(K_F e^{i\phi_F} + K_S e^{i\phi_S}\right) dr_1 dr_2 \qquad \textbf{(13.81)}$$

where the quantity in brackets, $\left[C_{L_\alpha}^* I_L\right]$, is the *nonlinear epicyclic swerve*.

Now, δ^2 may be written in the form:

$$\delta^2 = \xi\bar{\xi} = K_F^2 + K_S^2 + K_F K_S\left[e^{i(\phi_F - \phi_S)} + e^{-i(\phi_F - \phi_S)}\right] \qquad \textbf{(13.82)}$$

Substituting equation (13.82) into equation (13.81), and performing the double integration, we find:

$$\left[C_{L_\alpha}^* I_L\right] = -C_{L_{\alpha 0}}^* \left[\frac{K_F e^{i\phi_F}}{\phi_F'^2} + \frac{K_S e^{i\phi_S}}{\phi_S'^2}\right]$$

$$-C_{L_{\alpha 2}}^* \left[\frac{\delta_{eF}^2 K_F e^{i\phi_F}}{\phi_F'^2} + \frac{\delta_{eS}^2 K_S e^{i\phi_S}}{\phi_S'^2}\right]$$

$$-C_{L_{\alpha 2}}^* K_F K_S \left[\frac{K_F e^{i(2\phi_F - \phi_S)}}{(2\phi_F' - \phi_S')^2} + \frac{K_S e^{i(2\phi_S - \phi_F)}}{(2\phi_S' - \phi_F')^2}\right] \qquad \textbf{(13.83)}$$

Many projectiles known (from wind tunnel tests) to have nonlinear lift force coefficients have been fired in modern spark photography ranges, and in all cases, the swerving motions have been accurately fitted using the linearized swerve reduction. Therefore, we will neglect the mixed frequency swerve terms appearing in equation (13.83), and equate the quasi-linear and the nonlinear epicyclic swerve components.

$$C_{L_\alpha}^* \left[\frac{K_F e^{i\phi_F}}{\phi_F'^2} + \frac{K_S e^{i\phi_S}}{\phi_S'^2}\right] = C_{L_{\alpha 0}}^* \left[\frac{K_F e^{i\phi_F}}{\phi_F'^2} + \frac{K_S e^{i\phi_S}}{\phi_S'^2}\right]$$

$$+C_{L_{\alpha 2}}^* \left[\frac{\delta_{eF}^2 K_F e^{i\phi_F}}{\phi_F'^2} + \frac{\delta_{eS}^2 K_S e^{i\phi_S}}{\phi_S'^2}\right] \qquad \textbf{(13.84)}$$

Dividing both sides of equation (13.84) by (*see at right*), we obtain: $\left(\dfrac{\rho S d}{2m}\right)\left[\dfrac{K_F e^{i\phi_F}}{\phi_F'^2} + \dfrac{K_S e^{i\phi_S}}{\phi_S'^2}\right]$

$$C_{L_\alpha} = C_{L_{\alpha 0}} + C_{L_{\alpha 2}} \left[\frac{\phi_S'^2 \delta_{eF}^2 K_F e^{i\phi_F} + \phi_F'^2 \delta_{eS}^2 K_S e^{i\phi_S}}{\phi_S'^2 K_F e^{i\phi_F} + \phi_F'^2 K_S e^{i\phi_S}}\right] \qquad \textbf{(13.85)}$$

Equation (13.85) contains the complex epicyclic pitch and yaw arms in both the numerator and the denominator. However, this difficulty is easily resolved, by multiplying both the top and the bottom of the last term by the conjugate of the denominator, and again discarding the mixed frequency terms. The result is:

$$C_{L_{\alpha(R)}} = C_{L_{\alpha 0}} + C_{L_{\alpha 2}} \delta_{esw}^2 \qquad \textbf{(13.86)}$$

where
$$\delta_{esw}^2 = \frac{\phi_S'^4 K_F^2 \delta_{eF}^2 + \phi_F'^4 K_S^2 \delta_{eS}^2}{\phi_S'^4 K_F^2 + \phi_F'^4 K_S^2} \qquad \textbf{(13.87)}$$

For most spin-stabilized projectiles, $\phi_F' >> \phi_S'$, and equation (13.87) reduces to the simpler form:

$$\delta_{esw}^2 \approx \delta_{eS}^2 \qquad \textbf{(13.88)}$$

Equation (13.88) reminds us that for spin-stabilized projectiles with adequate gyroscopic stability, only the slow epicyclic pitch

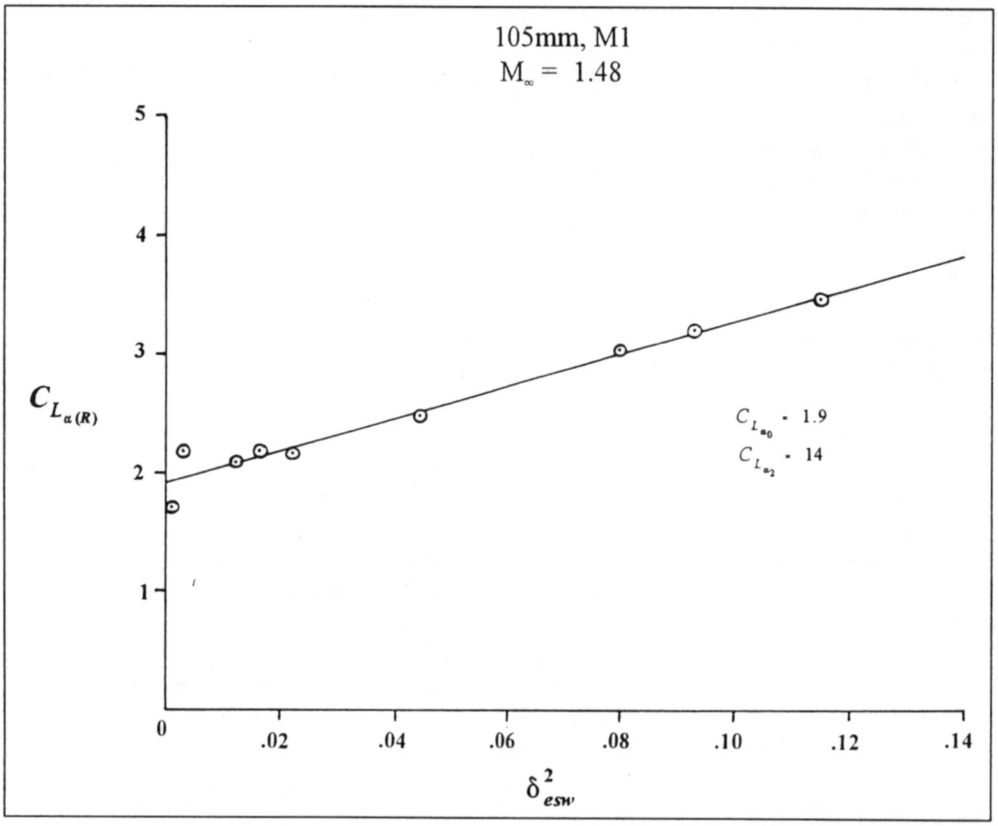

Figure 13.31 Lift Force Coefficient versus Effective Squared Yaw.

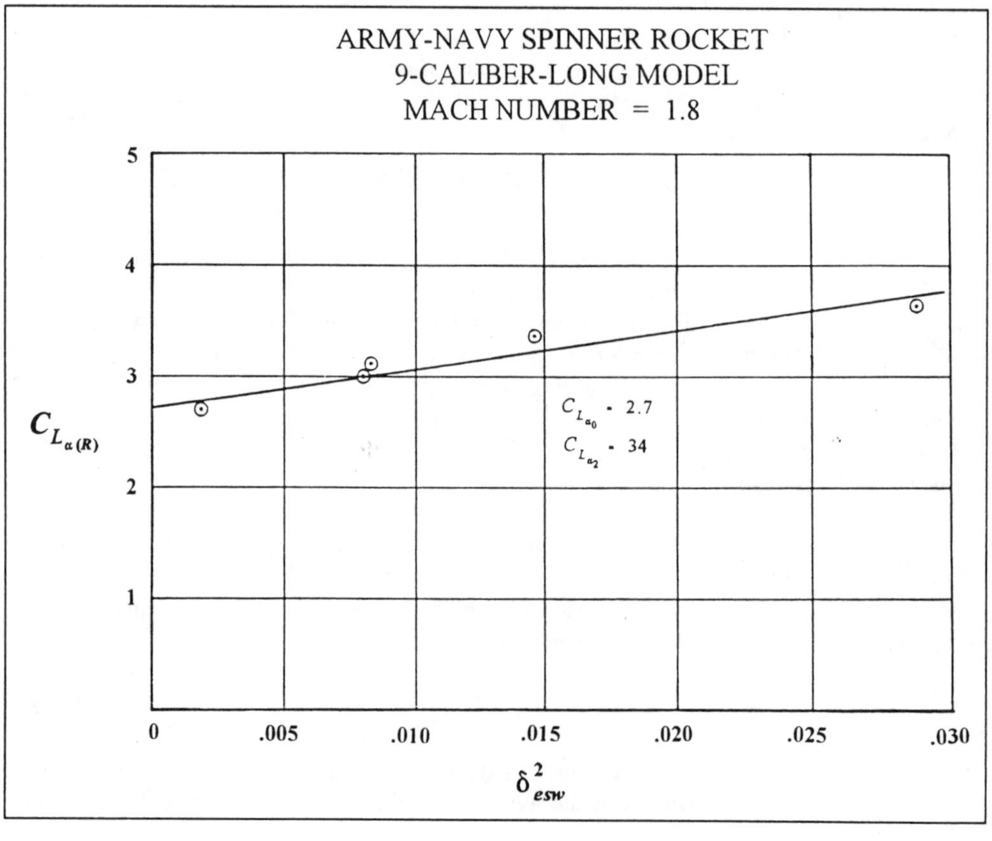

Figure 13.32 Lift Force Coefficient versus Effective Squared Yaw.

and yaw arm makes a measurable contribution to the epicyclic swerve.

Two examples of nonlinear lift force coefficient analysis from free-flight swerve reductions are illustrated in Figures 13.31 and 13.32. Figure 13.31 shows the range-determined values of the lift force coefficient, $C_{L_{\alpha(R)}}$, plotted against the proper effective squared yaw for swerve, δ^2_{esw}, for the 105mm, M1 shell at Mach 1.48. A straight line, fitted to the data by the method of least squares gives values of 1.9 for the zero-yaw lift force coefficient, $C_{L_{\alpha 0}}$, and 14 for the cubic lift force coefficient, $C_{L_{\alpha 2}}$.

Figure 13.32 is a similar plot for the 9-caliber-long Army-Navy Spinner Rocket, at Mach 1.8. A linear least-squares fit of the range-determined lift coefficient data gives a value of 2.7 for $C_{L_{\alpha 0}}$, and the cubic lift force coefficient, $C_{L_{\alpha 2}}$ is found to be 34. These values agree well with those obtained from the pitching moment versus CG analysis, and subsequent conversion of the normal force measurements to zero-yaw and cubic lift force coefficients.

At the end of section 13.3, it was noted that a negative value of the cubic pitching moment coefficient is a general characteristic of typical spin-stabilized projectiles. The reverse is usually true for the nonlinear lift force. The cubic lift force coefficient, for typical spin-stabilized shell, is nearly always a positive quantity.

As a final comment on the analysis of nonlinear swerving motion, we will consider two aerodynamic forces that were previously neglected. Although they are not included in the analysis of this book, the BRL swerve reduction retains the Magnus force for spinning shell, and the pitch damping force for non-rolling, statically stable projectiles. The Magnus force is generally of order of one-tenth the size of the lift force, and its contribution to the epicyclic swerving motion is therefore usually lost in the noise of the experimental data. The same comment applies to the pitch damping force, which seldom produces a detectable amount of swerving motion. On the rare occasions when a nonlinear Magnus *force* coefficient is well determined from swerve reductions, $C_{N_{p\alpha(R)}}$ should be plotted against δ^2_{esw} , the effective squared yaw for swerve.

The best method for measuring the Magnus *force* coefficient acting on spinning projectiles is the two-center-of-gravity technique. If models are fired in a modern spark photography range with forward and rear center-of-gravity locations, at a fixed nominal Mach number and several yaw levels, both the zero-yaw and the cubic Magnus moment coefficients can be determined, using the methods outlined in sections 13.5 and 13.6. $\hat{C}_{M_{p\alpha 0}}$ and $\hat{C}_{M_{p\alpha 2}}$ for the forward and rear center-of-gravity models are then plotted against CG location, and the slopes of the least-squares fitted straight lines then provide the zero-yaw and the cubic Magnus *force* coefficients, respectively.

The relationships used for the center-of-gravity analysis are adaptations of the Magnus moment-CG transformation equation listed in Table 2.1 of Chapter 2. Two equations are needed, one for the zero-yaw coefficients, and a second equation for the cubic Magnus coefficients:

$$\hat{C}_{M_{p\alpha 0}} = C_{M_{p\alpha 0}} + \Delta_{CG} C_{N_{p\alpha 0}} \quad \textbf{(13.89)}$$

$$\hat{C}_{M_{p\alpha 2}} = C_{M_{p\alpha 2}} + \Delta_{CG} C_{N_{p\alpha 2}} \quad \textbf{(13.90)}$$

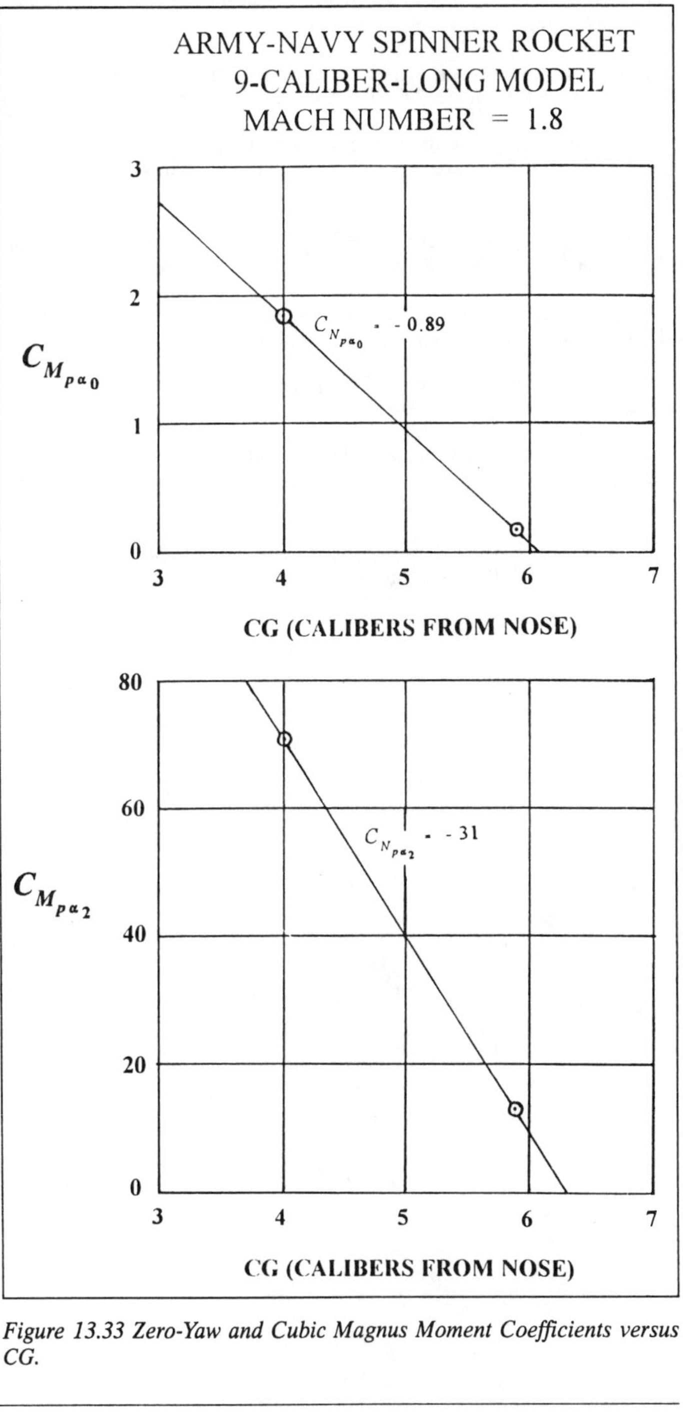

Figure 13.33 Zero-Yaw and Cubic Magnus Moment Coefficients versus CG.

An excellent example of the center-of-gravity method is provided by the spark range Magnus moment coefficient data shown in Figure 13.9 for the 9-caliber-long Army-Navy Spinner Rocket at Mach 1.8. If the zero-yaw and the cubic Magnus moment coefficients from Figure 13.9 are plotted against the CG location, the slopes of the straight lines passing through the data points yield the zero-yaw and the cubic Magnus *force* coefficients, respectively. Figure 13.33 shows the results. The value of $C_{N_{p\alpha_0}}$ from the center-of-gravity method is -0.89, and the cubic Magnus force coefficient, $C_{N_{p\alpha_2}}$ is -31. A value of $C_{N_{p\alpha_0}}$ = -0.87 was obtained from a small-yaw swerve reduction for the forward center-of-gravity model. The close agreement between such delicate measurements is indeed encouraging.

REFERENCES

1. Maple, C. G., and J. L. Synge, "Aerodynamic Symmetry of Projectiles," *Quarterly of Applied Mathematics*, Volume 4, 1949.

2. Buford, W. E., "Aerodynamic Characteristics of the 30mm Shell T306E10 HEI," Ballistic Research Laboratories Technical Note No. 1019, 1955.

3. Roecker, E. T., and E. D. Boyer, "Aerodynamic Characteristics of 30mm HEI Shell, T306E10," Ballistic Research Laboratories Memorandum Report No. 1098, 1957.

4. Murphy, C. H., "The Measurement of Non-Linear Forces and Moments By Means of Free Flight Tests," Ballistic Research Laboratories Report No. 974, 1956.

5. Wylie, C. R., Jr., *Advanced Engineering Mathematics*, Second Edition, McGraw-Hill Book Company, Inc., New York, New York, 1960.

6. Murphy, C. H., "Free Flight Motion of Symmetric Missiles," Ballistic Research Laboratories Report No. 1216, 1963.

7. Roecker, E. T., "Large Yaw Firings of the 20mm, HEI, T282E1 Shell, With Fuze T196, at Mach Number 2.3," Ballistic Research Laboratories Memorandum Report No. 888, 1955.

8. Kryloff, N., and N. B. Bogoliuboff, *Introduction to Nonlinear Mechanics*, (translated by S. Lefschetz), Princeton University Press, 1947.

9. Bradley, J. W., "RED: a Free Flight Reduction Program," Unpublished Report, June 1989.

10. McCoy, R. L., "Aerodynamic Characteristics of the 30mm, XM788E1 and XM789 Projectiles," Ballistic Research Laboratory Technical Report ARBRL-TR-02432, 1982.

11. McCoy, R. L., and A. J. Sowa, "Aerodynamic Characteristics of 40mm Ammunition for the MK-19 Grenade Launcher," Ballistic Research Laboratory Memorandum Report BRL-MR-3788, 1989.

12. Braun, W. F., "Aerodynamic Data for Small Arms Projectiles," Ballistic Research Laboratories Report No. 1630, 1973.

13. McCoy, R. L., "The Aerodynamic Characteristics of .50 Ball, M33, API, M8, and APIT, M20 Ammunition," Ballistic Research Laboratory Memorandum Report BRL-MR-3810, 1990.

14. Roecker, E. T., "The Aerodynamic Properties of the 105mm HE Shell, M1, in Subsonic and Transonic Flight," Ballistic Research Laboratories Memorandum Report No. 929, 1955.

15. Whiteside, J., "Interim Report on Projectile, 155 mm: HE, XM 549," Ballistic Research Laboratories Memorandum Report No. 2165, 1972.

16. Puhalla, R. T., Jr., "The Aerodynamic Characteristics of 155mm, M549 and M549A1 Projectiles, Ballistic Research Laboratory Memorandum Report BRL-MR-3899, 1991.

14

Measurement of Aerodynamic Forces and Moments

14.1 INTRODUCTION

Aerodynamic forces and moments acting on projectiles can be measured either directly or indirectly. Direct force and moment measurements utilize wind tunnels, in which a model of the projectile is mounted in the test section and airflow at the proper speed is established. Instrumentation is built into the model support system, which provides the force-moment measurements.

Indirect force and moment measurements are made by firing projectiles through instrumented free-flight ballistic test ranges. High-precision measurements are made of the projectile's time of flight, position in space, and the pitch, yaw and roll angles, at many points along the trajectory. Given the complete in-flight motion of the projectile, the forces and moments that produced the observed motion can be inferred.

In general, modern spark photography ranges provide the highest precision free-flight measurements, although direct photography has been successfully used for aeroballistic ranges. Yawsondes and radars are also used to make indirect measurements of the aerodynamic forces and moments that act on projectiles in flight, as are the traditional ballistic chronograph and yaw-card ranges. Illustrations and examples of the various experimental methods are presented in this chapter, and the measurement accuracy of the different facilities is discussed.

14.2 WIND TUNNEL METHODS

Some of the earliest wind tunnels were constructed around 1870 by Wenham of England, Irminger and Vogt of Denmark, and A. J. Wells of the United States. These early low-speed wind tunnels were initially used to measure the lifting effect of plane surfaces at various angles of attack. In 1901, the Wright brothers built and operated their first wind tunnel, and they used a balance that measured lift and drag. In their second wind tunnel, the Wright brothers achieved sufficient accuracy to permit the design of gliders, and then the first successful powered aircraft. All the early low-speed wind tunnels were used for airplane design, rather than for aeroballistic investigations of projectile flight. However, by 1920 several low-speed wind tunnel tests had been conducted on typical artillery shell configurations, and a wind tunnel test methodology for projectiles had been established.

By the 1930s, several small supersonic research tunnels had been built in England, Germany, Italy, and other nations. The beginning of World War II accelerated the development of larger and more efficient wind tunnels. In this section, we will discuss the characteristics of modern supersonic wind tunnels, and their capabilities to measure the aeroballistic forces and moments that act on spinning and finned projectiles.

There are basically four types of modern supersonic wind tunnels: (1) intermittent blowdown tunnels, (2) intermittent indraft tunnels, (3) intermittent pressure-vacuum tunnels, and (4) continuous-flow tunnels. Blowdown tunnels use a high-pressure air storage reservoir, which is discharged through a nozzle, diffuser and test section. Indraft tunnels operate on the reverse principle of pumping down a reservoir to a near-vacuum, then opening a valve and letting air flow through the nozzle, diffuser and test section, into the low-pressure reservoir. Pressure-vacuum tunnels combine the principles of blowdown and indraft tunnels, and can achieve very high test-section Mach numbers. Generally speaking, the useful run-times of all intermittent supersonic wind tunnels are measured in seconds.

Continuous-flow wind tunnels are more expensive to build, maintain and operate than are intermittent tunnels. However, given the choice, wind tunnel engineers always prefer several minutes of test time per run, instead of the few seconds available in an intermittent tunnel. Thus, continuous-flow wind tunnels are usually preferred for modern aeroballistic testing. The details of supersonic wind tunnel design, construction and calibration are beyond the scope of this book. Reference 1 contains an excellent description of modern wind tunnel facilities, and the interested reader may consult this reference.

In practice, the wind tunnel test engineer must have the means to accurately determine the properties of the air flowing through the test section. The free-stream static pressure, temperature, density, dynamic pressure, Mach number, Reynolds number, flow angularity and free-stream turbulence level must all be accurately measured. In addition, the dewpoint must be monitored, to insure that condensation does not occur in the nozzle. For some testing, heat transfer to the model surface must be measured. Model surface pressure measurements are often required. Finally, flow visualization methods, such as a shadowgraph or a schlieren system must be employed, so the design engineer can evaluate the flowfield past the projectile. The reader is referred to References 1 and 2 for detailed discussions of the installation, calibration and operation of wind tunnel airflow instrumentation.

The earliest balances used for measuring low-speed aerodynamic forces and moments were mechanical external balances. An external balance uses one or more structural members to transmit the aerodynamic forces and moments acting on the model to the balance, which is located outside the wind tunnel test section. External balances are seldom used for high-speed wind tunnels, because strut interference significantly affects the flowfield past the model, and also because modern strain gages provide more accurate measurements than mechanical external balances.

Notes on Modern Strain Gage Balances

Modern internal force-moment balances are designed to fit within a hollowed-out cavity in the base of the model. Figure 14.1 is an illustration of a spinning projectile model and a typical five-component balance, with two strain-gage bridges in the pitch plane for measuring the normal force and pitching moment, and *three* similar bridges in the yaw plane, for increased accuracy in determination of the smaller side (Magnus) force and moment. The aft end of the balance is attached to the wind tunnel angle of attack system, and the front end forms a cantilevered beam, with the spinning model supported at the free end.

The model is attached to the front end of the balance by means of a non-rotating sleeve. A tapered fit between the sleeve and the forward section of the balance insures a positive fit, and prevents movement of the sleeve during the tests. The sleeve serves as the mount for the bearing inner races, transfers the aerodynamic loads from the model shell to the balance, and supports the spring assembly, which axially preloads the bearings. The model shell, whose outer surface conforms to the test configuration, is mounted on the outer races of the bearing, and permits the model shell to spin relative to the balance.

An air turbine nozzle is mounted on the balance, just aft of the non-rotating sleeve. The air turbine is powered by an external air supply that is fed to the nozzle by means of a drilled hole through the center of the balance. The nozzle creates four sonic jets that impinge on the turbine blades attached to the model shell, and cause the model to spin. The model is first brought to the desired angle of attack, and is then spun up by means of the air turbine. The external air supply is then cut off, and data is taken during the spin coast-down phase. The spin rate of the model is monitored by means of two permanent magnets mounted to the shell of the model, and a pick-up coil mounted on the nozzle housing.

Most strain-gage balances are designed for the measurement of from two to six of the possible loading components. Maximum balance diameters range from less than ½ inch to 2 or more inches, and maximum aerodynamic loads vary from less than ten pounds to several hundred pounds. Six-component balances are often used; one strain-gage bridge is used to measure axial force, and another is used to determine the rolling torque. The other four bridges are used to measure normal force and pitching moment, and the side force and moment.

The strain-gage balance is calibrated before the balance and model are mounted in the test section. Calibration is accomplished by mounting a calibration sleeve on the balance, and hanging known weights at different axial locations, in both the pitch and yaw planes. The details of balance calibration techniques are discussed in References 1 and 2.

A Few Examples of Supersonic Wind Tunnel Measurements

A comparison of the wind tunnel and spark photography range drag coefficients for the 30mm, T306E10 shell at Mach 2.17, was shown

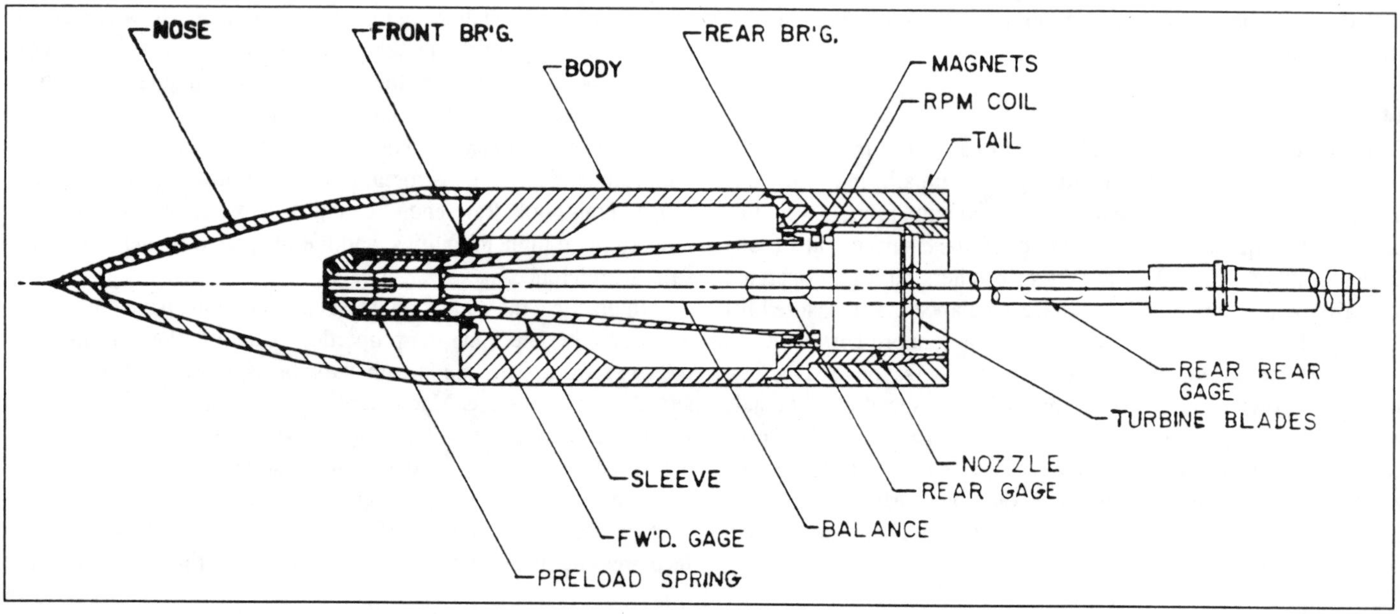

Figure 14.1 General Design Arrangement of a Spinning Model, for Wind Tunnel Magnus Measurements.

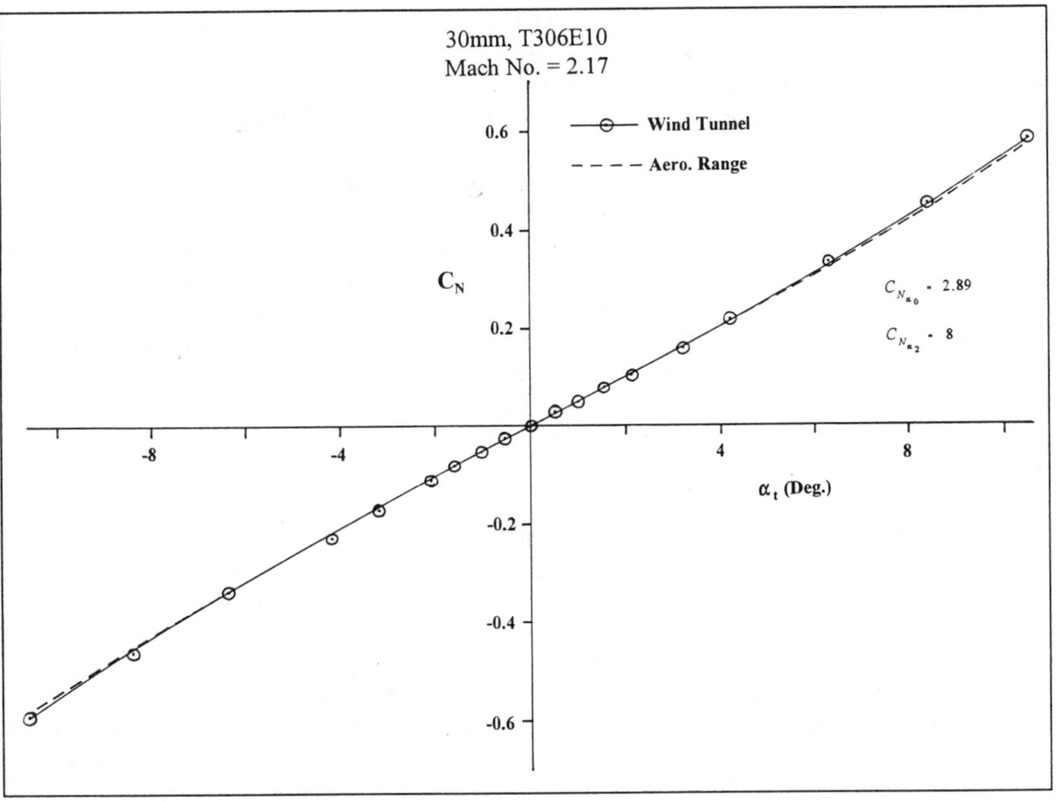

Figure 14.2 Comparison of Wind Tunnel and Spark Range Normal Force Coefficients.

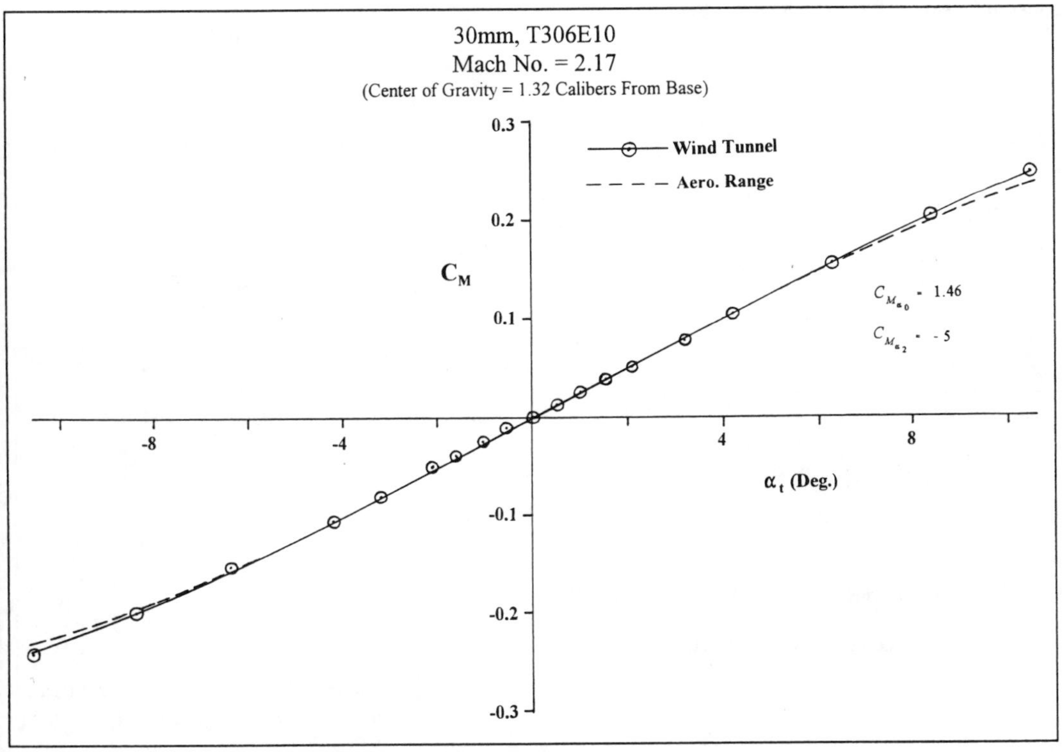

Figure 14.3 Comparison of Wind Tunnel and Spark Range Pitching Moment Coefficients.

in the previous chapter (see Figures 13.1 and 13.2). Figures 14.2 and 14.3 of the present chapter illustrate the same comparisons for the normal force coefficient (C_N) and pitching moment coefficient (C_M), of the T306E10 projectile (see References 3 and 4). We recall equations (2.16) and (2.20) from Chapter 2:

$$C_{N_\alpha} = C_{N_{\alpha_0}} + C_{N_{\alpha_2}} \delta^2 \qquad \textbf{(2.16)}$$

$$C_{M_\alpha} = C_{M_{\alpha_0}} + C_{M_{\alpha_2}} \delta^2 \qquad \textbf{(2.20)}$$

where $C_{N_{\alpha_0}}$ = linear normal force coefficient

$C_{N_{\alpha_2}}$ = cubic normal force coefficient

$C_{M_{\alpha_0}}$ = linear pitching moment coefficient

$C_{M_{\alpha_2}}$ = cubic pitching moment coefficient

$\delta = \sin \alpha_t$

α_t = total angle of attack

Given the linear and cubic normal force and pitching moment coefficients, the coefficients C_N and C_M are readily calculated:

$$C_N = C_{N_\alpha} \sin \alpha_t = C_{N_{\alpha_0}} \sin \alpha_t + C_{N_{\alpha_2}} \sin^3 \alpha_t \qquad \textbf{(14.1)}$$

$$C_M = C_{M_\alpha} \sin \alpha_t = C_{M_{\alpha_0}} \sin_{\alpha_t} + C_{M_{\alpha_2}} \sin^3 \alpha_t \qquad \textbf{(14.2)}$$

The wind tunnel measures the normal force and pitching moment, and the data reduction process calculates the coefficient C_N by dividing the force by the product of the free-stream dynamic pressure and the reference area, $\frac{1}{2}\rho V^2 S$. The pitching moment coefficient, C_M, is obtained by dividing the pitching moment by the quantity $\frac{1}{2}\rho V^2 Sd$. Figure 14.2 is a plot of the normal force coefficient, C_N, measured by the supersonic wind tunnel (Ref. 3), and it includes the same coefficient calculated from the spark range data (Ref. 4), using equation (14.1) Figure 14.3 illustrates the same comparison for the overturning, or pitching moment coefficient, C_M. The agreement between the wind tunnel values and the spark range measurements is observed to be excellent for total angles of attack up to 10 degrees.

Figure 14.4 shows the comparison between the wind tunnel (Ref. 5) and the spark range (Ref. 4) Magnus moment coefficients, $C_{M_{p\alpha}}$, for angles of attack up to 15 degrees at Mach 2. The largest total angles of attack achieved in the spark range firings were of order of 10 degrees. Reference 6 contains an excellent description and discussion of wind tunnel Magnus force and moment testing.

The wind tunnel data plotted in Figure 14.4 suggest a tri-cubic Magnus moment, whereas the spark range data show a bi-cubic behavior in the same angle of attack region. However, the overall trends of the two curves are similar. Since the measurement of the Magnus moment is a delicate proposition in both facilities, the agreement observed in Figure 14.4 is considered satisfactory.

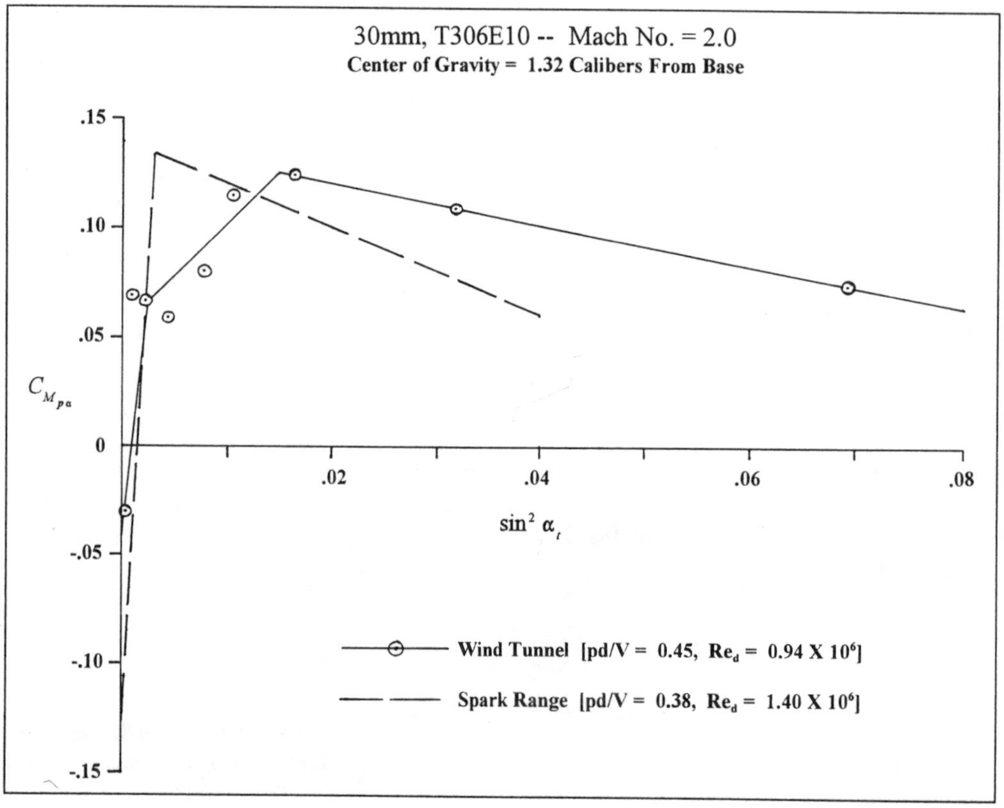

Figure 14.4 Comparison of Wind Tunnel and Spark Range Magnus Moment Coefficients.

Advantages and Disadvantages of Wind Tunnels for Projectile Aeroballistic Testing

The projectile designer is often faced with the need for aeroballistic testing. Given a specific (and usually quite limited) budget, should wind tunnels or spark photography ranges be selected? The use of either facility is expensive, and the design engineer must rely on his or her background and experience in making the selection. A few of the author's observations and comments, based on more than thirty years of aeroballistic test experience, may be of some assistance to the reader.

In the early design phase of a new projectile, one of the greatest advantages of wind tunnels over spark photography ranges is flexibility. The projectile designer can fabricate wind tunnel test models with a number of potentially useful variations on a basic configuration, and the wind tunnel quickly provides the effects of these variations on the aerodynamic forces and moments. Although the same configurational variations can also be tested in a spark range, each variation represents an entirely new set of firings, and the cost often becomes prohibitive.

If the projectile must fly at very large angles of attack, wind tunnels are often the only practical means of acquiring the necessary data. Average angles of attack up to thirty degrees have been achieved in free-flight ballistic ranges, using sophisticated yaw-induction techniques which will be described later in this chapter. However, in general, for total average angles of attack above twenty degrees, the necessarily severe yaw induction methods usually produce uncontrollable free-flight trajectories, and it is often no longer possible to keep the projectile within the instrumented test window.

A wind tunnel to be used for large angle of attack testing must have a sufficiently large test sectional area to prevent blockage and shock wave reflections, at the largest angles to be tested. At subsonic speeds, the blockage requirements are well known (see Reference 1). For high supersonic or hypersonic speeds, a discussion of both the blockage and the shock reflection requirements may be found in References 1 and 2. Transonic speeds present a difficult problem for most wind tunnels (and for spark ranges as well), because shock reflections off the tunnel walls and back onto the model are hard to avoid. In general, very large wind tunnel test-sectional areas are required for testing at transonic speeds.

If a spin-stabilized projectile is fired at sufficiently high gun elevation angles (usually greater than 70 degrees), the projectile will often "fail to trail," and will descend from the summit of the trajectory in a base-forward mode. In order to run six-degrees-of-freedom trajectories for the 105mm, M1 projectile at very high gun elevation angles, low-speed (Mach 0.2 to 0.3) pitch-plane and Magnus data were required at various spin-to-velocity ratios, and for angles of attack from zero to 180 degrees. The data for angles between 90 and 180 degrees were obtained by using a second spinning model, with a nose-mounted sting instead of the usual mounting in the projectile base. The data from these tests, conducted in the Army 7 X 10 foot subsonic wind tunnel at NASA Ames, is reported in Reference 7. Such very large angle of attack testing would have been impossible to conduct in spark photography ranges.

Unfortunately, there are also a few disadvantages to wind tunnel testing. One of the most critical is the measurement of the aerodynamic drag force. If a side-mounted sting is used, the model support system interferes with the flowfield past the model, and leads to incorrect drag readings. Usually, a base-mounted sting is used, and in this case the presence of the sting, or balance, affects the base pressure; e.g., the base pressure acting on the model is not the same as it would have been had the sting not been present. Thus conventional wind tunnel drag data always requires some "correction" for the sting effect, and there is a significant uncertainty about the proper correction. Recently, magnetic-suspension wind tunnel balances, which require no sting, have been developed, but due to the large electrical power requirements, they have proved feasible only for small test models.

The Reynolds numbers achieved in high speed supersonic wind tunnels are often significantly lower than free-flight Reynolds numbers, by factors that vary from three to ten. The normal force and pitching moment are usually insensitive to moderate changes in Reynolds number, but the skin friction component of the drag force is significantly affected by Reynolds number. The Magnus force and moment are the most sensitive aerodynamic force and moment to changes in Reynolds number, and if the wind tunnel Reynolds numbers are low by a factor of three or more, the measured Magnus characteristics are likely to be seriously in error.

Pitch damping moments are also difficult to measure accurately in wind tunnels. The model must be driven in either a planar sinusoidal pitching motion, or for spinning projectiles, in a coning motion about the central axis of the wind tunnel test section. The mechanical drive systems necessary for pitch damping data collection are expensive, and the wind tunnel data reduction is significantly more complicated than that required for static angle of attack testing.

Modern wind tunnels are still very useful facilities to the aeroballistician, despite the disadvantages mentioned above. Whenever many parametric projectile configuration changes need to be made, the wind tunnel is the most cost-effective test facility. In later design stages, the spark photography range often becomes a more useful tool than the wind tunnel. Free flight ranges and wind tunnels are not competitive facilities, but complementary ones.

14.3 FREE-FLIGHT BALLISTIC RANGES

The first free-flight ballistic range experiments were probably done by Isaac Newton of England. He was very interested in the motion of projectiles, and one of his early experiments consisted of dropping spheres of different sizes and densities from the top of St. Paul's Cathedral, and measuring their descent times from the ceiling to the floor. From these data, Newton made the first rough measurements of the aerodynamic drag force.

More accurate free-flight drag measurements were made around 1740 by Benjamin Robins of England. Robins invented the ballistic pendulum, which was capable of making reasonably accurate velocity measurements. He placed his ballistic pendulum at different distances from the gun, and thereby achieved the first reliable measurements of the projectile's remaining velocity versus distance.

Francis Bashforth of England developed an accurate chronograph for artillery projectiles, about the middle of the nineteenth century. Bashforth's chronograph received its start and stop signals when the projectile broke screens of fine copper wire, and the time interval between the two signals was measured by an electrical circuit, based on principles developed by Wheatstone. Bashforth made many good measurements of the drag of spherical cannon shot, as well as measurements of the drag forces acting on elongated cannon shell, which first appeared at about the same time.

A number of European investigators developed reasonably good experimental methods for free-flight drag measurements during the last quarter of the nineteenth century. In the late 1800s and early 1900s, Cranz in Germany (Ref. 9) had done the first free-flight yaw card experiments, and ballisticians had gained a rudimentary understanding of the nature of the pitching and yawing motion of spin stabilized projectiles. F. W. Mann, who worked in the first decade of the twentieth century (Ref. 10), used a yaw-card range to do an extensive study of the pitching and yawing motion of spin-stabilized small arms bullets.

The first definitive free-flight yaw-card experiment was conducted in 1919 by the English scientists Fowler, Gallop, Lock and Richmond (Ref. 11) at Portsmouth, England, using 3-inch English naval gun projectiles. The four English authors showed that the pitching and yawing motion of an elongated spinning shell is "epicyclic," with two characteristic frequencies. Their paper, titled *The Aerodynamics of Spinning Shell* is now considered a modern classic.

Ballistic chronograph and yaw-card firing ranges reached their zenith in the two decades preceding the Second World War. Many good measurements of the aerodynamic drag force and the overturning moment were made in such facilities, although the quality of results was necessarily lower than what would be achieved later in modern spark photography ranges. Reference 12 gives an excellent description of the methods used.

The beginning of World War II brought about a revolution in science and technology, that resulted in the simultaneous development of high-speed digital computers, continuous flow supersonic wind tunnels, and modern free-flight spark photography ranges. Since this section is about spark photography ranges, we will now explore them in detail.

Modern Spark Photography Ranges

The first spark photography range was built in 1924, at the National Physical Laboratory in England. According to J. W. Maccoll (Ref. 13), this small research ballistic range was 150 feet long, and the test section was large enough to permit firing one-inch diameter models. The range originally had eight spark photography stations; this number was later increased to nineteen. The triggering of the spark was accomplished by a fine wire grid, which was broken by the passing projectile.

R. H. Kent attempted to build a spark photography range at Aberdeen Proving Ground in 1938, using the recoil of the gun to trigger the spark sequence. Kent's range was unsuccessful, but it laid the foundation for A. C. Charters' efforts in the early 1940s. The Weapons Institute of the Luftwaffe Research Establishment constructed a spark photography range at Braunschweig, Germany, in the early years of the Second World War. However, the war ended before this range was completed, and it was never fully utilized for its intended purpose.

The BRL Aerodynamics Range was constructed under the direction of Dr. A. C. Charters, and it became operational in February, 1943. Initially, the range was equipped with six spark photography stations (Ref. 14), and it was used only for drag measurements. Later the number of stations was increased to sixteen, and by 1946, twenty-five stations were available for use. The first yaw reductions were done graphically, using a method developed by E. J. McShane. By 1948, analytical procedures for the yaw and swerve reductions had been developed independently by Z. Kopal (Ref. 15) and R. Turetsky (Ref. 16). Today, there are approximately forty operational spark photography stations distributed over the 300-foot length of the Aerodynamics Range.

A number of free-flight spark photography ranges are in use today, in the U.S., Canada, and various European countries. All of them trace their ancestry to the BRL Aerodynamics Range, which is still fully operational. A photograph of the Aerodynamics Range (circa 1958) was shown as Figure 1.11, in Chapter 1. The row of cylindrical cans to the left of the stations are the spark light sources. Today, triggering is done with infrared light screens; these have replaced the square-framed electrostatic inductance coils shown in Figure 1.11. Figure 1.12 of Chapter 1 shows the local and master coordinate systems used in the Aerodynamics Range. An excellent description of the range may be found in Reference 17.

The BRL Transonic Range was designed in 1944 and primary construction was finished in 1947. The instrumentation was completed, and full scale operation began, in the summer of 1950. Photographs of the exterior and interior views of the Transonic Range were shown as Figures 1.13 and 1.14 in Chapter 1. An excellent description of the range is given in Reference 18. This large (22 ft. by 22 ft.) free-flight spark photography range was designed to satisfy von Kármán's ratio for 3-inch diameter projectiles. (Theodore von Kármán had derived the theoretical result that for no choking at transonic speeds, the ratio of test sectional area to projectile cross-sectional area should be at least 10,000 to one). Although the range building is 1000 feet long, only 680 feet are fully instrumented. The same basic data reduction methods are used for both of the BRL free-flight spark photography ranges.

14.4 CLASSICAL DATA REDUCTION FOR SPARK PHOTOGRAPHY RANGES

The classical spark range data reduction procedure consists of the following steps: (1) measuring the photographic plates or film, (2) estimating certain critical flight motion parameters, (3) fitting the closed-form analytical solutions to the spark-range data by means of a nonlinear differential-corrections least-squares method, and (4) determining the aerodynamic force and moment coefficients from the least-squares-obtained values of the flight motion parameters. The mathematical details of these procedures are very complicated, and will not be discussed in this book. The interested reader may consult References 16 and 19, which go into considerable detail on the methodology. Reference 20 contains an excellent treatment of the classical spark range data reduction procedure.

For the relatively short segments of flat-fire trajectories encountered in spark range work, the variation in the drag coefficient over the length of the firing range is negligible, and C_D may therefore be treated as a constant. The velocity then decreases exponentially with increasing distance, according to equation (10.68) of Chapter 10:

$$V = V_o e^{-C_D^* s} \quad \textbf{(10.68)}$$

where V = projectile velocity at a given non-dimensional distance, s

V_o = initial velocity

$$C_D^* = \frac{\rho S d}{2m} C_D$$

The time of flight is related to the non-dimensional distance along the trajectory by the following equation:

$$t = t_o + \frac{d\left[e^{C_D^* s} - 1\right]}{V_o C_D^*} \quad \textbf{(14.1a)}$$

In practice, the right hand side of equation (14.1a) is expanded as a cubic in non-dimensional distance *s*, and the coefficients are then determined by a *linear* least squares fit:

$$t = t_o + \frac{d}{V_o} s + \frac{C_D^* d}{2V_o} s^2 + \frac{C_D^{*2} d}{6V_o} s^3 \quad \textbf{(14.1b)}$$

Murphy has noted [Ref. 20, and BRL Report No. 1216] that the cubic coefficient in equation (14.1b) absorbs any Mach number variation in C_D as well as errors in the expansion of the exponential term in equation (14.1a). In those cases where the cubic fits well, the resulting C_D agrees very closely with the value obtained from a nonlinear least squares fit of equation (14.1a) to the same data.

If the projectile is fitted with a roll pin in the model base, the roll angle at each spark photography station can be measured. If a finned missile has differentially canted fins, both a rolling moment and a spin-damping moment are present. For this case, the equation of rolling motion was derived as equation (10.74) in Chapter 10:

$$\phi = \phi_0 + \phi'_{(s/s)} s + A\left(e^{-K_p s} - 1\right) \quad \textbf{(10.74)}$$

where $K_p = -\left[k_x^{-2} C_{l_p}{}^* + C_D^*\right]$ **(10.72)**

$$K_\delta = k_x^{-2} \delta_F C_{l_\delta}{}^* \quad \textbf{(10.73)}$$

ϕ = roll angle at a given non-dimensional distance, s

ϕ_0 = initial roll angle

$\phi'_{(S/S)}$ is the steady-state spin, or rolling velocity, measured in radians per caliber of travel

$$\phi'_{(S/S)} = K_\delta / K_p$$

$$A = \frac{K_\delta - \phi'_0 K_p}{K_p^2} = \frac{\phi'_{(s/s)} - \phi'_0}{K_p}$$

Equation (10.74) is fitted to the observed roll angle data for a finned missile with canted fins, and if the drag coefficient is also known from the drag reduction, the values of the rolling moment coefficient, C_{l_δ}, and the spin damping moment coefficient, C_{l_p}, may be determined from the range flight.

For a spin-stabilized body of revolution (or a finned missile with uncanted fins), there is no rolling moment, and K_δ is therefore zero. For this case equation (10.74) reduces to:

$$\phi = \phi_0 - \frac{\phi'_0}{K_p}\left(e^{-K_p s} - 1\right) \quad \textbf{(10.77)}$$

In practice, the right hand side of equation (10.77) is expanded as a cubic in non-dimensional downrange distance, *s*:

$$\phi = \phi_0 + \phi'_0 s - \frac{1}{2}\phi'_0 K_p s^2 + \frac{1}{6}\phi'_0 K_p^2 s^3 \quad \textbf{(14.1c)}$$

The coefficients are determined by a *linear* least squares fit, and the value of K_p is determined from the range flight. With the help of equation (10.72), and the known value of the drag coefficient, the spin damping moment coefficient, C_{l_p}, is then readily determined. As in the drag reduction described previously, the cubic coefficient in equation (14.1c) absorbs any Mach number variation in C_{l_p}, as well as errors in the exponential expansion of equation (10.77). In cases where the cubic fits the data well, there is very little difference observed between values of C_{l_p} obtained from equation (14.1c) and the nonlinear equation (10.77).

The equation describing the linearized epicyclic pitching and yawing motion for a spinning projectile was derived as equation (10.94) of Chapter 10:

$$\xi = K_F e^{i\phi_F} + K_s e^{i\phi_s} + i\beta_R \quad \textbf{(10.94)}$$

where $\xi = \alpha + i\beta$

$K_F = K_{F_0} e^{\lambda_F s}$, the amplitude of the fast epicyclic yaw mode (or arm)

$K_S = K_{S_0} e^{\lambda_S s}$, the amplitude of the slow epicyclic yaw mode (or arm)

$$\phi_F = \phi_{F_0} + \phi'_F s$$

$$\phi_S = \phi_{S_0} + \phi'_S s$$

ϕ_{F_0} = initial phase angle of the fast epicyclic yaw arm

ϕ_{S_0} = initial phase angle of the slow epicyclic yaw arm

$$\beta_R = \frac{PG}{M + iPT} \quad \textbf{(10.95)}$$

$$\lambda_F + i\phi'_F = \frac{1}{2}\left[-H + iP + \sqrt{4M + H^2 - P^2 + 2iP(2T - H)}\right] \quad \textbf{(10.96)}$$

$$\lambda_S + i\phi'_S = \frac{1}{2}\left[-H + iP - \sqrt{4M + H^2 - P^2 + 2iP(2T - H)}\right] \quad \textbf{(10.97)}$$

After completing the drag and roll reductions, the next step in the data reduction procedure is to fit equation (10.94) to the pitch and yaw measurements, by means of a nonlinear least squares fitting process. The results of the least squares fit provide values of the two epicyclic arm lengths (amplitudes), as well as the two characteristic frequencies and the damping exponents of the observed epicyclic motion. The relationships between the linearized aerodynamic coefficients and the flight motion parameters were stated as equations (10.98) through (10.101) of Chapter 10. An expanded form of those equations is repeated here as equations (14.2) through (14.5):

$$P = \phi'_F + \phi'_S = \left(\frac{I_x}{I_y}\right)\left(\frac{pd}{V}\right) \quad \textbf{(14.2)}$$

$$M = \phi'_F\phi'_S - \lambda_F\lambda_S = k_y^{-2}C_{M_\alpha}{}^* \quad \textbf{(14.3)}$$

$$H = -\left[\lambda_F + \lambda_S\right] = C_{L_\alpha}{}^* - C_D^* - k_y^{-2}\left(C_{M_q}{}^* + C_{M_{\dot\alpha}}{}^*\right) \quad \textbf{(14.4)}$$

$$T = \frac{-\left[\phi'_F\lambda_S + \phi'_S\lambda_F\right]}{P} = C_{L_\alpha}{}^* + k_x^{-2}C_{M_{p\alpha}}{}^* \quad \textbf{(14.5)}$$

where a starred coefficient is always the coefficient multiplied by (*see at right*). $\left(\frac{\rho S d}{2m}\right)$

Note that in addition to the drag coefficient, we also need the lift force coefficient for the flight, before the Magnus and the pitch damping moment coefficients can be determined. The lift force coefficient can usually be obtained from the swerving motion in modern high-precision spark ranges. Another alternative is to fire models with more than one center-of-gravity location, at the same nominal Mach number and yaw level. The lift force coefficient can then be determined indirectly from the two-center-of-gravity pitching moment coefficient data (see section 13.8 of Chapter 13).

The classical linearized swerve reduction (neglecting the very small Coriolis force) is done by fitting equation (11.29) of Chapter 11 to the vertical (y) and horizontal (z) center-of-mass swerve data:

$$y + iz = \left(y_0 + iz_0\right) + \left(y'_0 + iz'_0\right)s - \frac{gds^2}{2V_0^2}\left[\frac{e^{2C_D^* s} - 2C_D^* s - 1}{2\left(C_D^* s\right)^2}\right] + C_{L_\alpha}{}^*\int_0^s\int_0^{r_2}\xi dr_1 dr_2 \quad \textbf{(11.29)}$$

where y_0 = initial value of y (calibers)

z_0 = initial value of z (calibers)

$y'_0 = \tan\phi_0$, the tangent of the trajectory's vertical angle of departure (positive upward)

$z'_0 = \tan\theta_0$, the tangent of the trajectory's horizontal angle of departure (positive to the right, when looking downrange)

s = downrange distance, measured in calibers

The double integral appearing in the last term of equation (11.29) was evaluated in Chapter 11. Writing the results of that double integration in a slightly different form leads to equations (14.6) through (14.11):

$$\int_0^s\int_0^{r_2}\xi dr_1 dr_2 = -\left[\left(\frac{\lambda_F - i\phi'_F}{\lambda_F^2 + \phi_F'^2}\right)K_{F_0}e^{i\phi_{F0}} + \left(\frac{\lambda_S - i\phi'_S}{\lambda_S^2 + \phi_S'^2}\right)K_{S_0}e^{i\phi_{S0}}\right]S + \left(R_{F_1} - iR_{F_2}\right)K_{F_0}e^{i\phi_{F0}}\left[e^{(\lambda_F + i\phi'_F)s} - 1\right] \quad \textbf{(14.6)}$$

$$+\left(R_{S_1} - iR_{S_2}\right)K_{S_0}e^{i\phi_{S0}}\left[e^{(\lambda_S + i\phi'_S)s} - 1\right] + i\left(\frac{PG_0}{M}\right)s^2\left[\frac{e^{2C_D^* s} - 2C_D^* s - 1}{\left(2C_D^* s\right)^2}\right]$$

where

$$R_{F_1} = \frac{\lambda_F^2 - \phi_F'^2}{\left(\lambda_F^2 + \phi_F'^2\right)^2} \quad \textbf{(14.7)}$$

$$R_{F_2} = \frac{2\lambda_F\phi'_F}{\left(\lambda_F^2 + \phi_F'^2\right)^2} \quad \textbf{(14.8)}$$

$$R_{S_1} = \frac{\lambda_S^2 - \phi_S'^2}{\left(\lambda_S^2 + \phi_S'^2\right)^2} \quad \textbf{(14.9)}$$

$$R_{S_2} = \frac{2\lambda_S\phi'_S}{\left(\lambda_S^2 + \phi_S'^2\right)^2} \quad \textbf{(14.10)}$$

$$G_0 = \frac{gd}{V_0^2} \quad \textbf{(14.11)}$$

The swerve reduction usually yields an excellent value of the lift force coefficient, C_{L_α}, and it thereby enables the Magnus moment and pitch damping moment coefficients to be determined [see equations (14.4) and (14.5)]. It is readily apparent that a good yaw reduction is a necessary prerequisite to a successful swerve reduction.

Criteria for the Quality of Spark Photography Range Results

The quality of aerodynamic coefficients obtained from spark photography ranges depends on the accuracy of projectile physical measurements, as well as the accuracy of position, time, pitch, yaw and roll measurements in the range itself. Modern spark photography ranges always include a high-precision physical measurements laboratory, and great care is taken to obtain the most accurate physical measurements possible. Reference 21 gives an excellent (although dated) description of the details. A list of precision measurement errors in the projectile's physical properties is given in Table 14.1:

Table 14.1
Precision in the Measurement of Projectile Physical Properties

Physical Property	Precision Measurement Error
Projectile Mass (Weight)	±0.03 %
Reference Diameter	±0.0002 Caliber
Center of Gravity Location	±0.0006 Caliber
Axial Moment of Inertia	±0.1 %
Transverse Moment of Inertia	±0.1 %

Measurements of the barometric pressure, air temperature and relative humidity are carefully made, using frequently-calibrated laboratory grade instruments, for each shot fired in modern free-flight ballistic ranges. The barometric pressure is not used directly, but is required for the determination of air density. Precision atmospheric measurement errors for enclosed, climate-controlled spark photography ranges are ±1 degree Fahrenheit in air temperature, and ±0.5 % in air density.

At each station, the position (X, Y, Z coordinates), time of flight, and the pitch, yaw and roll angles, are all very accurately measured in modern high-precision free-flight spark photography ranges. Precision measurement errors in the BRL Aerodynamics Range and the BRL Transonic Range are listed in Table 14.2 (*below*).

After all the rounds of a spark range program have been fired, and all the data has been reduced, values of the various aerodynamic coefficients are obtained for each round fired. Modern spark photography range data deserves a careful analysis, and the following guidelines, based on many years experience, are provided for the benefit of the inexperienced program engineer.

In addition to values of the aerodynamic coefficients and the flight motion parameters, the spark range data reduction provides a number of statistical error calculations, which prove helpful in the data analysis. The percent error in the drag coefficient, from the least squares fit of the time-distance data, turns out to be the most useful criterion for determination of the quality of a drag measurement. The root-mean-square (RMS) errors of the yaw and the swerve fits are excellent estimates of the "noise" in the yaw and swerve data, and turn out to be very useful in calculating several required "signal-to-noise" ratios. In addition, a certain minimum number of spark stations must always be present for a good quality data reduction. In general, a minimum data section length (usually stated either in calibers, or as a fraction of the period of one epicyclic yaw arm) must also be present, if the aerodynamic coefficients are to be well-determined.

Many years experience in the analysis of spark photography range data has shown that the ratios of the fast and the slow epicyclic yaw amplitudes (K_F and K_S, respectively) to the root-mean-square error of the yaw fit (RMS_Y), are the correct signal-to-noise ratios for determining the quality of the measured pitching moment coefficient and the Magnus and pitch-damping moment coefficients. Similarly, the ratio of the swerve radius due to lift, R_L (calibers) [for spin-stabilized projectiles, see equation (11.56) of Chapter 11] to the root-mean-square error of the swerve fit (RMS_{SW}), turns out to be the correct signal-to-noise ratio for appraising the quality of a lift force coefficient determination.

A tabular summary of the spark-range data quality criteria for several of the aerodynamic coefficients is presented in Table 14.3 (*see p. 308*).

Note 1 [(*) in Table 14.3]: If the spin has been measured, only *one* of the two epicyclic yaw arm amplitudes must be three times the RMS error in yaw, because the pitching moment coefficient may be accurately determined from one epicyclic frequency and the spin. However, the Magnus and pitch-damping moments, which are obtained from the observed damping exponents of the yaw fit, will not be of good quality unless *both* yaw arms meet the stated criteria.

Note 2: In Table 14.3, (??) denotes a questionable value of the coefficient. If a questionable coefficient is consistent with other good quality values from the same program, it should be retained; otherwise it should be discarded.

After a quality-of-results analysis has been conducted on the aerodynamic coefficients obtained from a spark range firing program, the poor quality coefficients are discarded, and the good quality (and initially the questionable quality) values are retained for further analysis. Precision measurements in the spark-range-determined aerodynamic coefficients are illustrated in Table 14.4 (*see p. 309*).

Table 14.2
Precision Measurement Errors in the Two BRL
Spark Photography Ranges

Quantity	Precision Measurement Error (Aerodynamics Range)	Precision Measurement Error (Transonic Range)
Position (X, Y, X)	±0.01 Inch	±0.1 Inch
Time of Flight	±0.5 Microsecond	±1 Microsecond
Pitch and Yaw Angles	±0.1 Degree	±0.1 Degree
Roll Angles (With Roll Pin)	±1.0 Degree	±1.0 Degree

Table 14.3 Summary of Criteria for Quality of Spark Range Measured Aerodynamic Coefficients

Coeff.	Min. No. Stations	Min. Data Section Length (Calibers)	Criteria for Data Quality *	Quality Rating
C_D	10	2000	% Error in $C_D < 1$ %	Good
	10	2000	% Error in $C_D > 1$ %	??
C_{M_α}	10	3/4 Cycle - Slow Arm	$\frac{K_F}{RMS_Y} \geq 3$ *and* $\frac{K_S}{RMS_Y} \geq 3$	Good
	10	1 Cycle - Slow Arm	$2 \leq \frac{K_F \text{ and } K_S}{RMS_Y} < 3$	??
	10	1 Cycle - Slow Arm	$\frac{K_F \text{ and } K_S}{RMS_Y} < 2$	Poor
$C_{M_{p\alpha}}$ *and* $C_{M_q} + C_{M_{\dot{\alpha}}}$	10	1.5 Cycle - Slow Arm	$\frac{K_F \text{ and } K_S}{RMS_Y} \geq 5$	Good
	10	2 Cycles - Slow Arm	$3 \leq \frac{K_F \text{ and } K_S}{RMS_Y} < 5$	??
	10	2 Cycles - Slow Arm	$\frac{K_F \text{ and } K_S}{RMS_Y} < 3$	Poor
C_{L_α}	10	3/4 Cycle - Slow Arm	$\frac{R_L}{RMS_{SW}} \geq 3$	Good
	10	1 Cycle - Slow Arm	$2 \leq \frac{R_L}{RMS_{SW}} < 3$	??
	10	1 Cycle - Slow Arm	$\frac{R_L}{RMS_{SW}} < 2$	Poor

Table 14.4
Percent Errors in Spark-Range
Measured Aerodynamic Coefficients

Aerodynamic Coefficient	Precision of Measurement (in Percent)
Drag Coefficient, C_D	1%
Pitching Moment Coefficient, C_{M_α}	2%
Lift Force Coefficient, C_{L_α}	5%
Magnus Moment Coefficient, $C_{M_{p\alpha}}$	15%
Pitch Damping Moment Coef., $C_{M_q} + C_{M_{\dot\alpha}}$	15%
Roll Moment Coefficients, C_{l_p}, C_{l_δ}	5%

Examples of Classical Spark-Range Data Reduction

In 1946, an Army-Navy joint service aeroballistic research program was started to investigate the dynamic stability properties of high fineness (length-to-diameter) ratio spin-stabilized projectiles, in supersonic and transonic flight. Of the six aerodynamic coefficients that affect dynamic stability, two — the Magnus moment coefficient and the pitch damping moment coefficient — had never been adequately measured, and information on these two coefficients was therefore of prime importance in the investigation. The program was called the Army-Navy Spinner Rocket program, and the firings were conducted in the U.S. Army's BRL Aerodynamics Range.

All of the Army-Navy Spinner Rocket test models had a two-caliber long, pointed secant ogive nose, whose generating radius was twice the tangent ogive radius for the same nose length. The nose section was followed by three, five, or seven-caliber cylindrical afterbody lengths, to give overall projectile fineness ratios of five, seven, and nine calibers. In addition, aluminum and bronze alloys were used in various combinations for the nose, centerbody, and tail sections, to give models with forward, middle, and rear center-of-gravity locations for each fineness ratio. Axial spin was imparted by means of a pre-engraved aluminum sabot placed immediately behind the model, and coupled to the model by means of a cruciform key. After firing, the sabot and key dropped away, and left the model alone in free flight. Twenty millimeter guns rifled one turn in ten calibers and one turn in fifteen calibers were used.

Average yaw levels for the ANSR program were between one degree and six degrees. The lower limit was imposed by measurement accuracy, and the top limit reflects the upper bound of linearized aerodynamic theory. The five-, seven-, and nine-caliber long models were tested at supersonic speeds (Ref. 22), to determine the effect of model length on the aerodynamic properties. In addition, the seven-caliber long models were tested at transonic and high subsonic speeds (Ref. 23). The aerodynamic data obtained for the seven-caliber long Army-Navy Spinner Rocket models is presented in this chapter, as an illustration of the high quality results that are

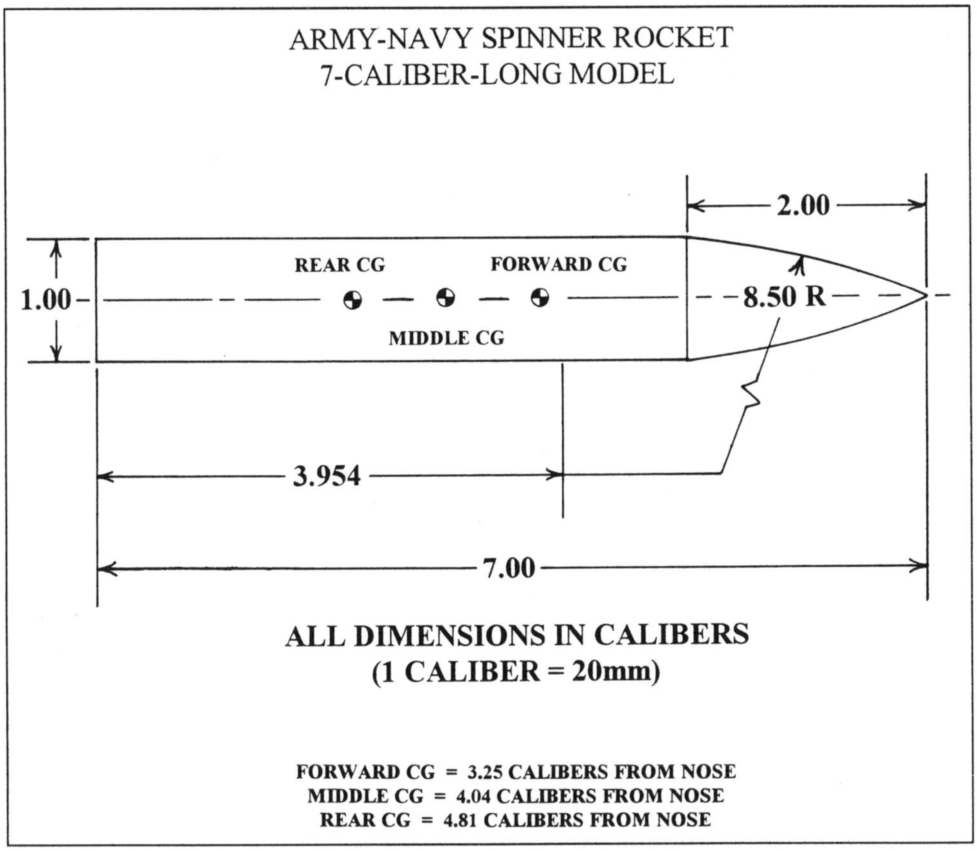

Figure 14.5 Sketch of the 7-Caliber Army-Navy Spinner Rocket Models.

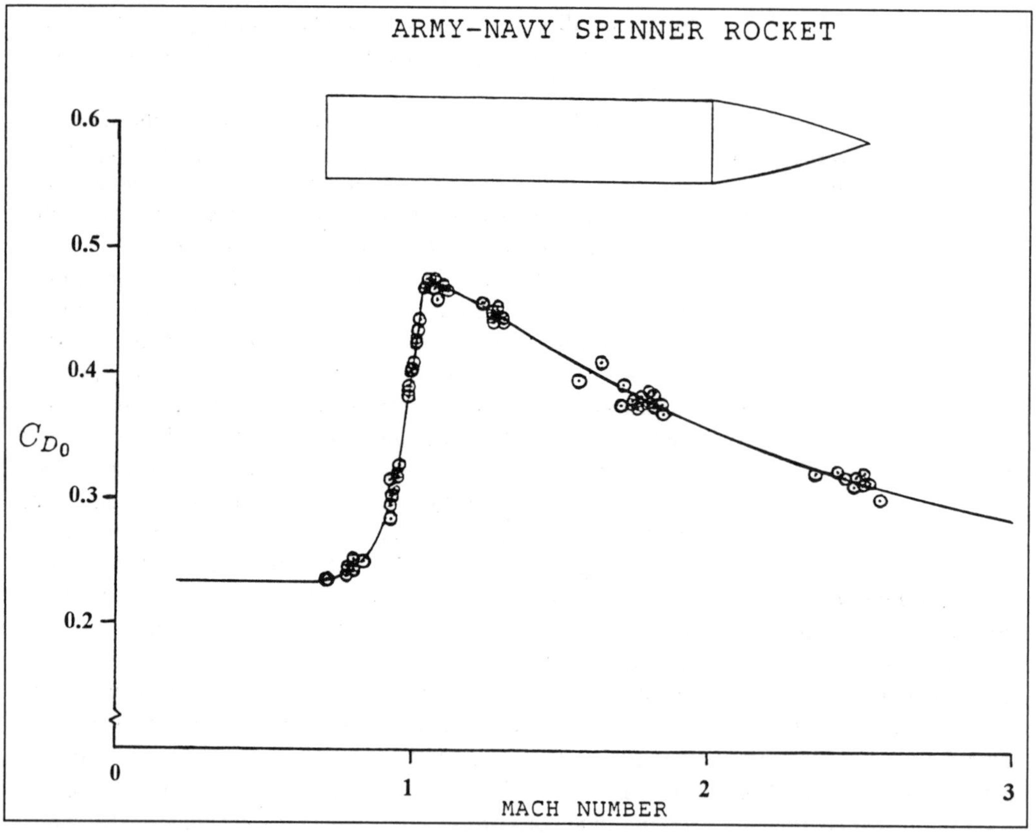

Figure 14.6 Zero-Yaw Drag Force Coefficient vs. Mach Number.

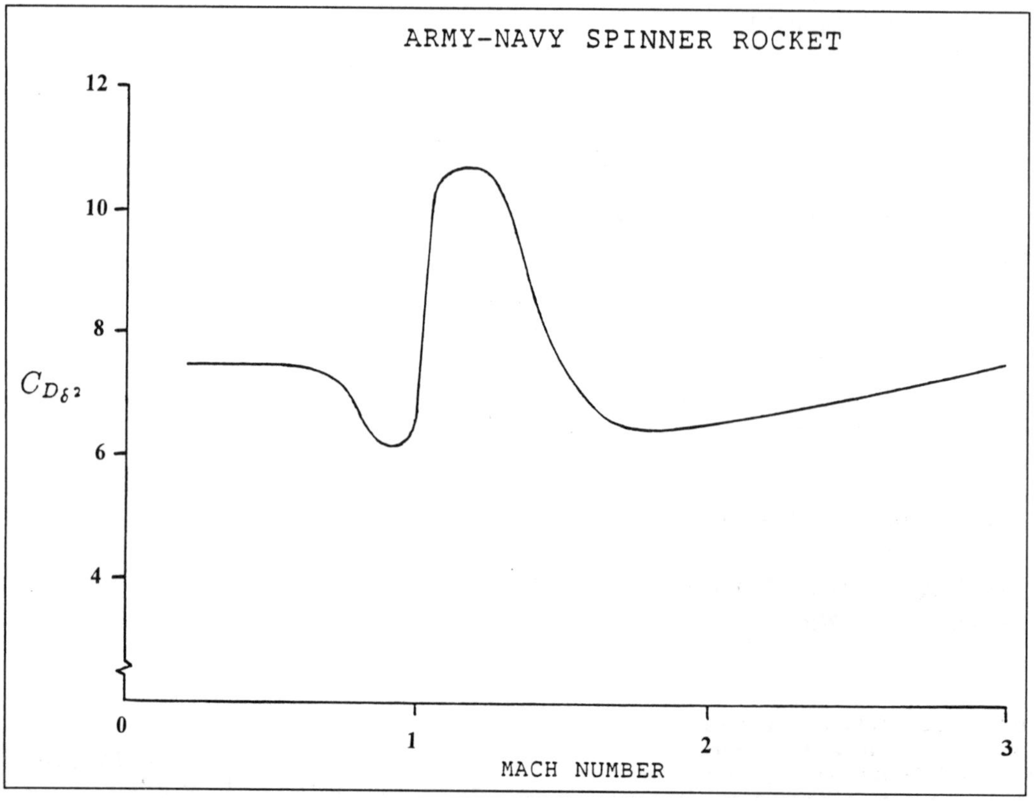

Figure 14.7 Quadratic Yaw-Drag Coefficient vs. Mach Number.

routinely obtained from firing a large program in a modern spark photography range.

A sketch of the 20mm, 7-Cal. ANSR (seven-caliber Army-Navy Spinner Rocket) model, showing the forward, middle, and rear center-of-gravity locations, is shown as Figure 14.5. Figures 14.6 and 14.7 illustrate the zero-yaw drag coefficient and the quadratic yaw-drag coefficient, respectively, for the 7-Cal. ANSR (these two plots were previously shown as Figures 4.39 and 4.38, in Chapter 4). The curve shown in Figure 14.7 was obtained from an analysis of the nonlinear drag coefficient data (see section 13.2 of Chapter 13), and was used to correct the range values of C_D to the zero-yaw values plotted in Figure 14.6. The standard deviation in the drag coefficient at supersonic speeds is 0.006, or about 1.7%.

Small roll pins were placed in the bases of some of the ANSR models, so the spin-damping moment coefficient, C_{l_p}, could be determined. Figure 14.8 is a plot of C_{l_p} versus Mach number. The spin-damping moment coefficient for the 7-Cal. ANSR shows no significant nonlinear variation with angle of attack (in general C_{l_p} exhibits no significant nonlinear behavior for any spin-stabilized projectile). Figure 14.8 shows that the spin-damping moment coefficient is negative at all speeds; it is more negative at subsonic speeds, and less negative at supersonic speeds (these same trends are normally observed for spin-stabilized projectiles). The standard deviation in C_{l_p} for the 7-Cal. ANSR models at supersonic speeds is 0.0005, or about 3%. Note that neither the drag force coefficient nor the spin-damping moment coefficient are affected by the model's CG location, therefore the data for all centers of gravity are combined in Figures 14.6 through 14.8.

The range-measured pitching (overturning) moment coefficients, C_{M_α}, for the forward, middle, and rear CG locations are plotted against Mach number in Figure 14.9. As expected, the value of C_{M_α} is smaller for the forward CG models, and larger for the rear CG projectiles. The pooled standard deviation in C_{M_α} for all CG locations at supersonic speeds is 0.11, or about 1.7%.

Figure 14.10 is a plot of the normal force coefficient, C_{N_α}, versus Mach number, for the 7-Cal. ANSR models. The individual round values shown in Figure 14.10 were obtained from the swerve reduction and the small-yaw relationship, $C_{N_\alpha} = C_{L_\alpha} + C_D$. The standard deviation of the swerve-determined normal force coefficient at supersonic speeds is 0.14, or about 4.8%. Note that values of C_{N_α} could also have been obtained by plotting the pitching moment coefficients at fixed Mach numbers against the CG location, and determining the slopes of the least-squares straight lines through the data. This analysis has been done and the results, at all test Mach numbers, fall on the solid curve drawn through the swerve data points of Figure 14.10.

The spark-range Magnus moment coefficient data for the 7-Cal. ANSR models is illustrated in Figures 14.11 and 14.12. Figure 14.11 is a plot of the range-measured $C_{M_{p\alpha}}$ versus CG location, at two fixed Mach numbers. (If more Mach numbers are added to this plot it becomes too cluttered, so only a sample of the spark range data is shown here). At Mach 0.8, most of the Magnus moment coefficients are negative, and the slope of the least-squares straight line fitted to the data is the Magnus force coefficient $C_{N_{p\alpha}}$, which in this case has the value -0.30. At Mach 1.3, the $C_{M_{p\alpha}}$ values are positive for the forward and middle CG models, and the Magnus force coefficient has the value -0.65.

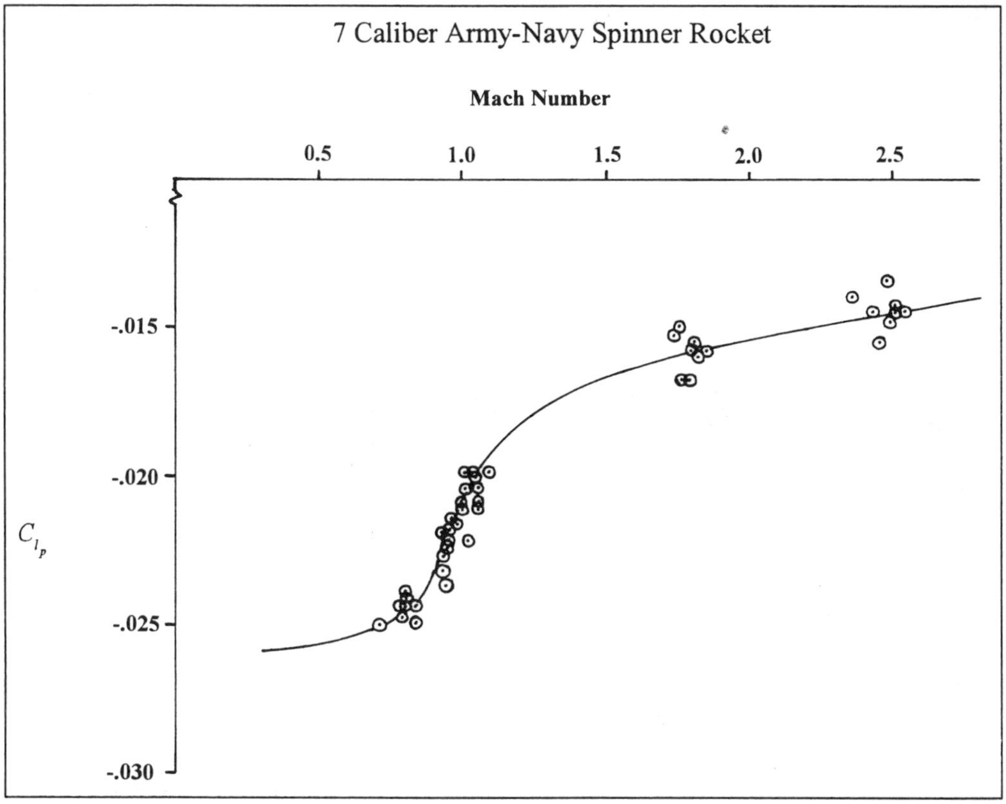

Figure 14.8 Spin-Damping Moment Coefficient vs. Mach Number.

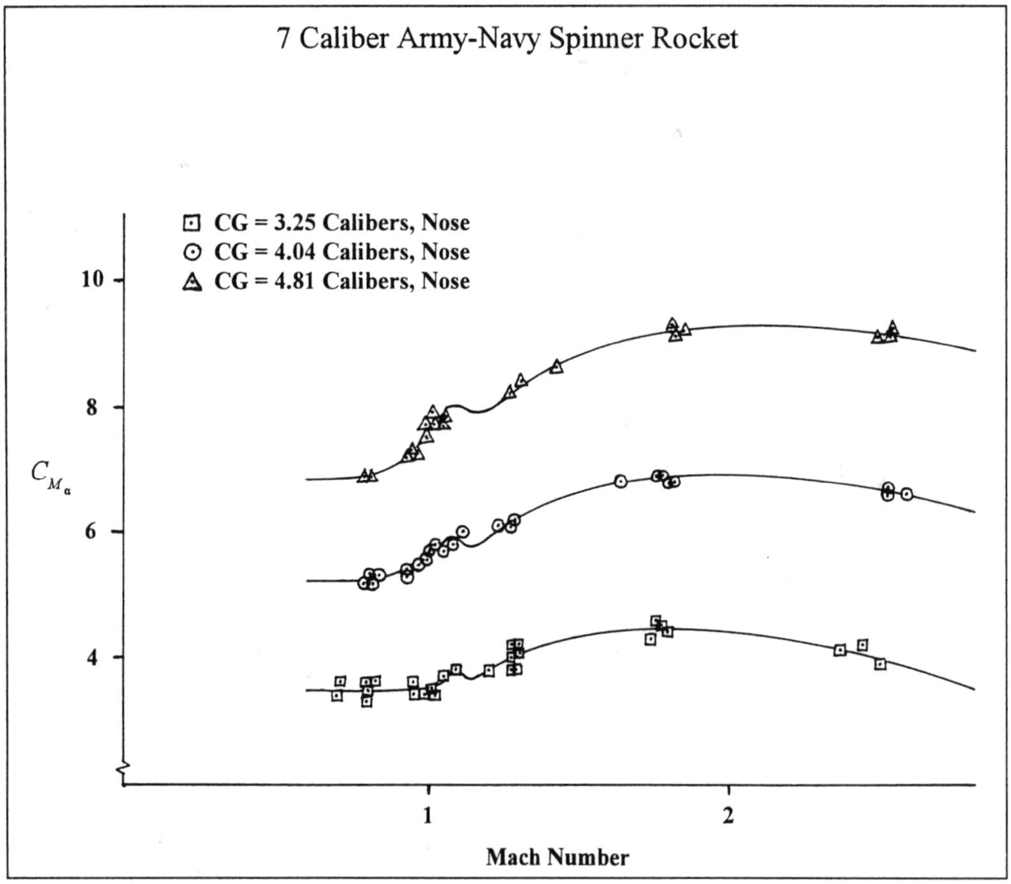

Figure 14.9 Pitching Moment Coefficient versus Mach Number, for Three CG Locations.

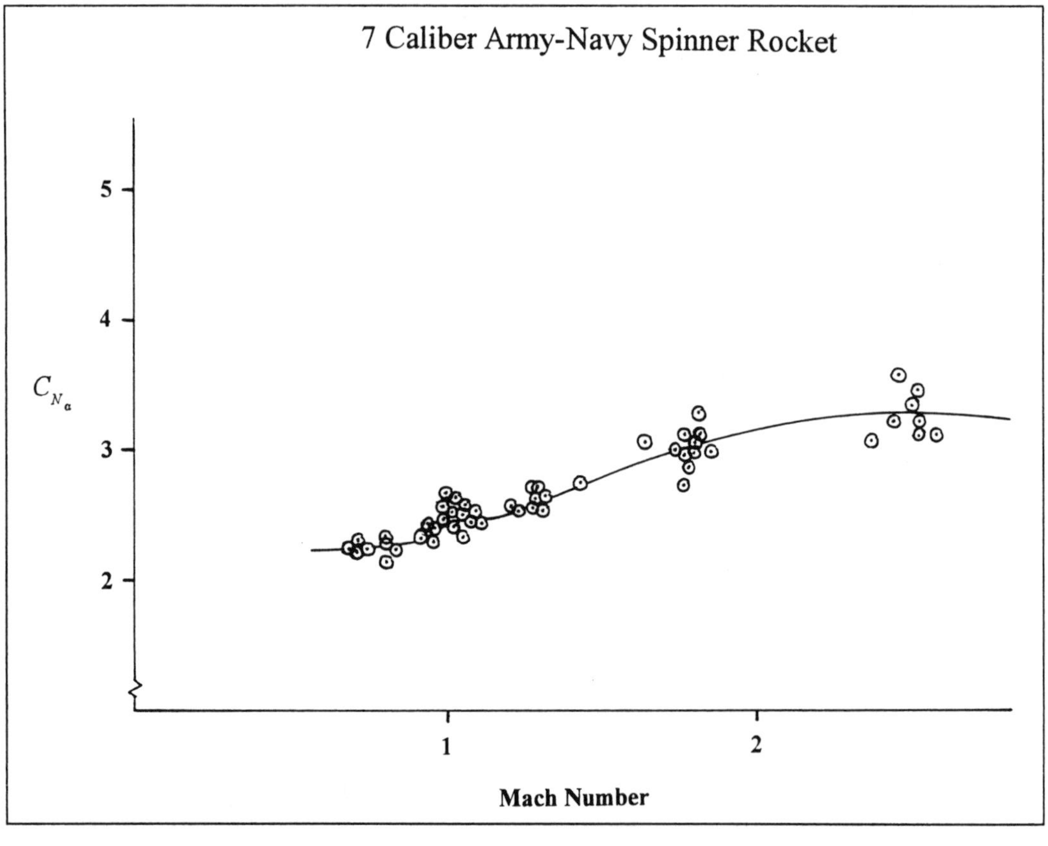

Figure 14.10 Normal Force Coefficient vs. Mach Number.

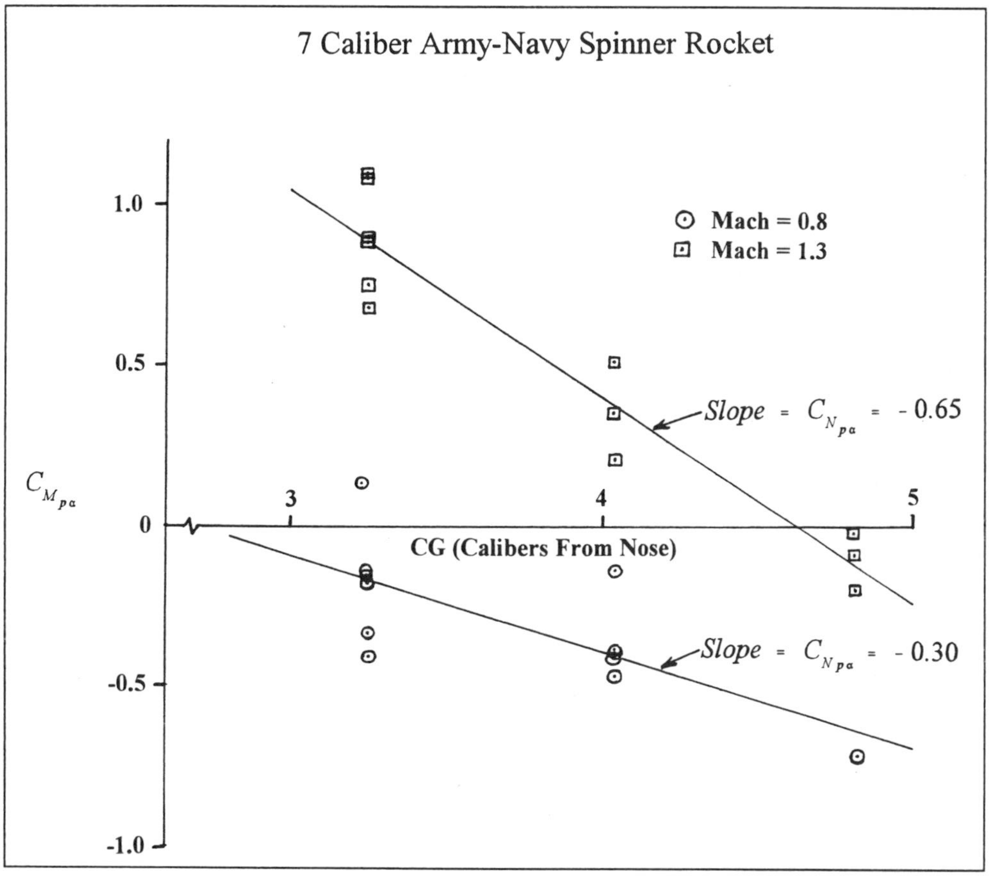

Figure 14.11 Magnus Moment Coefficient vs. CG Location, at Two Mach Numbers.

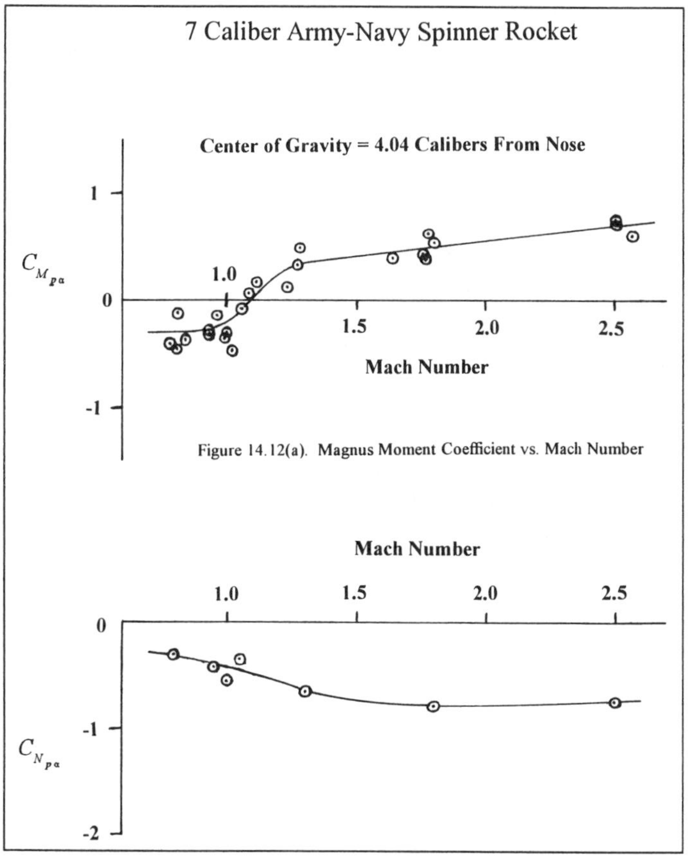

Figure 14.12 Magnus Force Coefficient vs. Mach Number.

The upper plot in Figure 14.12 shows the variation of the Magnus moment coefficient with Mach number for the middle CG, 7-Cal. ANSR models. Again, the plot would become too cluttered if the data for the other CG locations were included. The pooled standard deviation in the Magnus moment coefficient at supersonic speeds is 0.19. This represents an average standard deviation of about 30%, with all three center-of-gravity locations considered.

The lower graph in Figure 14.12 illustrates the values obtained for the Magnus force coefficient, $C_{N_{p\alpha}}$, at supersonic, transonic and subsonic speeds. Note that in almost all cases, the Magnus force has too small an effect on the swerving motion to provide reliable swerve-determined values. In general, if accurate values of the Magnus force coefficient are required, the only way to determine them is by firing models with two or more CG locations, and plotting the data as shown in Figure 14.11.

Figure 14.13 is a plot of the normal force and the Magnus force centers of pressure against Mach number, for the 7-Cal. ANSR models at supersonic, transonic, and subsonic speeds. The middle CG location (4.04 calibers from the nose) is also included, as a dashed line in the plot.

The center-of-pressure is a fictitious quantity that represents the point at which a concentrated force would have to act, in order to produce the observed moment. The defining equations for the normal force and the Magnus force centers of pressure (CP_N and CP_F, respectively) were given in Chapter 2, and are restated here as equations (14.12) and (14.13):

$$C_{M_\alpha} = C_{N_\alpha}\left(CG_N - CP_N\right) \tag{14.12}$$

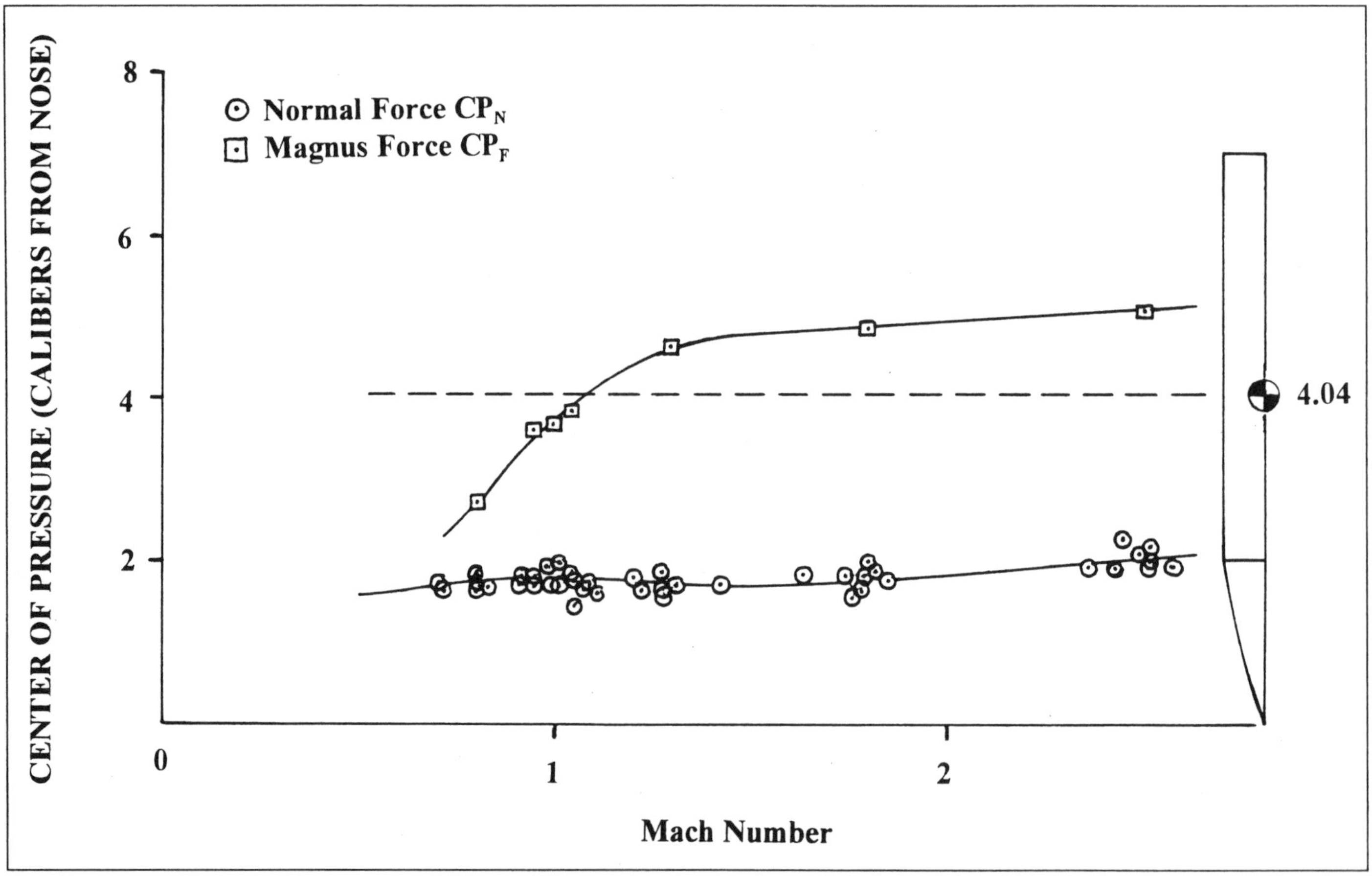

Figure 14.13 Centers of Pressure of the Normal and Magnus Forces vs. Mach Number.

$$C_{M_{p\alpha}} = C_{N_{p\alpha}}\left(CG_N - CP_F\right) \quad \textbf{(14.13)}$$

where CG_N = center-of-gravity (CG) location (calibers from nose)

CP_N = normal force center-of-pressure location (calibers from nose)

CP_F = Magnus force center-of-pressure location (calibers from nose)

Figure 14.13 shows that the locations of the normal force center-of-pressure and the Magnus force center-of-pressure are significantly different. At supersonic speeds, the Magnus force CP_F is located much farther aft than the normal force CP_N. This tells us that the Magnus force acts as if it were concentrated near the tail of the projectile, whereas the normal force acts as if it were concentrated near the junction of the projectile nose section and the cylindrical afterbody. The above observations are generally true for slender, flat-based, spin-stabilized projectile configurations, flying at supersonic speeds.

Before we can analyze the pitch damping moment coefficient data for the 7-Cal. ANSR models, we must return to Table 2.1 of Chapter 2, and recall several equations that describe the effect of a center-of-gravity shift on the aerodynamic coefficients. The relationships we will need are summarized below, and are given equation numbers:

$$\hat{C}_{M_\alpha} = C_{M_\alpha} + \Delta_{CG} C_{N_\alpha} \quad \textbf{(14.14)}$$

$$\hat{C}_{N_q} = C_{N_q} - \Delta_{CG} C_{N_\alpha} \quad \textbf{(14.15)}$$

$$\hat{C}_{N_{\dot\alpha}} = C_{N_{\dot\alpha}} \quad \textbf{(14.16)}$$

$$\hat{C}_{M_q} = C_{M_q} + \Delta_{CG}\left(C_{N_q} - C_{M_\alpha}\right) - \Delta_{CG}^2 C_{N_\alpha} \quad \textbf{(14.17)}$$

$$\hat{C}_{M_{\dot\alpha}} = C_{M_{\dot\alpha}} + \Delta_{CG} C_{N_{\dot\alpha}} \quad \textbf{(14.18)}$$

The coefficients with a circumflex (^) overscript are the values obtained after a center-of-gravity shift of Δ_{CG} (measured in calibers). Note that Δ_{CG} is considered positive if the CG shift is toward the tail of the projectile.

The pitch damping moment coefficient sum for a shifted CG location is given by the sum of equations (14.17) and (14.18):

$$\hat{C}_{M_q} + \hat{C}_{M_{\dot\alpha}} = C_{M_q} + C_{M_{\dot\alpha}} + \Delta_{CG}\left(C_{N_q} + C_{N_{\dot\alpha}}\right) - \Delta_{CG}\left(C_{M_\alpha} + \Delta_{CG} C_{N_\alpha}\right) \quad \textbf{(14.19)}$$

Note that the pitch damping moment coefficient sum exhibits an unfortunate *quadratic dependence* on the CG location, instead of the linear dependence observed for the static and Magnus coefficients. However, it turns out that the use of a *modified pitch damping moment coefficient* eliminates this difficulty.

We first substitute equation (14.14) into the last term of the right hand side of (14.19):

$$\hat{C}_{M_q} + \hat{C}_{M_{\dot\alpha}} = C_{M_q} + C_{M_{\dot\alpha}} + \Delta_{CG}\left(C_{N_q} - C_{N_{\dot\alpha}}\right) - \Delta_{CG}\hat{C}_{M_\alpha} \quad \textbf{(14.20)}$$

The quantity $\Delta_{CG}\hat{C}_{M_\alpha}$ is now added to both sides of equation (14.20), and the *modified pitch damping moment coefficient*, $\left[C_{M_q} + C_{M_{\dot\alpha}}\right]$, is *defined* as:

$$\left[\hat{C}_{M_q} + \hat{C}_{M_{\dot\alpha}}\right] = C_{M_q} + C_{M_{\dot\alpha}} + \Delta_{CG}\hat{C}_{M_\alpha} \quad \textbf{(14.21)}$$

where the Δ_{CG} for the modified pitch damping moment coefficient is measured from the location of the centroid of volume, which is the standard reference point in slender-body aerodynmic theory. Substituting (14.21) into (14.20) we find:

$$\left[\hat{C}_{M_q} + \hat{C}_{M_{\dot\alpha}}\right] = C_{M_q} + C_{M_{\dot\alpha}} + \Delta_{CG}\left(C_{N_q} + C_{N_{\dot\alpha}}\right) \quad \textbf{(14.22)}$$

The pitch damping *force* coefficient, found from the sum of equations (14.15) and (14.16), varies linearly with CG location, and therefore we do not need a "modified" pitch damping force coefficient.

$$\hat{C}_{N_q} + \hat{C}_{N_{\dot\alpha}} = C_{N_q} + C_{N_{\dot\alpha}} - \Delta_{CG} C_{N_\alpha} \quad \textbf{(14.23)}$$

In practice, the modified pitch damping moment coefficients are calculated from the measured spark range pitching moment coefficients and the pitch damping moment coefficient data, using the Δ_{CG} values measured from the volume centroid, and equation (14.21). To calculate the modified damping moment coefficients, note that for the 7-Cal. ANSR forward CG models, Δ_{CG} = (3.25 - 4.04) = - 0.79 caliber, and for the rear CG models, Δ_{CG} = (4.81 - 4.04) = + 0.77 caliber. The middle CG coincides with the centroid of volume, so Δ_{CG} = 0 for the middle CG models.

The modified pitch damping moment coefficients are then plotted against the CG location, and the slopes of the least-squares fitted straight lines are the pitch damping force coefficients, at the centroid of volume. If pitch damping force coefficients are required at other CG locations, they may be obtained by means of equation (14.23).

Figure 14.14 is a plot of the modified pitch damping moment coefficients for the 7-Cal. ANSR models, versus the CG location, for two Mach numbers. Adding data for other Mach numbers would make the graph too cluttered, so only a sample of the data is shown.

The variation of the pitch damping moment coefficient with Mach number, for the middle CG models, is shown in the upper plot of Figure 14.15. The behavior of the pitch damping *force* coefficient with Mach number, also for the middle CG models, is shown in the lower plot of the same figure. The pitch damping moment coefficient is everywhere negative, which is necessary for dynamic stability. The pitch damping *force* coefficient for the 7-Cal. ANSR with a middle CG location is positive at all test Mach numbers. However, the pitch damping force has little or no effect on projectile flight, so in general, its sign does not matter.

We will now present a second example of classical spark-range data reduction. Terminal ballisticians have always favored hemispherical-based high-explosive shell designs, because of their enhanced fragmentation characteristics. However, hemispherical-

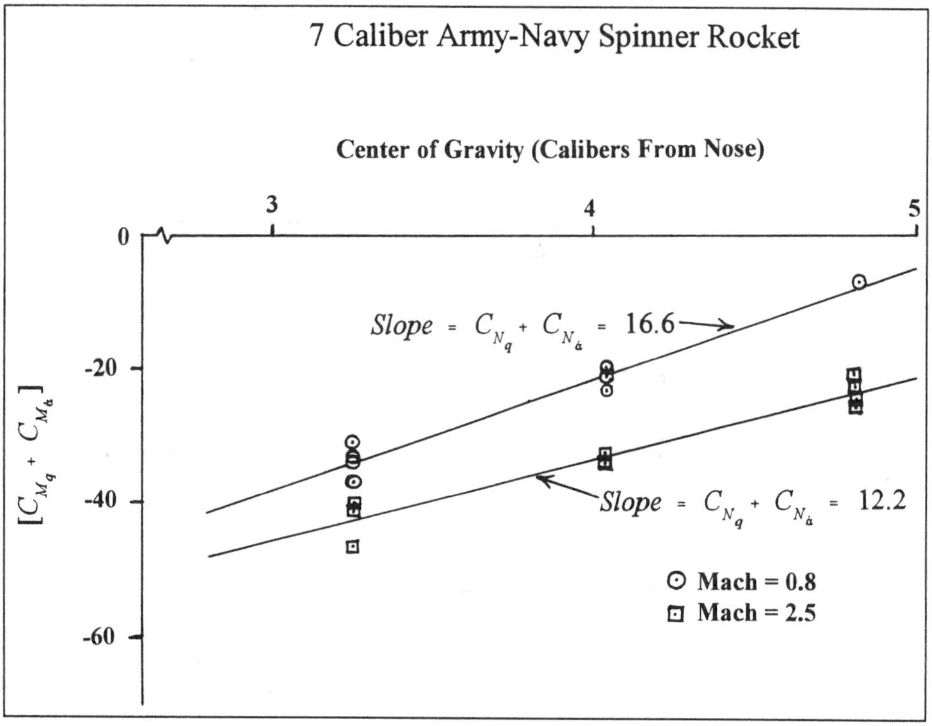

Figure 14.14 Modified Pitch Damping Moment Coefficient vs. CG Location.

based projectiles have historically exhibited severe dynamic instability, and very poor flight. In 1955 a test program was fired in the BRL Aerodynamics Range to determine the aeroballistic characteristics of hemispherical-based shell (Ref. 24), and to ascertain what particular aerodynamic properties caused the observed flight dynamic instability.

Flat-based and hemispherical-based 20mm models were machined from Tobin bronze, and each type was tested in two projectile lengths. The best comparison is between the short hemispherical-based model (fineness ratio equal to 5.68 calibers), and the long flat-based model (fineness ratio equal to 5.74 calibers). These two models have nearly identical fineness ratios, which eliminates projectile overall length as a variable.

The variation of the zero-yaw drag coefficients with Mach number is shown in Figure 14.16. An approximate value of the yaw drag coefficient, $C_{D_{\delta^2}} = 5.0$, was used to correct the range-measured drag coefficients to zero-yaw values. Across the Mach number range from subsonic to moderate supersonic speeds, the hemispherical-based shell shows about 10% higher average drag than the flat based model. The supersonic drag of a short, large-angled conical boattail is higher than that of a flat-based shell (Ref. 25), and the hemispherical base, in essence, behaves as a short, large-angled boattail.

The hemispherical-based model shows a higher lift force coefficient at all speeds than does the flat-based design, as illustrated in the upper plot of Figure 14.17. On the other hand, the pitching (overturning) moment coefficient for the hemispherical-based shell is everywhere lower than that of the flat-based projectile. The hemi-

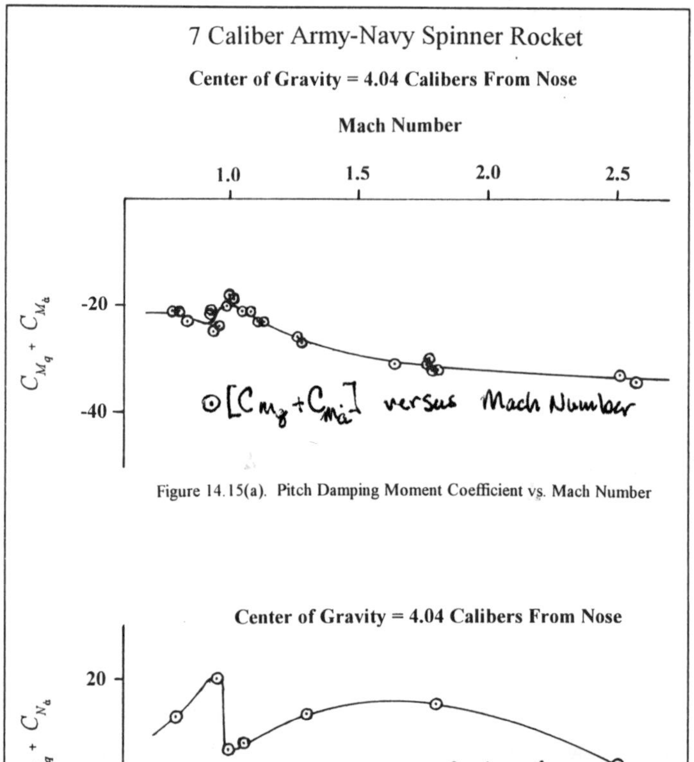

Figure 14.15(a). Pitch Damping Moment Coefficient vs. Mach Number

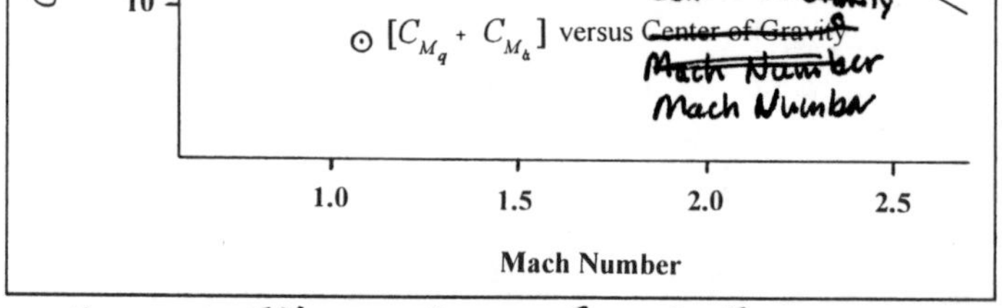

Figure 14.15 Pitch Damping ~~Force~~ Coefficient vs. Mach Number.

Figure 14.15(b) Pitch Damping Force Coefficient vs. Mach #

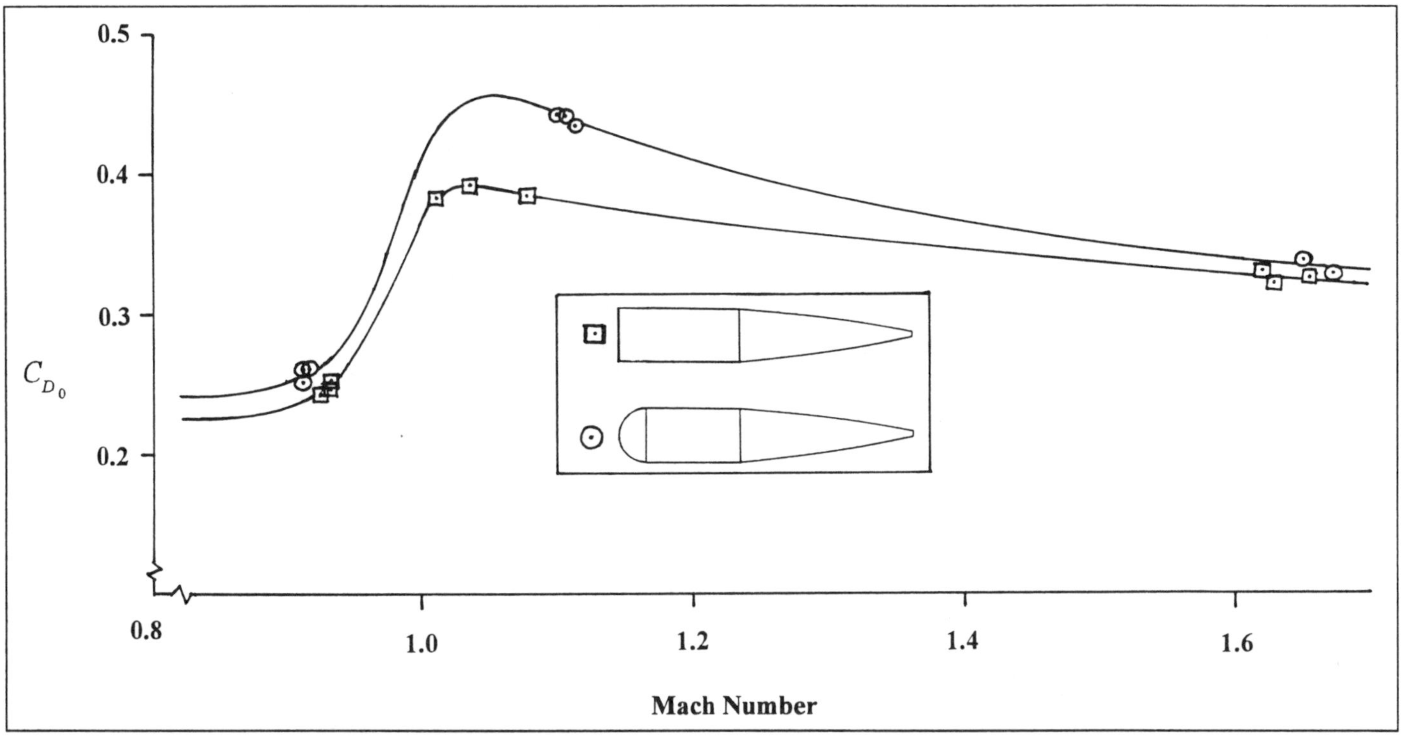
0.5
0.4
0.3
0.2
C_{D_0}
0.8
1.0
1.2
1.4
1.6
Mach Number

Figure 14.16 Zero-Yaw Drag Coefficient vs. Mach Number.

spherical base effectively shifts the normal force center-of-pressure farther toward the tail of the projectile, relative to the flat-based model. This effect is caused by the difference in the boundary layer separation point on the windward and leeward sides of the hemisphere.

Figure 14.18 (*p. 318*) illustrates the behavior of the Magnus moment coefficient and the pitch damping moment coefficient for the flat-based and the hemispherical-based shell. This figure clearly shows the reason for the observed poor flight characteristics of hemispherical-based projectiles. The upper plot of Figure 14.18 shows that the hemispherical based models have large negative Magnus moment coefficients at all flight speeds, and this condition alone is sufficient to cause slow-arm dynamic instability. In addition, the lower plot shows that the pitch damping moment coefficient for a hemispherical-based shell is positive at all speeds! The unfortunate combination of a large negative Magnus moment coefficient *and* a positive pitch damping moment coefficient produces a strong slow-arm dynamic instability. Projectile designers should therefore avoid hemispherical-based shell designs whenever possible.

14.5 SIX-DEGREES-OF-FREEDOM DATA REDUCTION FOR SPARK RANGES

The Chapman-Kirk 6-DOF data reduction method was first advanced in 1969, in a paper (Ref. 26) presented at the AIAA (American Institute of Aeronautics and Astronautics) 7th Aerospace Sciences meeting, followed by a journal article (Ref. 27). The Chapman-Kirk method numerically integrates the governing 6-DOF differential equations, rather than using approximate, linearized solutions of the equations of motion. Parametric differentiation is used to

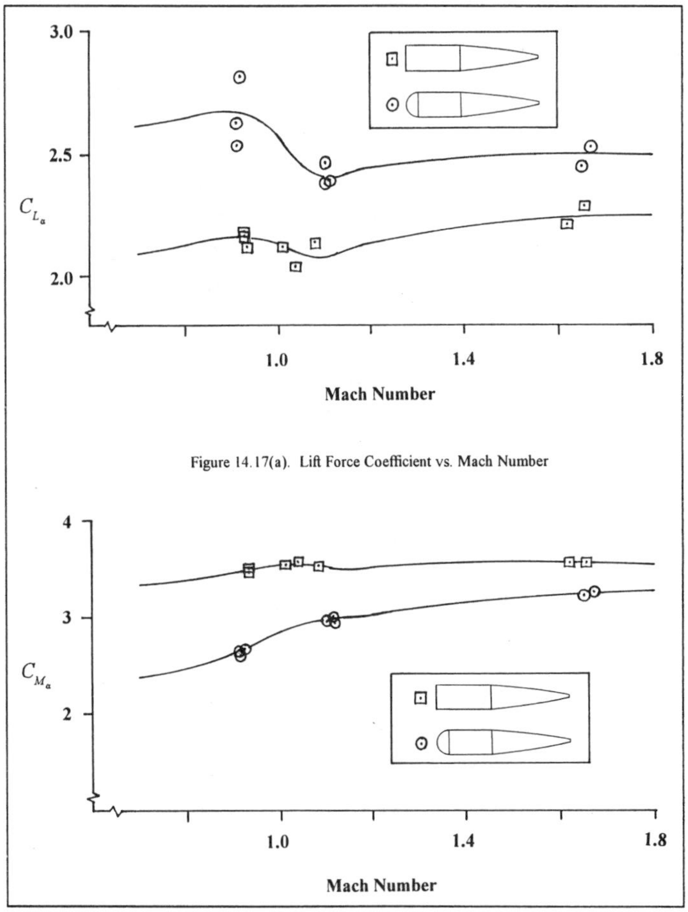

Figure 14.17 (a) Lift Force Coefficient and (b) Pitching Moment Coefficient vs. Mach Number.

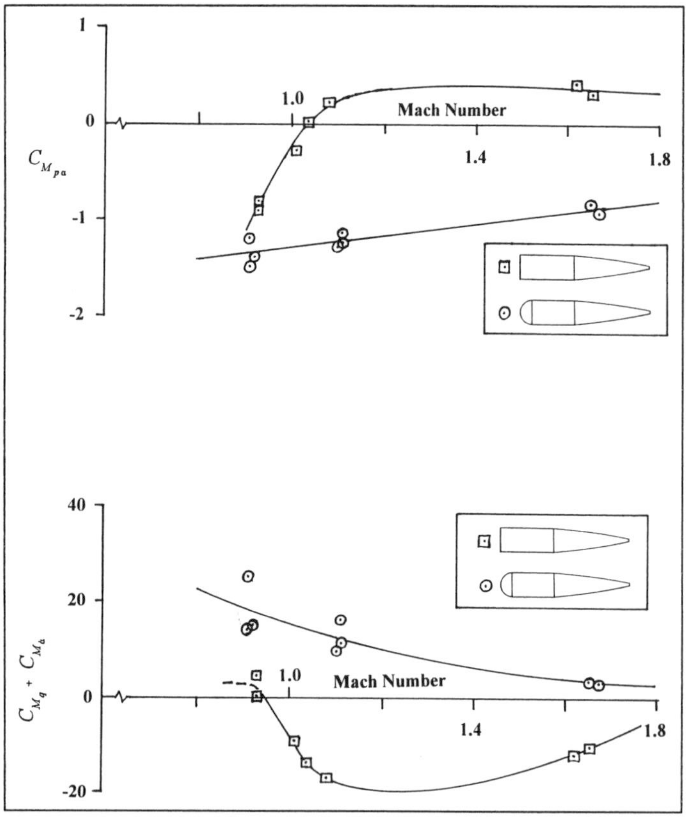

Figure 14.18 (a) Magnus Moment Coefficient and (b) Pitch Damping Moment Coefficient vs. Mach Number.

obtain accurate values of the required partial derivatives with respect to the unknown aerodynamic coefficients. In their original paper, Chapman and Kirk showed that the new technique permits accurate fitting of observed free-flight pitching and yawing motions, even when rapidly varying roll rates and large angles of attack are present in the data.

Whyte et al. (Ref. 28) extended the Chapman-Kirk method to include all significant nonlinear aerodynamic forces and moments, for spin-stabilized rotationally symmetric projectiles. More recently, Whyte's code has been revised to include the capability of simultaneously fitting data from several test rounds, fired at the same nominal Mach number. In addition, the latest version of the code has been extended to include a generalized "Airplane 6-DOF" data reduction that does not require the projectile to be rotationally symmetric.

The 6-DOF data reduction methods are the way of the future, and they will be used more extensively in the twenty-first century. The author has had little personal experience with these methods, and no further discussion is included in this book. For more information, it is suggested that the reader contact Mr. Robert H. Whyte, of Arrow Tech Associates, Inc., 1233 Shelburne Rd., South Burlington, Vermont, 05403.

14.6 MODERN DATA REDUCTION FOR YAW-CARD FIRINGS

Spark photography ranges have generally replaced yaw-card ranges for modern aeroballistic testing. The principal advantages of spark photography over yaw cards are an order of magnitude higher precision of measurement, no interference with the free flight of the projectile, and high quality flowfield visualization provided by the spark shadowgraphs. In spite of these advantages, however, yaw cards are still used, often because of the high cost of spark range testing, and sometimes because test configurations involve either discarding parts (sabots) that are hazardous to expensive instrumentation, or projectiles made of toxic materials that cannot be fired in spark ranges due to environmental restrictions.

The data obtained at a given yaw-card station consists of the total amplitude of yaw, which is determined from the shell geometry, the size and shape of the hole in the perforated card, and the orientation angle of the yaw, which is taken as the direction the projectile nose was pointing when it passed that station. The total amplitude of yaw and orientation angle are converted to pitch (α) and yaw (β) angles, and the data reduction then proceeds in the same manner as for spark range data. For finned missiles, one fin may be color-coated with a substance such as prussian blue, which allows the projectile roll angle to be accurately measured. Note that in general, yaw-card swerve measurements are seldom made, although there is no reason they cannot be done if one is willing to go through the effort of doing a high-precision survey of the yaw-card range. [Mann (Ref. 10) did this for spin-stabilized small arms bullets in the first decade of the twentieth century, and he made the first reasonably accurate measurements of aerodynamic jump and epicyclic swerve].

The older classical data reduction methods for yaw-card firings always used graphical techniques, because high-speed digital computers were not yet available. However, graphical methods are inherently less accurate than a modern differential-corrections, least-squares fit of the data. There is no reason today not to use a digital computer and a modern yaw reduction (such as that described for spark photography range firings in section 14.4 of this chapter) for yaw-card data. (One could even use a 6-DOF reduction, although such sophistication is probably undeserved).

The selection of an optimum material for the yaw cards has always been a problem. The card must survive the projectile impact without disintegrating, yet it must not be stronger or thicker than necessary to hold a good imprint. Traditional card materials for small arms and small cannon projectiles include plain white paper of various grades, and photographic paper, with the emulsion side placed toward the muzzle of the gun. For larger cannon artillery shell, various grades and thicknesses of cardboard and chipboard have traditionally been used. A study of modern card materials needs to be done, if serious yaw-card work is contemplated. The author has found that placing a sheet of carbon paper on the front of each card often increases the resolution of the projectile's imprint, regardless of the card material used.

The relative imprecision of measurement is one of the biggest drawbacks of yaw-card firings. Modern spark photography ranges determine pitch and yaw angles with errors of order of 0.1 degree. However, typical measurement errors from yaw-card firings are of order of 1.0 degree, which is an order of magnitude greater than typical spark-range errors. As we will see, this translates into a yaw-card data quality problem for small-yaw flight.

A summary of the criteria for the quality of spark-range measured aerodynamic coefficients was presented as Table 14.3 in section 14.4 of this chapter. The same criteria also apply to coefficients determined from yaw-card firings. However, note the results listed in the fourth column of Table 14.3. In order to have good determinations of the pitching moment coefficient, the amplitude of *each* epicyclic yaw arm must exceed the average measurement error by a factor of three, and for good determinations of the Magnus and pitch damping moment coefficients, *each* arm must be at least five times the noise amplitude. Thus for spark range data, good values of all coefficients can be obtained for maximum yaw amplitudes as small as one degree. However, for the poorer quality yaw-card data, maximum yaw amplitudes must be of order of *ten degrees*, if all aerodynamic coefficients are to be well determined. It is not difficult to induce such large levels of pitching and yawing motion, using a yaw inducer. *The problem is that accurate aerodynamic data at smaller yaw levels is also required and in general, it cannot be obtained from yaw card firings*!

There is a second major problem with the use of yaw cards. Unfortunately, the cards themselves often have a significant effect on the projectile's flight. In general, successive impacts with yaw cards have an analogous effect to an increase in air density. Several years ago, the author took a modern look at this problem (Ref. 29) for determination of the pitching moment coefficient, and the interested reader will find the details in this reference. A system of yaw-card forces and moments was added to the conventional aerodynamic force-moment system, and a solution was obtained to the resulting differential equation for the pitching and yawing motion. The solution showed that if projectiles were fired through both dense and sparse yaw-card arrangements, the card pitching moment coefficient and the "effective card density" could be determined. (Note that this doubles the number of test rounds that must be fired). The results of the yaw-card analysis were compared against spark range measurements for four sample projectiles, and excellent agreement was found. The corrections for the card effect are very significant for spin-stabilized small arms projectiles. For typical dense card distributions, the true, or corrected, value of the pitching moment coefficient can be twenty percent less than the uncorrected value!

The analysis of Reference 29 also shows that the presence of yaw cards tends to destabilize spinning projectiles, and it contains the warning that a very high effective card density may induce a gyroscopic instability! For test cases involving suspected marginal instability, the yaw-card firings should be conducted using a gun with a faster twist of rifling. The measured gyroscopic stability factors are then corrected to the desired twist rate.

For high length-to-diameter ratio finned projectiles, typical yaw card measurement errors can be much smaller than those discussed above. In 1991 the author did a few test firings of an experimental 25mm fin-stabilized, discarding-sabot, long-rod penetrator, at a flight Mach number of 4.05. Several rounds were fired in the BRL Aerodynamics Range, and a few additional rounds were fired through dense and sparse distributions of yaw cards. Photographic paper was used for the cards, and the card spacing was five feet for the dense distribution, and ten feet for sparse. A sketch of the test projectile, and the measured physical characteristics are shown in Figure 14.19.

The length-to-diameter ratio of this finned model is 16.4, and the very long baseline permits the measurement of pitch and yaw angles from yaw cards to within 1/4 degree error, rather than the 1.0 degree card measurement error typically observed for shorter, conventional spin-stabilized munitions. The spark range and the yaw card data were reduced and analyzed, and for this heavy, high velocity, finned projectile, no significant effect of the cards on the pitching and yawing motion could be detected. The linear and cubic pitching moment coefficients, and the pitch damping moment coefficients, all at Mach 4.05, are presented in Table 14.5.

25mm Fin-Stabilized Long-Rod Penetrator

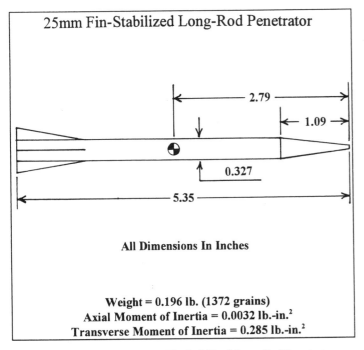

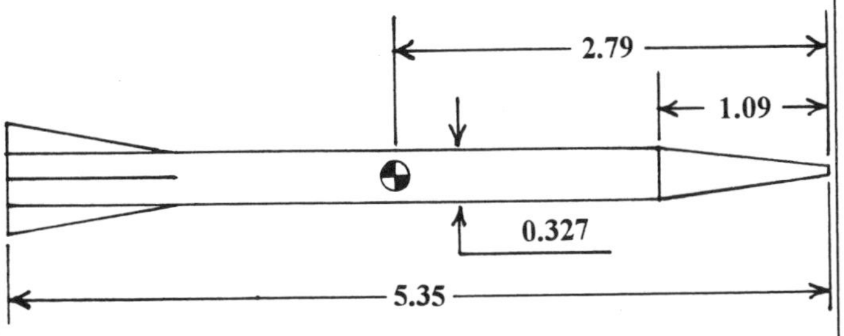

All Dimensions In Inches

Weight = 0.196 lb. (1372 grains)
Axial Moment of Inertia = 0.0032 lb.-in.²
Transverse Moment of Inertia = 0.285 lb.-in.²

Figure 14.19 Sketch of a 25 mm Fin-Stabilized Long-Rod Penetrator.

Table 14.5
Comparison of Spark Range and Yaw Card Results for a Finned Projectile

Quantity	Spark Range Average Value	Yaw Card Average Value
$C_{M_{\alpha 0}}$	-21.7	-22.4
$C_{M_{\alpha 2}}$	570	315
$\left(C_{M_q} + C_{M_{\dot{\alpha}}}\right)$	-346	-374

The linear pitching moment coefficients differ by 3%, and the pitch damping moment coefficient values differ by 8%. The disagreement in the cubic pitching moment coefficients is significantly larger, but this is not surprising, since the average total angle of attack of these flights varied between 2 and 5 degrees, and none of the cubic coefficients were well determined.

14.7 METHODS OF YAW INDUCTION

The determination of nonlinear aerodynamic forces and moments from free-flight spark photography range tests depends heavily on the ability to fire several rounds at a fixed flight Mach number, but with varying amplitudes of the pitching and yawing motion. Yaw induction has been mentioned on several occasions in this book, and it is now time to discuss how that is done. A number of different yaw induction techniques have proven to be useful in the BRL spark photography ranges over the past forty years, and we will look at several of them in this section.

There are three requirements that any successful yaw induction technique must meet, if it is to be generally useful: (1) the yaw inducer must not damage either the projectile or the gun used for firing it; (2) a means of systematically varying the induced amplitude of yaw must be provided, and for any given "setting" of the yaw inducer, the resulting yaw level must be relatively consistent from shot to shot, and (3) the projectile's flight path must be at least reasonably predictable after yaw induction, so the trajectory remains within the "instrumented window" of the firing range. The third requirement is often the most difficult to accomplish. As the amplitude of induced yaw increases, the trajectory usually becomes less and less "controllable."

Half-Lip Yaw Inducers

One of the most successful types of yaw inducer is the half-lip design. These devices are attached to the muzzle of the gun barrel, usually by means of threads or set screws. Figures 14.20 through 14.23 are photographs of half-lip yaw inducers, mounted on the muzzles of Mann barrels ranging in size from .50 caliber through 25mm, and they illustrate the devices very well. Scaled-down versions of these yaw inducers are used with small arms, and larger versions are successfully used for firing large cannon artillery shell. A variation of the half-lip principle, called a "break-away muzzle brake" is sometimes used to induce yaw for very high velocity cannon artillery firings. At top velocity zones, the transverse loading on the half-lip produces a bending moment that can be large enough to damage the cannon. The "break-away" feature contains a deliberately weak mechanical link, and it permits the yaw inducer to shear away and fall before damage to the gun can occur.

The inside of the half-lip, extending beyond the muzzle of the gun, is bored out to an inside diameter slightly greater than the barrel's groove diameter, before one-half of the lip is milled away. This insures that the projectile never makes direct physical contact with the yaw inducer, which might damage the model. The principle of operation of the half-lip yaw inducer is to create a highly asymmetric muzzle jet of propellant gas, which "kicks" the tail of the model away from the lip as it clears the muzzle. In general, the amplitude of induced yaw increases with increasing length of the half-lip extension, and with increasing muzzle exit pressure.

Figure 14.20 illustrates a .50 caliber yaw inducer, with provision for a variable-length lip extension. Lip sections of varying length may be added or subtracted, which permits "calibration" of the device. A 20mm yaw inducer with a short fixed-length lip is

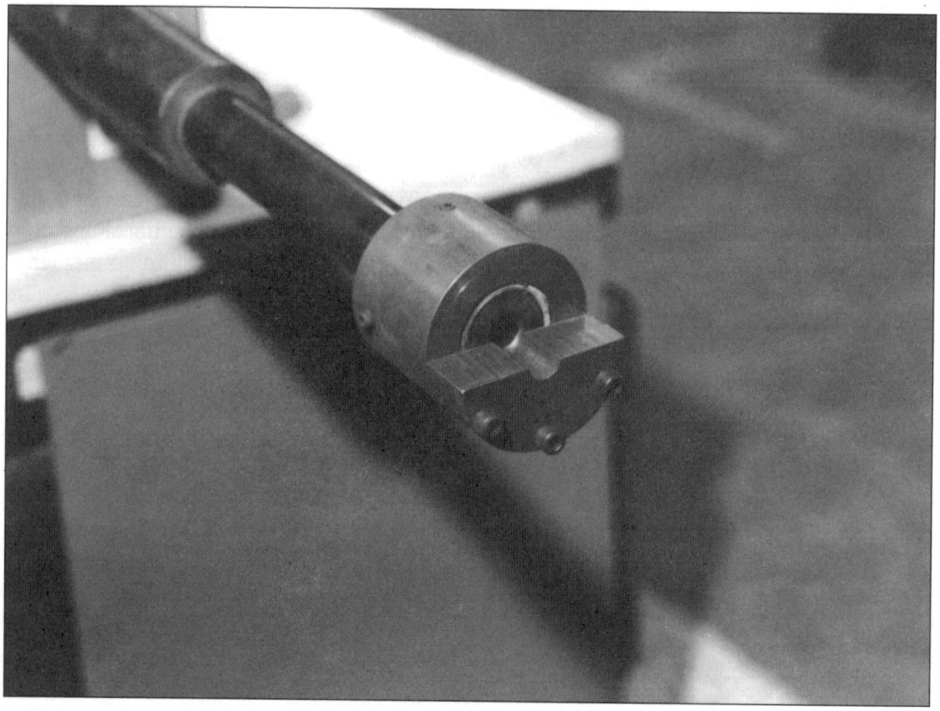

Figure 14.20 Photograph of a .50 Caliber Yaw Inducer, with Variable Lip Extension.

Figure 14.21 Photograph of a 20 mm Yaw Inducer, with a Fixed Short Lip Length.

shown in Figure 14.21, and Figure 14.22 is a similar 20mm device, but with a very long fixed-length lip. Another half-lip yaw inducer with provision for variable-length lip extensions is shown in Figure 14.23, mounted on the muzzle of a 25mm gun. In general, lip lengths between 1/2 caliber and 2 calibers have been found to be the most useful.

At moderate to high supersonic muzzle velocities, the muzzle exit pressures of modern guns have proved high enough to induce maximum yaw amplitudes between 10 and 15 degrees, with lip lengths between 1 and 2 calibers. At lower (transonic and subsonic) muzzle velocities, the muzzle exit pressure is often too low to induce significant yaw levels, and other techniques must then be used.

Oblique Impact Methods of Yaw Induction

Oblique impact methods are based on the physical principles of impulse and momentum. If the projectile experiences an in-flight oblique elastic collision with another body, the relative linear velocities and transverse angular velocities of both bodies will be changed. In simple terms, the mechanism is fundamentally that of a "controlled ricochet."

Figure 14.22 Photograph of a 20 mm Yaw Inducer, with a Fixed Long Lip Length.

The most commonly used oblique impact yaw-induction methods fall into two general categories. The first might best be described as a "tipping card" technique, in which the projectile is fired through a thicker-than-normal yaw card, mounted at an angle to the flight path. The oblique impact imparts transverse linear and angular momentum to the projectile. The transverse *linear* momentum alters the direction of the flight path after the impact, usually by a small angle. The transverse *angular* momentum imparted induces pitch and/or yaw rates after the impact, and the amplitude of the resulting maximum total angle of attack is directly proportional to the combined pitch and yaw rate. In general, the amount of yaw induced increases with increasing tipping card thickness, and with an increasing angle between the card and a plane normal to the flight path.

The second commonly used useful oblique impact method is to deliberately cause the ogive of the projectile to collide with another elastic (or partially elastic) body. This technique is often referred to as the "billiard-ball" method. As an illustrative example, we will assume that a table has been placed under the gun muzzle. We then place a long plastic right-circular cylinder standing vertically, some distance in front of, and off to the side of, the bore centerline. The cylinder is positioned so there is a small "interference," and when the gun is fired the projectile's ogive strikes the side of the plastic cylinder. The two bodies recoil away from each other; the plastic cylinder flies off the side of the table, and transverse linear and angular momentum are imparted to the projectile. The trajectory deflection and the amount of yaw induced increase with increasing weight of the cylinder, and with increasing "interference" between the two bodies. (Note that there is nothing magic about a *plastic* cylinder; plastic is often used because it is "soft" and is therefore less likely to damage the projectile).

One of the biggest problems with oblique impact methods of yaw induction is the potential for structural damage to the projectile. The tipping card method is less prone to cause damage than is the billiard-ball approach. Soft cardboard tipping cards have been used with fragile cast and swaged lead small arms bullets at transonic and subsonic speeds (where half-lip yaw inducers do not work well), without incurring detectable projectile damage. However, tipping cards are usually less effective as yaw inducers than other techniques.

If very large angle-of-attack flight is required, the billiard-ball method of yaw induction offers the highest potential for success. In section 13.6 of the previous chapter, large-yaw firings of the 105mm, M1 shell in the BRL Transonic Range were discussed, but no mention was made of the yaw-induction technique used. Average angles of attack up to *thirty* degrees were obtained during this firing program, using large nylon right-circular cylinders as the yaw inducers! However, it must be noted that the 105mm, M1 shell has thick steel walls, and is structurally strong. Several thinner-walled artillery shell designs have been observed to break apart after impact with a heavy plastic cylinder.

In general, the billiard-ball method is not a good choice for structurally weak projectile designs. Typical small arms bullets are good examples of soft, weak projectiles. Most modern small arms bullets consist of a gilding metal jacket surrounding a lead or lead-alloy core, and the use of a billiard-ball yaw inducer is quite likely to leave a dent in the bullet's ogive. Shadowgraphs show that in

Figure 14.23 Photograph of a 25 mm Yaw Inducer, with Variable Lip Extension.

extreme cases, the entire ogive appears to have been flattened on one side, and the projectile appears to be bent!

Additional Methods of Yaw Induction

Electromagnetic yaw induction has been successfully used in the BRL spark photography ranges. This method uses a high strength magnet embedded in the test projectile, which is then fired through the field of a powerful electromagnet. Ten-caliber long, 20mm-diameter finned projectiles, containing four-inch long, half-inch diameter Alnico V magnets, were launched through an armored electromagnet with a maximum field strength of 18,000 Gauss. Average yaw levels up to five degrees were obtained in these supersonic tests. However, other methods are easier and less expensive to operate, and the electromagnetic yaw induction technique has not been used in recent years.

For saboted projectiles, the inside diameter of the sabot can be shimmed on one side at the rear, and on the opposite side at the front, thus forcing the projectile to be canted, or tilted at a small angle, relative to the bore centerline. If the sabot and its projectile are rapidly spinning, this technique can in some instances, yield relatively large angle-of-attack flight. Even with nonrolling finned missiles, the eccentric model/sabot method will often produce sufficiently large yaw for many practical purposes.

Another method that has been used occasionally for spinning projectiles is a deliberately unbalanced pusher/obturator behind the projectile base. The pusher/obturator is initially coupled to the projectile by means of a mechanical key, that fits into a machined keyway in the projectile base. During the interior ballistic phase of the trajectory, the two units are mechanically coupled. Upon release at the gun muzzle, the unbalanced pusher/obturator experiences lateral throwoff, and it thereby imparts transverse angular momentum to the projectile. Soon after launch, the pusher/obturator falls away, and leaves the now-yawing projectile in free flight. This technique is more difficult to implement and calibrate in practice than some other yaw-induction methods, and it is therefore seldom used.

An artificial crosswind placed just in front of the gun muzzle has been used occasionally as a yaw-induction device. Large, high-speed fans are placed in front of, and just off to the side of, the gun, and the projectiles are fired through the effective crosswind. This method works fairly well for low- velocity finned projectiles, and it has been used for low-speed finned rockets. In general, it is not a very useful technique.

There are probably a number of additional yaw induction methods that have proved successful in other test facilities, but the author is unfamiliar with them. However, the techniques described in this section have all been found useful at one time or another, and they provide a starting point for the program engineer who is faced with a decision as to which method to use.

14.8 YAWSONDE TESTING

This section on yawsonde testing was kindly supplied to the author by Mr. Vural Oskay, an Aerospace Engineer with the Propulsion and Flight Division of the Army Research Laboratory (ARL), located at Aberdeen Proving Ground. Mr. Oskay and the author have been friends and colleagues for more than thirty years. He has had many years experience in both spark range and yawsonde testing, having been involved with yawsondes since the beginning of such work in the United States, in the late 1960s. Mr. Oskay's comments follow.

A solar yawsonde is a device that measures the angle between the axis of symmetry of a projectile, and a vector directed from the projectile toward the sun. It consists of a data gathering system, signal processing electronics, a transmitter and a power source. The solar yawsonde was first developed in England by Amery et al. (Ref. 30). Their design used a silicon solar cell behind a V-shaped mask, built into the body of a special fuze. The front of the device was designed to match the exterior contour of a standard artillery fuze, but it intruded about four inches into the projectile's payload volume. A pinhole had to be drilled through the projectile ogive, in such a way as to permit the sun's rays to impact on the silicon cell. Unfortunately, this procedure was very exacting and tedious.

During the late 1960s, the U.S. Army Harry Diamond Laboratories (HDL) improved on the British design by moving the solar cell to the ogival part of the fuze. This eliminated the necessity of machining the shell's ogive, and reduced the intrusion into the payload volume to about 2.5 inches.

By 1974, the entire yawsonde package had been housed within the confines of an artillery fuze (Ref. 31). The second generation BRL yawsonde separated the two legs of the V-shaped mask, so that the slits of the unit formed a "virtual V" in space, rather than a physical "V" on the surface of the silicon cell (see Figure 14.24). This new configuration had several advantages: (a) the excursions of the pulse from the second arm of the "V" were no longer limited to 1/3 the distance between the consecutive occurrences of the pulses from the first arm, as they were for both the British and the HDL designs; (b) since the two slits used two separate silicon cells, it was possible to invert one of the signals (usually one from the second arm) to make differentiation easier, and to permit the use of yawsondes at higher angles of attack, or near the edges of visibility of the sun, where signal cross-over was a possibility; (c) the reduced surface area of the silicon cells permitted a more compact unit, and reduced the payload intrusion to less than two inches; (d) it was possible to build units with more than two silicon cells, so that axial spin, or other aspects of the flight motion could be independently measured; (e) the use of multiple silicon cells permitted the use of yawsondes mounted on slowly rolling projectiles; and (f) the silicon cells could be placed in the most convenient geometric locations.

Operational Principle of a Yawsonde

When silicon cells are exposed to the sun, they generate a voltage. This voltage can be used to produce a pulse train for transmission to a ground receiving station. Figure 14.25 is a schematic of the electronic circuitry used to produce such a pulse train. The voltages from each solar cell are fed into a signal conditioner which inverts one of the voltages and adds the two signals. Its output is then sent to a voltage controlled oscillator (VCO). The VCO then modulates the frequency of the RF signal which is sent to the ground station.

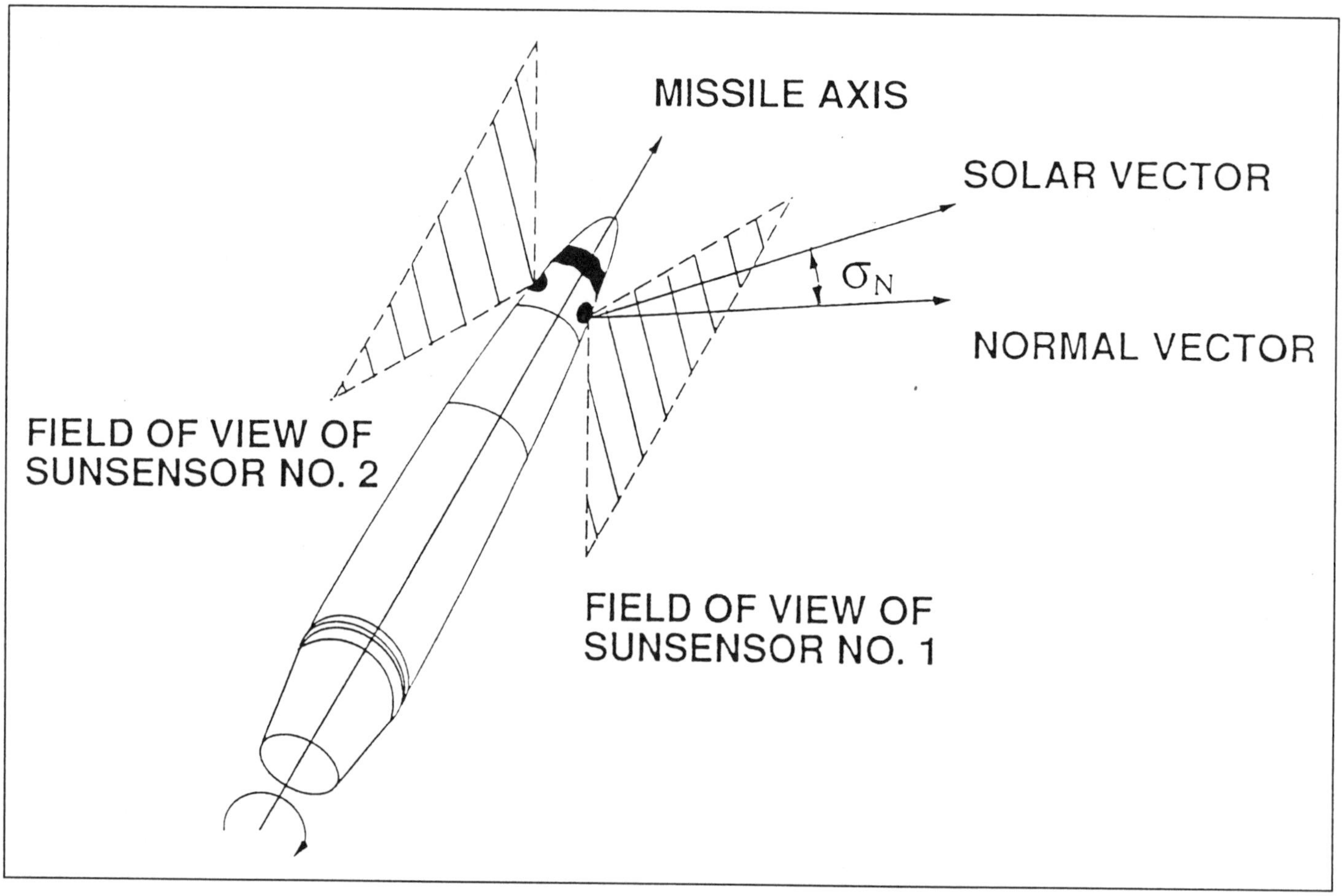

Figure 14.24 Sunsensor Field of View.

At the ground station, the signal is de-modulated to recover the original pulse train, which is used to determine the yawing behavior of the test projectile.

Referring back to Figure 14.24, as the projectile flies along its trajectory the solar cells are exposed to the sun's rays once each revolution. Since they are behind slits that form a "V," as the projectile pitches and yaws, the phasing between the two signals varies from one revolution to the next. The elapsed time between the signals from the second sensor to the first sensor depends on the times of exposure to the sun at each revolution. This is controlled by the geometric aspect of the sun with respect to the projectile's spin axis. Therefore, operation of a yawsonde is controlled by the date of the test (ephemeral position of sun), latitude of the test site, line of fire with respect to North, trajectory angle, and the total yaw angle between the spin axis and the velocity vector. The phasing of the resulting pulse train can then be translated into a single-plane yaw history, through the calibration of the yawsonde done after its manufacture.

The single-plane yaw history (called "Sigma-N") versus time is somewhat different from the pitch and yaw histories obtained in spark photography ranges. The shell is always flying along a curved trajectory, and Sigma-N versus time will be on a curved baseline. For long and/or high trajectories, it will have a distinct S-shape. Second, the measured data are values of the angle between the projectile's spin axis and a vector directed toward the sun, they do not correspond to the standard earth-fixed coordinate values.

In spite of these unusual data properties, yawsondes have proved to be very helpful in determining the flight characteristics of projectiles and other test items. Qualitatively, it is possible to observe a shell's fast and slow epicyclic frequencies, although they are presented as a function of time rather than the distance travelled, in calibers. The damping or growth of the modal epicyclic pitch and yaw arms is also observed, as is any limit-cycle yawing on the downleg, and the roll, or spin history is also measured. (Note that the spin measured by a yawsonde is slightly different from the usual spin rate; a yawsonde measures Eulerian roll rate rather than the spin about the projectile's axis of symmetry.)

Some Examples of Yawsonde Data

Figures 14.26 and 14.27 show the yawing behavior and spin history of a 155mm artillery shell, fired at a gun elevation angle of 18.5 degrees. Figure 14.26 is a plot of Sigma-N versus time. Nearly twenty-five seconds of the flight along this trajectory are illustrated. Note the downward slope of the Sigma-N versus time curve, which is caused by trajectory curvature. Both modal arms are observed in the shell's yawing motion. This test was conducted to determine the damping of the pitching and yawing motion at large angle of attack, and a yaw inducer was used to induce approximately twenty degrees first maximum yaw. We observe that the slow mode is strongly damped, whereas the fast mode is only weakly damped. During the entire observed twenty-five second flight, the fast arm amplitude damped to approximately half its initial value.

Figure 14.27 is a plot of the spin history for the same flight. As stated above, this plot is actually the Eulerian roll rate (Phi-Dot), rather than the ordinary axial spin rate. As such, it shows some of the crossfeed of the fast mode motion. However, the average of this plot at any instant is very close to the expected spin rate of the projectile.

Figure 14.28 is another example of spin measurement by means of a yawsonde. These data were obtained for a 2.75-inch rocket with wrap-around fins. Wrap-around fins are known to be very sensitive to changes in flight Mach number and yaw level. Therefore, a four-cell yawsonde (a "quadsonde" in our nomenclature) was used for this shot. It can be seen that during the motor burn over the first 0.8 second of flight, the rocket is spinning up due to canted nozzles. Once the burn phase terminates, the missile comes under the influence of the wrap-around fins, and it strongly changes its spin characteristics. Figure 14.28 shows three zero-spin crossings, as well as the fact that during most of its flight, the projectile is rolling in a direction opposite to that produced by the rocket motor.

Future of On-Board Instrumentation for Artillery Projectiles

Yawsondes have been very useful instruments in determining stability and flight characteristics of artillery shell. They have been used extensively by ARL (formerly BRL) and ARDEC, at Picatinny Arsenal, New Jersey. However, by their nature, there is only so much that can be done with their data. Through the use of appropriate algorithms and software, the data can be made to look more similar to what aerospace engineers are accustomed to. With some ingenuity, it is even possible to extract some of the aerodynamic coefficients (Ref. 32) from yawsonde flights. However, new systems require additional data besides yaw and spin. Standard projectiles need accurate drag information, and rockets need good thrust measurements. For a smart (guided) munition, the effects of canard motion and g-loading effects are also usually required.

With modern miniaturized electronic components, it will possible in the future to house accelerometers, vibration sensors, GPS detectors, etc., within the confines of a standard artillery fuze. At present, it is even possible to place electronic devices within the tracer cavity of a kinetic energy projectile, to observe its spin history.

D. G. Miller has kindly provided the author a final reference on modern exterior ballistics measurements and instrumentation. This is a British survey of experimental methods called *Textbook of Ballistics and Gunnery, Volume Two*, published by Her Majesty's

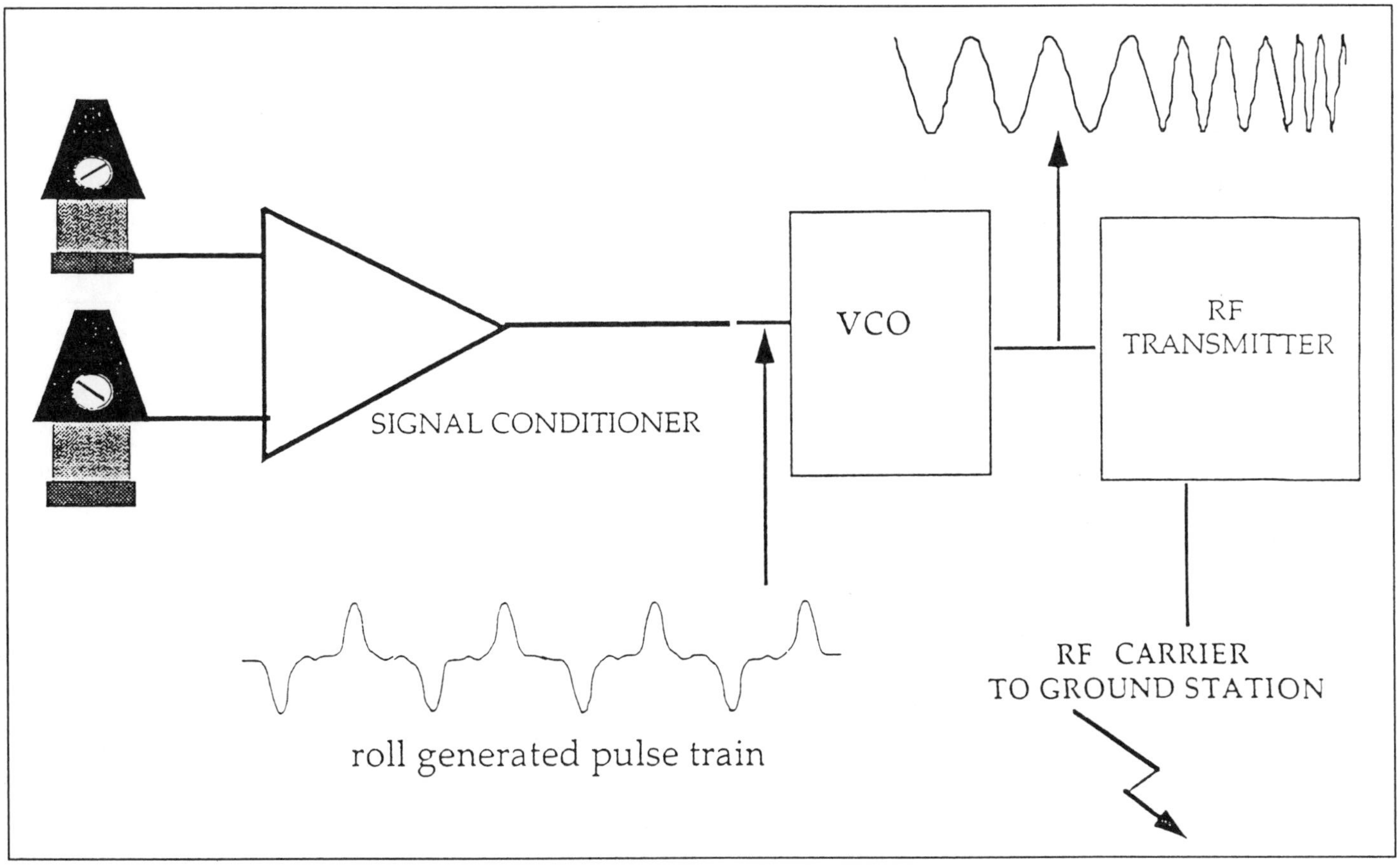

Figure 14.25 Yawsonde Telemetry Projectile Electronics.

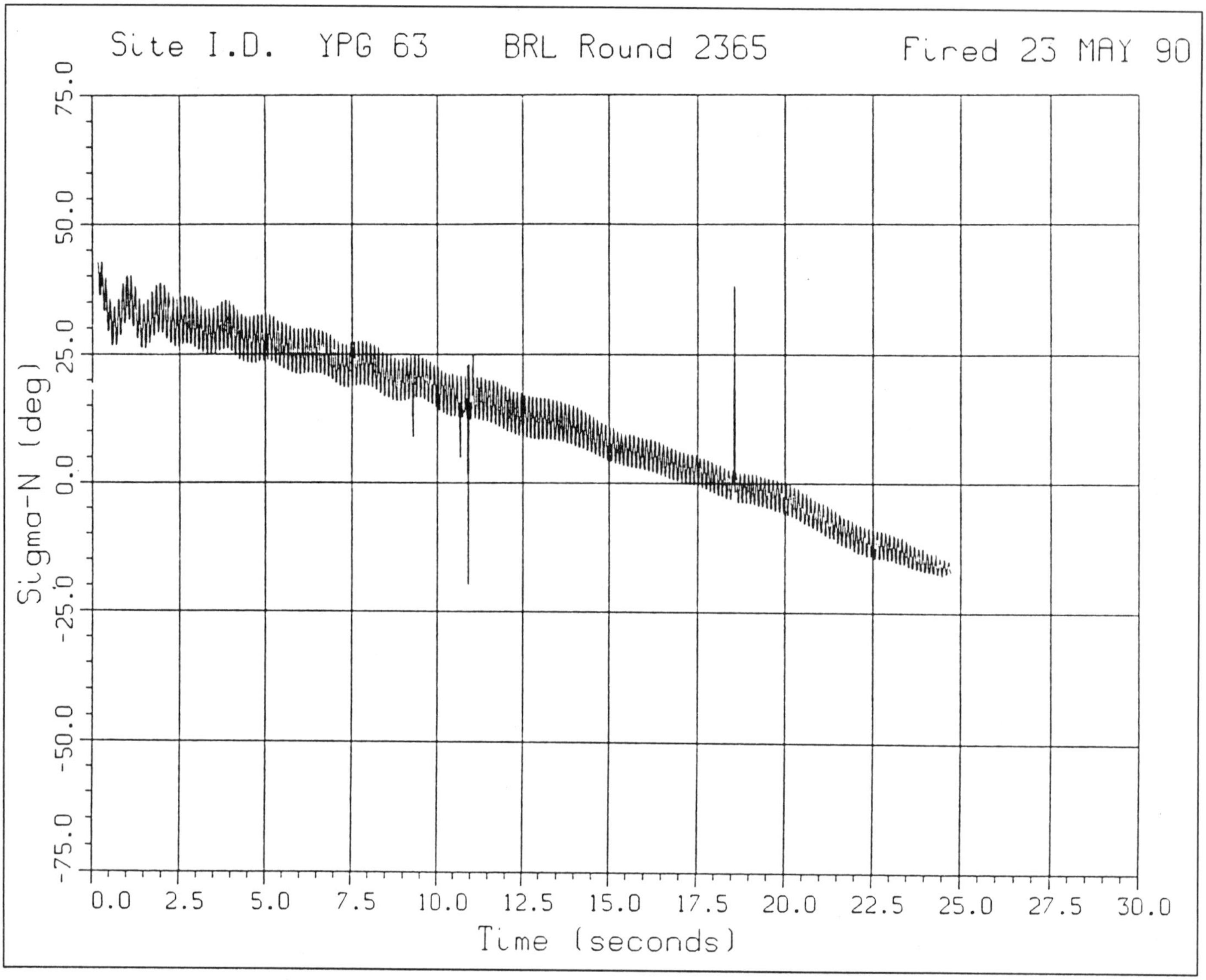

Figure 14.26 Sigma-N versus Time for a 155 mm Artillery Shell.

Stationary Office, London, 1984. The book includes wind tunnels, open and enclosed free-flight ranges, yawsonde testing, and Doppler radar velocimeter measurements. The author has not seen a copy of this reference, but according to Miller it is both very hard to get and very expensive. Volume One of this reference was published later, and it includes theoretical methods and design notes for interior, intermediate, exterior and terminal ballistics.

REFERENCES

1. Pope, A., and K. L. Goin, *High-Speed Wind Tunnel Testing*, John Wiley & Sons, Inc., New York, New York, 1965.

2. Volluz, R. J., *Handbook of Supersonic Aerodynamics*, Section 20, Wind Tunnel Instrumentation and Operation, Naval Ordnance Laboratory, 1961.

3. Buford, W. E., "Aerodynamic Characteristics of the 30mm Shell T306E10 HEI," Ballistic Research Laboratories Technical Note No. 1019, 1955.

4. Roecker, E. T., and E. D. Boyer, "Aerodynamic Characteristics of 30mm HEI Shell, T306E10," Ballistic Research Laboratories Memorandum Report No. 1098, 1957.

5. Platou, A. S., and J. Sternberg, "The Magnus Characteristics of a 30mm Aircraft Bullet," Ballistic Research Laboratories Report No. 994, 1956.

6. Platou, A. S., R. Colburn and J. S. Pedgonay, "The Design and Dynamic Balancing of Spinning Models and a Testing Technique for Obtaining Magnus Data in Wind Tunnels," Ballistic Research Laboratories Memorandum Report No. 2019, 1969.

7. McCoy, R. L., "The Subsonic Aerodynamic Characteristics of the 105mm HE Shell, M1 at Angles of Attack From Zero to 180 Degrees," Ballistic Research Laboratories Memorandum Report No. 2353, 1974.

8. Charbonnier, P., *Ballistique Exterieure Rationnele*, Paris, 1907.

9. Cranz, C., *Lehrbuch der Ballistik*, Berlin, 1927.

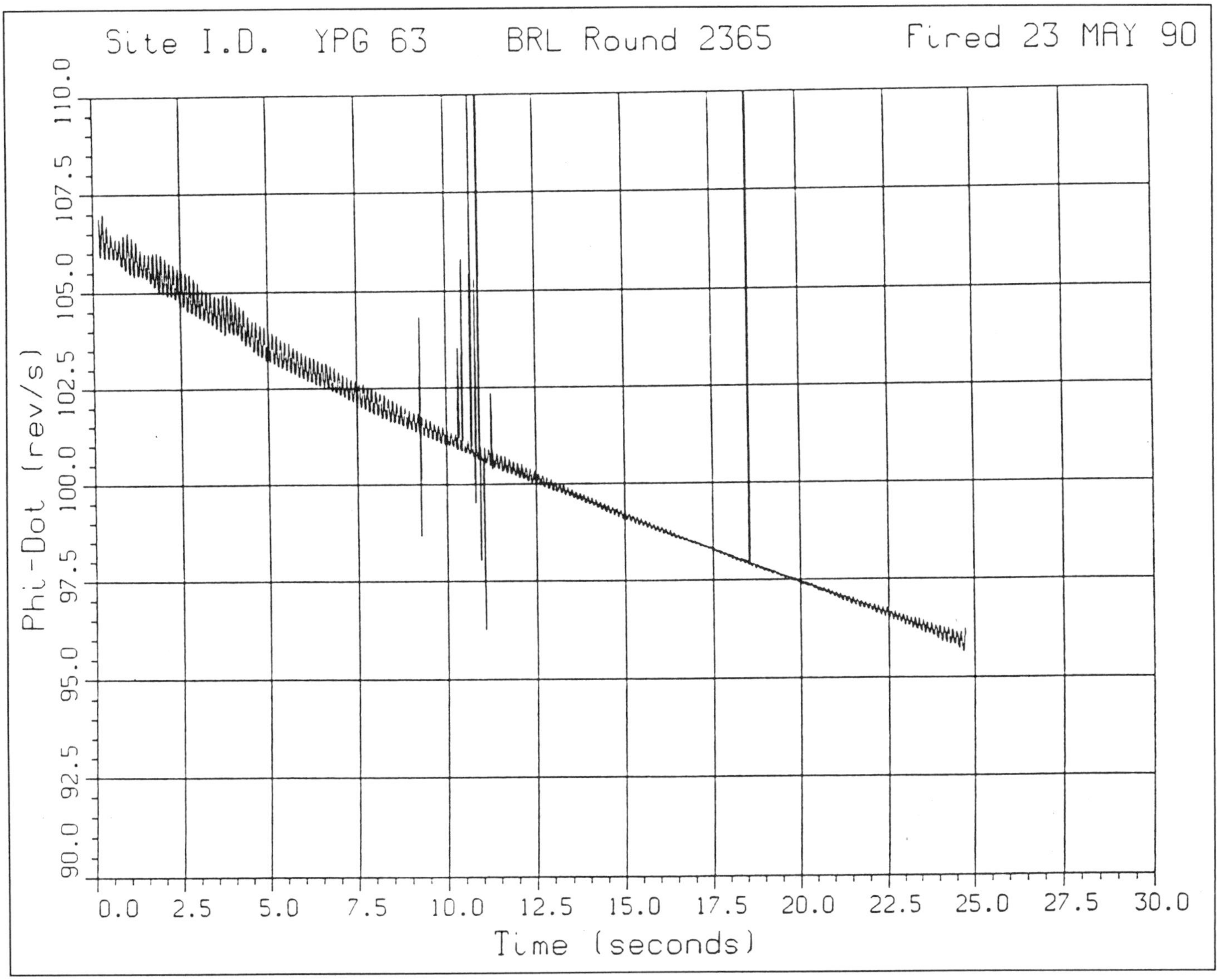

Figure 14.27 Phi-Dot versus Time for a 155 mm Artillery Shell.

10. Mann, F. W., *The Bullet's Flight from Powder to Target*, Munn & Company, New York, New York, 1909. (Reprinted 1942, 1952).

11. Fowler, R. H., E. G. Gallop, C. N. H. Lock and H. W. Richmond, "The Aerodynamics of a Spinning Shell," *Philosophical Transactions of the Royal Society of London*, Series A, Volume 221, 1920.

12. Hitchcock, H. P., "Resistance and Stability of Projectiles: Experimental Methods and Details of Computation," Ballistic Research Laboratories Report No. X-113 (BRL File A-IV-45), 1932.

13. Nelson, W. C., Editor, *Selected Topics on Ballistics - Cranz Centenary Colloquium*, Pergamon Press, New York, New York, 1959.

14. Charters, A. C., and R. N. Thomas, "The Aerodynamic Performance of Small Spheres from Subsonic to High Supersonic Velocities," Ballistic Research Laboratories Report No. 514, 1945.

15. Kopal, Z., K. E. Kavanagh and N. K. Rodier, "A Manual of Reduction of Spinner Rocket Shadowgrams," Massachusetts Institute of Technology, Center of Analysis, Technical Report No. 4, Cambridge, Massachusetts, 1949.

16. Turetsky, R., "Reduction of Spark Range Data," Ballistic Research Laboratories Report No. 684, 1948.

17. Braun, W. F., "The Free Flight Aerodynamics Range," Ballistic Research Laboratories Report No. 1048, 1958.

18. Rogers, W. K., Jr., "The Transonic Free Flight Range," Ballistic Research Laboratories Report No. 1044, 1958.

19. Conte, S., "On the Reduction of Shadowgrams, "Ballistic Research Laboratories Report No. 786, 1952.

20. Murphy, C. H., "Data Reduction for the Free Flight Spark Ranges," Ballistic Research Laboratories Report No. 900, 1954.

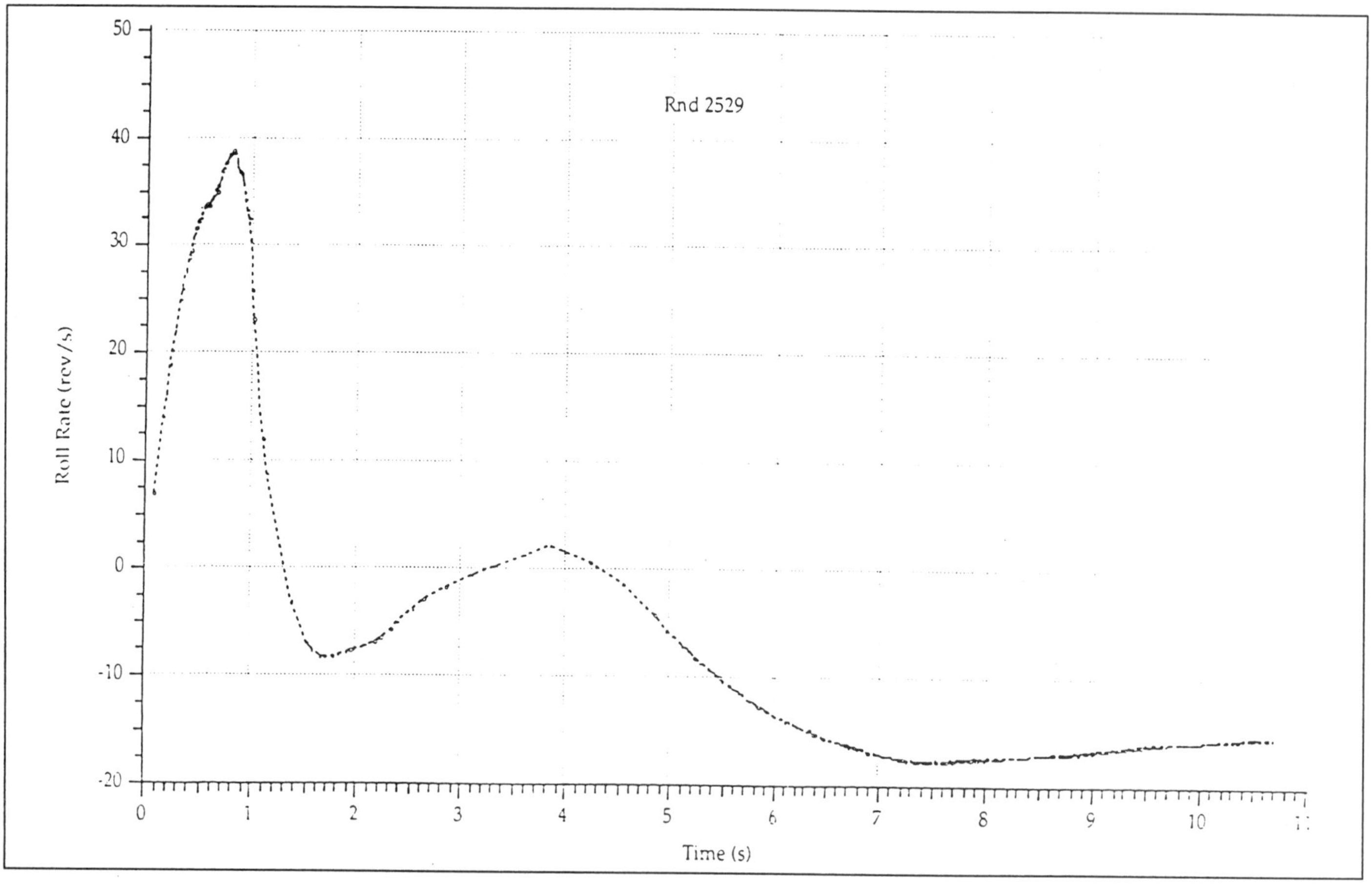

Figure 14.28 Roll Rate versus Time for a 2.75-Inch Rocket.

21. Dickinson, E. R., "Physical Measurements of Projectiles," Ballistic Research Laboratories Technical Note No. 874, 1954.

22. Murphy, C. H., and L. E. Schmidt, "The Effect of Length on the Aerodynamic Characteristics of Bodies of Revolution in Supersonic Flight," Ballistic Research Laboratories Report No. 876, 1953.

23. Schmidt, L. E., and C. H. Murphy, "The Aerodynamic Properties of the 7 Caliber Army-Navy Spinner Rocket in Transonic Flight," Ballistic Research Laboratories Memorandum Report No. 775, 1954.

24. Deitrick, R. E., "Effect of a Hemispherical Base on the Aerodynamic Characteristics of Shell," Ballistic Research Laboratories Memorandum Report No. 947, 1955.

25. Karpov, B. G., "The Effect of Various Boattail Shapes on Base Pressure and Other Aerodynamic Characteristics of a 7-Caliber Long Body of Revolution at M = 1.70," Ballistic Research Laboratories Report No. 1295, 1965.

26. Chapman, G. T., and D. B. Kirk, "A New Method for Extracting Aerodynamic Coefficients from Free-Flight Data," AIAA Paper No. 69-134, AIAA 7th Aerospace Sciences Meeting, New York, New York, 1969.

27. Chapman, G. T., and D. B. Kirk, "A New Method for Extracting Aerodynamic Coefficients from Free-Flight Data," *AIAA Journal*, Vol. 8, No. 4, 1970.

28. Whyte, R. H., A. Jeung, and J. W. Bradley, "Chapman-Kirk Reduction of Free-Flight Range Data to Obtain Nonlinear Aerodynamic Coefficients," Ballistic Research Laboratories Memorandum Report No. 2298, 1973.

29. McCoy, R. L., "The Effect of Yaw Cards on the Pitching and Yawing Motion of Symmetric Projectiles," Ballistic Research Laboratory Technical Report BRL-TR-3338, 1992.

30. Amery, I. O. F., "Flight Behavior of Projectiles. Yaw Telemetry Trial. 4.5" Naval Shell. Malta, April, 1967," Royal Armament Research and Development Establishment Memorandum 9/68, 1968.

31. Mermagen, W. H., and W. H. Clay, "The Design of Second Generation Yawsonde," Ballistic Research Laboratories Memorandum Report No. 2368, 1974.

32. Whyte, R. H., and W. H. Mermagen, "A Method for Obtaining Aerodynamic Coefficients from Yawsonde and Radar Data," *Journal of Spacecraft and Rockets*, Vol. 10, No. 6, 1973.